J.H. Balfour Browne

Wood´s Browne on the Law of Carriers of Good and Passangers by Land and Water

AF786373

Salzwasser

J.H. Balfour Browne

Wood´s Browne on the Law of Carriers of Good and Passangers by Land and Water

1. Auflage | ISBN: 978-3-84604-710-1

Erscheinungsort: Frankfurt, Deutschland

Erscheinungsjahr: 2020

Salzwasser Verlag GmbH

Reprint of the original, first published in 1883.

WOOD'S

BROWNE

ON THE

LAW OF CARRIERS

OF

GOODS AND PASSENGERS BY LAND AND WATER.

BY

J. H. BALFOUR BROWNE, Esq.,

OF THE MIDDLE TEMPLE AND MIDLAND CIRCUIT, BARRISTER-AT-LAW; AUTHOR OF "THE MEDICAL JURISPRUDENCE OF INSANITY," ETC.

WITH NOTES AND REFERENCES TO AMERICAN CASES

By H. G. WOOD,

AUTHOR OF "LANDLORD AND TENANT," "FIRE INSURANCE," AND "SLANDER AND LIBEL."

BANKS AND BROTHERS,

Law Publishers,

NEW YORK: 144 NASSAU ST. ALBANY, N.Y.: 473 AND 475 BROADWAY.

1883.

UNIVERSITY PRESS:
JOHN WILSON AND SON, CAMBRIDGE.

TO THE

HONORABLE SIR ROBERT LUSH, KNIGHT,

ONE OF THE JUSTICES OF HER MAJESTY'S COURT
OF QUEEN'S BENCH,

This Work is Dedicated,

BY PERMISSION,

AS A TRIBUTE OF PERSONAL ESTEEM,

AND PROFOUND RESPECT FOR HIS JUDICIAL CHARACTER
AND LEGAL ATTAINMENTS.

PREFACE TO THE AMERICAN EDITION.

No excuse is necessary for the reproduction of this admirable treatise in this country. It is indispensable to American lawyers, to enable them to determine the applicability of the decisions of the English courts to similar questions arising in our courts. The law relating to carriers is so largely regulated by statute in England, that, without a work pointing out the instances in which those statutes have varied the common-law rules relating thereto, it is impossible to determine whether the decisions of the English courts upon a given question relating to the rights and liabilities of carriers are entitled to any weight upon the determination of similar questions here. Mr. Browne has pointed out the instances in which these statutes have overridden or changed the common-law rules very clearly, and thus has performed a most excellent service for our lawyers and courts; and it is believed that, while the work may not supplant the various excellent American treatises upon this subject, yet it will be found to be a convenient and necessary adjunct thereto.

H. G. WOOD.

Boston, June 1, 1883.

PREFACE.

THE importance of any department of law is in direct proportion to the importance of the interests affected by its rules. The relative importance of various legal questions has consequently varied with the varying conditions of progressive civilization. The real-property law of this country is a museum of useless rules and regulations which, although admirable in their day, have as little meaning in these new times as the flint arrow-heads which are found in our bogs and marshes.

We see a reflected history of the past in the laws which were dictated by the necessities of the time, just as we can trace the tides of the sea which has retreated from some coast, by the breakwater which was at one time necessary to prevent its encroachments.

The old feeling, which was natural in lawless times, that real property was a much more eligible possession than property in chattels, has to some extent passed away before the inexorable facts of industrial times; but the respect which is still given to the owners of land is perhaps to be traced, as to its roots, to the feelings of that earlier and less civilized period. Now, however, the law in its relation to personal property, although it may have less historical interest, is not less important in the eyes of lawyers than that which has reference to property in land. The movable property of this country is at the present time of infinitely more value than the immovable; and as it is in the hands of a much larger number of proprietors, the interests affected by the laws relating to personal property are certainly not less important than those which have reference to real property.

But our personal property has, owing to the conditions of the period, become more movable than it was in times past. We are a commercial as well as an industrial people, and the more our manufactures increase, the more our commerce extends. The laws of action and reaction are visible in the vital phenomena of trade. Industry has not only increased the amount of traffic, but traffic has increased the amount of industry. Rapid means of conveyance have localized industries in those places which were most favorable for their advantageous prosecution, and this large-scale division of labor (large-scale because it is not only a division of employments among individuals but among cities and countries) has in its turn reacted upon traffic.

At the present time, therefore, our property is valuable by reason of its very movable character. As a money system is more excellent than a system of barter, because of the possibility of currency, so personal property has become more valuable in these days by reason of the facilities for exchange. And the tendency of our times is still further to divide the labor of the country, and consequently to make a still more extensive use of the means of trade conveyance. Hence the importance of the law of carriers.

These circumstances will indicate why the subject dealt with in this treatise has more importance now than it had in times gone by, and may serve to explain the reasons which induced the author to enter upon the task of writing it so soon after the publication of Messrs. Chitty and Temple's able work upon the Law of Carriers. Although it seems a short time since the publication of that work, it is not really a short time to a lawyer, who must judge of the necessity of a restatement of the law, not by the number of years since the publication of the last work, but by the number of cases which have been decided, or rather, to look at the subject with a deeper internal reference, to the number of important principles which have received illustration and elucidation since the publication of the previous text-book.

This leads the author naturally to speak of what might seem a defect in the following treatise, but which to him appears a positive merit. Some parts of the subject have received a greater amount of attention than others, and while every important question connected with the law of carriers has been alluded to, many have been much more fully treated than others, and that because the author found that the statement of the law contained in other text-books was sufficiently adequate in relation to certain rules, and could have done little more than transfer the statements contained in these to the pages of his own work. He was unwilling to do this, and he therefore left most of those portions of his subject which were adequately treated in other works with a less full exposition in his own, while he bestowed greater attention upon those questions which had received inadequate answers in other books upon the same department of law.

The author does not wish his book to seem to enter into competition with Mr. Angell's admirable work upon the Law of Carriers. That useful text-book must still be of service to the English practitioner, and invaluable to the American lawyer. In many connections, however, the text of that work cannot be regarded as an efficient statement of the law of England as it at present stands, and some subjects which must in future be of paramount importance in the eyes of English lawyers, are only alluded to. That being so, the work can never be all in all to the lawyer who has to practise in relation to English courts, and consequently there is still some necessity for a work on the law of carriers. But any treatise on the law in its relations to conveyance, written at the present time, would be wanting in a great excellence which Mr. Angell's work possesses, unless it contained references to cases decided in the United States.

The author has to express his deep sense of the obligation which he owes to his friend Mr. James P. Aspinall, of the Midland Circuit, for his careful revision of the manuscript of the first part of this work, and for the advice and assistance which he has afforded with reference to those portions which are devoted to questions of freight and shipping.

He has also great pleasure in acknowledging his indebtedness to his friends, Mr. Henry F. Makins and Mr. Lewis E. Glyn, both of the Home Circuit: the former, for his kindness in revising many of the proofs and correcting many inaccuracies; the latter, for the compilation of the Appendix of Pleadings, which will, he doubts not, be of the greatest service to the reader or practitioner.

5 Essex Court, Temple,
Oct. 23, 1872.

CONTENTS.

CHAPTER VIII.

CHAPTER IX.

CHAPTER X.

CHAPTER XI.

CHAPTER XII.

APPENDIX.

INDEX OF STATUTES.

TABLE OF CASES.

[THE FIGURES REFER TO THE PAGES.]

C.

D.

E.

H.

I.

J.

K.

L.

M.

Q.

R

S.

T.

U.

V.

W.

THE LAW OF CARRIERS.

CHAPTER I.

INTRODUCTORY.

THE PRINCIPLES OF THE LAW OF BAILMENTS.

SEC. 1. **The Principles of Law and Common-sense.** — The principles upon which all laws are founded are those of common-sense. The truth of such a statement may seem obvious, but it is not the less necessary to state it upon that account. Things that are very true are little better than things that are very false. Ordinary parlance would almost lead one to believe that "truism" is another name for a lie. There is some importance in the statement that the principles of law and the principles of common-sense are the same. True though it is, many people doubt it. Laymen are apt to regard the maxim that ignorance of law shall not excuse wrong-doing, as absolutely unjust. If, however, it could be proved that the principles of law and the principles of common-sense were the same, the injustice would disappear. It is within the power of each man, by means of ordinary intelligent attention to the conduct of others, to ascertain what his duties are. It is within the power of every sane man to conform his conduct to the laws which are deducible from human habit. It cannot, therefore, be unjust to hold that every man must know the law. True, the laws may be bad. Unless the laws have been formed with regard to the customs and habits of mankind, they are bad. Unless the needs of mankind have been had regard to, the laws are defective. But where this is not the case, where these considerations have regulated the legislature of a country, there can be no hardship in regarding ignorance of the law as no excuse for wrong-doing, for the law is founded on common-sense.

SEC. 2. **Of Bailments.** — These principles of common-sense would tell one that when one person delivered an article to another to use in any particular way, and when that other received the article with the understanding that it was to be used in a particular way, and that when it had been so used it was to be returned to the owner, a certain relation existed between the parties. That relation has been called a contract, and such delivery has been designated a bailment.[1] It is evident that it does not matter whether the delivery was made with a view to the simple custody of the article for a certain time, with a view to its being made use of, or with a view to its being carried to a particular place. The relation between the parties is obviously the same in all these cases. There is, first, the delivery which creates a trust in the person receiving the possession of the article;[2] there is then the express or implied contract by the party to keep or carry, as the case may be; and there is the express or implied condition to redeliver the chattel when the objects of the trust shall have been fulfilled.[3]

[1] The word "bailment" is derived from the French word *bailler*, to deliver. 2 Bl. Com. 451; Jones on Bailm. 90; Story on Bailm. § 2.

[2] An Essay on the Law of Bailments, by Sir William Jones, 4th ed., § 1, 117. See also 2 Bl. Com. 451.

[3] Cross *v.* Andrews, Cro. Eliz. 622; Corbett *v.* Parkington, 6 Barn. & Cress. 268; Ratcliffe *v.* Davies, Cro. Jac. 245; Walter *v.* Smith, 5 Barn. & Ald. 439.

SEC. 3. **The Importance of the Subject.** — When goods have been delivered in this way, the relationship which arises between the parties is one of the utmost importance. Any relationship which implies mutual rights and duties has importance in the eyes of lawyers; but a relationship which is constantly being entered upon, a relationship which has a permanent interest for the majority of mankind, is a subject of paramount importance.

SEC. 4. **Distinction between Duties of Finder of Chattel and those of a Bailee.** — Distinction is a kind of definition. To say what a thing is not, is one way of pointing out what it is. This trust-contract of bailment is easily to be distinguished from the relationship which exists between the finder of an article which has been lost, and the owner of the lost chattel. In the former case, there is an express or implied duty which binds the individual to do certain things, and to exercise certain faculties; in the latter, there is no very obvious duty connected with the found property. If it is not worth the owner's while to make diligent search for the lost article, it cannot be held to be the duty of the finder to be very diligent in his care of it. It was chance that bailed it to him, and the trusts of fortune are not to be construed strictly.

SEC. 5. **Different Kinds of Bailment.** — This delivery may, as we have seen, take place with a view to the carriage of the goods, and therefore the law of carriers is a branch of the law of bailments. For such carriage, an individual may be paid or unpaid, and the duties of the bailee must necessarily differ according to such circumstances.[1] It is evident that when a neighbor does one a favor, one must not expect such care in

[1] A person who keeps a ferry for his own convenience, and the convenicuce of customers to his mill, and transports persons to and from the mill free of charge, is only bonnd to exercise ordinary diligence. Self *v.* Dunn, 42 Ga. 528. And the same is true as to a gratuitous bailee. Lloyd *v.* West Branch Bank, 15 Penn. St. 172; De Haven *v.* Kensington Bank, 81 Penn. St. 95. But in all cases of this character the question as to what constitntes ordinary carc will depend upon the character of the property, and it is not always true that he is only bound to that degree of diligence whicb he exercises in reference to his own property. Bank of Carlisle *v.* Graham, 79 Penn. St. 106.

the doing as he has a right to expect when he has paid him for his labor, his time, and his diligence. A sense of honor might make a man more earnest in doing that for which he was not to be remunerated. But the common experience of mankind will teach every one that this scrupulousness is very rare, and that if you do not pay for care and diligence you are not likely to get them. Even where the labor is undertaken, for friendship's sake, without any remuneration, he who trusts his neighbor has a right to expect some exercise of prudence upon the part of him to whom he gives his property in keeping;[1] and the question which is involved in the law of bailments, and therefore in the law of carriers, is the amount of care which a man has a right to expect from another to whom his goods are intrusted, under the various circumstances of delivery, and the amount of the responsibility of him to whom the goods are given, for neglect.

SEC. 6. **Degrees of Care and Diligence.** — In deciding this question, several others must necessarily be considered. "There are," as SIR WILLIAM JONES remarks, "infinite shades of *care* and *diligence*, from the slightest momentary thought or glance of attention to the most vigilant anxiety and solicitude, but *extremes* in this case, as in most others, *are inapplicable to practice;* the first extreme would seldom enable the bailee to perform the condition, and the second ought not in justice to be demanded; since it would be harsh and absurd to exact the same anxious care which the greatest miser takes of his treasure from every man who borrows a book or a seal. The degrees, then, of care for which we are seeking must lie somewhere between these extremes; and by observing the different manners and characters of men we may find a certain standard which will facilitate our inquiry; for, although some are excessively careless and others excessively vigilant, and some through life, others only at particular times, yet we may perceive that *the generality of rational men* use nearly the same degree of diligence in the conduct of *their own*

[1] In the Roman Law, the mandatarius who failed to discharge faithfully his duty, although performed gratuitously, was stamped with infamy. D. iii. 2 I.

affairs; and this care, therefore, which *every person of common prudence and capable of governing a family* takes of *his own* concerns is a proper measure of that which would uniformly be required in performing every contract, if there were not strong reasons for *exacting* in some of them a *greater* and *permitting* in others a *less* degree of attention. Here, then, we may fix a constant determinate point, on each side of which there is a series consisting of variable terms tending indefinitely towards the above-mentioned extremes, in proportion as the case admits of indulgence or demands rigor; if the construction be *favorable*, a degree of care *less* than the standard will be sufficient; if *rigorous*, a degree *more* will be required; and, in the first case, the measure will be that care which *every man of common sense though absent and inattentive* applies to his own affairs; in the second, the measure will be that attention which a man *remarkably exact and thoughtful* gives to the securing of his personal property."[1]

SEC. 7. **Circumstances which determine the Kind and Amount of Diligence.** — But in deciding the question of what constitutes diligence, many circumstances must be taken into consideration. What is negligence in one set of circumstances is diligence in another. What would be carelessness in one climate would not be carelessness in another. These circumstances, which must be understood in deciding upon all questions as to the sufficiency of the care exercised in a bailee's trust, may be classed under four heads: 1. The nature and value of the article; 2. The customs of the place and trade; 3. The conditions of the country or climate; and 4. The conditions of the time and civilization.[2]

SEC. 8. **The Nature and Value of the Article.** — If an article is so large that it cannot be carried away, there is no necessity to fear theft. If it be of such a nature that it will not be damaged by rain, it is unnecessary to see that it is housed. And a man who has such articles in keeping will not be guilty of negligence for leaving them exposed to the night prowlers or the rain. Thus a block of marble is not without value, yet

[1] Jones on Bailm., 3d ed., pp. 4, 5.

[2] Bank of Carlisle *v.* Graham, 79 Penn. St. 106.

who can steal it? On the other hand, a bag of gold is likely to be stolen, because facility is a temptation. A bank note, although of greater value than a sovereign, is not so likely to be purloined, because it may, through stoppage at the bank, be valueless in the thief's hands, and might even lead to detection and punishment. Again, a man who carries glass with as little care as he would iron, is guilty of negligence. The same care need not be taken of the canvas upon which a picture is about to be painted as of that upon which a picture actually is painted. All these cases show that the amount of negligence, in any case, is not to be ascertained without a careful reference to the nature and condition of the article bailed, and also show that the amount of negligence is always proportioned to the possibly foreseen or foreknown degree of danger of loss or damage.

SEC. 9. **The Customs of the Place and Trade.**—If a man has been in the habit of using a certain stable without a lock, and the bailee of his horse, aware of this custom, used the same stable, he would not be guilty of negligence in case the horse was stolen. But not only have such individual habits an influence in the decision of the question as to negligence, but certain customs of trade will also upon occasion relieve a bailee who conformed to the custom from any culpability arising from the loss or damage of the bailor's chattel. What every one else does without danger, it is fair to argue, may be done by me without danger too. And when, in spite of the general safety of articles bestowed in a certain way, a chattel in the possession of a bailee, and bestowed according to the custom of the trade, is lost or damaged, it would be unjust to hold that the chance mishap had made him guilty of negligence, which is a certain condition of the mind of the individual, and is not the omission or act itself. What no ordinary man can foresee, no ordinary man is to be punished for not foreseeing. The habits and customs of a trade are a sufficient guide for the actions of most men; for we cannot suppose that a certain act in connection with business has become habitual without there being some reason for it. It is evident that a custom of trade, the course of business, or the practice of a place, may be sufficient to exonerate a bailee who has complied with one or other of these from any loss or damage which may have arisen in consequence of such compliance.

SEC. 10. **The Conditions of the Country or Climate.** — Men do not turn their horses into a quagmire any more than ants carry out their pupæ into the frost. It is such wisdom as is manifested in these acts that constitutes what is called diligence, and it is a want of the ordinary knowledge which each man acquires by means of experience which constitutes negligence. Thus there is no want of care in him who takes out a book in a summer day and leaves it on his own lawn. The same act done under clouds in mid-winter would be negligent. The man who lies on his back on a hill-side and stares up into the sky is running little or no risk if the weather is fine, but the same gazing at the same sky, where the stars ought to be, would be rash, if he had a rail under his neck and a rail under his feet and the express was due. Of course these are extreme cases, but they indicate the mental condition, in relation to certain external circumstances, which is the reason for there being such a thing as the law of negligence.

SEC. 11. **The Condition of the Time and Civilization.** — A man who left his front door open in a city would be extremely careless, but a man might do the same thing in the country without incurring censure. There is nothing more certain than that the value of facts varies in different ages and countries. What was regarded as negligence in the time of our great-grandfathers is not the same thing that is negligence to-day. What was diligence then may be negligence now. A circumstance is only to be rightly understood in its connection with other circumstances; and to ascertain what is negligence, one must understand to some extent the nature and spirit of the times. A gang of robbers in our neighborhood would make us more careful of our own property, and therefore those whose property we have in keeping have a right to expect an equal amount of care for their interests. In lawless times it might have been negligence not to have possessed a blunderbuss, but that cannot be said of to-day. Where the laws are bad, an individual's own care is the more necessary. A man on an island need not build a wall to keep out his neighbor's cattle, and so the police of a country are a kind of wall around a man's dwelling; the existence of such an institution will necessarily lighten the responsibility of each private individual for neglect. All these circumstances must be weighed and considered, if we would arrive at any correct conclusion with regard to the negligent conduct of an individual.

SEC. 12. **The Degrees of Negligence, slight, ordinary, gross.** — As negligence can only exist in the mind, it is well clearly to understand what it is, and in what degrees it may exist. Lawyers have distinguished (1) slight neglect[1] (the *levissima culpa* of the Roman lawyers), which is a want of very scrupulous carefulness, from (2) ordinary neglect (the *levis culpa* of the Roman law), which is a want of that ordinary care which a man bestows upon his own affairs, and from (3) gross neglect (the *lata culpa* of the civil law), which is a very great want of care, which, in consequence of the evil it causes and the mischief it does, has by many writers been considered as equivalent to fraud, or inconsistent with good faith;[2] but, on the other hand, it has sometimes been regarded as nothing more than ordinary negligence, with "a vituperative epithet" added to it.[3] It is, however, to be clearly distinguished from fraud. It is unphilosophical to confound two causes which differ widely from one another because their effects are the same; and there is no reason for regarding gross negligence as equivalent to fraud except in so far as it is a violation of good faith. But slight negligence and ordinary negligences are in the same way violations of good faith, although in a less degree and with consequences less hazardous. But the mental conditions which afford the truest ground of distinc-

[1] With each of these there was in the Roman law the correlation of its opposite: 1. *Levissima diligentia*, slight diligence; 2. *Diligentia*, ordinary diligence; and 3. *Exactissima diligentia*, extraordinary diligence.

[2] Jones on Bailm. 21; Story on Bailm. § 18.

[3] Campbell's Law of Negligence (London, 1871), § 11, p. 11; 1 Sm. L. Ca. 196; Grill *v.* Gen'l Iron Screw Collier Co., L. R. 1 C. P. 612; Wilson *v.* Brett, 11 M. & W. 115. See also Wyld *v.* Pickford, 8 M. & W. 461; Hinton *v.* Dibbin, 1 Q. B. 661; GIBBS, C. J., Broadwater *v.* Blot, Holt, 547, cf. Marfell *v.* S. Wales Railway, 29 L. J. 315 C. P.

tion between acts, in relation to gross negligence and to fraud, are totally different. In the one, the characteristic is a want of activity, a want of plan, a heedlessness and purposelessness; in the other, the characteristic is an activity in plotting, a secrecy of plan, a contrivance, and a carefulness which is undertaken with a view of bringing about a mischievous end. The end may be the same in both cases, but surely the means are different. A pistol is not a dagger, because they will both kill a man.

SEC. 13. **Distinction between Negligence and Misfeasance.** — There is a distinction between negligence and misfeasance. Negligence is some carelessness in the performance of a contract, while misfeasance is carelessness in contravening the contract. Thus when a parcel containing country bankers' notes was delivered to a carrier, without any notice of its value, to be carried by a mail coach, and was accepted by him to be so carried, and it was in contravention of this agreement sent by a different coach and was lost, this was held by BAYLEY, J., to be a case of misfeasance.[1] So when the master of a ship trading between Hull and Gainsborough — after notice by the proprietors of the vessel that they would not be responsible for any loss unless it was occasioned by a want of care in the master — took on board the plaintiff's goods to be carried from Hull to Stockwith, a place between Hull and Gainsborough, and the vessel passed Stockwith without delivering the goods, and sunk, without any negligence upon the part of the master, before it reached Gainsborough, this was held to be a case of misfeasance upon the part of the defendant's servant.[2]

SEC. 14. **Application of the Doctrine of Negligence.** — Negligence, then, being such as we have described it above, it is of importance to understand in what way the law adapts and applies these doctrines with regard to its degree. First, then, when the bailment is for the sole benefit of the bailor, it is evidently just that the law should demand only *slight* diligence upon the part of the bailee, and that consequently the bailee

[1] Sleat *v.* Fagg, 5 B. & Ald. 342. See also Garnett *v.* Willan, 5 B. & Ald. 53.
[2] Ellis *v.* Turner, 8 T. R. 531.

should, in case of the loss or damage of the article, only be liable for gross negligence.[1] Second, when the bailment is for the sole benefit of the bailee, a very great amount of care is properly demanded, and the bailee is properly held responsible for a very minor degree of negligence.[2] There is, of course, a kind of bailment which holds an intermediate place between these two. It is a delivery for mutual benefit. Each party is to be advantaged by the bailment. In this case the law expects ordinary diligence, or such attention to the object of the bailment as a man ordinarily bestows upon business matters, and therefore ordinary neglect will in such a case render the bailee liable for loss of or injury to the articles bailed.[3] This last kind of bailment is that which exists between those who deliver goods to be carried and those who carry goods for hire. In many cases it is evident that the determination as to the precise degree of negligence is a question which may be best left to the jury, and this is really what is done.[4] From all the principles which have been stated above, and from those principles of common-sense with which the principles of jurisprudence are indissolubly associated, it is evident that a bailee is not to be held responsible for that which no amount of care upon his part could have avoided. Thus unavoidable accident, a robbery, or other casualty which could in no way be attributable to the fault of the bailee, will relieve him from consequences of the loss or destruction of the property which is in his keeping.[5] A man can deprive himself of this immunity by special contract, as we shall see hereafter, and he is sometimes deprived of it by the special policy of the law.

[1] Doorman *v.* Jenkins, 2 Ad. & El. 256.

[2] Blakemore *or* Blackmore *v.* B. & Exeter Railway, 8 E. & B. 1035; 27 L. J. 167 Q. B.; M'Carthy *v.* Young, 3 L. T. Rep. N. S. 785.

[3] VAUGHAN, J., 3 Bing. N. C. 477.

[4] Clarke *v.* Earnshaw, Gow, 30.

[5] See Coggs *v.* Barnard, 2 Ld. Raym. 909; 1 Sm. L. Ca., 147, 4th ed.; Kettle *v.* Bromrell, Willes, 121; Shiells *v.* Blackburne, 1 H. Bl. 162; Dean *v.* Keate, 3 Camp. 4; Dartnall *v.* Howard, 4 B. & C. 345; Doorman *v.* Jenkins, 2 Ad. & El. 256; Cairns *v.* Robins, 8 M. & W. 258; Wilson *v.* Brett. 11 M. & W. 115; Syred *v.* Caruthers, 1 E. B. & E. 469; Finucane *v.* Small, 1 Esp. 315; Cailiff *v.* Danvers, 1 Peake's N. P. 155.

SEC. 15. **Division of Bailments.** — The division of bailments made by LORD HOLT, in Coggs *v.* Barnard,[1] has been modified more than once. He arranged bailments under six heads, as follows: 1. *Depositum:* A bare naked bailment of goods delivered by one man to another to keep for the use of the bailor. 2. *Commodatum:* When goods or chattels that are useful are lent to a friend gratis to be used by him. 3. *Locatio rei:* Where goods are lent to the bailee to be used by him for hire. 4. *Vadium*, or Pawn. 5. *Locatio operis faciendi:* Where goods are delivered to be carried, or something is to be done about them, for a reward to be paid to the bailee. 6. *Mandatum:* A delivery of goods to somebody who is to carry them, or do something about them gratis.

In this work we have only to do with the fifth and sixth of these classes, and we need not inquire whether LORD CHIEF JUSTICE HOLT'S classification is correct, as MR. SMITH[2] has asserted, or incorrect, as SIR WILLIAM JONES attempted to prove.[3] We will consider these in their order.

SEC. 16. **Locatio Operis faciendi.** — Where goods are delivered to be carried, or something is to be done about them, for a reward to be paid to the bailee.

Where one man pays another for his labor or care, he has a right to expect that the labor or care will be bestowed according to agreement. When this is not done, he has a cause of complaint and a cause of action. It is evident that a man can buy his neighbor's attentive diligence just as he can buy his cloth or hire his labor or services; but, as LORD CHIEF JUSTICE HOLT said in Coggs *v.* Barnard,[4] the bailment may be made to "one that exercises a public employment, or to a private person." If goods are placed in the hands of those who profess skill, the bailor has a right to expect skill; if he places his goods in the hands of an amateur, he must not be surprised if he gets bad workmanship. The same rule evidently applies to those who profess the trade of carriers, and it is prudent in the law to have declared that when goods are

[1] Coggs *v.* Barnard, 1 Sm. L. Ca. 147, 4th ed.

[2] 1 Sm. L. Ca., 6th ed., 189.

[3] Jones on Bailm. 36. See also Story on Bailm. §§ 4–7.

[4] 1 Sm. L. Ca. 177, 6th ed.

placed in the hands of such persons, who are to be paid for their trouble, they "are bound to answer for their goods at all events." "The law charges this person *thus intrusted to carry goods against all events but acts of God and of the enemies of the king.*"[1]

SEC. 17. **Duty of Carrier Bailees.**—The demands of the law on, and therefore the liabilities of, common carriers are much in excess of those which belong to other bailees. Wherever circumstances will induce one man to trust another, there is evidently a necessity for more severe penalties in case of the breach of trust than if those circumstances had not existed, and it is upon this ground that the above distinction has been drawn between professed carriers of wares and those who are not so professed. If a man hold himself out for employment, there is an implication in his act that he is fit to do the work. We have seen that the duties of ordinary bailees do not extend beyond ordinary diligence and care,[2] the measure of which might be the care which a prudent owner would take of his own goods; but exceptional cases require exceptional rules, and it is upon that account that law has distinguished between the cases of bailment to innkeepers and common carriers, and the cases of bailment to ordinary bailees. In every case, however, where the bailee is to be rewarded for his diligence, he must use reasonable precautions and take prudent care. Thus in one of the above-mentioned cases a chronometer was sent to a watchmaker to repair. The watchmaker allowed the chronometer to remain in his shop, where his servant was in the habit of sleeping. The chronometer was stolen by the servant, and the watchmaker was held liable for the larceny. The decision in this case was upon the ground that the watchmaker, as bailee, had not taken reasonable care of the bailor's property, and this was

[1] See Bennett *v.* The Peninsular Steamboat Co., 6 C. B. 775. See also, as to liabilities of common carriers, Marklin *v.* Waterhouse, 5 Bing. 212; Gatliffe *v.* Bourne, 4 Bing. N. C. 314; Cairns *v.* Robins, 8 M. & W. 258; Wyld *v.* Pickford, 8 M. & W. 443; Raphael *v.* Pickford, 5 Man. & G. 551. See also 19 & 20 Vict. c. 60, § 17.

[2] Clarke *v.* Earnshaw, Gow, 30; HOLT, C. J., Coggs *v.* Barnard, 1 Sm. L. Ca. 177, cf. notes 193; Dansey *v.* Richardson, 3 E. & B. 144; 23 L. J. 217 Q. B.

proved by the fact that he had been more careful to secure the safety of his own. He had placed the watches belonging to himself in a place where they were inaccessible to the servant.

SEC. 18. **Mandatum** is a delivery of goods to somebody who is to carry them, or do something about them gratis.

A very strict construction of such a contract as against the bailee would be eminently unjust. Therefore, no action will lie for the non-performance of the contract, because it is a *nudum pactum*, as it is not founded on a valuable consideration. To allow mere promises to be a foundation of an action at law would be impolitic; but where, in pursuance of such a promise, an individual has undertaken some labor for another, or where he has begun the performance of his empty agreement, there is every reason in the world why he should be held liable for any wanton negligence in such performance or such labor. The goods were trusted to his keeping upon the understanding that they were to be restored, and if, through his culpable carelessness, the articles are wasted or destroyed, in fairness he ought to be held liable for the loss sustained by the owner.[1] The case of Coggs *v.* Barnard[2] decided this point. The declaration was for the damage *in transitu*, by the defendant's negligence, of goods belonging to the plaintiff, and it was held that when a man undertakes to carry goods safely and securely, he is responsible for any damage they may sustain in the carriage, through his neglect, though he was not a common carrier, and was to have nothing for the carriage. So in another case, where the owner of a horse sent it for the night to a neighbor, who turned it out after dark into his pasture-field, which was separated from another field by a fence which the owner of the neighboring field was bound to repair. The fence, however, had not been repaired, and, during the night, the horse fell from the one field into the other through one of the gaps, and was killed. In this case, it was held that the owner of the field into which

[1] Lengridge *v.* Dorville, 5 B. & Ald. 117; Wheatley *v.* Low, Cro. Jac. 668; Whitehead *v.* Greetham, 2 Bing. 464; Shilliber *v.* Glynn, 2 M. & W. 143.

[2] 1 Sm. L. Ca., 177, 6th ed.

the horse was turned, although a gratuitous bailee, might maintain an action against the proprietor of the neighboring field whose duty it was to repair the hedge, and recover the value of the horse.[1] It is evident, from the whole circumstances of the case, that a mandatary of animals is bound to feed and take care of them during the bailment. A gratuitous bailee is also bound, if he has undertaken the performance of anything, to use such skill as he possesses.[2]

SEC. 19. **Division of Bailments.** — For convenience, bailments may be, and have already been,[3] divided into three classes: *First*, those in which the trust is exclusively for the benefit of the bailor; *Second*, those in which the trust is exclusively for the benefit of the bailee; and, *Third*, those in which the trust is for the mutual benefit of the bailor and the bailee. The first of these includes the carriage of goods without hire, and the last the carriage of goods for hire. We will speak of these classes in their order.

[1] Rooth *v.* Wilson, 1 B. & Ald. 59.

[2] Wilson *v.* Brett, 11 M. & W. 113. See, with regard to what amounts to such an undertaking, office, or employment as will make a performance of its duties necessary, Elsee *v.* Gateward, 5 T. R. 143; Balfe *v.* West, 13 C. B. 466; Fish *v.* Kelly, 17 C. B. N. S. 194.

[3] 1 Sm. L. Ca. 224, 6th English ed.

CHAPTER II.

CARRIERS WITHOUT HIRE.

SEC. 20. **Duty imposed upon Bailees by Law.** — Certain duties of care and prudence are imposed by law upon those who undertake to carry the goods of another gratuitously, and who, in performance of that agreement, begin the work that they promised to do.[1] It is a necessity of a trust which has

[1] It is held that a mere mandatary is only liable for *gross* negligence. Stanton *v.* Bell, 2 Hawks (N. C.), 145; Anderson *v.* Foresman, Wright (Ohio), 598; Sadowsky *v.* McFarland, 3 Dana (Ky.), 205; Beardslee *v.* Richardson, 11 Wend. (N. Y.) 25; Tracy *v.* Wood, 3 Mas. (U. S.) 132; Bland *v.* Wormack, 2 Murph. (N. C.) 373; Tompkins *v.* Saltmarsh, 14 S. & R. (Penn.) 275; Kemp *v.* Farlow, 5 Ind. 462; McLean *v.* Rutherford, 8 Mo. 109; Nabb *v.* Lockhart, 18 Ga. 495; Lampley *v.* Scott, 24 Miss. 528; Connor *v.* Winton, 8 Ind. 315; Jourdan *v.* Reed, 1 Iowa, 135; Skelly *v.* Kohn, 17 Ill. 170; Storer *v.* Gowen, 18 Me. 174. But under this rule it must be understood that *gross* negligence is the omission of such care as other mandataries of common prudence are accustomed to take of the class of property intrusted to them; and the question as to whether he was negligent or not, is dependent upon the *kind* of property, and the degree of care usually exercised by men of common prudence in keeping it. Money requires a higher degree of care than most other articles of property, because of its currency; and diamonds, government bonds, &c., and other articles having a great special value, and which can be readily removed and converted, require a higher degree of care from the mandatary than articles of equal or even greater value, but which, by reason of their

been placed in a man in consequence of his representations or promises, that, when the property which is in trust has been

bulkiness, cannot be readily removed. Bland *v.* Wormack, *ante;* Tracy *v.* Wood, *ante.* But even where money and other property of a portable and equally valuable character are received by a mandatary, he is only bound to the exercise of that degree of care which men of ordinary prudence usually exercise under similar circumstances in reference to similar property. Monteith *v.* Bissell, Wright (Ohio), 410; Ulmer *v.* Ulmer, 2 N. & M. (S. C.) 489. In the case last cited, money was placed by A in B's hands to buy goods for A, in a distant town. Before B left home, he used A's money and his own to redeem property of a neighbor, which had been seized on execution, and on arriving at the place where the goods were to be bought for A, he sold some of his own property, and received the money for it, and as he was about buying the goods for A, the whole of his money was stolen from him. It was held that he was liable to A for the amount of money received from him, because he, by using the money, had changed his relation from that of a mandatary to a borrower. See, also, Graves *v.* Ticknor, 6 N. H. 537, where it was held that where money is delivered to a person to be delivered to another, but which he fails to deliver, he is liable in assumpsit therefor upon an implied contract to deliver the money to the person directed, or return it to the person from whom he received it. It would be both unwise and unjust to hold that a person who received no pay therefor, but nevertheless voluntarily, gratuitously assumed the responsibility of caring for or transporting the property of another, was under no obligation to exercise any special care in executing his voluntary trust. Having undertaken the trust, he assumes the duty of executing it with that degree of care and skill which men usually exercise under similar circumstances in reference to the same kind of property, and having reference to its character and value. Graves *v.* Ticknor, *ante;* Tompkins *v.* Saltmarsh, 14 S. & R. (Penn.) 275. The confidence induced by undertaking any service for another is a sufficient legal consideration to create a duty in the performance of it. Whitehead *v.* Greetham, 2 Bing. 464; Shilliber *v.* Glynn, 2 M. & W. 143; Wilkinson *v.* Coverdale, 1 Esp. 74; Beauchamp *v.* Powley, 1 M. & R. 38. In some of the cases, it is said that he is liable only for the loss of the property when he has been guilty of such *gross* negligence as is equivalent to fraud. Foster *v.* Essex Bank, 17 Mass. 500; Edson *v.* Weston, 7 Cow. (N. Y.) 278. And, where he omits to use the species of ordinary care before referred to, he becomes liable; and if he *uses* the property, although he replaces it in kind, from that moment he becomes liable for it as for money had and received, if he fails to execute the trust, whatever may have been the degree of care exercised as to the *substituted* property. Ulmer *v.* Ulmer, 2 N. & M. (S. C.) 489. This rule was adopted in a case where money was deposited with the clerk, by order of court, and he used it. The money having depreciated between the date of its deposit and the date at which it should have been returned, it was held that, as he was entitled to have the *same* money returned to him, the clerk was liable for its value at the time of its deposit with him. Mott *v.* Pettit,

placed in his hands, the law should give the owner some right to enforce the performance of the trust in a proper manner. And by the leading case of Coggs *v.* Barnard,[1] as we have seen, it was decided that the bailor had this right. The declaration in this case stated that the defendant had undertaken to remove several hogsheads of brandy from one cellar to another, and that in so doing, through the negligence of the defendant and his servants and agents, one of the casks was staved, and a great quantity of brandy was spilt. The verdict was for the plaintiff, and the defendant moved in arrest of judgment that the declaration was bad, because it did not allege that the defendant was a common porter, nor did it aver that he had anything for his pains. The court were, however, of opinion that the action lay. In giving judgment, LORD HOLT drew a clear distinction between the case in which such an agreement is executory, and the case in which it is executed. In 11 Hen. IV., 33, "the action was brought against a carpenter for that he had undertaken to build the

1 N. J. L. 298. But, except where the relation of the parties is changed by an express contract, or by the act of the mandatary, he is only liable for *gross* negligence in respect to the property intrusted to him. Dartnall *v.* Howard, 4 B. & C. 345; Shiells *v.* Blackburne, 1 H. Bl. 158; Beauchamp *v.* Powley, 1 M. & Rob. 38. But the term "gross negligence," in this connection, is not to be understood, as is intimated in some of the cases, to mean that the act of the mandatary must be such as to amount to a fraud, as in that case it would be virtually impossible to fix his liability, unless the courts resort to another refinement of reasoning, and hold, as was stated in the commencement of this note, that the omission of such care as other mandataries of common prudence exercise in the care of such property, is evidence of fraud. Indeed, the refinements formerly indulged in, in reference to *gross* negligence, have ceased to commend themselves to intelligent courts; and when a person fails to exercise, in reference to the property of another, which is in his possession for the purpose of being by him gratuitously delivered to another, such a degree of care as men of ordinary prudence would exercise under similar circumstances, in reference to the kind of property intrusted to him, he is guilty of a breach of an implied duty in respect thereto, and of such negligence as renders him liable for any injuries thereto, or its loss or destruction (Tracy *v.* Wood, *ante*) without reference to the question whether his act was such that it could be said to be fraudulent or not. Fellowes *v.* Gordon, 8 B. Mon. (Ky.) 415; Tudor *v.* Lewis, 3 Met. (Ky.) 378.

[1] *Ante*, p. 13.

plaintiff's house within such a time and had not done it, and it was adjudged that the action would not lie."[1] However, the court was agreed that if he had built the house, and done the work unskilfully, an action would have lain. The reason of such a distinction has been already pointed out,[2] and is as easily appreciated as it is eminently satisfactory.

SEC. 21. **Gratuitous Bailee or Carrier without Hire chargeable for Gross Neglect.** — From this case it is evident that a gratuitous bailee, as a carrier without hire, is chargeable for gross negligence ; and it has been advanced that he ought to be held liable for negligence which may not deserve that name, it being argued that the contract[3] into which he has impliedly entered should necessitate his performance of the duties involved with the ordinary diligence which a man bestows upon his own business matters ; and it has been asserted that a general impression in favor of this view has tended towards the opinion — the prevalence of which is on the increase — that gross negligence is only negligence with a vituperative epithet added to it.[4]

SEC. 22. **Reason of the Distinction.** — There still seems to be some meaning in the distinction. That services which are not paid for are generally worthless, is a belief in the minds of many men. It seems to be a piece of practical wisdom to understand that if you want a thing, you must pay for it. It matters not whether it be talent or tallow, skill or skins. Nothing for nothing is the rule of business. If, in spite of such a belief, emphasized, as it must be, by the knowledge of the ordinary experience of mankind, a man trusts his property to another to be carried to a certain place, he surely ought to be satisfied with a modified care of his goods, as he saves the remuneration he would have paid to a common carrier. When a man has the means of being fully warned of the possible insecurity of a trust, and he still enters into it, there seem many reasons why law should not strengthen the securities in favor of the person trusting, and increase the liabili-

[1] 1 Sm. L. Ca. 191, 6th ed.

[2] *Ante*, p. 13.

[3] See Story on Bailm., p. 4, § 2, n.

[4] ROLFE, B., Wilson *v.* Brett, 11 M. & W. 115 ; Tudor *v.* Lewis, 3 Met. (Ky.) 378.

ties of the trustee. And, at the same time, there can be no question that a person having undertaken, out of good-will, to carry a neighbor's goods, and having actually entered upon the performance of his promise, is bound to use care in that performance, and that, in the event of gross negligence, he should be held liable to reimburse the bailor for the loss which his thoughtless imprudence has occasioned.[1] By his representations, or his accession to the wishes of his neighbor, he has led him to repose a confidence in him; he has induced him to believe, not only by his words, but by his acts, in undertaking what he promised, that he would actually accomplish what he undertook. If he does this — if he pays any attention to the duty which he has created to insure its faithful performance, perhaps that is all that the owner has a right to expect; and if, in spite of this minor degree of care, the property is injured, the gratuitous bailee would not be held liable. This proposition is true, whether — as in the case of Coggs *v.* Barnard — there is an undertaking to lay the goods down *safely*, or there is simply an undertaking to keep and carry the goods, although, in LORD HOLT'S judgment, there is a distinction drawn between two such agreements.

SEC. 23. **Gross Negligence, what it is. — Degrees of Attention. — Degrees of Negligence generally a Question for a Jury.** — Gross negligence is only negligence of an exaggerated kind. As negligence is constituted by a certain condition of mind, it is evident that it may exist in very many different degrees. The attention which a man pays to what is going on around him varies from what has been called "rapt attention," to the absolute inattention of reverie. And so does negligence vary in the inverse ratio to attention. A man's whole thoughts may be fixed upon some labor, or his whole thoughts may be turned entirely away from what his hands have found to do. The former properly deserves the name of extraordinary diligence, — the latter of gross negligence. In many cases it can be decided by a judge whether there has been gross negligence; in most, the question can be more

[1] Shiells *v.* Blackburne, 1 H. Bl. 159.

satisfactorily answered by a jury. In the case of Doorman *v.* Jenkins,[1] MR. JUSTICE TAUNTON said that gross negligence was "a great and exaggerated degree of negligence, as distinguished from negligence of a lower degree." The circumstances of this case illustrate the definition. It was an action against a gratuitous bailee of money. The defendant was a coffee-house keeper, and he made the following statement: that he had put the money of which he was the bailee into his cash-box, with a larger sum of his own. The box was kept in the tap-room, which had a bar in it. The tap-room was open on Sundays, but the rest of his house was not open on that day. The cash-box, with his own and the plaintiff's money, was stolen on that day. The judge left it to the jury to say whether there had been gross negligence, and he told them that the loss of the defendant's own money did not necessarily prove reasonable care. In this case there was an entire absence of proof of care. It was open to the defendant to show that the cash-box was in a place which most people would have thought secure. He might have proved that, although the tap-room was open upon Sunday, it was not generally frequented; or that he had taken some precaution for the safety of the box, by being in the tap-room the whole time it was open. But, in the absence of all such proof, the court refused to disturb the verdict of the jury, which was in favor of the plaintiff. It need scarcely be asserted that the terms "slight negligence," "ordinary negligence," and "gross negligence," have had a very definite connotation attached to them in courts of law by those judges who affirm a usefulness in the distinction between them. Indeed, all that we should desire would be, that the culpable negligence of gratuitous bailees should be judged of more leniently than the culpable negligence of those who undertake a similar work for hire. The many varying decisions in our courts prove that the usefulness of the distinction has, to some extent, been frustrated by the defective manner in which it has been appreciated. Thus, we find that CRESSWELL, J., in Austin *v.* Manchester, Sheffield,

[1] 2 Ad. & Ell. 256.

and Lincoln Railway,[1] says: "The term 'gross negligence' is found in many of the cases reported on this subject, and it is

[1] 10 C. B. 454. The distinctions which were formerly made in regard to negligence, and the recognition of three distinct *grades* of carelessness, namely, slight, ordinary, and gross, have been exploded; and in most of the States the simple question is, Was the defendant, in view of the circumstances, negligent? If so, he is liable; if not, he is not liable. Railroad Co. *v.* Derby, 14 How. (U. S.) 84; Steamboat New World *v.* King, 16 How. (U. S.) 474. CURTIS, J., in delivering the opinion in the latter case, said: "The theory that there are three degrees of negligence, described by the terms 'slight,' 'ordinary,' and 'gross,' has been introduced into the common law from some of the commentators on the Roman law. It may be doubted if these terms can be usefully applied in practice. Their meaning is not fixed, or capable of being so. One degree, thus described, not only may be confounded with another, but it is quite impracticable exactly to distinguish them. Their signification necessarily varies according to circumstances, to whose influence the courts have been forced to yield, until there are so many real exceptions, that the rules themselves can scarcely be said to have a general operation. In Storer *v.* Gowen, 18 Me. 177, the Supreme Court of Maine says: 'How much care will, in a given case, relieve a party from the imputation of gross negligence, or what omission will amount to the charge, is necessarily a question of fact, depending on a great variety of circumstances which the law cannot exactly define.' MR. JUSTICE STORY (Bailments, § 11), says: 'Indeed, what is common or ordinary diligence is more a matter of fact than of law.' If the law furnishes no definition of the terms 'gross negligence,' or 'ordinary negligence,' which can be applied in practice, but leaves it to the jury to determine, in each case, what the duty was, and what omissions amount to a breach of it, it would seem that imperfect and confessedly unsuccessful attempts to define that duty had better be abandoned. Recently the judges of several courts have expressed their disapprobation of these attempts to fix the degrees of diligence by legal definitions, and have complained of the impracticability of applying them. Wilson *v.* Brett, 11 M. & W. 113; Wyld *v.* Pickford, 8 M. & W. 443, 461, 462; Hinton *v.* Dibbin, 2 Q. B. 646, 651. It must be confessed that the difficulty in defining gross negligence, which is apparent in perusing such cases as Tracy *v.* Wood, 3 Mas. (U. S.) 132, and Foster *v.* The Essex Bank, 17 Mass. 479, would alone be sufficient to justify these complaints. It may be added, that some of the ablest commentators on the Roman law, and on the civil code of France, have wholly repudiated this theory of three degrees of diligence, as unfounded in principles of natural justice, useless in practice, and presenting inextricable embarrassments and difficulties. See Toullier's Droit Civil, 6th vol. p. 239, &c.; 11th vol. p. 203, &c.; Mackeldey, Man. de Droit Romain, 191, &c." As previously stated, the question now is, whether the defendant, in a given case, in view of all the circumstances, was negligent. Maynard *v.* Buck, 100 Mass. 40. And "gross" negligence, where the degrees of negligence, as stated above, are recognized, is held to be that entire want of care which

manifest that no uniform meaning has been ascribed to those words, which are more correctly used in describing the sort of negligence for which a gratuitous bailee is responsible, and have been somewhat loosely used with reference to carriers for hire;" and he refers to the words of LORD DENMAN, who, in giving judgment in the case of Hinton v. Dibbin,[1] said: "It may well be doubted whether between gross negligence and negligence merely, any intelligible distinction exists." These opinions, and others which have already been alluded to,[2] show that the distinction which has been spoken of as existing between gross negligence and negligence which is not gross, has not invariably found favor in the eyes of judges, and give some color to the opinion that the classification is useless. The mere fact, however, that a thing has not been used, does not prove that it is useless.

SEC. 24. **What constitutes Care or Negligence to be judged of in relation to Facts.—Illustration.**—It has already been pointed out that the question as to what is care or diligence, and what, consequently, constitutes negligence in any case, can only be determined by a reference to facts. Ordinary prudence tells

will raise a presumption of a conscious indifference to consequences. Southern Cotton Press, &c. Co. v. Bradley, 52 Tex. 587. Of course, in a given case, the circumstance that a gratuitous bailee took the same care of the property that he took of his own, of a similar character, may be sufficient to overcome the charge of negligence. Thus, if a bank receives a special deposit and places it in its vaults, where it keeps its own money and securities, it has been held not to be liable to the depositor, if its cashier fraudulently takes it away and converts it to his own use, unless it was guilty of bad faith. Smith v. Westfield Bank, 99 Mass. 605; Foster v. Essex Bank, 17 Mass. 479. But if a bailee violates his instructions in reference to the property (although he acted in perfect good faith), in consequence of which it is lost, he is liable therefor without reference to the question of diligence. Thus, where the plaintiff, who was upon the point of starting upon a long voyage, gave the defendant $1000, and requested him to purchase a government bond and keep it for him, for which service the defendant was to receive nothing, and the defendant, having kept the bond for about a year, without any directions from the plaintiff or his wife, sent it by mail to the plaintiff's wife, and it was lost on the way, it was held that he was liable therefor without reference to the question whether he had or had not used due diligence. See also Colyar v. Taylor, 1 Coldw. (Tenn.) 372, to the same effect.

[1] 2 Q. B., at p. 661; 2 Gale & D., at p. 43.

[2] *Ante*, p. 8.

a man that if he has undertaken the care of animals for another, he has at the same time undertaken the correlative duty of feeding them. Whether he is to receive remuneration for the care that he has, either expressly or by implication, undertaken to bestow, if he has become the bailee of cattle he is bound to see that they do not die of starvation. Men do not bail cattle that they may famish in the possession of another. So, if he has become the bailee of sheep or horses, he is bound not to allow them to stray and be lost.[1] Had that been the bailor's object in the bailment, he must have been insane; and no one but an insane bailee, or one who was grossly careless, could allow such an event to happen while the animals were in his possession. And so it is in every other case which could be put.

SEC. 25. **How the Amount of Care or Diligence is to be estimated.**—The kind and amount of the care to be taken, and the diligence to be required, is in the direct ratio to the necessity of such care and diligence, and to the probability of loss or damage to article which is bailed, in case of negligence. It must also necessarily depend upon the nature and value of the article,—to the circumstances of the times and place, as well as to the circumstances of the bailee.[2] Where

[1] But he is only bound to exercise ordinary care to prevent cattle from straying, even though he is an agistor. Rey *v.* Toney, 24 Mo. 600. And where a slave was delivered to the defendant to be kept by him upon trial, until he could determine whether he would buy him or not, and the slave was permitted to go a short distance from the house, and he ran away, it was held that he was not liable to the plaintiff for the loss of the slave. De Fonclear *v.* Shottenkirk, 3 John. (N. Y.) 170.

[2] In Jenkins *v.* Motlow, 1 Sneed (Tenn.), 248, money was intrusted to the owner of a steamboat by a passenger who paid no more than the ordinary fare.' There was a great crowd, and two boats lying near had just been robbed. The money was placed in a safe on the boat, and the safe was robbed, and the extra watchman employed about the boat was not produced as a witness to show the degree of care exercised by the boat-owner. It was held that the owner was liable as a mandatary, and that the evidence was sufficient to show such a want of ordinary care called for under the circumstances, as to sustain a verdict for the plaintiff. In Colyar *v.* Taylor, 1 Coldw. (Tenn.) 372, the defendant undertook gratuitously to receive for the plaintiff $1000 at a certain place, and to deliver it to him at another town where they both resided. After drawing the money he went to a pub-

a man undertakes a trust, fully believing that he will be able to perform the obligatory duties, and where circumstances occur contrary to all expectation, and, as it were, by the act of God, which render him unable efficiently to perform the work he has undertaken, there cannot be said to be any negligence upon his part. But this change may take place either in the circumstances of the individual himself, or in the circumstances of the article which was intrusted to him. If a man undertakes to carry an article of little or no value, without hire, upon the express understanding that it is worthless, and if subsequently, *in transitu*, through some unavoidable accident, he discovers that the article which he is carrying is an article of value, it would seem that it would be unjust to hold him liable for a want of care greater than that which his original contract necessitated. If, however, on the other hand, he undertook to carry a parcel, without inquiry as to its value, and without knowledge of its contents, and he subsequently became aware, through accident, that the value of the contents was considerable, he would properly be held liable for any want of care which was disproportioned to the danger of loss or injury. This was the case of Nelson *v.* Mackintosh.[1] The plaintiff's box was taken on board the "Arundel," of which the defendant was captain, at Trinidad. The plaintiff, who meant to work his way home to England on board ship, was accidentally left behind when the ship sailed, and soon after the departure of the ship the plaintiff's box was opened, upon the suggestion of the captain that there might be contraband goods

lic fair, where he met a neighbor who was going home before he was, and, stepping a little aside from the crowd, he gave him the money to carry to the plaintiff. While on his way home in a crowded car, the neighbor had his pocket picked, and the money was taken by the thief. The defendant was held liable, because he had violated his trust by delivering it to his neighbor, and was guilty of a conversion and gross negligence. So, too, it has been held that a gratuitous bailee of money which was lost while he was carrying it, while his own money was not lost, is liable for the loss, upon the ground that, at all events, the bailee is bound to exercise as much care in reference to such money as he exercises in reference to his own. Bland *v.* Womack, 2 Murph. (N. C.) 373; Delaware Bank *v.* Smith, 1 Edm. (N. Y.) Sel. Cas. 351; Anderson *v.* Forseman, Wright (Ohio), 598.

[1] 1 Stark. 237.

in it. When the contents were ascertained, the box was again closed and nailed down as before. Towards the termination of the voyage, however, the trunk was again opened, and the captain, in the presence of several passengers, put the contents into a canvas bag, which he deposited in his own chest, where his own valuables were generally kept. At Gravesend, the captain and one mate left the vessel when the river pilot was taken on board, and an excise officer and two young men belonging to the vessel were allowed to sleep in the cabin. The next morning the captain's chest, containing the valuables, was missing, and was not afterwards discovered. LORD ELLENBOROUGH, in his address to the jury, said: "Every person who delivers goods to another, to be carried for hire, has a right to the utmost care; the carrier stands in the situation of an insurer, and is liable for all losses except those occasioned by the act of God, or of the king's enemies; and where a person does not carry for hire, he is bound to take proper and prudent care of that which is committed to him;"[1] and he left it to the jury to say whether the captain had been guilty of negligence, telling them that as soon as he had discovered the valuable nature of the property he was bound to watch it with great care and diligence; and the jury, being of

[1] A bailee without reward, who receives money to transmit to a third person, is bound to perform his undertaking in good faith and with due diligence and attention adequate to the trust reposed in him. Where money was given to A to transmit to B, without reward, and, there being no bankers where he resided in Utah, he purchased a draft of the United States marshal upon the Treasury Department at Washington, with B's money and some of his own and of others uniting with him, in accordance with the usual method of transmitting money from that place, and the draft was refused payment, it was held that he was not liable. Eddy *v.* Livingston, 35 Mo. 487. Where one, as a bailee without hire, receives money to deliver to another, there is an implied contract that he shall deliver it, or return it, or account for it, in a reasonable time. If, in such case, the money is enclosed in a letter, and neither money nor letter is accounted for, a tort is not thereby proved so as to prevent the maintenance of assumpsit, but is merely evidence of gross neglect. Graves *v.* Ticknor, 6 N. H. 537. In the last case, it was held that assumpsit lay against the mandatary, but it must be upon the contract, as, except where an appropriation by him of the money is shown, an action on the common counts cannot be maintained. Beardslee *v.* Richardson, 11 Wend. (N. Y.) 25.

opinion that proper care had not been taken of the money, found a verdict for the plaintiff.[1]

SEC. 26. **Duties of Bailee relative to Nature of Article.** — In another case the duties of the bailee in relation to the value of the article are indicated. In this case the plaintiff intrusted a parcel to a carrier, who had given notice that he would not be answerable for parcels of value unless entered and paid for as such. The plaintiff, who was aware of the defendant's notice, delivered his parcel, which contained bank-notes to a large amount, without informing the defendant of its contents. The coach in which the box was conveyed from Berwick to Newcastle arrived in Newcastle at midnight, and stood for half an hour in a wide street. A porter was ordered to watch the coach, but this person was a considerable distance from it, and was so inattentive to his duty that the box was stolen. At the trial, BAYLEY, J., left two questions to the jury,—*viz.*, First, whether the plaintiffs dealt fairly by the defendants in not apprising them that the contents of the box were of value? Second, whether there was in the conduct of the defendants gross negligence? And it was held that the direction to the jury was right.[2] In this case the defendant was a common carrier, but it is quoted to show that the bailee ought in every case to proportion his care to the possible injury or loss which may be sustained by any improvidence or negligence upon his part, and, at the same time, to show that the negligence which makes him liable must be within the scope of the implied contract entered into at the time of the bailment.

SEC. 27. **The Amount of Care to be taken by Gratuitous Bailees.** — The measure, then, of the care which a gratuitous carrier of goods is to bestow, in order that, in case of loss or damage to the chattels bailed, he may be regarded as irresponsible for the injury or loss, is the care which a prudent man bestows upon similar work when undertaken on his own be-

[1] See Beauchamp *v.* Powley, 1 Mood. & Rob. 38.

[2] Batson *v.* Donovan, 4 B. & Ald. 21. See also Gibbon *v.* Paynton, Burr. 2298; Izett *v.* Mountain, 4 East, 371; Clarke *v.* Gray, 6 East, 564; Harris *v.* Packwood, 3 Taunt. 263; Bignold *v.* Waterhouse, 1 M. & S. 255; Bodenham *v.* Bennett, 4 Price, 31.

half. We have seen that the amount of care which a man takes of his own property will not be a standard by which, in all cases, we may judge of his duty as the bailee of the goods of another. For it is to be remembered that the loss of his own goods may be a comparatively trivial circumstance to him, while the loss of the bailed goods may be an irreparable injury to the bailor.

SEC. 28. **Another Criterion.** — Perhaps a better criterion would be the amount of care which ordinary bailees similarly circumstanced take of similar chattels.[1] It is certain that a man may be grossly negligent of his own goods, and if, through that gross negligence, he loses his own property at the same time that he loses that of which he is the gratuitous bailee, that loss would be no excuse in an action by the proprietor of the articles intrusted to him. The circumstances in all such cases require to be carefully considered. SIR WILLIAM JONES has put a case which is in some aspects not altogether satisfactory: "If Stephen desire Philip to carry a diamond ring from Bristol to a person in London, and he put it, with bank-notes of his own, into a letter case, out of which it is stolen at an inn, or seized by a robber on the road, Philip shall not be answerable for it, although a very careful, or perhaps a commonly prudent, man would have kept it in his purse at the inn, and have concealed it somewhere in the carriage. But if he were to secrete his own notes with peculiar vigilance, and either leave the diamond in an open room or wear it on his finger in the chaise, he would be bound in case of a loss by stealth to restore the value of it to Stephen." But is such a doctrine altogether satisfactory even in the case of a gratuitous bailee? May not the leaving the notes in the letter case arise from gross negligence? and does the loss of the bailee's own money prove the existence of sufficient care to exonerate him from liability to the bailor for the lost ring? If he was

[1] This was the rule adopted in Tracy *v.* Wood, 3 Mas. (U. S.) 132; Bland *v.* Womack, 2 Murph. (N. C.) 373; and Anderson *v.* Forseman, *ante;* the court, in these cases, holding that gross negligence is the omission of that care which bailees without hire, or other mandataries of common prudence, are accustomed to take of property of a like kind.

habitually a careless man, and Stephen, knowing this fact, trusts him with the ring, or if Stephen, without knowing anything about Philip, trusts him with the ring, which he wishes conveyed to London, then, perhaps, Stephen deserves to lose his ring. If, however, the whole of Philip's past life has held out the assurance to his neighbors that he is a prudent man, and if Stephen, being one of these neighbors, trusts Philip with the ring upon the strength of this knowledge of his character, then the leaving of the bank-notes, along with the ring in the letter case, ought, it seems, to be proved to be in conformity with the ordinary prudent conduct of the bailee, before it could be adduced as a ground for regarding him as irresponsible for the loss of the property. It has also been argued that this test, as to the care which is required from gratuitous bailees, is unsatisfactory, upon the ground that a man "might in respect of his own property be willing to encounter extraordinary risks or adventure upon mere gambling speculations, with a view to a particular advantage, or from a natural disposition to rashness, which would be entirely unjustifiable in respect to the goods of another put in his custody.[1] But this

[1] See Jones *v.* Matlow, 1 Sneed (Tenn.), 248; Colyar *v.* Taylor, 1 Coldw. (Tenn.) 372, where a higher degree of diligence than that named in the text was required. The rule is that if a mandatary undertakes the business submitted to him, he is bound to use a degree of diligence and attention adequate to the performance of his undertaking; and whether or not such diligence has been used, is a question for the jury. Kirtland *v.* Montgomery, 1 Swan (Tenn.), 452; Jones on Bailments, 62. This rule was adopted in Bland *v.* Womack, 2 Murph. (N. C.) 373. And a bailee who gratuitously undertook to carry money for the plaintiff, and lost it, while his own was not lost, was held liable therefor. See also, to the same effect, Anderson *v.* Forseman, *ante*, and Delaware Bank *v.* Smith, 1 Edm. (N. Y.) Sel. Cas. 351. See Monteath *v.* Bissell, Wright (Ohio), 598, where it was held that a gratuitous bailee who took as good care of the money intrusted to him as he did of his own, was not liable. But in Tracy *v.* Wood, *ante*, which was a case where the defendant undertook gratuitously to carry two bags of money, STORY, J., in charging the jury, said: "I agree, that in cases of bailees without reward, they are liable only for gross negligence. The language of the books as to what constitutes gross negligence, or not, is sometimes loose and inaccurate, from the general manner in which propositions are stated. When it is said that gross negligence is equivalent to fraud, it is not meant that it cannot exist without fraud. There may be very gross negligence, in cases where there is no pretence that the

scarcely seems an argument against the use of this test, for in every bailment the power of the bailee over the chattels bailed is limited by the definite objects of the trust,—the article has to be carried or kept. But if such acts as those indicated were not a contravention of the implied contract, then it is fairly to be presumed that the bailor may have trusted his property to the bailee, upon the ground of those very qualities which he constantly manifests with regard to his own property,—call it speculative energy or what you will. It is to be taken for granted that he who trusts knows something of the character of the person he trusts, and if he has done nothing to ascertain the trustworthiness of his bailee, he is himself guilty of a rashness which is as worthy of the punishment of the loss of his property as the speculative rashness of the bailee is worthy of the punishment of the loss of the value of the property bailed,—that is, under the supposition that the gratuitous bailee has not been guilty of gross negligence. In the case just supposed, the speculative ability may stand in the same relation to the bailment that skill does in other cases.

party has been guilty of fraud; though certainly such negligence is often presumptive of fraud. It appears to me that the true way of considering cases of this nature is to consider whether the party has omitted that care which bailees without hire, or mandataries of ordinary prudence, usually take of property of this nature. If he has, then it constitutes a case of gross negligence. The question is not, whether he has omitted that care which very prudent persons usually take of their own property, for the omission of that would be but slight negligence; nor whether he has omitted that care which prudent persons ordinarily take of their own property, for that would be but ordinary negligence: but whether there be a want of that care which men of common sense, however inattentive, usually take, or ought to be presumed to take, of their property, for that is gross negligence. The contract of bailees without reward is not merely for good faith, but for such care as persons of common prudence in their situation usually bestow on such property. If they omit such care, it is gross negligence" This was a bailment of money, of which, said the learned judge, much greater care is always taken than of other things. "He kept his own money in the same valise, and took no better care of it than of the plaintiff's. Still, if the jury are of opinion that he omitted to take that reasonable care of the gold which bailees without reward in his situation usually take, or which he himself usually took of such property under such circumstances, he has been guilty of gross negligence." Foster *v.* The President, Directors, and Co. of the Essex Bank, 17 Mass. 478.

And the bailee is bound, if he undertakes to do something requiring skill, to exercise whatever skill he possesses, or, at least, such an amount of skill as, by his profession, by his conduct, by his actions, by his ordinary business relations, he pretends to the public to possess.

SEC. 29. **Doctrine in Shiells v. Blackburne.**—This was made clear by HEATH, J., in Shiells *v.* Blackburne,[1] where he said: "If a man applies to a surgeon to attend him in a disorder, for a reward, and the surgeon treats him improperly, there is gross negligence, and the surgeon is liable to an action. The surgeon would also be liable for such negligence if he undertook gratis to attend a sick person, because his situation implies skill in surgery. But if the patient applies to a man of different employment or occupation for gratuitous assistance, who either does not exert all his skill, or administers improper remedies to the best of his ability, such a person is not liable. Although this argument is fallacious, it is still true that in many cases the care which a man will take of his own property would not afford a good criterion of the duty of diligence upon the part of a gratuitous bailee. And as we have said above, we would prefer to regard the amount of care which ordinary bailees similarly circumstanced bestow upon similar chattels, as a more accurate criterion of a bailee's duties and obligations.

SEC. 30. **Modification of Duties by Special Agreement.— Promises "to keep," and "to keep safely."**— But the character of the duties of a gratuitous bailee may be varied by the express words of the contract at the time the bailment was made. Notwithstanding what was said by LORD COKE in Southcote's Case,[2] there is a difference between the effects of two gratuitous promises,—the one to keep or carry goods, and the other to keep or carry them safely.[3] And there can be no reason why a man, if he contracts to take more care than that which is necessarily thrust upon him by the common law, should not be held liable for the breach of this contract. In the one case,

[1] 1 H. Bl. 159, at p. 162; Kuehn *v.* Wilson, 13 Wis. 104.

[2] 4 Rep. 84; Cro. Eliz. 815.

[3] Per HOLT, C. J., Coggs *v.* Barnard, 1 Sm. L. Ca., p. 183, 6th ed. See also Ross *v.* Hill, 2 C. B. 877.

therefore, the gratuitous bailee would be properly held liable only for gross negligence, while in the other an ordinary amount of negligence would make him liable to the owner of the chattel in case of loss or injury. On the other hand, there can evidently be no reason for holding that a carrier without hire may not stipulate for immunity from liability in case of damage or loss to the articles intrusted to him, although that loss or injury is occasioned by the grossest negligence upon his part. At the same time, no stipulation can do away with a bailee's liability in case the loss arises through his fraud, and it is also evident that no special contract of the parties at the time of the bailment can be binding if it is in defiance of morals or contrary to express legislative enactments.[1]

SEC. 31. **Duties of Bailee who promises to keep safely.** — In the case of Kettle *v.* Bromsall,[2] the distinction between the two promises made by gratuitous bailees referred to by LORD HOLT was well illustrated. There WILLES, C. J., said: "If the goods were delivered to be kept safely, though the defendant have been robbed of them, detinue will lie against him; for he must take his remedy against the thief or the hundred, as he can. But if the goods were delivered to the defendant to take care of them as his own proper goods,[3] &c., if he be robbed of them, that is a good plea."

Owing to various circumstances, actions at common law on the contract of mandate have been very few, and owing to this

[1] See 17 & 18 Vict. c. 31, § 7, and Wyld *v.* Pickford, 8 M. & W. 443; Hinton *v.* Dibbin, 2 Q. B. 646. With regard to the effect of conditions on liability of common carriers, Lord *v.* Midland Rail. Co., 36 L. J. C. P. 170; 2 L. R. C. P. 339; 15 W. R. 405; Rooth *v.* North-Eastern Rail. Co., 36 L. J. Exch. 83; 2 L. R. Exch. 173; 15 W. R. 695; 15 L. T. N. S. 624; Martin *v.* Gt. Indian Peninsular Rail. Co., 3 L. Rep. Exch. 9; 17 L. T. N. S. 349; 27 L. J. Exch. 27; Kirby *v.* Great Western Rail. Co., 18 L. T. N. S. 658; Pepper *v.* South-Eastern Rail. Co., 17 L. T. N. S. 469; Peninsular and Oriental Steam Navigation Co. *v.* Shand, 11 Jur. N. S. 771. By such a special acceptance, by a common carrier, or by a public notice to the effect that he will not be liable, he can place himself in the position of a private carrier for hire. See *post*.

[2] Willes, 118.

[3] Though even in such case the defendant is answerable for damage or losses arising from gross negligence. Mytton *v.* Cock, 2 Stra. 1099.

circumstance there are scarcely any decisions which enable one to form a satisfactory conclusion as to the common-law doctrine with regard to the rights of the bailee, as against the mandator, which arise out of the contract. MR. STORY, however, in his learned work upon the Law of Bailments, without endeavoring to discover how far the doctrines he states would be adopted by the laws of England or America, has given a clear statement of the civil law with regard to the obligations of the mandator.

First. *With regard to expense.* — If the mandator gives his goods to the bailee with a view to having something done to them, in the process of which the bailee must necessarily incur expense, he is bound to reimburse him; "for it can never be presumed that a gratuitous trust is designed to be a burden on the mandatary."[1] If, however, the expenses have been incurred wantonly, if they were unnecessary or in excess of what was necessary, if the necessity for the outlay arose from the gross negligence of the bailee, — from his fraud, or from an unwarranted departure from the duties imposed by the terms of the bailment, — they are not reimbursable.

Second. *With regard to indemnity for incidental contracts made by the mandatary.*[2] — A very similar principle is involved in this question. If, in the course of the performance of the duties imposed upon the bailee in the execution of the contract, he gives a bond to a third party on behalf of the mandator, the latter is bound to indemnify him therefor. If, however, anything in the original contract implied that the mandatary was to bear the expense, this obligation upon the part of the mandator would not arise. It is equally within the power of a man to undertake to pay money as to give labor.

Third. *With regard to the obligation of the mandator to indemnify the mandatary for any losses or injuries sustained by*

[1] Story on Bailm. § 197, p. 180; Domat, B. 1, tit. 15, § 2, art. 2, 3; Dig. Lib. 17, tit. 1, l. 10, § 9; Id. l. 27, § 4; Id. l. 12, § 9; Pothier, Pand. Lib. 17, tit. 1, n. 53, 54, 55, 56, 57; Pothier, Contrat de Mandat. n. 69, 78, 79.

[2] Story on Bailm. § 198, p. 180; Dig. Lib. 17, tit. 1, l. 45.

him in the execution of the trust. — If the proximate cause of the injury can be directly traced to the execution of the trust, then, by the civil law, the mandator was liable to the mandatary. If, however, the execution of the mandate was only the occasion of the injuries suffered by the mandatary, then the bailor was not liable.[1] The distinction between cause and occasion is of some importance. Thus, if a man asks his neighbor, who is about to travel from London to Newcastle, to carry some money for him to the latter place, and if, *in transitu*, the money with which he has been intrusted is stolen, together with his own, in such a case the mandator is not liable for the loss sustained by the mandatary. If, however, in order to perform the duties of a gratuitous bailment, the mandatary undertakes a journey through a part of the country which is infested with robbers, and whilst performing the journey he suffered some similar loss to that mentioned in the last supposition, in such a case, according to the civil law, the mandator would be liable. In the first case the mandate was only the occasion of the loss, in the second it is the cause. Similar cases are put by STORY; but he seems to overlook the fact that even in the first case, if the sum which the mandatary undertook to carry was so great as to excite the cupidity of robbers, — so great as to be bruited abroad, and to become well known, — the mandator would have been held liable to reimburse the mandatary for the loss he sustained. This shows that all the circumstances must be taken into consideration in deciding any such case. These are the principles upon which the Roman law decided questions in which the obligations of the mandatary arising out of the contract arose, and there seems every reason to regard it as probable that similar principles would guide the decisions of our judges in similar cases.

[1] Story on Bailm. § 200, p. 181; Dig. Lib. 47, tit. 2, l. 61, § 5; Pothier, Pothier, Pand. Lib. 17, tit. 1, n. 61; Contrat de Mandat. n. 75.

CHAPTER III.

CARRIERS FOR HIRE WHO ARE NOT COMMON CARRIERS.

SEC. 32. **Who are Private Carriers.** — *A person whose trade is not that of conveying goods from one place or person to another, may nevertheless, upon occasion, undertake to carry the goods of another, and receive a reward for so doing. Such a person is a private carrier.*[1] In this chapter we will consider

[1] An essential characteristic of a common carrier is that he holds himself out as such to the world, and undertakes generally, and for all persons indifferently, to carry goods and deliver them for hire, and that his public profession of his employment must be such that if he refuses to do so, without some just ground, for any one, in the course of his employment, and for reasonable and customary prices, he is liable to an action (3 Kent's Com. 597; Story on Bailm. § 495; Fish *v.* Clark, 2 Lans. (N. Y.) 178, affirmed 49 N. Y. 122; Allen *v.* Sackrider, 37 N. Y. 341); and a person who has never assumed or offered to carry goods of a certain class, *except upon special rates or terms exempting him from liability therefor as a common carrier*, is not, as to that class of property, a common carrier. Lake Shore, &c. R. R. Co. *v.* Perkins, 25 Mich. 329. As to such property, the carrier assumes only the relation of a private carrier; and such is the case in all instances where the carrier may take or refuse freight at his option, and only upon special rates or terms to be agreed upon. Thus the owner of a canal boat, used generally for transporting his own merchandise, entered into a contract with common carriers to transport a boatload of merchandise for them at an agreed price. The boat met with an accident on its way, on account of which, and without the fault or negligence of the defendants or their boat's crew, the boat and property were badly injured, and the latter partially lost. The court held that the defendants were not common carriers, and consequently could not be held chargeable for the loss of the goods. "*It is*," said the court, "*the business of carrying goods for others*, not a single act known to the consignor to be outside his usual em-

the liability of such carriers. We have seen that a mandatary is bound to exercise a certain amount of care in the execution

ployment, which fixes the liability of a common carrier." Fish *v.* Clark, 49 N. Y. 122. In Allen *v.* Sackrider, 37 N. Y. 341, PARKER, J., in delivering the opinion of the court, says: "The employment of a common carrier is a public one, and he assumes a public duty, and is bound to receive and carry the goods of any one who offers." He also quotes with approval MR. PARSONS's definition as to what constitutes a common carrier, as follows: "On the whole, it seems to be clear that no one can be considered a common carrier unless he has in some way held himself out to the public as a carrier, in such a manner as to render him liable to an action if he should refuse to carry for any one who wished to employ him." See Self *v.* Dunn, 42 Ga. 528. And it seems that any person who undertakes and holds himself out to carry for hire, without special contract, incurs the responsibility of a common carrier. Mass *v.* Bettis, 4 Heisk. (Tenn.) 661. In most of the States it is held that the owners of a tow-boat, who undertake to tow vessels and boats loaded with merchandise, are not common carriers as to such boats and merchandise. Caton *v.* Rumney, 13 Wend. (N. Y.) 387; Arctic Fire Ins. Co. *v.* Austin, 54 Barb. (N. Y.) 559; Varble *v.* Bigley, 14 Bush (Ky.), 598. But in Louisiana it is held that a tow-boat used in towing barges and water-crafts laden with merchandise is as much a common carrier of such merchandise as though it was laden on herself. Bussey *v.* Mississippi Valley Transportation Co., 24 La. An. 165. And a similar doctrine has been held in North Carolina. Walston *v.* Myers, 5 Jones (N. C.), 174. And in New Jersey (Ashmore *v.* Steam Towing, &c. Co., 28 N. J. L. 180) and in California (White *v.* Mary Ann, 6 Cal. 470) the courts intimate a tendency to adopt this view, although the question was not actually decided; while in New York (Wells *v.* Steam Navigation Co., 2 N. Y. 204), Pennsylvania (Brown *v.* Clegg, 63 Penn. St. 51; Taylor *v.* Campbell, 1 Pittsb. (Penn.) 459; Hays *v.* Millar, 77 Penn. St. 238; Leonard *v.* Hendrickson, 18 Penn. St. 40), and Kentucky (Varble *v.* Bigley, 14 Bush (Ky.), 428), it is held that they are not common carriers, nor subject to liability as such for injury to or loss of the vessels or property in tow; and such also is the doctrine of the United States Court (Transportation Line *v.* Hope, 95 U. S. 297). In Brown *v.* Clegg, 63 Penn. St. 51, READ, J., carefully reviewed the authorities, and said: —

"The common-law rule applies only to goods, and not to vessels or boats, to which it cannot be extended except by a forcible perversion of its terms and meaning. Towage by steam is a different and new business, to which should be applied the ordinary rules of bailees for hire; and this has been the clear understanding of the community in this State. In Leech *v.* The Owner of the Steamboat Miner, 1 Phila. (Penn.) 144, the action was for the loss of two boats loaded with coal, alleged to have been lost by the carelessness of the defendant, who had undertaken to tow them from the mines on the Monongahela to the landing at Pittsburgh. LOWRIE, J., charged the jury, 'that the owners of a tow-boat are not liable as common carriers for the safety of the boats and their contents which they undertake to tow.

of his gratuitous services, and that, should he prove grossly negligent, he will be liable to the mandator. But it would be

In the performance of the duty they are bound to exercise ordinary care and skill in directing their movements, and are liable if the accident arose from such want of care and skill.' In Leonard *v.* Hendrickson, which was the case of a raft taken in tow by a steamboat, HEPBURN, J., in the same court held that the owners of the boat were not common carriers. This case was taken to the Supreme Court, and there affirmed, and is reported in 18 Penn. St. 40. A very able opinion was delivered by CHAMBERS, J., considering the question upon reason and authority, rejecting the Louisiana doctrine, and adopting the New York rule as unanimously laid down by the Court of Appeals in Wells *v.* Steam Navigation Co., 2 N. Y. 207. In Hays *v.* Paul, 52 Penn. St. 134, the court below affirmed the defendant's point, 'that the owners of a steamboat employed in towing boats are not common carriers, and are only bound to take such reasonable degree of care and attention that the owner of the boat or raft towed shall incur no damage or loss through the negligence or default of the owner of such steamboat, or of his servant.' The case was tried and decided upon this principle, and affirmed by the Supreme Court. It appears, therefore, to be the settled rule in Pennsylvania that the owners of steam tow-boats are not common carriers. I am aware of the opinion of KANE, J., in Vanderslice *v.* The Steam Tow-boat Superior, in admiralty, in the District Court of the United States for the Eastern District of Pennsylvania, reported in 2 Am. L. J. N. S. 347, and in 13 Law Rep. 399. The learned judge agrees with CHANCELLOR KENT, and disagrees with STORY, J., and with the case in 3 Hill (N. Y.), 9, in holding steam-tugs common carriers. After stating various reasons for considering them common carriers, he says: 'These considerations urge us very strongly to hold the steam-tug to the rigid accountability of a common carrier; but I do not think it necessary to decide the question.' There is no date to this opinion; but as the libel was for damage done to a boat and her cargo in March, 1846, and as neither the case in 7 Hill (N. Y.), 533, nor that in 18 Penn. St. 40, is referred to, it must have been prior to the publication of those cases, the last of which would have had a controlling influence over the mind of the judge. In 1 Wharton's Dig. (6th ed. 1853) 203, under the head of Bailment, 1, *Common Carrier*, part 11, the digester, after stating the case of Vanderslice *v.* The Superior, as if it had been a positive decision that a steam-tug towing boats for hire was a common carrier, adds: 'This case was affirmed on appeal to the Circuit Court by GRIER, J., on the ground that there had been a want of ordinary care on the part of the steam-tug, but he declined to rule that she was a common carrier.' In the supplement of Wharton's Digest published in 1865, under the head *Bailments*, page 42, 'Who are Common Carriers?' '3. Steam-tugs are not liable as common carriers for the safety of vessels which they are towing, or of their cargo. Hinter *v.* Steam-tug Enterprise; Hinter *v.* The Steamer Napoleon, 3 Wall. (U. S.) 5.' It is clear the dictum of KANE, J., did not form the grounds of decision in the case before him, nor of any other case in the third circuit, so far as we know. The decisions on this

somewhat unreasonable only to expect the same amount of care in the case where the benefit to be derived from the bail-

point in the State courts and in those of the United States entirely harmonize. In Merrick *v.* Brainard, 38 Barb. (N. Y.) 574-585, the court say: 'One who contracts to tow a boat laden with merchandise for another is not a carrier, and does not assume, nor is he charged with, the duties and responsibilities of a carrier. Wells *v.* Steam Navigation Co., 2 Comst. 204. In the same case (4 Seld. 375) it was held that the owners of a tow-boat, in the absence of an express contract limiting their liability, are bound to exercise ordinary care and diligence, and are liable for the want thereof.' In the Court of Appeals, in Merrick *v.* Van Santvoord *et al.*, 34 N. Y. 208, this case was modified by reversing the judgment of the court below, as to the defendant Van Santvoord, who had been held liable as a mere stockholder in a Connecticut corporation, but affirming the judgment as against the defendant Brainard, upon the principle just stated. 'We have examined the questions raised by the appeal which affect the defendant Brainard, and think the judgment as to him should stand for the reasons assigned in the court below,' in which all the judges concurred. Betts, J., in Abbey *v.* Steamboat R. L. Stevens, 22 How. Pr. (N. Y.) 78, in the District Court of the United States for the Southern District of New York. The decision in The Princeton, 3 Blatchf. (U. S. C. C.) 54, by Nelson, J., one of the judges who decided the case of Alexander *v.* Greene, 3 Hill (N. Y.), 9, looks in the same direction, and can bear no other interpretation. In The Steamboat Angelina Corning, 1 Ben. (U. S. C. C.) 109, Benedict, J., of the United States District Court for the Eastern District of New York, held that a steam-tug is not a common carrier of the vessel she tows. In The Steamer New Philadelphia, 1 Black. (U. S.) 62, it seems to have been taken for granted in the District and Circuit Courts, and in the Supreme Court, that the steam-tug New Philadelphia was not a common carrier of the coal-barge she had in tow; and the ground of claim by the libellant for the damages to the tow was that they were occasioned by negligence and want of ordinary skill, care, and prudence on the part of those who were intrusted with the navigation of the tug. It may therefore be affirmed that by the law of Pennsylvania, and also of New York, as administered by the courts of those States, and by the courts of the United States in the second and third circuits, steam tugs or boats are not common carriers of the vessels they tow. The cases in England are generally in the admiralty, which has jurisdiction of towage, and which is often connected with salvage. In Symonds *v.* Pain, 6 H. & N. 709, which was an action by the owner of a smack against the owners of a steam-tug employed to tow his smack out of the harbor, for negligence of the master of the tug, by which the smack was stranded, the declaration was in the common form for negligence in towing the plaintiff's vessel out to sea. The defence set up was a special notice on the back of the printed receipts given by the defendants, exempting them from all liability for any loss or damage, whether arising from or occasioned by any supposed negligence or default of them or their servants, and the question was whether

ment is to be mutual, and therefore the law exacts what has been called ordinary diligence from a private carrier, and

the plaintiff had knowledge of this notice. The LORD CHIEF BARON expressed the opinion that the contract was upon the terms of the notice, and that it was evident the defendants did not undertake for the charge of seven shillings and sixpence to be insurers against accidents to the vessels they towed; and the plaintiff was then nonsuited. Upon a motion for a new trial in showing cause, defendants' counsel said: 'This is not the case of a common carrier. There was no common-law obligation on the defendants to tow the plaintiff's vessel, but the liability depends on contract.' BARON MARTIN said: 'I am of opinion that it was a question for the jury, what was the contract the plaintiff and defendants entered into, and that it was not a question of law for the judge to decide. Whether the plaintiff had knowledge of the notice by reason of having the receipts was essentially a question of fact, and ought not to have been withdrawn from the consideration of the jury.' A new trial was granted; and upon a second trial before ERLE, C. J., the learned judge left it to the jury to say whether the contract between the plaintiff and defendant was made on the terms printed on the back of the receipts, and, the jury having found in the affirmative, plaintiff elected to be nonsuited. In The Minnehaha, 1 Lush. 335, and in the Judicial Committee of the Privy Council, LORD KINGSDOWN said: 'When a steamboat engages to tow a vessel for a certain remuneration from one point to another, she does not warrant that she will be able to do so, and will do so, under all circumstances and at all hazards; but she does engage that she will use her best endeavors for that purpose, and will bring to the task competent skill, and such a crew, tackle, and equipments as are reasonably to be expected in a vessel of her class. She may be prevented from fulfilling her contract by a *vis major*, by accidents which were not contemplated, and which may render the fulfilment of her contract impossible, and in such case, by the general rule of law, she is relieved from her obligations. But she does not become relieved from her obligations because unforeseen difficulties occur in the completion of her task; because the performance of the task is interrupted or cannot be completed in the mode in which it was originally intended, — as by the breaking of the ship's hawser. But if in the discharge of her task, by sudden violence of wind, or waves, or other accidents, the ship in tow is placed in danger, and the towing vessel incurs risks and performs duties which were not within the scope of her original engagement, she is entitled to additional remuneration for additional services, if the ship be saved, and may claim as a salvor, instead of being restricted to the sum stipulated to be paid for mere towage.' In the cases on this subject the towage contract is generally spoken of as superseded by the right to salvage. In the case of The Julia, in the Judicial Committee of the Privy Council, 11 Moore P. C. 210, 1 Lush. 224, LORD KINGSDOWN said: 'When the contract was made, the law would imply an engagement that each vessel should perform its duty in completing it, that proper skill and diligence would be used on board of each, and that neither vessel by neglect or misconduct could create unnecessary risk to the other, or increase any risk which might be inci-

makes a private carrier responsible for ordinary neglect.[1] When, however, a man holds himself out to the public as a

dental to the service undertaken.' So, where a steam-tug, to avoid being crushed by collision, let go her tow and slipped out from between the two vessels, and dropped astern, 'it was admitted on all sides that this manœuvre was perfectly justifiable.' The Annapolis, P. C., 5 Law Times R. 38. It is clear from these authorities that steam tow-boats or tugs are not, by the law of England, common carriers of the vessels they tow. The cases in the United States which are supposed to express a contrary opinion are White *v.* Mary, 6 Cal. 462, October term, 1856, where JUSTICE HEYDENFELDT, delivering the opinion of the court, says: 'It is immaterial to consider whether the defendant was or was not a common carrier, although I think she was, according to the most striking analogies.' In Walston *v.* Myers, 5 Jones (N. C.), 174, JUDGE PEARSON said: 'We are inclined to the opinion that the defendants, John and Redding Myers, the owners of the steamboat, were common carriers, in respect to the plaintiff's flat they had in tow.' In Ashmore *v.* Penn. Steam Towing Trans. Co., 28 N. J. L. 180, one judge, upon a motion for a new trial, deemed it unnecessary to decide whether a tower was a common carrier. Another judge held, both upon principle and authority, that he was not a common carrier. A third seemed to be of the opinion that he was a common carrier; and the chief justice, who had tried the cause, and who had not charged the jury that the steamboat was a common carrier, concurred with the majority in dismissing the motion for a new trial. In Sproul *v.* Hemmingway, 14 Pick. (Mass.) 1, a brig which was towed at the stern of a steamboat, employed in the business of towing vessels in the river Mississippi, below New Orleans, was, through the negligence of the master and crew of the steamboat, over whom those in charge of the brig had no control, brought into collision with a schooner lying at anchor. It was held that the owner of the brig was not responsible for the damage sustained by the schooner. There is nothing in this case showing that the court regarded the steamboat as a common carrier; and this is remarkable because the case of Smith *v.* Pierce, 1 La. 349, in which the owners of steam tow-boats on the Mississippi were held liable as common carriers, had been decided in May, 1830, and published in 1831, two years before the decision of the Massachusetts case. Of the text-writers, Story on Bailm. 7th ed. § 496, says: 'The owners of a steamboat, who undertake to tow freight-boats for hire, or undertake to tow vessels in or out of port for hire, are not common carriers, but are responsible only for ordinary care, skill, and diligence in their undertaking.' And in 1 Parsons on Shipping and Admiralty, p. 247, it is said 'steam tow-boats are not generally considered common carriers in respect to the boats they have in tow.' The detailed examination we have made of the authorities upon this point shows conclusively that in Pennsylvania the law is definitely settled that steam tow-boats or tugs are not common carriers as regards the vessels they have in tow, and their cargoes.

[1] See *ante*, p. 8.

carrier by trade, or a common carrier, when those who trust him do it because he professes to devote his whole attention

There is nothing in any of the other specifications of error, and the judgment is therefore affirmed."

There is a class of cases in which the rule relative to common carriers has been apparently enlarged so as to embrace carriers who only incidentally exercise that employment; but upon examination it will be found that they do not essentially vary the rule. Thus, in Iowa, in Bruce *v.* Dubuque Street Railway Co., 53 Iowa, 278, 36 Am. Rep. 221, the proprietors of hacks used to convey passengers for hire were treated as being common carriers, and liable for injuries to passengers as such. In Sales *v.* Western Stage Co., 4 Iowa, 547, a similar doctrine was held as to stage companies transporting passengers from one point to another. But it is questionable whether hack proprietors can be regarded as common carriers strictly, unless by law, State or municipal, they are bound to transport passengers who apply to them, at certain rates fixed by law, or otherwise; nor indeed was it essential, in the case referred to, to hold them to be common carriers to bring them within the rule of liability stated in the case; nor is it directly held in the case that they are common carriers. But the court indirectly intimate that they are to be so regarded; but this doubtless is inadvertent, as they hardly come within the rule previously stated, as decisive of the question whether or not a person is a common carrier. The court doubtless intended to be understood that in the transportation of passengers they were under the same obligations as common carriers are, under the rule that a carrier of passengers is bound to exercise the highest degree of diligence in their transportation; but to hold that in any other respect hack proprietors are ordinarily subject to the duties and obligations of common carriers, is hardly believed to be accurate. In Gordon *v.* Hutchinson, 1 W. & S. (Penn.) 285, a wagoner who carried goods for hire was held to assume the responsibilities of a common carrier, whether it is his direct business or not; and, generally, the question as to whether such a carrier contracted as a common carrier is a question for the jury. Fuller *v.* Bradley, 25 Penn. St. 120. But it by no means follows, because in a given case the carrier has assumed the responsibilities of a common carrier, expressly or impliedly, that he is a common carrier within the technical meaning of the term. In all the cases a person is only regarded as *technically* a common carrier when he holds himself out as such, and places himself in such a position that he is bound to receive the goods of any person offering them for transportation, at the same rates that the same class of goods are transported for others, which is never the case where the carrier is at liberty in all cases to accept or refuse them at his option, and to make his own terms in every case. Fish *v.* Chapman, 2 Ga. 353; Jones on Bailm., 103, note (*d*), 3d London ed.; Jackson *v.* Rogers, 2 Show. 327; Fish *v.* Clark, *ante.* One of the distinctive tests for determining whether or not a person is a common carrier, and probably the decisive one, is, *whether he has consented to be bound as such.* By this, it is not to be understood that his assent to the taking upon himself of these onerous liabilities need be express, because it may arise as a necessary legal inference

and skill to the business of conveying goods, and because they naturally think that a man who does a thing often is more

from his acts, or may be imposed by statute, or may arise from the circumstance that he is licensed to act in that capacity, and is required to assume this relation as a condition to the granting of the license. "The liabilities of common carriers," says CAFER, J., in Varble *v.* Bigley, 14 Bush (Ky.), 698, "is upon contracts implied by law. No one can become bound by such contracts, *unless he has either consented to be bound in that character or has so acted as to justify the belief that he intended to be so bound.* Without actual consent or conduct from which it can be presumed, no one can become liable as a common carrier, any more than upon any other character of contract. The law applicable to them is extremely rigorous. It is founded in public policy and not in abstract justice." They are not permitted to shield themselves from liability by showing that they exerted the highest degree of care to avert the casualty. The law holds them in fault, however blameless they may show themselves to be, unless the casualty resulted from the act of God or the king's enemies. "When a person has assumed the character of a common carrier, either by expressly offering his services to all who will hire him, or by so conducting his business as to justify the belief on the part of the public that he means to become the servant of the public, and to carry for all, he may safely be presumed to have intended to assume the liabilities of a common carrier, for he was bound to know that the law would so charge him, and, knowing, must have intended it. But in order to impress upon him the character, and impose upon him the liabilities, of a common carrier, his conduct must amount to a public offer to carry for all who tender him such goods as he is accustomed to carry. When this is the case, then those who tender him goods to carry accept his offer, and he becomes bound to carry them; and if he refuses to do so, "having convenience," and being tendered satisfaction for the carriage, he is liable to an action, unless he has reasonable excuse for his refusal. Jackson *v.* Rogers, 2 Show. 327; Riley *v.* Horne, 5 Bing. 217; Cotton *v.* Frankland, 1 Ld. Raym. 646; 2 Kent's Com. 598.

This duty is inseparable from the character of a common carrier. By his conduct he induces the public to rely upon him to do their carrying. He is continually offering his services; and when his offer is accepted, he has no right to refuse performance. But when he has not held himself out in such way as to amount to an offer to carry for all shippers, no one has a right to depend upon him, or to demand that, as matter of duty, he shall carry his goods, and he may refuse, though he has room to spare, and his charge for carriage be tendered. If he is bound to carry for all who offer, then he is a common, a public, carrier, and whatever he receives as a common carrier, he is bound for in that character. The duty to receive and the liability to account are correlative, and a carrier must receive and transport in the same character. If he receives as a private carrier, he carries and is liable in that character, and that only; he is bound according to the tenor of his contract. If he receives as a common carrier, he carries and is liable in that character, unless he has contracted for a modified lia-

likely to do it efficiently and well than a man who does it only occasionally, then there is an implied contract that he will use his skill, and the law protects him only when the loss of or injury to the goods has been caused by the acts of God or the queen's enemies. At all events, he is bound to preserve them. He was applied to, and paid, that the owner of the goods might feel confidence that the goods would be safely delivered to the consignee, and his responsibility cannot be avoided by the proof of any amount of diligence upon his part. This distinction between carriers for hire who are not common carriers, and common carriers, is one of considerable importance. The latter, as it were, insures the safety of the goods either expressly or by implication; while the former, as being a bailee for valuable consideration, is bound only to use ordinary diligence, and avoid culpable neglect in his duties as carrier.

SEC. 33. **Ordinary Negligence.** — *Ordinary negligence is the absence of ordinary diligence; and ordinary diligence is that amount of care which a prudent man ordinarily takes of his own goods or his own business.*[1] The absence of this care,

bility. The result of this line of reasoning is, that *a carrier of goods is not liable as a common carrier, unless he was under a legal obligation to accept the goods and carry them, and would have been liable to an action if, without reasonable excuse, he had refused to receive them; and that he could not be liable to an action unless he had expressly and publicly offered to carry for all persons indifferently, or had, by his conduct and in the manner of conducting his business, held himself out as ready to carry for all.* See opinion of CAFER, J., *ante.* There is a class of cases where these rules have been ignored; but upon examination, it will be found that they were hastily decided, no reasons being given for the doctrine, and no authorities cited to sustain it. Thoughtful and intelligent courts are extremely careful in extending the law so as to embrace a class of persons who have not expressly assumed the character of common carriers, or, by their conduct and from the nature of their business, justified the belief on the part of the public that they intended to assume it; and CHIEF JUSTICE MARSHALL, in Boyce *v.* Anderson, 2 Pet. (U. S.) 150, well said: "Though to the extent to which the law has been applied we admit its necessity and its policy, we do not think it ought to be carried farther or applied to new cases."

[1] Ordinary care is such care as men of ordinary sense, prudence, and capacity would take under like circumstances in the conduct and management of their affairs, Shaw *v.* Boston, &c. R. R. Co., 8 Gray (Mass.), 45; Shrewsbury *v.* Smith, 12 Cush. (Mass.) 177, and has relation to the situation of the parties, the business in which they are engaged, and varies according

then, will, where it occasions loss or damage to the goods which have been placed in the hands of a private carrier with a view to their conveyance from one place to another, render him liable to the owner for such loss or injury. It follows, however, that the private carrier will not be liable if the goods which were under his care were taken from him by force. "If," says LORD ABINGER, C. B., "a man agrees to carry goods for hire, although not a common carrier, he thereby agrees to make good all losses arising from the negligence of his servants, although he would not be liable for losses by thieves or by any taking by force."[1] A distinction, however, is to be drawn between an open theft, which is effected by force, and a secret purloining. In the first of these the bailee is evidently relieved from all responsibility. The notoriety of the crime is sufficient proof that no vigilance upon the part of the bailee could have avoided the misfortune, any more than care upon his part could prevent a horse with which he is intrusted being killed by lightning. In the other case, however, where the theft has been accomplished by means of cunning, and not by means of force, there is a necessity for some proof upon the part of the bailee that he used the amount of care which a prudent man would use to protect his property from such casualties. Indeed, the fact that the goods have been stolen under such circumstances raises a presumption that the requisite amount of care has not been taken; and it is for the carrier to rebut this presumption if he can.[2]

to the circumstances, and must conform in degree to the circumstances under which it is to be exerted. Cunningham *v.* Hall, 4 Allen (Mass.), 268. And where the personal safety or life of a human being is concerned, a higher degree of vigilance is required than is required in other cases. Cazzer *v.* Taylor, 10 Gray (Mass.), 274. And the same sliding scale is applied to property, the degree of vigilance required varying according to the character and value of the property.

[1] Brind *v.* Dale, 8 C. & P. 207; 2 M. & R. 80.

[2] Hodgson *v.* Tullarton, 4 Taunt. 786; Montague *v.* Janverin, 3 Taunt. 442; Hatchwell *v.* Cooke, 6 Taunt. 576. This presumption exists also in cases where a passenger is injured by reason of the breaking of the machinery used in transportation. Yerkes *v.* Keokuk, &c. Packet Co., 7 Mo. App. 265; Eagle Packet Co. *v.* Defries, 94 Ill. 598; Lemon *v.* Chanslor, 68 Mo. 340. This presumption does not extend to all classes of property. Thus, where a horse in apparent good health was shipped on board a steamer, and was delivered in

SEC. 34. **The Loss of Goods raises Presumption of Negligence.** — That the loss of goods affords a *primâ facie* presumption of negligence and want of care will be evident from the two following cases. In the one, the declaration alleged that the plaintiff delivered to the defendant 3*l.*, to be carried to and delivered at the "Black Boy" Inn, in Southwark; that the defendant, in consideration of the premises, and "for that the plaintiff did undertake reasonably to content him for the carriage, promised safely to convey it thither and deliver it at the said inn to the plaintiff, but that he had not done so." It was held that the defendant, in that he had undertaken to carry the goods of the plaintiff to a certain place for hire, and had neglected to do so, was liable upon such a promise, although he was not a common carrier, and although no sum certain had been promised him as the price of the carriage.[1] In the other case, the defendant was a proprietor of cabs, and the plaintiff hired one of his cabs for the conveyance of himself and his luggage to the terminus of the Great Western Railway, at Paddington. On the arrival of the vehicle at the railway station, a portion of the plaintiff's luggage was found to be missing. It was held that the acceptance of the luggage by the cabman to be carried along with the passenger for hire implied a promise upon his part to carry "*safely and securely*," and that he was therefore liable for the portion of the luggage which was lost by the way.[2]

sick and dying condition, it was held that a recovery could not be had without showing some negligence on the part of the carrier, and that until such evidence is given the burden is not shifted upon the carrier to show that he was not in fault. The Sarragossa, 3 Woods (U. S. C. C.), 380. Nor does this presumption exist where the property has been delivered to the consignee some time before the injury or loss is discovered, and the injury or loss might have occurred after the delivery. Thus, in an action against a carrier to recover for a package of jewelry lost from a box, the loss not being discovered until after delivery to the consignee, but there was evidence that the box had been opened and the nails redriven, but there was no evidence as to the care taken of the box after its delivery down to the time the loss was discovered, it was held that the evidence was not sufficient to warrant a finding that the package was abstracted while in the carrier's possession. Canfield *v.* Baltimore & Ohio R. R. Co., 75 N. Y. 144.

[1] Rogers *v.* Head, Cro. Jac. 262.

[2] Ross *v.* Hill, 2 C. B. 877. See also Harris *v.* Costar, 1 C. &. P. 636; Dudley *v.* Smith, 1 Camp. 167; Cairns

It is clear, then, that the amount of care required from a private carrier for hire is what has been designated ordinary diligence; and, in many cases, it is a question entirely for the jury to answer, whether ordinary diligence has been used.[1] Thus, in the case of Beck *v.* Evans,[2] the defendant's wagoner was intrusted with a cask of brandy, to be carried for the plaintiff from Shrewsbury to London. Upon the way the wagoner was informed that the cask was leaking, and at the time he took no steps to ascertain the correctness of the information, or to stop the leak, if it existed. He remained three hours at Birmingham without doing so, and it was not until after he had passed through Wolverhampton that he took the cask out of the wagon and saved what remained of the brandy. The judge left it to the jury to consider whether the injury arose from the negligence of the defendant's wagoner in not examining the cask after he was informed of its leaky state. The jury found a verdict for the plaintiff. A rule to set aside the verdict, on the ground of misdirection of the judge, was moved for in the Court of King's Bench, but was refused, on the ground that the defendant was misconducting himself by not performing a duty which, by his servant, he was bound to perform.

SEC. 35. **Limitation of Liability.** — But we have seen that a special acceptance[3] may limit the liability of a carrier, and in this way, or by means of a public notice, to the effect that the carrier will not be liable, a great many common carriers become private carriers for hire, or occupy the same position to their employers as regards rights and liabilities.[4] Thus a common carrier becomes a private carrier for hire, and, in case of loss or damage to the goods of his bailor, he is liable only for gross neglect, and has satisfied the implied condition of the bailment if he has exercised ordinary care. Where the

v. Robins, 8 M. &. W. 258; Beauchamp *v.* Powley, 1 M. & Rob. 38; Mackenzie *v.* Cox, 9 C. & P. 632.

[1] Duff *v.* Budd, 6 Moore, 469; 2 B. & B. 177; Batson *v.* Donovan, *supra;* Beeford *v.* Crutwell, 5 C. & P. 242; 1 M. & Rob. 187.

[2] 16 East, 244.

[3] *Ante*, p. 25.

[4] Wyld *v.* Pickford, 8 M. & W. 446; Lake Shore, &c. R. R. Co. *v.* Perkins, 25 Mich. 329.

plaintiff had given the defendant, after a notice upon his part that he would not be answerable for any losses beyond the amount of *5l.*, a small box, containing plate of the value of *104l. 1s. 7½d.*, to be carried by the defendants' servants from Chester to London, the verdict was for the defendants; and when a new trial was moved for, the verdict was affirmed, on the ground that it is necessary to establish a case of gross negligence under such circumstances.[1] In another case, where the defendants were proprietors of carriages for the conveyance of goods upon a railway, and it was stated in the declaration that they had received nine horses of the plaintiff, to be safely and securely carried in their carriages by the railway for hire, and averred the loss of one of the horses by reason of the insufficiency of one of the carriages, it appeared that when the horses were received a ticket was given to the plaintiff, stating the amount paid by him for the carriage of the horses, and having at the bottom the following memorandum: "N.B. This ticket is issued subject to the owner's

[1] Lowe *v.* Booth, 13 Price, 329. See also Bodenham *v.* Bennett, 4 Price, 31, in which case the jury had found a verdict for the plaintiff for the full value of the parcel lost, on the ground that there had been gross negligence on the part of the defendant's servants. Smith *v.* Horne, 2 Moore, 18; 8 Taunt. 144; 5 B. & Ald. 57. But in such cases notice of the limitation must be given, or it will not be binding upon the shipper. Thus, where a traveller in a dimly lighted car delivered the check for his trunk to the agent of a baggage express company, taking, without reading it, a receipt designated upon the margin "domestic bill of lading," marked with the number of the check and place of delivery, and purporting to limit the carrier's liability, save in cases of special contract, to $100, and nothing was said as to the contents of the trunk, it was held that no contract upon the terms of the receipt arose as a matter of law from such acceptance, and that the plaintiff could recover the full value of the contents of the trunk. Madan *v.* Sherard, 73 N. Y. 329. Indeed, in all cases, in order to make such a restriction binding, it is incumbent upon the carrier to show that the condition was known or assented to by the consignor. Merchants' Despatch, &c. Co. *v.* Theilbar, 86 Ill. 71; Adams Express Co. *v.* King, 3 Ill. App. 316. But where the bill of lading or receipt containing the limitation is delivered *before* the goods are shipped, the shipper, by accepting such bill of lading without objection, will be treated as assenting thereto. Louisville, &c. R. R. Co. *v.* Brownlee, 14 Bush (Ky.), 590; Germania Fire Ins. Co. *v.* Memphis, &c. R. R. Co., 72 N. Y. 90; Morrison *v.* Phillips, &c. Construction Co., 44 Wis. 405.

undertaking all risks of conveyance whatsoever, as the company will not be responsible for any injury or damage (however caused) occurring to horses or carriages while travelling, or in loading or unloading." It was held that the terms contained in the ticket formed part of the contract for the carriage of the horses, and that the alleged duty of the defendants, safely and securely to convey the horses, did not arise upon that contract.[1] There has, however, been an alteration in the law since the decision of the case just quoted. The Railway and Canal Traffic Act of 1845,[2] enacted that companies are to be held liable for loss or injury of cattle, horses, goods, &c., "in the receiving, forwarding, or delivering thereof, occasioned by the neglect or default of such company, or its servants, notwithstanding any notice, condition, or declaration made and given by such company contrary thereto, or in any way limiting such liability; every such notice, condition, or declaration, being hereby declared to be null and void: Provided always, that nothing herein contained shall be construed to prevent the said companies from making such conditions with respect to receiving, forwarding, &c., the said animals, &c., as shall be judged by the court or judge before whom any question relating thereto shall be tried, to be just and reasonable." In the case of Allday *v.* The Great Western Railway Company,[3] a condition contained in a special contract, headed "Reduced Rates," that a railway company was not to be liable for any damage on the conveyance of cattle, from suffocation, or being trampled on or bruised, nor for any consequence arising from over-carriage, detention, or delay, however caused,

[1] Shaw *v.* York & North Midland Rail. Co., 6 Rail. Cas. 87; 13 Q. B. 347; 13 Jur. 385; 18 L. J. Q. B. 181. See also Austin *v.* Manchester, Sheffield, & Lincoln Rail. Co., 16 Q. B. 600; 15 Jur. 670; 20 L. J. Q. B. 440; Chippendale *v.* Lancashire & Yorkshire Rail. Co., 15 Jur. 1106; 21 L. J. Q. B. 22; Carr *v.* Lancashire & Yorkshire Rail. Co., 7 Exch. 707; 7 Rail. Cas. 426; 17 Jur. 397; 21 L. J. Exch. 261; Morville *v.* Gt. North. Rail. Co., 16 Jur. 578; 21 L. J. Q. B. 319; M'Cance *v.* London & North-Western Rail. Co., 7 H. & N. 477; 31 L. J. Exch. 65; Gannell *v.* Ford, 5 L. T. N. S. 604.

[2] 17 & 18 Vict. c. 31, § 7.

[3] 11 L. T. N. S. 267; 34 L. J. 5 Q. B. See also Maynard *v.* Syracuse, &c. R. R. Co., 71 N. Y. 180; Merchants' Despatch, &c. Co. *v.* Cornforth, 3 Col. 280.

was held to be unreasonable, and that as the injury to the plaintiff's cattle was the direct and proximate consequence of the delay, the defendants were liable in an action for the damage. So in a more recent case, in which the death of one of the cattle, which a railway company had undertaken to carry, was caused by the delay occasioned by the servants of the defendant company, the company was held liable for the injury and loss, notwithstanding that the servant of the plaintiff had signed a consignment note which was in the usual form, but which, among other conditions, contained one that the company would not be answerable for any consequences arising from over-carriage, detention, or delay in the conveying or delivering of the cattle in time for a particular market, however caused.[1] BARON MARTIN, in summing up, said: "As long as I can remember, and probably half a century before, there were always squabbles about carriers' notices. Railway companies continued these notices until they were put an end to by the Act.[2] If a railway company claims to make special conditions, they must make such as are reasonable as a whole." And the inference to be drawn from these cases, in so far as it concerns our present purpose, is, that *a common carrier may so far limit the extraordinary liability which the law imposes upon him, as to occupy the position of a private carrier for hire, by means of reasonable conditions which are known to the owner of the goods, and that in such a case a common carrier will be held liable for ordinary negligence.*[3]

[1] Kirby *v.* Great Western Rail. Co., 18 L. T. N. S. 658. But see Morrison *v.* Phillips, &c. Construction Co., 44 Wis. 405.

[2] 17 & 18 Vict. c. 31.

[3] Lake Shore R. R. Co. *v.* Perkins, 25 Mich. 329. There is now no question but that a common carrier may, by special contract, relieve himself from liability as a common carrier, and assume to the property transported the relation of a private carrier. Baltimore, &c. R. R. Co. *v.* Brady, 32 Md. 333; Shriver *v.* Sioux City, &c. R. R. Co., 24 Minn. 506; Ohio, &c. R. R. Co. *v.* Dunbar, 20 Ill. 623; Kimball *v.* Rutland & Burlington R. R. Co., 26 Vt. 247; East Tennessee, &c. R. R. Co. *v.* Whittle, 27 Ga. 535; Roberts *v.* Riley, 15 La. An. 103. But in a majority of the States it is held that they can impose no limitation which exonerates them from liability for loss resulting from their own want of care, or that of their servants, as such contracts are against public policy, and consequently void. School District *v.* Boston, &c. R. R. Co., 102

SEC. 36. **Assumption of Responsibility by Private Carrier.** — As a common carrier can, by express agreement, get rid of

Mass. 552; Hoadley *v.* Northern Transportation Co, 115 Mass. 304; Squires *v.* N. Y. Central R. R. Co., 98 Mass. 239; Evansville, &c. R. R. Co. *v.* Young, 28 Ind. 516; Penn. R. R. Co. *v.* Butter, 57 Penn. St. 335; Kallman *v.* U. S. Express Co., 3 Kan. 205; Seller *v.* Pacific R. R. Co., 1 Oreg. 409; Southern Express Co. *v.* Moon, 39 Miss. 822; Ashmore *v.* Penn. R. R. Co., 28 N. J. L. 180; Farnham *v.* Camden, &c. R. R. Co., 55 Penn. St. 53; Penn. R. R. Co. *v.* McCloskey, 23 Penn. St. 536; Indianapolis, &c. R. R. Co. *v.* Allen, 31 Ind. 394; Christenson *v.* Southern Express Co., 15 Minn. 270; Southern Express Co. *v.* Crook, 44 Ala. 468; Cleveland, &c. R. R. Co. *v.* Curran, 19 Ohio St. 1; Simon *v.* The Fung Shuey, 21 La. An. 363; Louisville, &c. R. R. Co. *v.* Brownlee, 14 Bush (Ky.), 590; Railroad Co. *v.* Lockwood, 17 Wall. (U. S.) 357; Express Co. *v.* Koutz, 8 Wall. (U. S.) 342. In other words, the rule generally adopted, and the one which seems best to accord with principle, good common-sense, and sound public policy, is that common carriers may protect themselves from liability as insurers, and for loss or injury in the transportation of property, which, in view of the nature of the property and the condition of the climate or country through which it is to be transported, is reasonable. "It is impossible," said LORD ELLENBOROUGH, in Lyon *v.* Mills, 5 East, 438, "without outraging common-sense, to allow carriers to say, 'We will receive your goods, but we will not be bound to take care of them, and will not be answerable at all for any loss occasioned by our own misconduct, be it ever so gross and injurious.' But they cannot, either by special contract or otherwise, absolve themselves from liability for loss resulting from their own want of reasonable care. This rule is well illustrated by an English case, — McManus *v.* Lancashire, &c. Rail. Co., 4 H. & N. 327. In that case a lot of horses were delivered to be forwarded by a cattle truck from Liverpool to York for reward, and the owner was required to sign a ticket containing a memorandum to the effect that the ticket was issued subject to the owner's undertaking all risk of conveyance, loading and unloading, as the company would not be responsible for any injury or damage, however caused, occurring to live-stock travelling upon the railway or in their vehicles, and the defendants' servants provided a truck which, in external appearance, and so far as the defendants' servants knew, was sound, and sufficient for the conveyance of the horses, but it was in fact unsound, and of insufficient strength for the purpose, and a hole was made in the bottom of the truck during the journey, and one of the horses got his leg through the hole and was injured, it was held that the railway was responsible for the damage done to the horse, notwithstanding the terms of the special contract signed by the owner of the horse. "We are of opinion," observes the court, "that the condition or special contract in this case is not just and reasonable. In order to bring the defendants within its protection, it is necessary to construe it as excluding responsibility for loss occasioned, not only by all risks of whatever kind directly incidental to the transit, but also for that caused by the insufficiency of the carriages provided by the de-

some of the responsibility which attaches to his trade by law, so a private carrier for hire can, by expressly warranting the

fendants, though occasioned by their own negligence or misconduct. The sufficiency or insufficiency of the vehicles by which the companies are to carry is a matter, generally speaking, which they, and they alone, have the means of fully ascertaining; and it would be unreasonable and mischievous if they were to be allowed to absolve themselves from the consequence of neglecting to perform properly that which seems naturally to belong to them as a duty. It is unreasonable that the company should stipulate for exemption from liability for the consequences of their own negligence, however gross, or misconduct, however flagrant; and that is what the condition under consideration professes to do. That condition is therefore void, and the case stands simply upon the ground that the plaintiff has employed the defendants to carry his horses safely, and that they have used an insufficient and improper vehicle for that purpose, whereby the horses have been injured." The rule in this case accords with the doctrine generally held in this country. Thus a common carrier may stipulate against liability for loss resulting from the breakage of goods transported by him; but he cannot exempt himself from liability for a loss resulting from a breakage occasioned by the negligence of himself or servants. Ketchum *v.* American Express Co., 52 Mo. 390; Missouri Valley R. R. Co. *v.* Caldwell, 8 Kan. 244. So he may reasonably stipulate against liability for loss from fire; but such a stipulation will not protect him from such a loss where the fire was caused by the negligence of himself or servants. Michigan, &c. R. R. Co. *v.* Heaton, 37 Ind. 448; York Company *v.* Central R. R. Co., 3 Wall. (U. S.) 107; Bankard *v.* Baltimore & Ohio R. R. Co., 34 Md. 197. And this is also the rule in those States where it is held that a carrier may by contract exempt himself from liability for injuries resulting from the negligence of his servants. Lamb *v.* Camden, &c. R. R. Co., 46 N. Y. 271; Caldwell *v.* New Jersey Steamboat Co., 47 N. Y. 282. And the same rule prevails as to carriers by water. They may by special contract exempt themselves from liability from the ordinary perils of navigation and transportation, but not from loss resulting from their negligence in navigating their vessel. Christenson *v.* American Express Co., 15 Minn. 270. And, generally, it may be said that a carrier may make any reasonable stipulation as to his liability for loss resulting during transportation; but all such contracts, being in derogation of the common law, are construed strictly, and will not be extended to cover a loss arising from any other or different cause than that specified. Thus it is held that a general exemption from liability for loss, "*from whatsoever cause arising*," does not, even in those States where it is held that the carrier may stipulate against loss arising from his negligence, extend to losses resulting from the negligence of his servants or agents, but that, in order to have that effect, the stipulation must be express and specific, or it will be treated as only exempting him from his liability as an insurer. Maynard *v.* Syracuse, &c. R. R. Co., 71 N. Y. 180. The words "at the owner's risk" in bills of lading only exempt the carrier from liability as an insurer, and do not exempt him from losses which

safety of the goods, assume the greater responsibility which devolves upon those who carry as a business or trade. Thus,

might have been prevented by the exercise of ordinary care and diligence. Baltimore, &c. R. R. Co. *v.* Rathbone, 1 W. Va. 87. The words "perils of the sea excepted," or "dangers of the river excepted," do not exempt the carrier from any of the perils within the scope of these phrases, if they could have been avoided by the exercise of ordinary care on his part. Williams *v.* Branson, 1 Murph. (N. C.) 417. Thus, if merchandise on board a vessel gets wet by accident, and the carrier makes no exertion to dry it, it has been held that such an exception does not save him from liability for the ensuing damage. Bird *v.* Cromwell, 1 Mo. 81; Ewart *v.* Street, 2 Bailey (S. C.), 157. So, where the goods were lost in consequence of the persons who were navigating the boat attempting to pass a dangerous bend in the river during a freshet, it was held that the loss could not be regarded as being within "the perils of the river." Williams *v.* Branson, *ante;* Spencer *v.* Daggett, 2 Vt. 92. But such exceptions save the carrier from liability from loss by accidents which are unavoidable, as where the boat is lost by reason of hidden obstructions newly placed in the river, such as human foresight could not discover or avoid; but if the carrier knew of the obstruction before the injury resulted, and failed to exercise a proper degree of vigilance to avoid it, he is chargeable. Gordon *v.* Buchanan, 5 Yerg. (Tenn.) 71. Where a common carrier stated in his bill of lading that he would not be liable for the breakage of goods in boxes, it was held that he was nevertheless liable for a breakage of the goods through the negligence of his servants. Reno *v.* Hagan, 12 B. Mon. (Ky.) 63. And it has been held that proof of injury to goods by breakage, under such a stipulation, is *primâ facie* evidence of negligence, and throws the onus upon the carrier of establishing the fact that the loss did not result from his negligence. Steele *v.* Townsend, 37 Ala. 247; United States Express Co. *v.* Backman, 2 Cinc. (Ohio) 251; Baltimore, &c. R. R. Co. *v.* Brady, 32 Md. 383; Lawrence *v.* New York, &c. R. R. Co., 36 Conn. 63. But in Adams Express Co. *v.* Lamb, 7 Bush (Ky.), 499, a contrary rule was adopted; and where the carrier stipulated that he should not be liable for a loss unless it arose from the fraud or gross negligence of the company, it was held that the plaintiff could not recover unless he proved that the loss arose from such fraud or gross negligence.

In some of the States, especially in New York, it is held that a carrier may, by special contract, exempt himself from liability for a loss arising even from his gross or wilful negligence. Maynard *v.* Syracuse, &c. R. R. Co., 71 N. Y. 180. And such ground was also taken in a West Virginia case. Baltimore, &c. R. R. Co. *v.* Rathbone, 1 W. Va. 87. But in both of these States such contracts are construed with the utmost strictness, and are not extended by inference to cover losses arising from the carrier's negligence, unless so expressly and in terms provided. Happily, too, as has already been stated, the great majority of our courts repudiate this doctrine, and entertain the idea that "sound public policy" should have some influence in the determination of questions of such vital importance to the vast commercial interests of the country,

where the plaintiff employed the defendant to carry goods, and the defendant said to the plaintiff at starting, "I will war-

and that common carriers, especially such as railroad companies, steamboat companies, &c., which derive all their power and vitality from the State, should not be permitted to place themselves in such a position that they can with safety divest themselves of all care in reference to the property transported, especially as to such property which, as common carriers, they are bound to transport. In England, by statute it is provided that a carrier cannot limit his liability by public notice or otherwise, except by contract; and in this country it is held that he cannot restrict his liability by public notice. Kimball *v.* Rutland & Burlington R. R. Co., 26 Vt. 247; Derwort *v.* Loomer, 21 Conn. 245. And it is now generally held, both in this country and in England, that the court is bound to look at the particular matter in each case, to see whether the condition is reasonable or not; and it has been held that a condition which seeks to relieve a railway company from the consequences of the loss or non-delivery of goods, by reason of insufficient or improper package, is not reasonable. Simons *v.* Gt. West. Rail. Co., 18 C. B. 830; 26 Law J.C. P. 25; LORD WENSLEYDALE, Peek *v.* North Staffordshire Rail. Co., 10 H. L. C. 473. And if the condition is framed without limitation or exception, so as to exempt the company from all responsibility for injury, however caused, it will be void, as being neither just nor reasonable. Peek *v.* North Staffordshire Rail. Co., *ante;* Gregory *v.* West. Mid. Rail. Co, 33 L. J. Exch. 155. But a condition qualifying their liability only — for instance, one annexed to the carriage of meat that the company will not be responsible for the loss of a market — is a reasonable one. Lord *v.* Midland Rail. Co., L. R. 2 C. P. 339.

In some of the States it is held that a common carrier, by a mere notice, cannot limit his liability as a common carrier, even though the notice is brought home to the knowledge of the shipper. Steele *v.* Townsend, 37 Ala. 247; Derwort *v.* Loomer, 21 Conn. 245; Hollister *v.* Nowlen, 19 Wend. (N. Y.) 234; Jones *v.* Voorhees, 10 Ohio, 145; Michigan Cent. R. R. Co. *v.* Hale, 6 Mich. 243; Southern Express Co. *v.* Newby, 36 Ga. 635.

In Railroad Co. *v.* Mfg. Co., 16 Wall. (U. S.) 318, this question was raised under the following circumstances: The plaintiff's agent delivered to the defendant a quantity of wool at Jackson, Mich., to be transported to the Mineral Springs Mfg. Co., at Stafford, Conn., and took a receipt for it as follows: —

MICHIGAN CENTRAL R. R. CO.,
JACKSON, Oct. 11, 1865.

Received from Wm. Bostwick, as consignor, the articles marked, numbered, and weighing as follows: —

(Here described.)

To be transported over said railroad to the depot in Detroit, and there to be delivered to ——, agent, or order, upon the payment of the charges thereon *and subject to the rules and regulations established* by the company, a part of which notice is given on the back hereof. — This receipt is not transferable.

HASTINGS, *Freight Agent.*

The notice on the back was as follows: —

"The company will not be responsible for damage occasioned by delays

rant the goods shall go safe," it was held that, although the defendant was "not a common carrier by trade, he had put

from storms, accidents, or *other causes . . .* and all goods will be at the risk of the owners thereof, *while in the company's warehouse, except such loss or injury as may arise from the negligence of the agents of the company.*"

Bostwick gave verbal instructions that the wool be sent from Detroit to Buffalo, by lake, in steamboats, which instructions were embodied in the bill of lading accompanying the wool. The wool reached Detroit and lay there *six* days, at the end of which time it was destroyed by an accidental fire, without fault on the part of the company. It was held by the court that while a company may limit its liability as a carrier by special contract, it cannot do so by a notice printed on the back of a receipt, though the receipt with such notice printed thereon may be accepted by the consignor without dissent. Kimball *v.* Rutland & Burlington R. R. Co., 26 Vt. 247. See also Moses *v.* Boston & Maine R. R. Co., 32 N. H. 323; Powell *v.* Myers, 26 Wend. (N. Y.) 591; Dwight *v.* Brewster, 1 Pick. (Mass.) 53; Cole *v.* Goodwin, 19 Pick. (Mass.) 251. But he may by such notice reasonably modify his liability. Sager *v.* Portsmouth, &c. R. R. Co., 31 Me. 228; Smith *v.* North Carolina R. R. Co., 64 N. C. 235. And by special contract he may restrict his liability. Michigan Central R. R. Co. *v.* Wood, 2 Mich. 538; Kimball *v.* R. & B. R. R. Co., 26 Vt. 247; Wallace *v.* Matthews, 30 Ga. 617; Ill. Cent. R. R. Co. *v.* Frankenberg, 54 Ill. 88; Thayer *v.* Alton, &c. R. R. Co., 22 Ind. 26; Hannibal R. R. Co. *v.* Swift, 12 Wall. (U. S.) 262. Thus a railroad company may restrict its liability to its own line, even though the goods are to be delivered to another line for shipment beyond. Chicago, &c. R. R. Co. *v.* Montfort, 60 Ill. 175; Detroit, &c. R. R. Co. *v.* Farmers', &c. Bank, 20 Wis. 122. And connecting lines are entitled to the benefit of the special provisions of the contract of shipment made with the first line. Babcock *v.* Lake Shore, &c. R. R. Co., 43 How. Pr. (N. Y.) 317; Maghee *v.* Camden & Amboy R. R. Co., 45 N Y. 514; Lamb *v.* Camden, &c. R. R. Co., 2 Daly (N. Y. C. P.), 454; Manhattan Oil Co. *v.* Camden R. R. Co., 54 N. Y. 197. But any such limitation is restricted to their liability as insurers, and does not excuse them from liability for loss or injury resulting from their actual negligence. Penn. R. R. Co. *v.* Butler, 57 Penn. St. 335; Stedman *v.* Western Trans. Co., 48 Barb. (N. Y.) 97; Evansville R. R. Co. *v.* Young, 28 Ind. 516; Farnham *v.* Camden, &c. R. R. Co., 55 Penn. St. 53; Ashmore *v.* Penn., &c. R. R. Co., 28 N. J. 180; Southern Express Co. *v.* Moon, 39 Miss. 822; Seller *v.* Pacific, 1 Oregon, 409; Mercantile Ins. Co. *v.* Chase, 1 E. D. S. (N. Y.) 115; Am. Trans. Co. *v.* Moore, 5 Mich. 368; Boorman *v.* Am. Ex. Co., 21 Wis. 152; Darr *v.* N. J. Steam Nav. Co., 4 Sand. (N. Y.) 174; York Co. *v.* Cent. R. R. Co., 3 Wall. (U. S.) 107; Harmony *v.* Bingham, 12 N. Y. 99; Parsons *v.* Monteath, 13 Barb. (N. Y.) 353. All such contracts are regarded as against public policy. Berry *v.* Cooper, 28 Ga. 543; Cincinnati, &c. R. R. Co. *v.* Pontius, 19 Ohio St. 221; Indianapolis, &c. R. R. Co. *v.* Allen, 31 Ind. 394; Michigan, &c. R. R. Co. *v.* Heaton, 37 Ind. 448; Farnham *v.* Camden, &c. R. R. Co., 55 Penn. St. 53; Lamb *v.* Same, 2

himself into the situation of a common carrier by his particular warranty."[1]

Daly (N. Y.), 454; York Manufacturing Co. *v.* Illinois Central R. R. Co., 1 Biss. (U. S.) 377; Union Mut. Ins. Co. *v.* Indianapolis, &c. R. R. Co., 1 Disney (Ohio), 480; Adams & Co. *v.* Reagan, 29 Ind. 21; School Dist. in Medford *v.* Boston, &c. R. R. Co., 102 Mass. 552; York Co. *v.* Ill. Cent. R. R. Co., 3 Wall. (U. S.) 107; Kansas Pacific R. R. Co. *v.* Reynolds, 8 Kan. 623; Reno *v.* Hagan, 12 B. Mon. (Ky.) 63. But *contra*, see Baltimore, &c. R. R. Co. *v.* Rathbone, 1 W. Va. 87. And the taking of a receipt limiting the carrier's liability, brought to the attention of the consignor, has been held binding as a part of the contract in the following cases: Ill. Cent. R. R. Co. *v.* Frankenberg, 54 Ill. 88. But the assent must be fairly established by showing full notice of the provisions of the receipt. Levering *v.* Union Transportation Co., 42 Mo. 88; French *v.* Buffalo, &c. R. R. Co., 2 Abb. (N. Y.) App. Dec. 176; Peck *v.* Weeks, 34 Conn. 145; Adams Express Co. *v.* Noak, 2 Duv. (Ky.) 562; Fillebrown *v.* Grand Trunk R. R. Co., 55 Me. 462. This question is ably discussed by BUSKIRK, J., in an Indiana case (Ohio, &c. R. R. Co. *v.* Selby, 47 Ind. 471), and the doctrine generally prevailing in this country ably stated. In that case the plaintiff sought to recover for personal injuries sustained by him while riding upon the defendants' road upon what is called a drover's or stock pass, upon which was an indorsement as follows: "In consideration of receiving this ticket I voluntarily assume all risk of accidents, and expressly agree that the company shall not be liable under any circumstances, whether by negligence of their agents or otherwise, for any injury to my person, or for any loss or injury to my property; and I agree that as for me, in the use of this ticket, I will not consider the company as common carriers, or liable to me as such. (Signed) George A. Selby." While riding upon this pass the plaintiff was injured by reason of the negligence of the defendants' servants; and in an action therefor the court held that he was not precluded from a recovery for such injuries, because of the stipulations in the contract.

"The question presented by the second paragraph of the answer is, whether the contract hereinbefore set out was sufficient to relieve the appellant from liability for the injury complained of. The appellant insists that by the terms of such contract she is exempted from responsibility for all accidents, including those occurring from negligence, at least the ordinary negligence of its servants. Is such a contract valid? This involves an inquiry into the law affecting the right of a railway company to exempt itself by special contract from the liability which ordinarily attaches to it as a common carrier of persons and property. There seems to be an irreconcilable conflict in the adjudged cases in England and in this country. We propose, therefore, to make a brief review of the leading cases, and classify them, so that it may be seen which sustain and which oppose the validity of the contract relied upon by appel-

[1] Robinson *v.* Dunmore, 2 Bos. & P. 416. See also Gibbons *v.* United States, Dev. C. C. 26.

SEC. 37. **Effect of continued Custody of Goods by Owner.** — A question arose in this case as to the effect which the pres-

lant. And we will, in the first place, examine the adjudged cases in this court. In Wright *v.* Gaff, 6 Ind. 416, it was held that a steamboat might, by special contract, be exempted from liability for injury resulting from ordinary negligence, but not for gross negligence. The ruling in the last case cited was referred to with approval in the case of The Indianapolis, &c. R. R. Co. *v.* Remmy, 13 Ind. 518.

"In the case of The Indiana Central R. R. Co. *v.* Mundy, 21 Ind. 48, Mundy was riding on a free pass, with conditions on the back, assuming all risks of personal injury, similar to the pass in the case at bar. The court in that case decided that Mundy did not assume any risks arising from acts of gross negligence, but approved the charge of the court below, 'that the railway company would not be liable except for wilfully gross negligence,' &c.; and in a note to that case, authorities are cited to sustain that ruling. The ruling in the above case was adhered to in the case of Thayer *v.* The St. Louis, &c. R. R. Co., 22 Ind. 26. The case of The Michigan Southern & Northern Indiana R. R. Co. *v.* Heaton, was decided by the late judges of this court at the May term, 1869. A rehearing was granted, not, however, upon the point under examination. In the case of The I., P., & C. R. R. Co. *v.* Allen, 31 Ind. 394, decided at the same term as the above case, the following reference is made to the ruling in such case: —

"'It is true that the language of the contract is broad enough to cover loss from any cause whatever; but in The Michigan Southern & Northern Indiana R. R. Co. *v.* Heaton, at this term, after a careful examination of the subject, this court came to the conclusion that a contract as broad in its terms as the one under consideration did not cover liability for loss occasioned by ordinary negligence. Indeed, it is held in that case that a common carrier cannot contract against liability for loss from his own ordinary negligence; that such a condition is void as against public policy.' The opinion of the court in that case is published in a note commencing on page 397. Such case, having been resubmitted and re-argued, came before the court as at present constituted, and will be found reported in 37 Ind. 448; s. c. 10 Am. Rep. 89. Upon the last hearing it was held that 'a common carrier cannot by contract relieve himself from liability for the loss of goods delivered to him for transportation, which has been occasioned by his own negligence, or that of his agents or servants, or where such negligence has in any degree contributed to such loss. A common carrier can no more stipulate for a slight degree of negligence than he can for gross negligence.' In the subsequent case of The Adams Express Co. *v.* Fendrick, 38 Ind. 150, the opinion of the court was delivered by the same judge who wrote the opinion in the case last cited. He says: 'The only question we need to consider is that presented by the ruling on the demurrer to the first paragraph of the answer. It will be seen that the loss is alleged to have occurred from one of the dangers of "river navigation," for which it was stipulated that the company should not be liable. Doubtless at common law, and independently of any contract to the contrary, the defendant, as a common carrier, would

ence of the plaintiff's servant, during the transit of the goods, would have upon the implied contract of the carrier. It is an

have been liable for the loss; a common carrier being regarded as an insurer against all casualties in the transportation of goods, except those arising from the act of God or the public enemy. But the great current of authorities has established the proposition that a common carrier may, by contract, limit the extreme liability which the law thus throws upon him. In the case of The Michigan, &c. R. R. Co. *v.* Heaton, 37 Ind. 448; s. c. 10 Am. Rep. 89, this court held that a common carrier might, by contract, exclude himself from liability for a loss not arising from or being contributed to by any degree of negligence on the part of the carrier, his servants or agents.' In many of the cases a distinction has been drawn between the degrees of negligence. In some it was held that a common carrier might contract against slight negligence, in others against ordinary negligence, and in a few against gross negligence. But the very decided tendency of modern decisions is to disregard this distinction.

"The Supreme Court of the United States, in the case of Railroad Company *v.* Lockwood, 17 Wall. (U. S.) 357; s. c. 10 Am. Rep. 366, uses the following language in reference to the degrees of negligence: 'The defendants endeavor to make a distinction between gross and ordinary negligence, and insist that the judge ought to have charged that the contract was at least effective for excusing the latter. We have already adverted to the tendency of judicial opinion adverse to the distinction between gross and ordinary negligence. Strictly speaking, these expressions are indicative rather of the degree of care and diligence which is due from a party and which he fails to perform, than of the amount of inattention, carelessness, or stupidity which he exhibits. If very little care is due from him, and he fails to bestow that little, it is called gross negligence. If very great care is due, and he fails to come up to the mark required, it is called slight negligence. And if ordinary care is due, such as a prudent man would exercise in his own affairs, failure to bestow that amount of care is called ordinary negligence. In each case the negligence, whatever epithet we give it, is failure to bestow the care and skill which the situation demands; and hence it is more strictly accurate perhaps to call it simply "negligence." And this seems to be the tendency of modern authorities. 1 Smith's Lead. Cas. 453, 6th Am. ed.; Story on Bailm. § 571; Wyld *v.* Pickford, 8 M. & W. 443; Hinton *v.* Dibbin, 2 Q. B. 661; Wilson *v.* Brett, 11 M. & W. 113; Beal *v.* South Devon Railway Co., 3 H. & C. 337; L. R. 1 C. P. 600; Philadelphia, &c. R. R. Co. *v.* Derby, 14 How. (U. S.) 486; The Steamboat New World, 16 How. (U. S.) 474. If they mean more than this, and seek to abolish the distinction of degrees of care, skill, and diligence required in the performance of various duties and the fulfilment of various contracts, we think they go too far, since the requirement of different degrees of care in different situations is too firmly settled and fixed in the law to be ignored or changed.'

"We do not mean to say that in no case does the distinction in the degrees of negligence exist. Such a distinction may exist in cases involving a question of contributory negligence.

evident principle, that *if the bailor does anything, while the goods are in the hands of the bailee, to conduce to their loss or*

We are now considering the degree of negligence that may be contracted against, and beyond that we decide nothing. We shall not attempt a review of the cases sustaining, or in conflict with, the recent decisions of this court, but will cite such cases.

"The following cases hold that a common carrier may be exempted from liability for a loss occasioned by ordinary negligence: Welles *v.* The New York Central R. R. Co., 24 N. Y. 181; Perkins *v.* The New York Central R. R. Co., 24 N. Y. 196; Smith *v.* The New York Central R. R. Co., 24 N. Y. 222; Bissell *v.* New York Central R. R. Co., 25 N. Y. 442; Poucher *v.* New York Central R. R. Co., 49 N. Y. 263; s. c. 10 Am. Rep. 364; Ashmore *v.* Pennsylvania, &c. Co., 28 N. J. L. 180; Kinney *v.* Central R. R. Co., 32 N. J. L. 407; Hale *v.* New Jersey, &c. Co., 15 Conn. 539; Peck *v.* Weeks, 34 Conn. 145; Lawrence *v.* The New York, &c. R. R. Co., 36 Conn. 63; Kimball *v.* Rutland, &c. R. R. Co., 26 Vt. 247; Mann *v.* Birchard, 40 Conn. 326; Adams Express Co. *v.* Haynes, 42 Ill. 89, 458; The Illinois Central R. R. Co. *v.* Adams, 42 Ill. 474; Hawkins *v.* Great Western R. R. Co., 17 Mich. 57; s. c. 18 Mich. 427; Baltimore & Ohio R. R. Co. *v.* Brady, 32 Md. 328; Levering *v.* Union, &c. Co., 42 Mo. 88. Many of the above cases were decided by divided courts. Some of them limit the exemption to cases of slight negligence, some of them to ordinary negligence, and a few of them extend the doctrine to cases of gross negligence.

"We now proceed to cite cases holding the opposite doctrine and fully sustaining the recent decisions in this court. Cole *v.* Goodwin, 19 Wend. 251; Gould *v.* Hill, 2 Hill (N. Y.), 623; Dorr *v.* The New Jersey Steam Nav. Co., 4 Sandf. (N. Y.) 136; Stoddard *v.* The Long Island R. R. Co., 5 Sandf. (N. Y.) 180; Parsons *v.* Monteath, 13 Barb. (N. Y.) 353; Moore *v.* Evans, 14 Barb. (N. Y.) 524; Laing *v.* Colder, 8 Penn. St. 479; Camden & Amboy R. R. Co. *v.* Baldauf, 16 Penn. St. 67; Goldey *v.* Pennsylvania R. R. Co., 30 Penn. St. 242; Powell *v.* The Pennsylvania R. R. Co., 32 Penn. St. 414; The Pennsylvania R. R. Co. *v.* Henderson, 51 Penn. St. 315; Farnham *v.* The Camden, &c. R. R. Co., 55 Penn. St. 53; American Express Co. *v.* Sands, 55 Penn. St. 140; The Empire Transportation Co. *v.* Wamsutta Oil Co., 63 Penn. St. 14; Jones *v.* Voorhees, 10 Ohio, 145; Davidson *v.* Graham, 2 Ohio St. 131; Graham *v.* Davis, 4 Ohio St. 362; Wilson *v.* Hamilton, 4 Ohio St. 722; Welsh *v.* The Pittsburgh, &c. R. R. Co., 10 Ohio St. 65; The Cleveland, &c. R. R. Co. *v.* Curran, 19 Ohio St. 1; The Cincinnati, &c. R. R. Co. *v.* Pontius, 19 Ohio St. 221; Knowlton *v.* The Erie Railway Co., 19 Ohio St. 260; Fillebrown *v.* The Grand Trunk Railway Co., 55 Me. 462; Sager *v.* Portsmouth &c. R. R., Co., 31 Me. 228, 238; School Dist., &c. *v.* Boston, &c. R. R. Co., 102 Mass. 552; Flinn *v.* The Philadelphia, Wilmington, & Baltimore R. R. Co., 1 Houst. (Del.) 469; Orndorff *v.* Adams Express Co., 3 Bush (Ky.), 194; Swindler *v.* Hilliard, 2 Rich. (S. C.) 286; Berry *v.* Cooper, 28 Ga. 543; Steele *v.* Townsend, 37 Ala. 247; Southern Express Co. *v.* Crook, 44 Ala. 468; Whitesides *v.* Thurlkill, 12 Sm. & M. (Miss.) 599;

damage, the bailee shall not be held liable for the injury which results directly from the bailor's conduct. Such a bailment is

The Southern Express Co. *v.* Moon, 39 Miss. 822; The New Orleans Mutual Insurance Co. *v.* The New Orleans, &c. R. R. Co., 20 La. An. 302.

"The ruling of the Supreme Court of the United States has been uniformly against the validity of all contracts to exempt a common carrier from liability for loss resulting from any negligence. The following are leading cases: The New Jersey St. Nav. Co. *v.* The Merchants' Bank, 6 How. (U. S.) 383; The Philadelphia, &c. R. R. Co. *v.* Derby, 14 How. (U. S.) 486; The Steamboat New World *v.* King, 16 How. (U. S.) 469; The York Company *v.* Central R. R., 3 Wall. (U. S.) 107; Walker *v.* The Transportation Co., 3 Wall. (U. S.) 150; Express Co. *v.* Kountze Brothers, 8 Wall. (U. S.) 342; New York Central R. R. Co. *v.* Lockwood, 17 Wall. (U. S.) 357; s. c. 10 Am. Rep. 366. The earlier English cases, such as Hinton *v.* Dibbin, 2 Q. B. 646, and Wyld *v.* Pickford, 8 M. & W. 443, were in entire accord with the decisions of the Supreme Court of the United States. But the later decisions, made between 1832 and 1854, held the opposite doctrine. See Carr *v.* The Lancashire Railway Co., 7 Exch. 707. This change of ruling is fully shown in the opinion of Mr. Justice Blackburn, in Peek *v.* North Staffordshire Railway Co., 10 H. L. C. 473.

"Parliament, in 1854, passed an act called 'The Railway and Canal Traffic Act,' declaring that railway and canal companies should be liable for negligence of themselves or their servants, notwithstanding any notice or condition, unless the court or judge trying the cause should adjudge the conditions just and reasonable. 1 Fisher's C. L. Dig. 1466. The condition written upon the back of the ticket given the appellee was in the following words: 'In consideration of receiving this ticket, I voluntarily assume all risk of accidents, and expressly agree that the company shall not be liable under any circumstances, whether by negligence of their agents or otherwise, for any injury to my person, or for any loss or injury to my property; and I agree that as for me, in the use of this ticket, I will not consider the company as common carriers, or liable to be as such.'

"The facts and principle involved in the case of Railroad Company *v.* Lockwood, *supra*, are very similar to those involved in the present case. The ruling there is an authority directly in point here. The facts of that case are thus stated: —

"'The plaintiff in this case was a drover, injured whilst travelling on a stock train of the defendant, proceeding from Buffalo to Albany, and the suit was brought to recover damages for the injury. He had cattle in the train, and had been required, at Buffalo, to sign an agreement to attend to the loading, transporting, and unloading of his cattle, and to take all risk of injury to them and of personal injury to himself, or to whomsoever went with the cattle; and he received what is called a drover's pass, certifying that he had shipped sufficient stock to pass free to Albany, but declaring that the acceptance of the pass was to be considered a waiver of all claims for damages or injuries received on the train. The agreement stated its consideration to be the carrying of the plaintiff's cattle at less than tariff rates. It was

intermittent. If a man has trusted his goods to another for a year, and during that time repeatedly has the goods in his own

shown on the trial that these rates were about three times the ordinary rates charged, and that no drover had cattle carried on those terms; but that all signed similar agreements to that which was signed by the plaintiff, and received similar passes. Evidence was given on the trial tending to show that the injury complained of was sustained in consequence of negligence on the part of the defendants or their servants; but they insisted that they were exempted by the terms of the contract from responsibility for all accidents, including those occurring from negligence, at least the ordinary negligence of their servants, and requested the judge so to charge. This he refused, and charged that if the jury were satisfied that the injury occurred without any negligence on the part of the plaintiff, and that the negligence of the defendants caused the injury, they must find for the plaintiff, which they did.' The court, after a very able review of the American and English authorities, uses the following language: 'It is argued that a common carrier, by entering into a special contract with a party for carrying his goods or person on modified terms, drops his character and becomes an ordinary bailee for hire, and, therefore, may make any contract he pleases. That is, he may make any contract whatever, because he is an ordinary bailee; and he is an ordinary bailee because he has made the contract.

"'We are unable to see the soundness of this reasoning. It seems to us more accurate to say that common carriers are such by virtue of their occupation, not by virtue of the responsibilities under which they rest. Those responsibilities may vary in different countries, and at different times, without changing the character of the employment. The common law subjects the common carrier to insurance of the goods carried, except as against the act of God or public enemies. The civil law excepts, also, losses by means of any superior force, and any inevitable accident. Yet the employment is the same in both cases. And if by special agreement the carrier is exempted from still other responsibilities, it does not follow that his employment is changed, but only that his responsibilities are changed. The theory occasionally announced, that a special contract as to the terms and responsibilities of carriage changes the nature of the employment, is calculated to mislead. The responsibilities of a common carrier may be reduced to those of an ordinary bailee for hire, whilst the nature of his business renders him a common carrier still. Is there any good sense in holding that a railroad company, whose only business is to carry passengers and goods, and which was created and established for that purpose alone, is changed to a private carrier for hire by a mere contract with a customer, whereby the latter assumes the risks of inevitable accidents in the carriage of his goods? Suppose the contract relates to a single crate of glass or crockery, whilst at the same time the carrier receives from the same person twenty other parcels, respecting which no such contract is made, is the company a public carrier as to the twenty parcels and a private carrier as to the one?'

"Again the court say: 'If the customer had any real freedom of choice, if he had a reasonable and practicable alternative, and if the employment of

possession, the liability of the bailee is not constant, and he can properly be held liable for the loss or injury only when

the carrier were not a public one, charging him with the duty of accommodating the public in the line of his employment, then, if the customer chose to assume the risk of negligence, it could with more reason be said to be his private affair, and no concern of the public. But the condition of things is entirely different, and especially so under the modified arrangements which the carrying trade has assumed. The business is mostly concentrated in a few powerful corporations, whose position in the body politic enables them to control it. They do, in fact, control it, and impose such conditions upon travel and transportation as they see fit, which the public is compelled to accept. These circumstances furnish an additional argument, if any were needed, to show that the conditions imposed by common carriers ought not to be adverse (to say the least) to the dictates of public policy and morality. The status and relative position of the parties render any such conditions void. Contracts of common carriers, like those of persons occupying a fiduciary character, giving them a position in which they can take undue advantage of the persons with whom they contract, must rest upon their fairness and reasonableness. It was for the reason that the limitations of liability first introduced by common carriers into their notices and bills of lading were just and reasonable, that the courts sustained them. It was just and reasonable that they should not be responsible for losses happening by sheer accident, or dangers of navigation that no human skill or vigilance could guard against; it was just and reasonable that they should not be chargeable for money or other valuable articles liable to be stolen or damaged, unless apprised of their character or value; it was just and reasonable that they should not be responsible for articles liable to rapid decay, or for live animals liable to get unruly from fright, and to injure themselves in that state, when such articles or live animals became injured without their fault or negligence. And when any of these just and reasonable excuses were incorporated into notices or special contracts assented to by their customers, the law might well give effect to them without the violation of any important principle, although modifying the strict rules of responsibility imposed by the common law. The improved state of society and the better administration of the laws had diminished the opportunities of collusion and bad faith on the part of the carrier, and rendered less imperative the application of the iron rule, that he must be responsible at all events. Hence, the exemptions referred to were deemed reasonable and proper to be allowed. But the proposition to allow a public carrier to abandon altogether his obligations to the public, and to stipulate for exemptions that are unreasonable and improper, amounting to an abdication of the essential duties of his employment, would never have been entertained by the sages of the law.

"'Conceding, therefore, that special contracts made by common carriers with their customers, limiting their liability, are good and valid so far as they are just and reasonable; to the extent, for example, of excusing them for all losses happening by accident, without any negligence or fraud on their part; when they ask to go still further, and to be excused for negli-

the goods are in his possession. There can be no carelessness in trusting an owner with his own goods. And it is only carelessness or want of thought which renders a bailee liable for negligence, and not the fact of the loss of the article intrusted to him, or the injury that is done to it. Thus, in a case where the defendant was a private carrier for hire, or a town carman, the plaintiff gave him certain goods to be taken care of, and safely carried from one wharf to another, it was proved that the plaintiff had agreed to go with the cart which was to carry the goods, and to look after them, as the driver had explained that he could not watch both the horse and the goods. Upon the arrival of the cart at its destination one of the parcels was missing, and the plaintiff, who had not followed the cart, brought an action for the loss of the package through the

gence, — an excuse so repugnant to the law of their foundation and to the public good, — they have no longer any plea of justice or reason to support such a stipulation, but the contrary. And then, the inequality of the parties, the compulsion under which the customer is placed, and the obligations of the carrier to the public, operate with full force to divest the transaction of validity.'

"In the above case, the court reached and stated the following conclusions of law: —

"'1. That a common carrier cannot lawfully stipulate for exemption from responsibility when such exemption is not just and reasonable in the eye of the law.

"'2. That it is not just and reasonable in the eye of the law for a common carrier to stipulate for exemption from responsibility for the negligence of himself or his servants.

"'3. That these rules apply both to carriers of goods and carriers of passengers for hire, and with special force to the latter.

"'4. That a drover travelling on a pass, such as was given in this case, for the purpose of taking care of his stock on the train, is a passenger for hire.'

"The recent case of Louisville, &c. R. R. Co. *v.* Hedger, 15 Am. Rep. 740, is in accord with the foregoing cases.

"We are of opinion that the facts stated in the second paragraph of the answer did not constitute a defence, and that the ruling of the court thereon was correct.

"The third paragraph of the answer proceeds upon the theory that the appellee was travelling on a free pass, and therefore the appellant was not liable. The only affirmative averment in this paragraph is, that appellee was travelling on a free pass. The other averments are denials of what the plaintiff was required to prove. But it is well settled that even in the case of a person riding on a free pass, common carriers of passengers are held to the same liability as for those paying fare. Pierce on Railways, 478, 483; Gillenwater *v.* The Madison, &c. R. R. Co., 5 Ind. 339; Indiana Central Railway Co. *v.* Mundy, 21 Ind. 48; Redf. on Railways, § 149, note."

negligence of the defendant's servant.[1] LORD ABINGER, C.B., in summing up, said: "The first objection that the defendant makes to the plaintiff's recovering in this action is that he is not a common carrier. My opinion is that the defendant is not a common carrier, and, if necessary, I will give leave to move to enter a non-suit on that point. The next point is whether the plaintiff delivered these goods to the defendant as a common carrier. Now a common carrier is in the nature of an insurer, and if he carries without any qualification of his liability, he becomes an insurer against all but fire, tempest, and the king's enemies, and he insures against thieves, and the frauds of his own servants. Still there are cases in which, although a person is not a common carrier, he is liable for the neglect of his own servants. I take it that *if a man agrees to carry goods for hire, although not a common carrier, he thereby agrees to make good losses arising from the negligence of his own servants, although he would not be liable for losses by thieves or by any taking by force;* or if the owner accompanies the goods to take care of them, and was himself guilty of negligence, — for it is a rule of law that a party cannot recover for his own negligence, — he was as much the cause of the loss as the defendant. It appears that the defendant lets out carts, which ply at different stands, and if, when his cart was let, the plaintiff agreed to go with the goods and watch them, it is manifest that he did not rely solely on the defendant's servant."

SEC. 38. **Rule in Whalley v. Wray.** — Doing negligently what it was not one's duty to do, will not be a ground of action. And the duty of each carrier is to be determined not only by the law, but by the circumstances which may modify the contract. The case of Whalley *v.* Wray[2] illustrates this point. This was an action in assumpsit against the defendant, as lighterman, for damage done to the plaintiff's goods, which had been intrusted to him to deposit in the plaintiff's warehouse. The declaration was in the common form, *viz.*, that the defendant, being a lighterman, &c., had undertaken to

[1] Brind *v.* Dale, 8 C. & P. 207; 2 M. & R. 80.
[2] 3 Esp. 74.

carry the plaintiff's goods, and to deliver them safely, and then averred a loss by negligence. The facts of the case were, that a quantity of rice had been delivered on board the defendant's lighter to be landed at the plaintiff's warehouse. Previous, however, to rice being permitted to be landed, it is necessary to present a petition to the commissioners of the customs, who refer it to the land-surveyor, upon whose report it is permitted to be landed. In this case a petition had been presented to the commissioners by Mr. Stevenson, who was the custom-house agent to the plaintiff; but no report having been made on it, the land-surveyor refused to permit the rice to be landed; in consequence of which it remained in the lighter undischarged, when it received the damage for which the action was brought. It appeared in evidence that the presenting the petition, &c., was usually done by the custom-house agent of the party to whom the rice belonged, and that it was not usually done by the lighterman. LORD ELDON said: "To entitle the plaintiff to recover, it must appear that the loss happened by the neglect of doing that which was the regular and common duty of the defendant. The law raises no presumption of what is his duty; that is a matter of evidence: here it is in evidence that the presenting the petition and the subsequent proceedings was the business of the custom-house agent of the plaintiff, not of the lighterman; if there had been any contract or undertaking on the part of the lighterman, by the neglect of which the goods were spoiled, it should have been the object of a special count; there is no such count, and the plaintiff has relied on the general liability of the defendant without making it out in evidence that it was the duty of the defendant to have done that from the neglect of which the loss has arisen."

SEC. 39. **Duty of Private Carrier enlarged by Terms of Contract.** — In a case already quoted for another purpose,[1] it was held that when a person sent goods by another person who said, "I will warrant they shall go safe," the individual who undertook to carry the goods safely was liable for any damage

[1] Robinson *v.* Dunmore, 2 B. & P. 416, *et supra.*

sustained by the goods, notwithstanding the owner sent one of his own servants along with the cart to look after them. CHAMBRE, J., in giving judgment, said: "It has been determined that if a man travel in a stage-coach and take his portmanteau with him, though he has his eye upon the portmanteau, yet the carrier is not absolved, but will be liable if the portmanteau be lost.[1] In this case the plaintiff, for greater caution, sends his servant with the goods, who pays for watching them because he apprehends danger of their being stolen. So the man who travels in a stage has some care of his own property, since it is more for his interest that the property should not be lost than that he should have an action against the carrier." This reasoning finds favor in the eyes of MR. POWELL,[2] who, in his work on carriers, makes use of MR. JUSTICE CHAMBRE'S illustration, and that upon the page opposite to that on which he quotes the dicta of LORD ABINGER in Brind *v.* Dale.[3] The opinion of MR. JUSTICE CHAMBRE, however, seems to be untenable, and his illustration was unfortunate. It is true that it may be more for the owner's advantage to keep his portmanteau than to have his cause of action against the carrier; but the fact that a thing is for a man's advantage does not go far to prove that he will do the thing. Ordinary experience every day proves that many men are grossly negligent of their own property, although it is certainly for their interest that they should exercise the greatest care. That being so, it would certainly be impolitic of the law to allow a carrier to be sued for the negligence of the owner of the property; and a recent case has shown that such is not the policy of the law. In that case the owner of a portmanteau, in travelling from Cheltenham to Reading by the Great Western Railway, took it with him into the carriage at Swindon. Having left the train for refreshment, he failed,

[1] So "it is no excuse for an innkeeper to say that he delivered the key of the chamber door to the guest, in which he is lodged, and that he left the chamber door open; but he ought to keep the goods and chattels of his guest in safety. And therewith agree 22 Hen. VI. 71; 11 Hen. IV. 41, 42; Edw. III. 11." Cayle's Case, 8 Co. 33.

[2] Powell on Carriers, p. 13, 2d ed.

[3] 8 C. & P. 207.

on returning, to find his carriage, and continued his journey in another part of the train. When the train arrived in London, the portmanteau was found in the carriage in which it had been placed at Cheltenham, but it had been cut open and the contents had been abstracted. In an action by the passenger against the company for the value of the articles, the jury found that there had been negligence on his part, but none on that of the company. It was held that the general liability of the company was, under the circumstances, modified by the implied condition that a passenger should use reasonable care, and that, as the loss was due to his neglect alone, the verdict was entered for the company.[1] So in another case, more nearly resembling that referred to by MR. POWELL, it was held that where the owner of a portmanteau allows his servant to carry it by train as his own personal luggage, the servant taking and paying for his ticket, and the owner travelling by a later train, he cannot, in case of the loss of the portmanteau, maintain an action against the company.[2] The true result of these decisions would seem to be that if the owner of the goods deliver them to the carrier in such a way that they are in the entire control of the carrier, the latter will be liable for them, even though the owner may exercise a certain supervision over their transport, and may, in the words of CHAMBRE, J., "have his eye upon them." But, on the other hand, if the owner goes by the same conveyance as his goods, and has them placed in such a part of the conveyance that they are in his entire control, and not in the control of the carrier, the duty of the carrier is modified, and in case of loss occasioned by want of reasonable care on the part of the owner, the carrier is not liable, as he cannot be said to have assumed any duty towards the owner.[3]

We have seen, then, that the liability of a private carrier may be increased by a special warranty, so that he becomes

[1] Great Western Railway Co. *v.* Talley, 19 W. R. 154; 23 L. T. N. S. 413, C. P.; s. c. Talley *v.* Great Western Railway Co., L. R. 6 C. P. 44.

[2] Beecher *v.* Great Eastern Railway Co., 22 L. T. N. S. 299; 18 W. R. 627; 5 L. R. Q. B. 241; 39 L. J. Q. B. 122.

[3] See Talley *v.* Great Western Railway Co., *ante*.

quoad a particular act a common carrier. We have also seen that a common carrier may, by entering into a modified contract, diminish his liability, and may relieve himself of any other duty than that which the law imposes upon a carrier for hire, who is not a common carrier. But it is further within the power of a private carrier for hire to modify the contract of bailment in such a way that, in case of loss or injury to the goods, he shall be held liable only in case such damage or loss has directly resulted from his gross negligence.[1] It is evident, from the very nature of bailment,[2] that as a man can intrust his property to another for a particular time, and for particular purposes, it must also be in the power of the parties to modify the terms almost infinitely, so long as neither the bailor nor the bailee attempts, by contract, to exempt himself from liability for his fraudulent acts, so long as the contract is not contrary to morals, or in defiance of legislative enactments.[3] This is evidenced by numerous decisions.[4] Other questions which might be considered in this place will be more conveniently treated of in another connection.

[1] Alexander *v.* Green, 3 Hill (N. Y.), 9.

[2] *Ante*, p. 2.

[3] *Ante*, p. 26.

[4] The words "safely and securely," when used in connection with a promise to carry goods or persons, are to be construed with reference to the promise implied by law from a bailee under certain circumstances. Thus, when used by a private carrier, they can only be considered to mean that he will use ordinary diligence. 2 Bl. Com. 452. When used by a common carrier, they mean that he will deliver the goods at all events, unless prevented by the act of God or the king's enemies. Ross *v.* Hill, 2 C. B. 877. Their meaning, therefore, depends on the relation between the parties.

CHAPTER IV.

WHO ARE COMMON CARRIERS.

SEC. 40. **The Duties of Common Carriers.** — We have already seen that the law imposes very onerous duties, and very considerable risks, upon a person who is designated a common carrier. As to his duty, he is bound by law to undertake the carriage of goods. Another man is free from any such duty until he has entered into a special agreement; but the law holds that the common carrier, *by the very fact of his trade and business, has, on his side, entered into an agreement with the public to carry goods, which becomes at once a complete and binding contract when any person brings him the goods, and makes the request that he should carry them to a certain person or place.* To make such a contract binding upon him as a common carrier, it is not necessary that a specific sum of money should be promised or agreed upon; but where that is not the case, there is an implied undertaking upon the part of the bailor that the remuneration shall be reasonable.[1] To make a person a common carrier, he must exercise the business as a public employment, and must undertake to carry goods for persons generally; he must hold himself out as ready to engage in the transportation of goods for hire, *as a business* and not as a casual occupation *pro hac vice.*[2] But a person may be a common carrier as to one class of property, and not as to another. Thus a railroad company, while a common carrier of most kinds of merchandise and property, is not necessarily a common carrier of money, and generally, in order to charge a person in a given case, as a common carrier, it must be shown that the usage of his business includes the goods carried, or that there was a special contract to carry them.[3] Thus, where a farmer undertook the carriage of goods to certain points at certain seasons of the year, but not at others, it was held that he did not necessarily assume the relation of a common carrier as to all contracts for the transportation of goods at other seasons, and under special circumstances;[4] and, generally, the question in all such cases, as to whether the person sought to be charged as such is a com-

[1] Citizens' Bank *v.* Nantucket Steamboat Co., 2 Story (U. S. C. C.), 16. In this case it was held that no person is a common carrier, within the meaning of the term, who is not a carrier for hire. "It is not necessary," says the court, "that the consideration should be a fixed sum; it is sufficient if it be in the nature of a *quantum meruit* inuring to the benefit of the owners. Nor is it necessary that the goods or property should be entered upon a freight list, or the contract be verified by any written memorandum."

[2] Samms *v.* Stewart, 20 Ohio, 69; Fish *v.* Chapman, 2 Ga. 349; Satterlee *v.* Groat, 1 Wend. (N. Y.) 272; Verner *v.* Sweitzer, 32 Penn. St. 208.

[3] Tunnell *v.* Pettijohn, 2 Harr. (Del.) 48; Powell *v.* Mills, 30 Miss. 231.

[4] Haynie *v.* Baylor, 18 Tex. 498. But see Chevallier *v.* Strahan, 2 Tex. 115, where two persons, whose usual business was farming, during certain seasons engaged in the business of hauling goods between certain places. The plaintiff employed them to haul a lot of cotton. They took the cotton, and while on the way some of the ropes broke, and the bales burst; and one night the wagon with the cotton was placed near the camp fire, and during the night was burned. It was held that they were liable as common carriers for the loss. But, according to the principal case, they would not have been liable if they had undertaken to transport the cotton by special agreement during a part of the season when they were not exercising this vocation. See also Harrison *v.* Roy, 37 Miss. 396.

mon carrier, is a question for the jury under proper instructions from the court.[1]

SEC. 41. **A Common Carrier is an Insurer at Law.** — As to his risk, we have already seen that a common carrier is regarded as an insurer at law,[2] and that consequently no amount of diligence or care upon his part will relieve him from the responsibility which, by the mere fact of his trade and the operation of the law, has devolved upon him. He is bound to deliver the goods at all events, and nothing but an act of God, or the violence of foreign foes, will excuse him from this imperative duty. That being the case, it is evidently a matter of the utmost importance to determine who are common carriers, as it is certain that in many cases much injustice would be done by regarding persons who had done nothing to hold themselves out to the public as persons acting in that capacity, as having assumed the duties and responsibilities of professional conveyers of goods; and, on the other hand, an equal amount of injustice might be done by failing to recognize those who had used inducements to make the public trust them with goods to be carried upon the strength in the belief in the insurance offered.[3] In the one case, to raise a private carrier to the position of a common carrier would, in case of loss or damage to the goods intrusted to him, be a gross injustice to him; in the other, to hold a man who had undertaken the duties of a carrier and an insurer as liable only in case of ordinary negligence would be as great a hardship to the proprietor of the damaged goods. The importance of arriving at a satisfactory decision on this point can scarcely be exaggerated.

SEC. 42. **The Meaning of the Phrase "Public Employment."** — According to LORD CHIEF JUSTICE HOLT,[4] a delivery to carry for a reward to be paid to the bailee "is either a delivery to one that exercises a public employment, or a delivery to a private person." Subsequently, the words "public employ-

[1] Gordon *v.* Hutchinson, 1 W. & S. (Penn.) 285.

[2] Forward *v.* Pittard, 1 T. R. 27.

[3] Citizens' Bank *v.* Nantucket Steamboat Co., 2 Story (U. S. C. C.), 16.

[4] Coggs *v.* Barnard, 1 Sm. L. Ca., p. 83, 6th ed.

ment" had a more definite connotation attached to them. In an early case it was decided that any person undertaking to carry for hire the goods of *all persons indifferently* is, as to the liability imposed, to be regarded as a common carrier.[1] In a more recent case it was held that if a person holds himself out to carry goods for every one as a business, he is a common carrier. ALDERSON, B., in summing up, said: "Every one who undertakes to carry for any one who asks him is a common carrier.[2] The criterion is, whether he carries for particular persons only, or whether he carries for every one. If a man hold himself out to do it for every one who asks him, he is a common carrier; but if he does not do it for every one, but carries for you or me only, that is a matter of special contract." [3]

[1] Gisbourn *v.* Hurst, 1 Salk. 249; Bac. Abr. (Carriers, A.).

[2] This is regarded as the test in this country; and a person who undertakes to carry goods or persons for hire, indifferently for all who may employ him, is a common carrier. Verner *v.* Sweitzer, 32 Penn. St. 208; Samms *v.* Stewart, 20 Ohio, 69; Fuller *v.* Bradley, 25 Penn. St. 120; Mershon *v.* Hobensack, 22 N. J. L. 372; Russell *v.* Livingston, 19 Barb. (N. Y.) 346. But he is only liable as such according to the usages of his business. Thus a person who confines his business to the carriage of money or of pianos, &c., is a common carrier only as to such goods. Tunnell *v.* Pettijohn, 2 Harr. (Del.) 48; Powell *v.* Mills, 30 Miss. 231. A horse-railroad company, which simply transports persons, is not bound to carry freight, nor can it be made liable for goods carried upon its cars, unless by usage it has been accustomed to do so, or unless it has specially contracted to do so; and the same is true as to the proprietors of stage-coaches. If they have made a practice of carrying parcels for hire, they become liable as common carriers therefor. Dwight *v.* Brewster, 1 Pick. (Mass.) 53; Robertson *v.* Kennedy, 2 Dana (Ky.), 430; Beckman *v.* Shouse, 5 Rawle (Penn.), 179. But the fact that the driver of a horse-car or of a stage-coach is shown to have been in the habit of carrying parcels for persons not passengers, does not necessarily charge the railroad company nor the stage company with liability therefor as common carriers. In order to have that effect, it must be shown that it was done with their knowledge or assent, express or implied. Sheldon *v.* Robinson, 7 N. H. 157. See as to the effect of the usages of a business upon this question, Harrington *v.* McShane, 2 Watts (Penn.), 44.

[3] Ingate *v.* Christie, 3 Car. & K. 61. In Pennewell *v.* Cullen, 5 Harr. (Del.) 238, it was held that a private carrier is one who, without being engaged in such business as a public employment, undertakes, in a particular case, to carry goods for hire, and that a person merely keeping a vessel for his own use does not become a common carrier by chartering her to a person by special agreement; and in all cases it

SEC. 43. **The Reason for the Distinction.** — The reason for such a distinction is easily appreciated. While a few acts may be undertaken by one who does not mean to prosecute the trade to which these acts properly belong, a great many acts undertaken, not at the request of particular individuals, but at the request of any indifferent person, shows that the person who does undertake thus to do a certain work is, to all intents and purposes, practising the business or employment which his conduct would lead a man of ordinary experience to suppose. The whole course of a man's life is often a much more secure promise of his future than a few words which may be forgotten as soon as they are spoken; and as the experience of mankind has taught them to rely upon the conduct of their fellow-men, any one who, by his acts, leads the public to suppose that he belongs to a certain trade or profession, is by law properly held to have assumed the duties and responsibilities of a member of the profession or trade to which he appears to belong. It is in each man's power to refrain from such a course of conduct as will impose these duties and liabilities upon him. If he does assume a certain position with his eyes open, he must fulfil the duties of that position, otherwise there would be injustice to the public.[1]

may be said that when a special contract is made with a common carrier *as to that transaction*, he becomes a private carrier. Moriarty *v.* Harnden's Express, 1 Daly (N. Y. C. P.), 227. In Allen *v.* Sackrider, 37 N. Y. 341, the owner of a sloop was specially employed to make two trips with her to carry grain. It was held that this was not sufficient to charge him as a common carrier. But the circumstance that a person usually transports goods only between certain points does not necessarily restrict his liability as a common carrier to the transportation of goods between those points when he specially undertakes to transport them beyond those points. Thus, where the defendants, who were common carriers between Newark and New York, agreed to carry a load of iron to Saugerties, which was a place *beyond* New York, it was held that they were common carriers for the whole distance. Tuckerman *v.* Stephens, &c. Transportation Co., 32 N. J. L. 320.

[1] Blossom *v.* Griffin, 13 N. Y. 369; Wilcox *v.* Parmalee, 3 Sandf. (N. Y.) 610. In Harrison *v.* Roy, 39 Miss. 396, a planter employed his wagons in hauling his crops to markets, and habitually loaded them with goods to be carried for hire on their return trip. It was held that by receiving such goods and receipting therefor, undertaking to deliver them in good order and without delay, at the customary charges, he became responsible as a common carrier.

SEC. 44. **Assumption of Duties of Common Carriers implies the Assumption of their Responsibilities.** — The case of Palmer *v.* Grand Junction Railway Company[1] throws light upon this subject. A railway company was incorporated by Act of Parliament,[2] with authority, if they should think fit, to carry goods and passengers on the railway; at the same time they were to be bound to keep the fences of the line in repair. The act also contained a clause that no action should be brought against them "*for anything done or omitted to be done in pursuance of that act*, unless fourteen days' previous notice in writing be given of such intention." The company undertook to carry some horses by the railway from Liverpool, and to deliver them safely at Birmingham, but in consequence of some of the fences being broken down, the train was overset by coming in contact with a horse which had strayed from a neighboring field, and one of the horses that the company had undertaken to carry was killed, and the rest were injured. The owner brought an action and declared against the company as common carriers. It was decided that although it was, in the first instance, optional with the company whether they should trade at all as common carriers, that, having elected to do so, and not having restricted their liability by any special contract, they were subject to the liabilities of carriers at common law, *viz.*, responsible for all losses which do not fall within the excepted cases of the act of God or of the queen's enemies; and it was also held that they were not entitled to notice of action when declared against as such. Whenever, therefore, an individual indicates, by his ordinary occupation, that he does carry goods or passengers for hire, and not simply by any casual acts he may have undertaken, he is, in so far as his duties and liabilities go, to be looked upon as a common carrier. But the question as to the kind of occupations which do imply a carriage of the goods of the public for hire is a question which it is sometimes difficult to answer.[3]

1 4 M. & W. 749; 7 Dowl. P. C. 232; 1 Horn & H. 489.

2 3 Will. IV. c. 34 (local and personal).

3 Harrison *v.* Roy, *ante;* Chevallier *v.* Strahan, *ante;* Witbeck *v.* Schuyler, 44 Barb. (N. Y.) 469; Wilcox *v.* Parmalee, *ante;* Haynic *v.* Baylor, 18 Tex.

SEC. 45. **Rule in Brind v. Dale.** — In Brind *v.* Dale,[1] it was held that a town carman, not conveying goods from any one known terminus to another, but plying for hire near the wharves, and undertaking jobs as he can get them, is not a common carrier. And in the same case, as we have seen,[2] it was held that the fact that the owner had promised to follow the cart in which his goods were being carried, and look after his baggage, made the delivery of the goods to the carrier a delivery of a modified nature, and not a delivery of goods to a common carrier. It is of course clear that, unless a person or company definitely holds himself or itself out to the public as a trader in the capacity of a common carrier, these liabilities cannot be imposed upon him or it. Thus, where a railway company posted up a list of tolls, including those taken for coals, at a particular station, such an advertisement was held of itself to be insufficient evidence of the alleged fact that the company held themselves out to the public as common carriers of coal from that station, or from any particular station.[3]

498; Hall *v.* Renfro, 3 Met. (Ky.) 51; Allen *v.* Sewall, 2 Wend. (N. Y.) 327. In the last case, a steamboat company, incorporated for the transportation of goods, wares, and merchandise, and made individually liable as common carriers, are not common carriers of packages of bank-bills, unless they make it a part of their ordinary business, and are not liable for loss of such packages intrusted to the master of the boat, if they had forbidden him to carry money, and he had never knowingly done it, and if the usage was for persons sending money to pay the masters, and for the steamboat company to charge freight only on specie. Sewall *v.* Allen, 6 Wend. (N. Y.) 335. Compare Citizens' Bank *v.* Nantucket Steamboat Co., 2 Story (U. S. C. C.), 16.

[1] 2 M. & Rob. 80; 8 Car. & P. 207. It is somewhat difficult to see why the circumstance that the goods are not conveyed from a known terminus should affect the liability of the individual who undertakes to carry them. Neither is it easy to understand why the circumstance that this carrier of goods plies in the streets for any job he can get, and that he has no fixed rate of charges, should prejudice the bailor's right to compensation in case any of his property is lost or injured.

[2] *Ante*, p. 43.

[3] Oxlade *v.* North-Eastern Railway Co., 9 W. R. 272; 3 L. T. N. S. 671, C. B. But if it is shown that he has publicly exercised this calling, and established a usage in that respect, it is sufficient. Haynie *v.* Baylor, *ante;* Dwight *v.* Brewster, 1 Pick. (Mass.) 53; Robertson *v.* Kennedy, 2 Dana (Ky.), 430. Thus, in the last two cases, it was held that the practice of conveying for hire, in a stage-coach,

SEC. 46. **What constitutes a Carrier a Common Carrier.** — So, where the declaration against the owners of a ferry stated that they were possessed of a ferry across the river Mersey, from Woodside to Liverpool, and that the plaintiff delivered to the defendants a phaeton, together with the jewelry and watches contained in it, to be conveyed by them in a steam-boat from Woodside to Liverpool, and there landed for the plaintiff, it also alleged the duty of the defendants to take care of the plaintiff's property while it was in their custody, and also alleged the breach of this duty through negligence. In this case it was held that a contract to carry and land the carriage and jewelry, as stated in the declaration, could not be implied from the mere character of the defendants as owners of the ferry, but that it was a question for the jury whether there was in fact a contract between the parties, either express or implied from usage, to take the carriage on board, and to land it again at the end of the transit across the river.[1] These cases will show that it is not always easy to say from what facts we are to infer the existence of the business of common carriers in each particular case. But there seems to be reason for regarding the above rule as a correct criterion, that when the acts or conduct of the individual in the ordinary course of business will lead the public to conclude that he is carrying on the business of a common carrier, and when such an understanding as the ground of an agreement is not modified by a special contract, the individual so acting will be held to be a common carrier.[2]

SEC. 47. **Hoymen and Barge-masters are Common Carriers.** — SIR WILLIAM JONES pointed out that although no substan-

parcels not belonging to passengers, constitutes the proprietors of the coach common carriers as to such parcels. But the proprietors must be shown to have had knowledge of such practice, or to have assented thereto, expressly or impliedly. Sheldon *v.* Robinson, 7 N. H. 157.

[1] Walker *v.* Jackson, 10 M. & W. 161; 12 L. J. Exch. 165.

[2] The carrier of messages, if it is his habitual occupation, may be a common carrier. M'Andrew *v.* Electric Telegraph Co., 17 C. B. 3; 25 L. J. 26, C. P. This is not true of the post-master-general. 12 Car. II., c. 35; but see Lane *v.* Cotton, 1 Ld. Raym. 646; Whitefield *v.* Lord Despencer, 2 Cowp. 754.

tial difference exists between "carriage by land and carriage by water, — or, in other words, between a wagon and a barge, — yet it soon became necessary for the courts to declare, as they did in the reign of James I., that a common hoyman, like a common wagoner, is responsible for goods committed to his custody, even if he be robbed of them.[1] All that has just been advanced, then, concerning a land carrier, may therefore be applied to a barge-master or boatman."[2]

This principle has, since that time, become the subject of judicial affirmation, it having been decided that a hoyman who undertakes to carry goods must deliver them safely, except damaged by the act of God or by the king's enemies;[3] so the liability of a wharfinger who undertakes to convey goods from his wharf to the vessel in his own lighter, is exactly similar to that of a common carrier.[4] In one case the carrier of goods by water was held liable for damage occasioned by running against an anchor to which no buoy appeared to be fastened;[5] and in this case LORD MANSFIELD and the other judges of the Court of King's Bench expressly declared that there was no distinction between a land and a water carrier.[6] Indeed, it could scarcely be otherwise. The laws of the country are founded on the thoughts of those who inhabit it, and in thought there can be no reason for distinguishing between the duties or liabilities of two persons who in the same way hold themselves out to the public as professed

[1] Hob. Ca. 30; 2 Cro. 330. Rich *v.* Kneeland. "The first case of this kind," says LORD HOLT, "to be found in our books." 12 Mod. 480.

[2] Jones on Bailm., 3d ed., pp. 106, q, r, s, t, v, w, 107, o, p, q, r. See also King *v.* Shepherd, 3 Story (U. S. C. C.), 349.

[3] Dale *v.* Hall, 1 Wils. 281; Richardson *v.* Sewell, 2 Smith, 205.

[4] Maving *v.* Todd, 1 Stark. 72; Goff *v.* Clinkard, 1 Wils. 282.

[5] Trent Navigation *v.* Wood, 3 Esp. 127; Abb. on Ship., 11th ed., p. 329; 4 Dougl. 287; 1 T. R. 28, n.

[6] The law with regard to this subject is the same in this country, although there have been conflicting decisions. See 2 Kent's Com. 600; Story on Bailm., § 489; Allen *v.* Sewall, 2 Wend. (N. Y.) 327; M'Arthur *v.* Sears, 21 Wend. (N. Y.) 189; Merritt *v.* Earle, 31 Barb. (N. Y.) 38; Hays *v.* Kennedy, 41 Penn. St. 378; McHenry *v.* Railroad Co., 4 Harr. (Del.) 448; The Gold Hunter, Blatch. & How. (U. S. C. C.) 300; Boney *v.* The Huntress, 4 Hunt's Merch. Mag. (Jan., 1841) 83. But see Lamb *v.* Parkman, 1 Sprague (U. S. C. C.), 343.

carriers of goods for hire, merely because the one conveys the wares with which he is intrusted in a cart, while the other conveys the goods placed in his hands by means of a barge; or because the journey of the one is over a road, and the other is over a river. To us there seems to be no possible ground upon which to distinguish between professed carriers for hire and professed bargemen, professed canal boatmen or professed ferry boatmen, in so far as duties and liabilities go.

SEC. 48. **Rule in Proprietors, &c. v. Wood.** — In The Proprietors of the Trent Navigation Company *v.* Wood,[1] BULLER, J., said, "As a general principle, there is no distinction between a land and a water carrier;" and in Richardson *v.* Sewell,[2] LORD ELLENBOROUGH suggested that at common law there was no difference between the liabilities of carriers by land and carriers by sea, "except that at sea the acts of God, which give rise to accidents excepted, are multiplied beyond those on land, and therefore many things at sea are excepted against, which cannot happen by land." It is true that the proof that the work in question is within the province of their ordinary avocations will differ in each one of these cases; but that can be no reason for making a distinction between the liabilities of those persons, when the fact that carriage of goods for hire is their ordinary employment, and that it is exercised publicly, has been satisfactorily proved. The same principle will hold with regard to any other kind of water carriage.[3] There can be no grounds for saying that carriage

[1] 3 Esp., at p. 132. See also Rich *v.* Kneeland, Cro. Jac. 330; Wardell *v.* Mourillyan, 2 Esp. 693.

[2] 2 Smith, 205.

[3] Morse *v.* Slue, 1 Vent. 190, 238; T. Raym. 220. See Jones on Bailm. p. 190; Trent Nav. Co. *v.* Wood, 3 Esp. 127. See also Dale *v.* Hall, 1 Wils. 282; Boson *v.* Sanford, 2 Salk. 439; Ellis *v.* Turner, 8 T. R. 531; Gale *v.* Laurie, 5 B. & C. 156; Bennett *v.* Peninsular & Oriental Steamboat Co., 6 C. B. 775; but see 17 & 18 Vict. c. 104, § 583. LORD HOLT, in the celebrated case of Coggs *v.* Barnard, 2 Ld. Raym. 909, in commenting upon the common-law liability of a common carrier, thus clearly states the rule as to the responsibility assumed by them: "The law charges every person exercising the public employment of a common carrier, common hoyman, master of a ship intrusted to carry goods, against all events but acts of God and enemies of the king. For though the force be never so great, as if an irresistible multitude of people should rob him,

by means of steam should in any way vary the liability of the owner of the steamboat from what it would be if the boat was

nevertheless he is chargeable. And this is a politic establishment contrived by the policy of the law for the safety of all persons, the necessity of whose affairs obliges them to trust this sort of persons, that they may be safe in their dealings. For else these carriers might have an opportunity of undoing all persons that had any dealings with them by combining with thieves, &c.; and yet doing it in such a clandestine manner as would not be possible to be discovered. And this is the reason the law is founded upon that point." The rule as stated by LORD HOLT has been somewhat modified, or rather it has been extended, so as to relieve the carrier from liability in certain cases where, perhaps upon a strict construction of the rule as stated by him, he might not be exempt; and it may be said that a common carrier is not only liable for negligence, but is an *insurer* against any loss not occasioned by the act of God, public enemies, *the fault of the party, or from the inherent qualities of the property itself*. Harris *v.* North Indiana R. R. Co., 20 N. Y. 232; Kohannan *v.* Hammond, 42 Cal. 227; Rixford *v.* Smith, 52 N. H. 355; Williams *v.* Grant, 1 Conn. 487; Harrell *v.* Owens, 1 D. & B. (N. C.) L. 273; Kemp *v.* Coughtry, 11 John. (N. Y.) 107; Ewart *v.* Street, 2 Bailey (S. C.), 273; Turner *v.* Wilson, 7 Yerg. (Tenn.) 340; Moses *v.* Morris, 4 N. H. 304; and the rule is the same whether the person is a carrier by land or by water. Daggett *v.* Shaw, 3 Mo. 264; Spencer *v.* Daggett, 2 Vt. 92; Harrington *v.* Lyles, 2 N. & McC. (S. C.) 88; Lea *v.* Stroud, 2 Binn. (Penn.) 74; Clark *v.* Richards, 1 Conn. 54; Emery *v.* Hersey, 4 Me. 411; Boyle *v.* McLaughlin, 4 H. & J. (Md.) 291; Harrington *v.* McShane, 2 Watts (Penn.), 443; Jones *v.* Pitcher, 3 S. & P. (Ala.) 135. In Boston & Albany R. R. Co. *v.* Shanley, 107 Mass. 568, a manufacturer of a blasting compound ordered one manufacturer to send him a quantity of dualin, and another to send him certain exploders. The plaintiffs as common carriers received both of these articles without knowing their nature, and neither manufacturer knew that the two articles were ordered or were to be shipped together; but the plaintiff, not knowing their nature, or that there was danger from combining the two, received them, and while being carefully transported they exploded, injuring the property of the carrier, and other property being transported by it. It was held that the two manufacturers were liable. In Barney *v.* Burnstinbinder, 64 Barb. (N. Y.) 612, where nitro-glycerine was shipped without notice to the carrier of its dangerous qualities, and having sprung aleak was taken to a warehouse at San Francisco for examination, and while being opened exploded, damaging the warehouse and freight, it was held that the shipper was liable, even though the immediate cause of the explosion was the opening of the package. Now, in these cases it would have been exceedingly unjust to have held the carrier chargeable for the loss of the property, when the injury resulted entirely from the inherent qualities of the property itself. If the shipper had been made acquainted with the nature of the goods, liability would not have attached for injuries to its property resulting from the explosion, neither would the carrier have

moved through the water by means of sails. And the standard by which we must judge of the liability in all these cases

been liable for the loss of the property itself. Ewart *v.* Street, 2 Bailey (S. C.), 157; Campbell *v.* Morse, Harp. (S. C.) 157; Gordon *v.* Little, 8 S. & R. (Penn.) 573; Colt *v.* McMechen, 6 Johns. (N. Y.) 160; Williams *v.* Grant, 1 Conn. 487; Spencer *v.* Daggett, 2 Vt. 92; Emerey *v.* Horsey, 4 Me. 411; Pemberton Co. *v.* New York Central R. R. Co., 104 Mass. 144; The Live Yankee, Deady (U. S.), 420. In Hall *v.* Renfro, 3 Met. (Ky.) 51, the plaintiff shipped cattle by the defendant's conveyance which by their own viciousness caused injury to each other. Held that the carrier was not liable. By the term "act of God" is meant something in opposition to the act of man, such as storms, lightning, tempests, and inevitable accidents not resulting from human agency. If the danger or the accident, though unavoidable, has been occasioned by the act of man, the carrier cannot avail himself of it as an excuse for the non-delivery of the goods. Oakley *v.* Portsmouth, &c. Steam Packet Co., 11 Exch. 622. Thus, where an action was brought against a common carrier for not safely carrying and delivering a quantity of hops, and it appeared that a fire broke out in a building adjoining a booth under which the carrier had placed the hops, and burnt with inextinguishable violence, and extended itself to the hops, and consumed them, without any neglect or default on the part of the carrier himself, it was held that inasmuch as the fire had not been occasioned by lightning, but by the act of man, the occurrence of the disaster constituted no answer to the action. Forward *v.* Pittard, 1 T. R. 33; Hyde *v.* Trent Nav. Co., 5 T. R. 399. If the goods have been destroyed or swept away by rains and floods, the circumstances attendant upon the loss must be regarded, in order to determine whether it has been occasioned by the act of God or the act of man. If the common carrier has neglected to provide proper coverings for the goods; if he has gone out of his way to meet the danger; if he has travelled by unusual roads, or crossed a plain subject to inundations when he might have kept the high ground and been safe, the loss occasioned thereby is a loss from the act or negligence of man, and the common carrier is consequently responsible therefor. Doct. & Stud. Dial. 2, c. 38; Noy, c. 43. Not only is a common carrier liable for all injuries to goods being transported by him, except such as arise from the act of God, public enemies, or the act of the party, but he is not relieved from liability, except for such injuries as *must* be attributable to the act of God; and the mere fact that they may be so attributed is not enough. Neither is it enough that they have been lost by the act of God, if his own act or neglect has in any measure contributed to bring about the injury. Thus, if he has departed from his line of duty, and has violated his contract, and while thus in fault, and in consequence of that fault, the goods are injured by an act of God, *which would not otherwise have occurred*, he is liable. Read *v.* Spaulding, 30 N. Y. 630; Michaels *v.* New York, &c. R. R. Co., 30 N. Y. 564. So, where a violent storm caused an unusually low tide, and the carrier's barge, while lying at the pier which was used by him, was pierced by a timber projecting from the wharf, which was covered at ordinarily low

is the same, *viz.*, the damage having been caused by the act of God or by the act of the queen's enemies.[1]

tide, but which was known by the carrier to exist, it was held that he was liable, notwithstanding that the fact of his leaving his barge there would not have produced the injury without the concurrence of the act of God, and the negligence of the wharf-builder. New Brunswick Co. *v.* Tiers, 24 N. J. 697. In Michaels *v.* New York, &c. R. R. Co., 30 N. Y. 564, the defendant received at Albany a box from the Hudson River R. R. Co., to be transported to Rochester. It did not forward the box at once, as it was its duty to do, but placed it in its freight-house, and kept it for some days, to await the rendering of a bill for back charges. While the box was in the freight-house, the goods were wet and injured by an unusual rise of the Hudson River. It was held that while the injury to the goods arose from the act of God, yet the negligence of the carriers having concurred in and contributed to the injury, they were liable therefor. The same question was involved and the same rule adopted in Read *v.* Spaulding, *ante*. But if the injury would have happened independent of his fault, his concurring act will not render him liable. Hill *v.* Sturgeon, 28 Mo. 323. And when a carrier sets up *inevitable* accident, or the act of God, as a defence, the burden is upon him to show not only that the injury resulted from a cause over which he had no control, but that his act in no wise contributed to the injury, the presumption being against him. Van Winkle *v.* South Carolina R. R. Co., 38 Ga. 32; Day *v.* Ridley, 16 Vt. 48; Lawrence *v.* McGregor, Wright (Ohio), 193; Spencer *v.* Daggett, 2 Vt. 92; Avend *v.* Liverpool Steamship Co., 64 Barb. (N. Y.) 118; The Rockett, 1 Biss. (U. S.) 354; Lewis *v.* Smith, 107 Mass. 374.

Anything may be said to result from the act of God *in the production of which man has no agency, immediate or remote*, as injuries resulting from lightning, the death of animals without fault on the part of man, or any cause which arises without the agency of mankind in any measure. Hall *v.* Renfro, 3 Met. (Ky.) 51. It is sometimes said that *inevitable* accident and the act of God are synonymous terms when used in reference to the liability of a common carrier. Neal *v.* Sanderson, 1 S. & M. (Miss.) 572; Fish *v.* Chapman, 2 Ga. 349. But this is not so where the carrier by means of public advertisements or otherwise has held himself out as insuring a safe delivery. In Morrison *v.* Davis, 20 Penn. St. 171, the defendants contracted to transport goods for the plaintiff upon a canal. There came on an extraordinary flood in a certain division of the canal, by reason of which the boat was wrecked. The plaintiff insisted that the defendant could not excuse himself from liability upon the ground of inevitable accident, because he started off his boat with one lame horse, and except for that would have passed the point where the accident happened, before the flood. But the court held that where nothing had been done by the carrier to insure an absolutely safe delivery,

[1] Sidoret *v.* Hall, 4 Bing. 607; 1 M. & P. 561; Gatliffe *v.* Bourne, 4 Bing. N. C. 314; 5 Scott, 667; 1 Arn. 366, 369. See 7 Geo. II. c. 15, and 26 Geo. III. c. 159.

SEC. 49. **Modifying Circumstances.** — But circumstances might arise, even in a case where the damage had arisen from

the law made an exception in favor of the carrier for all injuries resulting from inevitable accident, and the fact that the defendant's horse was lame, as connected with the injury, was a cause too remote to affect the question of liability. The striking of a steamboat or other vessel on a snag or on a rock, the existence of which was not known to the carrier, or was not *generally* known, is held as such an inevitable accident as will excuse a carrier from liability. Steamboat Co. *v.* Pason, Harp. (S. C.) 262; Williams *v.* Grant, 1 Conn. 487; Barnwell *v.* Hussey, 1 Tread. (S. C.) 114. But otherwise, where the snag or rock is known to exist, even though the boat is driven on to it by a tempest. Collin *v.* Valentine, 11 Miss. 287.

In Harris *v.* Rand, 4 N. H. 259, the plaintiff undertook to carry a lot of salt on his boat from Hartford to Haverhill, on the Connecticut River. He arrived with his boat within fourteen miles of Haverhill, when by reason of ice in the river he was compelled to land the salt, and a part of it was lost. In an action for the freight, it was held that the defendant was not liable to pay freight on the lost salt. When the carrier is excused from liability for the loss of goods by reason of inevitable accident, he cannot charge freight. If a barge-owner who carries goods for hire on a canal accepts certain goods to be carried for hire, and rats gnaw a hole in the barge, and cause a leak, and the goods are injured, the barge-owner is responsible for the damage. Dale *v.* Hall, 1 Wils. 281. He is not, of course, responsible for any deterioration in the value of the goods resulting from the negligence or want of care of the owner or the consignor, such as defective packing, nor for losses occasioned by an inherent defect in the article causing its destruction. If, however, the defective packing of goods is patent and visible, and easily remedied, and he accepts the goods for conveyance, he is bound to take all reasonable means to provide against the defect and secure their safety. Where a dog, with a string about his neck, was delivered to a common carrier to be carried, and was tied by the string in a watch-box, and shortly afterwards the dog slipped his head through the noose and escaped, and was never seen afterwards, and an action was brought to recover the value of the dog, and it was contended that the owner ought to have taken care that the cord was properly secured round the dog's neck, it was held that as the common carrier had the means of seeing that the dog was insufficiently secured, he ought to have locked him up, or taken other proper means to secure him, and that he was responsible for the loss. Stuart *v.* Crawley, 2 Stark. 324. Where, however, a greyhound, secured in the way ordinarily adopted and obviously intended by the owner to be used, namely, by a collar and strap, was delivered to a railway company to be carried, and the greyhound during the journey slipped his head through the collar and was lost, it was held that the company was not responsible. Richardson *v.* North-Eastern Railway, L. R. 7 C. P. 75.

If a cargo or load of goods weighing a certain weight be delivered to a common carrier to be carried for hire, and the cargo on its arrival at its destination is deficient in weight, there is

the act of God or the country's enemy, in which the carrier would not be relieved from his liability for loss or damage. If a carrier goes out of his way to meet the enemies of the queen, if, through his own evident carelessness, he has brought the goods with which he is intrusted into the jeopardy in which they suffer by the act of God, he would be properly held liable for the damage thence ensuing.[1] In an action against the

a *primâ facie* presumption of negligence on the part of the carrier, which the latter must rebut by showing that the deficiency of weight arose from causes over which he had no control. Hawkes *v.* Smith, C. & M. 72. So of all freight. The carrier's receipt stating the condition in which the goods are received, and the quantity, is *primâ facie* evidence that the goods were in good order when received, and that there was the quantity therein stated; and any injury thereto, or diminution in the quantity, throws the burden on the carrier of showing that the loss did not arise from any default or miscarriage on his part. Hastings *v.* Pepper, 11 Pick. (Mass.) 43; Rich *v.* Lambert, 12 How. (U. S.) 347; Clark *v.* Barwell, 12 How. (U. S.) 272; Warden *v.* Grear, 6 W. & S. (Penn.) 424; Nelson *v.* Woodruff, 1 Black (U. S. C. C.), 161; Murphy *v.* Stanton, 3 Munf. (Va.) 237; Alden *v.* Pearson, 3 Gray (Mass.), 342; Fenn *v.* Simpson, 4 E. D. S. (N. Y.) 276. The rule relative to a carrier's liability does not extend to the *time* of delivery. As to that, he is only answerable when he has failed to exercise due diligence. Parsons *v.* Handy, 14 Wend. (N. Y.) 215. Nor does it extend to injuries resulting from the inherent qualities of, or defects in, the property transported. Hall *v.* Renfro, 3 Met. (Ky.) 51.

[1] If a carrier departs from the line of duty and violates his contract, if the goods are lost while thus in fault, and in consequence thereof, by an act of God which would not otherwise have produced the injury, he is not protected. Michaels *v.* New York, &c. R. R. Co., 30 N. Y. 564. Thus, where the carrier was guilty of an unreasonable delay in forwarding goods, and while they were in a railroad depot at an intermediate point they were wetted and injured by an extraordinary flood, caused by the damming up of the water in the channel by ice, and setting the same back upon the freight depot, and it was held that the goods having been exposed to the peril by the fault and neglect of the carrier, he was liable for the injury. Read *v.* Spaulding, 30 N. Y. 630. So where a carrier attempted to ford a stream between sunset and dark, while a shower was approaching, without examining the state of the ford, and the wheels of his wagon stuck fast in the mud of the stream, and the water rose with extraordinary suddenness, and the goods were injured, it was held that he was liable therefor. Campbell *v.* Morse, Harp. (S. C.) 468. In order to excuse the carrier for injuries resulting from the act of God, it must appear that the injury occurred without fault on his part. Smith *v.* Whitman, 13 Mo. 352; Nettles *v.* Railroad Co., 7 Rich. (S. C.) 190; Blackstack *v.* New York, &c. R. R. Co., 1 Bosw. (N. Y.) 77. Where the act of God is relied upon to excuse a carrier, it must be shown to be not only the sole, but the immediate, cause of the loss;

proprietors of a steam vessel to recover compensation for damage done to goods sent by them as carriers, if, on the whole, it be left in doubt what the cause of the injury was, or if it may as well be attributable to the perils of the seas as to negligence, the plaintiff cannot recover; but if the perils of the sea require that more care should be used in the stowing of the goods on board than was bestowed on them, that will be negligence for which the owners of the vessel will be answerable.[1] In another case, where the defendant received on board his barge certain lime, which was to be conveyed for the plaintiff from Bewly Cliff to London, the master deviated from the usual and customary voyage without any justifiable cause, and while the barge was so out of her course, she encountered a storm, and the sea communicating with the lime caused it to ignite, and the barge and cargo were lost. In an action on the case for the loss of the lime, the declaration alleged that "it was the duty of the defendant to have carried and conveyed the lime by and according to the direct, usual,

and a loss occasioned by an obstruction in a river, produced by mixed causes, and which is not the result of the operation of natural forces upon natural objects alone, as the shores or the bottom, is not, in a logical or legal sense, the act of God. Thus, where a steamboat carrying property for hire, was wrecked in the Hudson by running upon the mast of a sunken vessel which had been capsized and sunk by a violent storm a day or two before, it was held that the owner of the steamboat was liable for the property lost by the sinking of the steamer. Merritt *v.* Earl, 31 Barb. (N. Y.) 38; affirmed, 29 N. Y. 115. So, while a carrier is not responsible for the loss of perishable property by natural decay in transportation, yet if in the transportation the carrier does that which hastens the natural process of decay, or if he neglects to take reasonable measures to prevent the loss of the property by the operation of the weather, he is responsible therefor. Thus, where potatoes were shipped over the defendant's road, and he failed to use due care to prevent their being frozen, and in consequence of which they were lost, the company was held liable therefor. Wing *v.* New York, &c. R. R. Co., 1 Hilt. (N. Y. C. P.) 235. So, where horses which were shipped on board a ferry-boat started and ran overboard, the defendant not having erected sufficient barriers to prevent such accidents, it was held that the accident could not be said to have happened by reason of any natural infirmity of the property, but rather from the ferryman's want of proper care in not having erected suitable barriers to prevent such accidents. Powell *v.* Mills, 37 Miss. 671.

[1] Muddle *v.* Stride, 9 Car. & P. 380. See also The Peytona, Ware (U. S. C. C.), 541.

and customary way, course, and passage, without any voluntary and unnecessary deviation or departure from, or delay or hindrance in the same;" and averred the loss to be by reason of the departure, delay, and deviation from such usual and customary course and passage: it was held that the damage sustained by the plaintiff was sufficiently proximate to the wrongful act of the defendant to form the subject of an action, and it was further held that the declaration was sufficient to support a judgment for the plaintiff.[1] It will be seen from these cases that a carrier will not be excused from liability for the loss of goods by reason of the loss having occurred through the act of God or the queen's enemies, unless those excepted perils are the proximate and sole cause of the loss. If the carrier by his own act contribute to the loss, he will still be liable.

SEC. 50. **Common Carriers not necessarily General Carriers.** — It will be clearly understood that a man may be a common carrier of one thing, while he is not a common carrier of another. An electric telegraph company, which holds itself out to the public as a carrier of messages,[2] is not to be held a common carrier of luggage, if it undertakes, through its servants, to convey a portmanteau; and is not to be regarded as liable for the loss or injury, should any arise, unless it can be traced to some negligence upon the part of the company, or their servants. The limitation of the character of common carriers is to be judged of by the profession of the individual, by words, advertisements, or by the overt acts of the trade or business. Thus it is allowable for the proprietors of a stage-coach or steamboat to advertise that they will only carry passengers. And if, when such an advertisement has been published, any person chooses to send luggage by such stage-coach or steamboat, the proprietors will, with regard to that luggage, occupy the position of private carriers for hire, and

[1] Davis v. Garrett, 4 M. & P. 540; 6 Bing. 716. See also Parker v. James, 4 Camp. 112; Max v. Roberts, 12 East, 89; Abbott on Ship., 5th ed., 239; The Niagara v. Cordes, 21 How. (U. S.) 7, 23; Lamb v. Camden, &c. R. R. Co., 2 Daly (N. Y. C. P.), 454.

[2] M'Andrew v. Electric Telegraph Co., 17 C. B. 3; 25 L. J. 26, C. P.

will only be liable in case they have been guilty of a want of prudent care. So it is competent for a man to avow his intention of carrying for hire the goods of any person who will pay him for so doing, and provided the goods be of a certain kind. In such a case the man who thus makes known his intentions to the public, and who, in pursuance of such intentions, plies his trade, always restricting his carrier's duties to goods of a certain class, is evidently a common carrier *quoad* that particular class of goods; and should he be induced by any one individual to carry an article of another description for hire, he is not, in regard to that article, to be regarded as an insurer or a common carrier, and the law of common carriers, in so far as it refers to the duty of undertaking the carriage of such articles, is not applicable to him.[1]

[1] Moriarty *v.* Harnden's Express, 1 Daly (N. Y. C. P.), 227; Tunnell *v.* Pettijohn, 2 Harr. (Del.) 48; Powell *v.* Mills, 30 Miss. 231. In Michigan Southern R. R. Co. *v.* McDonough, 21 Mich. 162, it was held that railroad companies are not common carriers of live-stock, or subject to the liabilities of common carriers when they assume to carry them. In passing upon this question, CHRISTIANCY, J., said: "For the purpose of this case it may be assumed that this company, by their charter and act of consolidation, are required to take upon themselves the business of common carriers, and to transport, as such, all such property tendered to them for that purpose as was usually transported by railroads, as common carriers, at the date of the charter of the Michigan Southern Railroad Company in 1846, and any other kind of property which, in the progress of invention and business, might be tendered for such carriage, which should not, from its nature, impose risks of a different character, or require an essentially different mode of managing their road, or the incurring of extra expenses on *account of the different character* of such *new kinds* of property. But the transportation of cattle and live-stock by common carriers by land was unknown to the common law when the duties and responsibilities of common carriers were fixed, making them insurers against all losses and injuries not arising from the act of God or of the public enemies. These responsibilities and duties were fixed with reference to kinds of property involving in their transportation much fewer risks, and of quite a different kind from those which are incident to the transportation of live-stock by railroad. Animals have wants of their own to be supplied; and this is a mode of conveyance at which, from their nature and habits, most animals instinctively revolt; and cattle especially, crowded in a dense mass, frightened by the noise of the engine, the rattling, jolting, and frequent concussions of the cars, in their frenzy injure each other by trampling, plunging, goring, or throwing down; and frequently, on long routes, their strength exhausted by hunger and thirst, fatigue and fright, the weak easily fall and are trampled

SEC. 51. **The Nature of Carriers' Business to be decided by a reference to Public Representations.** — We shall see that *the*

upon, and, unless helped up, must soon die. Hogs also swelter and perish. See per PARKE, B., in Carr *v.* Lancashire & York Rail. Co., 7 Exch. 712, 713; DENIO, J., in Clarke *v.* Rochester R. R. Co., 14 N. Y. 573. It is a mode of transportation which but for its necessity would be gross cruelty, and indictable as such. The risk may be greatly lessened by care and vigilance, by feeding and watering at proper intervals, by getting up those that are down, and otherwise. But this imposes a degree of care and an amount of labor so different from what is required in reference to other kinds of property that I do not think this kind of property falls within the reasons upon which the common-law liability of common carriers was fixed. In McManus *v.* Lancashire Rail. Co., 2 H. & N. 702, the court say: 'We are able to decide this case without referring to the second point made by the defendants, *viz.*, the alleged distinction between the liability of carriers as to the conveyance of horses and live-stock and ordinary goods; but should the question ever arise, we think the observation which fell from BARON PARKE, in Carr *v.* Lancashire & York Rail. Co., *ante*, is entitled to much consideration.' In the same case on appeal in the Exchequer Chamber, 4 H. & N. 346, EARLE, J., speaking of the condition of the contract in that case, says: 'This condition is imposed in respect of horses. And I find neither authority nor principle for holding that defendants were bound to receive living animals as common carriers.' In Palmer *v.* Grand Junction Rail. Co., 4 M. & W. 758, PARKE, B., interrupting counsel, asks: 'Does the rule as to negligence apply to live animals, as horses? Of course, if they are stolen, it would; but is it so when they are delivered, although hurt or damaged? If misdelivered, the carrier would be liable; but they would not be liable for a mere accident to an animal, supposing the carriage to be safe and good and properly conducted.' This case was decided in 1839, when the question was comparatively a new one. And it is quite manifest that BARON PARKE, in the above remarks, had reference to the question as one of common law merely; and when he comes to decide the case (on pp. 767, 768), holding that if the company choose to carry (horses), and do not take care to accept them with a limited responsibility, then, by accepting them, they must be held to have accepted as common carriers, it is equally manifest that the decision is rested wholly upon the statute which he cites, expressly enumerating '*cattle*' with 'other goods, wares, and merchandise articles, matters, and things,' which the company were authorized to carry, placing all apparently upon the same ground. The conclusion from the statute would seem to have been quite as broad, at least, as the premises would warrant. But it had the statute, such as it was, to rest upon. It may, however, well be doubted whether the decision would have been the same if the question had arisen for the first time after the decision in Oxlade *v.* Northwest Rail. Co., 15 C. B. N. S. 680, to be hereafter noticed, and that of Pardington *v.* South Wales Co., 38 Eng. L. & Eq. 432, decided in November, 1856. In the latter case the question arose upon the reasonableness of a notice given by the company to a shipper of cattle under 17 & 18 Vict.

representations which the carrier has made to the public are invariably *the guide to a proper decision as to the nature of his*

c. 31, § 7 (Railway Traffic Act of 1854), which expressly held the company liable for the loss of, or injury done to, 'any horses, cattle, or other animals,' or to any goods, &c., unless the conditions fixed by the notices, &c., should be held by the court to be just and reasonable. MARTIN, B. (interrupting counsel), says: 'The common-law liability of common carriers does not apply to cattle at all. In former days they were not carried. They might therefore, but for the statutes, make what conditions they pleased.' POLLOCK, C. B., also says: 'Why should they not say, "If you insist upon our carrying your cattle, we will carry them; but it must be upon the terms that we shall not be responsible for any injury which may happen to them"? They hold themselves out as carriers of horses and cattle, *sub modo.*' The drovers went with the cattle, as in the present case; and MARTIN, B., in giving his judgment, says: 'I doubt the liability of the company at all, even if there had been no stipulation on their part; for the fault, if any, was the fault of those who went by the train with the cattle.' All the judges held the notice reasonable.

"It will be noticed that in England, by the statute cited, railroad companies are common carriers of cattle, horses, &c., and bound to carry as such, if insisted upon by the shipper, except as they may limit their liability by notices or contracts which the court hold reasonable. And that the statute cited in Palmer *v.* Grand Junction Co., 4 M. & W. 758, was there held to have the effect to make them common carriers of such property, if they accepted it without conditions. (In that case, however, there was no evidence of their having held themselves out as doing such business *only* on special terms.) But this case has been frequently cited in this country, as if it had been made upon common-law reasons only, and applied to cases where there was no such statute as that upon which it was clearly rested by the court. Thus (without enumerating other instances) in Kimball *v.* Rutland Co., 26 Vt. 247, the court, after very correctly holding that the company by publicly offering to take cattle at one price with the common-law liability, and at another and less rate when the owner assumed the risk, thereby held themselves out and became common carriers of cattle, proceed to cite this case of Palmer *v.* Grand Junction Co., as proving the proposition that 'the fact that the company have undertaken such transportation for *hire*, and for such persons *as choose to employ them*, establishes their relation as common carriers.' The remark was correct enough, if applied to the facts of the case before them; but the language is much broader than is warranted by the case cited.

"Upon sound principle and upon the English authorities above cited, I think it clear the transportation of cattle by railroad does not come within the reasons of the law applicable to common carriers, so far as relates to the care of the property and responsibility for its loss or injury. Unless, therefore, there be something in the defendant's charter, or the act of consolidation, or some other statute applicable to the case (a question I shall hereafter consider), the company were not bound to receive or transport cattle or hogs, as common carriers, but they might

business. Thus, where a defendant company was declared against as common carriers for refusing to carry the plaintiff

legally refuse to carry them in that or any other capacity. And having the right to refuse altogether, they must have the right to refuse, except upon just such terms and conditions as they saw fit to require. And these conditions might, I think, be fixed by special contract, or by notice, or by their uniform course of doing that branch of business. They might, if they chose, undoubtedly assume the position of common carriers of such property; and if they held themselves out to the public or the parties employing them as acting in that capacity, and receiving and transporting such property in that character, as they do other property, they would be bound as such, and would thereby naturally assume the custody, care, and management of the cattle from the time of their delivery at the yard or depot for transportation, the loading and unloading, and certainly the feeding and watering, when necessary, getting them up when they get down in the cars, and their protection from injuries of that and the like kind. But to do this would obviously require them to provide yards or stables for them before put on board, with conveniences for watering and feeding, and the necessary supply of food there and at other stations, or at least at the terminus where they are unloaded (and their safety might sometimes require this to be done at stations along the route), or they must provide some mode, not yet invented, for feeding and watering on the train. They must employ a corps of men skilled in the care and management of stock, — a business quite foreign in its character from that of operating a railroad; and they must make many other provisions to guard against injury and risk which are not required for other property generally transported by railroads. Now we must shut our eyes to what is notorious to all business men, or we must take judicial notice, as I think we are bound to do, that *this is not the mode*, and such *are not the principles*, upon which this great and rapidly increasing business of transporting live-stock to an Eastern market is generally, if at all, done upon the railroads of this State (if, in fact, in any other of the Western States). Naylor *v.* Maugles, 1 Esp. 109; Spear *v.* Hartley, 3 Esp. 81; 3 Pars. on Cont. 240; Sisson *et al.* *v.* C. & T. R. R., 14 Mich. 489.

"I think we are also bound to know that if this business were done in this mode and upon these principles, and could be done in no other way, and the railroads were to be held responsible as insurers for all damages not caused by the act of God or the public enemies (which is strictly the common-law liability), or by the viciousness of some particular animal or animals in the mass (Walker *v.* London Railroad, cited Angell on Carriers, § 214, note, which would be a ludicrous distinction applied to a carload of cattle), or for all such as might be prevented by human agency (Clarke *v.* Rochester R. R., 14 N. Y. 570), the railroad companies, to indemnify themselves against such risks and the extraordinary expenses of this mode of doing the business, must of course demand a much higher freight; and if they can be compelled to carry at all in this way, they must provide themselves with all the conveniences I have mentioned, and keep on hand a special corps of experienced stock men;

in their regular packet-boat, which was advertised to carry passengers, on fixed terms, from Southampton to Gibraltar,

and being compelled to keep them, and having gone to the expense of the necessary conveniences, it would then be for their interest to charge the higher freight *in all cases*, and refuse to carry upon any other terms; and in this manner those who would prefer to take the care and risk upon themselves for a lower freight would be deprived of the opportunity.

"The law of common carriers is founded mainly upon considerations of public policy; and these considerations, therefore, should not be overlooked. On the other hand, if the drover, with a sufficient force of his own men experienced in the proper management of the cattle, goes upon the same train free of charge, in a drover's car provided for that purpose, and has the entire charge, care, and management of the cattle, and the responsibility for the loss and injury incident to that mode of transportation, the company only furnishing the proper cars and motive power, and being responsible only for their sufficiency and the proper mode of making up and running the train, it is manifest there will be much less liability to injury or loss, and that the companies can afford to carry the cattle at greatly reduced rates. This undoubtedly is substantially the mode in which this branch of business is generally carried on upon the railroads of this State, and probably other Western States, so far as relates to the transportation of cattle to an Eastern market; sometimes by special contract setting forth the terms, as in a bill of lading, receipt, or ticket, and sometimes only by the uniform course of business as adopted by the company and acted upon by their employers. But by reason of this diversity the particular terms and conditions upon which the business is actually done, in a particular case, cannot be judicially noticed without proof.

"It has been frequently held, and seems to be well settled, that companies incorporated under charters which simply permit, but do not require, them to undertake the business of common carriers, become such, as to any particular kind of property (though such as comes within all the reasons of the law of carriers), or as to any particular portion of their route, only so far as they hold themselves out as such to the public, and are under no obligations to carry otherwise, or other kinds of property than they publicly profess to carry. Oxlade *v.* Northwest Rail. Co., 15 C. B. N. S. 680; Johnson *v.* Midland Rail. Co., 4 Exch. 367; Farmers' & Mechanics' Bank *v.* Champlain Transportation Co., 23 Vt. 186, 206; 2 Redf. on Railways, 116. This was held in the first case above cited (decided in 1864), as to the carriage of coals, notwithstanding the Railway (and Canal) Traffic Act of 1854, already cited, which clearly made the railway companies common carriers as to all kinds of property, except as qualified by notices or contracts which the court should hold reasonable; all special contracts to be signed by the shipper, &c. And if the defendants in the present case were not bound, as common carriers, to receive cattle and hogs for transportation, and they do not come within the reasons of the law of carriers as applied to other property, then it must be very clear, under these authorities, that they were not common carriers of this species of property, unless, and only so far as, they professed to be and held themselves out

upon the defendant's side it was denied that they were common carriers, but the jury decided that they were. A new trial was moved for, and it was argued by the defendants that extra-territorial carriers were not common carriers; but the rule was refused on the ground that there was no substantial difference between a carrier who carried within the realm, and one who went from a place in the realm to a place beyond it.[1]

as such. If they have only held themselves out and professed to carry cattle on the terms that the property should be under the care and management of the owner, or not under the care of the company, the latter merely furnishing proper cars and motive power, and being responsible only for the proper making up and running of the trains, this would not be holding themselves out as common carriers. They would, doubtless, be under the same obligations to furnish suitable cars and properly to make up and run the trains. And the duties and obligations of the company in all matters not pertaining to the care, management, and risk of the stock, or to the mode of its reception and delivery, would be the same as those which attach to them in reference to other property generally. And all the provisions of the charter against partiality in the order of receiving and shipping property would probably apply.

"These obligations might arise under their charter from their holding themselves out and professing to transport this kind of property on the same terms for all persons alike who choose to employ them. But their professing to take property for all persons applying, upon the same terms, as to custody, care, and risk, would not make them common carriers in respect to such custody, care, and risk, unless those terms were the same as the law applicable to common carriers would have fixed without such terms; for this would be to hold that it would be incompetent for the company to enter into express contracts of the same kind with all persons who should choose to employ them, if such terms should vary the common-law liability; in other words, that while each contract would be good *by itself*, *all* would be rendered *void* by showing that *all* were *alike* in these particulars."

[1] Bennett *v.* Peninsular & Oriental Steamboat Co., 6 C. B. 775; 18 L. J. 85, C. P.; Johnson *v.* Midland Rail. Co., 4 Exch. 367; s. c. 18 Law J. Rep. N. S. Exch. 366; Muschamp *v.* Lancaster & Preston Rail. Co., 8 M. & W. 421; Scothorn *v.* South Staffordshire Rail. Co., 8 Exch. 341; 22 L. J. N. S. Exch. 121; Parker *v.* Great Western Rail. Co., 7 Man. & G. 253; 13 L. J. N. S. C. P. 105; and per ALDERSON, B., Johnson *v.* Midland Rail. Co., *supra;* 2 Kent's Com. 599, 600, 606, 608; Story on Bailm. §§ 497, 501, and the cases there cited; Richards *v.* Gilbert, 5 Day (Conn.), 415; Boyce *v.* Anderson, 2 Pet. (U. S.) 150; Clark *v.* Richards, 1 Conn. 54; Williams *v.* Grant, 1 Conn. 487; Bell *v.* Reed, 4 Binn. (Penn.) 127; Brown *v.* Clayton, 12 Ga. 564; Emery *v.* Hersey, 4 Me. 407; M'Clures *v.* Hammond, 1 Bay (S. C.), 99; Harrington *v.* Lyles, 2 Nott & M'Cord (S. C.), 88; Hastings *v.* Pepper, 11 Pick. (Mass.) 41; Dwight *v.* Brewster, 1 Pick. (Mass.) 50; De Mott *v.* Larraway, 14 Wend. (N. Y.) 225; Crosby *v.* Fitch, 12 Conn. 410.

This subject was, however, satisfactorily settled in a more recent case.[1] In this case the plaintiff was a small parcel collector and carrier. He employed agents in various towns, and he forwarded the parcels with which he was intrusted in London to his agents in the country, to be delivered to the parties to whom they were addressed. Before railways were introduced he had made use of wagons, or coaches, for the purpose of forwarding his parcels, and when these modes of conveyance ceased to exist, he had recourse to railways. In the ordinary course of his business, the plaintiff took parcels to the defendant company's stations to be forwarded by them to the plaintiff's agents in Sheffield and Glasgow, and tendered them the sum receivable and received by the company for parcels of the weight of those brought to them by the plaintiff, and to be forwarded to the destination which was written on the plaintiff's parcels. In consequence of certain orders which had been extracted from the minutes of a meeting of the company, the defendant's servants refused to receive and book the parcels to the places named in the address, and said that in the case of that which was addressed to Sheffield, it would not go further than Rugby, and that which was addressed to Glasgow would not go further than Preston, at which places the lines belonging to the defendant company ended. It was, however, proved that the defendant company had, by arrangement with other railway companies, been in the habit of booking, and receiving, and carrying goods beyond the limits of their own line to Sheffield and Glasgow, and of receiving the price of the carriage for the whole distance. It was also proved that the defendants had held themselves out as carriers of goods through from London to Glasgow, at certain rates which were to be found in their published tables. Upon these facts it was decided that the defendants must be regarded as common carriers for the whole distance.[2]

[1] Crouch *v.* London & Northwestern Rail. Co., 14 C. B. 255; 7 Rail. Cas. 717; 2 C. L. R. 188; 18 Jur. 148; 23 L. J. C. P. 73.

[2] In this country a common carrier, in the absence of a special contract, is only liable, as such, for the extent of his own route, and for the safe storage and delivery to the next carrier. McMillan *v.* Michigan Southern R. R.

JERVIS, C. J., said: "I think the defendants are liable on the first count; that, holding themselves out as common

Co., 16 Mich. 79; Baltimore, &c. R. R. Co. *v.* Schumaker, 29 Md. 176; Jacobs *v.* Hooker, 1 Edm. Sel. Cas. (N. Y.) 472; McDonald *v.* Western R. R. Co., 34 N. Y. 497. The rule in this respect is well stated in Lowell Wire Fence Co. *v.* Sargent, 8 Allen (Mass.), 189, to be that common carriers doing business between certain points, and not undertaking personally for their carriage to any further point, but merely engaging to forward them to their destination through the established lines of transportation beyond, are not liable, under their receipt for a bill of goods "for collection" from a person beyond the termination of their route, in the absence of any special contract creating an additional obligation, for the failure of other carriers, to whom in the ordinary course of their business the bill was intrusted for collection, to pay over the amount received by them upon the same. See also Darling *v.* Boston, &c. R. R. Co., 11 Allen (Mass.), 295; Crawford *v.* Southern R. R. Association, 51 Miss. 222; Gray *v.* Jackson & Co., 51 N. H. 9; Nutting *v.* Connecticut River R. R. Co., 1 Gray (Mass.), 502; Root *v.* Great Western R. R. Co., 45 N. Y. 524; Grindle *v.* Eastern Express Co., 67 Me. 317; Union, &c. R. R. Co. *v.* Hart, 30 Ga. 798; Hunt *v.* New York, &c. R. R. Co., 1 Hilt. (N. Y. C. P.) 228; Dillon *v.* New York, &c. R. R. Co., 1 Hilt. (N. Y. C. P.) 231. In Britnall *v.* Saratoga, &c. R. R. Co., 32 Vt. 665, a box of goods, marked and directed to B. at Boston, was delivered by B.'s agent, at Saratoga Springs, to a railroad company, to be transported over their road on its way to Boston. The defendants gave a receipt therefor in these words: "Received, Saratoga Springs, September 17, 1855, from B., in apparent good order, one box, to forward to Castleton, for B., Boston, Mass., at freight of —— per 100 lbs. weight." It appeared that Castleton was the terminus of their road toward Boston, and that with the Rutland and Washington Railroad, with which it connected at Castleton, and other roads, a line of railroad communication was formed between Saratoga Springs and Boston. It was held that the defendants were only liable for the safe delivery of the box of goods at the end of their own road in Castleton, and that it was their duty there to deliver it over to the railroad forming the next link in the chain in the line to Boston; and that it was sufficient to establish, *primâ facie*, a right of recovery on the part of B., in an action on the case against the defendants, for negligence as common carriers, for the loss of the box of goods, to show its delivery to them, and that it had not arrived at Boston, and was lost. In Burroughs *v.* Norwich, &c. R. R. Co., 100 Mass. 26, it appeared that by a contract between the defendant company and a steamboat company whose routes formed a continuous line, it was provided that each should furnish on its own route only connecting trains and boats respectively for the transportation of passengers and merchandise over the line at agreed rates of fare or freight, the proceeds to be divided between the contracting parties in an agreed proportion; and that "loss or damage occasioned by injuries to person or property on said line shall be borne by the party having possession of them at the time the injury was done." It was held that a person who delivered goods to one corporation, for

carriers in England, and professing, as such, to carry from London to Glasgow, they are liable for refusing to accept

transportation over the line to a point on the line of the other corporation, could not, by virtue of this contract, hold the first corporation liable for loss of the goods while on the route, and in the possession of the second. Judson *v.* Western R. R. Co., 4 Allen (Mass.), 520. The rule may be said to be that where a carrier receives goods to transport beyond the terminus of his route, his responsibility ceases on a delivery in good order to the next carrier in the regular course of transportation. Mullarkey *v.* Baltimore, &c. R. R. Co., 9 Phila. (Penn.) 114. In Grindle *v.* Eastern Express Co., *ante*, a person having a policy of insurance on his life delivered the premium thereon to defendant, an express company, to be forwarded to a certain point and there delivered to the agent of the insurance company. The money was not so delivered, and the policy lapsed. The defendant had knowledge of the purpose for which the money was sent. It was held that if the point of delivery was beyond the defendant's line, it would, in the absence of an agreement, express or implied, to the contrary, be discharged from liability by promptly delivering the money to the next carrier. And this is the rule in nearly all the States; the English rule to the contrary, being predicated upon the statute, has no application at common law, and is not recognized here. The fact that the goods to be carried are marked to a point beyond the terminus of the carrier's line does not import a contract to deliver them at their place of destination; but, under such circumstances, the rule is, that, in the absence of any special contract or circumstances, the law will merely imply an undertaking on the carrier's part to deliver them at the end of his route to the next succeeding carrier; and if he does not so deliver them or tender them, he is liable for any injury happening to them while in his custody; otherwise he is not. Rawson *v.* Holland, 59 N. Y. 611; 17 Am. Rep. 394. In this case the defendant was a common carrier of the goods in question, from the city of New York to Detroit, Michigan. It received them at New York "to be forwarded to Detroit only," and the express terms of the undertaking exclude any inference or implication that it was to carry them farther. But Detroit was not the final destination of the property. The box was marked "Day & Lathrop, Dryden, Michigan, *via* Ridgway," clearly indicating that Dryden was the ultimate destination, and that the transit was by some agency to be continued from Detroit *via* Ridgway, to the place of consignment. The defendant transported the goods to the terminus of its line, and without delivering or tendering them to the connecting road, stored them in its warehouse, where they were subsequently destroyed by fire. In an action for the loss the company was held responsible.

"The defendant," said ANDREWS, J., "was not bound to carry the goods beyond Detroit. It performed its contract in respect to the actual carriage upon carrying them to that place. But the obligation of a carrier is not fully discharged by transporting the goods from the place of shipment to the place of consignment, or, in case of an intermediate carrier, from the place of shipment to the end of his route. The undertaking to transport the goods to a particular place includes the duty of delivering them there in safety. De Mott

goods to be carried from the one terminus to the other. It is not denied now, although the authorities upon the subject

v. Larraway, 14 Wend. (N. Y.) 225. What is due delivery depends upon the nature of the carriage, whether by ship, rail, or other conveyance, and also upon the facts whether the carrier in the particular case is an intermediate carrier, or is the one who transports the goods to their final destination; and their mode of delivery may, in some cases, be controlled by custom and usage. In all cases, however, there must be a delivery by the carrier, or something tantamount to a delivery, before he rids himself of his responsibility as such. In the case of an intermediate carrier, who accepts goods to be carried to a point short of their final destination, directed to a place beyond the termination of his route, the law from such direction, in the absence of other special circumstance, implies an undertaking on his part to deliver them, at the end of his route, to the next succeeding carrier in the line of transportation; and if such carrier refuses or neglects to receive them, the first carrier may store the goods, and then the nature of the bailment changes, and he is relieved from the stringent responsibility originally assumed, and the liability of a warehouseman is substituted. Van Santvoord *v.* St. John, 6 Hill, 157; Goold *v.* Chapin, 20 N. Y. 259; McDonald *v.* Western R. R. Co., 34 N. Y. 497; Root *v.* Great Western R. R. Co., 45 N. Y. 524; Mills *v.* Michigan Central R. R. Co., 45 N. Y. 622; Nutting *v.* Connecticut River R. R. Co., 1 Gray (Mass.), 502.

"In this case the defendant did not, on the arrival of the goods at Detroit, offer them to any other carrier for transportation beyond that point, or give notice to any other carrier of their arrival. They were deposited in the defendant's warehouse, and remained there for about twenty days, when they were destroyed by an accidental fire which happened without fault or negligence of the defendant. The failure to deliver to another carrier did not result from the fact that there was no carrier on the route designated by the direction, to whom delivery could be made. The Grand Trunk Railway Company operated a line of railway from Detroit to Ridgway, a station on that road, and was the customary and usual carrier to Ridgway, of goods sent from Detroit to Dryden *via* Ridgway, and, so far as appears, there was no other public carrier between these places.

"The defendant, not having delivered or tendered the goods to the Grand Trunk Railway, is, under the general rule of law, liable for the loss, and it must be so adjudged unless the case is taken out of the rule by the special circumstances relied upon.

"There are, however, two grounds upon which it is claimed that the defendant was excused from delivering the goods to the Grand Trunk Railway: first, that by a regulation of that company, of which the defendant had notice, it would not remove goods for transportation unless the shipper would accept a receipt containing certain exemptions from the liability imposed upon carriers at common law; and, second, that by a custom of the defendant, goods carried by its line to *Detroit*, destined to points on the Grand Trunk Railway, were detained until notice was given to consignees, and their direction taken as to sending them by that road, and that such notice was given in this case, and the goods were

are not numerous, that if a person holds himself out as a common carrier from London to Oxford, both termini being

destroyed before any direction had been given. We do not think that either of these answers is sufficient, under the circumstances of this case, to relieve the defendant from liability.

"The direction on the box was a clear indication that Rawson, Buckley, & Co., the shippers, designed that it should be sent from Detroit to Dryden *via* Ridgway, and was, in effect, a direction to the defendant to send them by the usual mode of carriage from Detroit to that point. The defendant was entitled to regard the shippers as authorized to direct as to the mode of transportation, whatever their actual relation to the goods may have been; whether, in fact, they or the consignees were the owners. The direction that the goods should be sent *via* Ridgway, coupled with the fact that the Grand Trunk Railway was the usual carrier between Detroit and that place, authorized the defendant to deliver the goods to that company, upon the usual contract required, and in case of loss after such delivery, and while they were in possession of that company, the defendant would not have been liable, although the Grand Trunk Railway under its contract might have been exempted from liability also. Nelson *v.* Hudson River R. R. Co., 48 N. Y. 507; Squire *v.* New York Central R. R. Co., 98 Mass. 240; Barnett *v.* London & Northwestern Rail. Co., 5 H. & N. 604.

"There is nothing decided in the case of Lamb *v.* Camden & Amboy R. R. Co., 46 N. Y. 271; s. c. 7 Am. Rep. 327, which conflicts with this view. In that case there was no indication in the contract of the first carrier as to the particular route or company by which the goods were to be sent from Chicago; nor, so far as it appears, was it necessary that the first carrier should consent to a restricted liability in order to procure the goods to be carried from that point; and as he had guaranteed that they should be carried to the final destination at a specified through rate, it perhaps might justly be inferred that they were to be carried from Chicago under a contract as favorable as that made with the first carrier. We, however, confine our decision to the case presented on this record, and are of opinion that the defendant was not excused from tendering the goods to the Grand Trunk Railway, and that he would have been justified in delivering them to that road, and in accepting the usual contract required by the company.

"The defence founded upon the alleged custom is, we think, wholly insufficient. The proof is that, up to a short time before the shipment of these goods, the Grand Trunk Railway had not exacted of the defendant a compliance with the general rule of the company, but had received its goods on the *forms* used by the defendant. This had been changed in 1865 or 1866, and the regulation was thereafter enforced as to goods received from the defendant. The defendant, from that time, was accustomed to detain goods destined to points on the Grand Trunk Railway, and advise the consignees, and await their direction before sending them forward, and in this case written notice was sent to 'Day & Lathrop' of the arrival of the goods, but they gave no instructions.

"It is said in Van Santvoord *v.* St. John, 6 Hill (N. Y.), 160, that a carrier who receives a box marked in

within the realm, he is bound to carry, within reasonable limits, all goods that may be tendered to him to be carried

a particular way, without any directions, except such as may be inferred from the marks themselves, has a right to presume that the consignor intends that he shall transport and dispose of them in the usual and customary way. That was the case of a carrier by tow-boats on the Hudson River, who received a package marked 'J. Petrie, Little Falls, Herkimer County,' and it was held that the first carrier was justified in delivering it at the end of his route to a succeeding carrier by canal, and was discharged thereby from further responsibility, it being shown that there was a general, established, and uniform usage in the business, that such delivery might be made; and it was also held that the consignor was bound by it whether he knew it or not. And in Gibson *v.* Culver, 17 Wend. (N. Y.) 305, it was held that the general obligation created by law in respect to the mode of delivery by a carrier, may be controlled by a uniform usage and course of the business in which he is engaged. In this case the proof falls far short of establishing a custom superseding the general obligation of the defendant to make delivery of the goods to the next carrier. At most it was a usage recently established, and confined to the particular business of the defendant at a particular place, not known to the plaintiffs, and which they were not bound to ascertain.

"The usage relied upon in this case lacks the essential elements of a valid usage. It is neither general, established, uniform, nor notorious. It would be unreasonable to give it effect in this case to defeat a recovery by the plaintiff. The parties did not make their contract in reference to it, and cannot be presumed to have done so.

"It is the general rule, that a local usage must be shown to have been known to a party before he will be held to be bound by it. Smith *v.* Wright, 1 Cai. (N. Y.) 43; Stevens *v.* Reeves, 9 Pick. (Mass.) 198; Krechner *v.* Venus, 12 Moore's P. C. C. 361; Bartlett *v.* Pentland, 10 B. & C. 760; 1 Sm. L. Ca. 836; 2 Pars. on Cont. 541, note.

"The conclusion is, that the defendant, at the time of the fire, held the goods as a common carrier, and is responsible for the loss under the general rules of law. If the exemption in the bill of lading from liability for loss by fire can be construed as applying to the goods after the transit to Detroit was ended, the delay in delivering them to the Grand Trunk Railway was a violation of duty which deprived the defendant of the benefit of it. Michaels *v.* New York Central R. R. Co., 30 N. Y. 564; Read *v.* Spaulding, 30 N. Y. 630; Maghee *v.* Camden & Amboy R. R. Co., 45 N. Y. 514; Condict *v.* Grand Trunk Rail. Co., 54 N. Y. 500."

Where, however, the carrier, after reaching the end of his route, does all that can reasonably be expected of him to have the succeeding carrier take them, — as by giving notice to him of the arrival of the goods and their readiness for transshipment, — his liability as common carrier ceases, and he becomes liable merely as warehouseman or as bailee, according to the circumstances. Thus in Goold *v.* Chapin, 10 Barb. (N. Y.) 612, the proprietors of the Hudson River Line of tow-boats received on board one of their barges, in the city of New York, goods belonging to persons in Brockport, to be by them transported to Albany, and there

from London to Oxford. The only question on this part of the case is, whether the rule applies where one of the termini

delivered to the agent of a company for transporting goods on board the canal, styled "The Atlantic Line." The goods arrived safe at Albany on Monday, August 14th, and were put on board a float belonging to the owners of the barge, kept by them in the Albany basin, for the purpose of receiving goods brought by their barges, and then transferring them to the canal craft, which came alongside of the float to receive their loading. On the 15th of August the agent of the Atlantic Line was notified, on behalf of the owners of the Hudson River Line, that there were goods on their float for his line, and he was requested to take them away. On the next day the like notification and request was made to him, and again repeated on the 17th of August, when the agent said he was taking some goods from another line, and when he got them on he would shove up and take those goods from the float; but on the same afternoon the float with the goods in question was consumed by fire. Held, 1. That the float in the basin was not, in any proper or legal sense of the term, a warehouse. 2. That placing the goods upon this float was merely shifting them from one vessel of the carriers to another; and that it was clearly no delivery to the consignees, "The Atlantic Line." 3. That, had the carriers placed the goods in a warehouse at Albany, that being the place of delivery, so far as they were concerned, their liability as carriers would have been entirely discharged. 4. That by placing the goods in either of their own two warehouses, which it appeared from the evidence that they had at Albany, and giving notice to the consignees, their undertaking and duties as carriers would have entirely terminated, and those of warehousemen commenced. 5. That, inasmuch as they elected to retain possession of the goods after notice, without depositing them in a warehouse, they were not entirely discharged from their liability. 6. That after the repeated notices given by them to the agent of the Atlantic Line of the arrival of the goods, with requests that he would take them away, their liability as insurers did not continue until the destruction of the goods; that, under the circumstances, their strict liability as common carriers had ceased at the time of the fire, and that they were then holding the goods as bailees in deposit merely; and the goods having been destroyed without any fault on their part, that they were not liable.

In Alabama (Mobile, &c. R. R. Co. *v.* Copeland, 63 Ala. 625; 35 Am. Rep. 13) the English doctrine, as laid down in Muschamp *v.* Railway Co., 8 M. & W. 421, was adopted, to wit, that unless the carrier expressly limits his liability to his own route, he is liable for the delivery of goods at their place of destination. And such also seems to be the rule in Illinois. Erie R. R. Co. *v.* Wilcox, 84 Ill. 239; 25 Am. Rep. 451. See also Bradford *v.* Railroad Co., 7 Rich. (S. C.) 201; Carter *v.* Peck, 4 Sneed (Tenn.), 203. But the language of the judge in the last-named case favoring the English rule is mere *dicta;* and the doctrine is now settled in Tennessee in accordance with the current of American cases. Nashville, &c. R. R. Co. *v.* Spraybury, 8 Baxt. (Tenn.) 341; 35 Am. Rep. 705.

The reasons given by the court in the Alabama case, cited *ante*, for adopt-

is a place out of England; and I think it does. If a person holds himself out as a common carrier, accepts goods, the law

ing the English rule in relation to connecting carriers are much stronger against than in favor of the rule, and the opinions of the judges in Muschamp *v.* Railway Co., *ante,* do not evince that degree of logical reasoning which the questions in the case seemed to demand; and while it may be quite proper for legal writers to entertain different views upon the expediency or wisdom of the rule, yet the great current of authority upon a legal question in the courts of the country is decisive as to the rule, and affords a strong argument in favor of its expediency and wisdom. In Hadd *v.* United States and Canada Express Co., 52 Vt. 335, 36 Am. Rep. 757, the rule applicable to carriers of general freight was applied to express companies. In that case the plaintiff intrusted to the defendant, an express company, a parcel addressed to a point beyond the termination of its route. The defendant's agent told the plaintiff that the defendant could not bill beyond its own route, but at his request received the charges through, and delivered to the plaintiff a receipt limiting its liability to its own route. The plaintiff being unable to read, the defendant's agent read the receipt to him, *omitting* the limitation clause. The defendant carried the parcel to the termination of its own route, and delivered it to the connecting carrier, by whom it was lost. It was held that the defendant was not liable for the loss. "It has been repeatedly decided," said VEASEY, J., "in the American courts that, in the absence of a special contract, common carriers, *including express companies,* receiving parcels marked to a point beyond their own route, and having no special business relations with other carriers, are only responsible as common carriers to the end of their own route, and the safe and seasonable delivery to the succeeding carrier in the direction of transportation. Nutting *v.* Connecticut R. R. Co., 1 Gray (Mass.), 502; Root *v.* Great Western R. R. Co., 45 N. Y. 524; Railroad Co. *v.* Manufacturing Co., 16 Wall. (U. S.) 318; Morse *v.* Brainerd, 41 Vt. 550; Stewart *v.* Terre Haute, &c. R. R. Co. (U. S. C. C.) 10 Reporter, 618; Railroad Co. *v.* Berry, 68 Penn. St. 272; Converse *v.* Transportation Co., 33 Conn. 166; Farmers' & Mechanics' Bank *v.* Champlain Transportation Co., 23 Vt. 209; Phillips *v.* Railroad Co., 78 N. C. 294; Hoagland *v.* Railroad Co., 39 Mo. 451; Packard *v.* Taylor, 35 Ark. 402; 37 Am. Rep. 37; Gray *v.* Jackson, 51 N. H. 9; Elmore *v.* Naugatuck R. R. Co., 23 Conn. 457; Irish *v.* Railroad Co., 19 Minn. 376; Crawford *v.* Railroad Association, 51 Miss. 222. In Lawrence *v.* New York, &c. R. R. Co., 36 Conn. 63, the defendants were common carriers of passengers and freight by railroad from Providence, R. I., to Groton, Conn., connecting at Providence with a railroad from Boston and at Groton with steamboats for New York, the three having formed for several years, under a common arrangement, a through line for passengers and freight from Boston to New York. The line had a standing advertisement in a Boston newspaper that cars would leave the station there at half-past five P. M., every week-day, connecting on three days named with the steamboat Commonwealth, and on the alternate days with the steamboat Plymouth Rock, for New York, and that through tickets were furnished and baggage

of England — that is, the law founded on the custom of the realm — engrafts on such an acceptance a contract to take

checked through to sundry places beyond New York. The defendants, also, by hand-bills and placards, advertised those two boats as running between Groton and New York in connection with their railroad. The plaintiffs, who had for a long time been in the habit of sending freight by the line, shipped a quantity of goods by it at Boston for New York, on the 28th day of December, taking bills of lading signed by an agent of all the companies forming the line, by which it was provided that the companies should not be liable for any injury to freight in the course of transportation arising from accidental delays, and that no package of goods if lost should be deemed of greater value than $200, unless specially receipted for at a greater valuation. The plaintiffs procured the bills of lading printed, and kept them in blank, to be filled up by themselves as needed. The steamboat Plymouth Rock, which was the regular boat for December 28th, had been taken off for necessary repairs, and the Commodore — a much smaller boat, belonging to the same owners, and which they were accustomed to put on in the place of either of the regular boats when taken off for repairs — was running in her place. By reason of her small capacity a large quantity of freight, which came by railroad from Boston on the evening of the 28th of December, including a part of the goods of the plaintiffs, and which the Plymouth Rock would have been able to take, could not be carried, and had to be discharged, as was the custom in such cases, into the depot of the defendants at Groton to wait for the boat of the next day, and during the night was destroyed by fire, with the depot. In a suit brought by the plaintiffs for the value of the goods lost, in which the jury returned a verdict for the plaintiffs for the full value of the goods, without reference to the limitation in the bills of lading, it was held, on a motion of the defendants for a new trial, 1. That the advertisement was obviously published for the information of passengers, and not of freighters, and that therefore the court below erred in instructing the jury that, in determining whether there was a contract on the part of the defendants that the Plymouth Rock should be the boat for the night in question, they should particularly consider the advertisement. 2. That there was nothing in the representation of the defendants as to the boats regularly running in connection with their road that constituted a binding stipulation that one of the boats should not be taken off for necessary and usual repairs and another temporarily substituted for it. 3. That on the arrival of the goods at Groton the defendants were bound to forward by the boat of that evening only so much of the freight as the boat could take, and were not responsible for the delay of the rest. 4. That all that could be required of them was to take reasonable care of the goods left over until they should be taken by the boat of the next day. It is well settled, however, that a carrier may bind himself by contract to carry goods beyond the terminus of his own line, and when he does so he remains liable therefor as a common carrier until the goods have reached their destination, although they are in fact lost while being transported by an intermediate carrier. Morse *v.* Brainerd, 41 Vt. 550; Stewart *v.* Mer-

and safely carry the goods, and to deliver them as an insurer, with certain exceptions, *viz.*, the acts of God and the king's

chants' Despatch Transportation Co., 47 Iowa, 229. And the question as to whether such an agreement existed has been held to be a question of fact for the jury. Gray *v.* Jackson, 51 N. H. 9. A contract of this character may be implied from the language of the receipt or bill of lading. Thus, in Kyle *v.* Laurens R. R. Co., 10 Rich. (S. C.) L. 382, the defendant gave receipts for cotton "to be delivered on presentation of this receipt, at Charleston." The cotton passed over the Laurens Railroad, and was delivered to another road for transportation to Charleston, but was lost. Held, that the company was liable, the undertaking being special, — to carry to Charleston. But in Wright *v.* Boughton, 22 Barb. (N. Y.) 561, the defendants, who were common carriers between Lewiston and Niagara Falls, received from the plaintiffs two casks of brandy at the former place, to be forwarded to different points on the Michigan Central Railroad. Goods destined for such points were in the usual course of the business shipped at Buffalo for Detroit; and this usage, as well as the fact that the defendants had no interest in or connection with any of the carrying business or companies beyond the falls, was known to the plaintiffs. The defendants gave a receipt at follows: —

"Received, Lewiston, &c., the following packages of goods on board the L. & B. R. Line, in good order, to be delivered in like good condition: —

Israel Kellogg,
Kalamazoo, Mich. } 1 qr.-cask brandy.
M. C. R. R.

Also for

McCrea & Morton,
Battle Creek, Mich. } 1 qr.-cask brandy.
M. C. R. R.

R. H. Boughton."

The plaintiffs delivered to the defendants shipping bills as follows: —

"Shipped, Lewiston, &c., one qr.-cask brandy, marked Israel Kellogg, Kalamazoo, &c."

"Shipped, Lewiston, &c., 1 qr.-cask brandy, marked McCrea & Morton, Battle Creek, Mich., &c."

The brandy was lost on the lake between Buffalo and Detroit. Held, that the receipt did not contain any implied agreement to transport the brandy to Kalamazoo or Battle Creek, the address being only incorporated in the instrument for the purpose of identification; and that this construction of the contract was further fortified by the use of the word "marked" in the shipping bills. Where a railroad company have contracted to transport goods to the terminus of their road, the burden of proof that the goods were carried there and delivered or tendered for delivery is upon the company. Schroeder *v.* Hudson River R. R. Co., 5 Duer (N. Y.), 55 There is another ground upon which the first carrier may be made liable as a common carrier after they have been transported to the end of his route and delivered to another carrier, and that is where he, in violation of the orders of the shipper to send them by a certain route or carrier, sends them in a different manner, or by another and different route. Thus, if goods are shipped from Boston to Chicago, and the shipper marks "*Via* B. & A. and N. Y. Central R R. Co.," and the B. & A. Company, at the terminus of its route, delivers them to D. & H. Railroad, by whom they are lost, the B. & A. Company, by delivering the goods to the D. & H. Company, violates its duty, and remains an insurer until the goods are delivered to the consignee. The

enemies. It was admitted during the argument, and could not be denied, that if the defendants had accepted the goods in London, the common law would have engrafted on their contract an obligation to carry them to Glasgow, subject to the liability I have mentioned.[1] Then, if it is admitted that

same is also true where the goods are marked "*Via* N. Y. Central R. R. Co. and steamer Mary Ann from Buffalo to Chicago," and the first carrier, instead of following the shipper's directions, sends the goods by another railroad from Buffalo to Chicago. Johnson *v.* New York Central R. R. Co., 33 N. Y. 610. So, where a carrier contracts to carry goods to their place of destination in vehicles controlled or owned by it, without transfer or breaking bulk, if, upon reaching the terminus of its route, it unloads the goods and places them in its warehouse, and they are destroyed by fire, he will be liable for their loss, although there is an express provision in the bill of lading stipulating that he shall not be liable for the destruction of the goods by fire, because by unlading them he has violated his contract, and the provisions relative to exemption from liability do not apply while the goods are in his warehouse contrary to the contract of shipment. Stewart *v.* Merchants' Despatch Co., 47 Iowa, 229. But if transportation is obstructed by the act of God, — as if the goods are to be carried by water, and the river or lake freezes up before the goods can be got to their destination, and in consequence thereof they are deposited in his warehouse, and burned while there, without his fault, — he cannot be held liable therefor. Clark *v.* Needles, 25 Penn. St. 338.

[1] See the case of Morse *v.* Slue, Raym. 220; 1 Vent. 190. The rule is otherwise in this country; and while a common carrier is bound to accept and carry goods, although marked and destined for a point beyond the terminus of his line (Elmore *v.* Naugatuck R. R. Co., 23 Conn. 471), yet he is not bound to accept them in the capacity of common carrier for any portion of the distance beyond his line, and if he does not contract expressly or by necessary inference to deliver the goods at their place of destination, he is treated as only assuming liability as a common carrier to the end of his own route; in other words, he is treated as merely contracting to safely carry the goods over his own route, and to seasonably and safely deliver them to the next carrier, when his liability ends. Detroit, &c. R. R. Co. *v.* McKenzie, 43 Mich. 609; Stewart *v.* Terre Haute, &c. R. R. Co., 1 McCrary (U. S. C. C.), 312; Clyde *v.* Hubbard, 88 Penn. St. 358; Grover & Baker Sewing Machine Company *v.* Missouri Pacific R. R. Co., 70 Mo. 672; 35 Am. Rep. 444. And where an express contract is made by an agent to transport goods beyond the terminus of the carrier's line, it is not binding upon the principal, unless he was expressly authorized to make such a contract, or unless such authority may reasonably be inferred from previous dealings, or the company has held itself out as a carrier to such points. Grover & Baker Sewing Machine Company *v* Pacific, &c. R. R. Co., *ante.* In this case it appeared that the defendant's roads ran from Kansas City to St. Louis, which at Sedalia, Mo., connected with the Missouri, &c., Railroad, which ran from that point beyond Clinton, which was the shipping

when once they have held themselves out as common carriers, there is engrafted on their acceptance of the goods the com-

point on the road for Osceola, Mo. Neither of the railroads was shown to be a common carrier to Osceola, which was twenty-seven miles distant from Clinton. One Lee was admitted to have been the defendant's freight agent at Kansas City, and had general authority to act as such at that point, but the rules of the company did not permit him to enter into any contract for the transportation of freight beyond the terminus of the defendant's line "of railroad without special permission from defendant's general freight agent at St. Louis. It was expressly agreed that said Lee was the freight agent of defendant at Kansas City, and by his duly authorized clerk, Leonard, executed and delivered to plaintiff the following receipt: —

KANSAS CITY, MO., March 7, 1872.

Received of Grover & Baker Sewing Machine Company, in good order, by Missouri Pacific Railroad Company, to be delivered in like good order unto James M. Thompson, Osceola, Missouri.

Marks.	Articles.	Weight.
J. M. Thompson, Osceola, Mo.	box and frame containing one sewing-machine.	100 lbs.

(Signed) J. M. LEE, Agent, L.

"The box and crate containing the machine reached the town of Clinton, and there the crate containing the machine-frame and a certain box were delivered to Jacob Blinckenhoff, to be delivered to said Thompson at Osceola. Upon the delivery of said box to said Thompson, it proved to be a box containing leather and shoe-findings, shipped to him from St. Louis, and the machinery of said sewing-machine was never delivered to said Thompson or to plaintiff. The receipt sued on was furnished, filled out, and presented to said clerk of Lee by plaintiff for signature. It was not shown that plaintiff had ever before shipped over said road sewing-machines, or other goods to be delivered at Osceola, or that the defendant had ever held itself out as carrier of goods to that point. On this state of facts, was the plaintiff entitled to recover?

"That a railroad may, by contract, subject itself to the obligation of a common carrier beyond its own line, is well settled by the weight of authority; but, as was said in Railroad *v.* Pratt, 22 Wall. (U. S.) 124, the result of American authorities limits the carrier's liability as such to his own line, when no special contract is made. In Perkins *v.* P. S. & P. R. R. Co., 47 Me. 593, it was held that 'a railroad may be bound by special contract, but not otherwise, to transport persons or property beyond the line of its own road.' This remark was criticised in Lock Company *v.* Railroad. 48 N. H. 355; s. c. 22 Am. Rep. 342, in which we think it was shown 'that the term "express contract" could hardly have been used in its strict sense, to signify a contract in the form of a direct promise or undertaking, in language, oral or written, proper to show a positive agreement, since the judge who delivered the opinion of the court speaks of a case where the carriers would be liable on the ground that they held themselves out as common carriers to that place, in which case (remarks the judge in the New Hampshire case), as I understand it, the contract would not be express in the strict or usual sense of the term, but implied from the conduct of the party.'

mon-law liability to carry, even if they are to carry beyond the realm, it would seem also that they were subject to the

Taking the criticism as just, the doctrine may be stated that a railroad company may be bound by contract, express or implied, but not otherwise, to transport persons or property beyond the line of its own road. As thus declared, it is fully sustained by the authorities, both in the United States and England.

"The vital question, therefore, in the case is whether the defendant's freight agent at Kansas City had authority to make the contract sued on; and in this case that is to be determined by ascertaining whether or not the power to make the contract was within the general scope of the agent's apparent authority. If it was, then, although the regulations of the company forbade him from making such a contract, unless plaintiff was aware of such regulations, the company is bound. Here the agent was forbidden to make such contracts; but there is no evidence tending to show that plaintiff was informed of such regulations. The whole question then depends upon the character of Lee's agency, whether it was general or special.

"There is a marked distinction between special and general agents, with respect to the authority to bind the principal. The principal is bound by the act of the general agent, though such acts are in violation of the agent's instructions; while the principal is not bound by the unauthorized acts of a special agent. Story on Agency, § 1720. Smith, in his Mercantile Law, page 59, thus states the doctrine: 'The authority of a general agent to perform all things usual in the line of business in which he is employed, cannot be limited by any private order or directions not known to the party dealing with him.' The agreed statement does not show that Lee was a general freight agent of defendant, but is only to the effect that the testimony would show that the contract sued on was executed by Lee, then the freight agent of defendant's road at Kansas City; and the testimony of Lee was that he was then freight agent of defendant at Kansas City, that he had general authority to act as defendant's freight agent at that point, but that the rules and regulations of the company did not permit him to enter into any contract for the transportation of freight beyond the terminus of defendant's road without special permission from the defendant's general freight agent at St. Louis, and that he did not have at that time such special permission. In Wait *v.* Albany & Susquehanna R. R. Co., 5 Lans. (N. Y.) 477, the court held that, 'strictly speaking, the business of a carrier, such as defendant, is confined to its own line, and the general scope of its subordinate agents' authority must be limited to its business.' Some of the cases deny even to a general agent authority to bind the company by a contract to transport goods beyond its own line, unless expressly authorized to do so. But the doctrine announced by SUTHERLAND, J., in his dissenting opinion in the case of Burtis *v.* Buffalo & State Line R. R. Co., 24 N. Y. 274, we think the better doctrine, *viz.*, that, if defendant had the power to make or to authorize the making of such contract, then the person acting as the general freight agent should be deemed to have been clothed with all the power to make contracts for freight, or in respect to the carrying and delivery of freight, that the principal had. But here there was no proof whatever

other part of the common-law liability, namely, to accept, within reasonable limits, all goods that may be tendered to

that Lee was the defendant's general freight agent. The evidence for plaintiff only proved him a station agent; and Lee's testimony was that he was subordinate to a general freight agent at St. Louis, and by that agent was expressly forbidden to make such a contract. No course of dealing between plaintiff and the company's agent at Kansas City was shown from which the authority of the agent to make the contract might be inferred. It was not shown that the company had held itself out as a carrier of goods between Kansas City and Osceola. The naked question is presented, whether a local freight agent can make a contract for the company not only unauthorized, but expressly forbidden, for the transportation of goods beyond its line. We think that the company is not bound by such a contract made by the agent. In Railroad Company *v.* Pratt, *supra*, there was evidence that Graves, the station agent, had authority to make the contract, and that for five years he had been the company's agent at Pottsdam, and that the plaintiff had been in the habit of transporting horses over the defendant's railroad to Boston, — a point neither a terminus nor on the line of the road. The court held that 'the power in a railroad corporation to make contracts to carry beyond its line is coincident with the power to make contracts for transportation with other carriers, and is confined to the governing officer of the corporation, and that its subordinate agents do not possess that power unless it has been expressly conferred upon them, or has been so exercised by those who exercise the general authority as to have become the established business of the road.'

"In Burroughs *v.* Norwich & Worcester R. R. Co., 100 Mass. 26; s. c. 1 Am. Rep. 78, the plaintiffs relied upon a receipt signed and delivered to them by the defendant's station agent at North Oxford, by the terms of which the defendant 'promised to forward and deliver the goods to the order of Trumbull, Slade, & Co., New York.' The station agent had been accustomed to give to the plaintiffs precisely similar receipts for goods delivered by them to the defendant at North Oxford to be transported; but the blank forms of these receipts were furnished by plaintiffs themselves, and the officers of the defendant corporation did not know that such receipts were given by the station agent; and receipts supplied by those officers to the station agent, and which they were accustomed to fill up and deliver when requested, for goods to be transported to New York, were of a different form, stipulating that the goods should be transported by defendant to New London, and thence by steamboat of the Norwich & New York Transportation Co. to New York, and that in case loss or damage should be incurred, the company should be responsible therefor in whose actual custody the goods might be when such loss or damage occurred. The station agent at North Oxford was the proper person to receive and sign receipts for goods delivered at that station, but had no other authority to sign and deliver to plaintiff the receipt relied upon than was to be implied from the above facts. The court held that these facts were 'clearly insufficient to warrant a court or jury in inferring that he had authority to bind defendant as common carriers beyond the line of their own railroad.' That case is directly in

them to carry. If, therefore, being carriers within the realm, they are bound to take the goods offered to them to be carried within the realm, it follows, that if they profess to be carriers beyond the realm, being themselves, at the time they so profess, within the realm, they are bound to accept and to carry goods beyond the realm upon the terms on which they profess to contract." [1]

SEC. 52. **Liability for Servants.** — As a carrier cannot avoid the responsibility of his position, merely because of the accident that the destination of the goods with which he is intrusted is out of the realm, so long as he has held himself out to the pub-

point; but it is not necessary for this court to adopt so stringent a rule as was there announced, in order to determine against plaintiff the question of the authority of the agent Lee to make the contract relied upon in this case. There were several facts there from which authority in the agent might have been inferred, that are not in this case, which only presents, as before stated, the naked question whether or not the defendant is bound by such a contract as Lee signed for the company without express authority to do so, and against the explicit directions to the contrary from his superior officer, the general freight agent, there having been no previous dealings between the plaintiff and the company from which the plaintiff might reasonably have inferred such authority, and the company not having held itself out as a common carrier to a point beyond its line of road. On such a state of facts, there can be no doubt that the company is not liable on the contract made by the agent. The court below, by its first instruction for the plaintiff, left it for the jury on the above facts to determine whether the agent Lee had authority to make the contract with the plaintiff or not. It should have declared, as a matter of law, that on the facts the plaintiff could not recover, or have given the second instruction asked by the defendant, — that the contract sued on as a contract of the defendant to carry to the town of Osceola is void." The first carrier must seasonably deliver the goods to the next carrier, and until it has notified the next carrier that the freight is ready, and left it at the place where such freight is usually delivered to it, it remains liable as a carrier therefor. Thus, in Kentucky, &c. Ins. Co. *v.* Western, &c. R. R. Co., 8 Baxt. (Tenn.), 268, cotton was brought over the defendant's road, and left uncovered on a flat car for three hours, without notice to the connecting carrier that it was ready for delivery, and it was burned. It was shown that a freight train passed the car upon which the goods were loaded, and that there was a custom that there was no delivery until the freight was hauled to the transfer platform of the receiving company and examined, &c. It was held that the defendant was liable for the loss, and that the plaintiff, who had paid the consignee the insurance thereon, was entitled to recover the value of the property.

[1] 23 L. J. C. P., at p. 80.

lic as a carrier to that place, so it is equally certain that he cannot avoid the responsibility which devolves upon him, by the accident that some person employed by him does his work, so long as he holds himself out to the public as a carrier through, or by means of, this servant or agent.[1] The public has a right to rely upon an employer of labor who holds himself out or professes to do a certain thing, and that reliance or confidence is the same, in point of law, whether it is felt with regard to the skill of an individual to do a thing himself, or to employ others to do it for him. It is evidently the same thing in principle whether a man professes to carry luggage by a certain vehicle — *quoad* which mode of carriage he is a common carrier — or professes to carry luggage by means of the agency of his servants. In the latter case he is a common carrier as much as in the former, provided he does it as a public servant, ready to undertake the commission of any one who hires him. This has been affirmed by statute.

SEC. 53. **Carriers' Act, Section 8.** — An act for the protection of common carriers, passed in the reign of George IV.,[2] sets forth that "nothing in the act shall be deemed to protect any mail contractor, stage-coach proprietor, and other common carrier for hire, from liability to answer for loss or injury to any goods or articles arising from the felonious acts of any coachman, guard, book-keeper, porter, or other servant in his or their employ, nor to protect any such coachman, guard, book-keeper, or other servant from liability for any loss or injury occasioned by his or their own personal neglect or misconduct." And this is but the confirmation of the common-law rule.

SEC. 54. **The Reason of Liability.** — But in order to charge a master with such liability in consequence of the wrong done

[1] Cavenagh *v.* Such, 1 Price, 328; Williams *v.* Cranston, 2 Stark. 82; Middleton *v.* Fowler, 1 Salk. 282; Hyde *v.* Trent & Mersey Navigation Co., 5 T. R. 397; Ellis *v.* Turner, 8 T. R. 531; Boyce *v.* Chapman, 2 Bing. N. C. 222. See also 2 Bell Com. pp. 455, 465, 471; Story on Bailm. §§ 507, 550; and for Roman Law, Pothier, Pand. Lib. 19, tit. 2, n. 31; Dig. Lib. 19, tit. 2, l. 11; Grover & Baker Sewing Machine Company *v.* Pacific, &c. R. R. Co., *ante.*

[2] 11 Geo. IV. and 1 Will. IV. c. 68, § 8. In this country a common carrier is as liable for the felonious as for the negligent acts of his servants.

by his servant, it is of importance to ascertain who are a man's servants, and also the extent and scope of his authority as derived from the nature of his employment, or from the express authority conferred upon him. Any person who is employed by a common carrier is not necessarily authorized by such employment to carry goods. If a man engages a servant to wait at table he does not give him authority thereby to drive a coach. And should such a man undertake such a work without his master's knowledge, and should loss or injury to goods result therefrom, it seems certain that the owners would have no claim against the employer of this house servant, although he was a common carrier. The reason why a man is held liable for the injury arising from the felonious acts of his servants is, that he has chosen those servants; and if he has chosen those who were untrustworthy, while he held himself out to the public, by the very fact of his business and employment, as capable of choosing those that were trustworthy, he must suffer for it. But a common carrier does not hold himself out to the public, by any act or constructive advertisement, as capable of choosing house servants; and as the house servant, in driving the coach, was acting without the consent, and contrary to the implied command, which was a part of the contract for his service, it would be absurd to regard the master as in any way responsible for his misfeasance. If, however, such a common carrier employs a servant, whether it be under the name of sub-contractor or agent, to do any part of the work which he as carrier has undertaken to perform, that person is a servant within the meaning of the act.[1] It is evident that wherever the contract to carry exists, where it is implied on the one side by the regular occupation of the party, and expressed on the other by his trusting his property to the professional carrier, the same liability will arise whether this transaction

[1] Machu *v.* London & Southwestern Rail. Co., 2 Exch. 415; 5 Rail. Cas. 302; 12 Jur. 501; 17 L. J. Exch. 271. See also Pickard *v.* Sears, 6 Ad. & El. 469; Laugher *v.* Pointer, 5 B. & C. 547; 4 L. J. K. B. 309; Quarman *v.* Burnett, 6 M. & W. 499; Rapson *v.* Cubitt, 11 L. J. Exch. 271; Milligan *v.* Wedge, 12 Ad. & El. 737; 10 L. J. Q. B. 19.

takes place between principals or agents; or, to use the words of LORD DENMAN, C. J., "A carrier receiving goods undertakes to carry them to the party whose address is upon them; the fact of their coming to him through a series of agents does not prevent him being liable to the sender. He cannot throw back the liability upon the earliest agent."[1] In this case the plaintiff sent a parcel *directed* to a person in London, to the postmaster of Bradford (Wilts), to be forwarded to Milksham. The postmaster received twopence to book the parcel, and sent it by a mail-cart to the "King's Arms" Inn, at Milksham. He was in the habit of taking in parcels for the mail-cart. The innkeeper at Milksham booked the parcel for London, and charged twopence for so doing, and also charging on the parcel the demand for carriage from Bradford, which he had paid. The innkeeper used to receive parcels to be forwarded by the mails and other coaches, but he had no authority from the mail-coach proprietors to book, nor had he ever been applied to by them to receive parcels. He used his own discretion in sending on parcels which were sent to him. He sometimes sent them by the mail, and sometimes by other coaches. Several coaches used to call at the "King's Arms;" for two years and a half the mail had been accustomed to pull up there, but not to change horses. There was no regular booking-office at the "King's Arms." The plaintiff's parcel was delivered by the innkeeper to the coachman of the London mail, and it was lost. On these facts it was held that the carrier employed by the Bradford postmaster was the agent of the plaintiff, and that the innkeeper at Milksham was the servant of the defendants, the proprietors of the mail-coach, and that therefore the plaintiff was entitled to recover damages from him for the loss of the parcel.[2] In another case, where the plaintiff was the publisher of prints in London, and had an agent at Bristol, named Leese, who wished to send certain prints by van to the plaintiff in London, the question as to what constituted a man a servant or

[1] Syms *v.* Chaplin, 1 N. & P. 129; 5 Ad. & El. 634; 2 H. & W. 411.

[2] Cavenagh *v.* Such, 1 Price, 328; Brind *v.* Dale, 2 M. & Rob. 80; 8 C. & P. 207.

agent for a particular purpose was considered. It appeared that the defendants in this action were the proprietors of a van which carried goods from Bristol to London, and that Mr. Leese, the plaintiff's Bristol agent, went to their booking-office in that town, and desired that the box containing the prints should be sent for. This request was complied with, and a porter, belonging to the defendants' booking-office, took it from Mr. Leese's house to the office. It was proved that the box had arrived in London, and had been placed in the print-room of the plaintiff, where, upon being opened, it was found that the prints had got wet, and were damaged to the amount of 136*l.* It was further proved, by a clerk of the plaintiff, that when the box was delivered the carriage was charged 12*s.* 6*d.*, and on the plaintiff objecting, the porter, who brought the box, replied that, being pictures, it required more care. In this case it was held that the box was delivered at the defendants' booking-office, as for the purpose of taking it there the plaintiff's agent made the defendants' servant his servant. In this action the defendants were held liable for the injury done to the prints.[1] When the fact of employment for the purpose of conveyance has been satisfactorily proved, difficulty may still arise with reference to the misfeasance of the servant. A mere suspicion that the loss arose from the felony of the servant will not make the common carrier liable — the felony must be proved.[2] With regard to what proof is necessary in such circumstances, another case may be alluded to. A parcel was delivered to a porter of the Great Western Railway Company at their station, to be forwarded from Gloucester to London, after the way-bill and the guard's parcel-book had been made up. The parcel was placed by the porter in the usual receptacle, a locked box, in the luggage van, and entered by him on the way-bill, but the fact of his having so placed it was not communicated to the guard. After several stoppages between Gloucester and London, the train reached its ultimate destina-

[1] Williams *v.* Cranston, 2 Stark. 82; Powles *v.* Hider, 6 El. & Bl. 207; 2 Jur. N. S. 472; 25 L. J. Q. B. 331.

[2] Great Western Rail. Co. *v.* Rimell, 27 L. J. C. P. 201.

tion, when the parcel was missed. On these facts it was held that there was no evidence for the jury that the parcel had been stolen by a servant of the company.[1] On the other hand, in a case tried in Ireland, a more positive decision was arrived at.[2] In this case the plaintiff sued the defendants for the loss of a travelling case containing watches, which he was carrying with him as personal luggage. The company pleaded that the plaintiff had not made the requisite declaration as to the contents of the parcel, to which the plaintiff replied that the loss was occasioned by the felony of the servant of the company. It appeared at the trial that the case had been lost on a part of the journey, that the plaintiff had been prevented by a servant of the company from carrying the case in the same carriage with himself, on the pretence that the luggage van was the proper place for its conveyance. It was proved that the interference of the servant was no part of his duty, that the case was not afterwards forthcoming, and that the said servant denied all knowledge of the transaction. The jury found that a felony had been committed, and it was held that there was sufficient evidence to go to the jury of a felonious taking of the goods.[3]

SEC. 55. **Effect of Contract with Servant of Carrier.** — While the doctrine that the master common-carrier is liable for the defalcations of his servants whenever it can be proved that a real contract to carry for hire has been entered into between him, or some one authorized by him, and the owner of the goods is firmly established, it is equally certain that *if any owner chooses to send parcels by the driver of a wagon, or a stage-coach, by a ferryman, or the master of a steamboat, and pays him for so doing, which remuneration is the personal gain of the driver, wagoner, or ferryman, and does not reach their employers, such employers are not liable in case the parcels thus sent are lost or injured.*[4] A common carrier undertakes the

[1] Great Western Rail. Co. *v.* Rimell, 18 C. B. 575; Boyce *v.* Chapman, 2 Bing. N. C. 222; 2 Scott, 365; 1 Hodges, 338.

[2] Keys *v.* Belfast Rail. Co., 8 Ir. C. L. R. 167, C. P.

[3] See also Metcalfe *v.* London, Brighton, & South Coast Rail. Co., 4 C. B. N. S. 307; 27 L. J. C. P. 205.

[4] Butler *v.* Basing, 2 C. & P. 613. Where the conductor of a freight train promised that he would stop at a cer-

trade with a knowledge of its duties and liabilities for the sake of gain; and if the profits do not reach him, he is not, in fairness, to be held liable for loss or injury should it occur. A servant is his servant for the purposes of his trade, that he may make money by means of him, and not that his employee may make money on his own account while he has the responsibility for his negligence or faults.

SEC. 56. **The Rule of Law as to Partner Carriers.** — That the same rule should apply to the case of partners as applies to master and servant, or principal and agent, in so far as the law of carriers is involved, will not be disputed. Thus, where three men are in partnership, and drive coaches, of which they are the proprietors, from one place to another, and undertake the conveyance of goods, and where, through the misfeasance or malfeasance of one of the three, the goods of a bailor are lost, that the three should be held liable to make good the loss, is a doctrine deducible from the principles which have guided the determination of all those cases which have arisen in regard to this question. The sender of the goods intrusted them to the carriers upon the strength of the confidence he had in the acknowledged partnership. It would be unjust

tain point where there was no station, or freight agent, and take on goods of the plaintiff if they were left there, and accordingly the goods were left there, but the conductor did not stop for them, and they were destroyed, it was held that the defendant was not liable therefor, because the conductor had no authority, real or apparent, to bind him by any such agreement. Wells *v.* Wilmington, &c. R. R. Co., 6 Jones (N. C), L. 47. The obligation of a common carrier does not arise out of contract in the usual sense of that expression, but it is declared by law, and his responsibilities are fixed by considerations of public policy. Where common carriers set up to carry certain kinds of property from one given point to another, they cannot be compelled to receive such property at intermediate points; and if an agent in their employ receives property at an intermediate point, his right so to receive it is a proper subject of inquiry in an action against his principals, because the agent failed to deliver property so received, and it is erroneous not to admit evidence upon that point. An advertisement, by common carriers, that a faithful special messenger is sent in charge of each express, is no evidence of any authority of such messenger to engage for, or receive, freight. Whether or not an agent has authority to do certain acts for which it is sought to charge the common carrier, must be proved, and is a question of fact for the jury. Thurman *v.* Wells, 18 Barb. (N. Y.) 500; Blanchard *v.* Isaacs, 3 Barb. (N. Y.) 388.

that he should suffer in any way for the confidence which was warranted by the ordinary experience of mankind. In conformity with this principle, it has been enacted that "any one or more of mail contractors, stage-coach proprietors, or common carriers may be sued by his, her, or their name or names only; and no action or suit for damages for loss or injury to any parcel, package, or person shall abate for the want of joining any co-proprietor or co-partner."[1] In the case of Watland *v.* Elkins,[2] it appeared that the defendant and one Dyson were carriers from London to Gosport, and that, by an arrangement between them, Dyson horsed the wagon from London to Farnham, and the defendant then conducted it from Farnham to Gosport, and that at the time the mischief happened in consequence of which the action was brought, the wagon was drawn by Dyson's horses, and was driven by one of Dyson's servants, who had been hired by, and had received wages from, Dyson, and with whose employment the defendant had no concern whatsoever, but that the wagon itself was the property of the defendant. The defendant was, however, held to be liable, notwithstanding this division of the concern between them, for the damage done, and responsible for the misconduct and negligence of the servant who had been hired by his partner, who, according to GIBBS, C. J., might, "for inferior purposes, and as between the parties, be considered as the servant of Dyson, still he was, for all legal purposes, the servant of Elkins."[3]

SEC. 57. **Scope of Trade, how determined.** — The rule which determines who are common carriers also serves to determine the scope of their trade. It is allowable for a man to carry one kind of goods and not another; but if he has been accustomed to carry all kinds of goods, he cannot, by his own

[1] 11 Geo. IV. and 1 Will. IV. c. 68, § 5; Ansell *v.* Waterhouse, 2 Chit. 1; 6 M. & S. 385. See Powell *v.* Layton, 2 B. & P. 365.

[2] Watland *v.* Elkins, 1 Stark. 272; s. c. Weyland *v.* Elkins, Holt, 227. See Barton *v.* Hanson, 2 Taunt. 49; Smith *v.* Taylor, 2 Chit. 142.

[3] As to who are partners in the business of carriers, see Fromont *v.* Coupland, 9 Moore, 319; 2 Bing. 170; 1 C. & P 275; Helsby *v.* Mears, 8 D. & R. 289; 5 B. & C. 505; Wooley *v.* Batte, 2 C. & P. 417. But see Merryweather *v.* Nixan, 8 T. R. 186.

free will, limit his duty to one particular class of articles, or limit his liability to a responsibility for these only. But if an article is brought to him which he has been in the habit of carrying, he is bound in law to accept the duty. But in many cases this rule would fall short of the actual requirements of the circumstances. We must be aware of the daily practice which exists amongst shipmasters and agents of receiving and transporting certain kinds of goods which have never before been shipped, and which may previously have been unknown. It would be absurd to argue that in such a case the carriers are relieved of their common-law liability as insurers, and become liable for loss or damage only in case of a want of ordinary care or diligence upon their own part, or upon that of one of their servants. In such a case the rule would evidently be too narrow; and, under such circumstances, it seems the best opinion that courts of law will have regard rather to the kind or class of goods which the carriers have been in the habit of conveying than to the specific description of the articles. Thus the owner of a *passage* boat carrying light freight would not ordinarily be answerable for a cargo of coal or of marble, taken on board by the master, although he had been in the habit of carrying small pieces or specimens of either for hire,[1] because the carriage of goods of that class is not in accordance with the usage of his business;[2] but if a usage to carry that class of goods is once established, then liability therefor as a common carrier attaches.[3]

SEC. 58. **Passengers' Luggage.** — There is a wide distinction between contracts for the conveyance of passengers and those for the conveyance of goods. In the latter case the parties are liable at all events, except the goods are destroyed by the act of God or the king's enemies; whilst in the former, they are only responsible to their passengers in cases of express

[1] Sewall *v.* Allen, 6 Wend. (N. Y.) 346. And see King *v.* Lenox, 19 Johns. (N. Y.) 235; Tunnell *v.* Pettijohn, 2 Harr. (Del.) 48. See also Story on Bailm. § 501, p. 458, &c., 8th ed.

[2] Powell *v.* Mills, 30 Miss. 231; Tunnell *v.* Pettijohn, 2 Harr. (Del.) 48.

[3] Beckman *v.* Shouse, 5 Rawle (Penn.), 179; Kemp *v.* Coughtry, 11 John. (N. Y.) 107.

negligence.[1] This being the case, and there being evident reasons why it should be so, it became a question whether the

[1] PARKE, J., Crofts *v.* Waterhouse, 11 Moore, at p. 138; cf. Sorett *v.* Hobbs, 2 Show. 428. See also Stokes *v.* Saltonstall, 13 Pet. (U. S.) 181; The New World *v.* King, 16 How. (U. S.) 469. A carrier of passengers is required to use the utmost human care and foresight, and he is held responsible for the slightest negligence. Maverick *v.* Eighth Ave. R. R. Co., 36 N. Y. 378; Johnson *v.* Winona, &c. R. R. Co., 11 Minn. 296; Derwort *v.* Loomer, 21 Conn. 245: McClenaghan *v.* Brock, 5 Rich. (S. C.) 17; Southern, &c. R. R. Co. *v.* Kendrick, 40 Miss. 374; Jeffersonville, &c. R. R. Co. *v.* Hendrick, 26 Ind. 228; Frink *v.* Potter, 17 Ill. 406; Huelsenkamp *v.* Citizens' R. R. Co., 37 Md. 534; Redhead *v.* Midland Rail. Co, L. R. 2 Q. B. 412; Sayles *v.* Western Stage Co., 4 Iowa, 547. But this rule does not require the exercise of the *greatest* precautions of which the human mind is susceptible, but requires the use of the highest degree of practicable care and diligence under the circumstances of the case. Fuller *v.* Talbot, 23 Ill. 357. It is not required that he should exercise such precaution as it is apparent *after* an accident might have prevented the injury, but the utmost care of a cautious person, in view of the consequences, without knowledge that the accident might occur. Bowen *v.* New York Central R. R. Co., 18 N. Y. 408; Ingalls *v.* Bills, 9 Met. (Mass.) 1; Farrish *v.* Reigli, 11 Gratt. (Va.) 697; McKinney *v.* Niel, 1 McLean (U. S. C. C.), 540; M'Lane *v.* Sharp, 2 Harr. (Del.) 431; Edwards *v.* Lord, 49 Me. 279; Wheaton *v.* North Beach, &c. R. R. Co., 36 Cal. 590; Stockton *v.* Fray, 4 Gill (Md.), 406; Frink *v.* Coe, 4 Greene (Iowa), 555; Lockhart *v.* Lichtenthaler, 46 Penn. St. 151. For injuries resulting from patent defects in its vehicles or other appliances used in the carriage of passengers, or from defects which might have been discovered by the exercise of reasonable diligence, it is responsible, but not for injuries resulting from latent defects, or those which could not be discovered by the exercise of the degree of care demanded by the circumstances. Mier *v.* Pennsylvania R. R. Co., 64 Penn. St. 225. Thus, in Ingalls *v.* Bills, 9 Met. (Mass.) 1, it was held that a passenger on a stage-coach who was injured solely by reason of the breaking of an iron axle in which there was only a very small flaw, which was entirely surrounded by sound iron one fourth of an inch thick, and which could not be discovered by the most careful examination, could not recover for the injury; and the same doctrine was held in Mier *v.* Pennsylvania R. R. Co., *ante*, where the injury resulted from the breaking of the axle of a railroad car under similar circumstances. There is, of course, a wide distinction between carriers of passengers upon public highways and carriers of passengers by rail, as in the former case the carrier cannot justly be held responsible for the safe condition of the road, while in the latter instance the carrier is not only responsible for the safe condition of the vehicles and engines, but also of the roadway itself, as he has both under his sole care and control. The rule is, that a railroad company is bound to so construct its roadway and track as to avoid such dangers as could have been reasonably foreseen by the exercise of that degree of care

usual baggage taken by passengers when they travel in stage-coaches, railway trains, steamboats, and the like, should be

and skill which is demanded in view of the results likely to ensue in case of a failure to exercise it, and this extends to the protection of its road-bed from the ordinary rainfalls or freshets incident to the section of country through which it is located. In Railroad Co. *v.* Halloran, 53 Tex. 46, by a sudden and extraordinarily heavy rainfall, about dark, confined to a limited locality, a portion of a railroad bed was so undermined that it gave way under the weight of a train three or four hours afterwards, and the plaintiff was injured thereby. It appeared that the road-bed was in a safe condition before the rainfall, and that a train had passed over it safely two hours before the accident, and that the track and road-bed had been inspected between the passage of that train and the time of the accident, and that at that time the track was in an apparently safe condition, and at the time of the accident the road was apparently safe. It was held that there could be no recovery for the injury. "If," says BONNER, J., referring to an accident resulting from the sudden washing away of a road-bed by an extraordinary flood, "an accident should happen from such cause on a road-bed and track which had been properly constructed and kept in good repair, when the agents and employees in charge of the train were in the exercise of that degree of caution and prudence necessary at all times, and when they did not have, from information conveyed to them, or from their own personal observation, reasonable grounds to anticipate impending danger, and consequently ,did not use such extraordinary precautions as might have otherwise averted it, then the law characterizes it as an act of God, or inevitable accident as is incident to all human works, and which would relieve the company from liability. In Great Western Rail. Co. *v.* Braid, 1 Moore's P. C. N. S. 101, the accident occurred in Canada. An embankment was carried away by an extraordinary storm; the accident occurred at about two o'clock, A. M.; loaded trains had safely passed between eleven and twelve o'clock of the same night, and at ten minutes past one of the same morning; all appeared safe then, and there was nothing to attract attention; but the flood afterward made a gap of forty-five yards. From six o'clock of the preceding evening there had been an excessively heavy rain. The road had been used four years without accident, and was inspected daily. A verdict was found for the plaintiff. This was affirmed. LORD CHELMSFORD said: "The railway company ought to have constructed their works in such a manner as to be capable of resisting all the violence of weather which in the climate of Canada might be expected, though perhaps rarely, to occur. . . . In the whole of the evidence there is nothing more proved than that the night was one of unusual severity, but there is no proof that nothing similar had been experienced before, nor is there anything to lead to the conclusion that it was at all improbable that such a storm might at any time occur. It must also be borne in mind that although the embankment had stood firm for five years, and had possibly not been exposed to any storm of equal violence to that before which it gave way, yet it was evidently not constructed, or at least not maintained, in

regarded as in the custody of the proprietors of these conveyances, in such a way as to make them liable as common carriers in case of their loss or damage. Common carriers not being insurers of the safety of the passengers they carry, are they to be regarded as insurers of the luggage which these passengers take with them? Formerly it was held that the proprietors of conveyances which carried passengers were not responsible as common carriers for the baggage of passengers unless a distinct price were paid for it.[1] Now, however, it is held that, as the custody of the luggage is an accessary to the principal contract, those persons who carry the luggage of passengers should be regarded as liable at law as common carriers. There can be no injustice in such a doctrine, as it is in the power of all carriers to charge such

a manner to resist any unusual pressure. . . . It is evident that the embankment was insufficiently provided with means of resisting the storm, which though of unusual violence was not of such a character as might not reasonably have been anticipated, and which therefore ought to have been provided against by all reasonable and prudent precautions." But where due precautions have been taken, and for several years the road-bed has resisted the ordinary floods and freshets incident to the locality, this circumstance furnishes strong evidence exonerating the company from the charge of negligence. In Withers *v.* North Kent Rail. Co., 27 L. J. Exch. 417, there was evidence that the embankment ran through a country subject to floods, and had been constructed five years, of sandy soil, with insufficient culverts; that an extraordinary fall of rain of sixteen hours had caused a flood which had washed away the soil, leaving the sleepers unsupported; but there was no evidence that anything had been seen on the line to indicate danger. The plaintiff had a verdict. Held, that there could be no recovery. POLLOCK, C. B., said: "The line had lasted five years in a country subject to floods, and it does not appear that there had been any accident or objection to its construction until this extraordinary flood occurred. The company was not bound to have a line constructed so as to meet such extraordinary floods." MARTIN, B., said: "If the line had nevertheless lasted five years, that tends to show that there was no reason to apprehend danger from ordinary floods, and they were not to provide for extraordinary." BRAMWELL, B., said: "It is contended, on the part of the plaintiff, that the company's servants were bound to know the consequences which were likely to follow from the flood. That is not so. *They were bound to know only that which could be known by the exercise of ordinary skill and prudence.*" See also Brehm *v.* Great Western Rail. Co., 34 Barb. (N. Y.) 256.

[1] Middleton *v.* Fowler, I Salk. 282; Upshare *v.* Aidee, 1 Comyns, 25; Wolf *v.* Summers, 2 Camp. 631.

a rate as will compensate them for the risk which they run.[1] Cases in which this question has been raised have come before our courts. In one of these, the plaintiff, a passenger by the Great Western Railway, having taken and paid for a second-class ticket, delivered her luggage to a porter of the defendants, telling him to what station she was going, and after seeing him label it, took her seat in the train. On her arrival at her destination, one of her boxes was missing. By the defendants' charter, they were empowered to make by-laws, which were to be painted on a board and hung up at the stations, and were to be binding on all parties. One of the by-laws ran as follows: "Every first-class passenger will be allowed 112 lbs., and every second-class passenger 56 lbs. of luggage, free of charge; but the company will not be responsible for the care of the same unless booked and paid for accordingly." It did not appear that the plaintiff knew of the by-law, or that it had been affixed at the stations as required by the act. It was admitted by the defendants that the box had been stolen. The plaintiff having sued the defendants in a county court for the loss, the judge, on these facts, held the defendants liable, and gave the plaintiff the full value of the box. On appeal, it was held that the judgment must be affirmed, as the *primâ facie* liability of the defendants was not conclusively rebutted, and there was therefore evidence to support the finding.[2]

[1] It is held that a carrier of passengers is liable for the ordinary baggage of a passenger, though no distinct price is paid for its transportation. Bomar *v.* Maxwell, 9 Humph. (Tenn.) 621; Merrill *v.* Grinnell, 30 N. Y. 594; Prixotti *v.* McLaughlin, 1 Strobh. (S. C.) 468; Orange County Bank *v.* Brown, 9 Wend. (N. Y.) 75; Woods *v.* Devin, 13 Ill. 746.

[2] Great Western Rail. Co. *v.* Goodman, 12 C. B. 313; 16 Jur. 862; 21 L. J. C. P. 197; Williams *v.* Great Western Rail. Co., 10 Exch. 15; Marshall *v.* York, Newcastle, & Berwick Rail. Co., 11 C. B. 655; 16 Jur. 124; 21 L. J. C. P. 34; Richards *v.* London & South Coast Rail. Co., 7 C. B. 839; 6 Rail. Cas. 49; 13 Jur. 986; 18 L. J. C. P. 251; Butcher *v.* London & South-Western Rail. Co., 16 C. B. 13; 3 C. L. R. 805; 1 Jur. N. S. 427; 24 L. J. C. P. 137. In this case there was evidence of negligence upon the part of the company's servants. Midland Rail. Co. app., Bromley, resp., 17 C. B. 372; 2 Jur. N. S. 140; 25 L. J. C. P. 94; COCKBURN, C. J., in Le Conteur *v.* London & South-Western Rail. Co., 1 L. R. Q. B. 54, 59; Powell *v.* Myers, 26 Wend. (N. Y.) 591; Walsh *v.* The

SEC. 59. **Reason of the Common-law Duty.** — From the way in which the liability of carriers of passengers for their passengers' luggage came to be recognized, it might be inferred that this liability extended only to luggage, and no further. The facts which brought about this recognition were these: First, the necessity which each person who travels is under to carry luggage; and second, the fact that the contract to carry the baggage was necessary on the side of the proprietors of the conveyance to make the contract to carry individuals at all advantageous. In that way the law came to impose the common-law duty, with regard to baggage, upon carriers of passengers, and at the same time to impose the common-law liability to make good the loss or damage of luggage so carried. From such a beginning it might be inferred that this duty only extended to a person's personal luggage. Such is actually the case.[1] It is sometimes difficult to deter-

H. M. Wright, 1 Newb. 494; Camden & Amboy R. R. Co. *v.* Belknap, 21 Wend. (N. Y.) 354; Pardee *v.* Drew, 25 Wend. (N. Y.) 459; Hollister *v.* Nowlen, 19 Wend. (N. Y.) 234; Bomar *v.* Maxwell, 9 Humph. (Tenn.) 321; Hawkins *v.* Hoffman, 6 Hill (N. Y.), 586; Blanchard *v.* Isaacs, 3 Barb. (N. Y.) 388; Gore *v.* Norwich, &c. Co., 2 Daly (N. Y.), 254; Holdridge *v.* Utica, &c. R. R. Co., 56 Barb. (N. Y.) 191.

[1] Shepherd *v.* Great Northern Rail. Co., 8 Exch. 30; 7 Rail. Cas. 310; 21 L. J. Exch. 286; Brooke *v.* Pickwick, 4 Bing. 218; 12 Moore, 447. It is often a very difficult question to determine what constitutes ordinary baggage for which a carrier is liable, the general rule being that the implied obligation of a common carrier to carry the baggage of a passenger does not extend beyond *ordinary* baggage, or such as a traveller usually carries with him for his personal convenience. Merrill *v.* Grinnell, 30 N. Y. 594; Johnson *v.* Stone, 11 Humph. (Tenn.) 419; Whitmore *v.* Steamer Caroline, 20 Mo. 513; The Ionic, 5 Blatchf. (U. S. C. C.) 538; Collins *v.* Boston R. R., 10 Cush. (Mass.) 606; Bell *v.* Drew, 4 E. D. S. (N. Y. C. P.) 59; Dibble *v.* Brown, 12 Ga. 217; Richards *v.* Westcott, 2 Bosw. (N. Y.) 589; Smith *v.* Boston, &c. R. R. Co., 44 N. H. 325; Stimson *v.* Connecticut, &c. R., R. Co., 98 Mass. 83. It is not necessary that the articles should be simply such as are necessary or useful *during* the journey; it is enough if they are for use during the stay at the terminus thereof. Toledo, &c. R. R. Co. *v.* Hammond, 33 Ind. 379; New Orleans, &c. R. R. Co. *v.* Moore, 40 Miss. 39. And this includes all kinds of clothing for himself and family who travel with him, as well as articles of jewelry and personal adornment. American Contract Co. *v.* Cross, 8 Bush (Ky.), 472; McCormick *v.* Hudson River R. R. Co., 4 E. D. S. (N. Y. C. P.) 181; Mississippi Central R. R. Co. *v.* Kennedy, 41 Miss. 671; Smith *v.* Boston, &c. R. R. Co., 44 N. H.

mine what is a man's personal luggage; but some decisions enable us to say at least what does not fall under that descrip-

325; Hawkins *v.* Hoffman, 6 Hill (N. Y.), 586. And the question as to what constitutes articles of personal convenience has been variously decided, and depends largely upon the habits, manners, and customs of the people in the section of country in which the question arises, as well as the profession or rank and condition of the passenger, and the length of the journey, and the purposes for which it was undertaken. A person undertaking a *long* journey requires many more articles for his personal convenience than one undertaking a short one; and while a person undertaking a journey of only a few miles is entitled to put in his baggage a sum of money sufficient to defray the reasonable expenses of his journey, yet he would not be entitled to place there, at the risk of the carrier, so large a sum as a person undertaking a long journey, as in all cases the question of *reasonableness* in this respect is to be determined in view of the circumstances. This rule is well illustrated by a recent case decided in the United States Supreme Court (New York Central, &c. R. R. Co. *v.* Fraloff, 100 U. S. 24). In that case a Russian lady travelling in this country carried as a part of her baggage and for her personal use a large quantity of lace, used as a part of her wearing apparel on certain occasions, and which she valued at $75,000, and which the jury found to be worth $10,000. The trunk containing it was lost, and the court held that under the circumstances a recovery could be had therefor. "To the extent that articles taken by a traveller," say the court, "for his personal use when travelling exceed in quantity and value such as are ordinarily taken by passengers of like station and pursuing like journeys, they are not baggage for which the carrier is, by general law, responsible as insurers; whether he has taken such excess is a question of fact for the jury." It was also held in the same case that the carriers may be discharged from liability for the full value, if the passenger, by any artifice, evades inquiry as to such value, whereby a responsibility is imposed upon them beyond what they are bound to assume in consideration of the ordinary fare charged for the transportation of the person. But that in the absence of legislation, or of special regulations by the carriers, or of conduct by the passenger misleading them as to such value, his failure to disclose it, when no inquiry is made of him, is not, in itself, a fraud upon them. "Manuscript books," the property of a student, and used in the prosecution of his studies, have been held to be ordinary baggage; also a gun and fishing-tackle. Hopkins *v.* Westcott, 6 Hill (N. Y.), 589. So the instruments of an army surgeon travelling with troops, Hannibal R. R. Co. *v.* Swift, 12 Wall. (U. S.) 262; an opera-glass, Toledo, &c. R. R. Co. *v.* Hammond, 33 Ind. 379; a carpenter's tools, Porter *v.* Hildebrand, 14 Penn. St. 129; a pocket pistol and a pair of duelling pistols, Woods *v.* Denin, 13 Ill. 746, but see Chicago, &c. R. R. Co. *v.* Collins, 56 Ill. 212, where it was held that only one pistol could be recovered for as baggage; linen, cut into shirt-bosoms for the use of the passenger, Duffy *v.* Thompson, 4 E. D. S. (N. Y. C. P.) 178; McCormick *v.* Hudson River R. R. Co., 4 E. D. S. (N. Y. C.

tion. Thus it has been decided that a railway company whose charter enabled every passenger to take with him his articles

P.) 181; Torpey *v.* Williams, 3 Daly (N. Y.), 162; a watch, Jones *v.* Voorhees, 10 Ohio, 145; personal jewelry, Doyle *v.* Kyser, 6 Ind. 242; McCormick *v.* Hudson River R. R. Co., *ante;* Torpey *v.* Williams, 3 Daly (N.Y.C.P.), 162; a proper sum of money for travelling expenses, Merrill *v.* Grinnell, 30 N. Y. 594, but not for an amount beyond that which a prudent person would deem proper for the purpose, Jordan *v.* Fall River R. R. Co., 5 Cush. (Mass.) 69; Dunlap *v.* International Steamboat Co., 98 Mass. 371; nor for money belonging to another passenger, however reasonable in amount. Stewart *v.* International Steamboat Co., 98 Mass. 371. Money, in order to constitute baggage, must be confined to such a reasonable sum as is necessary to defray the expenses of the journey; consequently money placed in a trunk for the purpose of buying clothing at the place to which the passenger is going, has been held not to be recoverable as baggage. Hickox *v.* Naugatuck, &c. R. R. Co., 31 Conn. 281. Thus, in the case last cited, the plaintiff admitted that sixty dollars of the money lost from his trunk was taken with him for the purpose of buying clothing, and the court held that it was not recoverable. The amount of money which may be treated as baggage is to be measured by the object, length, and purpose of the journey, and is such a reasonable sum as a prudent person would deem necessary in view of all the circumstances, and is a question of fact to be found by the jury. Illinois Central R. R. Co. *v.* Copeland, 24 Ill. 332; Jordan *v.* Fall River R. R. Co., 5 Cush. (Mass.) 69. When an extra charge is made for baggage, even though it consists of articles not within the class of ordinary baggage, it is held, in the absence of any fraud or imposition on the part of the passenger, that the carrier is liable for its loss by fraud or negligence; and this was held to be the case where a passenger packed "specie" in his trunk, and procured it to be taken as baggage, although the company advertised that "passengers are prohibited from taking with them anything as baggage but their wearing-apparel, which will be at the risk of the owner." Camden, &c. R. R. Co. *v.* Baldauf, 16 Penn. St. 67. Among articles of necessity for which a carrier by water is liable as baggage, is such bedding as is carried by a steerage passenger for use on the voyage, Hirschshon *v.* American Packet Co., 2 J. & S. N. Y. Superior Ct.) 521, but not for bedding packed in a trunk or not used on the voyage. Connolly *v.* Warren, 106 Mass. 146. Whether bedding belonging to a person who is moving with his family, packed in a box or trunk, is baggage or not, is a question of fact for the jury in view of all the circumstances, and the use, quality, value, and kind of articles. Ouimit *v.* Henshaw, 35 Vt. 605. The rules adopted by the courts as to what constitutes ordinary baggage are not always consistent nor uniform; and the doctrine of some of the cases, carried out to their legitimate sequence, would almost admit of a passenger taking along with him his entire household furniture, if he is *a poor man,* and needs the furniture for use at the end of his journey, and it can be packed in trunks or boxes. Of this class are Ouimit *v.* Henshaw, 35 Vt. 604; and Parmalee *v.* Fischer, 22 Ill. 212. In the former of these cases it was held

of clothing, not exceeding a specified weight and dimensions, and which absolved the company from all liability or respon-

that a feather bed and the necessary accompaniments of bedquilts, pillows, &c., belonging to *a poor man* removing with his family, might properly be regarded as personal baggage; while in the latter case, "*two* feather beds and pillows, two coverlets, two bedspreads, or blankets, . . . one oil-cloth table-cover, . . . one German-silver or britannia teapot, one looking-glass, one new double-barrelled gun, one set of common dishes, two dozen German-silver spoons, one serving-box, . . . and six towels," together with considerable clothing, worth about one hundred and fifty dollars, were found by the jury to be such articles of necessity and convenience as are usually carried by passengers for their personal use and comfort, instruction and amusement or protection, having regard to the object and length of the journey. The verdict was upheld on appeal. These cases cannot be said to conform to the principles usually adopted in this class of cases, except they are put upon the ground that travellers of the class in question, in the section of country where the action was brought, usually carried such articles as baggage, and the carrier was bound to know of the usage, and therefore to assent to accept and take them as baggage. From what has been said and the cases given, it will be seen that the question as to what constitutes "ordinary baggage," within the legal significance of the term, depends entirely upon the circumstance whether the articles are "necessary or convenient" to the traveller under the circumstances of the case, or are such as are usually carried by travellers. As we have seen, jewelry for personal use, to a reasonable extent, is within the term; but jewelry intended for presents to a traveller's friends is not. Nevins *v.* Bay State, &c. Co., 4 Bosw. (N. Y.) 225. But it seems that articles purchased for his family are properly baggage, if such as are usually carried, although not necessary for his use or comfort on the journey. Dexter *v.* Syracuse, &c. R. R. Co., 34 N. Y. 326. Masquerade costumes furnished for use at a ball, Michigan, &c. R. R. Co. *v.* Oehm, 56 Ill. 293, Masonic regalia, engravings, valuable merchaudise, &c., do not come under the head of baggage, Nevins *v.* Bay State, &c. Co., *ante;* Pardee *v.* Drew, 25 Wend. (N. Y.) 459, nor indeed any articles which are not necessary or convenient for the use of the passenger on his journey; and in all cases the question as to what is reasonable, necessary, or convenient is a question of fact for the jury in view of the character of the journey and the special circumstances of the case. Merrill *v.* Grinnell, 30 N. Y. 594. The rule is, that when a traveller presents to a carrier of passengers, as his baggage, a trunk or carpet-bag without describing its contents, he impliedly represents that it only contains such articles as are usually carried as baggage, or such as are necessary for his convenience and comfort upon his journey. The carrier is not bound to inquire for articles of extraordinary value which it may contain; but if there are such, the passenger should disclose the fact, that the carrier may exercise the increased vigilance which such extraordinary value demands. Michigan, &c. R. R. Co. *v.* Carran, 73 Ill. 348.

The liability of a common carrier for the baggage of a passenger con-

sibility for articles other than and except articles of clothing, having, as they had power to do under their charter, made a

tinues until the baggage is ready to be delivered to the owner at his destination, and until he has had a reasonable opportunity of receiving and removing it. What constitutes such reasonable time and opportunity is a mixed question of law and fact, necessarily dependent upon the peculiar surroundings of each particular case. Louisville, &c. R. R. Co. *v.* Mahan, 8 Bush (Ky.), 135. See Torpey *v.* Williams, 3 Daly (N. Y.), 162; Klein *v.* Hamburg, &c. Packet Co., 3 Daly (N. Y.), 390. And where, for his own convenience, a passenger left his baggage in the carrier's depot over night and it was burned, it was held that the company was not liable therefor. Morris *v.* Third Avenue R. R. Co., 1 Daly (N. Y. C. P.), 202; Jones *v.* Norwich, &c. Transportation Co., 50 Barb. (N. Y.) 493. The obligation to exercise ordinary care in keeping and preserving property as to which they have been relieved from their peculiar liability as insurers, by the failure of the owner to call for his baggage within a reasonable time, is not a new and independent obligation, arising from the circumstance, accidental and unprovided for, of the property being left in the hands of the carrier. The duty is imposed by the contract of carriage, and therefore rests upon the carrier with whom the contract was made, although the place of destination is beyond its route, and upon the line of a connecting carrier. Burnell *v.* New York, &c. R. R. Co., 45 N. Y. 184. Where baggage which had arrived at its point of destination was left in the custody of the agent of the railroad company for the night, and during the same night the depot and contents, including the baggage, were destroyed by fire, held, that, in order to make the company liable for the baggage so destroyed, it was incumbent on the owner to show that the fire was the result of such negligence on the part of the employees of the company as would render liable a bailee for hire. Louisville, &c. R. R. Co. *v.* Mahan, 8 Bush (Ky.), 184. The rule may be said to be that common carriers of passengers, with their ordinary baggage, for hire, are liable for losses occurring from any accident to the baggage while it is in their keeping as carriers, except those arising from the acts of God or a public enemy; and this liability once commenced does not necessarily terminate with the transit, but *primâ facie* continues until the safe delivery of the baggage to its owner. But when the passenger refuses to receive his baggage, or neglects to call for it within a reasonable time after the transit, the responsibility of the carriers is changed to that of a bailee, liable only for loss occasioned by his own neglect. Roth *v.* Buffalo, &c. R. R. Co., 34 N. Y. 548. It makes no difference, so far as a common carrier's responsibility for the safety of a passenger's baggage is concerned, whether the passenger travels with his baggage, or whether it is carried without him. Wilson *v.* Chesapeake, &c. R. R. Co., 21 Gratt. (Va.) 654. But a carrier is not responsible for the loss of baggage which the passenger himself takes charge of. Thus, where passengers left a portion of the jewelry usually worn by them in the stateroom of a steamboat, and it was stolen, it was held that the carrier was not responsible therefor. The R. E. Lee, 2 Abb. (U. S.) 49. But see Mudgett *v.* Bay State Steamboat Co., 1 Daly (N. Y. C. P.), 151, where it was held

regulation requiring passengers, after taking their tickets, to claim their luggage on the platform, and to see it marked

that the mere supervision of his baggage by a passenger, or his having the means of entering the place of its deposit, is not sufficient to discharge the carrier from liability for its loss, and that there must either exist the *animus custodiendi* on the part of the passenger to the exclusion of the carrier, or he must be guilty of such negligence as excuses the latter from his general obligation, and that the proprietor of a steamboat is responsible for baggage of a passenger which he has locked up in his stateroom, but which is stolen therefrom on the journey. See also, to the same effect, where the boat-owner was held responsible for an overcoat hung up in his stateroom by a passenger, and which was stolen therefrom. Gore *v.* Norwich, &c. Transportation Co., 1 Daly (N. Y. C. P.), 254; S. P. Van Horn *v.* Kermit, 4 E. D. S. (N. Y. C. P.) 453; Crozier *v.* Boston, &c. Steamboat Co., 43 How. (N. Y.) Pr. 466; Duffy *v.* Thompson, 4 E. D. S. (N. Y. C. P.) 178. But where a passenger on an emigrant vessel retains his trunk in his own possession, and it is stolen, the owners of the ship are not liable. To render them liable it must be placed under their charge. Cohen *v.* Frost, 2 Duer (N. Y. Superior Ct.), 335. Nor is a railroad company responsible for the loss of baggage or any property taken by a passenger into the car with him. Tower *v.* Utica, &c. R. R. Co., 7 Hill (N. Y.), 47. But if the carrier interferes with a passenger's baggage while in a passenger-car, — as if his servants remove it from one car to another, or attempt to do so, — and it is lost by reason of their negligence, they are responsible therefor. Thus, in Kinsley *v.* Lake Shore R. R. Co., 125 Mass. 54, it appeared that the plaintiff, on leaving a sleeping-car to get his dinner, was informed by an employee of the defendant that his baggage, if left therein, would be safe; and upon his return he found the car locked and detached, and was informed that he could have a seat in another sleeping-car, and would find his baggage there, but upon going there he found only part of his baggage. No previous notice of the change had been given him, and there was no evidence that he knew that the first car was not owned by the defendant, but by another company, who, by a contract with the defendant, provided conductors and servants therefor. The court held that the jury were warranted in finding that the missing bag was lost through the negligence of the defendant, and that the defendant was liable therefor, although the first car was not owned by it.

So, while a carrier is not obliged to accept anything but ordinary baggage as baggage, yet, *if without extra compensation, and knowing that it is not personal baggage,* he permits it to be carried and treated as such, he is liable for its loss. Ross *v.* Missouri, &c. R. R. Co., 4 Mo. App. 582. In Waldron *v.* Chicago, &c. R. R. Co., 1 Dakota, 351, the plaintiff, after buying a ticket for himself, son, and two daughters, pointed out to the baggage-master as his baggage three trunks and two boxes, one of which was a rough pine box, twenty inches square and ten inches deep, having nothing to which a check could be fastened, whereupon the baggage-master said he would place it in the baggage-car, and it would go just as safely, only that it would have to be looked after at M., or it might

with the company's labels, and declaring that no luggage would be placed in the train until it was so marked, and

be taken beyond that station. On arriving at M. the pine box was missing. It appeared that one T. had bought a ticket to S., requesting the night baggage-master to check the box thereto; that T. unlocked and took from the box and presented to him a photograph of W.'s family; that T. then locked the box and put a rope around it, whereto a check to S. was attached, and at S. the box was delivered to T. There was no other evidence than that stated, that T. was the plaintiff's agent, and the plaintiff denied any such agency. It was held that the company having received the box upon the passenger train without the plaintiff's having concealed the fact that it was not personal baggage, the fact that it was not such in fact did not save them from liability therefor. In Minter *v.* Pacific R. R. Co., 41 Mo. 503, a passenger delivered his trunk and a piece of carpeting to the baggage-master of a passenger train, and received a check for his trunk, but was told that no check was necessary for the carpet, as it would go safely; it was held that the railroad company was liable for the loss of the carpet, although by the printed rules of the company the baggage-master was forbidden to receive as baggage any article of merchandise. Checks given for baggage are merely evidence of its having been received by the carrier, and of its non-delivery, but do not of themselves establish the carrier's liability therefor; because, if they are obtained under the pretence that the owner of the baggage is a passenger, and has obtained tickets for that journey, or is about to do so, when such is not the fact, the carrier cannot be held chargeable as such for the baggage. The contract from which his liability for the safe carriage of the baggage arises is the contract for the carriage of the passenger himself. Chicago, &c. R. R. Co. *v.* Clayton, 78 Ill. 616; Davis *v.* R. R. Co., 22 Ill. 278; Milnor *v.* New York & New Haven R. R. Co., 53 N. Y. 363; Dill *v.* R. R. Co., 7 Rich. (S. C.) L. 158; Wilson *v.* Chesapeake, &c. R. R. Co., 21 Gratt. (Va.) 654. Consequently a contract to carry a passenger to a certain place, although it involves his transportation over several lines of railroads, is also operative as a contract to carry his baggage to the same point. Wilson *v.* Chesapeake, &c. R. R. Co., 21 Gratt. (Va.) 654. And in the case last cited, where a railroad company had an arrangement with a stage company to carry passengers and baggage from a certain point on its line to another point, it was held that, having issued a ticket to such place, it was liable for the loss of the passenger's baggage by the stage company. See also, as to connecting lines of railroads, Le Sage *v.* Great Western R. R. Co., 1 Daly (N. Y. C. P.), 306; Hart *v.* Rensselaer R. R. Co., 8 N. Y. 37; Weed *v.* Saratoga, &c. R. R. Co., 19 Wend. (N. Y.) 534; Candee *v.* R. R. Co., 21 Wis. 582; Illinois Central R. R. Co. *v.* Copeland, 24 Ill. 332; Torpey *v.* Williams, 3 Daly (N. Y. C. P.), 162; Burnell *v.* New York Central R. R. Co., 45 N. Y. 484; Cary *v.* Cleveland, &c. R. R. Co., 29 Barb. (N. Y.) 35. Although, if the passenger elects to do so, he may proceed directly against the carrier by whom the baggage was lost; the only disadvantage in that latter instance being that he takes the burden of showing that the carrier sued lost the baggage, while if he proceeds against the first

further declaring that they would not be responsible for any article of luggage that was not so marked — it has been

carrier, he is only called upon to prove the loss of the baggage, without being required to show by which carrier. Barter *v.* Wheeler, 49 N. H. 9; Illinois Central R. R. Co. *v.* Frankenberg, 54 Ill. 88; Coates *v.* United States Express Co., 45 Mo. 238; Toledo, &c. R. R. Co. *v.* Merriam, 52 Ill. 88; Cincinnati, &c. R. R. Co. *v.* Pontius, 19 Ohio St. 222; McCormick *v.* Hudson River R. R. Co., 4 E. D. S. (N. Y. C. P.) 181; Kessler *v.* New York Central R. R. Co., 61 N. Y. 538. In Wilson *v.* Chesapeake R. R. Co., *ante*, it was held that railway checks given for baggage are admissible in evidence to show what the carrier's undertaking was. In other words, they are admissible to show that a contract was in fact made and issued in connection with a through ticket, an evidence to show that the carrier undertook to carry the passenger through or otherwise, accordingly as the check is given through, or only for its own line. But the mere circumstance that a carrier gives a through check is not sufficient to establish his liability beyond his own line, unless it is also shown that he issued a through ticket. Thus, in Green *v.* New York, &c. R. R. Co., 12 Abb. (N. Y.) Pr. N. S. 473, the defendant railroad issued to the plaintiff a check for baggage to the terminus of his journey, which covered its own line and a steamboat line which run in connection therewith; but it did not issue a ticket to the passenger beyond its own line, and it was held that it could not be held liable for the loss of the baggage by the steamboat company. But if a passenger takes his baggage in the car with him over the first line, but procures it to be checked and carried in the baggage-car over the second, the first line cannot be held chargeable for the loss of the baggage, because it never had it in its custody. Straiton *v.* New York & New Haven R. R. Co., 2 E. D. S. (N. Y. C. P.) 184. But if it received the baggage in the outset, the fact that it was rechecked at another point on the route and by another carrier does not change its liability. Candee *v.* Pennsylvania R. R. Co., 21 Wis. 582. See also Mobile, &c. R. R. Co. *v.* Hopkins, 41 Ala. 486. Holding that the first carrier, issuing a through ticket and checking the baggage through, is liable for its loss, see Chicago, &c. R. R. Co. *v.* Fahey, 52 Ill. 81; Illinois Central R. R. Co. *v.* Copeland, 24 Ill. 332; Glasco *v.* New York Central R. R. Co., 36 Barb. (N. Y.) 557; Check *v.* Little Miami R. R. Co., 2 Dis. (Ohio) 237; Kessler *v.* New York Central R. R. Co., 7 Lans. (N. Y.) 62; Najac *v.* Boston, &c. R. R. Co., 7 Allen (Mass.), 320. Or that the passenger may hold the line actually losing the baggage therefor. Burnell *v.* New York Central R. R. Co., 45 N. Y. 184; Check *v.* Little Miami R. R. Co., *ante;* Kessler *v.* New York Central R. R. Co., *ante;* Burtis *v.* Buffalo, &c. R. R. Co., 24 N. Y. 269; Root *v.* Great Western R. R. Co., 45 N. Y. 525.

The possession of a railway baggage-check, accompanied by evidence of the baggage-master that, when required by passengers, he put checks on their baggage and gave duplicates to the passenger, is sufficient evidence that a person was a passenger on the cars, and that he had the baggage checked. Davis *v.* Cayuga, &c. R. R. Co., 10 How. (N. Y.) Pr. 330. In Dill *v.* South Carolina R. R. Co., 7 Rich.

decided that a company, having done so, cannot refuse to place in their van and convey as passengers' luggage a

(S. C.) 158, a check in the possession of a passenger was held to be evidence that the passenger's baggage was delivered to the company, and, as a trunk is the usual receptacle for baggage, that a trunk with its contents was delivered to it. In Kansas Pacific R. R. Co. *v.* Moutelle, 10 Kan. 119, a passenger from New York to Junction City, Kan., delivered his checks for his baggage to the baggage-master of the defendant with the understanding that the defendant should forward it to Junction City, and this was held evidence to go to the jury to establish the fact that the defendant received the baggage. See also, holding that the delivery of a baggage-check is *primâ facie* evidence that the carrier issuing it has the baggage, Davis *v.* Michigan, &c. R. R. Co., 22 Ill. 278, and that the check is of no importance as constituting the contract of the company, it being merely in the nature of a receipt and intended as evidence of the ownership and identity of the baggage. Hickox *v.* Naugatuck R. R. Co., 31 Conn. 281. It is only *primâ facie* evidence that the carrier received the passenger's baggage. Chicago, &c. R. R. Co. *v.* Clayton, 78 Ill. 616.

Palace-car companies are not responsible as innkeepers for the loss of baggage which is retained by a passenger in his own possession, and is only liable, in the absence of a special contract, as an ordinary private carrier of passengers. Welch *v.* Pullman Palace Car Co., 16 Abb. (N. Y.) Pr. N. S. 352. In Blum *v.* Southern Pullman Car Co., 1 Flip (U. S. C. C.), 500, the rule adopted was, that a sleeping-car company is not responsible either as an innkeeper or common carrier for the passenger's baggage, but that it must take reasonable care to prevent the larceny of a passenger's property; and that, if it is negligent in this respect, it is liable for such articles as are usually carried by a passenger about his person, and such a sum of money as may be deemed reasonably necessary to defray the expenses of his journey.

In order to render a carrier liable for the loss of baggage, it is sufficient to show a delivery of the baggage to him; and from the time of such delivery, although some time in advance of the time when it will start upon its transit, the carrier is liable for it as a common carrier, and not as a warehouseman, from the time of delivery, and if it is lost *before* the time for it to start upon its transit, the carrier is liable. Thus, in Hickox *v.* Naugatuck R. R. Co., 31 Conn. 281, the plaintiff took his trunk to the defendant's depot at Waterbury, at eleven o'clock, A. M., and asked to have it checked to Bridgeport, on the train which started at three, P. M. He was told that it was not their custom to check baggage until fifteen minutes before the train started, whereupon he left his trunk with the agent in the baggage-room, and at the customary time it was checked and put on the cars for Bridgeport. It was rifled after its delivery to the defendant, but whether before or after it left the station did not appear. The defendant asked the court to charge the jury that if the trunk was rifled after it was taken to the depot and before it was checked, there could be no recovery. The court refused so to charge, and upon appeal, BUTLER, J., said: —

"The reasonable convenience of

package brought by a passenger and made up in a railway wrapper or horse-rug, on the ground that it consists of

travellers requires that they have an opportunity to deliver baggage at any reasonable time before the departure of the train, and it is therefore the duty of a railroad company to keep an agent at all important stations to receive and take charge of baggage. Jordan *v.* Fall River R. R. Co., 5 Cush. (Mass.) 69. For aught that appears, such was the custom of the defendants, and the agent who received the trunk was there for that purpose. In respect to passengers the company are carriers merely, and the trunk an article which ordinarily accompanies the passenger. If nothing had been said, therefore, in respect to the purpose for which it was delivered and received by the agent of the defendants, its reception for transportation would be implied. But the purpose and the hour were expressly indicated by the plaintiff, and it was received without objection, except that they could not then give him a check. Clearly it was received for the purpose indicated, and the time fixed when by their custom a check would be given him. The length of time which elapsed between its reception and the departure of the train could make no difference.

"In the case of Camden & Amboy R. R. Co. *v.* Belknap, 21 Wend. (N. Y.) 354, trunks were left with the company in the afternoon of one day to go with the owner by the boat of next morning, and one of them was taken from the office of the company through the negligence of the clerk or porter, before the departure of the next boat, and it was holden that they were in the possession of the company as *carriers*, and that they were answerable as such. See also Redfield on Railways, 242, 3. The custom of checking can have no effect upon the character of the delivery. That custom did not necessarily qualify the delivery and acceptance. The check is in the nature of a receipt, and may be given and received at any time when the convenience and custom of the company dictate. It is not the contract, but evidence of the ownership, delivery, and identity of the baggage. It is the delivery and acceptance, the abandonment of all care of the baggage by the passenger, and the assumption of it by the agents of the carriers, expressly or impliedly for the purpose of transportation, which fix the liability of the latter as such, and that liability begins when the baggage is delivered to the agent of the company for carriage. Redfield on Railways, 246.

"Inasmuch, therefore, as the plaintiff was entitled to a verdict upon the facts, and no injustice has been done, there can be no new trial on that ground. But there is error in respect to the amount of damages. The company were liable for money contained in the trunk required by the plaintiff for his personal use and travelling expenses. That is well settled and was conceded on the trial. But their liability extended no further. The plaintiff admitted that sixty dollars of the money in the trunk was taken with him for the purchase of clothing. That money was in no just sense taken for travelling expenses or personal use. So the defendants requested the court to charge the jury; and we think they were entitled to such charge, in explicit terms, and that on that point the charge and verdict are wrong. A new trial is therefore ad-

articles of clothing. In this case the plaintiff, who was a passenger by the South-Eastern Railway, required the

vised unless the plaintiff remits the sum of sixty dollars, which he was not entitled to recover."

In Rogers *v.* Long Island R. R. Co., 56 N. Y. 620, the plaintiff sent his trunk to the defendants' depot at Peck's Slip, by an expressman, at about noon, April 11, 1868. It was marked "Israel P. Rogers, Riverhead, L. I." The expressman found inside the depot gate, where he carried the trunk, two or three men unloading freight, of whom he inquired who took charge of baggage. They told him the man in the office. He saw the man in the office, and told him he had a trunk outside, and the man said "All right," and immediately sent two men to take care of it. The trunk was left by the expressman where the baggage was kept, and inside the defendants' enclosure and near their baggage crate, which at that time was locked. The man in the office had been the defendants' ticket agent for some years. The plaintiff went to the station at three o'clock, and bought a ticket to Riverhead, and called for his trunk, and it could not be found. The court held that these facts show a delivery to the defendants, and were sufficient to charge them with the loss of the trunk. Of course a passenger is entitled to a reasonable time in which to call for his baggage after its arrival at its place of destination; but the question as to what is a reasonable time is one of fact, in view of the customs of the country, the manner and facilities for transporting baggage from the station, and all the surrounding circumstances, and what would be a reasonable time in one case might not be so in another. Mote *v.* Chicago, &c. R. R. Co., 27 Iowa, 22. It may be shown that the depot was at a distance from a hotel or village, and that there were no conveyances obtainable to take the baggage away, or that the passenger was sick and lame and unable to take charge of the baggage personally, to excuse the passenger from calling for his baggage upon the arrival of the train; and if it is shown that the defendants' agents agreed to let the baggage remain until called for, the carrier remains liable for it, *as carrier*, if it is called for within a reasonable time. Curtis *v.* Avon, &c. R. R. Co., 49 Barb. (N. Y.) 148. But in the latter case it was held that if baggage is left with the carrier for an unreasonable time without being called for, and no arrangement is made that the carrier shall retain it for him, and it is lost without the fault of the carrier, he is not liable therefor. See Minor *v.* Chicago, &c. R. R. Co., 19 Wis. 40. A carrier of passengers is bound to deliver baggage to a passenger within a reasonable time after its arrival. Cary *v.* Cleveland, &c. R. R. Co., 29 Barb. (N. Y.) 35. And if the baggage is not left at the station for which it is checked, but is carried to another and there stored, and it is lost while there, he does not cease to be carrier and become a mere warehouseman as to the baggage, as would have been the case if it had been stored at the place to which it should have been carried. Toledo, &c. R. R. Co *v.* Hammond, 33 Ind. 379. In Dinning *v.* New York & New Haven R. R. Co., 49 N. Y. 546, the plaintiff's wife was a passenger upon the defendant road from N. to M. Immediately upon the arrival of the train at M. the depot-master placed the trunk in the baggage-room

company's porter at their station in London to label and take in the luggage van a package consisting only of his

aud went away. She waited fifteen minutes to get the trunk, but could find no one to deliver it. About three hours afterwards the plaintiff's son went to the depot for the trunk, but the depot-master was still absent. The son went in pursuit of him and returned with him, delivered the check, and the trunk was drawn out to the door; but meanwhile the conveyance which was employed to take the trunk had left and no other could be obtained, so it was left in charge of the baggage-master for the night. During the night it was stolen from the depot. It was held that the defendant's liability therefor as common carrier had not terminated. When baggage is lost, it is presumed to have been lost by the fraud or negligence of the carrier. Garvey *v.* Camden, &c. R. R. Co., 4 Abb. (N. Y.) Pr. 171; Camden, &c. R. R. Co. *v.* Baldauf, 16 Penn. St. 67.

While a carrier is only bound to carry for a passenger a reasonable amount of baggage, and may make proper regulations relative thereto, yet, if he accepts an extra quantity without objection or extra charge, he is equally liable therefor as though it was within the specified amount. Glasco *v.* New York Central R. R. Co., 36 Barb. (N. Y.) 557. A carrier cannot defeat his liability as a common carrier for the loss of a passenger's baggage by a simple notice that all baggage is at the risk of the owner, Camden, &c. R. R. Co. *v.* Belknap, 21 Wend. (N. Y.) 354, printed either upon the ticket or check, Rawson *v.* Pennsylvania R. R. Co., 48 N. Y. 212, as there is no presumption that a passenger read either before entering upon his journey. Malone *v.* Boston, &c. R. R. Co., 12 Gray (Mass.), 388; Brown *v.* Eastern R. R. Co., 11 Cush. (Mass.) 97. Nor can he place himself in the position of a private carrier as to liability for such baggage, unless notice that he will only be liable as such therefor is brought home to the knowledge of the carrier before he enters upon his journey, and has an opportunity to recede from his position of a passenger by the carrier's line, if he so elects. Logan *v.* Pontchartrain R. R. Co., 11 Rob. (La.) 24. Nor, except possibly in two or three States, can he limit his liability from the consequences of the negligence or wilful default or tort of himself or servants. Mobile, &c. R. R. Co. *v.* Hopkins, 41 Ala. 486; Indianapolis, &c. R. R. Co. *v.* Cox, 29 Ind. 360. "Notice in the usual form," says the court in Camden, &c. R. R. Co. *v.* Burke, 13 Wend. (N. Y.) 611, "'All baggage at the risk of the owners,' though brought home to the knowledge of a passenger, will not in such cases excuse the company. Common carriers cannot by such notice excuse themselves from the implied agreement that the vessel, coach, or other vehicle used for the transportation of goods or baggage, is sufficient for the business in which it is employed."

If a carrier of passengers, through the mistake of a connecting carrier, receives from such carrier baggage which should be transported over another line, he is liable for its loss although the person to whom such baggage belonged had no ticket and was not a passenger over such line. Thus, in Burnell *v.* New York Central R. R. Co., 45 N. Y. 184; 6 Am. Rep. 61, the plaintiff took passage, at Palmyra, on the defendant's road for New York,

wearing apparel; the whole was wrapped in a shawl, properly packed and addressed, and was within the allowed weight.

aud purchased a ticket and checked his trunk to the latter place. On his arrival in New York, the plaintiff, without calling for his baggage, went to Brooklyn, and the second day after his arrival presented his check and demanded his trunk, but it could not be found, and has not since been found. This action was brought to recover the value of the trunk and contents. The referee found that the trunk was lost through the negligence of the defendants and their servants, and that the plaintiff was entitled to recover, upon which a judgment was entered, which was reversed by the general term, in the first district, and a new trial ordered, from which the plaintiff appealed.

The Supreme Court placed its decision upon the ground that the defendants' liability ceased with the transportation of the trunk by the Hudson River Railroad Company to New York, and its readiness to deliver it within a reasonable time after arrival, and that whatever responsibility was incurred afterward in keeping or storing it was incurred by the latter company, for which the defendants were not liable.

The Court of Appeals held that the defendants were liable, and repudiated the ground taken by the Supreme Court. "Leaving baggage with a carrier by railroad," said CHURCH, C. J., "either for temporary convenience, from necessity, sickness, or accident, is not such an unusual or exceptional circumstance as to create a presumption that it was not within the contemplation of the parties at the time the contract was made. The duty of exercising care over property thus remaining in their possession is a part of the duty of carriers, incidental, it is true, to their principal or main duty, but nevertheless incumbent upon them; and it is no less a duty growing out of their relation of carriers, because their liability is mitigated to that of ordinary bailees for hire. Besides, this is the ordinary mode in which this business has been transacted, as the evidence in this case shows, and as all railroad companies are in the habit of doing. Baggage thus left is and always has been kept and cared for, and the manner of disposing of it, if not finally called for, was long since regulated by law (Laws of 1837, p. 311), and it is presumed that the parties contracted with reference to the existing state of facts, and to the customary manner of transacting such business.

"The other view terminates all relations between carrier and passenger immediately upon the expiration of the 'reasonable time' within which the baggage must be called for, and transforms the carrier into a mere accidental finder, or gratuitous bailee, liable only for gross negligence. In other words, it makes two contracts in every case where baggage is left, and complicates the rights and duties of the respective parties, and, while it essentially impairs the security of the public, confers no substantial benefit upon the carrier. Its tendency would be to induce carelessness and negligence, where care and vigilance is necessary. The fair construction of the contract is, that the defendants agreed for a consideration to transport the plaintiff and his trunk to New York, and deliver the latter to him on its arrival, if called for; if not, that it should be properly stored, and reasonable care exercised to prevent in-

The porter refused to do so, as the company had made a rule not to label shawls, but offered to put it in the carriage with the plaintiff, where it was to be under his charge. This the plaintiff objected to, unless it was at the company's risk, but did not prevent the company putting it there, or in any other part of the train. The package being left behind, in consequence of such refusal to label and carry it with the rest of the luggage, was taken by a porter to the lost-property office, and refused to be restored to the plaintiff except on payment of 6*d.* It was held that this was a wrongful act, for which the company were responsible, as the company were not, under the circumstances, justified in refusing to carry this parcel with the responsibility of carriers.[1]

SEC. 60. **Ordinary Luggage. — Definition.** — In another case, pencil sketches of an artist, placed in his portmanteau, were held not to form part of his ordinary luggage, so as to entitle them to be conveyed free of charge.[2] And the "ordinary luggage," for which a railway company would be held responsible, does not include a client's title-deeds, which an attorney may be carrying with him to produce in court; nor can the words be held to mean bank-notes (to a considerable amount), which may be packed in a bag or portmanteau by the said attorney, to be carried for the purpose of defraying the expenses of the trial.[3] It has, however, been definitely decided

jury or loss until it was called for, or was lawfully disposed of. This simplifies the transaction, carries out the intention of the parties, legalizes the uniform practice, and does justice to the carrier and the public. Although the rule on this subject has not been very definitely settled, yet the principles herein indicated are not new. Cary *v.* Cleveland & Toledo R. R. Co., 29 Barb. (N. Y.) 35; The Norway Plain Co. *v.* Boston & Maine R. R., 1 Gray (Mass.), 271, and cases cited.

"These views in effect determine the liability of the defendants in this action. The Hudson River Company being the agents of the defendants in performing the contract, and the contract of storage being a part of the original contract of carriage, it follows that the defendants are liable for the loss."

[1] Munster *v.* South-Eastern Rail. Co., 4 Jur. N. S. 738; 27 L. J. C. P. 308; 4 C. B. N. S. 676; Richards *v.* London, Brighton, & South Coast Rail. Co., 7 C. B. 839; 18 L. J. C. P. 251.

[2] Mytton *v.* Midland Rail. Co., 28 L. J. Exch. 385.

[3] Phelps *v.* London & North-Western Rail. Co., 19 C. B. N. S. 321; 11 Jur. N. S. 552; 34 L. J. C. P. 259;

that those articles only which travellers usually carry with them as part of their luggage come within the definition of ordinary or personal luggage, which a railway company is bound to carry with a passenger free of charge.[1] Thus, a child's toy, called a spring-horse, 78 lbs. in weight, and 44 inches in length, standing on a flat surface, is not within the regulation of a company allowing first-class passengers 112 lbs. of "personal luggage only (not being merchandise, or other articles carried for hire or profit) free of charge." [2]

SEC. 61. **Question for Jury.** — It may, in many cases, be a question for the jury what a man's personal luggage consists of, for it may be allowable that a man should carry different articles with him, and that articles which, at one time and under one set of circumstances, should not be considered personal luggage, might, at another time and under different circumstances, be looked at in that light. Thus, a man who was carrying in his portmanteau an article which was meant as a present to some one he was going to visit, might clearly regard that in the light of personal luggage while upon the journey to the residence of his friend, although it might not be such an article as "travellers usually carry with them as a part of their luggage." [3]

13 W R. 782; 12 L. T. N. S. 496. But see, where a different rule of law was laid down, Hopkins *v.* Westcott, 6 Blatchf. (U. S. C. C.) 64; Dunlap *v.* International, &c. Co., 98 Mass. 371.

[1] Hudson *v.* Midland Rail. Co., 4 L. R. Q. B. 366; 17 W. R. 705; 38 L. J. Q. B. 213; 20 L. T. N. S. 526.

[2] Hudson *v.* Midland Rail. Co., 10 B. & S. 504. See Zunz *v.* South-Eastern Rail. Co., 4 L. R. Q. B. 539; 38 L. J. Q. B. 209; 20 L. T. N. S. 873. See also, with regard to the arrangements of a company as to the amount of luggage to be carried by passengers travelling by cheap excursion trains, Rumsey *v.* North-Eastern Rail. Co., 14 C. B. N. S. 641; 3½ L. J. C. P. 244; 11 W. R. 911; 8 L. T. N. S. 666; 10 Jur. N. S. 208; Stewart *v.* London & North-Western Rail. Co., 10 Jur. N. S. 805; 33 L. J. Exch. 199; 12 W. R. 689; 10 L. T. N. S. 302; Walsh *v.* The H. M. Wright, 1 Newb. (U. S.) 494.

[3] Hudson *v.* Midland Rail. Co., 4 L. R. Q. B. 366; The Ionic, 5 Blatchf. C. C. 538. The baggage for which a carrier of passengers is liable is not limited to such apparel or other articles as are absolutely necessary or material for the use, comfort, or convenience of the passenger on his journey, or while away from his home. It may include articles of ordinary wearing apparel, purchased on a journey to be carried home for the use of the passenger *or for that of members of his*

SEC. 62. **Ordinary Passengers' Luggage.** — In a recent case which came before the Court of Queen's Bench, the general principle, that whatever a passenger takes with him for his personal use and convenience (and that is to be judged of in relation to his habits or wants[1] as a member of the particular class in society to which he belongs), either with a view to present necessities, or any purpose for which the journey is undertaken, is to be regarded as personal luggage, was affirmed. The circumstances were shortly these: The plaintiff was a passenger by the Great Western Railway from Liverpool to London, and took with him, as his personal luggage in a trunk, six pairs of sheets, six pairs of blankets, and six quilts. It appeared that he had given up his residence in Canada, and the articles contained in the trunk were intended for the use of his household when he should have provided himself with a home in London. The trunk was lost, and he sought to recover the value of the articles from the railway company. It was held that these articles could not be considered as personal or "ordinary passengers' luggage." COCKBURN, C. J., remarked that "the term ordinary luggage being thus confined to that which is personal to the passenger, and carried for his use or convenience, it follows that what is carried for the purposes of business, such as merchandise or the like, or for larger or ulterior purposes, such as articles of furniture or household goods, would not come within the description of ordinary luggage, unless accepted as such by the carrier. The articles as to which the question in the present case arises consisted of bedding. Now, though we are far from saying that a pair of sheets, or the like, taken by a passenger for his own use on a journey, might not fairly be considered as personal luggage, it appears to us that the quantity of articles of this description intended, not for the use of the traveller on the journey, but for the use of his household

immediate family. It should not be deemed to include articles purchased for a stranger, Dexter *v.* Syracuse, &c. R. R. Co., 42 N. Y. 326, nor presents for friends outside his immediate family. Nevins *v.* Bay State, &c. Co., 4 Bosw. (N. Y.) 225.

[1] Per ERLE, C. J., in Phelps *v.* London & North-Western Rail. Co., 19 C. B. N. S. 321; 34 L. J. C. P. 259.

when permanently settled, cannot be held to be so."[1] A feather bed, necessary for a steerage passenger on a boat, and used by him on the journey, is baggage;[2] but not when it is packed up and not intended for use on the voyage.[3]

SEC. 63. **Merchandise.** — But although this is true, it is certain that a railway company is not bound to carry, and is not liable for the loss of, merchandise delivered to them by a passenger as his personal luggage, and without notice that the luggage contains merchandise.[4] It would certainly be unfair

[1] Macrow *v.* Great Western Rail. Co., 6 L. R. Q. B. 612, at p. 622; 24 L. T. N. S. 619.

[2] Hirschshon *v.* Hamburg American Packet Company, 2 J. & S. (N. Y. Superior Ct.) 521.

[3] Connolly *v.* Warren, 106 Mass. 146.

[4] Cahill *v.* London & North-Western Rail. Co., 10 C. B. N. S. 154; 7 Jur. N. S. 1164; 30 L. J. C. P. 289; 9 W. R. 653; 4 L. T. N. S. 246. Affirmed on appeal, 18 C. B. N. S. 818; 8 Jur. N. S. 1063; 13 L. J. C. P. 271; 10 W. R. 391; Belfast & Ballymena Rail. Co. *v.* Keys, 9 H. L. Cas. 556; 8 Jur. N. S. 367; 9 W. R. 793; 4 L. T. N. S. 841; Great Northern Rail. Co. *v.* Shepherd, 8 Exch. 30; 7 Rail. Cas. 310; 21 L. J. Exch. 286. See Mississippi Central R. R. Co. *v.* Kennedy, 41 Miss. 671; Cincinnati, &c. R. R. Co. *v.* Marcus, 38 Ill. 219. The term "baggage," for which passenger carriers are liable if lost, does not include articles of merchandise not intended for personal use. Collins *v.* Boston R. R. Co., 10 Cush. (Mass.) 606; The Ionic, 6 Blatchf. (U. S. C. C.) 538; Dibble *v.* Brown, 12 Ga. 83; Bell *v.* Drew, 4 E. D. S. (N. Y. C. P.) 59; Stimson *v.* Connecticut, &c. R. R. Co., 44 N. H. 325; Hawkins *v.* Hoffman, 6 Hill (N. Y.), 586; Doyle *v.* Kyser, 6 Ind. 242. In Richards *v.* London, Brighton, & South Coast Rail. Co., 7 C. B. 839, it appeared that the plaintiff's wife, as a passenger, had intrusted her luggage to a company's porter, who had placed her other luggage in the van, but put her dressing-case under her seat in the carriage. On arriving at the terminus, the company's servants had placed, as she thought, all her luggage in a hackney-coach close to the platform; but it appeared subsequently that the dressing-case was missing, and that it had not been placed in the hackney-coach. The court supported a verdict for the plaintiff, on the ground that, according to the course of the company's business, there was no complete delivery to the plaintiff's wife until the company's servant had placed the dressing-case in the hackney-coach. If, however, the passenger voluntarily takes charge of his own luggage, the carrier will not be responsible. In the last-named case WILDE, C. J., said: "There is nothing more common than for persons to put part of their luggage into the same carriage with them; and that may be done under such circumstances as never to cast any responsibility on the carrier, but that must be proved. When this is done by the company's servants, the company are not relieved from their liability as carriers in respect of it. So a passenger taking a valuable article openly and notoriously into the same carriage in which he

to charge those who have liability imposed upon them by law with responsibility for articles which may be of great value,

travels will not save the company from responsibility. The case is quite different from that of goods which are about the person of a passenger, which are to be considered entirely under his personal control and custody. In that case there is no delivery to or acceptance by the company. Acceptance by the company is the legal result of goods placed in their hands in the ordinary way in which they consent to receive them."

So in Butcher *v.* London & South Wales Rail. Co., 16 C. B. 13; 24 L. J. C. P. 137. In that case the plaintiff on entering a railway carriage had his portmanteau placed in the luggage van, but kept with him the whole journey a small hand-bag containing money and valuables worth £240. When the train arrived at the terminus the plaintiff got out on the platform with the bag in his hand. A company's servant then inquired of him whether he should get him a cab, and, on receiving an affirmative reply, he took the bag, and, as he stated, subsequently placed it on the footboard of the cab which he had engaged. When, however, the plaintiff (who had remained to take care of his portmanteau) got there, he found that the bag had disappeared, and the driver denied that it had ever been put on the cab. It also appeared to be the usual course for the company's servants to assist gratuitously in removing passengers' luggage from the trains to the authorized cabs in attendance, of which the cab in which the plaintiff got was one. The jury found generally for the plaintiff, and the court held that there was evidence to support the verdict. See also Le Conteur *v.* London & South-Western Rail. Co., L. R. 1 Q. B. 54; 35 L. J. Q. B. 40.

By all railways passengers are permitted to take a certain weight of luggage, and by most of them this luggage is confined to that which is of a *personal* as distinguished from that which is of a *merchantable* description; where, therefore, in such a case, a passenger carries merchandise as personal luggage the company will not be liable for its loss. "If," says COCKBURN, C. J., in Cahill *v.* London & North-Western Rail. Co., 13 C. B. N. S. 818; 31 L. J. C. P. 271, Exch., "a railway company which, by the terms of its regulations, allows a passenger to take personal luggage, chooses to take as luggage that which it knows to be merchandise, I agree that it does not lie in the mouth of the company, if an article be lost, to say that they will be exempt from liability, on the ground of the article being merchandise and not luggage. On the other hand, if a passenger who knows that he is only entitled to take personal luggage takes merchandise, he cannot afterward claim to be compensated in respect of its loss by the company, to whom he has given no notice of the contents of his package. The question comes to this: Was there knowledge on the part of the company that that which the passenger was taking with him as luggage was in fact merchandise? What was said by LORD WENSLEYDALE in Great Northern Rail. Co. *v.* Shepherd, 8 Exch. 30; 9 L. J. Exch. 286, is in perfect conformity with the view which we now take of the question. The point is, whether we can from the facts stated come to the conclusion that there was knowledge on the part of the company — that is, of the company's servants — that this box was merchandise. I do not see my way to that conclusion. It is true that it had

when, to all appearance, the boxes contain only the articles of clothing belonging to an individual. There can be no rea-

a semblance as of merchandise, and was marked 'glass.' But persons often take with them very curious packages, and mark them 'glass' to protect them from injury. Probably the porter never thought about it at all. It is not found by the jury that the company's servants knew that it was merchandise; and I do not think that we ought to arrive at the inference that they knew it, as a fair and legitimate conclusion from the facts stated in the case." In the foregoing case the plaintiff, who was the traveller of Mr. Rimmell, the perfumer of London, travelled by the defendants' railway from Northampton to London. He took with him a box about three feet long, eighteen inches wide, and twelve inches deep, and two other packages. The box was covered with a black leather case, and had painted on the top of it the name "Mr. Rimmell," in large white letters, and also had painted across the top on each end the word "glass." It contained samples of perfumery and other articles sold by Mr. Rimmell. On his arrival at the Northampton station the box was given to one of the defendants' porters on duty at the station. No question was asked by any of the company's servants about the box, nor was any demand made for payment for the carriage of it. The plaintiff did not give any information as to its contents. The porter took it, placed it with the other luggage, and it travelled safe to the junction at Blisworth, where the line from Northampton joins the main line of the defendants' railway. The luggage from Northampton was taken out at Blisworth, in order to be put into the train for London. On the arrival of the train at London the box could not be found, and had never since been heard of. The plaintiff's luggage, including the box, was under the weight allowed by the company. Upon an action being brought, a verdict was taken for the plaintiff, subject to a special case. In the case of Great Northern Rail. Co. *v.* Shepherd, 8 Exch. 30; 21 L. J. Exch. 286, the same point was decided. In that case the plaintiff in the court below was journeying by an excursion train, and had with him goods which were not personal luggage, but merchandise.

As to what constitutes personal luggage no very certain definition has as yet been given. In the above-cited case of Great Northern Rail. Co. *v.* Shepherd, PARKE, B., remarked "that the term 'luggage,' according to the true modern doctrine on the subject, comprises clothing and such articles as a traveller usually carries with him for his personal convenience; perhaps even a small present, or a book for the journey, might be included in the term, but certainly not merchandise, or materials bought for the purpose of being manufactured and sold at a profit." And in Hudson *v.* Midland Rail. Co., L. R. 4 Q. B. 366; 38 L. J. Q. B. 213, LUSH, J., said: "It is extremely difficult to frame a definition of what is 'personal luggage,' which embraces everything which can come within the meaning of the words, or which is not excluded by them. I cannot say that I am satisfied with any of the definitions which are given in the books which have been referred to. Those definitions were quite good enough for the occasions upon which they were given, but none of them seem to me to be perfect. It would be very difficult, perhaps impossible, to frame a

son why people should not take risk if they are aware of it before they enter into a contract. At that time they are in

definition which would be suitable in any possible exigency; but I think that the interpretation put upon the rule by the company is not wide enough, for they contend that 'personal luggage' applies only to luggage which is carried by the passenger for his own use, and is personal to himself. But I do certainly think that any one using the words 'personal luggage' would mean more than is included by this description. It is also to be observed that the statute uses the words 'ordinary luggage,' meaning a class of articles which are ordinarily carried by passengers as luggage; so that we may construe the rule by the aid of this description, for the company would take it into account when they were considering what was the description of goods for the carriage of which the passenger had paid when he had taken his ticket, and they would have regard to the usual habits of passengers. Now the article in question, although called a child's toy, cannot to my mind come within this description. It cannot be considered as a mere toy, which suggests something which may be carried in the hand different from a sort of rocking-horse weighing seventy-eight pounds, and forty-four inches in length."

The personal luggage must be that of the actual traveller, and not of a person not really engaged upon the journey. In Becher *v.* Great Eastern Rail. Co., L. R. 5 Q. B. 241; 39 L. J. Q. B. 122, it appeared that the plaintiff and a party of friends arranged to go from London to Newmarket, for the purpose of attending the races there, and they took a man-servant of one of the party to attend on them in common during their stay at Newmarket. On the last day of the races, the servant being about to return by an early train on the defendants' line, and the plaintiff being desirous of returning later in the day, he intrusted his portmanteau and its contents with the servant, with directions to take it up to London with him. The plaintiff gave the servant a sovereign for his attention during his stay at Newmarket. The servant accordingly proceeded to the defendants' station at Newmarket, and obtained from the defendants and duly paid them for a ticket from Newmarket to London. The servant delivered over the portmanteau with its contents and his own luggage, as well as that of the other gentlemen, to the servants of the defendants at the Newmarket station, as his ordinary luggage, and the same was received by the defendants as ordinary luggage, for the purpose of being carried by the defendants as carriers, with the servant on his journey. The servant was carried by the defendants to London; but the portmanteau and its contents were lost during the journey by default of the defendants. The plaintiff himself proceeded from Newmarket to London by a later train by the defendants' railway on the same day, and he also duly obtained and paid the defendants for his ticket for such journey, and took no luggage with him. By the special act of the defendants, every passenger travelling upon their railways may take with him his ordinary luggage not exceeding one hundred and twenty pounds in weight for a first-class passenger, one hundred pounds in weight for a second-class passenger, and sixty pounds in weight for a third-class passenger, without any charge being made for its carriage. The baggage taken with

a position to make their rate of charges cover the possible losses, so as — even calculating on certain casualties — to give them a fair remuneration for their capital, time, and trouble. But where it has been clearly understood that individuals are only to carry their ordinary luggage with them, and where the rates of conveyance have been calculated upon the understanding of casualties to such kinds of luggage only, it would be most unfair to allow persons to carry merchandise or money to a large amount, and, in case of loss, to hold the company liable.

SEC. 64. **Meaning of Common-law Liability of Carriers.** — All that the common-law liability of carriers means is this, that all those who carry on the trade of common carriers shall, by the fact of that trade, be presumed to hold out to the public generally a permanent offer of carriage of goods and insurance of the same, which offer, whenever it is accepted by any individual, at once becomes a complete contract binding on both parties. But this permanent offer to carry goods is not to be presumed as an offer to carry any goods, or to carry certain goods, at any rate. Both these particulars are in the power of the carrier to stipulate. But having so modified his offer, whenever this modified offer is accepted, he is bound

the servant was delivered to the company as not exceeding the weight he was allowed to take, and was not weighed. Upon these facts coming before the court upon a special case, it was held that the company were not liable. In his judgment MELLOR, J., said: "We are not satisfied that this action cannot be maintained. There can be no doubt but that the portmanteau was received by the company as the luggage of the servant, and that he was regarded by them as an ordinary passenger. It is unnecessary to say that the case where a man says, 'This is not my luggage, but my master's,' may give rise to different considerations. But here there is nothing of the kind. The person with whom they legally contracted was the servant, and the only duty which is imposed upon them is founded on their contract with them." So, too, LUSH, J., observed: "The company are in this position: they are bound by law to receive a certain quantity of the luggage of each passenger by their railway. But if they had known that the luggage was not the luggage of the servant, they would have known that they were not bound to receive it, and they probably would have refused it. There is no evidence of any duty on the part of the company except that which is founded upon their contract, and the only person with whom they contracted was the servant. But see Grant *v.* Nelson, 1 E. D. S. (N. Y. C. P.) 95, *contra.*

by it, but so is the party accepting. Now, the implied offer and acceptance in the case of a passenger's luggage is, on the one hand, that the luggage shall be personal luggage; and, on the other hand, that the carrier will carry and insure all such personal luggage. Upon these grounds, it would be most unfair to regard a common carrier as liable in the case of the loss of merchandise which a passenger is carrying as if it was personal luggage.

SEC. 65. **Where Carrier will be Liable.** — If, however, a passenger packs merchandise in such a way that the servants of a railway company or common carrier can see that it is merchandise, and if these servants make no objection to carrying it, or if they do not demand an extra charge, or a special bargain with regard to it, the company will be responsible in case it is lost or damaged.[1] In such a case the railway company has, by its silence, modified its own permanent offer, and the contract is not the same as that which exists under ordinary circumstances; and, as the contract is not the same, the liability is different. It may be said that, if the carrier, through its servants or agents charged with the duty of receiving baggage, accept as baggage, articles of merchandise, or other property not personal baggage within the legal meaning of the term, *knowing* the nature of the property, they become liable therefor as baggage;[2] and according to the case first cited in the preceding note, this is the rule, even though the passenger fraudulently procured them to accept it as such.

[1] Great Northern Rail. Co. *v.* Shepherd, 8 Exch. 30; 7 Rail. Cas. 310; 21 L. J. Exch. 286. See Waldron *v.* Chicago, &c. R. R. Co., 1 Dakota, 351; Ross *v.* Missouri, &c. R. R. Co., 4 Mo. App. 582, where this rule is adopted and well illustrated.

[2] Ross *v.* Missouri, &c. R. R Co., *ante;* Waldron *v.* Chicago, &c. R. R. Co., *ante.* But *contra,* see Blumanth *v.* Fitchburg R. R. Co., 127 Mass. 322. If a carrier accepts and transports as baggage for a passenger, articles of merchandise, knowing them to be such, he assumes thereto the relation of a common carrier. Hannibal, &c. R. R. Co. *v.* Swift, 12 Wall. (U. S.) 262; Butler *v.* Hudson River R. R. Co., 3 E. D. S. (N. Y. C. P.) 571. A trunk or valise containing samples of merchandise belonging to a merchant, but taken along by an agent to be used in procuring orders for similar goods, is not baggage for which a carrier is liable, even though he has checked it as baggage, but in ignorance of its contents. Stimson *v.* Connecticut River R. R. Co., 98 Mass. 83.

SEC. 66. **Actual Knowledge upon Carrier's Part.** — To render a railway company or common carriers liable in such a case, however, it is necessary to attach them or their servants with actual knowledge that the thing carried was merchandise, and not personal luggage. It is not enough to show that there was sufficient apparent upon the article carried to have directed their attention to it, and to have caused them to make inquiries. In the case of Cahill *v.* The London and North-Western Railway Company,[1] it appeared that the plaintiff had taken to a station a box labelled "glass," and had given it to a porter, who had placed it in the luggage van; in the course of the journey it was lost, and the plaintiff brought the action to recover its value. The box contained merchandise, and not passengers' luggage; but it was contended, on behalf of the plaintiff, that the fact of the box being labelled "glass" was enough to indicate to the defendants that it contained merchandise, and that, as they accepted it without further charge, they were responsible. Judgment was given for the defendants, and ERLE, C. J., said: "It seems to me that it would be introducing a rule most pernicious to public convenience that a railway company, to avoid being fixed with liability, which, according to their regulations, they do not intend to take, should be bound to make inquiries where a package is brought which appears likely to contain merchandise, and, if they do not make those inquiries, that they should be taken to know the contents of such package." The whole court held that the company had not knowledge that this was merchandise by the fact of the box being so labelled, and this decision was upheld by the Exchequer Chamber.[2]

SEC. 67. **Custody of Luggage by Passenger.** — There is one other question with regard to the liability of common carriers for the luggage of passengers, which is of importance. It has been more than once held that the fact that the owner of the luggage is present during the transit, or that he sends his servant to look after it, does not affect the responsibility of the carriers. We have seen that in Robinson *v.* Dunmore,

[1] 30 L. J. C. P. 289; 10 C. P. N. S. 154.
[2] 31 L. J. C. P. 271.

CHAMBRE, J., said: "It has been determined that if a man travel in a stage-coach, and take his portmanteau with him, though he has an eye on the portmanteau, yet the carrier is not absolved from his responsibility." [1] In another case it has been decided that the luggage of a passenger by railway, although never delivered to any servant of the company, but kept by the passenger during the journey, is nevertheless in point of law in the custody of the company, so as to render them responsible for its loss.[2] And the doctrine laid down with regard to stage-coaches by CHAMBRE, J., was repeated with regard to railway trains in the case of Le Conteur *v.* The London and South-Western Railway Company.[3] But this is not the rule in this country,[4] except where the carrier interferes with the baggage in some manner.[5]

SEC. 68. **Implied Modification of Contract.** — The case of Brind *v.* Dale [6] suggested that under certain circumstances a common carrier might exercise his calling under a modified contract, even where that modification was only implied. In that case it was left to the jury to say whether the goods were delivered to the defendant as a common carrier, or whether the fact that the owner of the goods having promised to follow the defendant's cart and look after the luggage, did not show that the goods were put into the cart under a contract modified to the extent of the plaintiff's promise. If that case was correctly decided, it would seem that the circumstance of a passenger travelling in the same carriage with his luggage would modify the contract of a company, and that the common carrier would to some extent be relieved from his legal liability, in which case the dictum of CHAMBRE, J., and the judgments in the other cases quoted, in so far as they relate to this particular point, must be regarded as unsatisfac-

[1] Robinson *v.* Dunmore, 2 B. & P. 416.

[2] Great Northern Rail. Co. *v.* Shepherd, 8 Exch. 30; 7 Rail. Cas. 310; 21 L. J. Exch. 286.

[3] 35 L. J. Q. B. 40; 12 Jur. N. S. 266; L. R. 1 Q. B. 54; 14 W. R. 80; 13 L. T. N. S. 325. See also Butcher *v.* London & South-Western Rail. Co., 16 C. B. 24 L. J. C. P. 137.

[4] Tower *v.* Utica R. R. Co., 7 Hill, 47.

[5] Kinsley *v.* Lake Shore, &c. R. R. Co., 125 Mass. 54.

[6] 8 C. & P. 207.

tory. The subject was considered in the recent case of Talley *v.* The Great Western Railway Company.[1] The plaintiff in this case was a passenger by the defendants' railway upon a return journey from Cheltenham to Reading. He had, at his own request, his portmanteau put into the same carriage with him. At Swindon the train stopped, as all trains did, to allow the passengers to get refreshments, and remained there ten minutes. The plaintiff left the carriage he was in, and upon returning to the train failed to find it. The carriage he had travelled from Cheltenham to Swindon in remained part of the train until it reached Paddington. The plaintiff completed his journey in another carriage of the same train, and afterwards obtained his portmanteau, from which, however, a portion of its contents had been taken. The contents had been stolen by some one in the carriage after the train left Swindon and before it arrived in London. The verdict in the county court was given for the plaintiff. A new trial was granted, and was heard before a deputy judge and a jury, when the verdict was for the defendant. It was appealed against, and in giving judgment WILLES, J., said: "With respect to articles which are not put in the usual luggage van, and of which the entire control is not given to the carrier, but which are placed in the carriage in which the passenger travels, so that he and not the company's servants has *de facto* the entire control of them whilst the carriage is moving, the amount of care and diligence reasonably necessary for their safe conveyance is, in fact, considerably modified by the circumstance of their being, during that part of the journey in which the passenger might, under ordinary circumstances, be expected to be in the carriage, intended by both parties to be under his personal inspection and care. To such a state of things the rule which binds common carriers absolutely to insure the safe delivery of the goods, except against the act of God or the Queen's enemies, whatever may be the negligence of the passenger himself, has never, that we are aware of, been applied."

[1] 19 W. R. 154; 23 L. T. N. S. 413; L. R. 6 C. P. 44.

SEC. 69. **When Wide Liability attaches.** — "There is great force in the argument that when articles are placed with the assent of the passenger in the same carriage with him, and so in fact remain in his own control and possession, the wide liability of the common carrier, which is founded on the bailment of the goods to him, and his being intrusted with the entire possession of them, should not attach, because the reasons which are the foundation of the liability do not exist. In such cases the obligation to take reasonable care seems naturally to arise, so that when loss occurred it would fall on the company only in the case of negligence in some part of the duty which pertained to them;" and he was of opinion that "the circumstance of the portmanteau being put with the passenger's assent, and, of course, for his convenience, into the carriage in which he was to travel, and so out of the immediate and active control of the company's servants, instead of in the ordinary luggage van, where it would have been under such control, it was intended by both parties, and was an implied term in the contract of carriage, that, in return for the convenience of having his luggage at hand, the passenger should, during the journey, take such care of his own property as might be expected from an ordinarily prudent man, and should not by his own negligence expose it to more than the ordinary risk of luggage carried in a passenger carriage, and that the finding of negligence in not using such reasonable care was sustained by the evidence. Upon the ground that the liability of the company was, under the circumstances, modified by the implied condition that the passenger should use reasonable care, and that the loss was caused by his neglect to do so, and would not have happened without such negligence, we think that the judgment of the county court should be reversed, and the verdict entered for the defendants." [1]

[1] As to a ferryman who takes passengers along with his luggage, see Walker *v.* Jackson, 10 M. & W. 161. The statute 12 Charles II. c. 35, which established a General Post Office, was regarded as an act which limited the ordinary responsibility of the carriers of letters; formerly a private carrier of letters was exactly in a similar position to a carrier of any

SEC. 70. **Limitation of Liability for Luggage.** — Another case of some importance may be referred to here. In that case a passenger by an English vessel, which belonged to an English company, from Southampton to the Mauritius, *via* Alexandria and Suez, took and signed a ticket, in the body of which the engagement of the company was stated to be subject to the conditions and regulations indorsed thereon, among which was the clause: "The company does not hold itself liable for damage to, or loss, or detention of, passengers' baggage." A package of baggage belonging to the plaintiff, a passenger, being lost during the voyage, the passenger sued the company in the Supreme Court at Mauritius for damages for the loss, and it was held that it was a contract to be interpreted by the law of England, the place where the contract was made; and it was further held that the company, as carriers at common law, had a power to limit the liability imposed upon them by the law by special contract, and that the limitation imposed by the stipulations indorsed on the ticket with respect to any loss, exempted the company under the circumstances above alluded to.[1] Sufficient has been said to indicate who are to

other thing, but in the case of Lane *v.* Cotton, 1 Ld. Raym. 546, it was directed that the Postmaster-General was not responsible for the loss of a letter containing Exchequer bills. And LORD MANSFIELD, in the case of Whitfield *v.* Despencer, Cowp. 754, held that there was no analogy between the postmaster and a common carrier. He said: "The comparison between a postmaster and a carrier or the master of a ship seems to me to hold in no particular whatsoever. The postmaster has no hire, enters into no contract, carries on no merchandise or commerce. But the Post-Office is a branch of revenue, a branch of police created by Act of Parliament. As a branch of revenue there are great receipts, but there is likewise great surplus of benefit and advantage to the public arising from the fund. As a branch of police, it puts the whole correspondence of the kingdom (for the exceptions are very trifling) under Government, and intrusts the management and direction of it to the crown. There is no analogy, therefore, between the case of the postmaster and a common carrier."

[1] Peninsular & Oriental Steam Navigation Co. *v.* Sand, 3 Moore, P. C. C. N. S. 272. See also Mobile, &c. R. R. Co. *v.* Hopkins, 41 Ala. 486. But such limitation must be brought to the notice of the passenger in some way, and assented to by him. Thus, in Woodruff *v.* Sherrard, 9 Hun (N. Y.), 323, an action was brought to recover for the loss of a box and its contents, delivered to the New York Transfer Company as a common carrier. They were then owned by the assignor of the plaintiff, who was his

be regarded as common carriers. Under some circumstances those carriers, even while they carry, are, by the implicit or

daughter. She was on her way from Rahway, in New Jersey, to the city of Brooklyn, and left her check at the office of the transfer company, at the foot of Courtlandt Street, in the city of New York, to have her baggage, consisting of a box and its contents, taken from the railway company to the place of her destination in Brooklyn. After delivering the check for them to the clerk in the transfer company's office, she started to leave it, when her companion suggested the propriety of having a receipt for it. She then turned to the clerk and requested him to give her a receipt for the check. He wrote out and delivered her a receipt, and also a contract limiting, in terms, the liability of the company in case of loss to the sum of $100, unless further compensation was paid for the additional risk. She received it, supposing it to be merely a receipt, and did not read it, or become aware of its contents until after the box and its contents had been lost by the company. When it was delivered to her, nothing was said by the clerk indicating that it was anything more than the receipt applied for by her. Upon these facts the referee held that no contract between the parties had been established, by which the liability of the transfer company was limited to the sum of $100. He found that the box and its contents were of the value of $330, and for that directed judgment in the plaintiff's favor. The defendant insisted that the recovery, on these facts, ought not to have exceeded the sum of $100. Daniels, J., said: —

"When the check was delivered to the clerk of the transfer company, the plaintiff's assignor could have refused to surrender it on any other terms than that the carrier should be charged with the full measure of its common-law liability concerning it. She had a right to decline to receive a contract of the limited nature of that contained in the instrument delivered to her, and that was the import of her request made to the clerk. It was for a receipt merely, which was probably required for the sole purpose of identifying the transaction in case the property was not delivered. And when the paper was given to her in response to her request, nothing was said or intimated by the clerk that it was anything different from the instrument asked for; she was not told that it was a contract as well as a receipt. And the act of passing it over to her without explanation, in compliance with her request that she should simply have a receipt, authorized the inference upon her part, that such was its nature and excused her for her omission to read or examine it. In complying with a request for a receipt, persons unacquainted with the modes of transacting business, as this young lady evidently was, would not expect to be handed a special agreement. If the clerk could not properly have given what he was asked for, he should have explained that he could not give a mere receipt without further compensation for the risk, in case the property exceeded in value the sum of $100. Then the owner would have been in a position in which she could have provided for the complete safety or responsibility of and for her property. By not doing that, but handing her a paper in response to her request for a receipt, and which she was justified by the circumstances

explicit nature of the contract, made private carriers for hire in relation to the particular transaction. Under other circum-

in believing was nothing more than that, she was put off her guard and induced to leave her property under the control of the company, when she might not otherwise have done so.

"To make a binding contract in such a case as this requires at least the implied assent of the party receiving the instrument, and that was not made to appear. The fact was the other way, and the referee has so found it. A contract declaring the liability of the company was not requested, but merely a receipt, and it was that, in the absence of everything indicating it to be different, that she must have supposed was handed to her in answer to her request. The minds of the parties did not meet upon the subject of a contract, and the paper received was not accepted as such. The case, for this reason, seems to be within the principle declared by the learned chief judge of the Court of Appeals, in deciding the case of Blossom *v.* Dodd, 43 N. Y. 264. It was there said that 'the contract cannot be made by one party. If the traveller is informed of the charges graduated by value, he can have a voice in the bargain; but in this case he had none. While the carrier should be protected in his legal right to limit his responsibility, the public should also be protected against imposition and fraud. The carrier must deal with the public on terms of equality; and if he desires to limit his liability, he must secure the assent of those with whom he transacts business.' The case of Kirkland *v.* Dinsmore, 62 N. Y. 171, contains nothing different from this proposition, and in no way conflicts with what was decided in the other case. It was there said, by ANDREWS, J., in delivering the opinion of the court, that 'it is not claimed that there was any fraud or imposition practised by the defendant's agent. He did not represent that the paper was a bare acknowledgment of the receipt of the package, nor did he do anything calculated to mislead the plaintiff or put him off his guard.' 62 N. Y. 178. In the present case the agent did both the acts not shown there, and which it is to be implied would, if they had appeared, have sustained the carrier's liability. For in apparent compliance with a simple request for a receipt, he handed her a contract, and did it in such a manner as to induce the belief that it was only the instrument she had asked for. The present case, in this respect, also differs materially from that of Belger *v.* Dinsmore, 51 N. Y. 166, in which it was 'not shown, nor is there any evidence whatever warranting the inference that the wife of the plaintiff, when she took the receipt, did not know, and was not fully informed of what provisions it contained, and fully understood them.' And for the same reason it cannot be considered as controlled by Huntington *v.* Dinsmore, 4 Hun, 66. The existence of the instrument as a contract was not shown by the evidence. It cannot be inferred that it was intended to be assented to as being anything more than a simple receipt, which was all that the agent was asked to deliver. No implication beyond that can be made from what was shown to have transpired between the parties preceding its delivery and acceptance. The referee was right in the construction he gave to the transaction, and the judgment should, therefore, be affirmed."

stances those who do not ordinarily fall under the designation "common carriers," have, by the nature of the contract and the policy of the law, their responsibility enlarged, and become common carriers for the nonce. The principles of the law upon this subject have been sufficiently explained, and they will receive further explication and illustration from the cases which will more properly fall under our consideration in subsequent chapters.

CHAPTER V.

OF THE COMMON-LAW DUTY OF COMMON CARRIERS TO RECEIVE GOODS.

SEC. 71. **Duty to receive Goods.** — We have already seen that the common law imposes a duty upon persons professing to carry on the trade of common carriers to receive the goods of any one that offers them, provided the individual offers at the same time a reasonable compensation.[1] It is as important to notice this point in connection with a description of common carriers, as distinguished from private carriers for hire, or those carriers who undertake the duty of a common carrier without looking for or accepting the ordinary remuneration, as it is important to recognize the measure of their responsibility in case of the loss of, or injury to, the goods with which they are intrusted. BEST, J., thus stated the law and the qualification of the absolute rule in the case of Riley *v.* Horne:[2] "As the law makes the carrier an insurer, and as the goods he

[1] Munster *v.* South-Eastern Rail. Co., 4 C. B. N. S. 676; 27 L. J. 308, C. P.; Crouch *v.* Great Northern Rail. Co., 11 Exch. 742; Norton *v.* Tibbett, 15 Ad. & El. 428; New Jersey Steam Navigation Co. *v.* Merchants' Bank, 6 How. (U. S.) 341; Lafaye *v.* Harris, 13 La. Ann. 553; Cole *v.* Goodwin, 19 Wend. (N. Y.) 261.

[2] 5 Bing. 217.

carries may be injured or destroyed by many accidents, against which no care on the part of the carrier can protect them, he is as much entitled to be paid a premium for his insurance of their delivery at their place of destination as for the labor and expense of carrying them there. He *must* take what is offered to him to carry, to the place to which he undertakes to convey goods, if he has room for it in his carriage."[1]

SEC. 72. **Conditions of Performance.** — Here there are two important qualifications of the compulsory duty of acceptance of goods. First, he is not bound to convey goods to any place to which they may be addressed, but his past habit will be the criterion by which one is to judge of the extent of his duty. If he is in the habit of carrying goods from A to B, there is no duty incumbent upon him of carrying a parcel, even if it be such a parcel as he ordinarily conveys, to C, however slightly he might have to deviate from his ordinary road to execute the commission.[2]

SEC. 73. **Room in Conveyance.** — Another point is, that he is not to be compelled to carry goods, if the vehicle which he ordinarily employs for the transportation of goods is not able to contain the article which is offered. He has no duty to provide extra carts or carriages to satisfy the extra demands that may be made on them.[3]

SEC. 74. **Payment.** — A third point is, that he is not under the obligation to carry any goods, unless the person who wishes them conveyed offers a reasonable remuneration.[4]

[1] But he is only bound to take it when it is offered by the owner or his agent, and has a right to demand payment of the freight in advance. Fitch *v.* Newberry, 1 Doug. (Mich.) 1.

[2] Davis *v.* Garrett, 6 Bing. 716; Hales *v.* London & North-Western Rail. Co., 4 B. & S. 66; Crouch *v.* London & North-Western Rail. Co., 14 C. B. 255.

[3] Peet *v.* Chicago, &c. R. R. Co., 20 Wis. 594. Where two kinds of property, one of which is perishable and the other not, are delivered to a carrier at the same time by different owners for transportation, and he can only carry one at once, he may give the preference to the perishable property over that which is not perishable, and, if either must wait, it should be the latter. Marshall *v.* New York, &c. R. R. Co., 45 Barb. (N. Y.) 502.

[4] See *ante*, p. 147; Galena R. R. *v.* Roe, 18 Ill. 488; Skipper *v.* Pennsylvania R. R., 47 Penn. St. 338; Fitch *v.* Newberry, *ante*. But he must insist upon prepayment before

Common carriers are not to be regarded as philanthropists. They carry goods in order that they may get their living by so doing; and as it has been found that persons who work honestly for gain are of real service to the community, it is therefore of importance that the community should, by its laws, protect their rights as jealously as it protects those of individuals who contract with them.

SEC. 75. **Innkeepers, their Duty.** — The common-law duties of innkeepers are exactly similar to those of common carriers. The acts to be performed by these two classes of persons are different, but the principle of the imposed duty is the same. It is the duty of an innkeeper to receive and entertain a guest if he has room in his inn or hotel, just as it is a carrier's duty to convey a parcel if he has room in his cart.[1] That there exists this right to modify the common-law duties, and that this liability may be modified by the circumstances, has been pointed out by ERLE, C. J., in the case of M'Manus *v.* The Lancashire and Yorkshire Railway Company.[2] "If," he says,

the goods are received, else he cannot insist upon it. Parcher *v.* Railroad Company, 14 Rich. (S. C.) L. 181; Hannibal, &c. R. R. *v.* Swift, 12 Wall. (U. S.) 262; The David, 5 Blatchf. (U. S. C. C.) 266.

[1] Jackson *v.* Rogers, 2 Show. 554. Innkeepers often combine with the trade of keeping houses of public entertainment that of carrying goods for hire, in which case they are liable for any loss of goods sent to their inn to be forwarded which happens before they are sent off. The two liabilities are combined in such a trade. See Hyde *v.* Trent Navigation Co., 5 T. R. 389.

[2] 4 H. & N. 327; 28 L. J. 353, Exch. One of the distinguishing qualities requisite to make a person a common carrier is that he has placed himself in a position where he is bound to accept and carry goods for any person who offers, within the usages of his business, and subject to certain reasonable limitations; and the question as to whether the goods offered come within the class which he is accustomed to carry is one of fact for the jury.

A carrier, however, may lawfully refuse to accept or carry goods which are improperly packed, although they belong to the class usually carried by him; or where they are of a perishable nature, and likely to become worthless before, in the ordinary course of things, they can reach their destination; or where he has good reason to believe that they are of a dangerous nature, The Nitro-glycerine Case, 15 Wall. (U. S.) 524; Union Express Co. *v.* Graham, 26 Ohio St. 595; or where, by reason of a press of business, he will be unable to carry the goods within a reasonable time, Peet *v.* Chicago, &c. R. R. Co., 20 Wis. 94; or because the goods are not delivered to him seasonably, or at his usual place of receiving them, Cronkite *v.* Wells,

"a person chooses to profess to be a common carrier, the law creates a duty to receive things brought for carriage, and he may be liable *ex delicto* for a refusal to receive.[1] But his duty is regulated according to his will in many respects. He may choose the kind of conveyance, the times for transit, the mode of delivery, the articles that he will profess to carry, what price he will have, when it shall be paid, and the duty to convey is always limited by his convenience to carry.[2] This right to qualify the duty of receiving, according to terms and conditions fixed by the carrier alone, comprises the right to qualify the common-law duty of insuring safety." And BEST, C. J., in a case already quoted, said: "We have established these points, — that a carrier is an insurer of the goods which he carries; that he is obliged, for a reasonable reward, to carry any goods to the place to which he professes to carry goods that are offered to him, if his carriage will hold them, and he is informed of their quality and value; that he is not obliged to take a package the owner of which will not inform him what are its contents,[3] and of what value they are; that, if he does not ask for this information, or if, when he asks and is not answered, he takes the goods, he is answerable for their amount; that he may limit his responsibility, as an insurer, by notice; but that a notice will not protect him against the consequences of a loss by gross negligence." [4]

SEC. 76. **When bound to receive.** — Further, a carrier is not bound to receive goods until he is ready to carry them.[5] But this qualification of the common-law duty of carriers extends even further. We have seen that a learned judge[6] expressed the opinion that, as a common carrier was an in-

32 N. Y. 247; or if the way is exposed to extraordinary dangers, by reason of floods or tempests, or from strikes or other popular outbreaks, Edwards *v.* Sherratt, 1 East, 604.

[1] Pickford *v.* Grand Junction Rail. Co., 8 M. & W. 372; 10 L. J. Exch. 342.

[2] Jackson *v.* Rogers, 2 Shower, 327, case 330; Johnson *v.* North Midland Rail. Co., 4 Exch. 367.

[3] See Great Northern Rail. Co. *v.* Shepherd, 8 Exch. 30.

[4] Riley *v.* Horne, 5 Bing. p. 224; *ante*, p. 147.

[5] Lane *v.* Cotton, 1 Ld. Raym. 652. See also Pickford *v.* Grand Junction Rail. Co., 12 M. & W. 766.

[6] BEST, C. J.

surer, he was entitled to be paid a premium for his insurance besides what he received for his labor, and care, and expense. This principle is really involved in the whole law of the duty of common carriers; and it follows from this principle, that if, owing to any especial circumstances, the risk of the carrier in transporting the goods is greatly increased, he should be entitled to a higher premium. The object of the law is not to rob one man in order to pay another. If when the circumstances are known to both parties, and the ordinary risks and dangers of the road are greatly increased, the owner will still transmit his goods, it is only right that he should pay more highly for the insurance of them.[1]

SEC. 77. **Modification by Statute.** — The common-law duty of railway companies is not unfrequently modified by the act under which they are incorporated, or by general statute; and when the duties, rights, or liabilities of a carrier are thus qualified, the common-law rules to that extent are subverted, and cannot be enforced either for or against him. So far as the receiving of goods is concerned, custom or express notice will regulate the peculiar nature of their carriage, as it does that of other common carriers.

SEC. 78. **Rule of Construction.** — It is a rule of construction with regard to these acts, that they are to be construed strictly against the company, and liberally in favor of the public. The evident reason for this rule is that, when a company has the making of rules by which they are to be bound, they ought to be careful, and will probably be careful, only to make rules with which they are capable of complying. When a company has done so, and entered into a bargain with the public, it is only right that they should be held strictly to the terms of their agreement. As for the construction in favor of the public, there is reason for that too. It is not to be expected that the public is familiar with all the private Acts of Parliament incorporating different railway companies; and although a man is bound by an agreement which he has entered into, even if his eyes were shut at the time, there is some

[1] See Tyler *v.* Morrice, Carth. 485.

reason for construing it liberally as against him, if there was a difficulty in opening his eyes.

SEC. 79. **Duty to receive from all who offer to pay the Reasonable Charges.** — The case of Parker *v.* Great Western Railway Company [1] is instructive in this connection. By the Acts of Parliament under which this company was incorporated, it was provided that the carriage of goods should be reasonable and equal to all persons, and that no reduction or advance should be made either directly or in favor of or against any particular person. The company acted themselves as carriers for the public, and issued certain scales of their charges for carriage of goods, including the collection, loading, unloading, and delivery of parcels; and they also carried goods for other carriers, to whom they made certain allowances, as an equivalent for the trouble of collecting the parcels, such collection being performed by the carriers. But in their dealings with A, a particular carrier, they refused to make such allowances, but were willing to perform for him all the things which formed a consideration for such allowances. In this case it was held that the charges to A were not equal or reasonable. The company, in their transactions with the public, made the following distinction as to their charges for carriage. In the case of the public, if there were several packages from one consignor to several consignees, or from several consignors to one consignee, the charge was upon the aggregate weight. In the case of carriers, if there were several packages for several consignees, the charge was upon the separate weight of each package, unless more than one package belonged to the same consignor (not being the carrier), or was going to the same consignee, in either of which cases the charge was upon the aggregate weight. But in such cases the company recognized the carrier only as the consignor and consignee of the goods, the agent of such carrier, in fact, receiving the goods at the end of the transit. It was held that the company were bound to treat a carrier as the consignor and consignee for all purposes, including the mode of charging in the aggregate.

[1] 7 Man. & G. 253; Edwards *v.* Great Western Rail. Co., 11 C. B. 588.

And it was further held that A, having paid the extra charges in both of the instances above mentioned, might recover the amount of such payments in an action for money had and received against the company, such payments not being voluntary, but made in order to induce the company to do that which they were bound to do without requiring such payments.

SEC. 80. **Custom and Election often the Criterion.** — But the custom or election of a railway company forms the criterion in many cases. Thus where, under the Railway Clauses Consolidation Act,[1] a company had elected to carry goods, it was held that it was subject to the liability which attaches to carriers at common law, and that only. Therefore it was held that such a company is not bound to carry every description of goods, and between all places on their line, but that the duty only extended to such goods, and to and from such places, as they have publicly undertaken to perform. The convenience of the carrier is also to be considered. "At common law," said PARKE, B., in giving judgment, "a carrier is not bound to carry for every person tendering goods of any description, but his obligation is to carry according to his public profession. The law is thus stated by HOLT, C. J., in Lane *v.* Cotton:[2] 'Whenever any subject takes upon himself a public trust for the benefit of the rest of his fellow-subjects, he is *eo ipso* bound to serve the subject in all the things that are within the reach and comprehension of such an office, under pain of an action against him; and for this see Keilway, 50. If, on the road, a shoe fall off my horse, and I come to a smith to have one put on, and the smith refuse to do it, an action will lie against him, because he has made profession of a trade which is for the public good, and has thereby exposed and vested interest of himself in all the king's subjects that will employ him in the way of his trade.[3] If an innkeeper refuse to entertain a guest when his house is not full, an action will lie against him;[4] and so against a carrier, if his horse be not

[1] 8 & 9 Vict. c. 20, § 86.

[2] 1 Ld. Raym. 654.

[3] Keilway, 50, pl. 4. See a note to the case of Parsons *v.* Gingell, 4 C. B. 555, which shows that the authorities do not support this proposition.

[4] Dy. 158; Godb. 346.

loaded, and he refuse to take a packet proper to be sent by a carrier; and I have known such actions maintained, though the cases are not reported.'" BARON PARKE went on to say: "A person may profess to carry a particular description of goods only, — for instance, cattle or dry goods, — in which case he could not be compelled to carry any other kind of goods; or he may limit his obligation to carry from one place to another, as from Manchester to London, and then he would not be bound to carry to or from the intermediate places. Still, until he retracts, every individual (provided he tenders the money at the time, and there is room for the conveyance) has a right to call upon him to receive and carry goods, according to his public profession." [1]

SEC. 81. **Rule with reference to Acceptance.** — There are some rules with regard to the acceptance of goods, which are founded upon principles which have been approved by general consent, and by the ordinary conduct of mankind. All that our judges in most cases do, is to give expression to a rule which has been implicit in the conduct of men. Thus, that a carrier is entitled to be paid the amount of his hire before he undertakes the responsibility of having the goods in his possession, is what was always approved by opinion, and has now had judicial confirmation.[2] *A carrier is entitled to demand the payment of that sum which, by common law, he is entitled to claim for the carriage of the goods, before he undertakes the risk and trouble attaching to the custody of them.* If that sum is refused, he may avoid his common-law duty and liability, and make terms for the carriage of the goods, exactly as a private carrier for hire may.[3]

[1] Johnson *v.* Midland Rail. Co., 4 Exch. 367, at p. 373. See also Jackson *v.* Rogers, 2 Show. 332; Munster *v.* South-Eastern Rail. Co., 27 L. J. 308 C. P.; Oxlade *v.* North-Eastern Rail. Co., 15 C. B. N. S. 680; Pickford *v.* Grand Junction Rail. Co., 10 M. & W. 399, at p. 422.

[2] BEST, C. J., in Batson *v.* Donovan, 4 B. & Ald. 28; 1 P. & D. 4. It has, however, been held that in an action for refusing to pay it is enough to aver readiness and willingness to pay the hire, without alleging an actual tender. Pickford *v.* Grand Junction Rail. Co., 10 M. & W. 399; Wyld *v.* Pickford, 8 M. & W. 443.

[3] *Per* PARKE, B., in Wyld *v.* Pickford, 8 M. & W. 443.

SEC. 82. **Reasonable Remuneration.** — It is, however, to be understood that the payment, which is a condition precedent to the acceptance of the goods for carriage, and the demand which is made, must be reasonable. A man who, by his profession, holds himself out as a servant of the public, has no right to demand exorbitant remuneration for the services which he performs. This case differs from that of a person who only carries to oblige a friend, and who does not undertake to convey goods as an ordinary employment. In such a case it may be presumed that the labor is undertaken at a loss of time or money to the individual, and a higher rate of remuneration than that which is ordinarily paid may not reimburse him for the losses he may otherwise incur. But in the case of a common carrier no such presumption arises. It is to be supposed that he can afford to carry at much the same rate of hire as that which is exacted universally by carriers similarly situated, and which, if it has been found to remunerate them, may, upon the best grounds, be called reasonable.

SEC. 83. **Action for refusing to carry.** — The word *reasonable*, therefore, is to be the criterion of the price which a common carrier has a right to demand; and if a person brings him goods to be conveyed, and tenders him a reasonable amount of remuneration, and he refuses to convey the goods upon those terms, he will be liable to an action for having refused. Thus the Grand Junction Railway Company were authorized by their Act of Parliament[1] to carry and convey upon the railway all such passengers, goods, merchandise, &c., as should be offered to them for that purpose, and to make such *reasonable charges* for such carriage and conveyance as they might from time to time determine on. The plaintiff in this action tendered goods for conveyance by the said company, and offered a sum of money which to the court seemed, under the circumstances, reasonable. The defendants, having refused to convey the goods for this sum, were

[1] 3 & 4 Will. IV. c. 34, § 156. Power extended by 4 Will. IV. c. 64, § 19.

held liable in the action for the breach of their implied duty.[1]

SEC. 84. **When Liability arises.** — When, however, a reasonable sum has been paid, or the goods have been given into the custody of the carrier, without the carrier having insisted upon prepayment, his liability for loss or damage at once arises. Whenever the owner has parted with his possession of the goods, when he has ceased to take any care of them, they are wholly in the keeping of the carrier. But, as we have seen, the care which is to be bestowed is, as it were, a constant quantity; and when the owner still remains in partial possession of his goods, as when a passenger travels in the same carriage with his portmanteau, the responsibility is divided, as it were, between the owner and the carrier. Each is bound to be careful; but when goods are accepted under a condition of the continued care of the proprietor, the common-law liability of the carrier evidently does not arise.[2] When, however, an actual delivery of the goods has taken place, an actual transfer of the responsibility took place at the same time. Even although the transit of the goods may not take place immediately, the duty of the carrier is not postponed until the journey actually begins.[3] His duty is to keep safely and to carry safely.

SEC. 85. **When Performance must begin.** — In all cases the liability of the carrier commences at the instant of the acceptance. As reasonableness is a rule which must guide the

[1] Pickford *v.* Grand Junction Rail. Co., 10 M. & W. 399.

[2] See also East India Co. *v.* Pullen, Stra. 690.

[3] Randleson *v.* Murray, 8 Ad. & El. 109; Dale *v.* Hall, 1 Wils. 281; Boehm *v.* Combe, 2 M. & S. 172; Cobban *v.* Downe, 5 Esp. 41. See also with regard to customary acceptance at wharf or quay, &c., Abbott on Shipp., Pt. 3, c. 3, § 3; Fragano *v.* Long, 4 B. & C. 219; Hart *v.* Baxendale, 6 Exch. 769; Story on Bailm. § 584. The law is the same with regard to the acceptance by warehousemen as carriers (Forward *v.* Pittard, 1 T. R. 27; but see Roskell *v.* Waterhouse, 2 Stark. 461); with regard to ferrymen and wharfingers who at the same time carry on the trade of lightermen (Maving *v.* Todd, 1 Stark. 72); and we have already seen that an innkeeper who receives goods to be forwarded is held liable as a carrier (Hyde *v.* Trent Navigation Co., 5 T. R. 389). Grosvenor *v.* New York, &c. R. R. Co., 39 N. Y. 34; Packard *v.* Getman, 6 Cow. (N. Y.) 757; Trevor *v.* Rens. & Sar. R. R. Co., 7 Hill (N. Y.), 47.

amount of remuneration, so reasonableness must be a rule which will guide the amount of time which may elapse before the carrier performs the duty he has undertaken. Raphael *v.* Pickford, 5 M. & G. 558. And the same word will be found to contain a principle for the determination of the amount of time which may elapse between the offer of the goods by the owner and their acceptance by the carrier. Thus, in Crouch *v.* Great Western Railway Company, 9 Exch. 556, the declaration charged the defendants, as common carriers, with having refused to receive the plaintiff's goods for carriage within a reasonable time after the plaintiff had tendered them, with the hire, to be carried. The judgment was for the plaintiff in this case, upon the ground that the defendants' plea of the insufficiency of the hire tendered was bad on the facts of the case.

SEC. 86. **Reason of the Rule of Law.** — We have found that custom is the rule which, in most instances, must determine the questions which arise with regard to the duty and responsibility of carriers; and the ground for this is, that a man's habits may, under ordinary circumstances, be relied upon as a reason for inferring what his conduct will be in the future, and therefore, when that man is in a public employment, the law should make such conduct as may reasonably be inferred from his customs a duty, and the breach of that duty a cause of action.

SEC. 87. **Where a Carrier may receive.** — In this particular, as in others, the above rule is to guide. Thus, if a carrier directs that goods shall be left at a particular booking-office, or if he has been in the habit of universally undertaking the duty of carriage in reference to parcels left at a particular place, he is to be held as receiving goods at that place to keep and to carry safely, and he will consequently be answerable for the negligence of the keeper of the booking-office, or of the person appointed by him to receive the goods sent there to be forwarded.[1] Where, in an action against a carrier for

[1] Culpepper *v.* Good, 5 Car. & P. 380. And see Gilbert *v.* Dale, 6 Ad. & El. 543; Upton *v.* Slark, 2 C. & P. 181; 11 Geo. IV. and 1 Will. IV. c. 68, § 5; and Southern Express Co. *v.* Newby, 36 Ga. 635.

the loss of a parcel, the defendant pleaded that it was not delivered to him to be carried, it was held sufficient for the plaintiff to show that the parcel was delivered to a person and at a house where parcels were in the habit of being left for the carrier.[1]

SEC. 88. **Receiving-house.** — An inn, where a book was kept for booking parcels by a particular coach, which stopped there regularly to take in and deliver parcels, was held to be a receiving-house for parcels, within 11 Geo. IV. and 1 Will. IV. c. 68, although other coaches were in the habit of stopping there for the same purpose, and it was the habit of the innkeeper to send the parcels by any coach he chose.[2] And in the case of Davey *v.* Mason,[3] it was decided that if a message is left at the booking-office of a carrier, requesting him to send his van to a certain inn for the plaintiff's luggage, for the purpose of conveying it to the destination of the carrier's ordinary journey; and if, in consequence of this message, the carrier's servant and van go to the inn specified in the message, and the plaintiff's luggage is there put into the carrier's van and afterwards lost therefrom, the carrier is liable for the loss, just as he would be if the plaintiff's luggage had been taken to the defendant's booking-office. It is evident, then, that just as servants can do the actual duty of conveying the goods for a carrier who is liable for the loss or injury caused by their faults or negligence, so can a servant undertake for a master the duty of accepting or receiving goods to be conveyed, so as at once to invest the master with the whole of the common-law liability and duty which attaches to those who carry on the trade or business of common carriers.[4] From these cases it appears that a valid delivery can take place, although such a kind of delivery has not been sanctioned by the notices or custom of the carrier.

SEC. 89. **Hours of Receiving.** — Certain carriers limit the

[1] Burrell *v.* North, 2 C. & K. 681.

[2] Syms *v.* Chaplin, 1 N. & P. 129; 5 Ad. & El. 634; 2 H. & W. 411.

[3] 1 Car. & M. 45.

[4] Cobban *v.* Downe, 5 Esp. 41; Boys *v.* Pink, 8 Car. & P. 361. See also Rogers *v.* Long Island R. R. Co., 38 How. (N. Y.) Pr. 289; Adams Express Co. *v.* Haynes, 42 Ill. 89.

time during which they will receive goods to be forwarded, and if custom has given life to such a notice, the carrier will doubtless be warranted in refusing to receive such goods as are brought to him at a time during which he has, by express notice, laid aside the character of a common carrier. If, however, goods are brought to him at a time or to a place at which he has by notice, confirmed by custom, refused to receive goods for carriage, and without saying anything to the owner he receives the goods, he thereby resumes his character of a common carrier and his liability as such.[1] Thus, though a carrier has been in the habit of receiving goods at a particular booking-office, he may, by accepting goods from an individual whom he meets upon the way, receive the goods so as to raise his common-law liability as an insurer in case of their loss or damage.

SEC. 90. **Acceptance by Carrier necessary to raise Liability.** — But there must be either an actual or constructive acceptance by the carrier, or the contract of bailment will not arise. The essential element of such a contract is, that the bailee is to be trusted with the goods, and if he is not made aware of the intention of the party to trust the goods to his keeping, or if the party, instead of trusting the goods to him, still retains the care of them, the bailment to the carrier evidently does not arise, or arises only in a modified form. Thus, where a wharfinger delivered goods, which were sent to a wharf to go on board a vessel, to one of the crew, and did not deliver them to the captain of the vessel, or to some other person that he might reasonably presume to be in authority, it was held that he had not discharged his duty, and he, and not the shipowner (the carrier), was liable for the loss which occurred owing to his negligence.[2] Thus, if a traveller by coach keeps a parcel in his hand, and under his own care, the carrier is not responsible for its loss, as it has never really been delivered to him, or to any one of his servants authorized to accept

[1] Pickford *v.* Grand Junction Rail. Co., 12 M. & W. 766; Phillips *v.* Earle, 8 Pick. (Mass.) 182; Story on Bailm. § 533.

[2] Leigh *v.* Smith, 1 Car. & P. 638.

goods to be carried for him. So, in the case mentioned by STORY,[1] "where a coat was delivered to the driver of a stage-coach by a person not a passenger, to be delivered to another in a different place, but nothing was paid for the carriage of the coat, and the driver refused to put it on the way-bill, saying he had no right to do so; and there was no proof that the coat ever came to the possession of the proprietor of the stage-coach or any of his agents, except the driver, it was held that there was no delivery of the coat *to such proprietor*, and that he was not responsible as a common carrier for the loss thereof." The evident reason for all these rules is, that to charge a carrier with the loss of an article which has never come into his possession, or to hold him responsible for the loss of an article of which he has never had an opportunity of taking care, would be eminently unjust. The rule that a man must insure the safety of an article which is intrusted to him is founded upon a large experience of the usefulness of such a regulation.

SEC. 91. **Principles of Insurance.** — The meaning of the whole principle of insurance is involved in the liability which the common law imposes upon carriers. But no principle of insurance could possibly show any excellence in a system by which liabilities could be imposed upon individuals, whether common carriers or not, without their knowledge, or where responsibility could be held to devolve upon them in reference to articles concerning which they knew absolutely nothing. Thus, in a case where the plaintiff received a parcel from G, which he was to book for London, at the office of the defendant, who was a common carrier, — and where the plaintiff, instead of carrying out G's instructions, put the parcel into his own carpet-bag, intending to take it to London himself, — the defendants having lost the bag containing G's parcel, it was held that the plaintiff could not recover damages from them in respect of the parcel.[2] TINDAL, C. J., said: "The

[1] Bailm. § 533; Olive *v.* Eames, 2 Stark. 181; Blanchard *v.* Isaacs, 3 Barb. (N. Y.) 388. See Ford *v.* Mitchell, 21 Ind. 54. See also Tower *v.* Utica, &c. R. R., 7 Hill (N. Y.), 47.

[2] Miles *v.* Cattle, 6 Bing. 743; *per* TINDAL, C. J., in Miles *v.* Cattle,

evidence is, that the parcel was delivered to him (the plaintiff), not for the purpose of carrying it to London himself, but of booking it at the defendant's office in Stockton. In violation of that trust, the plaintiff thought proper not to deliver the parcel to the defendants, but to deposit it in his own bag, thereby depriving G of any remedy he might have had against the defendants in case the parcel had been lost by them, and becoming himself a wrong-doer towards the defendants by depriving them of the sum they would otherwise have earned for the carriage of the parcel."

6 Bing. 743. See also East India Co. *v.* Pullen, 1 Stra. 690; Buckman *v.* Levi, 3 Camp. 414; Selway *v.* Holloway, 1 Ld. Raym. 46; Hyde *v.* Trent Navigation Co., 5 T. R. 397; Davey *v.* Mason, 1 Car. & M. 45; Southern Express Co. *v.* Newby, 36 Ga. 635; Orange County Bank *v.* Brown, 9 Wend. (N. Y.) 86.

CHAPTER VI.

OF THE COMMON-LAW DUTY OF COMMON CARRIERS TO CONVEY AND DELIVER GOODS SAFELY AND SECURELY, OR OF THEIR RESPONSIBILITY.

SEC. 92. **Common Carrier an Insurer.** — A common carrier is regarded as an insurer by the law of England, and only when the loss or damage to the goods under his care arises from unavoidable accident is he to be regarded as irresponsible for the injury to the bailor.[1] As CHIEF JUSTICE BEST said, "to give due security to property, the law has added to that responsibility of a carrier which immediately arises out of his contract to carry for a reward — namely, that of taking all reasonable care — the responsibility of an insurer."[2] And

[1] Woodleif v. Curteis, 1 Roll. Abr. 2 E. pl. 5; Coggs v. Barnard, 1 Sm. L. Ca., 6th ed., 177; Dale v. Hall, 1 Wils. 281; Forward v. Pittard, 1 T. R. 27; Jones on Bailm. 103; Pazi v. Shipton, 1 P. & D. 4; 8 Ad. & El. 963; 1 W. W. H. 624.

[2] Riley v. Horne, 5 Bing. 217, at p. 220; Macklin v. Waterhouse, 2 M. & P. 319; 5 Bing. 212; Oakley v. Portsmouth, &c. Co., 11 Exch. 618; 25 L. J. 99 Exch.

Lord Holt, C. J., in the case of Coggs *v.* Barnard, says: "The law charges this person, the carrier thus intrusted, to carry goods against all events but the acts of God and the enemies of the king. For though the force be never so great, as if an irresistible multitude of people should rob him, nevertheless he is chargeable. And this is a politic establishment contrived by the policy of the law for the safety of all persons, the necessity of whose affairs obliges them to trust this sort of persons, that they may be safe in their dealings. For else these carriers might have an opportunity of undoing all persons that had any doings with them, by combining with thieves, &c., and yet doing it in such a clandestine manner as would not be possible to be discovered. And this is the reason the law is founded in that point.[1]

Sec. 93. **The Principle of Law considered.** — There is undoubted reason that in order that people may transmit goods with a feeling of confidence as to their safety, there should be some system by which they should be enabled to insure their goods, but it is to be questioned whether it is equally expedient that a carrier should by the mere fact of his office become an insurer, and that he should be entitled to charge the premium for the insurance, together with the charge for his trouble and expense in carrying the goods. There is much to be said in favor of allowing all persons to know what they are paying for, and it might in many instances be better to make it necessary that a special contract should be entered into for the insurance of goods sent by a common carrier, while the law might impose a duty upon those carriers who had held themselves out to the public as insurers as well as carriers, similar to the common-law duty to carry which is imposed upon all common carriers at the present time. At the same time, even if common carriers were not insurers by the mere force of the common law, they would be responsible for all damage caused by their servants, or by others in their employ or confidence, or under their protection, but they would be exempted, except in the case of special contract for insurance, or unless they

[1] Coggs *v.* Barnard, 2 Ld. Raym. 909; 1 Sm. L. Ca., 6th ed., p. 177.

were professed insurers of goods as well as common carriers, from all responsibilities for thefts and for loss occasioned by mere accident or inevitable casualty. Such, however, is not at the present time the law. The principles of the English law, as it at present stands, seem to have been approved in this country.[1]

[1] Per BRONSON, J., in Hollister *v.* Nowlen, 19 Wend. (N. Y.) 234; and in Fairchild *v.* Slocum, 19 Wend. (N. Y.) 331; and in Cole *v.* Goodwin, 19 Wend. (N. Y.) 251; and the opinion of COWEN, J., 21 Wend. (N. Y.) 198. See also Crosby *v.* Fitch, 12 Conn. 419; Hale *v.* New Jersey Steam Nav. Co., 15 Conn. 539; Klauber *v.* American Express Co., 21 Wis. 21; Southern Express Co. *v.* Newby, 36 Ga. 635. See also Howe *v.* Oswego, &c. R. R. Co., 56 Barb. (N. Y.) 121; and in 1869, The Maggie Hammond, 9 Wall. (U. S.) 435. Common carriers are liable for every injury to property intrusted to them for transportation, except such as arises from inevitable accident, the act of God, public enemies, or the act of the owner. Harrell *v.* Owens, 1 D. & B. (N. C.) L. 273; Colt *v.* McMechen, 6 John. (N. Y.) 60; Moses *v.* Norris, 4 N. H. 304; Kemp. *v.* Coughtry, 11 John. (N. Y.) 107; Ewart *v.* Street, 2 Bailey (S. C.), 157; Williams *v.* Grant, 1 Conn. 487; Turner *v.* Wilson, 7 Yerg. (Tenn.) 340; Campbell *v.* Morse, Harp. (S. C.) 469; Gordon *v.* Little, 8 S. & R. (Penn.) 533. And this rule extends to carriers by water as well as by land. Daggett *v.* Shaw, 3 Mo. 264; Harrington *v.* Lyles, 2 N. & McCord (S. C.), 88; Clark *v.* Richards, 1 Conn. 54; Emery *v.* Hersey, 4 Me. 411; Boyle *v.* McLaughlin, 4 H. & J. (Md.) 291. And the destruction of goods by fire is not such an act of God, unless occasioned by lightning, as excuses the carrier's liability. Graff *v.* Bloomer, 9 Penn. St. 114; Parker *v.* Flagg, 26 Me. 181; Miller *v.* Steam Navigation Co., 10 N. Y. 431. But the rule does not extend to the *time* of delivery. Parsons *v.* Hardy, 14 Wend. (N. Y.) 215. A common carrier is only relieved from liability for such injuries as *must* be attributed to the act of God, and not merely for such as *may* be so attributed. If the injury is not the direct effect of the act of God, but is such as might not have happened but for the negligence of man, the carrier is liable. Therefore, where a violent storm caused an unusually low tide, and the carrier's barge, lying at the pier which he used, was pierced by a projecting timber, covered at ordinary tides, and known by the carrier to exist, it was held that he was liable, notwithstanding that his individual negligence in leaving his barge there would not have produced the injury, without the concurrence of the act of God and the negligence of the wharf-builder. New Brunswick Co. *v.* Tiers, 24 N. J. L. 697.

If he has departed from the line of duty, and has violated his contract, and, while thus in fault, and in consequence of that fault, the goods are injured by an act of God, which would not otherwise have produced the injury, then the carrier is not protected. Michaels *v.* New York, &c. R. R. Co., 30 N. Y. 564; Read *v.* Spaulding, 30 N. Y. 630. Thus, in the latter case, where there was an unreasonable delay on the part of a carrier in forward-

SEC. 94. **Same, continued.** — In order, then, rightly to understand the extent of a carrier's responsibility, it is necessary to understand what occurrences may be said to be the acts of God, or, as SIR WILLIAM JONES would prefer to call them, "inevitable accidents,"[1] and who are the queen's enemies. His objection to the phrase "acts of God" is, that the expres-

ing goods, and while they were in a railroad depot, at an intermediate point, they were wetted and injured by an extraordinary flood, caused by the damming up of the water in the channel by ice, and setting the same back upon the freight depot, it was held that, the goods having been exposed to the peril by the fault and neglect of the carrier, he was not excused.

In another New York case the defendant, a common carrier, received at Albany, from the Hudson River R. R. Co., a box of goods to be transported to Rochester and delivered to the owners, for hire. Instead of forwarding the box immediately, it detained the same in its freight house at Albany, to await the rendering of a bill for back charges by the Hudson River R. R. Co. While so detained the goods were injured by being wetted by an unusual and extraordinary rise in the waters of the Hudson River. It was held, —

1. That the detention of the goods was negligence on the part of the defendant; and that such negligence having concurred in, and contributed to, the injury of the goods, the defendant was precluded from claiming the exemption from liability, which the law would otherwise extend to it.

2. That the judge, on the trial, properly refused to direct a verdict for the defendant, on the ground that the injury complained of was caused by the act of God, and without any fault or negligence on the part of the defendant; or because the goods were in the possession of the defendant at the time, in the character of a warehouseman, and not as a common carrier.

3. That the judge properly instructed the jury that, under the evidence, the defendant was liable as a common carrier for the damages sustained by the plaintiffs, and that the only question to be considered was the amount of damages. Michaels *v.* New York, &c. R. R. Co., 30 N. Y. 564. Nor can he excuse his liability upon the ground that the loss resulted from the act of a third person. Thus, where a carrier employs a tow-boat to tow his vessel, and by the negligence of those in charge of the tow-boat damage is done to the property, and the carrier has not in his contract excepted such risks, he is liable to the owners of the property. Merrick *v.* Brainard, 38 Barb. (N. Y.) 574. Where property in the hands of a carrier is lost or destroyed through his negligence, the fact that it is insured does not *pro tanto* relieve him from liability. Burnside *v.* Union Steamboat Co., 10 Rich. (S. C.) 113.

A common carrier, or a private person, who undertakes for hire to carry and deliver goods safely, is bound to pursue the usual and ordinary route. If he unnecessarily deviates from that route he will be liable for any injury to the goods which may be occasioned thereby. Powers *v.* Davenport, 7 Blackf. (Ind.) 407.

[1] Jones on Bailm. 104, 105.

sion is not seemly and reverent. But there is a stronger argument against the phrase he proposes to substitute, and that is, that it is not adequate; for it has been held, and properly so, if we read the meaning of the word "insurance" aright, that a common carrier is liable for "inevitable accident,"[1] and there must therefore be some distinction between the occurrences which would fall under the one head and those which would fall under the other. The case put by LORD HOLT, and quoted above, "where the force is never so great, as if an irresistible multitude should rob him," might fairly be called an "inevitable accident;" "nevertheless," says his Lordship, "he is chargeable." LORD MANSFIELD, in distinguishing between "inevitable accidents" and the "acts of God," calls the latter a "natural necessity," and illustrates what he means by the phrase "natural necessity" by instancing "winds and storms which arise from natural causes," and a "sudden gust of wind."[2] From these judicial examples of the casualties which fall under the definition "acts of God," it is evident that ***physical occurrences which cause loss or damage are to be classed amongst acts of God if they are of so stupendous a character that no act of man could do anything to avoid them.***[3] In one

[1] Per MANSFIELD, C. J., in Forward *v.* Pittard, 1 T. R. 27, at p. 33.

[2] Trent Nav. Co. *v.* Wood, 3 Esp. 127; Amies *v.* Stevens, 1 Stra. 128. See Ballentine *v.* North Missouri R. R. Co., 40 Mo. 491.

[3] A carrier may always excuse himself, where the loss or damage resulted from *vis major;* and where such proof is given, he is not under obligation to show that he was not guilty of any negligence in respect thereto. If the plaintiff makes any such claim, he must prove it. Railroad Co. *v.* Reeves, 10 Wall. (U. S.) 176. The maxim, *causa proxima non remota spectatur*, applies in such cases; and if the carrier exercised ordinary diligence he is excused, the rule being that where the act of God is the *proximate* cause of the loss, the carrier is excused, although his own negligence may have contributed as a *remote* cause. Thus, where a freshet destroyed a railroad bridge and caused delay in the shipment of cotton, and where the cotton was injured by bad handling, it was held that the company was not liable for the injury caused by delay, as that was *vis major*, but that it was liable for the injury caused by bad handling. Lifford *v.* Charlotte, &c. R. R. Co., 7 Rich. (S. C.) L. 409; Barber *v.* Brace, 3 Conn. 9. See also Ballentine *v.* North Missouri R. R. Co., 40 Mo. 491, where it was held that a carrier could not be held responsible for a delay occasioned by the road being blocked up by snow. But in all cases it is the duty of the carrier to use reasonable diligence to relieve himself from obstructions, &c., occasioned by such causes, and the

sense every event is caused by God; but yet a carrier would not be exempted from responsibility — indeed, he would be guilty of culpable carelessness — if he allowed goods that would spoil to remain exposed to a shower of rain. Those acts of God, then, only are called "acts of God" in law which cause damage which no act of man could prevent. If "inevitable accident" was allowed to be an excuse for the loss of goods in the possession of a carrier, and inevitable accident was understood to include robbery, which, under certain circumstances, might be an unavoidable accident, it has been pointed out that the carrier might be in league with the robbers, and thus intentionally put the owner's goods in jeopardy with a feeling that he was perfectly safe in so doing. Such a result would be disastrous to trade, and it is therefore well that the exceptions to the liability of the insurer should be very few, and that they should be well understood, so that those persons who trust their goods to carriers may know exactly the risk they run.

SEC. 95. **Waste.** — In the older books there is a distinction drawn similar to that mentioned above. There, under the head of "Waste," the falling down of a house caused by a tempest, or the burning of a house caused by lightning, is said to be no waste; but the burning of a house by negligence or by mischance is, according to the same authority, waste.[1] A similar distinction is, as we have seen, to be drawn between acts which are and acts which are not the acts of God. Thus, if goods be lost or damaged owing to a storm, a flood, lightning, or the sudden and unlooked-for death of the servants that were in charge of them, the carrier would not be held liable. *If, however, they were damaged owing to their having been placed in a house which was insecure, and tumbled of its own decrepit nature, if they were trusted to an insecure ferry-boat, or if they were burned while in the possession of the carrier, the fire not being caused by lightning, the carrier would be held*

burden is upon him to show that the loss or damage resulted from the act of God. Winne v. Illinois Central R. R. Co., 18 Iowa, 555; Bausemer v. Toledo, &c. R. R. Co., 25 Ind. 434.

[1] Co. Litt. 53, a, b.

responsible for the loss.[1] The case of Forward *v.* Pittard is in point. LORD MANSFIELD, in delivering the opinion of the court

[1] The Northern Belle, 9 Wall. (U. S.) 526; Cardwell *v.* New Jersey Steamboat Co., 56 Barb. (N. Y.) 425. If, however, the building, being secure, is destroyed by a tempest, or is set on fire by lightning, or if an earthquake should swallow it up, or prostrate it, the loss would be clearly attributable to the act of God, and the carrier would be exonerated. But if the building should be prostrated by reason of the act of a third person excavating upon an adjoining lot, or should be destroyed by an incendiary fire, or torn down by a mob, the loss and damage, being wholly attributable to the acts of man, would not exonerate the carrier. If by a violent storm, freshet, or other convulsion of nature, obstructions are suddenly thrown across a railway track at a point and under such circumstances that the carrier could not, by any reasonable degree of diligence, have discovered it in season to avoid, whereby the train is wrecked and the goods destroyed, it would seem that, at least, upon the principle of some of the cases, the company would be exonerated. Thus, in South Carolina, it has been held that where a vessel runs upon a snag placed in the channel of a navigable stream by a sudden freshet, the carrier cannot be held chargeable for the loss. Faulkner *v.* Wright, Rice (S. C.), 107; Smyrl *v.* Malin, 2 Bailey (S. C.), 421. In Williams *v.* Gould, 1 Conn. 487, this principle was recognized under the following state of facts. The plaintiffs shipped four hundred and fifty bushels of salt, by a vessel belonging to the defendants, from Providence to New York. While the vessel was on her voyage she ran against a hidden rock in the Providence River. At the time the injury occurred the vessel was sailing under a moderate breeze, the weather being fair. The vessel, running upon the rock, bilged, and the salt was thereby destroyed. The plaintiff contended that the existence of the rock was well known to people in the neighborhood and those concerned in the navigation of the river; that the vessel at the time the injury occurred was out of her usual course, and that the master was not acquainted with the navigation of the river, and that there was no pilot on board as was usual, and produced witnesses to prove these facts. The defendant, however, produced witnesses to prove that the existence of the rock was not generally known. The court charged the jury that if they should find from the evidence that the rock was generally known, the loss would be imputable to the negligence of the defendants, and the plaintiff would be entitled to recover; but that if they should find *that it was not generally known*, then the loss was occasioned by the perils of the sea, and the defendants were not liable. Upon appeal, SWIFT, C. J., said: —

"Common carriers are liable for the loss of goods intrusted to their care in all cases, except where the loss arises from the act of God, the enemies of the state, or the default of the party sending them. Under the term *act of God* are comprehended all misfortunes and accidents arising from inevitable necessity, which human prudence could not foresee or prevent; and in cases of this description they may be liable for a loss arising from an inevitable necessity existing at the time of the loss, if they had been guilty of a previous negligence or miscon-

in that case, said: "The question is whether the common carrier is liable in this case of fire. It appears, from all the

duct, by which the loss may have been occasioned.

"If the rock on which this vessel struck had been generally known, then it was the duty of the master to have known and avoided it, and the loss would be imputable to his negligence. If the situation of the rock was not generally known, and the master did not actually know it, then if he conducted properly in other respects, and no fault was imputable to him, his striking on the rock would be an act of God, an unavoidable accident, and he would not be liable for the loss. For, though the rock had been there for ages, yet if it had never been discovered before, it is the same thing as if it had been created and placed there immediately before the accident happened. See M'Arthur *v.* Sears, 21 Wend. (N. Y.) 190. The charge of the court to the jury on this point was correct.

"In this case, however, the plaintiffs offered evidence to prove that the master was ignorant of the navigation; that he had no pilot, as was customary; and that the vessel went out of the usual course. It does not appear but that the running of the vessel on the rock may be attributed to this negligence. Of course, the court should have submitted these facts to the jury, and should have instructed them that though the situation of the rock was not generally known, yet if they found the other facts to be true, so that the loss was imputable to the negligence of the master, then he was liable for it, and they must find a verdict for the plaintiffs. For this reason I would advise a new trial."

Gould, J., said: "It is very clear that a common carrier is liable, under a general acceptance, for all losses, except such as are occasioned by inevitable accident, the act of the public enemies, or the act or default of the bailor himself. In the case now before the court, neither any act of public enemies, nor any act or default of the plaintiffs, is in question. With respect to the other ground of exemption (inevitable accident), the defendants are indeed, by an express exception in the bill of lading, excused, so far as regards losses caused by 'dangers of the sea.' This exception, however, does not seem at all to qualify their liability; for by 'dangers of the sea' are meant no other than *inevitable* perils, or accidents, upon that element, and by *such* perils or accidents common carriers are *primâ facie* excused, whether there is any such express exception or not. In either case, however, it is a condition precedent to their exoneration that they should have been in no *default;* or, in other words, that the goods of the bailor should not have been *exposed* to the peril, or accident, which occasioned the loss by their own misconduct, neglect, or ignorance. For though the immediate, or proximate, cause of a loss, in any given instance, may have been what is termed *the act of God,* or inevitable accident, yet, if the carrier unnecessarily exposed the property to such accident, by any culpable act or omission of his own, he is not excused. I recollect a case put in some book to this effect: That if a common hoyman unnecessarily puts to sea under circumstances which render a loss of the goods on board probable, — as in very tempestuous weather, — he is liable in the event of a loss, although it were *im-*

cases for a hundred years back, that there are events for which the carrier is liable independent of his contract. By the nature of his contract he is liable for all due care and diligence, and for any negligence he is suable on his contract. But there is a further degree of responsibility by the custom of the realm, that is, by the common law; a carrier is in the nature of an insurer. . . . In this case it does not appear but that the fire arose from the act of some man or other. It certainly did arise from some act of man, for it is expressly stated not to have happened by lightning. The carrier, therefore, in this case, is liable, inasmuch as he is liable for inevitable accident."[1]

mediately occasioned by the elements over which he had no control. This I take to be law. In the present case the plaintiff claimed, and attempted to prove at the trial, that the master unnecessarily deviated from the ordinary course; that he was ignorant of the navigation of the river; and that it was usual in that navigation to have a pilot (whom he confessedly had not). Now such a deviation would certainly have been misconduct; the alleged ignorance of the master, there being no pilot on board, would have been a species of deficiency in the nature of unseaworthiness; and the want of a pilot, where one is, by common usage, employed, and the master ignorant of the navigation, is manifestly a culpable neglect. And as the plaintiffs made it a ground of claim that this misconduct, deficiency, and neglect contributed to occasion the loss, by bringing the property on board within the reach of the peril, the existence of the facts on which the claim was founded should have been left to the jury, and the legal effect of them, upon the supposition of their existence, explained." A similar doctrine was held in an early New York case, Colt *v.* McMechen, 6 John. (N. Y.) 160, where a vessel which was sailing in shore under a light wind which, if it had continued, would have carried her safely, failed, and the vessel was thereby run ashore. See also Hays *v.* Kennedy, 41 Penn. 378, where it was held that a loss resulting from a collision of vessels upon the river without the fault of the master or crew, was such unavoidable danger of river navigation as excused the carrier under a bill of lading containing this exception.

[1] Forward *v.* Pittard, 1 T. R. 27. See Abbott on Ship., pt. iv. ch. 6. p. 343; Hyde and Another *v.* Trent and Mersey Navigation Co., 5 T. R. K. B. 389. But a warehouseman is not answerable for loss by fire. Garside *v.* Trent and Mersey Navigation Co., 4 T. R. K. B. 581. But see 26 Geo. III. c. 86, § 2, which enacts "that no owner or owners of any ship or vessel shall be subject or liable to answer for or make good to any one or more person or persons any loss or damage which may happen to any goods or merchandise whatsoever which, from and after the first day of September, 1786, shall be shipped, taken in, or put on board any such vessel by reason or means of *any fire* happening to or on board the said ship

SEC. 96. **Applicability of Rule to Carrier by Water.** — There can be no reason why the rule that is applicable to loss which is caused by fire upon land should not also apply to the carriage of goods upon water, whether the carriage is effected by means of vessels which sail or vessels which are moved by steam. It may be argued that, as ships which are moved by steam require to make use of fire, the same rule should not apply to them that holds with regard to other ships, and that, in case of the loss of the goods which they carry by means of fire, the owner should not be held liable any more than he is if the loss is caused by means of a tempest. But the only inference which can be drawn from these facts seems to us to be that possibly the owner of the steamboat, if the risk of loss by fire is proved to be greater in consequence of the necessary use of furnaces on board of a steamship, might be entitled to charge a higher rate of premium, which the owner of the goods might be willing to pay in return for the greater rapidity with which his goods would be carried, and which, in consequence of the time thus saved, he might be enabled to pay without diminishing his profits. In America it has been solemnly decided that the liability of steamboat owners as common carriers extends to destruction by fire on board their boats, and that no exemption exists in favor of those vessels.[1]

SEC. 97. **Where Act of God does not relieve from Liability.** — But it is evident, from all that has been said, that an act of

or vessel." But this section does not protect shipowners from liability for loss by fire in the case of freighted goods burned in a lighter employed by them to take the goods on board their ship. Morewood *v.* Pollock, 1 E. & B. 743. This act has been repealed by 17 & 18 Vict. c. 120. See the case of Oakley *v.* Port of Portsmouth and the Ryde United Steam Packet Co., 11 Exch. 618; 25 L. J. Exch. 99. See also Amies *v.* Stevens, 1 Stra. 128.

[1] Patton *v.* Magrath, Dudley (S. C.), 184, which case is approved in Swindler *v.* Hilliard, 2 Rich. (S. C.) 286. The Act of Congress of March 3, 1851, provides, however, that no owner of any ship or vessel shall be liable to answer for any loss or damage which may happen to any goods shipped by reason of fire on board, unless such fire is caused by design or neglect of such owner, with a proviso that the parties may make such contract between themselves on the subject as they please. Construed and applied, Moore *v.* American Transportation Co., 24 How. (U. S.) 1; Walker *v.* Transportation Co., 3 Wall. (U. S.) 150.

God will not under all circumstances relieve the common carrier of his liability. He is by his contract bound to use due care and diligence.[1] *If*, therefore, *the act of God would not have caused damage or loss of the goods but for some carelessness or negligence upon the part of the carrier, the mere fact that the proximate cause of the injury was an act of God will not relieve the carrier of his liability to make good such loss or injury to the owner.*[2] A carrier is always bound to use an ordinary amount of forethought and prudence in the exercise of his trust. And if a master of a ship left the harbor when all nautical experience would have warned him to remain in shelter, if he push out to sea in spite of the warnings of others who are in a position to read the face of the sky, the fact that the ship is lost through the dire force of the tempest, which is an act of God, will not excuse the master for his error, or the proprietors of the ship of their liability for the goods they undertook to carry safely and securely. This is only an instance, but the same principle is universally applicable.[3]

SEC. 98. **Where Carrier's Act is Primary Cause of Loss.**— Where a carrier goes to meet a danger which can only be due to the act of God, or can only come about in the course of physical nature, the injury or mischief which arises therefrom cannot be said to be caused by the act of God, but by the carelessness or temerity of the carrier. Now this may be brought about in many different ways. *If a carrier goes a road that he has been unaccustomed to go, and it should not be so safe as that he was in the habit of travelling, he has gone, as it were, to meet the*

[1] *Per* MANSFIELD, C. J., in Forward *v.* Pittard, 1 T. R. 27.

[2] See Williams *v.* Grant, *ante.*

[3] Siordet *v.* Hall, 4 Bing. 607; Davis *v.* Garrett, 6 Bing. 716. See Powell *v.* Layton, 2 N. R. 365; Goff *v.* Clinkard, 1 Wils. 282; Ellis *v.* Turner, 8 T. R. 531; Sutton *v.* Mitchell, 1 T. R. 18. But see, with reference to this case, 26 Geo. III. c. 86; Muddle *v.* Stride, 9 Car. & P. 380; Birkett *v.* Willan, 5 B. & Ald. 356; Bodenham *v.* Bennett, 4 Price, 31; Lowe *v.* Booth, 13 Price, 329; Smith *v.* Horne, 2 Moore, 18; 8 Taunt. 144; Holt, 643; Beckford *v.* Crutwell, 5 Car. & P. 242; 1 M. & Rob. 187; Dale *v.* Hall, 1 Wils. 281; Cailiff *v.* Danvers, 1 Peek, 155; Hunter *v.* Potts, 4 Camp. 203; Laveroni *v.* Drury, 8 Exch. 166; Oakley *v.* Steam Packet Co., 11 Exch. 618; Lyon *v.* Mells, 5 East, 428; Hollingworth *v.* Brodrick, 7 Ad. & El. 40.

dangers of that road, and any calamity which he might encounter would be brought about as much by his own act as by the act of God.[1] So, if he delays an unreasonably long time on the

[1] Williams *v.* Grant, *ante.* This is in obedience to the universal rule that, in order to excuse the carrier, the act of God must be the proximate cause of the loss, McArthur *v.* Sears, 21 Wend. (N. Y.) 190; Mershon *v.* Hobensack, 22 N. J. L. 372; Ewart *v.* Street, 2 Bailey (S. C.), 157; Backhouse *v.* Sneed, 1 Murph. (N. C.) 173; King *v.* Shepherd, 3 Story (U. S. C. C.), 349; Hart *v.* Allen, 2 Watts (Penn.), 114; and that where human agency intervenes and operates in conjunction with the act of God, the carrier is not excused, Merritt *v.* Earle, 29 N. Y. 115. BLACKBURN, C. J., in Nugent *v.* Smith, L. R. 1 C. P. Div. 19, — a case decided since the text of this work was written, — in commenting upon the species of losses and damage which may be said to be occasioned by the act of God, said: "It is obvious, as was pointed out by LORD MANSFIELD, in Forward *v.* Pittard, 1 T. R. 27, that all causes of inevitable accident — *casus fortuitus* — may be divided into two classes: those which are occasioned by the elementary forces of nature, unconnected with the agency of man or other cause; and those which have their origin, either in whole or in part, in the agency of man, whether in acts of omission or commission, of nonfeasance or misfeasance, or in any other cause independent of the agency of natural forces. It is obvious that it would be altogether incongruous to apply the term 'act of God' to the latter class of inevitable accident. It is equally clear that storm and tempest belong to the class to which the term is properly applicable. On the other hand, it must be admitted that it is not because an accident is occasioned by the agency of nature, and therefore by what may be termed the 'act of God,' that it necessarily follows that the carrier is entitled to immunity. The rain which fertilizes the earth, and the wind which enables the ship to navigate the ocean, are as much within the term 'act of God' as the rainfall which causes the river to burst its banks and carry destruction over a whole district, or the cyclone that drives a ship against a rock and sends it to the bottom. Yet the carrier, who by the rule is entitled to protection in the latter case, would clearly not be able to claim it in case of damage occurring in the former. For here another principle comes into play. The carrier is bound to do his utmost to protect the goods committed to his care from loss or damage; and if he fails herein, he becomes liable from the nature of the contract. In the one case he can protect the goods by the proper care; in the other it is beyond his power to do so. If by his default, in omitting to take the necessary care, loss or damage ensues, he remains responsible, though the so-called 'act of God' may have been the immediate cause of the mischief. If the ship is unseaworthy, and hence perishes from the storm which otherwise it would have weathered; if the carrier, by undue deviation or delay, exposes himself to the danger which he otherwise would have avoided, or if by his rashness he unnecessarily encounters it, as by putting to sea in a raging storm, the loss cannot be said to be due to the act of God alone, and the carrier cannot have the benefit of the exception." As to

journey, and it is proved that but for such unreasonable waste of time he would have been able to deposit the goods in safety,

the effect of deviation, see Powers *v.* Davenport, 7 Blackf. (Ind.) 497; Express Company *v.* Kountz, 8 Wall. (U. S) 342.

This question was carefully considered by the Supreme Court of Connecticut in Crosby *v.* Fitch, 12 Conn. 410. In that case the defendants, who were common carriers by water between Norwich and New York, undertook to carry for the plaintiffs fifty-two bales of cotton from New York to Norwich. The usual route of vessels was through Long Island Sound, in summer and winter. In the winter of 1836 the navigation of the Sound was obstructed by ice for a longer period than usual, to wit, from January to March, and in February the defendants, without waiting for the ice in the Sound to break up, took the outside passage by way of the open sea, and in a severe storm the cotton was thrown overboard to save the vessel and crew. It was not denied that the Sound was frozen over at the time the vessel sailed, so that it was impracticable for the vessel to sail by that route at that time; but the plaintiffs insisted that the defendants should have waited until the Sound was freed from the obstruction, and that in taking the route by the open sea they had invited the loss, and were therefore liable therefor. The defendants claimed that if, at the time the vessel sailed with the cotton, the navigation of the Sound was so obstructed by ice as to render it impracticable for the vessel to proceed by way of the Sound, and there was a reasonable prospect that the Sound would not be open soon so as to permit her to sail through it, the master had a right, at his discretion, to proceed on his voyage on the outside of Long Island, and especially if other vessels similarly situated did so, and that it was necessary that the usage to do so should be general or universal in order to justify the master in taking that course.

The court charged the jury, 1. That the defendants, being owners of the sloop Maria, were common carriers, and as such were liable for all losses or injuries not occasioned by public enemies, the act of God, such as perils of the sea, or the act of the plaintiffs themselves; that if the cotton in question was thrown overboard and lost, in consequence of imminent danger produced by a storm, to save the vessel and the lives of the crew, it was a loss by the act of God; and in such case the defendants would not be liable, unless such danger was encountered, or such perils produced, by reason of the unseaworthiness of the vessel, the want of a proper number of able men to manage her, or some negligence or improper conduct of the master or owners. 2. That it was the duty of the master of the vessel to perform his voyage from New York to New London by the usual and ordinary route; and if, without a reasonable necessity, he neglected this duty, and adopted another and an unusual route, it was such misconduct on the part of the master as would subject the owners of the vessel for all losses sustained by reason thereof; and if the jury believed that the master of the Maria departed from the usual route in pursuing his voyage, without reasonable necessity, as claimed by the plaintiffs, or that the vessel was unseaworthy and not sufficiently manned for such a voyage, and that the loss of which the plaintiffs com-

it will not be a good defence to an action for the amount of injury done to the goods of an owner who intrusted them to

plained was occasioned thereby, they ought to render a verdict for the plaintiffs; and that the fact that Long Island Sound was obstructed by ice, under the circumstances claimed by the defendants, did not constitute such necessity as would justify the master in prosecuting his voyage by an unusual route, on the south side of Long Island, unless a usage was proved to exist sufficient to justify it.

3. That no practice or usage for vessels bound from New York to New London and Norwich, and ports to the eastward, to perform their voyage on the south side of Long Island when the Sound is frozen and the navigation thereof obstructed, would justify the master in prosecuting his voyage in that manner, instead of waiting in New York until the navigation of the Sound became free, unless such usage was general, and of so long standing as to have become generally known. But if such usage was general, and well known, the master had a right and would be justified in prosecuting such voyage.

4. That the fact that insurance had been effected upon the cotton in question, and that the plaintiffs had, before the commencement of this action, demanded payment of the insurance office for the loss sustained, furnished no defence to this action.

The jury returned a verdict for the plaintiffs; and the defendants moved for a new trial.

In passing upon the question of deviation and its effect upon the liability of the carrier, CHURCH, C. J., said: —

"It was claimed by the defendants that if the cotton was thrown overboard to save the vessel and the lives of those on board, this was a loss by dangers of the seas, within the exception of the bill of lading, and not the consequence of the master's misconduct. If this were all, this claim of the defendants could not be resisted; and so the jury were instructed. This raised the question of deviation, which the plaintiffs insisted the master had been guilty of; for if there had been a deviation in the voyage from New York to New London and Norwich, by reason of which the storm was encountered and the danger incurred, it was such misconduct as would subject the defendants, and deprive them of the justification which they would have had if the same loss had been incurred in the prosecution of a voyage properly conducted.

"There was a deviation, if the master without reasonable necessity, either physical or moral, departed from the usual route of vessels between the ports of New York and New London; and of such deviation freighters, as well as insurers, may take advantage. 3 Kent's Com. 165; Williams *v.* Grant, 1 Conn. 492; Davis *v.* Garrett, 6 Bing. 716; Read *v.* Commercial Insurance Co., 3 Johns. (N. Y.) 348; Urquhart *v.* Barnard, 1 Taun. 456; Hughes on Ins. 197. It was conceded in this case, and the fact is too notorious for dispute, that the usual track of vessels from New York to New London and other Eastern ports is through Long Island Sound, both summer and winter. Was the master, in the present instance, justified in departing from this route, and performing his voyage through the open sea, on the south side of Long Island, in the month of *February?* Was there any reasonable necessity for this? We think there

him to be carried, to say that the injury was caused by a flood, which was the act of God. The flood was the act of God, but

was not. The claim is, that the navigation of the Sound was obstructed by ice, and so continued longer than had been usual in former seasons. Still we see no necessity for the sailing of this vessel while these obstructions continued. The obstruction was of such a nature that the master and all concerned knew that at a day not very remote it must be removed. This was known when the goods were placed on board. There was no contract which rendered it the duty of the master to sail by a given time, or to complete his voyage before a specified day. And if there had been, the freezing of the Sound, and the unusual continuance of the obstruction, was such an act of God as would probably have justified a longer stay in the port of departure. The distinction is a very obvious one between the present case and one in which a vessel already on her voyage and *in transitu*, departs from the usual route by reason of obstructions of this nature, or of blockades, &c. In such cases the master must act; a necessity is thrown upon him; and if he is governed by a sound discretion, he stands justified. But here it may as well be claimed that the master would be justified in leaving a safe port during the existence of a violent tempest, or in the face of blockading or embargo restrictions, because it might be uncertain how long these impediments would be in his way. The port of destination in this voyage was Norwich; and it is conceded that the obstruction caused by ice to the navigation of the river Thames usually continues several days longer than the Sound continues frozen. The master knew, therefore, that he could not complete his voyage earlier in consequence of the course he adopted.

"But it is said that the danger from fire, thieves, &c., while lying in the port of New York, created such a necessity of sailing as justified the master in taking the outside passage. It is true that danger of this sort to some extent existed, and does always exist, in all ports, and perhaps very nearly as much at one port as another, — as much at Norwich and New London as at New York. This pretended danger certainly could not be esteemed imminent or uncommon, and could not justify any unusual or hazardous experiment. Oliver *v.* Maryland Insurance Co., 7 Cranch (U. S.), 487. No fact appears from which we can infer any necessity for the sailing of this vessel on the outside of Long Island; and by adopting that route we think the master was guilty of a deviation. It is claimed, to be sure, that this was a question of *fact*, and as such ought to have been submitted to the jury. We have ever supposed that, upon given facts, whether deviation or not, was a question of law, and so we find it treated in all the cases. Suydam *v.* Marine Insurance Co., 2 Johns. (N.Y.) 138; Graham *v.* Commercial Insurance Co., 11 Johns. (N. Y.) 352; Brown *v.* Betts, 9 Cow. (N. Y.) 208; Newell *v.* Hoadley, 8 Conn. 381.

"Although it was not denied that the general usage of vessels bound from New York to New London and Eastern ports was to sail through Long Island Sound, as well in the winter as at other seasons, yet the defendants claimed that there was to some extent a practice for such vessels, when the Sound was obstructed by ice, to sail on the south side of the island, or at least that the exceptions from the general usage were so frequent as that the master in the present

the negligent delay which exposed the goods to it was the act of the carrier. The act of God alone then will not excuse,—whether it be "perils of the sea," "dangers of the river," a "want of seaworthiness,"[1]—unless it can be shown that no gross negligence upon the part of the carrier contributed to expose the goods injured or lost to the dangers by means of which they suffered. These rules are so well established that it seems unnecessary to do more than to mention them in this place, as their principle has already been fully explained. It must always be a question for the jury to decide whether the loss or injury done to goods while in the possession of a carrier has resulted from natural causes which followed upon misconduct, negligence, or incompetence upon his part, or upon that of his servants or agents. And in many cases there must be the utmost difficulty in arriving at a satisfactory answer to this question.

case could take the outside voyage without being guilty of a deviation. On this point the jury were instructed that no practice or usage for such vessels to perform their voyages on the south side of Long Island, when the Sound is frozen, and the navigation for that season obstructed, would justify the master in prosecuting his voyage on said south side, instead of waiting in New York until the usual navigation became free, unless such usage was general, and of so long standing as to have become generally known.

"If the question in the case had been one of care and prudence merely, perhaps such partial usage might have been material to show a want of gross negligence on the part of the master; but that was of no avail to show there had been no deviation. Freighters and insurers, in all their commercial transactions, are presumed to act and to contract in reference to known and general usage, and to submit to it; and such general usage may be well enough said to become a part of all their contracts. And if without consent a partial practice is substituted as governing a voyage or other commercial operation, it operates as interposing a new contract, not agreed to by the parties, and perhaps as a fraud. Indeed, usage should not be regarded at all, unless it be of such a character as may be supposed to influence parties; and none can be ordinarily presumed to do this but such as is public and continued. And therefore it is not sufficient to prove a few instances, not amounting to general practice, as an excuse of what otherwise would have been a deviation. Martin *v.* Delaware Insurance Co., 2 Wash. (U. S. C. C.) 254; 1 Condy's Marsh. on Insurance, 186, note; Hughes on Insurance, 145; Gabay *v.* Lloyd, 3 B. & C. 793; Trott *v.* Wood, 2 Gallison, 444; Barber *v.* Brace, 3 Conn. 10; Lawrence *v.* Stonington Bank, 6 Conn. 521; Gibson *v.* Culver, 17 Wend. (N. Y.) 305."

[1] The Niagara *v.* Cordes, 21 How. (U. S.) 7.

SEC. 99. **Queen's Enemies, Who are?** — The next question which arises with regard to the limitation of the insurance liability of a common carrier is, who are to be regarded as the queen's enemies? Those who steal are certainly enemies to the state to which they belong, yet we have seen that the policy of the law has made it refuse to recognize loss arising from theft,[1] as in any way exculpating the carrier, or freeing him from the liability to make good the loss. This rule had its origin in more troublous times than those in which we live; but although order is not in the habit of being rudely broken, although our highways are to some extent hedged in from danger by the efficiency of some of our institutions, there seems little reason to devise a change in this respect, except in the direction which has been indicated on a previous page;[2] and it is to be remembered that many things which, at first sight, seem to be hardships, are in reality nothing of the sort, as people can, and do, so suit their actions to their circumstances as to make what might seem unjust perfectly equitable. Thus, in reference to this very subject of the insurance of safety against robbers, or losses by theft, which devolves by law upon a carrier, it might be very unjust if the carrier was not made aware that such was his liability; but as he is aware of the risks, he has an opportunity of proportioning his charges in such a way that he may be enabled to make good the losses of his customers, at the same time that he has fair remuneration for his trouble, and a fair interest for the capital he has expended.

SEC. 100. **Pirates.** — But law does not look upon criminals as "enemies of the Queen," in so far as the question of the liabilities of common carriers goes, but confines that phrase to public enemies with whom the state is at open war.[3] But pirates on the high seas are also to be regarded as enemies of the state and of mankind.[4] The reason for this is, that, to some extent, the government of a country must be looked upon as the bailee of the goods of all its subjects, for the pur-

[1] Gibbon *v.* Paynton, 4 Burr. 2299.

[2] *Ante*, p. 120.

[3] See Story on Bailm. § 526.

[4] Pickering *v.* Barclay, 2 Roll. Abr. 248, & Style, 132; Barton *v.* Wolliford, Comb. 56.

pose that they may be kept in safety, and this bailment ought to extend to insurance against the aggressions of a foreign state, or against the robberies which may take place on the high seas; for, in both these instances, the government has an absolute duty, as it may be regarded as a bailee for hire, seeing that the taxes are imposed with the purpose that the country may be protected from public enemies, and that property, whether it is abroad or at home, may be secure. This rule has been, more than once, stated in courts of law,[1] and it is the same rule which was adopted by the Roman jurists.[2] But, as may be gathered from what has already been said, this rule is to be understood to apply only where the ship does not fall into the hands of pirates by any negligence or fault of the master.[3] These two causes of disaster may sometimes conspire to bring about mischief. The act of God may throw a ship into the hands of an enemy. A tempest may carry a ship on to an enemy's shore, and in these cases it is to be remembered that the proximate cause of the loss or capture is that to which it is to be ascribed in law. Thus, if the winds carry a ship to a coast where she is captured by the enemy, this is to be looked upon, according to authority, as a loss by capture of the enemy — this, however, under the supposition that she is captured before she has been stranded. If, on the other hand, the tempest should strand the ship, and she should subsequently be ransacked by the inhabitants, the loss is to be ascribed to the perils of the sea.[4] So far, however, as the common-law liability of common carriers is concerned, these somewhat fine distinctions are useless, as it is evident that the irresponsibility of carriers is the same, whether the loss or damage has been caused by one or both of these circumstances, which are excepted from the carrier's implied contract of insurance. Where, however, there is a special contract, as, for

[1] Pickering *v.* Barclay, *ubi supra;* Barton *v.* Wolliford, *ubi supra;* Morse *v.* Slue, 1 Vent. 190.

[2] Dig. 4, 9, 31.

[3] Emerigon, tom. 1, p. 532; Bexer *v.* Tomlinson, Easter Term, 36 Geo. III.

[4] Story on Bailm. § 526; Hayn *v.* Corbett, 2 Bing. 205; Greene *v.* Elmslie, Peake, 278. See also American cases, Syckel *v.* The Thomas Euring, Crabbe, 405; Curence *v.* Minturn, 17 How. (U. S.) 100; King *v.* Shephert, Story (U. S. C. C.), 349.

instance, that the owner of the goods shall bear the loss, if any is occasioned by the perils of the sea, but that the carrier shall be responsible for any loss or injury caused by the Queen's enemies, the determination of this question may be a matter of much importance. It is also to be noticed that the words "Queen's enemies" include something more than the meaning they at first sight bear. They do not mean exclusively the enemies of the sovereign of England, but also include the enemies of the sovereign or state of the carrier;[1] so that, if goods be intrusted to a foreign carrier, whose sovereign is at war with another, and his ship is captured, he is excused from performance of his contract, in the same manner as a British carrier would be if his vessel were captured by the enemies of this country. This rule was applied in reference to the capture of goods by the Confederate forces during the Rebellion; and in such cases the carrier was excused, upon the ground that the rebels were belligerents, and "enemies of the Queen" within the rule.[2]

SEC. 101. **Carrier's Liability in case of Loss where the Loss was otherwise Inevitable.** — A question of as much difficulty as interest may be considered in this place. A carrier may sometimes seem to anticipate fate. The goods may be lost through some casualty, for which, under the present law, the carrier is undoubtedly liable; and yet it may be capable of proof that, had they not been lost in the one way, they must inevitably have perished in another, for which the carrier would not have been liable. The question is, under these circumstances, is the carrier to be held responsible for the loss? Thus, suppose a master of a ship to deviate from his course to such a degree that his journey is prolonged for a day, and suppose that it is capable of proof that even had the

[1] Russell *v.* Nieman, 34 L. J. 10 C. P.; 17 C. B. N. S. 163; 10 L. T. N. S. 786. See also The Patria, 3 L. R. Adm. 436; 1 Asp. Mar. Law Cas. 71; The Teutonia, 3 L. R. Adm. 394; 24 L. J. N. S. 21; 1 Asp. Mar. Law Cas. 32; The Heinrich, 3 L. R. Adm. 424; 1 Asp. Mar. Law Cas. 79; The Wilhelm Schmidt, 1 Asp. Mar. Law Cas. 82.

[2] Southern Express Co. *v.* Wormack, 1 Heisk. (Tenn.) 256; Bland *v.* Adams Express Co., 1 Duv. (Ky.) 232; United States *v.* Palmer, 3 Wheat. (U. S.) 610; Thorington *v.* Smith, 8 Wall. (U. S.) 1.

delay of a day not taken place, the storm which wrecked the ship and caused the damage of the goods must inevitably have taken place, and caused the loss or damage. In this case is the carrier to be regarded as responsible for the loss?

SEC. 102. **Roman Law concerning this Matter.** — The Roman law would, under such circumstances, have held *that the carrier was not liable, and that the mere anticipation of the act of God, by the act which was negligent, careless, or wrong upon the part of the carrier, gave it a character resembling that of the inevitable and natural accident which would have done what it did.* "If the bailee, to use the Roman expression," says SIR WILLIAM JONES, "be *in mora* — that is, if a *legal demand* have been made by the bailor, he must answer for any casualty that happens after the demand, unless in cases where it may be strongly presumed that the same accident would have befallen the thing bailed, even if it had been restored at the proper time, or unless the bailee have legally tendered the thing, and the bailor have put himself *in mora* by refusing to accept it. This rule extends, of course, to every species of bailment."[1] *Opinion seems rather to be in favor of adopting this rule of the civil law.*

SEC. 103. **Negligence which does not cause Loss.** — The rule that, if negligence conduces to the loss which is proximately occasioned by an act of God, the carrier who has been negligent shall be held responsible, is not more firmly established than that which states the doctrine that no amount of carelessness upon the part of the carrier, which did not lead to the loss, or which had no effect in placing the goods in such a position that they could suffer by an act of God, will render him liable in case of their loss by such a casualty. The doctrine under consideration seems to have gained some of that approval which attaches to it,[2] from an estimate of this principle.

SEC. 104. **Rule where there is Doubt as to Cause of Loss.** — The negligence which causes a loss which would otherwise have happened, seems to resemble negligence which was

[1] Jones on Bailm. 70.

[2] See Story on Bailm. § 413, c. and d.

totally apart from the casualty in question; thus the courts have been careful in all cases to demand a clear proof that there was some connection between the loss and the carelessness; and in the case of Muddle *v.* Stride,[1] which was an action against the proprietors of a steam vessel to recover compensation for damage done to goods sent by them as carriers, it was held that if, on the whole, it be left in doubt what the cause of the injury was, or if it may as well be attributed to perils of the sea as to the negligence of the carrier, the owner of the goods is not entitled to recover. It seems a very insignificant advance from the doctrine stated in this case to that which holds the carrier, although the actual cause of the loss, irresponsible for that loss, if it was inevitable through an accident, such as lightning, for which he would not have been held liable. In an action against the proprietors of a barge, who had, by means of that barge, undertaken the conveyance of some lime belonging to the plaintiff from Bewly Cliff, in Kent, to the Regent's Canal, in London, and whose servant, the master of the barge, had deviated unnecessarily from the usual course, in consequence of which deviation the barge had encountered a tempest, which caused the lime to be wet and consequently to take fire, the defendants were sued for the loss by the owner of the lime. It was proved that in this way the lime and the defendants' ship were both destroyed. It was argued, however, for the defendants that the deviation of the master of the barge was not a cause of the loss of the lime sufficiently proximate to entitle the plaintiff to recover, inasmuch as the loss might have been occasioned by the same tempest if the barge had proceeded in her direct course. TINDAL, C. J., in giving the opinion of the court, after stating the case, said, with reference to this argument: "If it were to prevail, the deviation of a master, which is undoubtedly a ground of action against the owner, would never, or only under very peculiar circumstances, entitle the plaintiff to recover; for if a ship is captured in the course of deviation, no one can be certain that she might not have been captured

[1] 9 C. & P. 380.

if in her proper course. And yet, in Parker *v.* James,[1] where the ship was captured whilst in the act of deviation, no such ground of defence was even suggested. Or, again, if the ship strikes against a rock, or perishes by storm in the one course, no one can predicate that she might not equally have struck upon another rock, or met with the same or another storm, if pursuing her right and ordinary voyage. The same answer might be attempted to an action against a defendant who had, by mistake, forwarded a parcel by the wrong conveyance, and a loss had thereby ensued, and yet the defendant in that case would undoubtedly be liable. But we think the real answer to the objection is, that no wrong-doer can be allowed to apportion or qualify his own wrong, and that, as a loss has actually happened whilst his wrongful act was in operation and force, and which is attributable to his wrongful act, he cannot set up, as an answer to the action, the bare possibility of a loss if his wrongful act had never been done. It might admit of a different construction if he could show, not only that the same loss *might* have happened, but that it *must* have happened if the act complained of had not been done; but there is no evidence to that extent in the present case."[2]

SEC. 105. **Necessary Evidence.** — From this it would appear that there can be little doubt that the principle of the common law is the same as that of the civil law, but that in every case there must be clear proof that the act of God would inevitably have occurred, and that it was not in the power of man, by any forethought or care, to have avoided it. And the reason for the establishment of the rule upon this basis is, that an action, in case of loss, is founded upon the principle that there must be some connection between the injury and the carelessness, and that carelessness of itself, which did not cause loss or damage to the goods of the bailor, never could be a ground of action.

SEC. 106. **"Act of God" and "Queen's Enemies." — "Natural Decay." — Leakage.** — With reference to these two exceptions to the common-law liability of common carriers, something more may be said. It is evident that the phrase "act of God,"

[1] 4 Camp. 112.

[2] Davis *v.* Garrett, 6 Bing. 716.

may be extended to many cases other than those in connection with which it has most frequently been used. Men are too apt to hear God in the thunder and storm, and ignore his existence in the still small voice of the calm. But the acts of God are not always cataclasms, and "natural decay" may as reasonably be classed under this head as "tempests" or "lightnings." That a carrier should not be held liable for the loss of goods which have been delivered to him, if he has not been guilty of any delay which might contribute to their loss, might be deduced from the principles laid down in an earlier part of this work, but this has actually been decided in courts of law. The person consigning perishable goods ought to make himself aware of their qualities so thoroughly, and of the time that must be spent in transit between the place from which they are sent and their destination, as to guard against the casualty of their natural decay.[1] Where he fails to take such obvious and necessary precautions there is every reason why he should suffer the loss, as there is no rule which would make it necessary that a carrier should be more careful of the future of the goods consigned to him than their owner. The carrier does not by his trade or business profess to know how long oranges will keep on board ship, or how long the meat will be preserved in jars. And so long as he does what he professes to do, and arrives at his destination without any delay and by his ordinary course, he is not to be held liable for the losses occasioned by the act of God, "natural decay," and the carelessness of the owner in not ascertaining how long the goods would keep. All liquids are liable to some diminution by means of evaporation during a journey, and there is generally a certain amount of leakage, for neither of which can the carrier, with any propriety, be held liable. The owner who possesses and sends such goods should be aware that such occurrences universally take place, and ought to make his charges cover such inevitable loss.[2] So if, through

[1] See "The Gudion," ch. 7, arts. 7, 10. See Davidson v. Gwynne, 12 East, 381; Abbott on Ship. pt. iv. ch. 9, p. 380.

[2] Hudson v. Baxendale, 2 H. & N. 575; 27 L. J. Exch. 93; Ohrloff v. Briscall, 1 L. R. P. C. 231; and see Hunnewell v. Taber, 2 Sprague (U.S.

no fault of the carrier's, the wine he is carrying should turn sour, the owner, it seems to us, would have as much right to claim damages from him on account of the loss, as the owner of a ship in which Madeira was sent a voyage to improve it, would have a right to claim from the owner of the wine an amount equal to its enhanced value. At the same time it is the duty of the carrier to take all reasonable precautions to prevent deterioration; and if a diminution in value can be clearly traced to the negligent or wilful act of the carrier, he will be held liable for such loss.[1]

SEC. 107. **Natural Causes.** — But the principles involved in such cases are not to be used rashly. There are circumstances under which a mere change would raise a presumption of negligence upon the part of the carrier. Thus, where a cargo weighing a certain weight is delivered to a carrier to be carried, and when the cargo arrives at its destination the weight is different, it has been held that this is evidence from which a jury may infer negligence in the carrier, and it is incumbent upon him to show that the deficiency did not arise from his negligence.[2] So in an action against carriers for injury to casks of oil, alleged by them to have arisen from defects in the casks, it was left to the jury to say whether it arose from such defects, and whether, even if it did, the carriers knew or ought to have known thereof, and had acted negligently in sending them on in that state.[3] It is therefore to be understood that this rule only extends to cases in which the injury arises from natural causes, without the intervention of man.

SEC. 108. **Negligent Packing.** — Negligent packing upon the part of the owners of the goods, of which the carrier cannot be aware or could not obviate, will exonerate the carriers from their liability for losses which were caused by such negligent packing. But even such a rule is to be looked at strictly, for

C. C.), 1; Farra *v.* Adams, Bull. N. P. 69; Warden *v.* Greer, 6 Watts (Penn.), 424; Nelson *v.* Woodruff, 1 Black (U. S.), 156; Clark *v.* Barnewell, 12 How. (U. S.) 272; Tysen *v.* Moore, 56 Barb. (N. Y.) 442.

[1] Notara *v.* Henderson, 5 L. R. Q. B. 346; 22 L. T. N. S. 577; 3 Mar. Law Cas. O. S. 419, affirmed, L. R. 7 Q. B. 225, Ex. Cham.

[2] Hawkes *v.* Smith, Car. & M. 72.

[3] Cox *v.* London & North-Western Rail. Co., 3 F. & F. 77.

it has been decided that, in an action against a carrier for damage to goods, it is enough to prove the condition and value of the goods when delivered to him, and when received by the consignee, and if damaged in the hands of the carrier he is entitled to recover; and it was also held in this case, that the fact that the damage was partly caused by the packing goes only to the amount of the damage.[1] So, where a greyhound was delivered to a carrier, who gave a receipt for it, and the greyhound was subsequently lost, it was held that the carrier could not set up a defence that the dog was not properly secured when delivered to him.[2] In the case of Goff *v.* Clinkard, the defendant, a carrier, had undertaken to carry the plaintiff's goods from London to Amsterdam, and they were accidentally damaged in their being let down into the hold of the ship; the defendant was held liable for such damage.[3]

SEC. 109. **Where Responsibility begins and ends.**—This case seems to indicate where the responsibility of the owner ends and where that of the carrier begins. The duty of packing may, in the first instance, lie upon the owner, and in case of a neglect of this duty, which is not discoverable by the carrier, he may himself have to be responsible for the injury thus occasioned; but the duty of packing in the second instance, or storing in such a way that the goods shall not be damaged in the transit, lies on the carrier, and in case of injury caused by his neglect of this obvious duty he will be held liable.[4] But there are other questions of packing, which are of importance in this connection.

[1] Higginbotham *v.* Great Northern Rail. Co., 2 F. & F. 796; 10 W. R. 358 Q. B.; Peck *v.* Weeks, 34 Conn. 152; Clark *v.* Rochester & Syracuse R. R. Co., 14 N. Y. 570; Adrian *v.* The Live Yankee, 33 Hunt's Merch. Mag. 707; Ireguist *v.* Morewood, 33 Hunt's Merch. Mag. 706.

[2] Stewart *v.* Crawley, 2 Stark. 323.

[3] Goff *v.* Clinkard, cited 1 Wils. 282; Baxter *v.* Leland, Abb. Adm. (U. S.) 348; The Ree Side, 2 Sumn. (U. S.) 567.

[4] Sack *v.* Ford, 13 C. B. N. S. 90; 32 L. J. N. S. C. P. 12. See Wellwood, p. 29; Abbott on Ship. pt. iv. ch. 5, p. 308. But see Swanston *v.* Garrick, 2 L. J. 267, Ex. 255; and the judgment of WILLES, J., in Blakie *v.* Stembridge, 6 C. B. N. S. 894, Ex. Ch. Ib. 911; 28 L. J. C. P. 329; S. C. in error, 29 L. J. N. S. 212 C. P.; The Peytona, Ware (U. S. C. C.), 2d ed., 541: Zerega *v.* Poppe, Abb. Adm. (U. S.) 397; compare The Colombo, 3 Blatchf. (U. S. C. C.) 521.

SEC. 110. **The Carriage of Cattle.** — One of the most important parts of the traffic upon our railway lines at the present time is the conveyance of cattle. The division of labor has gone so far, that not only does every man work at a different trade, but every town or district has its own peculiar kind of business or manufacture, and depends for every other necessity and luxury of life upon its neighbors. This fact, which may to some extent be due to the facility with which food and other things can be brought from a distance, has brought about an amount of traffic which is totally unprecedented. As this is the case, it is of much importance to determine under what circumstances, when injury occurs to cattle, the loss shall be borne by the owner of the animals or the carrier. We have seen that, in a case where a greyhound was given to a carrier to be conveyed, and where it was lost, he was not allowed to set up the assertion that when it was delivered to him it was not properly secured;[1] and under like circumstances, a similar rule would hold with regard to other kinds of animals; upon the principle that where the carrier has every means of ascertaining whether the animal is well secured or not, he ought to use those means, and not trust exclusively to the care of the owner. His duty is to keep and carry safely.[2] When, however, the carrier has taken every reasonable precaution, and some circumstance, which may fairly be regarded as an act of God, causes damage to animals, he is not to be held liable in this case, any more than he would in that of damage done to any goods which are not animate. The cases on this point only show the similarity of the principle which is to be applied to all these cases. In one of these the declaration stated that a policy of insurance was effected on horses "warranted free from jettison and mortality," on the ship "Aimwell," at and from Liverpool to Jamaica. In the course of the voyage, in consequence of the laboring of the vessel in a storm, the horses broke their slings, and one of them, by kicking, broke down the partition between it and the next horse. Subsequently the other partition was broken down in a similar manner, and the

[1] Stewart *v.* Crawley, 2 Stark. 323.

[2] Pozzi *v.* Shipton, 1 P. & D. 4; 8 Ad. & El. 963; 1 W. W. & H. 624.

three horses having nothing to support them were unable to stand, on account of the rolling of the vessel. In this way it came to pass that the horses kicked, and bruised and wounded each other, in such a way that they all died. In this case it was held that the loss thus caused was a loss by a peril of the sea.[1] And the same thing was decided in a case almost precisely similar in every respect.[2] It has been held to be a question, whether the common-law liability of railway companies extends to live-stock conveyed by them.[3] And it has been expressly held that a railway company carrying living animals is not bound to provide fences or guards at the station where the animals may be landed, between the line and the station yard, so as to prevent them straying on the line.[4] These cases would seem to show that the rule is universal, and that the mere animacy of the goods conveyed can make no difference in the responsibility of the carriers;[5] but a recent decis-

[1] Gabay *v.* Lloyd, 3 B. & C. 793.

[2] Lawrence *v.* Aberdeen, 5 B. & Ald. 107. See also Tatham *v.* Hodgson, 6 T. R. 656; and Walker *v.* London & South-Western Rail. Co., Kingston Spring Assizes, 1843; quoted in "Walford's Summary of the Law of Railways," London, 1845.

[3] M'Manus *v.* Lancashire & Yorkshire Rail. Co., 2 H. & N. 693; 4 Jur. N. S. 144; 27 L. J. Exch. 201.

[4] Roberts *v.* Great Western Rail. Co., 4 Jur. N. S. 1240; 4 C. B. N. S. 560; 27 L. J. C. P. 266; Shepherd *v.* Bristol & Exeter Rail. Co., 37 L. J. Exch. 113; 3 L. R. Exch. 189; 16 W. R. 982; 18 L. T. N. S. 528; Page *v.* Great Northern Rail. Co., 2 Ir. R. C. L. 228, C. P.

[5] The American law with regard to slaves was different from that which was in force with regard to animals. Boyce *v.* Anderson, 2 Pet. (U. S.) 150; Stokes *v.* Saltonstall, 13 Pet. (U. S.) 181; Clark *v.* M'Donald, 4 M'Cord (S. C.), 223; Williams *v.* Taylor, 4 Port. (Ala.) 234; Hawkins *v.* Phythian, 8 B. Mon. (Ky.) 515; Swigert *v.* Graham, 7 B. Mon. (Ky.) 662. In Michigan it has been held that railroads are not common carriers of live animals. Michigan, &c. R. R. Co. *v.* McDonough, 21 Mich. 165. But in all the other States the rule is as stated in the text. Kansas Pacific R. R. Co. *v.* Nichols, 9 Kan. 235; Evans *v.* Dunbar, 117 Mass. 546. But they may limit their liability by special contract so as not to be liable except for loss resulting from their negligence, or may stipulate that they shall only be liable in any event to pay more than a certain sum for each animal injured or lost. Squire *v.* New York Central R. R. Co., 98 Mass. 239. But, failing to limit their liability, they are liable as carriers. Sager *v.* R. R. Co., 31 Me. 228; Rixford *v.* Smith, 52 N. H. 355; Lee *v.* R. R. Co., 72 N. C. 236; Louisville, &c. R. R. Co. *v.* Hedger, 9 Bush (Ky), 245; Illinois Central R. R. Co. *v.* Hall, 58 Ill. 409; Pennsylvania, &c. R. R. Co. *v.* Buffalo, &c. R. R. Co., 49 N. Y. 204; Cragin

ion[1] has made it evident that such is not the case. They indicate, however, that if there is no carelessness in the individual carrier in contributing to the loss or injury of the goods by the act of God, he shall not be held liable; and that where injury is caused by the natural and ordinary circumstances of the transit and the necessities of the road, together with the culpable negligence of the sender of the goods, the carrier shall in that case also be held to be free from the necessity of making good the loss.

SEC. 111. **"Circumstance of Transit," and "Necessity of Road."** — *The question as to what is a natural and ordinary circumstance of the transit, or what is a necessity of the road, is a question of fact.* In one case, which, as SIR WILLIAM JONES says, "has some appearance of hardship," "a box of jewels had been delivered to a ferryman, who knew not what it contained, and, a sudden storm arising in the passage, he threw the box into the sea, yet it was resolved that he should answer for it."[2] SIR WILLIAM JONES, in commenting on this case,[3] says: "I cannot help suspecting that there was proof in this case of culpable negligence, and probably the casket was both small and light enough to have been kept longer on board than other goods; for in the case of Gravesend barge, cited on the bench by LORD COKE, it appears that the pack which was thrown overboard in a tempest, and for which the bargeman was holden not answerable, was of great value and great weight, although this last circumstance be omitted by ROLLE, who says only "that the master of the vessel had no information of its contents."[4]

v. New York Central R. R. Co., 51 N. Y. 61; Evansville, &c. R. R. Co. *v.* Young, 28 Ind. 516; Kimball *v.* Rutland, &c. R. R. Co., 26 Vt. 247; Hall *v.* Renfro, 3 Met. (Ky.) 51; Betts *v.* The Farmer's Loan and Trust Co., 21 Wis. 80; Ohio, &c. R. R. Co. *v.* Dunbar, 20 Ill. 623; Toledo, &c. R. R. Co. *v.* Thompson, 71 Ill. 434; St. Louis, &c. R. R. Co. *v.* Downer, 72 Ill. 504.

[1] Kendal *v.* London & South-Western Rail. Co., Law Times, June 15, 1872.

[2] Per ROLLE, C. J., in Bancroft's Case; All. 93.

[3] On Bailm. 108.

[4] 2 Bulstr. 280; 2 Roll. Abr. 567; Story on Bailm. § 531; Abbott on Ship. pt. iii. c. 8.

CHAPTER VII.

THE LIMITED RESPONSIBILITY OF COMMON CARRIERS. — RESTRICTION OF THEIR COMMON-LAW LIABILITY BY STATUTE OR BY SPECIAL CONTRACT.

SEC. 112. **Limitation of Liability.** — Before it becomes necessary to consider the duties and liabilities of carriers with regard to the delivery of the goods bailed to them, it is necessary to examine how and to what extent their common-law liability may be modified. We have in the last chapter pointed out that the law which imposes such extensive liability upon common carriers, at the same time imposes certain restrictions upon it, and that, although they are insurers, they are not insurers against the act of God or of the king's enemies; and that, under certain circumstances, carelessness upon the part of the consignor of the goods may avoid their responsibility, even while the circumstances which caused the loss could not properly be classed either with natural physical events, or acts of the enemies of the country.[1] But there is another limitation of responsibility, as we have pointed out, which might either be looked upon as one of the common-law limitations, and therefore have been treated of in the last chapter, or be regarded as a kind of special contract made with the public generally, and therefore fall for consideration in this place.

SEC. 113. **By Custom.** — That limitation is the limitation which arises from the custom of the carrier's trade. The reason that the common law imposes such stringent duties upon public carriers is, *that they have held themselves out to the public as servants of all men, and such a profession is a profession of skill.* But this reason is equally true and effective with regard to the limitations of a man's trade as it is with regard to its scope, for these two mean exactly the same thing. Therefore, *where a man professes only to carry one species of article, and the public has sufficient means of knowing that such is his custom, this will limit his responsibility, if he undertakes the carriage of goods other than those which he is in the habit of conveying, to that of a private carrier for hire.*[2] But although this is in one aspect a limitation of the carriers' trade by custom, it is in another aspect nothing but a profession of the trade of a common carrier with regard to special articles or kinds of articles, and the special contracts which we have to refer to in this chapter are rather those which are expressed by notice or agreement than those which are implied by custom.

SEC. 114. **Qualified Acceptance.** — From very early times it has been understood that *a common carrier has a right to accept goods under a qualified or modified contract for carriage.* In a note to *Southcote's Case*, LORD COKE says that if goods are delivered to one person to be delivered over to another, it is good policy to provide for himself in special manner for doubt of being charged with his general acceptance.[3] This, however, seems to be only a warning that it is well, when the

[1] McKean *v.* McIver, 18 L. T. N. S. 410, Exch.

[2] See *ante*, p. 46 *et seq.*

[3] Southcote's Case, 4 Co. 84.

duty of the bailment is to bail, to use special precaution in case the duty of the second should be confounded with the duty of the first, and consequently a much larger amount of service be demanded of a man than he expressly or impliedly undertook to perform. Neither was the doctrine that a man can by a special acceptance limit his liability, definitely acknowledged by SIR MATTHEW HALE in Morse *v.* Slue,[1] as some writers seem to think. In the case of Gibbon *v.* Paynton,[2] however, the doctrine although not declared was assumed. In this case the plaintiff had concealed 100*l.* in a bag of hay and intrusted the bag to the defendant, a common carrier, to be conveyed to A. The plaintiff was aware of the fact that the defendant had published notices declaring that he would not be liable for the loss of money unless it was delivered to him as such; but the plaintiff, notwithstanding this knowledge, did not communicate the fact that a hundred pounds was concealed in the hay to the defendant. The court held this concealment to be constructive fraud upon the part of the plaintiff, and that the defendant was therefore not liable for a loss during the transit. LORD MANSFIELD said: "If the owner of the goods has been guilty of fraud upon the carrier, such fraud ought to excuse the carrier."[3] Fraud vitiates all contracts, and, upon principle as well as authority, where a shipper of goods fraudulently conceals the value or character of goods, the carrier is released from his liability as an insurer; and this is so whether the fraud is practised by his silence or by actual representations, or whether the shipper *intends* to practise a fraud upon the carrier or not.[4] If a shipper places money or other valuable articles in a bale of wool or cotton, or in a barrel ostensibly containing an ordinary species of freight, so that the vigilance of the carrier is relaxed as to its care or custody, it would be

[1] Morse *v.* Slue, 1 Vent. 190.

[2] 4 Burr. 2301.

[3] Gibbon *v.* Paynton, 4 Burr. 2301. See also, per LORD ELLENBOROUGH, in Leeson *v.* Holt, 1 Stark. 186; De Rothschild *v.* Royal Mail Steam Packet Co., 7 Exch. 734; Batson *v.* Donovan, 4 B. & Ald. 21.

[4] Pardee *v.* Drew, 25 Wend. (N. Y.) 459; Warner *v.* Western Transportation Co., 5 Robt. (N. Y. Superior Ct.) 490; Southern Express Co. *v.* Everett, 37 Ga. 688; Chicago, &c. R. R. Co. *v.* Thompson, 19 Ill. 578.

exceedingly unjust to hold him responsible for the loss of the money, unless it resulted from such negligence as would make him responsible for the loss of the wool, &c. if he was merely a private carrier. Therefore, where a carrier receives a package from a shipper of such a size or shape as is naturally calculated to throw him off his guard and lead him only to exercise, with reference to it, that degree of diligence which is exercised in reference to ordinary freight, no recovery can be had for its loss.[1] This rule was illustrated in an early New York case,[2] in which an action was brought to recover for the loss of a trunk, owned by a passenger, containing a large amount of money. The defendant was the owner of a steamboat, upon which the passenger and trunk were transported for hire, but no notice was given to the defendant or the officers of the boat that the trunk contained anything more than the ordinary baggage of passengers, and no extra compensation was paid for its carriage. It was held by the court that, while in the absence of any restrictions upon his liability, or any conditions imposing upon the passenger the duty of disclosing the value of the contents of the trunk, it became the duty of the carrier, if he desired to be informed of such value, to make inquiry relative thereto, yet that if any means were used to conceal the value of the article, and thereby the owner escaped the payment of a reasonable compensation for the risk, such unfairness and its consequences to the defendant, upon the principles of common justice, would exempt him from liability. It was held, therefore, that the delivery of the trunk to the defendant without any information as to its value, or anything calculated to put him upon inquiry, justified the carrier in treating it as only containing the ordinary baggage of a passenger, and with the failure to compensate him for his extraordinary risk, operated as a fraud upon him, which prevented a recovery for the loss of the money.[3] In the case of

[1] Chicago, &c. R. R. Co. *v.* Shea, 66 Ill. 471; Hayes *v.* Wells, 23 Cal. 185; Oppenheimer *v.* United States Express Co., 69 Cal. 62; Phillips *v.* Earle, 8 Pick. (Mass.) 182; Relf *v.* Rapp, 3 W. & S. (Penn.) 21; The Ionic, 5 Blatchf. (U. S. C. C.) 538.

[2] Orange County Bank *v.* Brown, 9 Wend. (N. Y.) 85.

[3] See, to the same effect, Relf *v.* Rapp, *ante;* Phillips *v.* Earle, 8 Pick. (Mass.) 182.

Nicholson *v.* Willan,[1] however, the law was expressly stated by LORD ELLENBOROUGH in these words: "It was also contended on the part of the plaintiffs that such a special acceptance of goods by a common carrier, as is contained in the defendant's notice, is contrary to the policy of the common law, which has made common carriers responsible to an indefinite extent for losses not occasioned by the only excepted causes of loss, viz., the act of God and the king's enemies. But considering the length of time during which, and the extent and universality in which, the practice of making such special acceptances of goods for carriage by land and water has now prevailed in this kingdom under the observation and with the allowance of courts of justice, and with the sanction also and countenance of the legislature itself, which is known to have rejected a bill brought in for the purpose of narrowing the carrier's responsibility in certain cases, on the ground of such a measure being unnecessary, inasmuch as the carriers were deemed fully competent to limit their own responsibility in all cases by special contract; considering also that there is no case to be met with in the books in which the right of the carrier thus to limit by special contract his own responsibility has ever been by express decision denied,[2] we cannot do otherwise than sustain such right in the present instance, however liable to abuse and productive of inconvenience it may be, leaving the legislature, if it shall think fit, to apply such remedy hereafter as the evil may require."[3] And LORD KENYON in another case said: "When no rate is fixed by law, the carrier is entitled to say on what terms he will carry; he is not obliged to take everything that is brought to his warehouse, unless the terms on which he chooses to undertake the risk are complied with by the person who employs him. The old mode of declaring used to be on the custom of the realm, but this is in *assumpsit*, it is founded on contract, and the contract must therefore govern the parties."[4]

[1] Nicholson *v.* Willan, 5 East, 513.

[2] But see, per LORD KENYON, in Hyde *v.* Proprietors of the Trent & Mersey Navigation, 1 Esp. 36; and in the King's Bench, 1 T. R. 389.

[3] New Jersey Steam Navigation Co. *v.* Merchants' Bank, 6 How. (U. S.) 344; York Co. *v.* Central R. R. Co., 3 Wall. (U. S.) 107.

[4] Anonymous *v.* Jackson, Peake's

SEC. 115. **Carriage by Sea. — Bill of Lading.** — In the case where the goods are to be carried by sea the law is, of course, precisely similar to that which applies to the carriage of goods by land. In this case the terms of the limitation are usually incorporated in the bill of lading, which is in fact a formal acknowledgment of the receipt of goods, and an engagement upon the part of the carrier to deliver them to the consignee or his assigns. That is, of course, the natural place in which to incorporate any formal agreement that the goods mentioned therein shall be carried upon certain conditions, but although this is usually done, still the carrier may be bound by other announcements. Thus, if a ship is advertised in the newspapers, and certain conditions are stated as an inducement to the owners of goods or merchants to make use of that particular ship, as for instance, that the owner of the ship will carry articles up to the value of 5,000*l.*, while in fact he did not so mean, but meant to limit his liability to articles of a much less considerable value, he will be bound by such advertisements, the terms of which may be incorporated into the contract.[1]

SEC. 116. **Express Contracts and Implied Agreements.** — Little difficulty will arise as to express agreements which limit the common-law liability of carriers, but there will be some difficulty felt in relation to implied contracts, which may do the same thing. There have been some statutory limitations upon this power of qualified acceptance; but, even before these acts were passed, several cases had done something to make definite the extent to which notice might affect these common-law obligations.

SEC. 117. **Exclusion of Responsibility by Notice. — Rule in Riley v. Horne.** — In one case it was held that a carrier might not only limit but exclude all responsibility by giving

Add. Cas. 185. See also Clay *v.* Willan, 1 H. Bl. 298; Izett *v.* Mountain, 4 East, 371; Harris *v.* Packwood, 3 Taunt. 264; Smith *v.* Horne, 8 Taunt. 144; Riley *v.* Horne, 5 Bing. 217; Ranger *v.* Great Western Rail. Co., 1 Rail. Cas. 1; Maving *v.* Todd, 1 Stark. 72; 4 Camp. 225; Hyde *v.* Trent & Mersey Navigation Co., 5 T. R. 389; 1 Esp. 36; Clarke *v.* Gray, 6 East, 564; 2 Smith, 622; 4 Esp. 177; Covington *v.* Willan, Gow. 115; Munn *v.* Baker, 2 Stark. 255.

[1] See Abbott on Ship., pt., iii. c. 4; Phillips *v.* Edwards, 3 H. & N. 813.

notice.[1] In another case the defendants had given notice that they would not be accountable for the loss or damage of goods unless the terms of the notice were complied with, and it was held that this notice protected them as well against loss by robbery as against accidental loss.[2] In a case where a carrier had given two notices, he was held to be bound by the least beneficial to himself.[3] And where a carrier placed a board in his office, giving notice that he would not be answerable for jewels, however small their value, unless entered as such, but circulated handbills stating generally that he would not be answerable for any article above the value of 5*l.*, unless entered as such, it was decided that he was answerable for the loss of jewels, although they were not entered as such, if they were under the value of 5*l.*[4] In the case of Riley *v.* Horne,[5] which was an action brought to recover damages for the loss of goods which had been intrusted to the defendants, as common carriers, to be conveyed by them from Kettering to London, and which had, according to the declaration of the plaintiff, been lost through the defendants' negligence, the question of the effect of a notice came before the court.

SEC. 118. **To what Notice applies.** — It appeared that the plaintiffs were silk-weavers, residing in London, and carrying on business there and at Kettering; that the defendants' coach ran from the "George and Blue Boar," London, to Kettering and back; and that, at the "George and Blue Boar," there was a notice to the effect that the proprietors of coaches which set out from that office would not be responsible for goods above the value of 5*l.*, unless entered as such, and paid for accordingly. It was further proved that the plaintiffs were aware of this notice, and were in the habit of sending goods up and down by the defendants' coach; that the goods in question — silks, to the value of about 46*l.* — were delivered to the defendants by the plaintiffs' servant, at the defendants' office, at Kettering, to be conveyed to London, and that

[1] Maving *v.* Todd, 1 Stark. 72; 4 Camp. 225. And see Hill *v.* Trent & Mersey Navigation Co., 5 T. R. 389; 1 Esp. 36.

[2] Covington *v.* Willan, Gow, 115.

[3] Munn *v.* Baker, 2 Stark. 255.

[4] Cobden *v.* Bolton, 2 Camp. 108.

[5] Riley *v.* Horne, 5 Bing. 217; 2 M. & P. 331.

the servant saw no such notice in the office at Kettering; and, finally, it was proved that the goods never were delivered to the plaintiffs. In this case it was decided that the notice in the "George and Blue Boar" applied, not only to the journey from London to Kettering, but also to the return journey from Kettering to London. BEST, C. J., in giving judgment, said: "As the law makes the carrier an insurer, and as the goods he carries may be injured or destroyed by many accidents against which no care on the part of the carrier can protect them, he is as much entitled to be paid a premium for his insurance of their delivery at the place of their destination, as for the labor and expense of carrying them there."

SEC. 119. **Principle of.** — Now it seems to us that this principle underlies the whole law with regard to notice. Insurance may be a trade, just as carrying is, and these two trades may be conjoined or combined, either by the will of the individual or by the force of the common law. When by the force of the common law these two trades are necessarily associated, the carrier has evidently a perfect right to his remuneration from both. He is entitled to be paid for carrying the goods, which cannot be done without time, trouble, and expense, and he is entitled to ask an amount which will enable him to make good the losses of his customers' goods, when any such loss occurs. All such matters come to be questions of arithmetic. It is not difficult to ascertain what amount of premium a carrier will have to demand from his customers, as the number of casualties is an ascertainable fact, if he has any knowledge of the value of the articles intrusted to him. If he has no means of discovering the value, if he is precluded by law from demanding, by notice, a statement of the value of the articles given to him to be carried, all he could do would be to consider the value of the goods which are ordinarily sent by mankind, and from that knowledge to arrive at a rough average of the value of every package or parcel. As, however, the value of many parcels which are at the present time intrusted to carriers is exceedingly great,[1]

[1] BEST, C. J., in Riley *v.* Horne, said: "By means of negotiable bills immense value is now compressed into a very small compass. Parcels con-

the average value of every package would be very high. Under these circumstances, a very high premium would have to be charged upon every closed parcel of which the carriers did not know the contents, and that circumstance would put an end to the traffic in articles of comparatively little value, for it would evidently be unjust that an individual who was sending a pair of gloves should pay such a premium for their insurance as would cover the loss of a parcel of negotiable bills. As this would inevitably have resulted from carrying the common-law doctrine of insurance to its fullest extent, the practice of notices became general. By their use a carrier can demand to know what risk he is to take upon every article, and make each one pay in proportion to the actual risk which is undertaken in connection with the goods which they bring to him to be conveyed. This is evidently an advantage to the public. A uniform rate of payment may be admirable for the carriage of letters and messages, but it will no more do in connection with insurance than it would do with regard to the purchase of articles generally. It has not as yet been argued that a uniform rate of payment for pianos, pinafores, estates, or eatables would be an advantage. The greatest good arises to the community from the system which allows every one to pay in proportion to the risk which the insurer runs, that risk being calculable from the number of known casualties and the amount of the business of the insurer.

SEC. 120. **Former Doctrine.** — Yet this doctrine has not always found favor in the eyes of lawyers. In the case of Hyde *v.* The Proprietors of the Trent and Mersey Navigation,[1] LORD KENYON said: "There is a difference where a man is chargeable by law generally and where on his contract. Where a man is bound to any duty, and chargeable to a cer-

taining these bills are continually sent by common carriers. As the law compels carriers to undertake for the security of what they carry, it would be most unjust if it did not afford them a means of knowing the extent of their risk. Other insurers (whether they divide the risk, which they generally do, amongst several different persons, or one insurer undertakes for the insurance of the whole) always have the amount of what they are to answer for specified in the policy of insurance."

[1] 1 Esp. 36. See also 1 T. R. 387.

tain extent by the operation of law, in such a case he cannot by any act of his own discharge himself. As in the case of common carriers, who are liable by law, in all cases of losses except those arising from the act of God or of the king's enemies, they cannot discharge themselves from losses happening under these circumstances by any act of their own; as by giving notice, for example, to that effect."[1] It is impossible to see upon what principle this rule was laid down, and upon what grounds it was for a considerable time received, without doubt or question, by the English judges. But even after the rigor of this rule had ceased, and when it was replaced by the more equitable doctrine that we have indicated above, many judges seemed to regret that the power of a carrier to limit his liability had ever been admitted. This doctrine still prevails in the United States, and neither a public nor a general notice by a carrier that he will not be responsible for freight, or that it will be at the risk of the owners, will vary the carriers' liability.[2] Notice by publication in newspapers, or printed upon receipts given for freight, or tickets sold to passengers, does not have the effect to vary the carriers' liability, unless it is proved that the person against whom it is asserted had knowledge of the terms thereof, the burden of establishing which is always upon the carrier.[3] Nor will such notice,

[1] The May Queen, 1 Newb. (U. S. C. C.) 464; New Jersey Steam Navigation Co. *v.* Merchants' Bank, 6 How. (U. S.) 344.

[2] Dewort *v.* Loomer, 21 Conn. 245; Kimball *v.* Rutland, &c. R. R. Co., 26 Vt. 247; Moses *v.* Boston, &c. R. R. Co., 32 N. H. 523; Dorr *v.* New Jersey Steam Navigation Co., 11 N. Y. 485; Southern Express Co. *v.* Newby, 36 Ga., 635; Smith *v.* North Carolina R. R. Co., 64 N. C. 235; Hollister *v.* Nowlen, 19 Wend. (N. Y.) 234; Jones *v.* Voorhees, 10 Ohio, 145; Clark *v.* Faxon, 21 Wend. (N. Y.) 153; Camden Transportation Co. *v.* Belknap, 21 Wend. (N. Y.) 354; Powell *v.* Myers, 26 Wend. (N. Y.) 591; Michigan, &c. R. R. Co. *v.* Hale, 6 Mich. 243; Judson *v.* Western R. R. Co., 6 Allen (Mass.), 486.

[3] Southern Express Co. *v.* Newby, 36 Ga. 635; Hollister *v.* Nowlen, 19 Wend. (N. Y.) 234; Cole *v.* Goodwin, 19 Wend. (N. Y.) 251. In Pennsylvania the carrier's liability may be restricted by general notice, but the *onus* of establishing it is upon the party setting it up, and must be such as amounts to *actual* notice, and merely emblazoning the general object on a check, ticket, or notice in large letters, but stating the restriction in small ones, is held insufficient. Verner *v.* Sweitzer, 32 Penn. St. 208.

even when its contents are known to the shipper of goods, be operative, unless it is shown that he assented thereto, nor in any case can such a notice be operative to restrict the carriers' liability unreasonably.[1] In New York it is held that the liability of a carrier cannot be limited by a mere notice, even though it is brought home to the knowledge of the shipper, unless the circumstances are such as to establish the shipper's assent thereto, so that it can be said to form a part of the contract between the parties; and mere notice affords no evidence of assent on the part of the owner, and he has a right to repose on the common-law liability of the carrier, who cannot relieve himself from such liability by any act of his own.[2] In all such cases the question of assent is one of fact for the jury, upon evidence *aliunde*, and all the circumstances attending the giving of the receipt in which the notice is contained, may be given in evidence to enable the jury to decide

And, according to the same case, the effect of such a notice is no more than to render the bailee a private carrier for hire. In Michigan the carrier may restrict his liability as an insurer by *special* notice; but the carrier must establish the shipper's assent thereto, and mere proof that the shipper has seen a notice restricting the carrier's liability is not sufficient to establish his assent thereto. McMillau *v.* Michigan Southern R. R. Co., 16 Mich. 79.

[1] Farmers', &c. Bank *v.* Champlain Transportation Co., 23 Vt. 186; Fillebrown *v.* Grand Trunk Rail. Co., 55 Me. 462; Sager *v.* Portsmouth, &c. R. R. Co., 31 Me. 228; Southern Express Co. *v.* Crook, 44 Ala. 468.

[2] Cole *v.* Goodwin, 19 Wend. (N. Y.) 251; Camden Co. *v.* Belknap, 21 Wend. (N. Y.) 354. See also Clark *v.* Faxon, 21 Wend. (N.Y.) 153; Hollister *v.* Nowlen, 19 Wend. (N. Y.) 234; Powell *v.* Myers, 26 Wend. (N. Y.) 591; Alexander *v.* Greene, 3 Hill (N. Y.), 9; 7 Hill (N. Y.), 533; Dorr *v.* New Jersey Steam Navigation Co., 11 N. Y. 485; Gott *v.* Dinsmore, 111 Mass. 52. Thus it has been held that notice that all baggage is at the risk of the owners, although it is brought home to the owner, does not excuse the carrier from losses arising from the acts of himself or his servants, nor from actual negligence, nor the inefficiency of his machinery or vehicles, though it cannot be discovered by the eye. Camden R. R. & T. Co. *v.* Burke, 13 Wend. (N. Y.) 611. And evidence that a notice is placarded in all the offices of the carrier in conspicuous places will not warrant an inference that the shipper or passenger had knowledge of its terms. Hollister *v.* Nowlen, 19 Wend. (N. Y.) 234; Cole *v.* Goodwin, 19 Wend. (N. Y.) 251. Nor is such assent established by the circumstance that the shipper accepted a receipt for the goods, in which such notice was written or printed, without dissent. Railroad Co. *v.* Manufacturing Co., 16 Wall. (U. S.) 319; Southern Express Co. *v.* Armstead, 50 Ala. 350.

the question.[1] The rule generally adopted is, that no notice, general or special, can operate as a limitation upon the carrier's liability, unless the shipper assents thereto *before* the goods were shipped, and in such a manner and under such circumstances that it can be said to enter into and form a part of the contract between the parties.[2] But as it is now universally known that neither individuals nor companies engaged as carriers undertake to assume the common-law liabilities of a common carrier, but issue receipts or give bills of lading containing certain limitations upon their liability, it seems to be generally conceded that the giving of such a receipt or bill of lading containing such limitations raises a presumption that the shipper knew of and assented to such limitations, and throws the burden upon him of proving his lack of knowledge thereof.[3]

[1] Field *v.* Chicago, &c. R. R. Co., 71 Ill. 458; Woodruff *v.* Sherrard, 16 N. Y. s. c. 322; Madan *v.* Sherrard, 73 N. Y. 329; Merchants' Despatch Co. *v.* Theilbar, 86 Ill. 71; Adams Express Co. *v.* King, 3 Ill. App. 316. In Merchants' Despatch Co. *v.* Cornforth, 3 Cal. 280, a common carrier orally contracted, in winter, to transport a lot of oranges, lemons, and bananas in a refrigerator car through from New York to Denver without change. After the fruit was loaded in the car, the carrier delivered to the owner's agent a bill of lading containing a printed condition not to be liable for injury occasioned by the weather, over which was written the words "general release." The fruit reached Denver in an ordinary box car, and badly frozen. Held, that the carrier was liable for the damages. A consignee had a special contract with the carrier to carry at reduced rates at the owner's risk. Where the owner shipped the goods himself, the court held, in an action by him against the carrier for an injury to the goods, that he might recover if it was not shown that he had notice of the consignee's contract for carriage at the owner's risk, even if he had accounted with the consignee for the freight paid by the latter at the reduced rates. White *v.* Goodrich Transportation Co., 46 Wis. 493. A railroad company accustomed to carry live-stock at the owner's risk delivered to a shipper of certain horses a receipt therefor, marked "O. R." It was held that the presumption of the owner's assent to the risk, raised by his possession of such receipt, was not overcome by his testimony that he did not "see" the letters "O. R." — not that he did not understand their meaning to be "owner's risk." Morrison *v.* Phillips, &c. Construction Co., 44 Wis. 405.

[2] Brown *v.* Adams Express Co., 15 W. Va. 812; Michigan, &c. R. R. Co. *v.* Boyd, 91 Ill. 268; American Express Co. *v.* Spellman, 90 Ill. 455; Merchants' Despatch Co. *v.* Leyser, 89 Ill. 43; Merchants' Despatch Co. *v.* Jaesting, 89 Ill. 152.

[3] Bank of Kentucky *v.* Adams Express Co., 93 U. S. 174; Squires *v.* New York Central R. R. Co., 98 Mass.

SEC. 121. **Modifications in the Principle.** — However, the doctrine did prevail, and we have seen that it was not only firmly established, but that the extent of its applicability had been somewhat clearly defined by the various cases which came before the courts, even before the legislature made a law to the effect. But other cases indicate other modifications in the principle. Where a carrier by water had given notice "that he would not be answerable for any damage unless occasioned by want of ordinary care in the master or crew of the vessel, in which case he would pay 10*l.* per cent upon such damage, so as the whole did not exceed the value of the vessel and freight," he was held to have given an implied promise that the vessel should be tight and fit for the purpose, and that he would be answerable for the damage arising from leakage, upon the ground that a loss happening by the personal default of the carrier himself (such as the not providing a sufficient vessel) was not within the scope of such a notice

239; Hoadley *v.* Northern Transportation Co., 115 Mass. 304; Pemberton Co. *v.* New York Central R. R. Co., 104 Mass. 144; Grace *v.* Adams, 100 Mass. 505; Gott *v.* Dinsmore, 111 Mass. 45. In these cases, as indeed in all of them, a distinction is made between restrictions contained in a mere receipt for goods and a bill of lading; and while actual knowledge of and assent to the restrictions in the case of a receipt is necessary, and the mere circumstance that the receipt contains such restrictions is not conclusive that the plaintiff *knew* thereof, Gott *v.* Dinsmore, *ante*, yet in the case of a bill of lading, as it embodies the contract between the parties, the plaintiff will not be permitted, in the absence of fraud, to show that he did not read the bill of lading or know of such restrictions. Grace *v.* Adams, *ante*. See, on general proposition in the text, Evansville, &c. R. R. Co. *v.* Androscoggin Mills, 22 Wall. (U. S.) 594; Farnham *v.* Railroad Co., 55 Penn. St. 53; King *v.* Woodbridge, 34 Vt. 565; Steers *v.* Steamship Co., 57 N. Y. 1; Huntington *v.* Dinsmore, 4 Hun (N. Y.), 66; Sneider *v.* Adams Express Co., 63 Mo. 376; Kallman *v.* Express Co., 3 Kan. 205; Kirkland *v.* Dinsmore, 62 N. Y. 171; Robinson *v.* Merchants' Despatch Co., 45 Iowa, 470; Swindler *v.* Hilliard, 2 Rich. (S. C.) 286; McMillan *v.* Railroad Co., 16 Mich. 112; Boorman *v.* American Express Co., 21 Wis. 154; Steele *v.* Townsend, 37 Ala. 247. But in Illinois the rule is otherwise; and the mere acceptance of a receipt containing limitations upon the carrier's liability does not raise any presumption that the bailor knew thereof, and the carrier assumes the burden of establishing such knowledge and assent. Adams Express Co. *v.* Haynes, 42 Ill. 89; United States Express Co. *v.* Haynes, 67 Ill. 137; Anchor Line *v.* Dator, 68 Ill. 369; Adams Express Co. *v.* Stettaners, 61 Ill. 184.

which was meant to exempt the carrier from losses by accident or chance, &c., even if it were competent to a common carrier to exempt himself by a special acceptance from the responsibility cast upon him by the common law for a reasonable reward to make good all losses not arising from the act of God, or the king's enemies."[1]

SEC. 122. **Extent of Limitation. — Express Agreement.** — Much difficulty has been felt in the decision of questions which have arisen as to the extent to which carriers can limit their liability, not by special contract, but by general notice. Where the limitation of the responsibility is effected by means of an express agreement between the parties, no reason can be suggested why there should be any restrictions upon the right a man has to bind himself to do or to suffer anything which is not in contravention of some law, and is reasonable when looked at in relation to the duty which a man has imposed upon him by law to accept goods to carry. Such contracts are, of course, binding upon both parties. While they indicate the extent of responsibility undertaken by the carrier in connection with any particular articles intrusted to him, they also indicate under what circumstances the consignor shall be entitled to recover for loss or injury done to his goods by events which do not fall under the description of those things which limit a carrier's responsibility at common law. But why a man should not, for some commensurate advantage, forego his right to recover from the bailee in case of loss or damage being done to his goods under other circumstances than those which are produced in the ordinary course of nature, or by a national foe, it is impossible to say. Why a carrier should not, by special contract, denude himself of the character of an insurer which the common law imposes, if the other party clearly understands that the contract is to the effect that the carrier shall simply convey the goods, and have no responsibility in connection with them, is a question which it would be difficult to answer. Every consideration points to the expediency of making the connection which

[1] Lyon v. Mells, 5 East, 428; 1 Smith, 418; Hutton v. Bolton, 3 Dougl. 59.

exists at common law between the trade of a common carrier and an insurer, a connection which may be dissolved by the express wish of both the parties to a contract of bailment.[1]

SEC. 123. **General Notice.** — But much difficulty is felt in regard to the limitation of the carriers' obligations and responsibilities by means of a general notice.[2] General notice can be given in so many ways, it may assume so many forms, that a mere definition is a matter of difficulty. But when one considers that a notice, which is to have the effect of doing away with an important responsibility which is imposed upon a certain class of men by law, must, in order to have that effect, be brought to the knowledge of the party for whose advantage the responsibility was imposed, the difficulty of the subject is increased.

SEC. 124. **Must come to Knowledge of Owner of Goods.** — A notice, to affect a man's conduct, must have been in his thoughts. It is unfair to allow ignorance to prejudice a man in his social relations, and it must be remembered that it is for the sake of the ignorant and weak that the laws exist. In one aspect the law itself seems to ignore this principle, by the existence of its fiction that all men are supposed to be acquainted with the law. The absolute expedience, and the possibility which each man enjoys of becoming acquainted with the law, justifies this presumption. And the fact that all good laws are expressions of moral conceptions with regard to acts goes far, in a country where the laws are admirable, to raise the presumption into a truth. But under no conceivable circumstances could it be just to allow an individual

[1] New Jersey Steam Navigation Co. *v.* Merchants' Bank, 6 How. (U. S.) 344; York Co. *v.* Central R. R. Co., 3 Wall. (U. S.) 107; Wallace *v.* Mathews, 39 Ga. 617; Express Co. *v.* Kountze, 8 Wall. (U. S.) 341; Simon *v.* The Fung Shuey, 21 La. Ann. 363; Lamb *v.* Camden, &c. R. R. Co., 2 Daly (N. Y.), 454; Indianapolis, &c. R. R. Co. *v.* Allen, 31 Ind. 394; Michigan, &c. R. R. Co. *v.* Heaton, 31 Ind. 397, n.; Baltimore, &c. R. R. Co. *v.* Skeels, 3 W. Va. 556; New Orleans, &c. Ins. Co. *v.* New Orleans, &c. R. R. Co., 20 La. Ann. 302. As to proof of such contract, see Southern Express Co. *v.* Purcel, 37 Ga. 103; Evansville, &c. R. R. Co. *v.* Young, 28 Ind. 516; McMillan *v.* Michigan Southern, &c. R. R. Co., 16 Mich. 79.

[2] Smith *v.* North Carolina R. R. Co., 64 N. C. 235.

trusting in the legal assurance that a carrier is to be responsible for all loss and damage done to the goods intrusted to him except in cases of loss by the enemies of the state or the act of God, to be prejudiced by a notice which had been given by the carrier, but which had never come to his knowledge. In each case, therefore, the existence of such a notice must be brought to the knowledge of the party consigning the goods, in order that it may debar him from his right to recover in the event of loss or injury.[1]

SEC. 125. **Factual Limitation.** — In some cases the facts bring a knowledge of limitation of responsibility home to the individual.[2] Thus, if a man is known generally as a carrier

[1] Hollister *v.* Nowlen, 19 Wend. (N. Y.) 234; Cole *v.* Goodwin, 19 Wend. (N. Y.) 251; Southern Express Co. *v.* Newby, 36 Ga. 635; Sager *v.* Portsmouth, &c. R. R. Co., 31 Me. 428; Fillebrown *v.* Grand Trunk Rail. Co., 55 Me. 462; Prentice *v.* Decker, 49 Barb. (N. Y.) 21; Limburger *v.* Westcott, 49 Me. 283; Farmers' &c. Bank *v.* Champlain Transportation Co., 23 Vt. 186; Southern Express Co. *v.* Purcell, 37 Ga. 103. Notwithstanding notice on the passage-ticket that "passengers are not allowed to carry baggage beyond $100 in value, and that personal, unless notice is given, and an extra amount paid, at the rate of the price of a ticket for every $500 in value," held, that the plaintiff was entitled to recover the value of his trunk, and of such portion of the contents as is customarily known and carried as travellers' baggage, being reasonable in amount and value, although worth more than $100, and although nothing extra was paid for baggage exceeding in value that sum. In considering what amount of baggage the plaintiff might reasonably have had, the jury were allowed to take into view his residence, business, station in life, the place from which he came and whither he was going.

Passage-tickets, given to passengers by railroads and steamboats, are rather tokens or vouchers that the passengers have paid their fare, and are entitled to their seats, and to be surrendered when that right is recognized, than special contracts fixing and regulating the terms of passage, amount of baggage, &c. Nevins *v.* Bay State, &c. Co., 4 Bosw. (N. Y.) 225.

In Pennsylvania a carrier may limit his liability by a general notice, but its terms must be clear and explicit; and the party with whom the carrier deals must be fully informed of the terms and its effects. The exception goes on the ground of a contract, express and implied; and where the notice was in the English language, and the passenger was a German, who did not understand the English language, it was held to be incumbent on the carrier to prove that the passenger had knowledge of the limitation; and if tickets, without anything more, are evidence of a special contract, yet they must be printed in a language which the passenger understands, or their terms must be explained to him. Camden, &c. R. R. Co. *v.* Baldauf, 16 Pa. St. 67.

[2] See Macklin *v.* New Jersey Steamboat Co., 7 Abb. Pr. (N. Y.) N. S. 229.

of one kind of article, and he, at the request of the consignor, receive goods of a different description from those in connection with which he generally plies his trade, he does not necessarily thereby assume the same responsibility in connection with these articles which he has in other cases. This is only fair. His trade is carrying articles of little value. All his business is conducted with reference to these. He has not to take the same precautions that would be necessary if he undertook the conveyance of valuables. When, therefore, an individual who is aware of the nature of his trade requests him to convey a parcel containing jewelry, he must do so at his own risk. It would be as unjust that the carrier should under such circumstances be held an insurer, as it would be to regard him in that light with reference to a table or a chair which he was allowing to remain in his house. The doctrine of insurance is limited in relation to the man's trade if the trade is limited, and the limitation is a fact which is known to all; the insurance is also limited in relation to the scope of the profession that a man makes to the public. Another consideration would point to the same conclusion. If a man undertakes a greater risk, he ought to be paid at a higher rate. The risk itself is a thing for which remuneration is not only possible but equitable. But, further, it is reasonable to suppose that the precautions which will be necessary in the cases where the risk is great will be more expensive than the ordinary means which are taken to secure safety where the probability of loss or damage is inconsiderable. This indicates the right that the carrier has to demand such information from the owner of the goods as will enable him to decide upon the proper amount of compensation which he will require for his services and risk, and the amount of care which will be necessary to an efficient performance of his task. This demand is in every respect reasonable. And it is one of the limitations which it is allowable for a carrier to make of his common-law responsibility. There can be no hardship upon the party intrusting his goods to the carrier, for his own sense of prudence ought to have informed him of the necessity of some such demand, and a truthful compliance with the request.

SEC. 126. **False Statement of Value, Effect of.** — Therefore, if the owner of the goods gives an answer false in a material point, the carrier is absolved from his responsibility for any loss except such as may be due to negligence or misconduct.[1] It, however, leaves the duty of inquiry upon the shoulders of the carrier.[2] Where, however, the question as to the extent to which, and the circumstances under which, a general notice will limit a carrier's liability comes to be considered, we shall find less reason to congratulate ourselves on the certitude of the law. Some decisions even go the length of allowing a carrier, without express contract, but simply by means of a general notice, to free himself entirely from the duty and responsibility which attach to his calling at common law.[3]

SEC. 127. **Rule in Maving v. Todd.** — In the case of Maving *v.* Todd,[4] LORD ELLENBOROUGH, speaking of the power which wharfingers and carriers have of limiting their responsibility, said, "Since they can limit it to a particular sum, I think they may exclude it altogether, and that they may say we will have nothing to do with fire;" and while, in answer to a suggestion from one of the counsel, he admitted that they were bound to receive the goods, he added, "but they may make their own terms." In another case, where the question as to what was sufficient notice to limit a carrier's responsibility, and in which it was decided that it was inadmissible to read in evidence an advertisement in a newspaper, by which notice of such limitation had been given, unless it was first proved that the plaintiff was in the habit of reading the paper in which the advertisement appeared, the same learned judge, in summing up, said: "If this action had been brought twenty years ago, the defendant would have been liable, since by the common law a carrier is liable in all cases, except two, where the loss is occasioned by the act of God, or of the king's enemies, using an overwhelming force, which persons with

[1] Gibbon *v.* Paynton, 4 Burr. 2298.

[2] Phillips *v.* Earle, 8 Pick. (Mass.) 182; Brooke *v.* Pickwick, 4 Bing. 218.

[3] Camden, &c. R. R. Co. *v.* Baldauf, 16 Penn. St. 67.

[4] Maving *v.* Todd, 1 Stark. 72; 4 Camp. 225; and see Hill *v.* Trent Mersey Navigation Co., 5 T. R. 389; 1 Esp. 36.

ordinary means of resistance cannot guard against." And he further remarked that, "if the carriers notified their terms to the person bringing the goods by advertisement, which, in all probability, must have attracted the attention of the person who brought the goods, they were delivered upon those terms."[1] A few other cases may be mentioned to show in what condition the law was before the passing of the statute 1 Will. IV. c. 68, of which we shall hereafter have occasion to speak.

SEC. 128. **Extinction of Common-law Duties by Notice.** — These cases show that there existed a doctrine that, notwithstanding the admitted duty which devolved upon a carrier to carry and to insure, he could by notice throw off both those duties, and so defeat the well-considered policy of the common law. It seemed that the existence of a notice which had come, or which might have come, to the knowledge of the party intrusting his goods to the carrier raised the presumption of a special contract as against him. This doctrine ignored the important fact that there was, even before any contract, a duty upon the part of the carrier to accept the consignor's goods, and looked upon the two parties as equal in every respect, and the contract as if it had been entered into by persons having an entirely voluntary relation. This was evidently unjust, and was a denial of the doctrine of the expediency of the duties devolved upon a carrier by the common law in relation to his public employment. It looked upon a general notice as proof of a special contract instead of regarding it as a proposal for a special contract upon the part of the carrier, which it was in the power of the consignor to refuse or accept.

SEC. 129. **Onus of Proof.** — Had it done the latter, the *onus* of proving the acceptance of these terms would have been upon the carrier. As it did the former, the *onus* of proving that there was no special contract was upon the owner of the goods. The following cases will also indicate the circumstances under which a notice could in these pre-statute times be regarded as

[1] Leeson *v.* Holt, 1 Stark. 186, and § 1; Hopkins *v.* Westcott, 5 Blatchf. (U. S. C. C.) 64.

binding the owner in the same way that a special contract would.

SEC. 130. **Rule in Macklin v. Waterhouse and Cobden v. Bolton.** — Thus it was held that a notice by carriers, that they would not be accountable for the loss or damage of goods, unless the terms of the notice were complied with, protected them where the goods were stolen, as well as against loss caused by accidental circumstances.[1] Where a carrier gave notice that he would not be liable for goods lost beyond the value of *5l.*, it was held that that condition extended to the property of passengers going by the coach, or other carriage, as well as to goods sent to be carried only.[2] A notice that the proprietor of a general coach-office would not be responsible for the carriage of parcels of more value than *5l.*, unless entered as such, was, in the case of Macklin *v.* Waterhouse,[3] held to be of no avail for the proprietor of a coach, who took the parcel from the office, unless it was otherwise shown that he was connected with the office. This case only shows that one man's notice is not a protection for another man. It would scarcely seem to have required argument. In the case of Cobden *v.* Bolton,[4] the defendant, a carrier, placed a board in his office, giving notice that he would not be answerable for jewels, however small their value, unless entered as such, but circulated handbills stating generally that he would not be answerable for any article above the value of *5l.*, unless entered as such; it was held that he was answerable for the loss of jewels, although they had not been expressly entered as such, if under the value of *5l.* Even in those days, it was necessary to prove that the notice had come to the knowledge of the owner of the goods, or that there was at least every probability that it had come to his knowledge.[5] This is the rule in this country, and the carrier takes the burden, not only of proving

[1] Covington *v.* Willan, Gow, 115.

[2] Clarke *v.* Gray, 6 East, 564; 2 Smith, 622; 4 Esp. 177.

[3] 5 Bing. 212; 2 M. & P. 319. See also Newborn *v.* Just, 2 C. & P. 76.

[4] 2 Camp. 108. See Munn *v.* Baker, 2 Stark. 255.

[5] Kerr *v.* Willan, 6 M. & S. 150; 2 Stark. 53. But a notice to the vendor was held to be equivalent to a notice to the vendee who directed the goods to be sent. Maving *v.* Todd, 1 Stark. 72.

the shipper's knowledge of the restrictions, but also of his assent thereto,[1] as in all cases, in order to make such notice available, it must be such that it operates as a special contract between the parties, changing the carrier's liability from that raised by the common law to that of a contract liability.[2]

[1] Blossom *v.* Dodd, 43 N. Y. 264; Baltimore, &c. R. R. Co. *v.* Brady, 32 Md. 333; Lawrence *v.* New York, &c. R. R. Co., 36 Conn. 63; Millan *v.* Michigan, &c. R. R. Co., 16 Mich. 79; Judson *v.* Western R. R. Co., 6 Allen (Mass.), 486.

[2] In Blossom *v.* Dodd, 43 N. Y. 264, this doctrine was well illustrated. In that case the plaintiff was a passenger on the New Jersey Central Railroad on the 17th of October, 1866, travelling toward New York. Before reaching Jersey City a messenger of Dodd's express — a baggage express company, doing business in the city of New York, and of which defendant is president — passed through the train upon which plaintiff was, asking and receiving baggage-checks of passengers and agreeing to deliver the baggage in such parts of New York as they should direct. The plaintiff was asked if he had any baggage to be delivered, and he thereupon handed the messenger two checks, and received a printed slip with blank places in which the numbers of his checks were written with a lead-pencil. With the exception of a large advertisement at the top, the printed parts of the slip were as follows: —

DODD'S EXPRESS.

N. J. R. R. DEPOT, PIER 13, N. R., No. 944 BROADWAY, N. Y.

Articles or checks numbered as below (for Dodd's Express): —

It is mutually agreed, and is part of the consideration of the contract, that Dodd's Express *shall not be liable* for merchandise or jewelry *contained in baggage*, nor for loss by fire, nor for an amount exceeding ONE HUNDRED DOLLARS upon any article unless specially agreed for in writing on the receipt *and the extra risk paid therefor*, nor for baggage to railroad, steamboat, or steamship lines after the same has been left at the usual place of delivery to such lines; and the owner hereby agrees that Dodd's Express *shall be liable only as above;* and it is further agreed that said express shall not be liable for loss or damage *unless the claim therefor* be made in writing at their principal office, with this receipt annexed, within thirty days thereafter.

Read this receipt.

At the time of plaintiff's receiving the slip it was eleven o'clock at night, and the cars were so dark that the print could not be read.

One of the parcels of baggage represented by the checks was delivered. The other, worth $260, was lost while in the hands of the express company. This action was brought for its value, and the defendant set up the stipulation in the receipt as a limitation upon his liability. The referee found for the plaintiff, awarding him the full value of the lost baggage.

The judgment was affirmed upon appeal, CHURCH, C. J., saying: "The common-law liability of common carriers cannot be limited by a notice, even though such notice be brought to the knowledge of the persons whose property they carry. Dorr *v.* New Jersey Steam Navigation Co., 1 Kern. 485. But such liability may be limited by express contract. Ib.; Bissell

SEC. 131. **Notice to Principal.**—As notice to the principal is, upon obvious legal principles, notice to all the agents, it

v. New York Central R. R. Co., 25 N. Y. 442; French *v.* Buffalo, New York, & Erie R. R. Co., 4 Keyes, 108.

"The principal question in this case is, whether there was a contract made between the parties limiting the liability of the defendants to a loss of $100 for the valise and its contents, which the plaintiff intrusted to their care. A *fac-simile* of the card upon which the alleged contract was printed has been furnished in the papers. It does not appear, on examination, like a contract, and would not, from its general appearance, be taken for anything more than a token or check denoting the numbers of the checks received, to be used for identification upon the delivery of the baggage. The larger portion of the printed matter is an advertisement, in large type. The alleged contract is printed in very small type, and is illegible in the night by the ordinary lights in a railroad car, and is not at all attractive, while other parts of the paper are quite so.

"Considerable stress is laid upon the fact that the words 'Read this receipt' were printed on the card in legible type. The receipt reads, 'Received of M—— articles or checks numbered as below, 368–319.' 'For Dodd's Express.' The blank is not filled, nor is the receipt signed by any one. The invitation is not to read the contract, but the receipt. In order to read it the paper must be turned sideways; and no one, thus reading the receipt, would suspect that it had any connection with the alleged contract, which is printed in different and very small type across the bottom of the paper. It is no part of the receipt, is not connected with it, and is not referred to in any other part of the paper. The defendants are dealing with all classes of the community; and public policy, as well as established principles, demand that the utmost fairness should be observed. This paper is subject to the criticism made by LORD ELLENBOROUGH, in Butler *v.* Heane, 2 Camp. 415, in which he said that 'it called attention to everything that was attractive, and concealed what was calculated to repel customers;' and added, 'If a common carrier is to be allowed to limit his liability, he must take care that any one who deals with him is fully informed of the limits to which he confines it.' Nor did the nature of the business necessarily convey the idea of a contract to the traveller in such a manner as to raise the presumption that he knew it was a contract expressive of the terms upon which the property was carried, or limiting the liability of the carrier. Baggage is usually identified by means of checks or tokens, and such a card does not necessarily import anything else. At all events, to have the effect claimed, the limitation should be as conspicuous and legible as other portions of the paper. In Brown *v.* Eastern R. R. Co., 11 Cush. (Mass.) 97, where the limitation was printed upon the back of a passenger ticket, the court says: 'The party receiving it might well suppose that it was a mere check, signifying that the party had paid his passage to the place indicated on the ticket.' In the cases of Prentice *v.* Decker, 49 Barb. (N. Y.) 21, and Limburger *v.* Westcott, 49 Barb. (N. Y.) 283, limitations were claimed upon the delivery of similar cards of another express company; and the court held, in both cases, that such delivery did not charge the persons

was, in the case of Mayhew *v.* Eames,[1] held that if a stage-coach proprietor has given the usual 5*l.* notice to principals

receiving them with knowledge that they contained contracts. A different construction was put upon the delivery of a similar card in Hopkins *v.* Westcott, 6 Blatchf. (U. S. C. C.) 64; but I infer that the learned judge who delivered the opinion intended to decide that something short of an express contract will suffice to screen the carrier from his common-law liability, and that a notice, personally served, which could be read, would have that effect. The attention of the court does not seem to have been directed to the distinction between such a notice and a contract. The delivery and acceptance of a paper containing the contract may be binding, though not read, provided the business is of such a nature and the delivery is under such circumstances as to raise the presumption that the person receiving it knows that it is a contract containing the terms and conditions upon which the property is received to be carried. In such a case it is presumed that the person assents to the terms, whatever they may be. This is the utmost extent to which the rule can be carried without abandoning the principle that a contract is indispensable. The recent case of Grace *v.* Adams, 100 Mass. 560, relied upon by the defendant's counsel, was decided upon this principle. The plaintiff delivered a package of money to an express company, and took a receipt containing a provision exempting the company from liability for loss by fire; and the court held that he knew that the paper contained the conditions upon which the money was to be carried, and was, therefore, presumed to have assented to them, although he did not read the paper. The court says: 'It is not claimed that he did not know, when he took it, that it was a shipping contract, or bill of lading.' So, in Van Goll *v.* South-Eastern Rail. Co., 104 Eng. C. L. 75, the same principle was decided. WILLES, J., said: 'Assuming that the plaintiff did not read the terms of the condition, it is evident she knew they were there.' KEATING, J., said: 'It was incumbent on the company to show that such was the contract. . . . I think there was evidence that the plaintiff assented to those terms.'

"As to bills of lading and other commercial instruments of like character, it has been held that persons receiving them are presumed to know, from their uniform character and the nature of the business, that they contain the terms upon which the property is to be carried. But checks for baggage are not of that character, nor is such a card as was delivered in this instance. It was, at least, equivocal in its character. In such a case a person is not presumed to know its contents, or to assent to them. The circumstances under which the paper was received repel the idea of a contract. No such intimation was made to the plaintiff. He did not, and could not if he had tried, read it in his seat. It is found that he might have read it at the end of the car, or by the lights on the pier or in the ferry-boat; and it is claimed that he should have done so, and, if dissatisfied, should have expressed his dissent. If he had done so, and, in the bustle and confusion incident to such occasions, could have

[1] 4 D. & R. 484; 3 B. & C. 601; 1 C. & P. 550.

in London in the month of January, and a traveller for the said principals, who proves that he was ignorant of such notice, sends them from Downham a parcel containing 87*l.*, which he has received for them, in the month of February, by a coach belonging to the said proprietors, and it is lost, the coach proprietors will not be responsible. But where an agent of a carrier informed the female servant of the owner of a parcel above the value of 5*l.*, that it ought to be insured, it was regarded as insufficient notice of the limitation of a carrier's responsibility to protect him from the consequences of loss or damage done to the parcel.[1] In one case, where there was an agreement between the plaintiff and one of the defendants, who were proprietors of stage-coaches, to the effect that the plaintiff's parcels of a certain kind should be carried by the defendant's coaches free of expense, and this agreement was in force for two years, but no evidence was offered to prove that the other defendants had any knowledge

found the messenger and demanded his baggage, the latter might have claimed, upon the theory of this defence, that the contract was completed at the delivery of the paper, and that he had a right to perform it and receive the compensation. It is impossible to maintain this defence without violating established legal principles in relation to contracts. It was suggested on the argument that the stipulation to charge according to the value of the property is just and proper. This may be true; but the traveller should have something to say about it. The contract cannot be made by one party. If the traveller is informed of the charges graduated by value, he can have a voice in the bargain; but in this case he had none. While the carrier should be protected in his legal right to limit his responsibility, the public should also be protected against imposition and fraud. The carrier must deal with the public upon terms of equality; and if he desires to limit his liability, he must secure the assent of those with whom he transacts business.

"My conclusion is, that no contract was proved, —

"1. Because it was obscurely printed.

"2. Because the nature of the transaction was not such as necessarily charged the plaintiff with knowledge that the paper contained the contract.

"3. Because the circumstances attending the delivery of the card repel the idea that the plaintiff had such knowledge, or assented in fact to the terms of the alleged contract.

"The order granting a new trial must be affirmed, and judgment absolute ordered for the plaintiff, with costs. All the judges concurring, upon the ground that no contract limiting the liability of defendants was proved."

[1] Macklin *v.* Waterhouse, 5 Bing. 212; 2 M. & P. 319.

of this agreement, and it was proved that the defendants had given notice that they would not be accountable for parcels above the value of 5*l.*, unless entered and paid for. Here it was held that the defendants were not liable for the loss of a parcel above the value of 5*l.*, which was sent by the plaintiff under this agreement, of the value of which no notice had been given to the defendants.[1] In the case of Palmer *v.* Grand Junction Railway Company, which was an action against common carriers, for the loss of goods intrusted to their care, there was conflicting evidence as to whether a ticket limiting their responsibility had been delivered by them to the plaintiff at the time of taking the goods in charge. The judge left it to the jury to say whether that ticket had been delivered to the plaintiff, and not whether it had been read over to him and explained; and upon a motion for a new trial, upon the ground of misdirection, he was held to have rightly directed the jury.

SEC. 132. **Means by which Notice is brought to Owner's Knowledge.** — With regard to the means by which the knowledge of such a notice is to be brought to the party, we have seen[2] that in one case LORD ELLENBOROUGH said it was not enough to prove that it had been advertised, and that it was necessary to prove that it had been advertised in a newspaper which the party whose rights were to be limited by the notice was in the habit of reading.[3] In that case, however, it was held that an advertisement in the Gazette might be read in a trial of such a nature without such a proof as that indicated. In one case, however, in which evidence that the newspaper, in which the proprietor of coaches had frequently inserted a notice of the limitation of his responsibility, had been taken in by the plaintiff for three years, was given, the jury gave a verdict in favor of the plaintiff, and the court refused a new trial.[4] In this country, notice by publication in a newspaper or otherwise is not sufficient, but actual notice must be shown.[5]

[1] Bignold *v.* Waterhouse, 1 M. & S. 255.

[2] *Ante*, p. 208.

[3] Leeson *v.* Holt, 1 Stark. 186.

[4] Rowley *v.* Horne, 3 Bing. 2; 10 Moore, 247.

[5] Southern Express Co. *v.* Newby, 36 Ga. 635; Prentice *v.* Decker, 49 Barb. (N. Y.) 21.

SEC. 133. **Notice by Placards.** — The most ordinary form, however, in which notice was wont to be given, was by means of placards stuck up in the office at which parcels were booked; and there were cases which decided under what circumstances these notices should have the effect of limiting the responsibility of the carrier, and defeating the objects of the common law. It was decided in one case that a notice stuck up in an office, to be available, must have been in such large characters that a person delivering goods at the office could not fail to read without gross negligence;[1] and this principle was explained more in detail in another case, in which a bill, speaking of the advantages of adopting his mode of conveyance, had been posted on an office door by a carrier, to which advertisement a notice was at the bottom added, to the effect that he would not be answerable for goods above the value of 5*l.*, unless entered as such, and paid for accordingly. This notice was printed in small letters, and it was held to be an insufficient notice of the limitation of the carrier's responsibility.[2] In this country, such placards, however printed or however conspicuously posted, afford no evidence that the shipper knew of the restrictions imposed by the carrier.[3]

SEC. 134. **Notice on Board in Office.** — In Kerr *v.* Willan,[4] already cited, which was an action of special assumpsit against the defendant, as a carrier, for negligence in losing a truss of goods committed to his care, this matter was under consideration. The defendant relied upon a notice put up in his office, intimating that he would not be liable for more than the rate of 20*l.* per hundred-weight for any goods whose weight ex-

[1] Clayton *v.* Hunt, 3 Camp. 27.

[2] Butler *v.* Heane, 2 Camp. 415. It has been correctly held in this country, that when an owner of goods seeks to charge a railway company as carriers for the loss of goods intrusted to them, by proving the terms of one of their own notices as to the rates and rules of transportation, he must take the notice as a whole, and that the defendants are entitled to the benefit of any exception which it contains. Burroughs *v.* Norwich, &c. R. R. Co., 100 Mass. 26; Squire *v.* New York Central R. R. Co., 98 Mass. 239.

[3] Hollister *v.* Nowlen, 19 Wend. (N. Y.) 234. But in Pennsylvania the rule is otherwise. Whitesell *v.* Crane, 8 W. & S. (Penn.) 369

[4] 2 Stark. 53; 6 M. & S. 150; S. P. Davis *v.* William, 2 Stark. 279.

ceeded 28 lbs. In order to affect the plaintiff with knowledge of this notice, it was proved that such a notice was painted on a board, and hung up in the defendant's coach-office; and a witness was called, who stated that he was a porter to the wagon by which the goods had been conveyed to town, and that he had taken them to the defendant's office; that he had frequently been at the office before, and had seen the board there, but that he did not suppose there was anything upon it, and, although he could read, had never, in fact, read what was upon it until after the loss of the truss.

SEC. 135. **Effectual Notice.** — LORD ELLENBOROUGH said: "You cannot make this notice to this non-supposing person; it is difficult to struggle with the common law; and it is incumbent upon a person, who wishes to rid himself of his responsibility at common law, to give effectual notice. The hardship of the case cannot alter the liability of the party. By the common law, the carrier is responsible for the loss of goods, unless he enter into a special contract by which he limits that responsibility. This he may do by giving notice in the public papers, or by any other medium by which the party with whom he deals is effectually apprised of the terms upon which he proposes to deal. If the person who carried the goods to the office, in this case, had read the notice, the plaintiff would have been bound by the limitations which it contained."[1] And it was decided, in another case, that a notice of certain limitations on a general liability, suspended at the *termini* of the journey, will not attach upon the delivery of goods at intermediate places, where no such notice is given.[2]

SEC. 136. **Limitation to a certain Value.** — Upon grounds which have been alluded to above, it has always been considered fair that a carrier might limit his liability to a certain value. The reasons of this rule were somewhat fully explained. Some of the cases in which these principles have been carried into effect may be mentioned in this place, before we consider the action of the legislature in this matter of

[1] Fillebrown *v.* Grand Trunk Rail. Co., 55 Me. 462.
[2] Gouger *v.* Jolly, Holt, 317.

notice. Where the usual notice had been given by carriers, exempting them from liability for the loss of goods above the value of 5*l.*, it was not held that they were thereby exempted from responsibility for the loss of the goods, although the value was above the sum named in the notice, if the appearance of the goods necessarily indicated their nature and the fact that the value exceeded the sum stated in the notice.[1] The object of the law is not to protect men from the effects of their own carelessness.

SEC. 137. **Bulky Goods.** — But such a notice would apply to goods which, from their bulk, may be supposed to exceed the specified value.[2] In such a case there is a strife of suppositions; for while the bulk may lead one to suppose that the value exceeds the amount stated in the notice, the sender of the parcel may be supposed to be honest, and the latter supposition should prevail. Therefore, if goods above the value of 5*l.* had, after the usual notice, been sent, and only from their bulk indicated their excessive value, the carrier would not be liable. The existence of such a notice does not preclude a variation in the terms of any special agreement. In a case where a notice that the carriers would not be "accountable for any china, glass, or contents, plate, watches, cash, bank-notes, bills, jewels, or writings, however small the value, nor for any other article of more than 5*l.* value, if lost or damaged, unless specified and *paid for as such when delivered* at their offices in town, or to their agents in the country," was relied upon to protect the carriers from the consequences of a looking-glass having been broken while in their possession, the facts were these: The looking-glass was packed in a case directed to the plaintiff, and marked "glass." It was delivered to the defendants' booker, at the "Saracen's Head," Snow Hill. The book-keeper, being told what it was, said he would charge 4 cwt. for it, although, in point of fact, it only weighed 3 cwt. The person who brought it answered, "Charge what you please; you shall be paid for it, provided you take care of it. It is worth 80*l.* It is in your care, and I am done

[1] Down *v.* Fromont, 4 Camp. 40.

[2] Thorogood *v.* Marsh, Gow, 105.

with it." No money was paid at that time, except 6*d*. for booking. The looking-glass, when unpacked, was found to be broken. In this case, notwithstanding the provision in the notice, it was held that, as the book-keeper knew what the article was, and had been told its value, and desired to charge what he pleased, "the payment of the money was dispensed with, and the notice was unavailing."[1] But if no such communication had been made by the person bringing the goods to the booking-office, and the plaintiff had relied upon the fact that the book-keeper who received the goods did happen to know what was in the parcel, or if he had relied upon a presumption that the book-keeper might, from the size of the case, from its shape or make, or some other circumstance, have inferred the value of the articles contained in it, such a notice as that alluded to above would have protected the defendant carriers.[2] It is, evidently, only just that what is explicit should only be rendered of non-effect by something which is equally explicit.[3]

The cases quoted above are sufficient to show in what condition the law was before the passing of the Carriers' Act.[4] That condition was, as we have seen, eminently unsatisfactory in many respects. At the time the anomalies above alluded to existed, there were many judicial recognitions of their true nature; but anomalies have deep roots and no judge had the courage to stub them up. Thus, with regard to the question of notice, we find BEST, C. J., making some excellent remarks in the case of Brooke *v.* Pickwick.[5]

SEC. 138. **Proper Way to limit Liability.** — "If," he says, "coach proprietors wish honestly to limit their responsibility, they ought to announce their terms to every individual who

[1] Wilson *v.* Freeman, 3 Camp. 527.

[2] Levi *v.* Waterhouse, 1 Price, 280. See also Harris *v.* Packwood, 3 Taunt. 264; Marsh *v.* Horne, 5 B. & C. 322; 8 D. & R. 223; Beck *v.* Evans, 16 East, 244; 3 Camp. 276. See also Warner *v.* Western Transportation Co., 5 Rob. (N. Y.) 490.

[3] Yet the construction of such notices ought always to be strict as against the person who seeks to limit his liability by such means. See Earle *v.* Cadmus, 2 Daly (N. Y.), 237; Hopkins *v.* Westcott, 6 Blatchf. (U. S. C. C.) 64; Perry *v.* Thompson, 98 Mass. 249.

[4] 1 Will. IV. c. 68.

[5] 4 Bing. 218.

applies at their office, and, at the same time, to place in his hands a printed paper, specifying the precise extent of their engagement. If they omit to do this, they attract customers under the confidence inspired by the extensive liability which the common law imposes upon carriers, and then endeavor to elude that liability by some limitation which they have not been at the pains to make known to the individual who has trusted them."[1] Still, as we have seen, principles other than these were acted upon, and necessarily caused endless litigation. That of itself is sufficient criticism upon the condition of the law. The excellence of a law, or of a rule of law, is in the inverse ratio to the amount of work lawyers get out of it.

SEC. 139. **11 Geo. IV. and 1 Will. IV. c. 68.** — At last, however, the legislature interfered, and passed the Carriers' Act.[2] It is entitled "An Act for the more effectual protection of mail contractors, stage-coach proprietors, and other common carriers for hire, against the loss of or injury to parcels or packages delivered to them for conveyance or custody, the value of which shall not be declared to them by the owners thereof." It recites that, "by reason of the frequent practice of bankers and others, of sending by the public mails, stage-coaches, wagons, vans, and other public conveyances by land, for hire, parcels and packages containing money, bills, notes, jewelry, and other articles of great value in small compass, much valuable property is rendered liable to depredation, and the responsibility of mail contractors, stage-coach proprietors, and common carriers for hire is greatly increased; and that, through the frequent omission, by persons sending such parcels and packages, to notify the value and nature of the contents thereof, so as to enable such mail contractors, stage-coach proprietors, and other common carriers, by due diligence, to protect themselves against losses arising from their legal responsibility, and the difficulty of fixing parties with knowledge of notices by such mail contractors, stage-coach propri-

[1] The judgment of BRONSON, J., in Hollister v. Nowlen, 19 Wend. (N. Y.) 236, is worth reading in this connection.

[2] 11 Geo. IV. and 1 Will. IV. c. 68.

etors, and other common carriers, with the intent to limit their responsibility, they have become exposed to great and unavoidable risks, and have thereby sustained heavy losses."

SEC. 140. **Declaration of Value.** — This act, in its 1st section, enacts that no mail contractor, stage-coach proprietor, or other common carrier by land, for hire, shall be liable for the loss of, or injury done to, any of the articles therein mentioned,[1] if the value of such property exceed 10*l.*, "unless at the time of the delivery the value and nature be declared, and an increased charge, or an engagement to pay the same, be accepted."

SEC. 141. **Public Notice.** — The 2d section enacts that, with a view to the carriers' trade in the conveyance of parcels containing some of the articles specified in the 1st section, the value of which shall exceed 10*l.*, the rate of the increased charge is to be notified by a public notice affixed to a conspicuous part of the office, warehouse, or receiving-house, that such notice is to be in legible characters, and that this notice shall bind the senders of such parcels, without further proof of its having come to their knowledge.

SEC. 142. **Carrier's Receipt.** — By the 3d section, carriers are required to give receipts for packages, after the requirements of the foregoing sections have been complied with, if they are asked to do so, and such receipt is to be an acknowledgment of the insurance of the goods which have been intrusted to them. And by the same section they are deprived of the benefit of the act if they do not give such a receipt when required to do so, or if the notice is not affixed to a con-

[1] These are bank-notes of any bank in England, Scotland, or Ireland, bills of exchange, checks on bankers, china, clocks, coins (gold or silver) of any country, deeds, engravings, foreign coins (gold or silver), furs, glass, gold coin, or other gold, manufactured or not, plate or plated articles, jewelry, lace, maps, money (gold or silver), notes, bills, orders or securities for payment of money, notes of any bank of the United Kingdom, or for the payment of money, orders for payment of money, paintings, pictures, plate or plated articles, gold or silver, precious stones, promissory notes, securities for payment of money, silks in a manufactured or unmanufactured state, and whether wrought up or not wrought up with other articles, silver, coin, or plate or plated articles, stamps, stones (precious), timepieces of any description, title-deeds, trinkets, watches, writings.

spicuous place, and does not fulfil the requirements of section 2, under which circumstances the liability of the carrier, in case of injury or damage, will be determined by the common-law rule.

SEC. 143. **As to Limitation of Liability by Notice.** — The 4th section provides that no public notice or declaration shall limit or in any wise affect the common-law liability of any such carriers for or in respect of any goods to be carried or conveyed by them, but that they shall be liable, as at common law, to answer for the loss of or damage done to any articles or goods, unless they are mentioned in or covered by the act, and that in spite of any public notice or declaration made by them contrary thereto.

SEC. 144. **Office.** — The 5th section provides that every office used by the carrier as a receiving-house shall be deemed to be such, and that any one of several carriers, who are partners or joint proprietors, may be sued separately.

SEC. 145. **Special Contracts.** — By section 6 it is expressly provided that nothing in the act is to extend, or be construed, to annul or in any wise affect any special contract between parties for the conveyance of goods.

SEC. 146. **Recovery of Loss.** — By the 7th section, a party who has delivered a parcel and paid for it as a valuable parcel under the act, is entitled to recover the amount of a loss or damage, including the increased charges for value and insurance.

SEC. 147. **Felonious Acts of Servants.** — The 8th section provides that nothing in the act shall protect any mail contractor, stage-coach proprietor, or other common carrier for hire from liability to answer for loss or injury to any goods or articles whatsoever, arising from the felonious acts of any coachman, guard, book-keeper, porter, or other servant in his employ, nor protect any such coachman, guard, book-keeper, or other servant from liability for any loss or injury occasioned by his own personal neglect or misconduct.

SEC. 148. **Proof of Value.** — By the 9th section it is provided that carriers shall be entitled to require from the plaintiff proof of the actual value of the contents by the ordinary legal evidence, and that they shall be liable only to such damages as are thus proved, not exceeding the declared value, together with the increased charges. The 10th section enables carriers, in actions brought against them, to pay money into court, as in ordinary actions.

SEC. 149. **Modification of these Provisions.** — These are the principal provisions of this act, but in some respects the generality of these provisions has been removed by the decisions which have from time to time been made in our courts of law. Thus it was held, in the case of the Peninsular and Oriental Steam Navigation Company *v.* Shand,[1] that neither the Carriers' Act[2] nor the Railway and Canal Act[3] applied to carriers by sea.[4]

SEC. 150. **Divisibility of Contract.** — It is important, however, to notice that where a carrier has entered into a contract for the carriage of goods from a foreign port to a port in England, and thence by land in England, the contract is divisible, and he is entitled to the protection of the 1st section of the Carriers' Act, in so far as the carriage by land is concerned.[5] It has further been decided that where, in an action against a common carrier for the loss of a parcel, it was pleaded, under this act, that the value exceeded 10*l.*, and was not declared at the time of delivery to the carrier, a replication that the loss arose from the felonious acts of the defendant's servants was good.[6] It also appears that to all goods other than those mentioned in the act, the common-law liability remains, in spite of any public notice or declaration made by the carrier with a view to limit such liability; and that his responsibility for goods which are specifically mentioned in the act, but whose value is under 10*l.*, remains as at common law.

SEC. 151. **Decisions on the First Section.** — Some decisions have been arrived at as to what is included under the descriptions of goods contained in the 1st section of the act.

[1] 3 Moore, P. C. N. S. 272.

[2] 11 Geo. IV. and 1 Will. IV. c. 68.

[3] 17 & 18 Vict. c. 81.

[4] See also Pianciani *v.* London & South-Western Rail. Co., 18 C. B. 226.

[5] Baxendale *v.* Great Eastern Rail. Co., 10 B. & S. 212, Exch. Ch.

[6] Metcalfe *v.* London, Brighton, & South Coast Rail. Co., 4 C. B. N. S. 307.

Thus the words "timepieces of any description" have been held to include a chronometer for use on ship-board.[1]

SEC. 152. **Trinkets.** — In another case, while it was admitted to be impossible to define with precise accuracy the word "trinkets," within the meaning of the 1st section of this act, it was asserted that the closest approximation to a definition is this, that they must be articles of *mere ornament*, or, if ornament and utility be combined, the former must be the predominating quality. And COCKBURN, C. J., in giving judgment, instanced "bracelets, shirt-pins, rings, and brooches," and held that ornamental portemonnaies and smelling-bottles "may fairly and properly fall within the description of trinkets."[2]

SEC. 153. **Manufactured Silks, Glass, Furs, Securities, Lace, &c.** — So silk watch-guards are "silks in a manufactured state," within the meaning of the act.[3] And smelling-bottles will fall under the description "glass;" so a looking-glass will be held to be "glass."[4] "Furs," according to TINDAL, C. J., in Mayhew *v.* Nelson,[5] within the meaning of the statute, are "articles made entirely of fur, and not articles in which there is only a portion fur." A security for money, to be within the act, must be of the intrinsic value of 10*l.* when it is delivered to the carrier. Therefore an imperfect bill of exchange for 11*l.* 10*s.*, which was lost before the name of the drawer was inserted, was held, in an action against a carrier-company for the loss, to be a "writing," but not a bill, note, or security for money within the meaning of the 1st section of the Carriers' Act.[6] In a more recent case

[1] Le Conteur *v.* London & South-Western Rail. Co., 1 Law Rep. Q. B. 54.

[2] Bernstein *v.* Baxendale, 6 C. B. N. S. 251.

[3] Bernstein *v.* Baxendale, 6 C. B. N. S. 251; Hart *v.* Baxendale, 6 Exch. 769. "Elastic silk webbing" is composed of silk and India-rubber. It was held that this webbing was "silks wrought up with other materials" within the meaning of the Carriers' Act. Brunt *v.* Midland Rail. Co., 2 H. & C. 889; 33 L. J. Exch. 187. See also Butt *v.* Great Western Rail. Co., 11 C. B. 140; 20 L. J. 241 C. P. See also Davey *v.* Mason, C. & M. 50.

[4] Owen *v.* Burnet, 4 Tyr. 133.

[5] 6 C. & P. 58.

[6] Stoessiger *v.* South-Eastern Rail. Co., 23 L. J. Q. B. 293; 3 El. & Bl. 549; 2 C. L. R. 1595; 18 Jur. 605. See as to jewelry, Smith *v.* London & Brighton Rail. Co., 7 C. B. 782.

the plaintiff was the owner of a valuable piece of lace (intended for use in celebrating the Holy Communion), which, together with a certificate of the novelty of the pattern, was put in a gilt frame and covered with glass, for the purpose of being shown at an exhibition of ecclesiastical articles. The whole was put in a packing-case, and sent — without any declaration within the Carriers' Act — by the defendants' railway, and lost. In this case it was held that, though the plaintiff was not entitled to recover the values of the lace, certificate, and glass, he was entitled to recover the values of the gilt frame and packing-case.[1]

SEC. 154. **Special Contracts still Admissible.** — It is also to be understood that this act does not in any way preclude the parties from entering into any special contract as to the conveyance of goods of any description or value; but the notice given under the act, although known to the consignor, does not of itself constitute a special contract for this purpose. Where, however, a notice was served by a railway company on a fishmonger that fish would not be taken for conveyance except on certain terms, and that no one had power to vary those terms, it was held that the fact of his sending his fish showed that he assented to a special contract to carry on those terms, and that the company were in that case protected under the Carriers' Act.[2]

SEC. 155. **Payment of Carriage.** — Of course, a carrier is not bound to convey goods except on payment of the full price for the carriage, according to their value. The common-law duty to carry is to be regarded as dependent upon the willingness of the owner of the goods to pay for their conveyance,

[1] Treadwin *v.* Great Eastern Rail. Co., 3 L. R. C. P. 308; 37 L. J. C. P. 83; 17 L. J. N. S. 601; 16 W. R. 365. See also Flowers *v.* South-Eastern Rail. Co., W. N. 1867, p. 155. See also Wyld *v.* Pickford, 8 M. & W. 443. As to pictures, see Boys *v.* Pink, 8 C. & P. 361. When framed pictures are sent by a carrier, the frames as well as the pictures are within the Carriers' Act. Henderson, or Anderson, *v.* London & North-Western Rail. Co., 5 L. R. Ex. 90; 18 W. R. 352; 21 L. T. N. S. 756; 39 L. J. Exch. 55. A silk dress, forming part of the wearing apparel of a railway passenger, is within the act. Flowers *v.* South-Eastern Rail. Co., 16 L. T. N. S. 321.

[2] Walker *v.* York & North Midland Rail. Co., 2 El. & Bl. 750; 18 Jur. 143; 23 L. J. Q. B. 73.

and if in any case the amount chargeable according to the value of the goods is not paid, it is competent for the carrier to limit his liability by special contract. And, therefore, where a carrier receives valuable goods to carry, after a notice to the bailor that he will not be responsible for loss or damage done to them unless a higher than the ordinary rate of insurance be paid for the carriage, he receives them on the terms of such notice, which amounts to a special contract.[1] In the case in which that was decided, it was, however, at the same time, laid down that he is not exempted thereby from all responsibility, but is, notwithstanding the notice, bound to take ordinary care in the carriage of goods, and is liable not only for any act which amounts to a total abandonment of his character of carrier, or for wilful negligence, but also for a conversion by mis-delivery arising from inadvertence or mistake, if such inadvertence or mistake might have been avoided by the exercise of ordinary care.[1]

SEC. 156. **Effect of Statute.** — The effect, then, of the statute, in so far as it relieved land-carriers from liability for the loss of or damage to valuable articles mentioned therein, unless the nature of the articles was declared, and a higher rate of insurance paid, must now be perfectly clear. The duties of the consignor and of the consignee must be ascertainable from what has been said by a very ordinary effort of thought. And the liabilities of each, when the duties thus imposed upon them by statute and by the common law have not been performed on the one side or the other, where these have not been enumerated, are of easy inference. It need scarcely be stated in this place that where both the owner of the goods

[1] Wyld *v.* Pickford, 8 M. & W. 443; Southern Express Co. *v.* Moon, 39 Miss. 822; Farnham *v.* Camden, &c. R. R. Co., 55 Penn. St. 53; American Express Co. *v.* Sands, 55 Penn. St. 140; Stedman *v.* Western Transportation Co., 48 Barb. (N. Y.) 97; Evansville, &c. R. R. Co. *v.* Young, 28 Ind. 516; Baltimore, &c. R. R. Co. *v.* Skeels, 3 W. Va. 556; New Orleans, &c. Ins. Co. *v.* New Orleans, &c. R. R. Co., 20 La. Ann. 302; Orndorff *v.* Adams Express Co., 3 Bush (Ky.), 194; Express Co. *v.* Kountze, 8 Wall. (U. S.) 342; Simon *v.* The Fung Shuey, 21 La. Ann. 363; Lamb *v.* Camden, &c. R. R. Co., 2 Daly (N. Y.), 454; Indianapolis, &c. R. R. Co. *v.* Allen, 31 Ind. 394; Michigan, &c. R. R. Co. *v.* Heaton, 31 Ind. 397, n.

and the carrier to whom they are intrusted have complied with the statutory requirements with regard to articles above the value of 10*l.*, that compliance has replaced the carrier in the position that was imposed upon him by the common law, *viz.*, the position of an insurer. And in case of the loss of or damage to such goods the owner will recover from the carrier the value of the property lost, or the difference between its value before and after the accident, in case of injury, from the carrier.[1]

SEC. 157. **Receiving-house.** — With regard to two sections of the act, however, something more may be said with advantage. Section 5, as we have already seen,[2] enacts that every office, warehouse, or receiving-house, which shall be used or appointed by a mail contractor or stage-coach proprietor, or other such common carriers, for the receiving of parcels to be conveyed, shall be deemed and taken to be the receiving-house, warehouse, or office of such mail contractor, stage-coach proprietor, or other common carrier. Under this section an inn where a book was kept for booking parcels by a particular coach which was in the habit of stopping there regularly to take up and deliver parcels, was held to be a receiving-house, and that, although it was proved that other coaches stopped at the same inn for the same purpose, and that the innkeeper sent the parcel by which coach he pleased.[3]

SEC. 158. **Rule in Gilbert v. Dale.** — In Gilbert *v.* Dale,[4] it was held that the contract entered into by a booking-office keeper, who takes in parcels to be forwarded by carriers, is only to deliver them safely to a carrier. If a common carrier, to whom goods are brought for conveyance, demands a certain sum for booking, and refuses to take charge of the goods unless such sum is paid, he is not liable to an action if they are left without being paid for and are lost.[5] So, as to this point, it has been decided that if a carrier directs goods to be sent to

[1] M'Manus *v.* Lancashire & Yorkshire Rail. Co., 4 H. & N. 327; 28 L. J. 354 Exch.

[2] *Ante*, p. 222.

[3] Syms *v.* Chaplin, 1 N. & P. 129; 5 Ad. & El. 634; 2 H. & W. 411.

[4] 1 N. & P. 22; 5 A. & E. 543; 2 H. & W. 383.

[5] —— *v.* Jackson, Peake, 185.

a particular booking-office, he is to be held liable for the negligence of the booking-office keeper.[1] The case of Davey *v.* Mason [2] also has a direct bearing upon this section of the act. In this case it appeared that the plaintiff, Miss Davey, had been staying at the "Horse Shoe Inn," at the Stone's End in the borough of Southwark, and, wishing to forward her luggage to Lindfield, she had sent to the "Talbot Inn," in the borough from which the van of the defendant, who was the Lindfield carrier, started, to desire that the van might be brought to call for her luggage at the "Horse Shoe Inn." It appeared that upon a certain day the defendant's van, driven by a servant of the defendant named Allen, was brought to the door of the "Horse Shoe Inn," when the luggage of the plaintiff was put into the van, from which it was afterwards lost while the van was on the way to Lindfield, and while the driver of the van was asleep. It was held that the defendant carrier was liable for the loss. LORD ABINGER, C. B., in summing up, said: "The defendant's servant and van called for these things at the 'Horse Shoe,' just as it is the custom of carriers to do. If you are satisfied that this luggage was delivered to the defendant's servant, as has been proved, I am of opinion that the defendant is just as liable in this action as if he had taken up these goods at the 'Talbot' instead of having taken them up at the 'Horse Shoe.'" In another case in which an action was brought against a carrier for the loss of a parcel, he pleaded that it had not been delivered to him to be carried, and it was held sufficient for the plaintiff to show that it was delivered to a person and at a house where parcels were in the habit of being left for the carrier. It was decided that it was immaterial whether this person was paid any money or not, and that in such an action the person who so left the parcel may be asked on cross-examination what direction was on the parcel.[3]

SEC. 159. **Rule in Baxendale v. Hart.** — The case of Baxendale *v.* Hart,[4] where the plaintiff sent to the defendant's

[1] Colepepper *v.* Good, 5 C. & P. 380.

[2] 1 Car. & M. 45.

[3] Burrell *v.* North, 2 C. & K. 680.

[4] 21 L. J. 123 Exch.; 6 Exch. 769; 16 Jur. 126.

office, to request him to call for goods, and the defendant accordingly sent and received them at the plaintiff's residence, is, in many respects, similar to that of Davey *v.* Mason.[1] In this case no communication was made as to the nature or value of the goods to be conveyed; and no increased charge, according to the value, was paid or tendered by the plaintiff. Some of the goods were lost during the transit, and POLLOCK, C. B., after taking the opinion of the Court of Exchequer, ruled that, as the package was not delivered at the defendant's office, the defendant could not claim the benefit of the statute. Upon error, however, this ruling was held to be incorrect. PATTESON, J., in delivering the judgment of the court, said: "We think the fair meaning of the statute, and in accordance with the first object of the legislature, is, that all persons who send goods of the particular description exceeding 10*l.* in value (they being the persons who know whether they are such goods or not, and the package not being open, and its contents unknown to the carrier), whenever they deliver them to the carrier, are bound to give information of the nature and value of the articles, whether they are delivered at the office of the carrier, at the sender's home, on the road, or anywhere else; and the rest of the clauses of the act follow after with certain provisions as to what is *then* to be done." And this case naturally leads us to the other section of the 11 Geo. IV. and 1 Will. IV. c. 68, about which something must be said. And that is the clause which makes a declaration of the nature and value of the goods, and an increased charge paid thereon, conditions precedent to the imposition of the character of an insurer upon a common carrier, when the value of the goods is over 10*l.*[2]

SEC. 160. **Necessity of Notice.** — The judgment of PATTESON, J., in the case of Baxendale *v.* Hart, which has been referred to above, continues to bear upon this question, and is worthy of quotation. "Then it is," he goes on to say, "that the carrier is entitled to have and to demand a larger charge, which is in the nature of a premium for insurance; he cannot,

[1] *Ante*, p. 228.

[2] See Hinton *v.* Dibbin, 2 G. & D. 36; 2 Q. B. 646; 6 Jur. 601.

indeed, have a larger charge (or, if it be not paid, save himself from responsibility) merely by saying that he must have such and such a sum of money, varying in cases of different persons; but he must have a tariff, or notice, stuck up in his office of the sums which he means to charge above the usual charge for carriage for the different articles, to all the world who send articles of that kind. No doubt, therefore, it is made necessary by the section that he should put a notice or tariff in his office; but then it must be observed that that notice is not a notice. 'I mean to take the benefit of this act, and I mean to require that every person who gives me articles of a particular description and of a particular value shall tell me that they are of that description and value;' it assumes that the Act of Parliament has made it necessary for the sender to state the contents and the nature and value of the articles in the first instance; and the tariff is only to notify to persons what is the extra charge the carrier intends to make in such case."

SEC. 161. **Information to be given by Owner.** — In a subsequent part of his judgment he says: "We think that the Act of Parliament requires the person who sends the goods to take the first step, by giving the information to the carrier which he alone can give; and that if the sender does not take that first step, then he cannot maintain this action, by the force of the 1st section of the Act of Parliament, which expressly says that the carrier shall not be liable unless the declaration is made. Such declaration, when made, will lead to other consequences. The carrier will know what he is to have more according to the tariff which he has stuck up in his office: if that sum is paid, and the goods are lost, then, of course, he would be liable; on the other hand, if he refuses to give a receipt, as provided by the statute, or has omitted to comply with any provision of that kind on his part to be performed, he would lose the protection given by the act; but in no case can the sender recover, unless he has taken the first step, by giving the information which the legislature intended he should give, as we think, in the very first instance."

SEC. 162. **How Owner's Duty to be performed.** — It was

upon these grounds they thought the ruling of the Chief Baron wrong. But it is to be clearly understood that the duty which, under this act, devolves upon the owner of goods above the value of 10*l.* to declare the nature and value of the articles which he delivers to a carrier to be conveyed, is not to be performed in a slovenly and informal manner. And it is not enough to prove that the carriers had a conviction as to the contents of a package, or as to the real nature and value of the goods conveyed, to show that a formal declaration was unnecessary, under the 1st section of this act.[1] With regard to this question of the declaration of the nature and value of the goods delivered, and the payment of the extra charge, the case of Behrens *v.* The Great Northern Railway Company[2] may be noticed.

SEC. 163. **Demand of Payment of Increased Charge.** — Every duty gives rise to a number of subsidiary duties. The performance of a duty is one thing; the manner of its performance is another. With regard to this matter, the question naturally arose, as to whether, when the declaration as to the nature and value of goods had been made by their owner, in a case where the value exceeded 10*l.*, he was bound to tender the increased charge mentioned in the notice affixed to the office of the carrier, or whether it is the duty of the carrier to demand the payment of the increased charge. A further question, of course, was dependent upon the decision of the last question, namely, the effect of a breach of the duty of either party upon whom the duty was cast, in case of the loss or damage of the articles. These questions were decided in the case above alluded to, which was heard in the Court of Exchequer, on the 30th of January, 1861, and the decision there given was affirmed, on appeal to the Exchequer Chamber, on the 5th of February, 1862.

SEC. 164. **Behrens v. The Great Northern Rail. Co.** — In that case the defendant company were common carriers of

[1] Boys *v.* Pink, 8 Car. & P. 361.

[2] 7 H. & N. 950; 8 Jur. N. S. 567; 31 L. J. Exch. 299; 10 W. R. 389; 8 L. T. N. S. 328, Exch. Cham., affirming the decision in the Exch. 6 H. & N. 366; 30 L. J. Exch. 153; 9 W. R. 338; 3 L. T. N. S. 863.

goods for hire, from London to Newcastle-on-Tyne, and the plaintiff, who was a picture-dealer in Coventry Street, London, delivered to the defendants, as such carriers, certain pictures to be carried from the former to the latter place. The place of delivery was the house of the plaintiff, at which the defendants' van called for the purpose of receiving the pictures, at the request of the defendants. At the time that the goods were delivered to the carman, he read, signed, and returned to the plaintiff, a book containing the following receipt:—

"MAY 29, 1860.

"Received of Mr. J. B. Behrens one case, containing a large valuable oil-painting, directed, with great care, to Mr. S. Sesser, 'Turk's Head Hotel,' Gery Street, Newcastle-upon-Tyne. Declared over the value of one hundred and ten pounds.

"(Signed) HARDING."

It appeared that the carman did not demand any increased charge or premium, that nothing was said upon the subject, and that no carriage at all was paid by the plaintiff. The case was conveyed by the defendants' railway from London to Newcastle, and after delivery at its destination, and the ordinary carriage paid, it was discovered to have been seriously injured. Upon application the defendants refused to compensate the plaintiff for the injury, on the ground that the additional rate of 15*l.* per cwt. had not been paid. When the case was before the Court of Exchequer, BRAMWELL, B., said: "To my mind the object of the 2d section was this: Having prescribed by the 1st section a declaration of value, and of the non-liability of the carrier, the 2d section enables the carrier, if he thinks fit, to notify that he will take an increased rate of charge, and thereupon to demand it from the person sending the articles; but if he does not think fit to notify the increased rate of charge, he cannot demand it, and although he does notify it, if he does not think fit to demand it, he is not entitled to demand it;" and CHANNELL and WILDE, BB., were also of opinion that the demand of the carrier is a condition precedent to the payment. In the Court of Exchequer Chamber, WIGHTMAN, J., delivered the judgment. In doing so, he said: "We think that the respondent, having declared the value of the picture to the carman, who was the agent of the appellants, and who received the same to be carried by them, was entitled, upon the loss of it by the appellants, to recover its value, though he did not pay, or offer to pay, any increased rate in proportion to the value, no such payment having been required either at the time of delivery to the carman, or at any other time before the loss. The case of Hart *v.* Baxendale [1] decides that in such a case as the present, the person delivering the goods to the carrier must, in the first instance, declare their value, in order to fix the carrier with responsibility, and the carrier may then require him to pay an increased rate of charge, according to a tariff put up in the office; but there is nothing in the statute which protects him from liability, if, after the value is declared to be such as would entitle him to demand an increased rate of charge, he chooses to accept the goods to be carried without making any demand of such increased rate, or requiring it to be either paid or promised. The carrier is not bound to receive such goods for carriage without payment of such increased rate, if required; but if he choose to do so, and the value is declared, he will not be protected by the act."

SEC. 165. **Declaration, Effect of.** — The declaration which is necessitated by this act being a formal declaration, the person making it is to be held bound by it even when it will prejudice his interests. He had the opportunity of representing the facts accurately or inaccurately as he pleased, and it would be injustice to allow him to be advantaged by repudiating his misrepresentation. Thus, where horses, each of which was above the value of 10*l.*, were delivered to a railway company to be conveyed by them for hire, the owner previously to such delivery having signed a declaration that each of the horses was under the value of 10*l.*, and where, through the negligence of the company, the horses were injured, it was held, in an action against the company for the damage actually sustained, that the parties having agreed to act upon an assumed state of facts, both parties were bound by it, and the owner of the

[1] 6 Exch. 769; 16 Jur. 126.

horses was therefore concluded by his statement of their value.[1]

SEC. 166. **Meaning of the Word "Loss."** — Only one other point will require mention in connection with this act, and that refers to the conditions under which, in connection with the articles mentioned in the 1st section of the act, above the value of 10*l.* the carrier becomes an insurer, and is liable or not liable, for their loss or injury. This is only the case when the *loss* or injury can be referred to the *article* as occasioned by the carrier or by his servants, when the act does not amount to a felony,[2] not when it can be referred to the *owner*. Thus, PARKE, B., in the case of Hearn *v.* The London and South-Western Railway Company,[3] defined the term "loss," such as would give the owner of the goods a right to recover, "as 'loss' of a parcel by the carrier, such as the abstraction of it by a stranger, or by his own servant, not amounting to a felonious act, or by the carrier or his servants losing them from the vehicle when in the course of carriage, or by mislaying them, so that it was not known where to find them when they ought to be delivered." The word "loss," then, as used in the statute, is not held to include "loss" which is occasioned by the non-delivery or delay of the delivery by the carrier or his servant, not pecuniary loss to the owner, but to some *loss* incidental to the ordinary business of a common carrier for hire, by which the article has gone astray or is missing.

SEC. 167. **Effect of Statute. — Private Notices.** — All that the Carriers' Act (11 Geo. IV. and 1 Will. IV. c. 68) did was to

1 M'Cance *v.* London & North-Western Rail. Co., 3 H. & C. 343; 10 Jur. N. S. 1058; 12 W. R. 1086. With regard to the effect of fraud, concealment, or misrepresentation, see Riley *v.* Horne, 5 Bing. 217; Harris *v.* Packwood, 3 Taunt. 264; Bull. N. P. 71; Miles *v.* Cattle, 6 Bing. 743, *ut suprà*. See also Story on Bailm. §§ 565, 565*a*; and see American Express Co. *v.* Perkins, 42 Ill. 458. There is, however, no presumption of fraud to be founded on the silence of the person sending the goods. He is not bound to disclose the contents of any parcel or box sent by him. See judgment of PARKE, B., in Walker *v.* Jackson, 10 M. & W. 168; Brooke *v.* Pickwick, 4 Bing. 218; Sleat *v.* Fagg, 5 B. & Ald. 342; Batson *v.* Donovan, 4 B. & Ald. 21; Webb *v.* Page, 6 Man. & G. 196.

2 Hinton *v.* Dibbin, 2 Q. B. 646.

3 24 L. J. Exch. 180; 3 Cl. R. 597; 10 Exch. 793; 1 Jur. N. S. 236.

take away from the validity of public notices. It did not in any way affect the right that parties had to enter into special contracts, nor did it affect the validity of those contracts when they were entered into. The fact that a system of private notices had come into use, necessarily led to litigation on the question as to whether an owner of goods is bound by a private notice; whether it becomes the terms of a special contract when such notice has been delivered to him, or to his agent personally, before the acceptance of the goods by the carrier. The result of the decisions, to some of which we shall have immediate occasion to call the reader's attention, seems to be that the delivery of such a notice under such circumstances does not create a contract[1] between the parties, but that it is evidence from which a jury will be bound to infer the existence of a contract of a nature parallel to that of the notice.[2]

We have already had occasion to allude to the case of Walker *v.* York and North-Midland Railway Company,[3] which was an action against the said railway company for not duly carrying fish from Scarborough to Manchester. It was averred that the fish had been received at the former place, to be carried as common carriers by the defendant company to Manchester. The pleas were, that the company did not receive the fish as common carriers, and that they received them on certain terms set out in the plea. It appeared, on the trial, that the company printed many notices, declaring that they would not carry fish, except on terms relieving them of all liability, and declaring also that none of their servants had power to vary those terms. It was further proved that a parcel of those notices had been sent to Scarborough, and served on the fish-merchants there, and also that the plaintiff had told the company's station-master at Scarborough that they (meaning the notices) were not of any use. Subsequently, it appeared that fish had been sent by railway, and were not duly carried. Upon these facts, the judge left it to the jury to say, first, whether the notice

[1] Crouch *v.* London & North-Western Rail. Co., 2 Car. & Kir. 789.

[2] See Prentice *v.* Decker, 49 Barb. (N. Y.) 21; Limburger *v.* Westcott, 49 Barb. (N. Y.) 283; Belger *v.* Dinsmore, 51 Barb. (N. Y.) 69.

[3] *Ante*, p. 225; 2 El. & Bl. 750; 23 L. J. Q. B. 73.

had been served upon the plaintiff; secondly, whether a special contract existed between the plaintiff and the company, that the fish should be carried on the terms stated in the notice; and he directed them that if the plaintiff had been served with the notice, and afterwards sent the fish by the company's railway, they ought to infer an agreement, on the plaintiff's part, to such terms, unless there was shown an unambiguous refusal by the plaintiff to be bound, and an acquiescence in that refusal on the part of the company. It was held that this direction was right, under the circumstances, that 11 Geo. IV. and 1 Will. IV. c. 68, § 4, is confined to public notices, and that the jury might rightly infer, from the plaintiff having special notice, that the fish would not be taken, except on certain terms, and that no one had power to vary the terms, and from his afterwards persisting in sending his fish, that he assented to a special contract to carry on these terms, and the company was in that case protected by this special contract under section 6.[1]

SEC. 168. **Limitation of Liability by Private Notices.** — From the decision and judgment in this case, we gather that it is competent for carriers, notwithstanding the Carriers' Act, to limit their liability by any private notice given to the owner before the acceptance of the goods, so long as the owner does not repudiate the notice, and that the act refers only to public general notices which are stuck up in the offices of carriers, or otherwise publicly given. It struck at the root of the contracts, which had formerly been implied from the constructive knowledge of a public notice upon the part of the sender. It did not forbid any special contract which the parties might think proper to enter upon previous to the acceptance of the articles by the carrier. With regard to the means by which such a contract can be entered upon, there was guidance in various decisions of our courts, even before 1854, when the legislature passed an act which applies to two classes of carriers, *viz.*,

[1] 2 El. & Bl. 750; 18 Jur. 143; 23 L. J. Q. B. 73. See also as to the necessary knowledge of owner of goods, Belger *v.* Dinsmore, 51 Barb. (N. Y.) 69; Fillebrown *v.* Grand Trunk Rail. Co., 55 Me. 462; Perry *v.* Thompson, 98 Mass. 249.

railway companies and canal traffickers.[1] And as that act is confined to two classes of carriers, and does not refer to all common carriers, it will be necessary to consider those cases, as they have a direct bearing upon some of the practice connected with this subject at the present time. At the same time, there is cause for regret in the fact that the 17 & 18 Vict. c. 31 is limited in its application. There seems to be no compensatory advantage gained by this legislation for a class of a class, and there are evident disadvantages in a system of law-making which tends to individualize instead of to generalize. The more individualization there is in our laws, the more litigation there will be in our courts, and the more injustice there will be in the world. The whole object of legislation is the reverse of this. To make courts of law unnecessary is the function of a court of law. To unify this process is the function of a legislative assembly. Any such process as that which has been indicated above is necessarily retrograde and anomalous.

SEC. 169. **Special Contracts by Tickets or Notices.** — The cases, then, which were decided before the statute above referred to, show that a special contract limiting the responsibility of the carrier, and his liability for loss or damage, may be entered into by the delivery of a ticket, or written or printed notice, to the sender of the goods, containing a statement of the terms upon which he consents to carry; and that the acceptance of this notice by the owner of the goods, without express repudiation, will be evidence from which a jury ought to infer, or are justified in inferring, the existence of a contract in the terms of the notice.[2]

SEC. 170. **Subject Considered.** — It may at first sight seem rather hard upon the sender of goods that he, in whose favor the common law imposed upon those persons who held them-

[1] 17 & 18 Vict. c. 31.

[2] M'Manus *v.* Lancashire & Yorkshire Rail. Co., 28 L. J. Exch. 353, per ERLE, J. See also Baltimore, &c. R. R. Co. *v.* Skeels, 3 W. Va. 556; Adams Express Co. *v.* Haynes, 42 Ill. 89; Farnham *v.* Camden R. R. Co., 55 Penn. St. 53; Hopkins *v.* Westcott, 6 Blatchf. (U. S. C. C.) 64; Smith *v.* North Carolina R. R. Co., 64 N. C. 235.

selves out as carriers to the public the duty of carrying, should thus, as it were, be forced into agreeing to the limitation of that liability which has also been imposed by the common law. The reason why the first of these duties was imposed was evidently this, that no man ought, by a public profession, to be led to take his goods to a certain place, from whence he believes he can have them transmitted to the destination he designs for them, merely to be told that the carrier will not convey them. This would have been an injustice to the owner of the goods who had taken the trouble to have them conveyed to the carrier's office, and this injustice would have been caused by the public profession of the carrier. It was right, therefore, that a duty towards the public should be associated with a declaration of a trade, whether that declaration was made in words or by acts. And therefore it was that the common law said, a man who professes to carry for the public shall not refuse to carry for any individual. This of course presupposed a fair remuneration to the carrier. But now it would almost seem as if by this system of private notices carriers could defeat the object that the common law had in view by imposing this duty upon them. The means by which this might apparently be accomplished would be by offering to each owner of goods who brought them goods to be conveyed, a ticket limiting or entirely divesting themselves of all responsibility in connection with the transit of goods. In this way they avoid one of their common-law duties.

SEC. 171. **Repudiation by Owner.** — If the owner receives the ticket without distinctly repudiating it, he is held to have acquiesced in its terms. If he does repudiate it, the carrier must acquiesce in such repudiation, or the owner will be held bound by a special contract in the terms of the notice. If again he refuses to assent to the terms, and the carrier refuses to carry on any other, the owner has to remove his goods, and find some other carrier with whom he can make other terms. But in that case the carrier would have divested himself by means of the notice of the duty imposed on him by the common law, and the person who was anxious to have his goods transmitted would have suffered the injustice which has been spoken of above. But the law does give the public some remedy, although the question still arises whether, if the doctrine with regard to tickets and notices had not been carried so far as it has been, as we have explained above, and as we shall have occasion to illustrate below, the remedy might not have been more direct, and in every way better for the owner and sender of the goods. That remedy, as explained by PARKE, B., in Carr *v.* Lancashire and Yorkshire Railway,[1] is this. "If," he says, "it had been the intention of the plaintiff to make the defendants liable as common carriers, he ought to have rendered them a reasonable sum for the carriage of the chattel, and upon their refusal to carry, to bring an action against them for not carrying. Most certainly every common carrier is bound only to carry goods of that description which his public calling requires him to carry. This is established in the case of Johnson *v.* The Midland Railway Company." [2]

SEC. 172. **Owner's Remedy.** — The remedy, then, is an action for a breach of the duty of the carrier, if the goods which were tendered with a reasonable sum were such as the carrier, by the known facts of his ordinary business, has bound himself to carry. And in this place we say again, that the inconvenience of having to withdraw the goods, the trouble of finding another carrier, the delay which the person to whom the goods are sent has to suffer, and other circumstances, indicate that the system of tickets and notices, which has been carried to such an extreme in some of the cases which we are about to mention, and which has been, to a great extent, the cause of the limitation of the owner's remedy, may not be an unmitigated good.

SEC. 173. **A Private Notice, What constitutes.** — In one case, where the plaintiff was a veterinary surgeon and dealer in horses, residing at Wakefield, and the defendants, the Great Northern Railway Company, were common carriers by railway[3] for hire from (among other places) Kirkstead, in

[1] 7 Exch. 707; 7 Rail. Cas. 426; 17 Jur. 397; 21 L. J. 261 Exch.

[2] 4 Exch. 367.

[3] This case came before the Bail Court in the month of May, 1852.

Lincolnshire, to Wakefield, in Yorkshire, it appeared that the plaintiff, Morville, had, upon a certain day of August, brought a horse to the Kirkstead station of the Great Northern Railway Company, for the purpose of having it conveyed from thence by railway to Wakefield. After the horse had been placed in a horse-box attached to the down train from London, the plaintiff went into the company's office and paid the charge demanded for the carriage of the horse to Wakefield, and upon the payment being made he signed a memorandum or ticket, in a book kept by the company's clerk. It was to the following effect: "The Great Northern and Lincolnshire Railway Company. Ticket for horses, cattle, sheep, pigs, dogs, and live-stock of every description. — No. 17. Date, August 15, 1851. From Kirkstead to Wakefield, 1 horse, at 19*s.* & 6*d.* — Paid. This ticket is issued subject to the owner's undertaking to bear all the risk of injury by conveyance and other contingencies, and the owner is required to see to the efficiency of the carriage before he allows his horses or live-stock to be placed therein; the charge being for the use of the railway carriages and locomotive power only, the company will not be responsible for any alleged defects in their carriages or trucks unless complaint is made at the time of booking or before the same leave the station, nor for any damages, however caused, to horses, cattle, or live-stock of any description travelling upon their railway or in their vehicles. *I have examined the carriages, and am satisfied with their efficiency and safety.* (Signed) JOHN MORVILLE, Owner or on the owner's account."

A ticket or duplicate of that signed by the plaintiff, with the exception that the part printed in italics in the above was missed out, was handed to him by the clerk. When the train reached Knothingly, the horse-box containing the plaintiff's horse was detached from the London train and shunted upon the Wakefield line by the servants of the defendants, and in so doing a concussion took place between the horse-box and a truck or carriage on the latter line, which caused an injury to the horse. In this case it was held that there was a special contract between the parties which was valid under 11 Geo.

IV. and 1 Will. IV. c. 68, § 6, and that the ticket was not a mere public notice, in which case it would no longer, under section 4 of the said act, be of any avail. And it was therefore held that the terms of the contract protected the company from liability in respect of injury to the horse.[1] In the course of the above case, two other cases were mentioned which deserve some attention in this place. In the first of these the declaration alleged that the defendants were proprietors of a railway and carriages for the conveyance of passengers, cattle, &c., for hire; that the plaintiff delivered to and that they received horses from the plaintiff to be carried for the plaintiff in their carriages for reward, and that one of the wheels of a carriage in which some of the horses were being conveyed caught fire from friction; that the plaintiff at the first station requested the defendants to change the carriage and not to persist in further conveying his horses in the same; that in spite of such request they did so persist; that the wheel afterwards, from want of precaution against friction and not otherwise, was snapped asunder, whereby the carriage was thrown off the rails and the horses were injured. It appeared that the plaintiff, at the time of agreeing for the carriage of the horses, was informed by the station-master that he would have to run all risk of carriage, to which he assented; and he also signed a ticket in the ticket-book of the company, which contained a memorandum that the owner of the horses was to be required to see to the efficiency of the carriages, that the company was not to be responsible for any alleged defects in their carriages or trucks, unless complaint was made at the time of booking or before leaving the station, nor for any damage, however caused, to the horses or live-stock travelling upon the railway.

SEC. 174. **Special Terms in Memorandum Part of Contract.** — Here it was held that the special terms of the memorandum disproved the bailment alleged in the declaration which was material to the breach, and therefore that the defendants were entitled to the verdict upon the above plea. In dis-

[1] Great Northern Rail. Co. *v.* Morville, 7 Rail. Cas. 830; 21 L. J. Q. B. 319; 16 Jur. 528.

charging the rule, WIGHTMAN, J., said: "The allegation is framed either upon contract or upon the duty arising out of the defendants' character as common carriers. If the latter, it has been disproved by the special terms upon which the horses were received. If upon contract, then the evidence shows that the horses were received by the defendants upon very different terms. Then it is said that the whole allegation of the delivery and acceptance is immaterial, or that the breach makes it so. But it is quite possible to reject the allegation consistently with the breach. The breach states 'being conveyed as aforesaid,' and therefore that which is alleged as the ground of the liability cannot be rejected." [1]

In the other case the plaintiff, being the owner of a horse, delivered it to the defendants, a railway company, to be carried on their railway subject to conditions which stated that the owners undertook all risks of conveyance whatsoever, as the company would not be responsible for any injury or damage, howsoever caused, occurring to live-stock of any description travelling on the railway. The horse having been injured by the horse-box being propelled against some trucks through the gross negligence of the company, it was held that the company under the terms of the contract were not liable for the injury.[2] But in this country, in a great majority of the States, while the carrier may, by special contract, limit his liability as an insurer, as for loss of the goods by fire, and other casualties which do not result from his negligence, yet it is held that he cannot restrict his liability so as to excuse himself from loss or damage resulting from the negligence of his servants or agents.[3] In New York, however, it is held

[1] Austin v. Manchester, Sheffield, & Lincolnshire Rail. Co., 20 L. J. Q. B. 440; 16 Q. B. 600; 15 Jur. 670; Hawkins v. Great Western R. R. Co., 17 Mich. 57; Illinois, &c. R. R. Co. v. Adams, 42 Ill. 474.

[2] Austin v. Manchester, Sheffield, & Lincolnshire Rail. Co., 10 C. B. 454; 7 Rail. Cas. 300; 16 Jur. 763; 21 L. J. C. P. 179.

[3] Ohio, &c. R. R. Co. v. Selby, 47 Ind. 471; Berry v. Cooper, 28 Ga. 543; Reno v. Hogan, 12 B. Mon. (Ky.) 63; Pennsylvania R. R. Co. v. Butler, 57 Penn. St. 335; Ashmore v. Pennsylvania R. R. Co., 28 N. J. L. 180; Southern Express Co. v. Moon, 39 Miss. 822; Hoadley v. Northern Transportation Co., 115 Mass. 304; Perry v. Thompson, 98 Mass. 249;

that the carrier may, by an explicit special contract, limit his liability against loss or damage resulting even from the gross or wilful negligence of his agents or servants.[1] But in most of the States, while the carrier may impose reasonable limitations upon his liability, he cannot by any provision, however explicit or direct, screen himself from liability for loss or injury resulting from his own or his servants' negligence.[2]

SEC. 175. **Constructive Knowledge.** — The constructive knowledge which, previous to the Carriers' Act,[3] was sufficient to make the provisions of a public notice binding upon a sender of goods, is under the present system sufficient to bind a man in a contract with terms similar to those of a notice, if the notice has been delivered to him at the time that the goods were accepted for conveyance. It is not necessary in such a case that the statement made in the notice or ticket should be read over to the sender of the goods, in order that he may be held constructively to know what its contents

Judson *v.* Western R. R. Co., 6 Allen (Mass.), 486; Pemberton County *v.* New York Central R. R. Co., 104 Mass. 144; Grace *v.* Adams, 100 Mass. 505; Medfield School District *v.* Boston, &c. R. R. Co., 102 Mass. 552; New Orleans, &c. R. R. Co. *v.* Faler, 58 Miss. 511; Shriver *v.* Sioux City, &c. R. R. Co., 24 Minn. 506; Louisville, &c. R. R. Co. *v.* Brownlee, 14 Bush (Ky.), 590; Chicago, &c. R. R. Co. *v.* Hale, 2 Ill. App. 150; Kansas Pacific R. R. Co. *v.* Reynolds, 17 Kan. 251; United States Express Co. *v.* Bachman, 28 Ohio St. 144; Clark *v.* St. Louis, &c. R. R. Co., 64 Mo. 440; Camp *v.* Hartford, &c. Steamboat Co., 43 Conn. 333; Bank of Kentucky *v.* Adams Express Co., 93 U. S. 174; American Express Co. *v.* Shier, 55 Penn. St. 140; Southern, &c. R. R. Co. *v.* Henlim, 52 Ala. 606; Nashville, &c. R. R. Co. *v.* Johnson, 6 Heisk. (Tenn.) 271.

[1] Maguin *v.* Dinsmore, 56 N. Y. 168; Westcott *v.* Fargo, 61 N. Y. 542; Poucher *v.* New York Central R. R. Co., 49 N. Y. 263; Spinotti *v.* Atlas Steamship Co., 81 N. Y. 71; 36 Am. Rep. 579; Bissell *v.* New York Central R. R. Co., 25 N. Y. 442; Baltimore, &c. R. R. Co. *v.* Rathbone, 1 W. Va. 87.

[2] Pennsylvania R. R. Co. *v.* Butler, 57 Penn. St. 335; Pennsylvania R. R. Co. *v.* McClosky, 23 Penn. St. 536; Farnham *v.* Camden, &c. R. R. Co., 55 Penn. St. 53; American Express Co. *v.* Sands, 55 Penn. St. 53; Evansville, &c. R. R. Co. *v.* Young, 28 Ind. 516; Seller *v.* Pacific, &c. R. R. Co., 1 Oregon, 409; Kallman *v.* United States Express Co., 3 Kan. 205; Davidson *v.* Graham, 2 Ohio St. 131; Southern Express Co. *v.* Moon, 39 Miss. 822; Ashmore *v.* Pennsylvania, &c. R. R. Co., 28 N. J. L. 180; Stedman *v.* Western Transportation Co., 48 Barb. (N. Y.) 97; Dorr *v.* New Jersey Steam Navigation Co., 4 Sandf. (N. Y.) 97.

[3] 11 Geo. IV. and 1 Will. IV. c. 68.

are.[1] In all such cases there is a greater or less amount of constructive knowledge. Even were such a notice read over to the owner of the goods there could be no certainty that he had a knowledge of the provisions. Even if reading over was thought necessary before such a notice was held to be binding, fault might be found with this rule on the ground that in some cases explanation was an absolute necessity.

SEC. 176. **Doctrine of Rules.** — But the doctrine of rules is that they do minor injustices with a view to the maximum of justice. And so, in deciding that the mere delivery of the ticket affects the owner with constructive knowledge, the doctrine may have been decided in consonance with the weight of expediency. One thing may be said with regard to this rule, and that is that any person of ordinary prudence, who was sending goods by means of a carrier, upon being presented with a notice or ticket would make a point of becoming cognizant of its contents. The case of the York, Newcastle, and Berwick Railway Company *v.* Crisp[2] is instructive in this connection. The facts as stated by the witnesses were these: That the respondents were partners as cattle jobbers, and the appellants were common carriers by railway from Alnwick to Newcastle. That upon a certain day the respondent brought some sheep and pigs to Alnwick, one of the stations on the appellants' railway, with the view of having them conveyed to Newcastle. Further, that he engaged trucks for the conveyance of his live-stock, and paid for their hire. That a certain ticket was given to him which contained terms exonerating the railway company from liability in case of injury to the animals, or delay in the delivery. There was proved to have been considerable delay before the stock was despatched from Alnwick, owing to the fact that no trucks were there, by means of which they could be forwarded. Owing to this delay the cattle were too late for the Newcastle market, with a view to which they had been destined by the owner, and were also injured by reason of the long time which they had

[1] Slim *v.* Great Northern Rail. Co., 14 C. B. 647; 8 Jur. 1119; 23 L. J. C. P. 166.

[2] 14 C. B. 527; 2 C. L. R. 1357; 18 Jur. 606; 23 L. J. C. P. 125.

been without food. It was further admitted by the witnesses for the appellants that no duplicate of the ticket was given, that it was not read to the respondent, nor was his attention called to the contents or meaning. The county court judge of Northumberland had declined to non-suit the plaintiffs, and left it to the jury to say whether the railway company were common carriers of cattle for hire, and whether they received the plaintiff's cattle for carriage as common carriers for hire, or whether they received them under a special contract on the terms contained in the ticket. This was held to be a misdirection, JERVIS, C. J., remarking: "I do not see that there was any evidence that the railway company were common carriers of cattle, or that they were bound to carry these animals. The only evidence is, that they took cattle upon a special contract, or that they offered to take them upon special terms, which were accepted. The judge ought to have told the jury that there was either a special contract, or no contract at all." [1]

SEC. 177. **Reconciliation of Cases.** — The decision in this case seems to have been misunderstood by some of our text-book writers.[2] They seem to have regarded the last sentence of the Chief Justice's judgment as a general rule applicable to all cases in which a ticket was presented to the sender of goods. If that were the case, the rule with regard to the effect of private notices would be much wider than it has been stated to be.[3] If such were the case the presentation of the private notice would create the special contract. As the law stands, however, it seems to us that the presentation and acceptance of a private notice limiting a carrier's responsibility, leaves the question as to whether the acceptance of, or acquiescence in the terms contained in it, constitutes a binding special contract in so far as the sender of the goods is concerned, a question of evidence for the jury.[4] And it seems evident to us that the last sentence of the judgment quoted

[1] Cleveland, &c. R. R. Co. *v.* Perkins, 17 Mich. 296.

[2] See Powell on Carriers, 2d ed., p. 107.

[3] *Ante*, p. 192.

[4] Walker *v.* York & Midland Rail. Co., 2 El. & Bl. 750. See *ante*, p. 193.

above is to be taken in conjunction with the first part of it. There the Chief Justice said that there was no evidence that the railway company were common carriers of cattle. It is evidently necessary, before you can establish the fact of a carrier's duty to carry a particular class of goods, to prove that he was a common carrier of such articles. If you take a cow to a man who only carries letters, no duty arises upon his part out of your act. In such a case, then, if a man carries the cow, it is quite evident that there must be a special contract, or no contract at all. And so in the absence of all proof that the railway company were in the habit of acting as common carriers of cattle, the only question that can be left for the jury to answer is that which was in this case indicated by the Chief Justice. If the railway company were not common carriers of live-stock, they could only have carried under some special contract, and the plaintiff was either bound by that contract, or if he had signed the ticket, not knowing its contents, or believing it to contain only an undertaking to pay, he might reasonably be held to have entered into no contract at all, because the parties to the contract were not, under those circumstances, *ad idem*. There is, therefore, no difficulty in reconciling these two cases; the difficulty arose out of the misunderstanding of one of them.

SEC. 178. **Rule in Shaw v. York, &c. Railway Co.** — The case of Shaw *v.* York and North Midland Railway Company [1] bears upon this subject. The declaration averred that the defendants, who were proprietors of a railway and carriages for the conveyance of passengers, cattle, and goods, received nine horses of the plaintiff to be safely and securely carried in their carriages by the railway for hire. It also asserted that it was thereupon the duty of the defendants safely and securely to carry and convey and deliver the horses. It also averred the loss of one of the horses through the insufficiency of one of the carriages. It appeared, however, that a ticket had been delivered to the plaintiff at the time the horses were received. This ticket was in the nature

[1] 6 Rail. Cas. 87; 13 Q. B. 347; 13 Jur. 385; 18 L. J. Q. B. 181.

of a receipt, but it had at the bottom the following memorandum: "N. B. This ticket is issued subject to the owner's undertaking all risks of conveyance whatsoever, as the company will not be responsible for any injury or damage, however caused, occurring to horses or carriages while travelling, or in loading or unloading."

Before the plaintiff received this ticket at the York Station he had been shown three horse-boxes and had objected to one of them, and one of the defendants' servants had attempted to remedy the defect and had assured the plaintiff that the box was quite safe. On the journey it was discovered that one of the plaintiff's horses was dead. It had fallen owing to the defective partition, which the company's servant had attempted to repair, and had been killed. In this case it was held, as we should have expected, that the duty alleged in the declaration of the plaintiff did not arise, and that the terms contained in the ticket formed part of the contract for the carriage of the horses. In ruling, the court said: "It may be that, notwithstanding the terms of the contract, the plaintiff might have alleged that it was the duty of the defendants to have furnished proper and sufficient carriages, and that the loss happened from a breach of that duty; but the plaintiff has not so declared, but has alleged a duty which does not arise upon the contract as it appeared in evidence."[1]

SEC. 179. **Carrier's Duty, how laid aside.** — It seems to us most important to bear this fact in mind. The suggestion of LORD DENMAN, in that case, shows that the law is jealous of the duty of a common carrier, and will not allow him to divest himself of it without express words indicative of an agreement to that effect. The imposition of this duty is not a light thing, and has been sanctioned by the accumulated wisdom of many years. It is therefore not to be shuffled off, but is only to be laid aside under circumstances which import a clear agreement upon the part of the other party to the contract that the common carrier should be divested of his character

[1] See Great Western R. R. Co. v. Hawkins, 18 Mich. 427; McDaniel v. Chicago, &c. R. R. Co., 24 Iowa, 412.

of common carrier and become a private carrier for hire.[1] Where, therefore, the terms of the contract are express and cover the question of negligence, they will protect the carrier from liability for losses or injuries which are clearly due to his want of care.[2] There is no hardship in this in so far as the owner is concerned. If he chooses to intrust goods to carriers who will not be responsible for loss, and who protect themselves from the liability for losses to others which may be due to their carelessness, he cannot complain of hardship if he loses his goods. It is a man's duty to employ such persons as he can trust; if he feels unwilling to repose a trust in them prudence would advise him to exact a guarantee, and if they will not give such an assurance of care he is not bound to employ them. The law cannot make a man prudent. All it can do is to protect prudence when it does exist. In the last-cited case the injury was found to have been occasioned by the gross negligence of the defendants in managing their trains, but, as we have seen, the terms of the notice were held binding against the plaintiff and therefore protected the defendants. The question, as ALDERSON, B., remarked, is, what are the terms upon which the defendants undertook to carry the goods? "It is clear," he went on to say, "that they were such as the defendants might make. It is plain to me that they undertook to carry the horse at the risk of the plaintiff. The words are, 'the owner undertaking all risk of conveyance whatsoever.' Now, under these terms, a question might be raised whether the injury contemplated was such as must issue in injury to the thing conveyed; so that a doubt might arise whether the case of the horse being stolen was contemplated, as under such circumstances the accident would not issue in

[1] Chippendale v. Lancashire & Yorkshire Rail. Co., 7 Rail. Cas. 824; 15 Jur. 1106; Hughes v. Great Western Rail. Co., 14 C. B. 637; 2 C. L. R. 1360; 18 Jur. 1001; 23 L. J. C. P. 153; Great Western Rail. Co. v. Goodman, 12 C. B. 313; 21 L. J. 197 C. P.; White v. Great Western Rail. Co., 2 C. B. N. S. 7; 26 L. J. 158 C. P.; Phillips v. Edwards, 28 L. J. 52 Exch.; M'Andrews v. Electric Telegraph Co., 17 C. B. 3; 25 L. J. C. P. 26; Streeter v. Horlock, 7 Moore, 287, per PARK, J.

[2] Carr v. Lancashire & Yorkshire Rail. Co., 7 Exch. 707; 7 Rail. Cas. 426; 17 Jur. 397; 21 L. J. Exch. 261.

damage to the horse. . . . The result is that, if there has been gross negligence upon the part of the defendants, they are protected against liability by virtue of the words of the contract." [1]

SEC. 180. **Interpretation of Private Notices.** — This judgment shows that the private notice will be interpreted strictly as against the carrier, as the learned judge seemed to imagine that the notice, which asserted that the company would not be liable for "any injury or damage (however caused)," would not protect them against a liability for a loss of the horse by its being stolen.

In the same case, PLATT, B., seemed to regard the interpretation there given to the notice as too lax, in so far as the defendants were concerned, and expressed his opinion that the owner of the horse never dreamed that the ticket absolved the company of all liability for damage when he signed it. The principle of the decision is, however, as it has been stated above. This principle will be further illustrated when we come to speak of the carriers of passengers.[2]

SEC. 181. **Carriers' Act protects Carriers who carry by Special Contract.** — Another point of importance is to be

[1] But see, per BEST, C. J., in Newborn *v.* Just, 2 Car. & P. 76, and per LORD ELLENBOROUGH, Lyon *v.* Mells, 5 East, 428; and see the American cases noted below. It is now certain that no notice or contract will discharge a common carrier from liability for negligence, misfeasance, or ordinary want of care. New Jersey Steam Nav. Co. *v.* Merchants' Bank, 6 How. (U. S.) 340; York Company *v.* Central R. R., 3 Wall. (U. S.) 107; Mobile, &c. R. R. Co. *v.* Jarboe, 41 Ala. 644; Montgomery, &c. R. R. Co. *v.* Edmonds, 41 Ala. 667; New Orleans, &c. Ins. Co. *v.* New Orleans, &c. R. R. Co., 20 La. Ann. 202; Farnham *v.* Camden, &c. R. R. Co., 55 Penn St. 53; American Express Co. *v.* Sands, 55 Penn. St. 140; Stedman *v.* Western Transportation Co., 48 Barb. (N. Y.) 97; Evansville, &c. R. R. Co. *v.* Young, 28 Ind. 516.

[2] See Great Northern Rail. Co. *v.* Hawcroft, 21 L. J. 178 Q. B.; Denton *v.* Great Northern Rail. Co., 5 El. & Bl. 860; 25 L. J. 129 Q. B.; cf. Warlow *v.* Harrison, 29 L. J., 14 Q. B. In the case of Winkfield *v.* Packington, 2 C. & P. 600, LORD TENTERDEN said: "If a person goes to the office of a carrier and asks what a thing will be done for, and he is told by a clerk or servant who is transacting the business there that it can be done for a certain sum, the master can charge no more." The point seemed to be that the goods were sent on the faith of what the clerk said, and his not being authorized to make charges or statements of the kind was immaterial.

noticed in relation to special contracts, and that is the fact that the carrier, who enters into such a contract for the carriage of goods, does not lose the protection of the 1st section of the Carriers' Act,[1] except in so far as the contract he has entered into is inconsistent with the goods being received by him in the character of a carrier.[2] For example, if a carrier receives goods upon the special contract that he shall not be liable in case of their injury, damage, or loss, that he is not to be held accountable for any delay in their delivery, in such a case he evidently does not receive the goods as a carrier, and the act cannot be held to apply to him. And from the same case it is to be gathered, as KELLY, C. B., remarked, "that section 6 applies only to contracts, the terms of which are inconsistent with the exemption claimed by the carriers under section 1."[3]

SEC. 182. **Distinction between Classes of Carriers.** — As we have seen, the law which refers to special contracts, as entered into by common carriers, is not the same for all classes of those who carry on this trade. We have seen that the method in which contracts of such a nature shall be entered into by railway and canal companies has been determined by legislative enactment, while the rules which apply to the contracts of carriers, other than those just mentioned, have to be gathered from the cases which we have just been considering.

SEC. 183. **Modification of these Rules.** — It seems expedient, therefore, to consider in this place in what way the "Railway and Canal Traffic Act, 1854,"[4] modified the general rules as laid down prior to that year, in so far as railway and canal traffic is concerned. The preamble of that act recited the expediency of making better provisions for regulating the traffic on railways and canals; and in its 7th section, with

[1] 11 Geo. IV. and 1 Will. IV. c. 68.

[2] Baxendale v. Great Eastern Rail. Co., 10 B. & S. 212 Exch. Ch.

[3] See further with regard to the question of special contracts, Martin v. Great Indian Peninsula Rail. Co., 37 L. J. Exch. 27; 3 L. R. Exch. 9; and some cases decided in the Courts of Ireland. Alexander v Malcomson, 2 Ir. R. C. L. 621; affirmed, 3 Ir. R. C. L. 578; 20 L. T. N. S. 930, Exch. Ch.; M'Court v. London & North-Western Rail. Co., 3 Ir. R. C. C. L. 107 Q. B.; affirmed, 3 Ir. R. C. L. 462 Exch. Cham.

[4] 17 & 18 Vict. c. 31.

which we, in this place, have more particularly to do, enacted that a railway or canal company "shall be liable for the loss of, or for any injury done to any horses, cattle, or other animals, or to any articles, goods, or things, in the receiving, forwarding, or delivering thereof, occasioned by the neglect or default of such company, or its servants, notwithstanding any notice, condition, or declaration made and given by such company thereto or in any wise limiting such liability, and every such notice, condition, or declaration is hereby declared to be null and void."

SEC. 184. **Reasonable Conditions.** — It provides, however, in the first place, that nothing contained in the act "shall be construed to prevent the said companies from making such conditions, with respect to the receiving, forwarding, and delivering of any of the said animals, articles, goods, or things, as shall be adjudged by the court or judge, before whom any question relating thereto shall be tried, to be just and reasonable."[1]

SEC. 185. **Amount Recoverable.** — It provides, in the second place, "that no greater damages shall be recovered for the loss of or for any injury done to any of such animals beyond the sums hereinafter mentioned (that is to say), for any horse, 50*l.*; for any neat cattle, per head, 15*l.*; for any sheep or pigs, per head, 2*l.*; unless the person sending or delivering the same to such company shall, at the time of such delivery, have declared them to be respectively of higher value than as above mentioned; in which case it shall be lawful for such company to demand and receive, by way of compensation for the increased risk and care thereby occasioned, a reasonable percentage upon the excess of the value so declared, above the respective sums so limited, as aforesaid, and which shall be paid in addition to the ordinary rate of charge, and such percentage or increased rate of charge shall be notified in the manner prescribed in 11 Geo. IV. and 1 Will. IV. c. 68, and shall be binding upon such company in the manner therein mentioned."

[1] See Adams Express Co. *v.* Reagan, 29 Ind. 21.

SEC. 186. **Proof of Value. — Contract to be signed.** — It provides, in the third place, "that the proof of the value of such animals, articles, goods, and things, and the amount of the injury done thereto, shall in all cases lie upon the person claiming compensation for such loss or injury." And it provides, in the fourth place, "that no special contract between such company and any other parties respecting the receiving, forwarding, or delivering of any animals, articles, goods, or things, as aforesaid, shall be binding upon, or affect any such party, unless the same be signed by him, or by the party delivering such animals, articles, goods, or things respectively for carriage;" and, lastly, it is provided that nothing contained in that act "shall alter or affect the rights, privileges, or liabilities of any such company, under 11 Geo. IV. and 1 Will. IV. c. 68, with respect to articles of the descriptions mentioned in the said act."[1]

SEC. 187. **Railway and Canal Carriers can still make Special Contracts.** — In a case decided in 1856, the provisions above alluded to came under the consideration of the Court of Common Pleas.[2] And it was held that while the 7th section of the Railway and Canal Traffic Act makes notices by railway and canal companies which limit their liability void, it does not prevent them from entering into special contracts for the carriage of goods, provided the conditions contained in such contracts are such as are held reasonable by the judge or court before whom any question relating thereto is tried, and provided the contract is signed by the party delivering the goods to be carried.[3] Some light was thrown upon this section of this act by another case, to which it will be well to refer. There it was shown that all the provisions of the 7th section of the 17 & 18 Vict. c. 31, must be read together, and that the limitations which under that section a carrier is entitled to make by contract of his liability must not only be just and reasonable, but must also be embodied in a special

[1] See American Session Laws, 1855, p. 173.

[2] Simons *v.* Great Western Rail. Co., 18 C. B. 805; 26 L. J. C. P. 25.

[3] See McMillan *v.* Michigan Southern, &c. R. R. Co., 16 Mich. 79.

contract in writing, signed by the owner or sender of the goods. As there were other points, the decision of which bore upon the provisions of the statute under consideration, it may be well to enter somewhat fully into the circumstances of the case.

SEC. 188. **Act Construed.** — It was an appeal to the House of Lords from a judgment of the Court of Exchequer Chamber, which had reversed a decision of the Court of Queen's Bench, in an action in which the appellant (Peek) was plaintiff, and the respondents (the North Staffordshire Railway Company) were defendants.[1] The appellant's agent was in the habit of sending goods by the respondents' railway, and had received printed notices from them, stating that the company would receive, forward, and deliver goods solely subject to the conditions thereunder stated; and among the conditions thereunder stated, was a condition that the company should not be responsible for the loss of, or injury to any marbles, unless declared and insured according to their value. The agent, being directed to do so by the appellant, sent certain marbles to one of the company's stations, and instructed the carter to inquire what the insurance would be, who was told by the clerk of the company that he did not know, unless the value of the goods was stated. Some correspondence ensued as to the rates of insurance for marbles, and the agent was informed verbally what the respondents' charge for the carriage of the marbles would be at the insured rate, and what at the uninsured rate. The agent subsequently by letter instructed the company to forward the marbles "not insured." He had, before he wrote the letter instructing the company to forward the marbles as directed, again received a notice from the respondents, stating that they would receive, forward, and deliver goods subject to the condition (amongst others) that they would not be responsible for loss of, or injury to any marbles unless declared and insured according to their value. The marbles were forwarded as directed, and when delivered were found to be damaged by exposure to rain. In an action

[1] Peek v. North Staffordshire Rail. Co., 10 H. L. Cas. 473; 9 Jur. N. S. 1023; 8 L. T. N. S. 768. 914; 32 L. J. Q. B. 241; 11 W. R.

for the damage thus caused, brought by the appellant against the company as common carriers under the 7th section of the Railway and Canal Traffic Act,[1] the company pleaded that the marbles were delivered to be carried by them subject to a certain special contract, whereby it was agreed that they should not be responsible for loss of, or injury to, marbles, unless declared and insured according to their value, and that the same were not, nor was any part thereof, so declared or insured. The company also pleaded that the marbles were delivered and received on the above condition, and that such condition made by the respondents, and assented to by the appellant, was a just and reasonable condition. The Court of Exchequer Chamber (reversing the decision of the Queen's Bench) directed that the defendants were entitled to a verdict on these pleas. In the House of Lords the following questions were put to the judges, and were answered by BLACKBURN, WILLES, CROMPTON, JJ., MARTIN, B., WILLIAMS, J., the Lord Chief Baron, and the Lord Chief Justice:[2] —

SEC. 189. **Reasonable Condition.** — First. Is the condition that the company should not be responsible for injury to the goods (that is, the marbles) unless the same were declared or insured to their value, a just and reasonable decision, within the true intent and meaning of the 17 & 18 Vict. c. 31, § 7?

Secondly. Is the plaintiff entitled to have the verdict entered for him upon the fourth plea (the first of those quoted above)?

Thirdly. Is the plaintiff entitled to have the verdict entered for him upon the fifth plea (the second of those quoted above)?

SEC. 190. **Effect of Notice. — Special Contract must be signed. — Unjust and Unreasonable Condition.** — The House of Lords reversed the decision of the Exchequer Chamber, and affirmed the judgment of the Queen's Bench, holding that no general notice given by a railway company is valid in law for the purpose of limiting the common-law liability of carriers, but that such liability may be limited by such conditions as the

[1] 17 & 18 Vict. c. 31.

[2] These answers are worthy of careful perusal.

court or judge shall determine to be just and reasonable, and that such conditions must be embodied in a special contract, signed by the owner or person delivering the goods. In this case, therefore, the condition, as stated above, was not just or reasonable. The Lord Chancellor (WESTBURY), in referring to this point, said: "If the present condition were introduced in a contract between the company and the owner of the goods delivered to be carried by that company, the necessary effect of such a contract would be, that it would exempt the company from responsibility for injury, however caused, including, therefore, gross negligence, and even fraud and dishonesty on the part of the servants of the company, for the condition was expressed without any limitation or exception. I am, therefore, in the first place, clearly of opinion that the condition insisted upon by the company, even if it had been duly embodied in a special contract between the parties to this appeal, is a condition which it would be the duty of a court or judge to hold to be neither just nor reasonable."

SEC. 191. **Such Contract, What is.** — In considering the other point, as to whether the letter from the appellant's agent to the respondent company, requesting them to forward the marbles to London, "not insured, as directed," constituted a special contract, embodied in writing, and signed by the owner or the person delivering the goods, his lordship said: "It is insisted by the company that that requisition of the statute is answered and fulfilled by the letter of the 1st August, 1857, and it is contended by the company that the words 'not insured' do refer to and incorporate the condition. I am clearly of opinion that there is no foundation for that condition on their part, and I am also of opinion that it is not competent, by any description of parol evidence, so to interpret the words 'not insured' as to embody or incorporate the condition itself into the letter, and thereby make it a special contract in writing. Such special contract in writing, signed by the party delivering the goods, must itself, either in terms or by distinct reference, set out or embody the condition. But I am of opinion that those words 'not insured' do not refer to the written condition, or afford any ground upon which the written condition can be regarded as incorporated with the letter. In order to embody in the letter any other document, or memorandum, or instrument in writing, so as to make it part of a special contract contained in that letter, the letter must either set out the writing referred to, or so clearly and definitely refer to the writing, that by force of the reference the writing itself becomes part of the instrument it refers to."[1]

SEC. 192. **Reasonable Conditions.** — In the case of Aldridge *v.* The Great Western Railway Company,[2] the decision of which was suspended until the publication of the judgment of the House of Lords in the case just referred to,[3] a person of the name of Smith, a general carrier, had signed for the plaintiff a printed contract, containing, amongst other conditions, the following: 1. The company will not be answerable for the loss or detention of, or damage to, wrappers or packages of any description, charged by the company as empties; 2. Nor in respect of goods destined for places beyond the limits of the company's railway; and, as respects the company, their responsibility will cease when such goods shall have been delivered for further conveyance. Any money which may be received by the company as payment for the conveyance of goods beyond their own limits, will be so received only for the convenience of the consignors, and for the purpose of being paid to the other carrier. This was an action against the defendants as carriers. It appeared that certain goods, consisting of empty packages, which had already traversed the line of railway of the defendants, were sent back, and for the return carriage of which, when empty, it was the custom not to make any further charge. It also appeared that the packages were, at the time the printed contract, already referred to, was signed, delivered to the defendants at a station on their line of railway; that the packages were addressed to a station on another line of railway, to which station the defendants were not carriers; that

[1] LORD CHELMSFORD dissented from the opinions expressed by the LORD CHANCELLOR and LORDS WENSLEYDALE and CRANWORTH throughout.

[2] 15 C. B. N. S. 588; 33 L. J. C. P. 161.

[3] Peek *v.* North Staffordshire Rail. Co., 10 H. L. Cas. 473.

the goods were safely carried by the defendants to the termination of their own line of railway, and that they were there delivered to another company. It further appeared that subsequent to such delivery the packages were lost.

SEC. 193. **Questions Raised. — Unreasonable Condition.** — The questions for decision in this case were three: 1. Was the first condition quoted above just and reasonable? 2. Was the second condition above quoted just and reasonable? 3. Was the special contract in this case duly signed? The first condition was held to be unreasonable, and upon sufficient grounds. The company was not conveying the packages for nothing. A charge had actually been made for the return carriage of empty packages at the time they were despatched full. That empty packages were returned free of charge was one of the inducements held out to the public to send full packages by means of that mode of conveyance. The expense of the return was evidently covered by the amount paid for the journey out.[1]

SEC. 194. **Signature of Agent.** — The second condition was held to be reasonable and legal. It, therefore, protected the defendants in this case. The company had no control, could exercise no care, and received no compensation for the transit of the goods upon the line beyond the limits of their own railway. There was, therefore, nothing unreasonable or unjust in refusing to be liable for a loss occurring, which they had no means of preventing, and occurring during a part of the transit for which they received no remuneration.[2] The third question was decided in the affirmative. The man Smith, who signed the contract in the name of the plaintiff, was a carrier employed both by the plaintiff and by the defendants. There was no reason why his signature should not bind the plaintiff. The suggestion that he was employed by both was not a good reason. The fact was, he was employed by the plaintiff, and

[1] Pierce *v.* Milwaukee, 23 Wis. 387.

[2] As to the American law as to through traffic on connecting routes, see Manhattan Oil Co. *v.* Camden R. R. Co., 52 Barb. (N. Y.) 72; Salinger *v.* Simmons, 8 Abb. (N. Y.) Pr. N. S. 409; Gass *v.* New York, &c. R. R. Co., 99 Mass. 220; Lamb *v.* Camden, &c. R. R. Co., 2 Daly (N. Y.), 454.

in general the signature of a common agent binds either party. This has been over and over again decided both on the construction of the 4th and 17th sections of the Statute of Frauds.[1]

SEC. 195. **Special Contracts must be Reasonable.** — Another case decided that the 7th section of this act, which makes void all notices, conditions, and declarations, made or given by a railway or canal company limiting their liability, unless such as the court or judge trying the cause may adjudge to be just or reasonable, extends to the case of a special contract signed in conformity with the subsequent provision in the same section.[2] In that case the plaintiff brought three horses to the cattle station of the Lancashire and Yorkshire Railway Company, at Liverpool, for conveyance by cattle truck to York. The defendants' servants provided a truck for the purpose, which, to all external appearance, and so far as the servant knew, was sufficient for the purpose. The plaintiff signed a ticket which contained the following memorandum: "This ticket is issued subject to the owners undertaking all risk of conveyance, loading, and unloading, whatsoever; as the company will not be responsible for any injury or damage (however caused) occurring to live-stock of any description travelling upon the railway or in their vehicles." The truck proved to be insufficient for the carriage of the horses. A hole was made in it on the journey, and the horses were injured. It was held by the Court of Exchequer Chamber, reversing the decision of the Court of Exchequer, first, that the condition that the company "would not be responsible for any injury or damage howsoever caused" was not just and reasonable and therefore void; secondly, that it did not protect the defendants from liability in respect of the defect in the truck.[3]

SEC. 196. **As to signing Contract.** — A case in which a

[1] See cases collected in Sugden's Vendors and Purchasers, 14th ed., p. 147. See also, as to the binding effect of an agent's signature, Kirby *v.* Great Western Rail. Co., 18 L. T. N. S. 658.

[2] M'Manus *v.* Lancashire & Yorkshire Rail. Co., 4 H. & N. 327; 5 Jur. 651; 28 L. J. Exch. 353; 33 L. T. 259 Exch. Ch.

[3] East Tennessee R. R. *v.* Whittle, 27 Ga. 535. See also Welsh *v.* Pittsburg R. R., 10 Ohio St. 65.

plaintiff delivered to a railway company goods which he described as "furniture," and signed a paper on which under the head "conditions" there was the following note: "No claim for deficiency, damage, or detention will be allowed unless made within three days after the delivery of the goods, nor for loss unless made within seven days of the time they should have been delivered, and that the company will not be answerable for the loss of any goods which may be untruly or incorrectly described in the receiving note,"— may be referred to, as it bears both upon the question of signing the special contract and of what will be considered just and reasonable conditions. In this case the plaintiff said, "He was told to sign the paper, and he did so. He might have seen the word 'conditions,' but he did not read them, and did not know and was not told what they were." One of the packages consisted of a sack of clothes which was not delivered, but no claim was made until more than seven days from the time when the same should have been delivered had elapsed. It was held, first, with regard to the signing, that there was nothing to rebut the presumption arising from the signature of the paper by the plaintiff, that he understood that the contract was subject to the conditions; and it was held, with regard to what are just and reasonable conditions within the meaning of the Railway and Canal Traffic Act, that the conditions contained in the paper signed by the plaintiff were just and reasonable, and therefore that the company had a defence to the action on the ground that the claim was not made within the seven days specified.[1] There was another point in this case. It was proved that the bag of clothes was misdescribed, and that would have been a defence, the negligence of the plaintiff having contributed to cause the loss of his goods.[2]

SEC. 197. **When Signature not Conclusive Evidence of Contract.**—But the signature of the individual is not always

[1] A condition that the carrier should not be liable for any loss unless a claim therefor should be presented within thirty days after date of the receipt was held to be unreasonable and void in a contract to carry a valise from Indiana to Georgia. Adams Express Co. *v.* Reagan, 29 Ind. 21. But see Wier *v.* Adams Express Co., District Court of Philadelphia.

[2] Lewis *v.* Great Western Rail. Co., 5 H. & N. 867; 29 L. J. Exch. 425.

conclusive evidence that the goods were delivered upon a special contract, the terms of which are expressed or referred to in the paper to which that signature is attached. It is a presumption, and it is liable to be rebutted. In the case just referred to there was no evidence to rebut the presumption. But where an individual delivering goods to a company's servant was asked to sign a paper, and had expressed an unwillingness to do so, upon the ground that he could not see to read it, but who, upon being assured by the clerk that it was of no consequence, and that the signature was a mere matter of form, signed it, it was held that there was evidence to show that the goods had not been delivered to the company to be carried under the special contract, the terms of which were contained in the paper signed by the plaintiff.[1]

SEC. 198. **Unsigned Contract binding upon Railway or Canal Carrier.** — It has been decided that a special contract to carry goods, though not signed by the consignor, is binding upon the railway or canal company by the 7th section of 17 & 18 Vict. c. 31, which, as we have seen,[2] provides that no contract shall be binding upon the party unless signed by him or the person delivering the goods to be carried.[3]

SEC. 199. **What are Just and Reasonable Conditions?** — It will be evident, from what has been said above, that it is of much importance to ascertain what general principles have guided our judges in the decision of the question, what conditions are just and reasonable? Unless we can discover that, the 7th section of the Railway and Canal Traffic Act will have done harm rather than good. The elements of uncertainty which exist in legislative enactments are to be removed by the decisions of courts of law. The process is as if laws were, by the legislature, made by contract for humanity, as clothes might be made by contract for a regiment of soldiers. After that has been done, there requires to be a good deal of trying on and adjustment to individual peculiarities of size and shape. So our judges fit the laws to the shape of humanity. Our

[1] Simons *v.* Great Western Rail. Co., 2 C. B. N. S. 620.

[2] *Ante*, p. 252.

[3] Baxendale *v.* Great Eastern Rail. Co., 10 B. & S. 212 Exch. Ch.

judicial procedure is a process of trying on. The legislature does well to leave, as in this case, much to the discretion of judges; but the discretion of judges is good for nothing if it cannot discover some general principles, which shall guide their decisions in particular cases. If they cannot do so with regard to their decisions, how are those whose conduct is to be regulated by law to discover such principles for themselves? Even if they could discover such principles, the advantage would not be obvious unless they could calculate with some degree of certainty that a parallel course of reasoning would guide the opinion of the judge. In this instance, what judges have deemed just and reasonable in times past will, as in every other department of case-law, be a guide to those who wish to limit their liability by conditions which will be held to be just and reasonable in time to come. But two cases are very seldom on all fours, and this fact indicates the necessity that exists to extract from past decisions the principles upon which they were given, that we may have a general rule to guide us in the ever varying circumstances of life. The difficult question to solve in all these cases is as to the amount of generality which is expedient. The rule may be so general as to be useless, just as it may be so particular as to be practically valueless. We shall, in the first instance, point out what has been held reasonable or unreasonable, just or unjust, in regard to the conditions in various cases, and we shall then be in a position to point out the general grounds of these decisions.

SEC. 200. **Unaccountable for Loss of badly packed Parcels, an Unreasonable Condition.** — It has been held that a condition that a railway company will not be accountable for the loss, detention, or damage of any package insufficiently or improperly packed is not a just or a reasonable condition.[1] In the same case, as we should have argued from the case of Lewis *v.* The Great Western Railway Company,[2] it was fur-

[1] Simons *v.* Great Western Rail. Co., 18 C. B. 805; 26 L. J. C. P. 25; s. P. Garton *v.* Bristol & Exeter Rail. Co., 1 B. & S. 112; 7 Jur. N. S. 1234; 30 L. J. Q. B. 273; 9 W. R. 734.

[2] 5 H. & N. 867; 29 L. J. Exch. 425; *ante*, p. 259.

ther held that a condition that no claim for damage will be allowed unless made within three days after the delivery of the goods, nor for loss unless made within seven days from the time that they should be delivered, was just and reasonable.

SEC. 201. **Loss of Market. — Delay, however caused. — As to a Horse.** — So a condition that a railway company should not be liable for loss of market or other delay arising from detention is a reasonable condition.[1] A condition not to be liable for delay, however caused, is unreasonable.[2] We have already seen that a condition that a railway company will not be responsible for injury to a case of marbles unless the same are declared according to their value, is not just and reasonable as a condition.[3] And in the case of Wise *v.* The Great Western Railway Company,[4] the subject came under consideration. There a horse was sent by railway, directed to the owner at Eton. The sender signed a document in the following terms: "Mr. Wise paid for one horse 12*s.* 6*d.* Newbury to Windsor. Notice: The directors will not be answerable for damage to any horse conveyed by this railway."[5] The horse arrived in safety at Windsor Station, but the owner not appearing to claim it, it was forgotten and left tied up in a horse-box in an exposed situation for twenty-four hours, and was injured by such neglect. As the condition was held reasonable, the company was held not responsible for the injury done.[6]

SEC. 202. **Reasonable Conditions as to Animals.** — In the case of Pardington *v.* South Wales Railway Company,[7]

[1] White *v.* Great Western Rail. Co., 2 C. B. N. S. 7; 26 L. J. C. P. 158.

[2] Kirby *v.* Great Western Rail. Co., 18 L. T. N. S. 658. See also Allday *v.* Great Western Rail. Co., 11 L. T. Rep. N. S. 267; 34 L. J. 5 Q. B.

[3] Peek *v.* North Staffordshire Rail. Co., 10 H. L. Cas. 473; 9 Jur. N. S. 914; 32 L. J. Q. B. 241; 11 W. R. 1023; 8 L. T. N. S. 768.

[4] 1 H. & N. 63; 25 L. J. Exch. 258.

[5] But see decision in M'Manus *v.* Lancashire & Yorkshire Rail. Co., 4 H. & N. 327; *ante*, p. 258.

[6] Even had not the plaintiff been bound by the special contract which had been signed for him, the company would not have been held responsible, as the injury arose from the negligence of the owner in not being at the Windsor Station to receive the horse.

[7] 1 H. & N. 392; 2 Jur. N. S. 1210; 26 L. J. Exch. 105.

which was tried a few months after the case we have just referred to (in 1856), a contract containing the following condition (amongst others) was signed by a person sending cattle by the railway of the defendant company. The condition was: "A pass for a drover to ride with his stock will be given. The company is to be held free from all risk in respect of any damage arising in the loading or unloading, from suffocation, or from being trampled upon, bruised, or otherwise injured, in transit, from fire, or from any other cause whatsoever."[1] It appeared that the plaintiff's servant in charge of the cattle received a free pass from the company. He travelled in the same carriage with the guard, and did not get out to look at the cattle during the journey, but on arriving at Gloucester, the destination of the cattle, he heard them making a noise, and found that the lid of one of the vans had become closed, and that of the sixteen oxen in it ten were dead, or dying, from suffocation, and four were very much injured. Some evidence was given to show that the lid could not have become closed by the motion of the train, but must have been purposely shut down by the servants of the railway company.

SEC. 203. **Where Drover went along with Animals.** — The learned judge (ALDERSON, B.) asked the jury whether they thought that the cattle were suffocated during the transit, and, the jury having found that question in the affirmative, he directed a verdict to be entered for the defendants, giving leave to the plaintiff to move to enter a verdict for 135*l.*, if the court should be of opinion that the conditions were unreasonable. The opinion of the Court of Exchequer was, that the ruling of the judge was correct, and that it was quite reasonable for the company to make such stipulations as those contained in the special contract set forth above. "The company provided free passes for the drovers, to enable them to go with the cattle for the express purpose of taking care of them. The drover had the means of knowing whether the cattle could travel safely in the carriages provided for them,

[1] It is a question whether such a condition is reasonable. See M'Manus *v.* Lancashire, &c. Rail. Co., *ante*, p. 258.

and he had no right to acquiesce in what was done and then throw the responsibility of failure upon the company." [1] It is also reasonable to stipulate that horses shall be carried by the company at the owner's risk.[2] A case sent by a county-court judge for the opinion of the Court of Common Pleas, stated that goods were removed by the railway company (The London and North-Western) under the following condition contained in a note signed by the plaintiff: "Risk-note. London and North-Western Railway Company, Park Lane Station, December 19, 1855. Hay, straw, furniture, glass, marble, china, castings, and other brittle and hazardous articles conveyed at the risk of the owners. Delivered to London and North-Western Railway Company from R. C., Dunham, three crates of beef, to be forwarded from Liverpool to London, at owner's risk."

SEC. 204. **Effect of Statutory Provisions.** — The court, after stating that the result of the 7th section of the Railway and Canal Traffic Act was, that "A general notice is void, but the company may make special contracts with their customers, provided they are just and reasonable, and signed; and whereas the monopoly created by the railway companies compels the public to employ them in the conveyance of their goods, the legislature have thought fit to impose the further security that the court shall see that the condition or special contract is just or reasonable," went on to say, that in the case before them, which was referred to them to say whether the conditions contained in the risk-note were unjust and unreasonable, it was impossible to come to any conclusion on the point, as they had not been told as to the circumstances under which the contract was made, or what the nature or the reason of the particular risk was.[3]

[1] Per POLLOCK, C. B., Pardington *v.* South Wales Rail. Co., 1 H. & N. 392. But see some American cases on this subject. Smith *v.* New Haven R. R., 12 Allen, 531; Hall *v.* Renfro, 3 Mct. (Ky.) 51; Conger *v.* Hudson River R. R., 6 Duer, 375; Harris *v.* Northern Indiana R. R., 20 N. Y. 232; Ohio R. R. *v.* Dunbar, 20 Ill. 623.

[2] M'Cance *v.* London & North-Western Rail. Co., 7 H. & N. 477; 31 L. J. Exch. 65; Gannell *v.* Ford, 5 L. T. N. S. 604 Q. B.; Harrison *v.* London, Brighton, & South Coast Rail. Co., 2 B. & S. 122; 8 Jur. N. S. 740; 31 L. J. Q. B. 113 Exch. Ch.

[3] Dunham *v.* London & North-Western Rail. Co., 18 C. B. 826.

We have, in another place,[1] had occasion to consider the reasonableness of a condition by which a company attempts to limit its liability to loss, or damage, occurring on its own line, when it receives goods to be transmitted to a station beyond the limits of its own plant, but receives no money for the transit of the goods upon the line of the neighbor company; and in the same place we considered the unreasonableness of a condition attempting to exonerate a railway company, under this section, from damage done to packing cases, and the like, when returned as empties. But there are still some other cases which require notice, because of the light they throw upon this question of the reasonableness or unreasonableness of a condition contained in a special contract.

SEC. 205. **Special Conditions necessitated by Kind of Goods.** — Certain kinds of wares naturally necessitate special conditions. And the reasonableness in every case may, to a certain extent, be ascertained by the ordinary experience of mankind. The circumstances of railway construction and traffic necessitate a man to make use of that mode of conveyance, and generally limit him to the choice of one company. It is well, then, that he should be protected from the power which the position of railway companies with regard to traffic gives them, to exact in a way which would be unjust. The law does this. But it is also to be remembered that these very circumstances necessitate, in some instances, a certain amount of protection to the railway company.

SEC. 206. **Perishable Goods.** — In the case of very perishable or fragile goods this may be the case. And, consequently, where a company gave public notice that fish would only be conveyed on their line by special agreement, and by particular trains, and that the sender should sign conditions to the effect that the company should not be held responsible, under any circumstances, for loss of market, or for other loss or injury arising from delay, or detention of train, exposure to weather, stowage, or from any cause whatever, other than gross neglect or fraud, the conditions were held just and reasonable.[2] On

[1] *Ante*, p. 256; Aldridge *v.* Great Western Rail. Co., 15 C. B. N. S. 582; 33 L. J. C. P. 161.

[2] Beal *v.* South Devon Rail. Co., 3 H. & C. 337; 12 W. R. 1115; 11 L. T. N. S. 184; affirming decision of

the other hand, in another case,[1] a condition excluding all risks of conveyance, loading, and unloading whatsoever, upon the ground that the company refused to be responsible for any injury or damage (however caused) occurring to live-stock of any description, was held to be unreasonable. And the facts being that, the truck provided for the conveyance of the plaintiff's horses being defective, and the horses having in the course of the journey knocked a hole in it, by means of which they injured themselves, the company was held liable for the damage done. Another important decision may be quoted to show in what cases the section of the Railway and Canal Traffic Act,[2] at present under consideration, is applicable. A passenger by the London, Brighton, and South Coast Railway, from London Bridge to Worthing, took with him two horses and a retriever dog; the horses were put into a horse-box, and a servant of the defendants (the company) proposed that the dog should be placed in the horse-box, to which the plaintiff assented. The dog was fastened by means of a leather collar round its neck, and a strap thereto which passed through a ring fastened to the side of the horse-box. The collar and strap were furnished by the plaintiff, and were his property. The plaintiff's agent signed a ticket which contained the following conditions: "The company will not be liable, in any case, for loss or damage to any horse or other animal above the value of 40*l.*, or any dog above the value of 5*l.*, unless a declaration of its value, signed by the owner or his agent at the time of booking the same, has been given to them, and by such declaration the owner shall be bound, the company not being in any event liable to any greater amount than the value so declared. The company will in no case be liable for injury to any horse or other animal, or dog, of whatever value, when such injury arises wholly or partially from fear or restiveness. If the declared value of any horse or other animal exceed 40*l.*, or any dog 5*l.*, the price of conveyance will, in addition to the

the Exchequer, 4 H. & N. 875; 29 L. J. Exch. 441; 8 W. R. 651 Exch. Ch.

[1] M'Manus *v.* Lancashire & Yorkshire Rail. Co., 4 H. & N. 327; 5 Jur. N. S. 651; 28 L. J. Exch. 353; 3 L. J. 259 Exch. Ch.

[2] 17 & 18 Vict. c. 31.

regular fare, be after the rate of 2½ per cent, or 6*d.* in the pound, upon the declared value above 40*l.* (or 5*l.*), whatever may be the amount of such value, and for whatever distance the horse or other animal is to be carried."

SEC. 207. **Liability for Negligence. — Excessive Charge. — Misconduct on Part of Company.** — The plaintiff made no declaration of the value of the dog, and paid 3*s.* for the carriage of it. When the train arrived at Worthing, a window of the horse-box was found open, through which the dog had escaped, and was lost. When this case was before the Court of Queen's Bench, it was held by COCKBURN, C. J., and BLACKBURN, J., that the conditions were not just and reasonable, within the 7th section of the Railway and Canal Traffic Act, in two respects: first, because the meaning of the ticket was that, if the value of the dog exceeded 5*l.*, and its value was not declared, the company would not be liable for the loss or injury occasioned by their own negligence; secondly, because in the absence of evidence by the company showing the contrary, the extra charge of 2½ per cent was excessive, and therefore, the conditions being void, the company were liable as common carriers for the full value of the dog. WIGHTMAN, J., on the other hand, held that the meaning of the ticket was, that the company would not, in any case, be liable for loss or damage beyond 5*l.*, unless the value was declared, and that this was a reasonable condition; that the court had no means of knowing whether the extra charge of 2½ per cent was reasonable or not, and therefore the plaintiff was not entitled to recover more than 5*l.*

When the case came before the Court of Exchequer Chamber (ERLE, C. J., WILLIAMS and KEATING, JJ., and CHANNEL, B.), the judgment of the Queen's Bench was reversed, and it was held that, assuming section 7 applied to the case, the conditions in the ticket were just and reasonable within that section, because the effect of the first condition was not to exempt the defendants from liability for loss or injury occasioned by wilful wrong; and if it exempted them from any negligence, it was severable, and valid to exempt when there was no negligence, and it lay upon the plaintiff to show that the extra charge in the third condition was exorbitant or unfair, and the question whether it was so was for a jury, and not for a court. And further, it was held by ERLE, C. J., and KEATING, J., that the 7th section of the act was confined to cases in which the loss or injury was occasioned by misconduct on the part of the company, and did not apply where it occurred through pure accident.[1]

SEC. 208. **Conveyance of Goods by Passenger Trains.** — It is usual for railway companies to charge more for transmitting goods by means of a passenger train than for transmitting them by means of an ordinary goods train. This is reasonable. The saving in time to the owner of the goods is often worth a great deal of money. Besides, the trouble to the company of forwarding goods by means of a passenger train is greater than it would be of sending them by means of the trains which are set apart for the conveyance of things rather than men.

SEC. 209. **Alternative Method of Carriage.** — In a case where the owner of horses knew that there was a certain rate for carrying horses, in horse-boxes, by a passenger train, and a lower rate for their conveyance by a goods train, in wagons, and he sent his horses by the latter after having signed a declaration that they were carried "at owner's risk," it was held that, as there was an alternative method of carriage, this condition was reasonable. Therefore, it was decided that such a condition, while it would not protect the company in case of a failure to carry in a reasonable time, did protect it in case the horses were injured on the journey.[2]

SEC. 210. **Reasonable Regulations by Telegraph Company. — Unrepeated Messages.** — Where an act, incorporating a telegraph company, provided that the public, without preference, should have the use of the company's telegraph, subject to reasonable regulations to be made by the company, it was regarded a reasonable regulation that, when a person wished to transmit a message by the telegraph, a message paper was

[1] Harrison *v.* London, Brighton, & South Coast Rail. Co., 2 B. & S. 122; 8 Jur. N. S. 740; 31 L. J. Q. B. 113; 6 L. T. N. S. 466 Exch. Ch.

[2] Robinson *v.* Great Western Rail. Co., 14 W. R. 206; 1 H. & R. 97; 35 L. J. C. P. 123; 1 L. R. C. P. 329.

handed to him for his signature, on the back of which there was a notice that messages of consequence ought to be repeated from the station to which they are addressed, that a higher rate was charged for repeating messages, and that the company would not be responsible for mistakes in the transmission of unrepeated messages. It was held that the company was not liable for the consequences of mistakes in unrepeated messages, and that, even had this regulation not been authorized as a reasonable regulation under the act, it was such a limitation as the company, in their character as common carriers, was entitled to create by notice to their customers.[1] In this latter aspect the case has already been considered,[2] but, as showing what is a reasonable condition, it is not unworthy of consideration in its present connection.

SEC. 211. **Company cannot free itself from all Risk. — Assumption of Risk by Owner.** — It cannot be doubted that where a company tries, by notice attached to their cattle-ticket, to free itself from all risk with respect to any loss or damage arising in the loading or unloading, or injury in the transit from any cause whatever, — where it endeavors to do this by the agreement with the owner, that he shall have all the risk, and see to the efficiency of the wagons before his cattle are placed therein, and that in case of insufficiency, complaint must be made in writing to the company's office before the wagon leaves the station, such an attempt will not succeed, and such conditions will be held neither just nor reasonable.[3] But from

[1] M'Andrew *v.* Electric Telegraph Co., 17 C. B. 3; 1 Jur. N. S. 1073; 25 L. J. C. P. 26.

[2] *Ante*, p. 228.

[3] Gregory *v.* West Midland Rail. Co., 2 H. & C. 944; 10 Jur. N. S. 243; 33 L. J. Exch. 155; 12 W. R. 528. In Kimball *v.* Rutland, &c. R. R. Co., 26 Vt. 247, it was held that a common carrier may, by special contract with the owner of property, become a private carrier, and his liabilities will be measured by the contract; but a general notice to the public, even if brought home to the party, will afford no evidence of such a contract; and A having declared against B, as a common carrier, in a case where B was a private carrier under a special contract, the question whether such contract was made was purely one of law. When, by special contract, the relation is changed from that of common carriers to private carriers, an action must be brought on the contract, or for a breach of duty, and not against them as common carriers. Where a railroad company

what has been said above, it must not be understood that the owner can, under no circumstances, assume the risk and re-

offered to become common carriers for a given hire, and, for a less sum, offered to furnish cars, motive power, &c., that the owner might be his own carrier, and assume the risk, it was held that the plaintiff who elected to pay the lower rate was bound by his election, and could not hold the company as common carriers, for damage; and that, *pro hac vice*, the railroad company were private carriers merely. In all cases, in order that a special contract limiting the carrier's liability may be operative, it must be just and reasonable; and a contract that relieves him from the consequences of his own gross negligence, or that of his servants or agents, is treated as unreasonable and void, as being opposed to the policy of the law. The rule is, that any limitation allowed to be imposed by common carriers upon their liability must be restricted to their liability as insurers. The carrier cannot impose a limitation which will protect him from responsibility for loss arising from his own want of care, or the negligence of his servants. Evansville, &c. R. R. Co. *v.* Young, 28 Ind. 516; Kallman *v.* U. S. Express Co., 3 Kan. 205; Southern Express Co. *v.* Moon, 39 Miss. 822; Ashmore *v.* Pennsylvania, &c. Co., 28 N. J. L. (4 Dutch.) 180; Dorr *v.* N. J. Steam Nav. Co., 4 Sandf. (N. Y.) 136; Stedman *v.* Western Trans. Co., 48 Barb. (N. Y.) 97; Davidson *v.* Graham, 2 Ohio St. 131; Seller *v.* Pacific, 1 Oreg. 409; Pennsylvania R. R. Co. *v.* McClosky, 23 Pa. St. 526; Farnham *v.* Camden, &c. R. R. Co., 55 Pa. St. 53; American Express Co. *v.* Sands, 55 Pa. St. 140; Pennsylvania R. R. Co. *v.* Butler, 57 Pa. St. 335.

In Farmers, &c. Bank *v.* Champlain Transportation Co., 23 Vt. 186, the defendants, a corporation, were common carriers upon Lake Champlain, and their charter extended to the carrying of all goods, wares, and merchandise, and "all other articles and things usually transported by water" on that lake; and it appeared that bank-bills were usually carried by the water craft upon that lake, at the time the corporation received their charter and went into operation; and it was held that the defendant's powers, as a corporation, extended to the carrying of bank-bills, but that the charter did not of necessity constitute them common carriers of bank-bills, so as to preclude them from the right of declining to assume the risk of carrying such articles, if they so elected. And it is not necessary, in such case, to show, by positive proof, that the company consented that the captain of their boat should carry money on their account, in order to hold the company responsible for the loss of the money. The captain of the boat is to be regarded as the general agent of the owners; and, *primâ facie*, the owners are liable for all contracts for carrying, made by the captain or other general agent for that purpose, within the powers of the owners themselves; and the burden rests upon them to show that the plaintiffs had made a private contract with the captain, which it was understood should be kept from the knowledge of the defendants, or else had given credit exclusively to the captain. The mere fact, in such case, that the captain was, by the company, permitted to take the perquisites for carrying such parcels, will not be sufficient to exonerate the company from liability. Their suffering him to continue to

sponsibility of the transit of his goods. In many cases it might be much more convenient for the owner to insure his own goods, and have them sent by the railway company at a lower rate. The question of ready money is sometimes more important to a man than that of security. If the legislature forced security upon a man, it would do much evil. Law must still allow freedom for the exercise of prudence or speculation. This is actually what the law does. Thus we have seen that the House of Lords, in the case of Peek *v.* The North Staffordshire Railway Company,[1] recognized the doctrine that

carry bank-bills ought to be regarded as fixing their responsibility, and the allowing him to take the perquisites as a mere arrangement among themselves. But it is not competent for the plaintiff, in order to charge the company with the loss of a package of bank-bills, to prove by his agent, who delivered the package to the captain of the boat, that he intended to intrust the money to the captain in his official capacity, and not in his private capacity, — without evidence that this was in some way made apparent at the time.

A common carrier may, by his express contract, limit his common-law responsibility; but a mere general notice, when brought to the knowledge of the owner of the goods carried, will not have that effect unless there is very clear proof that the owner expressly assented to that, as forming the basis of the contract. But a carrier may, by general notice brought to the knowledge of the owner of the goods, limit his responsibility for carrying certain commodities beyond the line of his general business, or he may make his responsibility depend upon certain reasonable conditions. When a common carrier, by steamboat or other vessel, in the due and common course of his business, delivers his goods, or parcels, into the custody of the wharfinger, upon the wharf, the transit is ended, and his responsibility as carrier ceases, unless he have, either expressly or by fair implication, undertaken to do something more; and the question, as to the time and place, when the duty of the carrier ends, is one of contract, to be determined by the jury from a consideration of all that was said by either party, at the time of the delivery and acceptance of the parcels by the carrier, the course of the business, the practice of the carrier, and all other attending circumstances, the same as any other contract, in order to determine the intention of the parties.

Upon the trial, in 1847, of an action against a common carrier to recover the value of goods lost, the plaintiff offered in evidence a printed advertisement, issued by the defendants in 1839, a portion of which had been accidentally torn and lost; and it appearing that search had been made by the plaintiff, at the places in the vicinity at which copies of the advertisement had been posted by the defendants, for another copy, without success, it was held that the part produced might be read in evidence, and parol evidence given as to the contents of the part which had been lost.

[1] 10 H. L. Cas. 473; 9 Jur. N. S. 914; 32 L. J. Q. B. 214; 11 W. R. 1023.

it is reasonable for a railway company to have two modes of carriage, — one by which they take a great responsibility, and carry by horse-boxes, and another by which they carry at a cheaper rate, but at a greater risk to the bailor; and we have seen that this doctrine was expressly confirmed by the Court of Common Pleas in a case which has been considered above.[1]

SEC. 212. **Delay caused by Negligence.** — In another case this question was considered, — in Allday *v.* The Great Western Railway Company,[2] where it appeared that the defendants had issued a consignment note for the carriage of cattle from Oxford to Birmingham, one of the conditions of which was, "The company are not to be amenable for any consequences arising from detention or delay in or in relation to the conveying of the said animals, however caused." This condition was held unreasonable, although it appeared that the rate charged for carriage had been reduced below that ordinarily demanded. COCKBURN, C. J., in refusing the rule, said: "Is that contract reasonable? Certainly not; for it is not merely that the company will not be responsible for delay, not only from over-carriage generally, and not limited to accidental circumstances independent of delay caused by the company, but they claim absolute immunity from all injury arising from delay caused by their own negligence. This I take to be an unreasonable condition, unless something appears which might make it inequitable in the sender to seek to exact from them the full extent of the ordinary carrier's liability. Suppose a company say, 'We are entitled to charge a certain rate of carriage; if so, of course they are liable to the liability of common carriers. But then this company say, 'We make this special contract; we will carry these animals for a lower price if you will release us from the liability attached to carriers, and will take your chance of goods arriving at their destination.' If a man enters into such a contract as that, it is unreasonable to say that he is not bound by it. But although the expression 'reduced

[1] Robinson *v.* Great Western Rail. Co., 14 W. R. 206; 1 H. & R. 97; 35 L. J. C. P. 123; 1 L. R. C. P. 329.

[2] 5 B. & S. 903; 34 L. J. Q. B. 5; 11 Jur. N. S. 12; 11 L. T. N. S. 267.

charges' occurs in this contract, it does not appear to have been used with reference to a greater rate, by which the sender might have gained additional security."[1] With reference to the second proviso in this section, it has been decided that it will protect a railway company against liability for the carriage of animals, although no complete contract for the carriage of the animals has been entered into, and no complete delivery of it has taken place. Its protective power arises if the animal was in the course of being delivered to or received by the company.[2]

SEC. 213. **"Proper Vice" of Animals.** — In reference to the common-law liability of carriers as insurers, a case of considerable importance has recently been decided. Just as the fact that man's intelligence introduces an element into the contract of a carrier who undertakes his conveyance, which was not to be considered in the case of the carriage of inanimate goods, so it has been held that the animacy of live animals must be a reason for a modification of the contract of insurance entered into by a carrier who conveys them. If a carrier has packed goods intrusted to him, which of their own nature will spoil before the journey can be completed, he is certainly not to be regarded as having insured against this inevitable circumstance. Insurance has to do with possibilities, not with certainties. Now, the principle which applies to the inherent nature of goods has been extended to the "proper vice" of animals. The case in which this was done was that of Kendal *v.* The London and South-Western Railway Company.[3] It appeared that the plaintiff booked his horse from Waterloo Station to Ewell, signing a note on the counterfoil of his ticket.

SEC. 214. **Condition.** — The conditions on the ticket were, that the company would not be responsible for any injury or

[1] See also Lloyd *v.* Waterford & Limerick Rail. Co., 15 Ir. C. L. R. 37; 9 L. T. N. S. 89 Q. B.

[2] Hodgman *v.* West Midland Rail. Co., 5 B. & S. 173; 10 Jur. N. S. 673; 33 L. J. Q. B. 233; 12 W. R. 1054; 10 L. T. N. S. 609. Affirmed on appeal, 13 W. R. 758; 35 L. J. Q. B. 85 Exch Ch.

[3] Reported in The Times for June 12, 1872; Law Times, June 15, 1872.

damage to any horse in the receiving, forwarding, or delivering thereof, if such injury or damage were occasioned by the kicking, plunging, or unruliness of the same. The horse was placed in a box by one of the defendants' porters, the saddle remaining on, and the stirrups being allowed to hang down. The box was placed at the extreme end of the train. On the horse's arrival at Ewell, he was found to be much frightened and greatly cut about, more especially about the forearms and fetlock joints. The plaintiff sued the company for the damage occasioned to his horse, and the case was tried before BARON MARTIN, at Guildhall.

SEC. 215. **Whether Railway Company an Insurer of Live Animals.** — It was admitted that the defendants had been guilty of no negligence, and the point involved was, whether the defendants are insurers for the safety of live animals intrusted to their care, as they are in the case of inanimate goods. The defendants called some stud-grooms to show that the sending of a riding-horse saddled and with the stirrups hanging down was the best mode of carrying him; and it appeared that this mode of conveying saddle-horses was general with railway companies. The verdict was entered for the plaintiff for 39*l.*, the question of liability being reserved for the full court, who were to have power to draw inferences of fact.

SEC. 216. **Company not Liable for Injury caused by "Proper Vice." — Defendants' Negligence.** — BRAMWELL, B., said: "No doubt the horse was the immediate cause of its own injuries, *i. e.* no person got into the box and injured it. It slipped, or fell, or kicked, or plunged, or in some way hurt itself. If it did so from no cause other than its inherent propensities, 'its proper vice,' — that is, from fright, or temper, or struggling to keep its legs, — the defendants are not liable. But if it so hurt itself from the defendants' negligence, or any misfortune happening to the train, though not through any negligence of the defendants, as, for instance, from the horse-box leaving the line through some obstruction maliciously laid upon it, then the defendants would, as insurers, be liable. If perishable articles, say soft fruits, are damaged by their own weight and the inevitable shaking of the carriage, they are injured through their own intrinsic qualities. If through pressure of other goods carried with them, or by an extraordinary shock or shaking, whether through negligence or not, the carrier is liable.

SEC. 217. **Burden of Proof.** — "Since this judgment was agreed upon, the case of The Great Western Railway *v.* Blower has been decided in the Common Pleas to this effect. Now, it might be a question on whom, in such a case as the present, the burden of proof lay; but in the actual case each gave evidence. The defendants' witnesses stated that the train proceeded without disturbance or interruption, and that there was nothing to excite the horse to do what he did to his own damage — no cause for the mischief except his own inherent disposition. If this is so, the defendants are not liable. On the other hand, the plaintiff's witnesses proved the horse was quiet, used to railway travelling, and therefore, they say, there must have been something extraordinary to excite the animal. This is a question of fact properly for a jury, but referred to us. If I am to decide it, I find for the defendants. The evidence of the plaintiff's witnesses renders it improbable that it was the 'proper vice' of the horse. The evidence of the defendants makes it impossible it was otherwise. It will be observed I take no notice of the saddle and stirrups being on the horse, as described. First, I am satisfied they were not the exciting cause of the mischief; secondly, it appears it was proper to carry the horse so caparisoned; and if so, and if this horse was affrighted by their being there, it was his own inherent and peculiar disposition that made him so — 'his proper vice.' At all events, I cannot find for the plaintiff on this ground. I cannot trace the injury to this cause. Nor do I notice the special conditions, because I understand the learned judge who tried the cause to report that the defendants did not show that the damage arose thus. For these reasons I think the rule ought to be made absolute."

SEC. 218. **The Law of Carriers.** — MARTIN, B., concurred. PIGOTT, B., differed in opinion from his learned brothers, — "The court is to draw inferences of facts, and I infer (there being no negligence on either side) that the animal either was thrown or got down in the box, or in struggling to get up again received the injuries in question. In my opinion, the cut on the forearm was caused by its lying on the stirrup, and the injuries on the hocks and fetlocks by struggling and kicking on the floor of the box, the result of some accident or casualty, without evidence to show how caused. The law of carriers, I apprehend, is clearly this,—that, in the absence of any special contract, they undertake to carry safely, and they insure against, and bear the risks of, all casualties of the transit, except such as result from the *vis major*, *i. e.* acts of nature, otherwise termed acts of God and of the Queen's enemies,—and that since the case of M'Manus *v.* The Lancashire and Yorkshire Railway Company,[1] there is, in this respect, no distinction between live and other ordinary merchandise. The present case," said his lordship, "is thus reduced to one of *onus* of proof; and upon whom is such *onus* cast, for it can be but pure speculation how this particular mischief occurred? There may have been an accidental jerk at a curve of the line, or a jolt of the train by sudden stoppage; or, on the other hand, possibly (though there is no evidence of it) the animal itself may have been the cause of its own injuries by some intrinsic propensity of its own nature. In this state of things it seems to me only reasonable that the carrier, who has sole control of the article, and who alone can know what has occurred, and certainly has the means of knowing, which the sender of the goods has not, should, if he rely upon any exception to his common-law liability, show by affirmative proof that the case is brought within the exception. This the defendants have failed to do, and their liability to insure against a casualty of the journey is unremoved. Therefore, I think, the plaintiff is entitled to recover."[2]

SEC. 219. **Inferences from these Decisions.—Reasonableness.**—The majority of the court being in favor of the company, the rule was made absolute. The inferences to be drawn

[1] 4 H. & N. 327.

[2] Clarke *v.* Rochester & Syracuse R. R. Co., 14 N. Y. (4 Kernan) 570; Betts *v.* Farmers' Loan, &c. Co., 21 Wis. 80; Evansville, &c. R. R. Co. *v.* Young, 28 Ind. 516; Ballentine *v.* North Missouri R. R. Co., 40 Mo. 491.

from these cases, notwithstanding the difference of opinion that took place in reference to several of them,[1] with regard to what conditions will be regarded as just and reasonable, seem to be, that the ordinary principles which would guide the conduct of mankind have been applied to the several sets of circumstances which have come before the courts,—that the word "reasonableness," as it will be applied by a court or judge, before whom any cause is brought involving a question with regard to a special contract between a bailor and a carrier, will not be interpreted technically, but that what ordinary men would deem to be a reasonable condition under the circumstances will be deemed a reasonable condition by the court. This, looking at the function of a court of law, and having regard to the way in which our courts of law have been constituted, is exactly what we should have been led to expect. That law gives only an authority to certain principles which had operated on people's practice long before the existence of the law, is surely true. In this sense laws may be said to bind society even antecedent to their expression. And when the question is one of interpretation of an express enactment, as it was in this case, judges must endeavor to anticipate the interpretation which will be put upon the enactment by the ordinary human beings who have to live under it as a law. Our written laws are, in the truest sense, not creations, but observations.

SEC. 220. **Railway or Canal Company cannot free itself from Consequences of Negligence.**— The results then seem to be, that general conditions and special conditions, by which a railway or canal company endeavors to divest itself from all responsibility for wilful or gross negligence, are void, on the ground of their unreasonableness.[2] It was evidently not the

[1] Peek *v.* North Staffordshire Rail. Co. (see *ante*, pp. 253, 262); Harrison *v.* London, Brighton, & South Coast Rail. Co., and Hodgman *v.* West Midland Rail. Co., *ante*, p. 273; Harrison *v.* London & South Coast Rail. Co., 2 B. & S. 122.

[2] Indianapolis, &c. R. R. Co. *v.* Allen, 31 Ind. 394; Michigan, &c. R. R. Co. *v.* Heaton, 31 Ind. 397; The Express Co. *v.* Konntze, 8 Wall. 342; Simon *v.* The Fung Shuey, 21 La. Ann. 363; Lamb *v.* Camden, &c. R. R. Co., 2 Daly (N. Y.), 454. And see cases cited pp. 191–205.

intention of the legislature, when it enacted the 7th section of the Railway and Canal Traffic Act, 1854, which has been so severely criticised in our courts of law,[1] to encourage any negligence upon the part of railway and canal companies,—it was rather, as we have seen, to protect the public from being injuriously affected by notices, which they may never actually have seen, and, at the same time, to leave parties free to enter into express contracts with carriers for the transmission of their goods.

SEC. 221. **Reason of Proviso.** — The fact that, as traffic is at present constituted, railway companies have a monopoly of the trade of carrying to given places, and that it is scarcely within the power of a man in business to refuse to employ them, made the legislature introduce the proviso that all conditions contained in such special contracts should be just and reasonable, and that if they were not it should be void. The law is for the protection of the weak, and the bailor is, in so far as he wishes to have goods transmitted by railway or canal companies, weak, by reason of their strength derived from this system of monopoly. These being, doubtless, the reasons of the legislative action in this matter, it behooved the judges, when they were called upon to say what was to be regarded as just and reasonable, to follow the dictates which were to be gathered from a consideration of the thoughts and opinions of mankind as to justice and reasonableness. This they have, for the most part, done.

SEC. 222. **Sufficient Declaration of Value.** — One other question arises in connection with the 7th section of this act,[2] and that is as to what will constitute a sufficient declaration of value upon the part of the sender of the goods. It is evident that, as the declaration of value was meant to be with a view to the insurance of the goods, to be sufficient it must be made with the intention upon the part of the sender that it shall be understood as made with the view to insurance.[3]

[1] COCKBURN, C. J., 29 L. J. 215 Q. B.; JERVIS, C. J., 26 L. J. 32 C. P.; LORD CAMPBELL, C. J., 27 L. J. 474 Q. B.

[2] 17 & 18 Vict. c. 31.

[3] Robinson *v.* London & South-Western Rail. Co., 19 C. B. N. S. 51; 11 Jur. N. S. 390; 34 L. J. C. P. 234.

SEC. 223. **Casual Statements.** — A mere casual statement of value will not be sufficient. So, where an individual was sending a horse by railway, the value of which was known by the company on whose line it was to be conveyed, through a telegram sent from the seller to the buyer, the company refusing to carry it without insurance, the owner wrote the following letter, and the question was whether he had given notice within the 17 & 18 Vict. c. 31, § 7: "If the man who goes for the mare finds that she is dangerous in the train, or if he finds that she has been in before, and anything has happened to her through her own vice, then I think she ought to be insured, but not otherwise. Mr. Ayling, the man I bought her of, told me she never had been in the train in her life. I have had horses of 300*l.* and 400*l.* value often by train, with nobody with them; I never insured a horse in my life, and never had an accident with one. It appears to me that your station-master at Liss is exceeding his powers. The value of this animal is 135*l.*" That was held to be no declaration of value.[1]

SEC. 224. **Personal Risk of Carrier.** — One subject deserves attention before we turn from a consideration of the limitation of the carrier's responsibility. The carrier is, as we have seen, exposed to considerable risk of pecuniary loss by the very nature of his employment, as that nature has been defined by the common law, but a carrier may in some cases be exposed to personal risk in the pursuance of his calling. Many of the goods which he may be called upon to convey from place to place may, from their very nature, expose him to imminent peril.

SEC. 225. **Goods of a Dangerous Nature.** — The 105th section of the Railway Clauses Consolidation Act[2] enacts, that "no person shall be entitled to carry, or to require the company to carry, upon the railway, any aquafortis, oil of vitriol,

[1] See also M'Cance *v.* London & North-Western Rail. Co., 3 H. & C. 343; 34 L. J. Exch. 39. Affirming decision in the Exchequer, 7 H. & N. 477; 10 W. R. 154. With regard to limitation of value, see Harrison *v.* London, Brighton, & South Coast Rail. Co., 29 L. J. Q. B. 209; 2 B. & S. 122.

[2] 8 Vict. c. 20.

gunpowder, lucifer matches, or any other goods, which in the judgment of the company may be of a dangerous nature, and if any person send by the railway any such goods without distinctly marking their nature on the outside of the package containing the same, or otherwise giving notice in writing to the book-keeper or other servant of the company with whom the same are left, at the time of so sending, he shall forfeit to the company twenty pounds for every such offence; and it shall be lawful for the company to refuse to take any parcel that they may suspect to contain goods of a dangerous nature, or require the same to be opened to ascertain the fact."[1] Thus we see another statutory limitation of the liability of a common carrier. To protect the carrier from such risks, an Act of Parliament was passed in 1866, which made it necessary that dangerous goods — such as nitro-glycerine or glonoine oil — should be marked as dangerous by the person delivering them to the carrier, and that notice should be given to the carrier of the nature of the goods. And it also enacted that no carrier (which the act defined as "all persons or bodies of persons carrying goods or passengers for hire by land or water") shall be bound to carry goods which are specially dangerous.[2] The principle involved in this statute is evidently just and reasonable. In the first place, experience of such materials has shown that the risks attendant upon their conveyance are very great, and consequently, to avoid as far as possible accidents through their agency, due notice ought obviously to be given to the carrier whose life, without such notice, would be seriously endangered. But, in the second place, the difficulty of safely conveying such materials is so great, and the precautions which must be taken to prevent explosion are so many, that very few carriers, who are in an ordinary business, could easily undertake the conveyance of such goods; and all these circumstances combine to show

[1] See Crouch *v.* London & North-Western Railway, 14 C. B. 255; 23 L. J. 73 C. B; 2 Car. & Kir. 389; Johnson *v.* Midland Railway, 4 Exch. 367; 18 L. J. 366 Exch.

[2] 29 & 30 Vict. c. 69. See also American law as to this subject, Act of July 3, 1866, 14 Stat. at Large, 81, and sec. 3.

that, with regard to such specially dangerous goods, the common-law duty to carry should not devolve upon the carrier, and that the legislature has done well to limit their liability in that direction.

SEC. 226. **Liability of Owner who does not declare Dangerous Character of Goods.** — One or two cases will serve to show the duties of the carrier in relation to goods, the conveyance of which is attended with danger. It has been decided that one who employs to carry an article of such a dangerous nature as to require extraordinary care in its conveyance, must communicate the fact to the carrier, or he will be responsible for any injury which may result to the carrier or his servants from his omission to do so. Thus, where a person caused a carboy containing nitric acid to be delivered to a servant of a carrier, in order that it might be conveyed by such carrier for him to Croydon, and he did not take reasonable care to make the servant aware that the acid was dangerous, but only informed him that it was an acid, and the servant was burned and injured by reason of the carboy bursting whilst, in ignorance of its dangerous character, he was carrying it on his back from the carrier's cart, it was held that the sender was liable to the servant in an action for damages for such injury.[1] In giving judgment in that case, ERLE, C. J., said: "It was the duty of the defendant, who knew the danger, to take care that the dangerous character of the article should be made known to all persons who were to be concerned in it." And in another case LORD ELLENBOROUGH remarked: "In order to make the putting on board wrongful, the defendants must be conversant of the dangerous quality of the article put on board; and if, being so, they yet give no notice, considering the probable danger thereby occasioned to the lives of those on board, it amounts to a delinquency in the persons concerned in so putting such dangerous articles on board, for which they are criminally liable as for a misdemeanor at least."[2]

[1] Farrant *v.* Barnes, 11 C. B. N. S. 553; 8 Jur. N. S. 868; 31 L. J. C. P. 137; Brass *v.* Maitland, 6 E. & B. 470; Williams *v.* The East India Company, 2 East, 192; Hutchinson *v.* Guion, V. C. B. 149.

[2] Williams *v.* The East India Company, 2 East, 192.

SEC. 227. **Rule in Hearne v. Garton.** — The case of Hearne v. Garton[1] is also in point. There it was proved that a railway act enacted that every person who should send or cause to be sent by the railway any vitriol, or other goods of a dangerous quality, should distinctly mark or state the nature of the goods on the outside of the package, or give notice in writing to the servant of the company with whom the same were left at the time of sending, on the pain of forfeiting 10*l.* for every default, or being imprisoned. It was held that the act made the sending of dangerous goods, without notice, a criminal offence, and that, therefore, a guilty knowledge on the part of the sender was necessary to render him liable under the act. The facts were these. The respondents received from N. some cases containing vitriol, and sent them by the railway. The nature of the goods was not marked on the packages, or known to the respondents when they received the packages. N., in answer to an inquiry by the respondents, informed them that the cases contained gun-stocks and other goods of a harmless nature, and respondents so described them in the receiving note sent by them with the goods to the railway, in which note they described themselves as the consignors. It was held on these facts that, as the respondents had been misled by N. as to the nature of the goods, and had no guilty knowledge of their dangerous character, they were not liable as senders of the goods within the meaning of the act, although they would have been civilly liable to the company for any damage arising from the sending.[2]

SEC. 228. **Carrier's Right to know the Character of the Goods.** — We have already inquired into the principles which are involved in the right which a carrier has in certain cases to know the contents of the parcels which are delivered to him to be carried.[3] All these principles are arguments in this

[1] 2 El. & El. 66; 5 Jur. N. S. 648; 28 L. J. M. C. 16; 33 L. T. 256.

[2] See, as to the right which masters and owners of ships have to refuse to carry goods of such a nature as would endanger the safety of the ship in which they are to be carried, or other portions of the ship's cargo, 17 & 18 Vict. c. 104, § 329.

[3] *Ante*, p. 210; and see Walker *v.* Jackson, 10 M. & W. 161; Crouch *v.* London & North-Western Rail. Co., 14 C. B. 255; Rail. Cas. 717; 2 C. S. R. 188.

place for the necessity of a clear and distinct notice upon the part of the sender of the nature of the goods sent, if that is of a dangerous character. But in the latter case not only the considerations of expediency as to the combination of the two trades of a carrier and an insurer, but considerations of the higher expediency of the safety of human life, make such a disclosure absolutely necessary. There can be little doubt of the excellence of these modifications in the common-law liability of carriers.[1]

The 12th section of the Regulation of Railways Act, 1871,[2] enacts that, "where a railway company, under a contract for carrying persons, animals, or goods, by sea, procures the same to be carried in a vessel not belonging to the railway company, the railway company shall be answerable in damages in respect of loss of life, or personal injury; or in respect of loss of, or damage to, animals or goods, in like manner, and to the same amount as the railway company would be answerable if the vessel had belonged to the railway company, provided that such loss of life, or personal injury, or loss or damage to animals or goods happens to the person, animals, or goods (as the case may be) during the carriage of the same, the proof of the contrary to be upon the railway company."

[1] As to this subject generally, see Martin *v.* Great India Peninsula Rail. Co., 3 L. R. Exch. 9; 37 L. J. Exch. 27; Kirby *v.* Great Western Rail. Co., 18 L. T. N. S. 658; Peper *v.* South-Eastern Rail. Co., 17 L. T. N. S. 469.

[2] 34 & 35 Vict. c. 78.

CHAPTER VIII.

ON DELIVERY AND NON-DELIVERY.

SEC. 229. **Arrangement of Subjects.**—The natural course of the transaction has determined our method of dealing with it. The simplest form of narrative is that which follows the course of events. And, with a view to simplicity and clearness, we have treated of the various duties of a carrier in the order in which they arise in any work that he may, in pursuance of his public calling, undertake. With that view we devoted our attention in the first instance to the duty which is imposed upon the carrier by the common law to receive goods that are delivered to him. We then considered his responsibility with regard to the goods when they were in his possession, and showed that here, too, the law had imposed a duty upon the carrier, — that of becoming an insurer with regard to the goods that were intrusted to him, — and that that fact necessitated that he should carry goods safely and securely at all events, except the loss or injury was caused by an inexorable event of nature's production, or by loss through the interposition of the queen's enemies. At that stage it was natural to consider how that duty could be modified at the will of the parties, and how it had been modified by legislative enactment. So far we have followed the progress of the circumstances in any transaction between a bailor and a carrier, and we are now in a position to consider the third duty which devolves upon a carrier, and that is, the duty to deliver the goods which have been placed in his hands for that purpose.[1]

SEC. 230. **Duty of Carrier to deliver, What amounts to. — Where Delivery must be made.** — It is his duty not only to carry, but it is his duty to deliver.[2] It is a part of the peculiar bailment which constitutes the contract into which a carrier enters. It is evident that the delivery is to be made at the place directed by the consignor of the goods; and it would seem just and reasonable that, even should that place be

[1] Forward *v.* Pittard, 1 T. R. 27; Garside *v.* Trent Navigation Co., 4 T. R. 581; Hyde *v.* Trent Navigation Co., 5 T. R. 389.

[2] The Mary Washington, 1 Abb. (U. S. C. C.) 1; Solomon *v.* Philadelphia Steamboat Co., 2 Daly (N. Y. C. P.), 104; Lamb *v.* Camden, &c. R. R. Co., 2 Daly (N. Y. C. P.), 454; Shenk *v.* Philadelphia Steam Propeller Co., 60 Penn. St. 109; Harris *v.* Rand, 4 N. H. 259; Eagle *v.* White, 6 Whart. (Penn.) 505; Gibson *v.* Culver, 19 Wend. (N. Y.) 305; Ludwig *v.* Meyre, 5 W. & S. (Penn.) 434; Erskine *v.* Thames, 6 Miss. 371; Parker *v.* Flagg, 26 Me. 181.

beyond the ordinary limits of the carrier's operations, he is still bound, having undertaken the work, to see it carried out. He would not, in the first instance, have been necessitated to receive the goods for conveyance. His duty to receive is defined by his usual custom, and by the public knowledge of that custom; his duty to deliver, by the general course of his trade.[1] It would be absurd to make a man who travelled to and fro between London and Oxford undertake the carriage of goods which were to be forwarded to Birmingham; but if such a carrier, without any special understanding between himself and the consignor, undertook such a duty, he would be bound to deliver the goods at their destination.[2] Formerly, when goods were transported by land, with teams, it was held to be the duty of carriers, unless a contrary usage had been established, to deliver freight to the consignee personally at his residence or place of business, according to the circumstances;[3] and such is still the rule as to that class of carriers[4] and express companies.[5] But the carrier may show a well-

[1] Golden *v.* Manning, 2 W. Bl. 916; 3 Wils. 429; Baltimore, &c. R. R. Co. *v.* Schumaker, 29 Md. 176.

[2] Duff *v.* Budd, 6 Moore, 469; 3 B. & B. 177; Morse *v.* Brainard, 41 Vt. 550; Tuckerman *v.* Stephens, &c. Transp. Co., 32 N. J. L. 320; Baltimore, &c. R. R. Co. *v.* Green, 25 Md. 72; Mosher *v.* Southern Express Co., 38 Ga. 37; Southern Express Co. *v.* Shea, 38 Ga. 519.

[3] Storr *v.* Crowley, 1 McC. & Y. 129; Gibson *v.* Culver, 17 Wend. (N. Y.) 305; Fisk *v.* Newton, 1 Den. (N. Y.) 45; Hemphill *v.* Chenie, 6 W. & S. (Penn.) 62.

[4] Gibson *v.* Culver, *ante;* Schroeder *v.* Hudson River R. R. Co., 5 Duer (N. Y.), 55; Eagle *v.* White, 6 Whart. (Penn.) 505.

[5] American Union Express Co. *v.* Robinson, 72 Penn. St. 274; Baldwin *v.* American Express Co., 23 Ill. 197; Witbeck *v.* Holland, 45 N. Y. 13; Southern Express Co. *v.* Armstead, 50 Ala. 350; American Express Co. *v.* Wolf, 79 Ill. 430; Packard *v.* Earle, 113 Mass. 280; American Union Express Co. *v.* Schier, 55 Ill. 140; Sullivan *v.* Thompson, 99 Mass. 259; Marshall *v.* American Express Co., 7 Wis. 1. But this rule may be changed by usage, in localities where the business is so small as to render it impracticable for them to keep a messenger, in which case they may absolve themselves by giving notice to the consignee. Baldwin *v.* American Express Co., *ante;* Haslam *v.* Adams Express Co., 6 Bosw. (N. Y. Superior Ct.) 235; Gulliver *v.* Adams Express Co., 38 Ill. 503. And where the business at a place on its line is too small to warrant the employment of an agent, it may show a usage to deliver packages addressed to persons at that point to the station agent, and if such usage is established it absolves it from liability. Sullivan *v.* Thompson, *ante.* And even a usage to leave goods at a station with notice

established usage to deliver at a certain place, and if such usage is sufficiently uniform and notorious to raise a presumption that the shipper knew or ought to have known of it, he is discharged from his liability as a common carrier by a delivery at such place.[1] But in reference to vessels and railroads, a different rule is held, and, unless a different usage is established, they are only bound to deliver at their wharves or warehouses at the place of destination, and, after having given the consignee notice of their arrival, and the lapse of a reasonable time for the consignee to take them away, their liability as common carriers ceases, and they are only liable as warehousemen for the goods.[2] It is as much a part of the contract of shipment that the owner or consignee of freight shall be ready at the place of destination to receive the goods, upon reasonable notice of their arrival, as that the carrier shall transport them. But if the carrier undertakes to deliver to his own agent instead of to the owner, he becomes liable as a warehouseman therefor after the arrival of the goods.[3] If the goods arrive upon Sunday or upon a legal holiday, the owner is not bound to take them away upon that day, but is entitled to a reasonable time after that day, in which to take them away.[4] But if he begins to take goods away which arrived *before* such day, but leaves the balance until the day *after* such holiday, and they are burned, the carrier is not responsible therefor unless such fire was occasioned by his negligence.[5] In the case last cited a ship was ready to discharge, and, the consignees being notified, she began to discharge on Monday. The consignee took the freight away

to the consignee, if known to the consignor, is sufficient. Packard *v.* Earle, 113 Mass. 280.

[1] Loveland *v.* Burke, 120 Mass. 139; F. & M. Bank *v.* Champlain Transportation Co., 23 Vt. 186; Van Santvoord *v.* St. John, 6 Hill (N. Y.), 157; Houston *v.* Peters, 1 Met. (Ky.) 558; Broadwell *v.* Butler, 6 McLean (U. S.), 296.

[2] Alabama, &c. R. R. Co. *v.* Kidd, 35 Ala. 209; Gould *v.* Chapin, 10 Barb. (N. Y.) 612; affirmed, 20 N. Y. 259; Rowland *v.* Miln, 2 Hilt. (N. Y. C. P.) 150; Dean *v.* Vaccaro, 2 Head (Tenn.), 288; Schales *v.* Ackerland, 15 Ill. 474.

[3] Alabama, &c. R. R. Co. *v.* Kidd, *ante.*

[4] Russell Manufacturing Co. *v.* New Haven Steamboat Co., 50 N. Y. 121.

[5] Richardson *v.* Goddard, 23 How. (U. S.) 28.

up to Wednesday night, leaving then a few bales on the wharf. Thursday was the annual fast-day appointed by the governor. During the forenoon of that day more cargo was unloaded, and in the afternoon all that was on the wharf was burned. The plaintiff claimed to hold the defendant responsible as a common carrier for the cotton burned upon the wharf, because Thursday was a day upon which by law he was not required or expected to perform any labor. The court held that although the consignee might refrain from labor upon that day, yet he did it at his own risk, and could not compel the carrier to refrain from delivering the goods where there is no statute forbidding labor upon such day, or custom compelling the carrier to observe such day, and that the carrier's liability as a common carrier ceased when the goods were placed upon the wharf and the consignee had had a reasonable time in which to take them away. But the carrier must, in the absence of any contract or local usage to the contrary, not only notify the consignee that the goods will be delivered at a certain wharf at a certain time, but also, if he is not at the place to receive them, the carrier should not leave them exposed on the wharf, but should store them for and on account of the owner.[1] The rule may be said to be, that, in order to relieve

[1] Rowland v. Miln, 2 Hilt. (N. Y. C. P.) 150. Where the distance on a railroad over which a commodity was carried was very short, and the consignee lived sixteen miles from the road, and no agent was present to receive it on its arrival, it was held that the depositing of the commodity in the company's warehouse at the point of delivery exonerated it from the liabilities of a common carrier, and that it was thenceforth only bound as a warehouseman. Hilliard v. Wilmington, &c. R. R. Co., 6 Jones (N. C.) L. 343. If goods are shipped upon a railroad to a point beyond the first carrier's line, and directions are given as to the line by which they shall be shipped from that point, the carrier should obey such directions; but if the line named will not accept them, then the carrier may exercise his discretion. Thus, where goods were shipped by the defendants' line to a point beyond their line with instructions to ship them from that point by the P. line, and the P. line refused to accept them, and the defendants, upon the refusal of the P. line, held the goods as forwarders without any direction as to lines, it was held that it was their duty to exercise their discretion and select the best that presented and was reasonably safe; that the established usage and course of business should govern their actions; and that, having forwarded the goods by the customary method, they were not liable for their loss. Johnson v. New York, &c. R. R. Co., 31 Barb. (N. Y.) 196. A carrier

the owners of vessels from responsibility, there must be a delivery on the wharf to some person authorized to receive the goods, or some act must be done, which is an equivalent to a delivery, and that, in order to constitute a delivery, there must be a notice given to the consignee, and a reasonable time given him to make the usual and necessary preparations to receive the goods. The manner of delivering the goods, and consequently the period at which the responsibility of the master and owners will cease, depend upon the custom of the particular place and the usages of the particular trade,[1] or between the parties. Thus, in a Wisconsin case,[2] it was held

gave a receipt for goods directed to a point beyond his route, and informed the shipper that the goods would be forwarded from the end of his route. Held, upon the evidence, that there was no agreement to carry to the destination, and that the liability of the carrier ended with his route. Dillon *v.* New York, &c. R. R. Co., 1 Hilt. (N. Y. C. P.) 231. Goods came by rail, were deposited on the platform in the usual place ready for delivery, the consignee notified thereof, and he paid the freight. Held, that the liability of the railroad as carriers was thereby at an end, and even if the delivery and acceptance were not complete by the payment of freight and the lapse of a reasonable time for removal, yet that the liability of the railroad was thereafter only that of warehousemen, and as the goods were destroyed by fire without negligence on the part of the company, the owner must bear the loss. New Albany, &c. R. R. Co. *v.* Campbell, 12 Ind. 55. Carriers by railroads, or steamboats engaged in the internal coasting and river trade, in the absence of a contract for a particular mode of delivery, must deliver freight received by them to the owner, consignee, or some authorized agent, or safely land it upon the wharf at the place of destination, or deposit it in their depot houses, and promptly notify the consignee. If delivered to a drayman, cartman, or any other person not authorized by the consignee to receive it, it is at the risk of the carrier. The usage or custom of a port cannot dispense with delivery, or notice of the landing of the goods; nor will the fact that the consignee and others had submitted to a delivery of goods to a drayman before, when no loss occurred, bind him to yield his legal right to notice when it is for his interest to assert it. Dean *v.* Vaccaro, 2 Head (Tenn.), 488. The carrier of goods by railway is not bound to seek out the consignee and make an offer to deliver them. It is the business of the consignee to repair to the depot to receive the goods, and if the carrier refuse to deliver them without valid excuse, an action will lie. The fact that some of the goods have been damaged in their transit does not authorize the consignee to reject the goods entirely and hold the carrier liable as for a total loss; neither does it devolve on the carrier any obligation to make an offer to deliver, otherwise than as if the goods had arrived uninjured. Michigan, &c. R. R. Co. *v.* Bivens, 13 Ind. 263.

[1] Sleade *v.* Payne, 14 La. Ann. 453.

[2] Marshall *v.* Wells, 7 Wis. 1.

that as between a consignee (a bank) and an express company in the habit of carrying their packages, it is competent for the carrier to prove that after banking-hours the bank is closed only as to banking business, and not as to the reception of packages, but that the latter have habitually been received on the arrival of the trains after "banking-hours," and, that fact being proved, a tender of the package to the bank, an hour and a half after banking-hours, at half-past five o'clock, P. M., in summer, is a good and reasonable tender; and that even in the absence of such proof, "banking-hours" are established only for banking business, and that such a tender, made to the agents then present in the usual discharge of their duties, is good. It was also held, even though it is the duty of the expressman, under those circumstances, to make such a tender, that after a proper tender made, the carrier is liable only for gross negligence.

SEC. 231. **When Carrier's Responsibility ceases, Question for Jury.** — Whenever delivery has taken place, the responsibility of the carrier for the goods ceases; but, in order that he may free himself from the responsibility, he must deliver the goods as they were intended to be delivered. The address will be a sufficient guide as to the intention[1] of the bailor, and if the carrier deliver the parcel at a place to which it is not addressed, an action of trover lies against him.[2] But other circumstances must be considered before we can say definitely what will constitute a competent delivery, and in that way terminate the responsibility of the carrier. As might have been anticipated, this is, in many cases, a question rather for the jury than for the court.[3]

SEC. 232. **Delivery within Reasonable Time.** — Other duties with regard to delivery, however, devolve upon a carrier.

[1] Stephenson *v.* Hart, 1 M. & P. 357; 4 Bing. 676. See Add. on Con. 810.

[2] Perkins *v.* Smith, 1 Wils. 328; Youl *v.* Harbottle, Peake, N. P. C. 68; Devereux *v.* Barclay, 2 B. & A. 702; Stephens *v.* Elwall, 4 M. & S. 259; and, as distinguished from these, Ross *v.* Johnson, 5 Burr. 2825. See also Bonney *v.* The Huntress, 4 Hunt's Merch. Mag. (Jan. 1841) 83; The Ben Adams, 2 Ben. (U. S. C. C.) 445; Meyer *v.* Chicago, &c. R. R. Co., 24 Wis. 586.

[3] See Hedges *v.* Hudson River R. R. Co., 6 Robt. (N. Y.) 119.

The place is not only a matter of importance, but the time is an element of the contract. Goods are not delivered to a carrier that he may deliver them at his own good pleasure, but that he may deliver them in such time as, looking at the length of his ordinary journey, the mode of the conveyance, and the circumstances of which the bailor might be cognizant before he intrusted his goods, shall be deemed reasonable.[1] In a case where the defendants received goods to be carried from London to Seaham Harbor, near Sunderland, and sent them by Newcastle instead of by Sunderland, it was held that they had not fulfilled the obligation to carry goods by the usual route professed by them.[2] And as there was a considerable delay in forwarding the goods from Newcastle, it was held that they had violated another obligation, which arises in the absence of any express contract, and that is, to deliver within reasonable time.[3]

SEC. 233. **Delay occasioned by Act of God.** — It would, however, be unfair to hold that the carrier had violated any duty in regard to the time of delivery, if the delay was proved to be occasioned by the act of God or by the enemies of the country of the carrier. The loss of the goods by any casualty which can be classed under either of these heads would not make him liable as an insurer[4] to the owner, and the loss of time arising in the same way should not subject him to any liability for a breach of his duty to deliver in a reasonable time. Indeed, the expression "reasonable time" might suggest the impossibility of imputing a delay thus occasioned to the carrier as a ground for recovery of any loss suffered by the owner of the goods. It would appear, therefore, that the question as to what will be considered a reasonable time is to be looked at in relation to all the circumstances of the case, — the weather, the state of the roads, the season of the year, and other matters of a like sort, might be considered with a view to a satisfactory answer.[5] Thus, where the defendants,

[1] Hughes *v.* Great Western Rail. Co., 14 C. B. 637; 2 C. L. R. 1360; Raphael *v.* Pickford, 6 Scott, N. R. 478; 5 M. & G. 558.

[2] But see, per TINDAL, C. J., Davis *v.* Garrett, 6 Bing. 725.

[3] 2 B. & S. 66.

[4] *Ante*, pp. 164–173.

[5] Briddon *v.* Great Northern Rail. Co., 28 L. J. Exch. 51; Broadwell *v.* Butler, 6 McLean (U. S.), 296; 1 Newb. 171.

a railway company, were prevented, by an unavoidable obstruction on their line, from carrying the plaintiff's goods within the usual (a reasonable) time, — the obstruction having been caused solely by the negligence of another company who had running-powers over their line, — the defendants were held not to be liable to the plaintiff for damage to his goods caused by the delay.[1] While, therefore, it is the carrier's duty to convey goods by means of the ordinary route, and without any unnecessary delay, both these duties may be obviated by the circumstances, and where either delay or deviation is necessary for the safety of the goods, it will be held to have been a part of the primary duty of the carrier.[2] It is the carrier's duty to deliver the goods to the consignee upon his presenting himself in reasonable time and at a proper place to receive them. If the consignee does this, or until he has had an opportunity to do so, there seems to be no good ground for reducing the liability of the carrier to that of a warehouseman.[3] The rule may perhaps be better stated to be, that *the liability of a carrier as such, continues until the goods are ready to be delivered at their place of destination, and the consignee has had a reasonable opportunity, during the hours when such goods are usually delivered, in which to examine them so far as to judge of their outward appearance, and to remove them.*[4] As to what constitutes a reasonable opportu-

[1] Taylor *v.* Great Northern Rail. Co., 1 L. R. C. P. 385.

[2] Davis *v.* Garrett, 6 Bing. 725.

[3] Graves *v.* Hartford, &c. Steamboat Co., 38 Conn. 143; TINDAL, C. J., in Gatliffe *v.* Bourne, 4 Bing. 333.

[4] Shenk *v.* Philadelphia Steam Propeller Co., 60 Penn. St. 109; The Mary Washington, 1 Abb. (U. S.) 1; Lamb *v.* Camden, &c. R. R. Co., 2 Daly (N. Y. C. P.), 454; Solomon *v.* Philadelphia Steamboat, &c. Co., 2 Daly (N. Y. C. P.), 104. In Graves *v.* Hartford, &c. Steamboat Co., *ante*, an action was brought against the defendants as common carriers by water for the loss of twelve bales of cotton which were transported by them from New York to Hartford. The steamer which carried the cotton to Hartford arrived, and on the day of arrival notice was sent to the plaintiff that the cotton was on the boat at the wharf in Hartford. The notice was sent between 8.30 and 9 o'clock in the forenoon, and at about 11.30 of the same forenoon the plaintiff's cartmen arrived at the boat with a team and assistants to help load the cotton, when they were told by the defendants that it was not off the boat, and that there was so much freight, and it was so far back in the boat, that they could not

nity, it may be said that no reference is to be had to the peculiar circumstances of the consignee, but is such as would give

get at it. The carmen then went to dinner, and between 12.30 and 1 o'clock of the same day started again for the cotton. The defendants' warehouse and freight upon the dock were then in flames.

The defendants had a commodious warehouse, with suitable and convenient open and covered platforms, situated upon their wharf, for the reception, delivery, and storage of freight transported by them; and freight-owners were accustomed to receive their freight from the platforms, the company leaving their freight on the platforms during the day, for convenience of delivery, and at night removing it into their warehouse, where it was stored without charge till called for. The plaintiffs' consignee had been accustomed to receive goods from the warehouse and platform. The cotton was discharged from the steamer between 11 and 12 o'clock, and placed on the platform in front of defendants' warehouse, at a place where, in the usual course of business, that kind of freight was usually deposited for delivery, at which place it remained in waiting until about 1 o'clock, when the warehouse took fire without fault of the defendants, and the cotton was mostly consumed.

The judge was requested by the plaintiffs' counsel to charge the jury that "the defendants' responsibility as carriers continued until the goods had been landed at the usual wharf, and notice given to the consignee, and the goods had been kept safely a sufficient time to give the consignee reasonable access to them to examine them, and reasonable time to remove them." The judge refused such instruction, and charged them as follows: "There is but one question in this case for you to determine. It is this. Was the cotton deposited by the defendants upon their wharf in Hartford? A common carrier making known and regular transits, and having a warehouse and platforms for the delivery of goods at the end of the transit, is discharged from liability as a carrier on placing the goods either on such platform or in such warehouse, for delivery to the owner or consignee, and thenceforth is only a warehouseman. If the jury shall find that in this case the defendants had provided a proper platform and warehouse at the end of their route for the delivery of freight, and in the usual course of business were accustomed to deliver goods on such platform, storing them in their warehouse only in case they were not called for during the day, or within a reasonable time, then the defendants would not be liable as common carriers for any goods safely discharged from their boat and deposited on said platform for delivery to the consignee." A verdict was had for the defendants, but upon appeal it was set aside; SEYMOUR, J., saying:

"The decisions of courts upon the questions involved in this case are conflicting, and we shall not attempt to marshal them and decide upon their weight. The authorities are so divided that we feel at liberty to decide the case upon our views of its merits, and of the principles which ought to govern it. The receipt given by the defendants does not attempt to specially define their duties. It simply acknowledges that the goods are received by the boat for W. F. Willard, agent, Hartford. It is of course to be construed in reference to the defend-

to a person residing in the vicinity of the place of delivery and informed of the usual course of the business, and of the

ants' mode of transportation, which being by water, their duty, so far as the carriage of the goods is concerned, is limited by that mode of conveyance. They are not required, as carriers by wagon under a like receipt would be, to seek the consignee on the land and make delivery at his place of business. The usual course of business of carriers by water, in general, and of the defendants in particular, may properly be referred to in giving a construction to the writing. The defendants made regular trips, and had their platforms and warehouses upon a wharf of their own in Hartford, where they were accustomed to deliver, and where consignees were accustomed to receive, their goods. Upon these facts the defendants claimed, and the plaintiffs conceded, that the wharf and platforms were the *proper places* of delivery. But the plaintiffs claimed, upon the fair and reasonable construction of the receipt, in connection with the admitted facts, that, if the consignee presents himself to receive his goods at the proper place and in proper time, the defendants are bound as common carriers to deliver the goods to him, and that in such a case the delivery to the consignee is a clear duty belonging to the defendants as common carriers under their contract. We think the plaintiffs are right in this proposition, and that, if the consignee is on hand in proper time and at the proper place, there is no room, nor any occasion, for the interposition of a warehouseman.

"We are not certain that the judge's charge to the jury was intended to apply to the case where the consignee is present and ready to take his consignment; but his language is general, and in terms is applicable to such a case. He says: 'A carrier making known and regular transits, and having a warehouse and platform for the delivery of goods at the end of the transit, is discharged from liability as a carrier on placing such goods either on such platform, or in such warehouse, for delivery to the owner and consignee, and thenceforth is only a warehouseman.' This charge, as applied to a case where the consignee or his agent is present to receive his goods, is, we think, clearly erroneous. In such case it is the duty of the defendants not only to place the goods on the platform '*for delivery*,' but it is their duty to make delivery, and that duty pertains to them as carriers. The parties have entered into only one contract, and that is a contract by the defendants as common carriers, and the contract cannot be changed to one of warehousemen, unless the plaintiffs, by neglect to be present to take their goods, make the interposition of the relation of warehousemen necessary. The placing the goods on the platform in the manner these defendants are accustomed to do, is rather a preparatory step toward a delivery, than in itself a delivery. The transfer of the possession and custody of the goods to the consignee is regarded as an important part of the duty of the carrier. During this transfer the goods are pointed out and selected, and their condition is examined in the presence of both parties, that it may be seen whether they have come safely, without injury or depredation. The goods are usually placed upon the platform for the mere convenience of the carrier, and are there assorted and arranged by him before he is ready to commence delivery. And, surely, until

time when the goods are expected to arrive, suitable opportunity *within the usual business hours*, to take them away.[1]

the consignee can get his goods, they must be regarded as in the defendants' possession as carriers. Cases were cited by counsel to show that, in some instances, delivery to a wharfinger or warehouseman has been held to be a good substitute for delivery to the owner. But this is only in cases where the owner has failed to come in due time to take the goods himself. If he thus fails, then indeed the carrier discharges his duty by leaving the goods with a warehouseman for the owner. But it is only because the owner is not ready to take his property that it may be left in a warehouse for him.

"But the case in the court below does not appear to have been tried upon the precise question thus far discussed. The plaintiffs did not put themselves upon the ground that their carman was actually present and waiting for the goods at the time of the fire, but on the broader ground that he used due diligence to get his goods, and that he was entitled to a reasonable time after their arrival to take them away, and that the defendants remained chargeable as common carriers until such reasonable time had expired. And the important point still remains to be considered, whether the plaintiffs are or are not correct in this broader claim. We have already said that, in our judgment, the consignees are entitled to receive their goods from the defendants as common carriers, if they present themselves at the proper place and at the proper time for that purpose. The point now to be considered is, what is that proper time. In order to avail themselves of their rights in this respect, must the consignees be on hand immediately on the arrival of the boat, and remain there constantly, without being absent even for their meals, until their goods are ready, and must they then immediately take them, or is a reasonable time to be allowed for these purposes? We suppose it is generally more convenient for the carrier that there should be no rush immediately upon his arrival. We suppose it is more convenient for him that he should examine and arrange his lading, and compare it with his bills, and place it in order on his platform, before he commences to deliver goods to consignees. Where the amount of freight is large, and for a large number of persons, it is not unreasonable for the carrier to refuse to commence the delivery until the steamer is unladen, and the goods properly arranged for the owners. And, this being so, it seems to us that consignees should also be allowed a reasonable time to take away their goods, so that they shall not be subjected to vexatious and irritating delays and waste of time in waiting for their turns. It is for the interest and convenience of both parties that the delivery should be deliberate, in order that mistakes may be avoided, and that the goods may be subjected to a careful examination, that it may be known whether the carrier has or has not carefully and properly discharged his duty in the transportation. In cases where the carrier has no warehouse or conveniences for keeping the goods, he may properly require that the consignee should be quite prompt, or be visited with the consequences of a deposit in a warehouse. But where, as in this case, the defendants have

[1] Moses *v.* Boston & Maine R. R. Co., 32 N. H. 523.

Thus, in the case last cited, ten bags of wool were delivered by the plaintiff to the defendant to be transported from Exeter,

commodious warehouses and platforms, and are doing an extensive business, consignees ought to have a fair and reasonable opportunity to take their property, and until they have had such opportunity and time, the goods do and ought to remain in the care of the carrier as such. Whatever reasons there are for imposing a strict rule of responsibility during the transit, exist and continue in full force until the consignee has reasonable time to take the goods into his own care and custody. The rule adopted in Massachusetts has the merit of being definite and of easy application, and may, in many cases, avoid a painful controversy as to what, under the circumstances, is a reasonable time within which the consignee must appear and take his goods. But, on the other hand, that rule puts an end to the carrier's responsibility as such, just where that responsibility is of the highest value to the shipper. Between the deposit of the goods on the platform and their delivery to the consignee, they are exposed to theft, depredation, and injury by strangers, and by the carriers' employees. In making delivery care is needed to avoid mistakes, and attention required to see if the goods are uninjured. During the whole process of delivery until fully completed, the goods should remain in the care of the carrier upon the full responsibility pertaining to him as such, and he ought not to be allowed to lay aside that responsibility, until the owner of the goods has had a fair and reasonable time and opportunity to receive them.

"In the case of Gatliffe *v.* Bourne, 4 Bing. 333, the defendants, being common carriers by water, interposed a defence similar to that made by these defendants, by way of a special plea, which was demurred to; and in deciding the demurrer well taken, CHIEF JUSTICE TINDAL says: 'The next special plea contains indeed the averment that, after the steam vessel had arrived in the port of London, the defendants were ready and willing to deliver the goods to the plaintiff, but that he was not there ready to receive them, whereupon the defendants landed the goods at the wharf. But this allegation is open to the objection that it does not appear that the plaintiff had a reasonable time or opportunity for receiving his goods from the vessel's side. The statement in the plea is compatible with the supposition that the steamboat arrived in the port at midnight, and proceeded at full speed to the wharf, and there immediately deposited the goods; facts which, whatever might be the readiness or willingness of the defendants to deliver, would make it impracticable for the plaintiff to receive them, if he had been there, and unreasonable to expect him to be there.'

"There are indeed particulars in which the case of Gatliffe *v.* Bourne differs somewhat from the case under our consideration. But we think CHIEF JUSTICE TINDAL expresses the true general rule governing the duty of carriers, to wit, that they are bound as carriers to deliver the goods to the consignee, provided the consignee appears within a reasonable time to receive them, and that the consignee is entitled to a fair and reasonable opportunity to receive his goods, before the carrier can deliver them over to himself, or to another as warehouseman. A new trial is therefore advised."

N. H., to Boston, and there delivered to a consignee. The wool was carried over the defendants' road on a train which arrived at their freight-house in Boston between one and three o'clock in the afternoon. In the usual course of business, from two to three hours were required to unload the freight from the cars into the warehouse, and the gates were closed at five o'clock, so that no goods could be removed from the warehouse after that hour until the next morning. During the night the warehouse and most of its contents, including the wool, were consumed by fire. It was held that upon these facts the jury were warranted in finding that the consignee had not a reasonable opportunity to take the wool into his possession before the fire, and that the defendants were liable as common carriers therefor, notwithstanding it might be proved by them that before the fire the wool had been placed upon the platform in the warehouse, from which such goods were usually delivered, separate from other goods, and ready for delivery.[1] In a New York case,[2] the defendants,

[1] Leaveuworth, &c. R. R. Co. *v.* Maris, 16 Kan. 333; Blumenthal *v.* Brainard, 38 Vt. 402; Winslow *v.* Vermont, &c. R. R. Co., 42 Vt. 700; Ouimit *v.* Heushaw, 35 Vt. 604; Porter *v.* R. R. Co., 20 Ill. 407; Alabama and Tennessee Rivers R. R. Co. *v.* Kidd, 35 Ala. 209; Chicago, &c. R. R. Co. *v.* Bensley, 69 Ill. 630; Wood *v.* Cracker, 18 Wis. 345; Lemke *v.* Chicago, &c. R. R. Co., 39 Wis. 449; Hirsch *v.* Quaker City, 2 Dis. (Ohio), 144; Morris, &c. R. R. Co. *v.* Ayres, 28 N. J. L. 393; Maignan *v.* New Orleans, &c. R. R. Co., 24 La. An. 333. A common carrier has not performed his contract as carrier until he has delivered, or offered to deliver, the goods to the consignee, or done what the law esteems equivalent to delivery. When the consignee is unknown to the carrier, a due effort to find him and notify him of the arrival of the goods, is a condition precedent to the right to warehouse them; and if a reasonable and diligent effort is not made, the carrier is liable for the consequences of the neglect. Zinn *v.* New Jersey Steamboat Co., 49 N. Y. 442. A common carrier, by water, of goods consigned to one not the owner, is not bound to deliver to the consignee in person, or at his warehouse. He may land them at a wharf at the port of destination, but before unlading he must give the consignee due notice of their arrival and unlading, and yield him a reasonable time after notice to take charge of and secure them; and reasonable time is such as gives the consignee time enough, under all proper and ordinary circumstances, and by proceeding in the ordinary mode of those engaged in the same business, to provide for the care and removal of the goods. McAndrews *v.* Whetlock, 52 N. Y. 40.

[2] Solomon *v.* Philadelphia, &c. Steamboat Co., 2 Daly (N. Y. C. P.), 104.

as common carriers, had in charge goods of the plaintiff which arrived Thursday, and were discharged on the dock Friday. Notice was mailed to the plaintiff Thursday evening of the arrival of the goods, but did not reach the plaintiff until Saturday forenoon. Saturday was a very stormy day, and the goods were not called for until Monday, when they were found to be badly damaged by the rain. The court held that the defendants remained liable as common carriers until notice of the arrival of the goods, and the plaintiff had had a reasonable opportunity for removing them; and that, under the circumstances, Monday was a reasonable time to remove the goods. And this rule also applies to carriers by water.[1] But a consignee cannot, after he has notice of the arrival of goods, defer taking them away while he attends to other affairs, or because it is inconvenient for him to do so, and thus prolong the carrier's liability as insurer. It is his duty at once, with diligence, to act upon the notice, and to seek delivery and continue it until the delivery is complete; and the time he gives to his other business after receiving the notice cannot be allowed him in determining what is a reasonable time in which to take delivery.[2] In Massachusetts,[3] however, it is held that the liability of the carrier as such, ceases when the goods have reached their place of destination and have been safely deposited upon the platform or in their warehouse, and that from that time, without notice to the consignee of their arrival, he is liable only as a warehouseman for their safe keeping; and this rule is adopted in North Carolina, Pennsylvania, Iowa, California, Indiana, Illinois, Alabama, and Georgia,[4] except that in the latter States the liability of the

[1] Shenk *v.* Philadelphia Steam Propeller Co., 60 Penn. St. 109; The Mary Washington, *ante;* Lamb *v.* Camden, &c. R. R. Co., *ante.*

[2] Hedges *v.* Hudson River R. R. Co., 49 N. Y. 223.

[3] Thomas *v.* Boston & Providence R. R. Co., 10 Met. (Mass.) 472; Norway Plains Co. *v.* Boston & Maine R. R. Co., 1 Gray (Mass.), 263; Stowe *v.* New York, &c. R. R. Co., 113 Mass. 521; Barron *v.* Eldredge, 100 Mass. 455.

[4] Neal *v.* Wilmington, &c. R. R. Co., 8 Jones (N. C.), L. 482; McCarty *v.* New York & Erie R. R. Co., 30 Penn. St. 247; Mohr *v.* Chicago, &c. R. R. Co., 40 Iowa, 579; Jackson *v.* Sacramento Valley R. R. Co., 23 Val. 269; Chicago, &c. R. R. Co. *v.* Mc-

carrier is not changed to that of a warehouseman until the goods have been placed in the warehouse or other place of safe deposit. Where the consignee *knows* that the goods have arrived, and of their readiness for delivery, or is present when they arrived, the carrier is excused from giving notice; and if he neglects to take them away within a reasonable time, the carrier is absolved from liability therefor, as such.[1] If the carrier is ignorant of the whereabouts of the consignee, it is his duty to make due inquiry to ascertain it, and if, after due inquiry, he fails to ascertain the fact, he is excused from giving notice; and after a reasonable time for removal has elapsed, his liability as a carrier ceases, if he has stored the goods, and he is only liable as a warehouseman.[2] From what has been said, it will be seen that the Massachusetts doctrine, that the carrier's liability terminates when the goods are unloaded from the train, does not obtain any sanction from the courts of the other States, and that the doctrine that the liability ceases when the goods are safely stored, without notice to the consignee, only prevails in a few of the States.

In one case in which a carrier did not deliver within reasonable time, the bailor was not only allowed to recover for that breach of duty upon the part of the carrier, but for the expenses to which the latter was put in consequence of the delay.[3]

Cool, 26 Ind. 140; Chicago, &c. R. R. Co. *v.* Scott, 42 Ill. 132; Alabama, &c. R. R. Co. *v.* Kidd, 35 Ala. 209; South-Western, &c. R. R. Co. *v.* Felder, 46 Ga. 433.

[1] Fenner *v.* Buffalo, &c. R. R. Co., 44 N. Y. 505; Pelton *v.* Rensselaer & Saratoga R. R. Co., 54 N. Y. 214. In Pinney *v.* First Division St. Paul, &c. R. R. Co., 19 Minn. 251, the rule was stated to be that, "if the consignee is present on the arrival of the goods, he must take them without unreasonable delay. But if he is not present, but lives at the place of delivery, the carrier must notify him of the arrival of the goods, and then he has a reasonable time to take and remove them." See also, adopting the same rule, Buckley *v.* Great Western R. R. Co., 18 Mich. 121; Culbreath *v.* Philadelphia, &c. R. R. Co., 3 Houst. (Del.) 392; Sprague *v.* New York Central R. R. Co., 52 N. Y. 637. In Mississippi it is held that where it is the custom of the company to give notice of the arrival of the freight, it is his duty to do so. New Orleans, &c. R. R. Co. *v.* Tyson, 46 Miss. 729.

[2] Pelton *v.* Rensselaer & Saratoga R. R. Co., *ante.*

[3] Black *v.* Baxendale, 1 Exch. 410; 17 L. J. Ex. 50. See also Adams *v.* Midland Rail. Co., 31 L. J. Exch. 35;

SEC. 234. **Loss of Profit.** — In the case of Hadley *v.* Baxendale,[1] however, the rule that only such damages can be recovered for the breach of a contract as were reasonably within the contemplation of the parties at the time the contract was made, was laid down, and in a case which came before the Court of Common Pleas soon afterwards it was acted upon. In that case it was held that a loss of profit by reason of the plaintiff, a commercial traveller, having left the town before the goods arrived, where the lateness of arrival was caused by the tardiness of a carrier company, could not be recovered.[2] And in another case, where it was proved that a commercial traveller delivered, in Oxford, a parcel of samples to a common carrier to be conveyed to Liverpool, but did not state the contents of the parcel, or the purpose for which it was required, and where, by the negligence of the carrier, the parcel was delayed, and the traveller spent three days at Liverpool, unemployed, waiting for it, in an action against the carrier for negligence, in which the hotel expenses of the traveller during the time he was waiting for the parcel were claimed as damages, it was held that he could not recover, on the ground that the damages were too remote, and that the profit which was lost by the delay in the case of The Great Western Railway Company *v.* Redmayne [3] would seem more naturally within the contemplation of the parties than hotel expenses. This case [4] overruled that of Black *v.* Baxendale, referred to above.[5]

SEC. 235. **Delivery must take Place as Early as Possible.** — With regard to the excuses for delay which have been mentioned above, we may mention in this place that any such retardation in the performance of the duty of the carrier only excuses delay, and does not relieve him from the duty of delivering at the earliest opportunity.[6]

Hamlin *v.* Great Northern Rail. Co., 1 H. & N. 408; 26 L. J. Exch. 20; Bodley *v.* Reynolds, 8 Q. B. 779; 15 L. J. Q. B. 219.

[1] 9 Exch. 341; 23 L. J. Exch. 179.

[2] Great Western Rail. Co. *v.* Redmayne, L. R. 1 C. P. 329.

[3] Great Western Rail. Co. *v.* Redmayne, L. R. 1 C. P. 329.

[4] Woodger *v.* Great Western Rail. Co., L. R. 2 C. P. 318.

[5] 1 Exch. 410.

[6] Hudley *v.* Clarke, 8 T. R. 259; Evans *v.* Hutton, 5 Scott, N. R. 670; Story on Bailm., 4th ed., § 545.

SEC. 236. **Delivery at a Reasonable Time and at Proper Place.** — But not only must delivery be made within a reasonable time, but, in order to exonerate the carrier from further responsibility in connection with the goods, it must be made at a reasonable time, in a reasonable manner, and at the proper place.[1] Unless these three requisites of a delivery are complied with, the responsibility of the carrier cannot be said to cease whenever he has got the goods out of his hands, any more than he could be said to terminate it by pitching the goods out of the conveyance during the journey.

SEC. 237. **Proper Time.** — As to a proper time: if perishable goods were delivered at the consignee's warehouse after the hour of closing, and, in consequence of that circumstance, were refused by some servant of the consignee, and the carrier, believing that his whole duty was discharged by such delivery, took no further care of the goods, — if in such a case injury was done to the goods by reason of the carrier's negligence, he would be liable to the bailor.

SEC. 238. **The Manner of Delivery.** — As to the manner in which goods are to be delivered, a consignee would be entitled to refuse to receive goods from a drunken man. And further, as to the manner of delivery, if it is customary for the carrier by water to carry merely from port to port, or from wharf to wharf, and for the owner to fetch the goods from the vessel itself, or from the wharf, as soon as the arrival of the ship has been reported, the carrier must give such owner due no-

[1] Goodwin *v.* Baltimore & Ohio R. R. Co., 50 N. Y. 154; but in this case it was held that the duty of the carrier ceases by the landing of bulky articles upon a public wharf *in the customary manner, with due notice to the consignee.* If a carrier lands perishable articles upon a wharf upon an unsuitable day, without reasonable notice to the consignee, he is liable for the damages resulting. McAndrews *v.* Whetlock, 52 N. Y. 40. See also, upon the general proposition in the text, Rowland *v.* Miln, 2 Hilt. (N. Y. C. P.) 150. The carrier is bound to provide a suitable place for delivery, and to provide suitable safeguards to prevent loss. Sunderland *v.* Westcott, 40 How. Pr. (N. Y.) 270; Cleveland, &c. R. R. Co. *v.* Sargent, 19 Ohio St. 438; Propeller Mohawk, 8 Wall. (U. S.) 153; Hill *v.* Humphreys, 5 W. & S. (Penn.) 123; Haslam *v.* Adams Express Co., 6 Bosw. (N. Y. Sup. Ct.) 235. But the consignee may, by accepting the goods at another and different place from that to which they are consigned, discharge the carrier from liability. Jewell *v.* Grand Trunk R. R. Co., 55 N. H. 84; Parsons *v.* Hardy, 14 Wend. (N. Y.) 215.

tice of the arrival of the said goods, in order to discharge himself from further liability. He cannot land the goods without such notice, and so discharge himself, but is bound to keep the goods on board at his own risk for a reasonable time to enable the consignee to come and fetch them.[1]

SEC. 239. **Merchant Shipping Act.** — The Merchant Shipping Amendment Act, 1862,[2] empowers the shipowner to enter and land the goods, in default of entry and landing by the owner; and notwithstanding the landing the shipowner may, by giving notice for that purpose, preserve his lien for freight.

SEC. 240. **Proper Place.** — As to place, it has been held that coach proprietors are not relieved from their responsibility, as carriers, by leaving goods at the coach-office, or at an inn at which the coach was in the habit of stopping; and where a parcel of goods was directed to "Mr. James Parker, High Street, Oxford," who, on being applied to, said he expected no such parcel, and it was afterwards delivered to a person who called at the defendant's office, claiming it as his, and who paid the carriage for it, the carrier was held responsible.[3]

[1] Bourne v. Gatliffe, 3 Scott, N. R. 44; 11 Cl. & Fin. 45.

[2] 25 & 26 Vict. c. 63, § 67 *et seq.*

[3] Duff v. Budd, 6 Moore, 469; 3 B. & B. 177. There were two men in St. Charles named H. H. A merchant at a distance received an order for goods, signed H. H., and, knowing of H. H. No. 1, to whom he was willing to sell, forwarded the goods by railroad. The company tendered the goods to H. H. No. 1, who said he had not ordered them, and refused them, and the company then stored them as warehousemen. H. H. No. 2 then appeared, produced bill of lading, and demanded the goods. The company delivered them to him, and he absconded with them, the price remaining unpaid to the seller, who then sued the company on the ground of misdelivery. It was held that the company, as warehousemen, were liable for due diligence only; that they were not chargeable, under the circumstances, with negligence; and there had not been a misdelivery. Bush v. St. Louis, &c. R. R. Co., 3 Mo. App. 62.

The delivery of goods to an agent of the consignee or owner relieves him from liability, but he is bound at his peril to know whether such person is authorized to receive them as agent. Adonis v. Blankenstein, 3 Cal. 413. They must at their peril deliver the goods to the right person, and if they make a wrong delivery they will be liable for the loss occasioned thereby. The Huntress, Davies (U. S. C. C.), 82. Indeed, a misdelivery is treated as a conversion by the carrier. Claflin v.

SEC. 241. **Liability of Carriers for Misdelivery.** — Where also a carrier, with the intention of delivering goods at the

Boston, &c. R. R. Co., 7 Allen (Mass.), 341.

On Feb. 20, 1869, plaintiffs shipped by defendant's line a quantity of butter to be carried from New York to Georgetown, consigned to plaintiffs' order; the packages were unmarked. One S. presented to defendant's delivery clerk a letter written by plaintiffs to him, containing this clause, "The roll sent you to-day you will find of very good quality;" and upon this the clerk delivered the butter to S. It was held that, as a question of law, the letter was not a sufficient authority to justify a delivery of the butter to S.; nor was the writing of it negligence *per se;* but it was a question of fact for the jury to determine, from the letter and the other facts of the case, whether by plaintiffs' negligence or otherwise the defendant was excused or justified in the delivery of the property. Viner *v.* N. Y., &c. Steamship Co., 50 N. Y. 23. Where a common carrier, without requiring evidence of identity, delivers to a stranger goods which have been fraudulently ordered by the latter in the name of a fictitious firm, and which have been shipped in compliance with the order directed to the fictitious firm, he is liable to the consignor for their value. Price *v.* Oswego, &c. R. R. Co., 50 N. Y. 213. In a case where the defendants received goods for transportation, accompanied by a manifest containing the instructions: "Order A, B, & Co., notify C," and they delivered the same to C, without the order of A and B, who were the plaintiffs, it was held that the defendants were liable for the loss incurred by the plaintiffs by such delivery. The defendants might perhaps decline to receive such shipments, but after they receive them they must obey the written directions of the consignor. Wright *v.* Northern Central R. R. Co., 8 Phil. (Penn.) 19.

In a Wisconsin case, where a carrier who, without authority from the consignor or consignee, delivered to B a package directed to A (and not to care of B), and it was never delivered to A, it was held that the carrier remained liable to A, although B was the consignor's agent in respect to other business, at the place of delivery. Ela *v.* American M. U. Exp. Co., 29 Wis. 611.

If a custom as to the place and manner of delivery of goods to a certain person has been established, the carrier is justified in pursuing that method; but if he deviates therefrom, and, as a result, the goods are lost, he is liable therefor. Thus, in an action against an express company for the loss of a diamond pin consigned to a student at a college, it was held that if it was the custom of the president of the college to receive from the defendant parcels directed to the students therein under his charge, and receipt therefor, or if it was in accordance with the rules of the college that he should do so, then he might properly be considered as the authorized agent of the students for that purpose, and the jury might presume a good delivery to the student to whom it was addressed, when delivered to the president. Southern Express Co. *v.* Everett, 37 Ga. 688. In an Illinois case the defendants, who were common carriers, had a written order from the plaintiff "to deliver to F. or Dane County Bank any packages that might come for him." They received at their express office, which was in the same building with the

address to which they were directed, made inquiries for the consignee at that place, but could not hear of him, and upon

bank, a package of $1,000 for the plaintiff, and, the bank clerk being in, while the defendants were distributing their goods, they said to him, "Here is a package for D. J. B. [the plaintiff]; will you take it?" He answered, "I will ask the bank," and returning immediately said, "Let F. have it." The defendant's agent left word at the store of F. that the package was at the office, and F.'s clerk said that F. was absent, and that he would come over and see about it. He afterwards went over and said that "F. was away and had the key of the safe, and that the defendants would have to keep it." But the package was not offered to him, nor was it entered on the delivery book according to the custom of the company. It was held that the package had not been delivered, and that the company was liable. Baldwin *v.* American, &c. Co., 23 Ill. 197.

The strictness of the rule requiring a delivery to the consignee or owner, or his agent, is illustrated by a New York case. In that case the plaintiff occupied a room in the fourth story of a building, and a carrier brought a box, weighing about sixty pounds, and placed it within the outside door of the building at the foot of the stairs, and then went up and notified a boy whom he found in the office, that the box was there and must be taken care of. The boy was not authorized to receive packages. The court held that there was not a sufficient delivery to discharge the carrier. Haslam *v.* Adams Express Co., 6 Bosw. (N. Y. Sup. Ct.) 235.

If the carrier, when bound to make a personal delivery, as in the case of an express company, tenders or offers to make delivery to the consignee at a proper time and place for delivery, and the consignee declines, for a cause which does not involve any fault on the carrier's part, to accept delivery, the carrier from that time stands only in the relation of a warehouseman. Thus in Weed *v.* Barney, 45 N. Y. 344, 6 Am. Rep. 97, the plaintiff consigned an express package marked "C. O. D." from New York to San Francisco. Defendants, an express company, received it, conveyed it to San Francisco, and on the 17th of March tendered it to the consignee, and demanded payment. The consignee said he would receive the package and pay at some other time. The tender of the package and demand of payment were repeated by the company several times until the 16th of April, when the package was destroyed while in defendants' warehouse without their fault. It was held that defendants' liability was that of warehousemen only, and that plaintiff could not recover the value of the package.

PECKHAM, J., in delivering the opinion of the court, said: "Whether Wells, Fargo, & Co. were liable as common carriers, or otherwise, for the package received at New York for San Francisco, as between those two cities, is not material to the controversy. The defendants received the package at the ship's tackles at San Francisco, and their responsibility confessed by them then commenced. They were to deliver the package to Finch & Co., at San Francisco, and collect the amount marked thereon, together with charges and commissions. The package was received by the defendants on the 17th of March, and put in their

receiving letters ordering them to be sent elsewhere, delivered them at the place mentioned in the letters, upon the transac-

warehouse, and it was tendered to the consignees and payment demanded. This was repeated several times, until on the 16th of April, when the package was destroyed, without fault of the defendants. Let it be remembered that this package could not have been delivered by the defendants. It was to be delivered only upon payment of the money; and the money was not paid. There was no refusal to receive or to pay. The consignees promised to receive and pay each time, and their delay in so doing was not unusual.

"Thus the package remained in the defendants' warehouse until it was destroyed, without their fault. We have lately held that a passenger's baggage, arriving at the end of the journey, and not called for until three days thereafter, was then held by the carriers as warehousemen. Burnell *v.* New York Central R. R. Co., *ante*, 128; and see Roth *v.* Buffalo and State Line R. R., 34 N. Y. 548; Goold *v.* Chapin, 20 N. Y. 259; Northrup *v.* Railroad, 2 Trans. App. 183; *In re* Webb, 8 Taunt. 443. After the defendants had tendered the package to the consignees and demanded the money, and after the consignees had had a reasonable time to call for and receive it, I think the defendants held the package as warehousemen, and not as common carriers, and were thereafter responsible for the care of warehousemen merely, whatever their attitude before. As warehousemen, it is not pretended they were liable.

"But it is insisted that the defendants should have given notice to the consignor, when the consignees did not receive and pay for the package. Was there any contract to do so? All there was on that subject was a mere direction from the defendants here to their agents there 'to notify this office' 'if the goods are refused or the parties cannot be found.' This could scarcely be regarded as a contract with the consignor. Nor did either contingency happen. The goods were not 'refused;' but the consignees promised to take and pay for them, within the time usual at San Francisco. What was there to notify, so long as these consignees were acting as others usually did at that place, if the practice were reasonable and valid? Neither counsel has questioned the validity of this practice, and I do not propose to pass upon it. The situation and location of the parties must be considered in reference to notice. Mail-time, then, between New York and San Francisco was twenty-two days. The defendants, of course, expected to get pay for the goods before a letter could be answered. Telegraphing was expensive; and there does not seem to have been occasion for its use. There is no statement that it was usually or ever resorted to under such circumstances. The authorities would not seem to require notice under the facts of this case, though notice may be sometimes necessary. Expressmen are not required to do unreasonable or absurd things. Heugh *v.* London & North-Western Rail. Co., L. R. 5 Exch. 51; London & North-Western Rail. Co. *v.* Bartlett, 7 H. & N. 400; Kremer *v.* Southern Express Co., 6 Coldw. (Tenn.) 356; Gulliver *v.* Adams Express Co., 38 Ill. 503.

"In the case at bar, what had the expressmen to communicate if they had given notice? Nothing unusual, as nothing unusual had occurred.

tion proving to be a fraud on the consignor by some person, and upon action being brought against the carrier for the goods, he was held liable for their loss, having been guilty of negligence in so delivering the goods.[1]

SEC. 242. **What constitutes Delivery.** — This subject was discussed in some of its relations in the case of Hyde *v.* Trent and Mersey Navigation Company.[2] At the trial it appeared that the goods were put on board the defendants' barges at the respective places mentioned in the declaration, and conveyed therein along the defendants' navigation and the Duke of Bridgewater's Canal to Manchester, where they were landed upon the quay and lodged there in the Duke of Bridgewater's warehouse, in which place they were consumed by an accidental fire the same night. In bills made out by the defendants, there were charges of so much for tonnage on the river Trent, so much for tonnage on the Trent and Mersey Navigation, so much for the Duke of Bridgewater's Canal, so much for warehouse-room for the Duke of Bridgewater; besides which, in the bill, there was a charge for the cartage from the Duke of Bridgewater's warehouse to the plaintiff's own warehouse in Manchester, and which was paid by the plaintiff when the goods were put on board the defendants' barges; but the charge for the warehouse-room was merely received by the defendants as agents for the duke, and they had no share of the profit. It appeared also to be the practice of many persons in Manchester, for whom goods were brought by the

But suppose they had notified the home office of the whole facts, and they had directly come to the knowledge of the consignor? He had thus become aware that some days had elapsed and the money had not been paid, but had been promised, and no doubt would be paid in a few days, as was usual at that place. Would the consignor have given any directions at war with the course pursued by defendants? In all probability he would not. But if he had given directions by mail to return the goods forthwith to New York, the order would have arrived too late; it would not have prevented the loss. Thus it was not the lack of giving notice that caused the loss; hence defendants are not liable for omitting to give it. Morrison *v.* Davis, 20 Penn. St. 171; Denny *v.* New York Central R. R. Co., 13 Gray (Mass.), 481."

[1] Stephenson *v.* Hart, 1 M. & P. 357; 4 Bing. 476; American Express Co. *v.* Stack, 29 Ind. 27; Winslow *v.* Vermont, &c. R. R. Co., 42 Vt. 700; The Ben Adams, 2 Ben. 445.

[2] 5 T. R. 389; 1 Esp. 36.

defendants, to send their own carts for the goods to convey them from the quay to the warehouse, but the usage had uniformly been for the cotton-merchants to have their goods conveyed to their own warehouse in carts furnished by the defendants. The question in the case was, whether a carrier was discharged from liability by delivery to a porter at the inn in the place of the destination of the goods, or whether he was bound to deliver to the individual at his house.

SEC. 243. **Delivery at House of Consignee.** — The majority of the court held that the carrier's liability continued until a personal delivery at the house or place of deposit of the consignee had taken place; and in giving his judgment, BULLER, J., said: "According to the defendants' argument there must be two contracts in all cases; but I think the same argument tends to establish a much greater inconvenience, the necessity of three contracts, in all cases where the goods are sent by a coach or wagon, — one with the carrier, another with the innkeeper, and a third with the porter. But in fact there is but one contract; there is nothing like any contract or even communication between any other person than the owner of the goods and the carrier; the carrier is bound to deliver the goods, and the person who actually delivers them acts as the servant of the carrier. . . . It has been said, too, that the place of a porter is valuable and the subject of purchase, but who sells it? Not the person to whom the goods are sent, but the carrier or innkeeper, whom I consider as the same person. If the innkeeper have no share in the profits of the carriage, and receive the goods for the purpose of delivering them to the owners, then the innkeeper is the servant of the carrier as well as the porter. Therefore, whether there be the innkeeper and the porter, or the porter only, the carrier is liable in all cases where the goods are lost after they get into the hands of the innkeeper or porter, because they are delivered to those persons with the consent and as the servants of the carrier. The different proprietors may divide the profits among themselves in any way they choose; but they cannot, by their own agreement with each other, exonerate themselves from their liability to the owner of the goods. They may fill the two different characters of warehousemen and carriers at different times, but I deny that they can be both warehousemen and carriers at the same instant. If the undertaking was to carry and deliver, then the goods remain in their custody as carriers the whole time."

SEC. 244. **Confirmation of Decision.** — This opinion has more than once been confirmed since the time at which the above case came before the court. Thus, where carriers received goods from the plaintiff in London on an undertaking to carry them to Worcester, and deliver them there to the plaintiff for his use on payment of the hire; the goods were carried to Worcester, and sent from the warehouse nearly half a mile to the house of the plaintiff, but, the hire not being ready to be paid, were taken back to the warehouse. Applications to send the goods again to the house were refused, not on the ground that the contract had been performed by the proffer of the goods at the place to which they were sent, but until satisfaction of a lien set up on one side and resisted on the other, and which proved to be unfounded in fact. In this case it was held that, under these circumstances, the carriers had waived the benefit which would probably have resulted to them from insisting on the proffer as an execution of the undertaking; that both parties had treated the contract as one continuing contract from the commencement of the transaction till an actual delivery should have taken place; and that the carriers not having performed their part of the agreement, the consignee was entitled to recover.[1] Although the judges who decided that case did not think it necessary either to enter into the question as to whether it is or is not necessary that the carrier should find out the consignee of the goods intrusted to his conveyance, and deliver them at his residence, nor the question as to whether a carrier is bound to bring goods for delivery more than once, they seemed to be under the impression that the answer to both these questions should be in the

[1] Storr *v.* Crowley, M'Clel. & Y. 129. See also Garnett *v.* Willan, 5 B. & Ald. 53; Bodenham *v.* Bennett, 4 Price, 34; Birket *v.* Willan, 2 B. & Ald. 356; Stephenson *v.* Hart, 4 Bing. 476; Duff *v.* Budd, 3 B. & B. 177.

affirmative. In one case, however, while the latter was not discussed, a point somewhat analogous to it was decided.

SEC. 245. **Return of Parcel to Consignor.** — In that case the plaintiff delivered in London to the defendants, who were common carriers, a parcel addressed to the plaintiff's agent, at Plymouth. The defendants' railway terminated at Bristol, from whence they forwarded the parcel to Plymouth by the South Devon Railway, and shortly before noon on the day of its arrival, a porter tendered it to the plaintiff's agent, who refused to pay the sum charged for its carriage, whereupon the porter took it away, saying that it would be returned to London; and it was accordingly sent back to London at eight o'clock on the morning of the following day. About two hours afterwards, the plaintiff's agent tendered, at the office of the South Devon Railway, the amount of the carriage, and demanded the parcel, when he was told that it had been that morning returned to London. The parcel remained in the custody of the defendants, at their office, in London, and it did not appear that the plaintiff had applied for it there. The jury found that the parcel was sent back to London unreasonably soon, and that the demand of the parcel and tender of the charge for the carriage was made within a reasonable time after the parcel had been refused. When the case came before the Court of Exchequer Chamber, on appeal from the Court of Exchequer, it was held that, under these circumstances, the defendants were liable for a breach of duty, even supposing their duty *qua* carriers ended with the tender of the parcel.[1]

SEC. 246. **Duty of Carrier after Consignee's Refusal of Goods.** — This decision indirectly supports the opinion to which allusion was made above, that a carrier is not bound to offer the goods more than once; but it also establishes the fact that a single refusal upon the part of the consignee to pay the charge, which is consequently a refusal to receive the goods, will not discharge all the duties which may devolve upon a carrier in relation to goods which have been intrusted to him. There seems to be little doubt that the tender of the goods did

[1] Great Western Rail. Co. *v.* Crouch, 3 H. & N. 183.

terminate his relation to them as a carrier; but the fact that he had goods in his possession created other duties in regard to them, which, in the case just considered, the defendants did not properly perform.[1]

SEC. 247. **Duties of Carrier as Bailee.** — It is to be taken for granted that it may, upon occasion, be inconvenient for a consignee to pay carriage or to receive goods from a carrier; but the accident of its being inconvenient is not to deprive him of all legal right with regard to the goods in question, although it may properly deprive him of some of that security which he had while the goods were in the possession of the carrier *qua* carrier. The rule which must regulate such a case must be that which is applicable to a bailee. And the carrier, as bailee, has certain duties to perform in relation to the goods in his charge.[2] One of these is to keep them for a reasonable time to give the consignee an opportunity of claiming them. In the above case, according to the verdict, that was not done. If, during that period, the goods were, through the negligence of the carrier, lost or stolen, he would, it seemed the best opinion, be held liable.

SEC. 248. **When Liability ceases. — Distinction between their Duties as Bailees and Carriers.** — If, however, he has kept them for a reasonable time, — and the decision of the question as to what a reasonable time would be must be decided upon all the circumstances of the carrier's knowledge, or want of knowledge, of the nature of the goods, — his duties as bailee will wear themselves out, and his liability for the goods would cease. If, however, in this case,[3] the parcel had been retained until the plaintiff's agent tendered the amount of the carriage at the office of the South Devon Railway, and demanded it, and it had then been given up to him, and lost by him between the said office and his own residence, the

[1] Eagle *v.* White, 6 Whart. (Penn.) 505; Kremer *v.* Southern Express Co., 6 Coldw. (Tenn.) 356.

[2] Adams Express Co. *v.* Cressap, 6 Bush (Ky.), 572. His relation to the goods is similar to that he would occupy with regard to them if he retained them at the request of the consignor. St. Louis, &c. R. R. Co. *v.* Montgomery, 39 Ill. 335. See also Rose *v.* Allen, 3 Blatchf. (U. S. C. C.) 289.

[3] Great Western Rail. Co. *v.* Crouch, 3 H. & N. 183.

defendants would not have been held liable on the ground that it is their duty to deliver at the residence of the consignee,[1] for the delivery was not made by them as carriers, — their duty in that respect having come to an end at the time the parcel was tendered by the company's servant to the plaintiff's agent.[2]

SEC. 249. **Liability of Carrier for Loss in Warehouse.** — In a case where four persons, who were partners as carriers, agreed with Messrs. Shepherd, of Frome, to carry goods from London to that place, where they were to be deposited in a warehouse belonging to the partnership at Frome (where one of the partners in the said firm of carriers resided), without any charge for warehouse-room, till it should be convenient to Messrs. Shepherd to take the goods home; some goods of Messrs. Shepherd were carried by the partners from London to Frome under this agreement, and were deposited in the warehouse at the latter place, and destroyed by fire. Under these circumstances, it was held that the partners were not liable to Messrs. Shepherd.[3] The court seemed to think that Messrs. Shepherd had made two contracts with the defendants, — one for carrying, and the other for warehousing, — and that the duty of the defendants as carriers ceased not on delivery, but upon the inception of their character as warehousemen, and that as the loss occurred while the goods were in the possession of the defendants as warehousemen, they could not be held liable for their loss by fire. This may be the correct view of the case. It has, however, another aspect. The agreement that the goods shall be stored until the convenience of the Messrs. Shepherd might be regarded only as a delay in the delivery. The warehousing could not be looked upon as gratuitous any more than the return of empties is gratuitous upon the part of a railway company.[4] All bargains are synthetic wholes. They may be analyzed. Thus this bargain con-

[1] Golden *v.* Manning, 2 W. Bl. 916; 3 Wils. 429; Duff *v.* Budd, 6 Moore, 469; 3 B. & B. 177; Stephenson *v.* Hart, 4 Bing. 476; 1 M. & P. 357.

[2] See also Winslow *v.* Vermont, &c. R. R. Co., 42 Vt. 700.

[3] *In re* Webb, 8 Taunt. 443; 2 Moore, 500.

[4] Aldridge *v.* Great Western Rail. Co., 15 C. B. N. S. 582; 33 L. J. C. P. 161.

tained, as it were, an offer upon the part of the partner-carriers for the custom of the Messrs. Shepherd. This offer was the offer of greater facility and convenience, and it was accepted. The partner-carriers may be supposed to have been in competition with other carriers, and to have offered this extra inducement to the public, or to Messrs. Shepherd, to deal with them,—in which case the whole transaction might be looked upon as one, and the warehousing as in no way different from the placing a parcel upon a shelf before an offer of delivery has been made.[1] As the case stood, however, the duty of the partners as carriers was doubtless suspended by the special contract between them and Messrs. Shepherd.[2]

SEC. 250. **When Warehousing is a Part of the Duty of Carrying.**— But, as the above exposition may have indicated, when a carrier has been intrusted with goods to convey from one place to another, and to be forwarded from the latter of the two places to a third place, and, before thus forwarding them, puts them in a warehouse where they were destroyed by fire, he will be answerable for the loss. The question as to whether he had or had not had an opportunity of forwarding them is not material.[3]

SEC. 251. **Modification of Duty of Delivery.**— Where the plaintiff's declaration stated a contract by the defendants safely and securely to carry and convey by a steam vessel certain goods of the plaintiff from Belfast to Dublin, and from thence to London, and to deliver the same at the port of London to the plaintiff or his assigns on payment of freight, a plea that the goods were put on board under a bill of lading, by which they were made deliverable to the plaintiff or his assigns, on payment of freight,—that after the arrival of the vessel at London with the goods on board, the defendants caused them to be unshipped, and safely and securely landed

[1] Garside v. Trent Navigation Co., 4 T. R. 581; Buckley v. Great Western Rail. Co., 18 Mich. 121. But see Chicago & A. R. R. Co. v. Scott, 42 Ill. 132.

[2] Per GIBBS, C. J., *In re* Webb, 8 Taunt. 443.

[3] Garside v. Trent Navigation Co., 4 T. R. 581; Buckley v. Great Western Rail. Co., 18 Mich. 121. But see Chicago & A. R. R. Co. v. Scott, 42 Ill. 132.

and deposited in and upon a certain wharf called Fenning's Wharf, at the port of London, there to remain until they could be delivered to the plaintiff according to the tenor of the bill of lading, the said wharf being a place at which goods conveyed in steam vessels from Dublin to London were used and accustomed to be landed and deposited for the use of the consignees thereof, and a place fit and proper for such purpose, and that afterwards, while the goods remained upon the said wharf, and before a reasonable time for the delivery thereof, according to the tenor and effect of the bill of lading, had elapsed, the goods were destroyed by an accidental fire, — was held by the House of Lords to be a good plea to the count.[1]

SEC. 252. **Other Modifications of Duty.** — We have seen, then, that the duty of the carrier to deliver the goods may be modified, — that the refusal of the consignee to receive the goods when they are offered discharges him from the necessity of making another offer to deliver, and makes the relation of the carrier to the goods that of a bailee for hire,[2] — that a special agreement entered into between the bailor and the carrier may modify this duty,[3] — and also that a usage of the trade may modify the duty which is imposed upon the carrier to deliver the goods at a certain place.[4] The latter principle necessarily follows from the very nature of a carrier's employment. His duties are thrust upon him by the fact that he is accustomed to exercise them. When a man does a thing in a certain way, the law rightly says you shall do it in that way, so long as you do it at all. No man is compelled to be a carrier; but every man is compelled to make his acts conform to his professions when he pretends to be a public servant, other-

[1] Bourne *v.* Gatliffe, 8 Scott, N. R. 604; 11 C. & F. 45. See also Gatliffe *v.* Bourne, 4 Bing. N. C. 314, and 1 Scott, N. R. 1.

[2] *Ante*, p. 310.

[3] *In re* Webb, 8 Taunt. 443; 2 Moore, 500; Robinson *v.* Turpin, Wilson *v.* London Steam Navigation Co., L. R. 1 C. P. 61. A bill of lading is only an agreement to carry from port to port; per BULLER, J., in Hyde *v.* Trent & Mersey Navigation Co., 5 T. R. 389.

[4] Bourne *v.* Gatliffe, 8 Scott, N. R. 604; Catley *v.* Wintringham, Peake, N. P. Cas. 140; Rowe *v.* Pickford, 8 Taunt. 83; Garside *v.* Trent Navigation Co., 4 T. R. 581; Abbott on Ship. But see Wardell *v.* Mourillyan, 2 Esp. 693.

wise the public would be misled. As custom has shaped his trade in every particular, we should expect it to modify his duty in this particular as well as in others. A carrier may be a warehouseman as well as a carrier, and in many cases the question of his liability will depend upon that other question, as to whether delivery has been dispensed with on the part of the owner of the goods, and whether, in consequence of such dispensation, the bailee is a warehouseman, or whether, there being no such dispensation, and consequent discharge, he still holds the goods as a common carrier.[1]

SEC. 253. **Due Notice of Arrival.** — With reference to the carriage of goods by water, we have already seen that bills[2] of lading very commonly modify the duty which exists at common law to deliver personally to the consignee, or at his residence; we have seen that, as BULLER, J., said,[3] "when goods are brought from foreign countries, they are brought under a bill of lading, which is merely an undertaking to carry from port to port." And we may add that if it is the custom of the carrier to carry from port to port, or from wharf to wharf, and for the owner to receive the goods at the vessel, or at the wharf, as soon as the arrival of the vessel is reported, due notice must be given to the owner, in order to give him the opportunity of receiving in safety, if the carrier would be discharged from his responsibility by such delivery.[4] Otherwise, such delivery would or might invariably result in loss of or damage to the goods, for which the owner would have no remedy, and which he could take no means of preventing.[5]

[1] Garside *v.* Trent Navigation Co., 4 T. R. 581; Forward *v.* Pittard, 1 T. R. 27. See *ante*, p. 298.

[2] *Ante*, p. 310. And see Brettan *v.* Barnaby, 21 How. 528; Howland *v.* Greenway, 22 How. 491.

[3] Hyde *v.* Trent & Mersey Navigation Co., 5 T. R. 389.

[4] Wardell *v.* Mourillyan, 2 Esp. 693; Quiggen *v.* Duff, 1 M. & W. 174; Gatliffe *v.* Bourne, 4 Bing. N. C. 314; Herman *v.* Goodrich, 21 Wisc. 536. See also The Peytona, Ware (U. S. C. C.), 541; The Grafton, Olc. (U. S.) 42; affirmed on appeal, Abb. Adm. (U. S.) 552 N.; Ostrander *v.* Brown, 15 Johns. (N. Y.) 39; Chickering *v.* Fowler, 21 Mass. 371; Gibson *v.* Culver, 17 Wend. (N. Y.) 305; Merwin *v.* Butler, 17 Conn. 138; The Peytona, 2 Curt. (U. S. C. C.) 21; Blossom *v.* Smith, 3 Blatchf. 316; Redmond *v.* Liverpool, &c. S. S. Co., 56 Barb. 320.

[5] See Withers *v.* New Jersey, &c. Co., 48 Barb. (N. Y.) 455.

This would not so much injure the owners of goods as the carriers of such articles. If there was no security in transmitting, men would not transmit. It would, of course, to a certain extent, paralyze trade.

SEC. 254. **Construction of Bill of Lading.** — The question of the duty of delivery came under the notice of the Court of Common Pleas, in the case of Wilson *v.* London and Italian and Adriatic Steam Navigation Company,[1] in which the question turned upon the construction to be placed upon a bill of lading. In a bill of lading there was a proviso that simultaneously with the ship being ready to unload the whole or any part of the goods (forty pipes of lemon juice), the consignee was bound to be ready to receive the same from the ship's side, and in default the master or agent of the ship was authorized to enter the goods at the custom house, and land, warehouse, or place them in lighters, at the risk and expense of the consignee. After part of the goods had been landed by the shipowner, but not before, the consignee was ready and offered to receive the remainder, but the shipowner refused to deliver them to him, and landed them himself. Here it was held that the contract was divisible, and that, unless the shipowner had been prejudiced by the delivery of the remainder, by the default of the consignee in not being ready to receive the whole, he was bound to deliver them. Therefore, in this case there could, by the means the shipowner adopted, be no discharge of his liability as a carrier with regard to that portion of the goods which he entered, landed, and warehoused himself, after the plaintiff was ready and offered to receive them, unless he could prove that by changing the mode of delivery he would be, in some way, prejudiced.

SEC. 255. **Delivery of Passengers' Luggage.** — Two cases may be referred to as showing the duty to deliver which is incumbent upon carriers with regard to passengers' luggage. In one of these the London, Brighton, and South Coast Railway Company were the defendants, and the plaintiff's declaration stated that the wife of the plaintiff had become a

[1] L. Rep. 1 C. P. 61.

passenger on the defendants' line of railway, to be carried, together with her luggage, from Woodgate Station in Sussex to Southwark Station in Surrey, and to be, *at the latter station, delivered* safely and securely for reasonable reward. And it alleged that the defendants, not regarding their duty, did not use due and proper care in and about the carriage or conveyance of the dressing-case (part of the luggage of the plaintiff's wife), but took so little and such bad care in and about the carrying and conveying the same, that through the carelessness, negligence, and improper conduct of the defendants, the dressing-case was lost. It appeared that the plaintiff's wife became a passenger by a first-class carriage, to be conveyed from the first to the second of the above-mentioned stations, — that the dressing-case was placed in the carriage under the seat, — that on the arrival of the train at the latter station, the porters of the company took upon themselves the duty of carrying the lady's luggage from the railway carriage to the hackney carriage which was to convey her to her residence, — and that on her arrival there, the dressing-case was missing.

SEC. 256. **Continuance of Duty.** — And it was decided that the duty of the defendants, as common carriers, continued until the luggage was placed in the hackney carriage.[1] Although the principle laid down in this case is perfectly correct, exception might be taken to the ruling, that the plaintiff was entitled to recover. The other case was somewhat similar. There the plaintiff was a passenger by the defendants' railway, and brought with him a carpet-bag containing a large sum of money, and kept it in his own possession until the arrival of the train at the London terminus. On alighting from the carriage with the bag in his hand, the plaintiff permitted a porter of the company to take it from him for the purpose of securing a cab. The porter, having found a cab (within the station), placed the carpet-bag on the foot-board thereof, and then returned to the platform to get some other luggage belonging to the plaintiff, when the cab disappeared, and the carpet-bag and its contents were lost. It was held

[1] Richards *v.* London, Brighton, & South Coast Rail. Co., 7 C. B. 839.

that this was a loss by the negligence of the company for which they were responsible in damages.[1]

SEC. 257. **Modification of Carriers' Duty.** — To this case, like that last quoted, exception might, with some force, be taken since the decision in the case of The Great Western Railway Company *v.* Talley,[2] in which it was held that the general liability was, under the circumstances (the owner of a portmanteau had taken his portmanteau into the carriage with him, and having left his carriage the portmanteau was discovered to have been cut open and its contents had been removed), modified by the implied condition that a passenger should use reasonable care, and that, as the loss was due to his neglect alone, the verdict must be entered for the railway company. No doubt both of the above-quoted cases are very similar to that just referred to. In each the duty of the railway company was modified by the duty which the owners had taken upon themselves, and the only circumstance which could make the company liable would be the delivery of the articles to the porters, who were servants of the company. If that was argued with regard to these cases, the implied duty of a company by its servants, to see after luggage of passengers when they have left the carriage in which it was deposited, might be asserted on the other side.

SEC. 258. **When Delivery takes Place.** — And as in the one case the company's duty was modified by the personal superintendence upon the part of the passenger, so it ought to have been held modified in the other. If the passenger, in the latter case,[3] regarded the bag containing the money as too valuable to be trusted out of his sight during the transit, — if he would not trust it to the company's servants, during the journey, to be placed in the van, — there is a presumption that, even when he gave it to the porter to carry, he meant himself to see it safely deposited, and that it was lost through some negligence of his own. Although it seemed necessary to point

[1] Butcher *v.* London & South-Western Rail. Co., 16 C. B. 13. See also Le Conteur *v.* London & South-Western Rail. Co., 6 B. & S. 961.

[2] 19 W. R. 154; 23 L. T. N. S. 413.

[3] Butcher *v.* London & South-Western Rail. Co., 16 C. B. 13.

out the want of uniformity in the decisions on this point, we have already said that the principles laid down in the cases cited were perfectly satisfactory. These principles were, that where a railway company employ porters to carry luggage, belonging to passengers, from the train to the carriages or hired vehicles of passengers, delivery cannot be held to have taken place, and therefore the liability of the company continues, until the luggage has been so conveyed.[1] The question in these two cases was, whether there had been an actual delivery to the carriers as carriers,[2] or whether the plaintiffs had not, by their acts, implied a contract that they would take the care and risk of their own goods.

SEC. 259. **Claim of Passenger.** — In every case, however, where luggage is to be delivered to a passenger by a company, the claim must be made within reasonable time. It would be a hardship upon a railway company to compel its servants to discover the owners of all the luggage in the van, and in many cases it would be impossible to do so. Under these circumstances, it is evidently the duty of the passenger to facilitate such delivery by demanding his goods. If such a demand is not made within reasonable time, the carrier will be divested of his character of insurer, and will, as we have already seen, with reference to goods not passengers' luggage, become a bailee for hire, or a gratuitous bailee, as the case may be. But this rule will apply only to cases where the luggage is unclaimed by the passenger, through the passenger's own neglect, and not where it remains unclaimed through some negligence upon the part of the carrier, as, for instance, in causing the passenger to go into a wrong train, whereby he was prevented claiming his luggage at his and its destination.[3]

[1] See also Great Western Railway *v.* Goodman, 12 C. B. 313; 21 L. J. 197 C. P.

[2] An overcoat was held never to have been delivered to the carriers; per CHAMBRE, J., in Robinson *v.* Dunmore, 2 Bos. & P. 416.

[3] The question as to whether delivery has taken place while the goods are still in the possession of the carrier is a somewhat difficult one to answer, and it seems to us that the answers which have been given are not altogether satisfactory. See Shepherd *v.* Bristol & Exeter Rail Co., 37 L. J. Exch. 113; 3 L. R. Exch. 189. See also Jeffersonville R. R. Co. *v.* Cotton, 29 Ind. 498; Buckley *v.* Great Western R. R. Co., 18 Mich. 121; Francis *v.* Dubuque, &c. R. R. Co., 25 Iowa, 60.

SEC. 260. **Delivery to Person.** — Having considered the question as to what delivery of goods, in so far as place is concerned, will discharge the carrier's liability, we may now consider what delivery of goods, in so far as the person is concerned, will effect the same object. We have seen that it is the carrier's duty to deliver to the consignee;[1] but just as the duty to deliver at the place to which the goods are addressed is subject to modification, so this other duty is not binding in all cases, and under all circumstances.

SEC. 261. **Delivery to Consignee's Agent.** — A delivery to an agent of the consignee authorized by him to receive the goods will free the carrier from further responsibility. It is just as important, however, for the carrier to ascertain that he delivers to an agent duly authorized to receive, as, in case of loss and compensation, he should ascertain the proper person to whom compensation is due before he pays.[2]

SEC. 262. **Delivery to Right Person.** — The duty of the carrier is imperatively to deliver to the right person, and no amount of care will excuse him from delivering to a person other than the right one. The case of Sanquer *v.* The London and South-Western Railway Company[3] is in point. There the plaintiff, a provision merchant at Morlaix, sent 314 casks of butter by the defendant's railway, marked A, and addressed, "To order, at Brewer's Quay." The defendants, concluding, from the fact of their having been in the habit of carrying butters similarly marked, consigned to Messrs. Allen & Anderson, factors, in London, that these butters were intended for them, and having received directions from Messrs. Allen & Anderson to send all butters, coming to them from Morlaix, to Hibernia Wharf, delivered 154 of the casks at that place, the remaining 160 having, by accident, got to Brewer's Quay. Goodchaux & Co., the holders of the bill of lading, had received directions not to let Messrs. Allen & Anderson

[1] See p. 314.

[2] Coombs *v.* Bristol & Exeter Rail. Co., 3 H. & N. 1. See also Russell *v.* Livingstone, 16 N. Y. 515; 19 Barb. 346; Ostrander *v.* Brown, 15 Johns. (N. Y.) 39; Adonis *v.* Blankenstein, 2 Cal. 413; Blossom *v.* Smith, 3 Blatchf. (U. S. C. C.) 316.

[3] 16 C. B. 163; 13 C. L. R. 811.

have the butter, unless they accepted certain drafts at sight, which they declined to do; and when Goodchaux & Co. applied to the defendants as to the 154 casks, they referred them to Messrs. Allen & Anderson, who took no further notice of the transaction. Messrs. Allen & Anderson afterwards sold the butter at the fair market price, and rendered account-sales to the plaintiff, but before the money was handed over, they suspended payment. Here, then, it was held that the defendants were liable to the plaintiff for this misdelivery, and that, notwithstanding that he had so far adopted the act of Messrs. Allen & Anderson as to endeavor to obtain from them the proceeds of the sale.[1]

SEC. 263. **Misdelivery.** — So, in an earlier case, where the plaintiff, having been imposed upon by a swindler, consigned a box at Birmingham, by the defendants, as common carriers, to J. West, 27 Great Winchester Street, London. The defendants found that no such person resided there; but upon receiving a letter signed "J. West," requesting that the box might be forwarded to a public-house at St. Albans, they delivered it there to a person calling himself West, who showed that he had a knowledge of the contents of the box; that person having disappeared, and the box having been originally obtained from the plaintiff by fraud, it was held that the defendants were liable to him in an action of trover, and that it had been properly left to the jury to say whether the defendants had delivered the box according to the due course of their business as carriers.[2]

[1] See also the recent case of McKean *v.* McIver, 24 L. J. N. S. 559; and in 6 L. R. Exch. 36; and see further Heugh *v.* London & North-Western Rail Co., 21 L. J. N. S. 677; 39 L. J. 48 Exch.; 5 L. R. Exch. 51; Cork Distilleries Co. *v.* Great Southern & Western Rail. Co., 5 Ir. R. C. L. 177 Exch.

[2] Stephenson *v.* Hart, 4 Bing. 476; 1 M. & P. 357. See also Ross *v.* Johnson, 5 Burr. 2825; Youl *v.* Harbottle, Peake, N. P. C. 68, per LORD KENYON; Devereux *v.* Barclay, 2 B. & A. 702; Duff *v.* Budd, 6 Moore, 469; 3 B. & B. 177; Brown *v.* Hodgson, 4 Taunt. 189; Bonney *v.* The Huntress, 4 Hunt's Merch. Mag. 83; American Express Co. *v.* Stack, 29 Ind. 27; Winslow *v.* Vermont, &c. R. R. Co., 42 Vt. 700; Meyer *v.* Chicago, &c. R. R. Co., 24 Wis. 566; The Ben Adams, 2 Ben. (U. S. C. C.) 445. But see Ten Eyck *v.* Harris, 47 Ill. 268. The carrier, at his peril, must deliver the goods to the right party;

SEC. 264. **Duty with respect to Delivery.** — But although the duty of the carrier to deliver to the right person is impera-

and neither fraud, imposition, nor mistake will excuse him from liability, if he delivers them to the wrong person. Therefore he has a right to require reasonable evidence of the identity of the consignee, and of his title to the goods; and although the real owner applies for the goods, but, being unknown to the carrier, is required to prove his identity, or right to the goods, before delivery, the carrier cannot be charged for their conversion. Thus in McEntee *v.* New Jersey Steamboat Co., 45 N. Y. 34, the defendants received at Albany several bundles of sash and blinds, to be carried to New York. The bundles were directed to "McEntee, New York." The goods reached their destination, and the plaintiff demanded the goods of the defendant, who refused to deliver them to him upon payment of charges. The defendant declined to deliver them to him unless he would produce some paper showing his ownership of the goods, or authority to receive them as the consignee. The judge presiding at the trial ruled that the only question for the jury was whether freight-money was tendered, and charged them that, under the circumstances, the defendants were justified in delivering the goods to any person calling for them; and that common carriers are not responsible for wrong delivery, and therefore had no right to insist upon any person proving ownership. The plaintiff had a verdict, but it was set aside upon appeal; ALLEN, J., saying: "The defendants were charged for the conversion of the goods, upon evidence of a demand and a refusal to deliver them. If the demand was by the person entitled to receive them, and the refusal to deliver was absolute and unqualified, the conversion was sufficiently proved, for such refusal is ordinarily conclusive evidence of a conversion; *but if the refusal was qualified, the question was whether the qualification was reasonable; and if reasonable, and made in good faith, it was no evidence of a conversion.* Alexander *v.* Southey, 5 B. & Ald. 247; Holbrook *v.* Wright, 24 Wend. (N. Y.) 169; Rogers *v.* Weir, 34 N. Y. 463; Mount *v.* Derick, 5 Hill (N. Y.), 455. *If at the time of the demand a reasonable excuse be made in good faith, for the non-delivery, the goods being evidently kept with a view to deliver them to the true owner, there is no conversion.*

"This action is not upon the contract of the carriers, but for a tortious conversion of the property; but the rights and duties of the defendants as carriers are, nevertheless, involved. The defendants were bailees of the property, under an obligation to deliver it to the rightful owner. They would have been liable had they delivered the goods to a wrong person. Common carriers deliver property at their peril, and must take care that it is delivered to the right person; for if the delivery be to the wrong person, either by an innocent mistake or through fraud of third persons, as upon a forged order, they will be responsible, and the wrongful delivery will be treated as a conversion. Hawkins *v.* Hoffman, 6 Hill (N. Y.), 586; Powell *v.* Myers, 26 Wend. (N. Y.) 290; Devereux *v.* Barclay, 2 B. & Ald. 702; Guillaume *v.* Hamburgh & Am. Packet Co., 42 N. Y. 212; Duff *v.* Budd, 3 B. & B. 177. The duties of carriers may be varied by the differing circumstances of cases as they arise; but it is their duty in all cases to be diligent in their

tive, as we have shown, still it is liable to such modifications that in some cases his responsibility as a carrier will be dis-

efforts to secure a delivery of the property to the person entitled, and they will be protected in refusing delivery until reasonable evidence is furnished them that the party claiming is the party entitled, so long as they act in good faith, and solely with a view to a proper delivery. The circumstances of this case, the very defective address of the parcels, and the omission of the plaintiff to produce any evidence of title to the property or identifying him as the consignee, justified the defendants in exercising caution in the delivery; and it should have been submitted to the jury whether the refusal was qualified, as alleged by the defendants, and if so, whether the qualification was reasonable, and was the true reason for not delivering the goods. The judge also erred in his instructions to the jury as to the duty of the defendants, as common carriers, in the delivery of goods. They may not properly, or without incurring liability to the true owner, deliver goods to any person who calls for them, other than the rightful owner. The judgment must be reversed and a new trial granted, costs to abide event." See also Southern Express Co. *v.* Crook, 44 Ala. 468; 4 Am. Rep. 140; Stevenson *v.* Hart, 4 Bing. 476; Chapman *v.* New Orleans, &c. R. R. Co., 21 La. Ann. 224; Ten Eyck *v.* Harris, 47 Ill. 288; McKean *v.* McIver, L. R. 6 Exch. 36; Meyer *v.* Chicago, &c. R. R. Co., 24 Wis. 566; 1 Am. Rep. 207; Jones *v.* Earl, 37 Cal. 630; The Ben Adams, 2 Ben. (U. S. C. C.) 445; Jeffersonville R. R. Co. *v.* White, 6 Bush (Ky.), 251; Dunlap *v.* Hunting, 2 Den. (N. Y.) 643; Carroll *v.* Mix, 57 Barb. (N. Y.) 215; Roberts *v.* Riley, 15 La. Ann. 103; Burrell *v.* North, 2 C. & K. 680; Bradley *v.* Waterhouse, 3 C. & P. 318; Packard *v.* Getman, 4 Wend. (N. Y.) 615; Michigan Central R. R. Co. *v.* Day, 20 Ill. 375; Ball *v.* Liney, 48 N. Y. 6; Wilson *v.* Vermont Central R. R. Co., 42 Vt. 200; 1 Am. Rep. 365; American Merchants Express Co. *v.* Milk, 73 Ill. 224; Dufour *v.* Murphy, 37 Miss. 577; Willard *v.* Bridge, 41 Barb. (N. Y.) 361; Dudley *v.* Hawley, 40 Barb. (N. Y.) 397; Dean *v.* Vaccaro, 2 Head (Tenn.), 485; Guillaume *v.* Hamburgh Co., 42 Vt. 212; Hempstead *v.* New York Central R. R. Co., 28 Barb. (N. Y.) 485; Rogers *v.* Weir, 34 N. Y. 463; Ostrander *v.* Brown, 15 Johns. (N. Y.) 40; Tuttle *v.* Gladding, 2 E. D. S. (N. Y. C. P.) 157.

It is for the jury to say whether, in requiring evidence of identity or title, the carrier acted in good faith. Watt *v.* Porter, 2 Mas. (U. S.) 77; Sargent *v.* Gile, 8 N. H. 325; Leighton *v.* Shapley, 8 N. H. 359; Dent *v.* Chiles, 5 S. & P. (Ala.) 383. The fact that the goods are delivered on a forged order is no defence. Gasling *v.* Higgins, 1 Camp. 451; Lubbock *v.* Inglis, 1 Stark. 104. Nor will the circumstance that the carrier acted in good faith in delivering the goods, and was deceived, as was also the plaintiff, by the person to whom they were delivered. Thus in an Indiana case, American Express Co. *v.* Stack, 29 Ind. 27, a person who had by some means ascertained that there were goods in the possession of the wife of James Stack, who was then absent, which he might obtain by falsely personating him, telegraphed to the wife, in the name of her husband, to send to James Stack, at the place from which the telegram was sent. The goods were

charged without any delivery upon his part. In the case of Barker *v.* Taylor,[1] circumstances which might modify the car-

forwarded by the wife, by the defendant carrier, she at the same time writing a letter addressed to James Stack, which the swindler obtained upon demanding the goods and presenting the letter aforesaid. The company were not satisfied as to his identity by this proof, and he produced a person who was known to the defendant's agent, who identified him as being James Stack, and who really believed him to be that person, and without making any further inquiry, the goods were delivered to him. In an action by James Stack, to recover for the goods, it was held that the defendant was guilty of gross negligence in the delivery of the goods, and that they were liable therefor.

In Southern Express Co. *v.* Van Meter, 17 Fla. 783, 35 Am. Rep. 107, a person sent a forged telegram, in the name of another, requesting a National Bank to forward to Gainesville, Fla., $500, to the address given in the telegram, to wit, Dr. Samuel Van Meter. This telegram was shown to Dr. Van Meter's son, who executed his note for the amount, and the same was sent by express, by the bank to which the telegram was addressed, directed to "Dr. Samuel Van Meter, Gainesville, Fla., at the Arlington House." The defendant company received the package from the American Express Co. for transportation and delivery. The defendant's agent expected the party to whom the package was addressed, to arrive from another place, as he was not a resident of the town where the package was to be delivered. The agent met the party assuming to be Dr. Samuel Van Meter at the train, at the depot. While there, the proprietor of a hotel *other* than the one at, or to the care of which the package was directed, asked the agent if he had a package addressed to Dr. Samuel Van Meter, and, the agent having said that he had, the hotel-keeper told him that he was here now. The agent was asked to bring the package to the hotel kept by the hotel-keeper aforesaid; but he declined to do so, not for want of identification, but because he had not the time to do so, but told the hotel-keeper that if he would bring Dr. V. to his office, he would deliver the package; and upon the impostor calling at the office, with the hotel-keeper, the agent delivered the package to him without any further identification. The hotel-keeper was known to the agent to be a reliable man, but no inquiries were made of him as to how he knew that the person was Dr. Van Meter. The company was, upon these facts, held liable for the money. "Had the agent," says WESTCOTT, J., "asked the hotel-keeper whether he knew the party to be the person he represented himself to be, he would have been at once informed of the extent of the hotel-keeper's knowledge, and that he only knew that the man so represented himself. The express company was a bailee of the property, under an obligation to deliver to the rightful owner; and its delivery to a stranger, not the rightful owner, cannot be justified upon the ground that the keeper of a hotel at the point of destination — known to the agent, and in whom he has confidence — simply treated the party as the person entitled to delivery;

[1] 1 C. & P. 101.

rier's duty in this respect came under the notice of the court. It appeared that a box, containing clothes, had been intrusted

the agent at the same time knowing the party to whom he delivered the package was a stranger who had just arrived in town. . . . Notwithstanding the forged telegram, this carrier, in making a personal delivery, was bound by law to deliver to the person to whom the package was addressed, he being the true owner. American Express Co. *v.* Fletcher, 25 Ind. 492; 29 Ind. 27. An express company belongs to that class of carriers who undertake to make a personal delivery of the goods to the consignee, and it is held to great strictness in the performance of this duty."

In another Indiana case, American Express Co. *v.* Fletcher, 25 Ind. 492, a similar rule was adopted, under circumstances which illustrate the extreme rigor of the rule. In that case a person calling himself J. O'Riley sent a message to the plaintiff, by telegraph, requesting the remittance of a considerable sum to his address. The message was received, and the money forwarded to J. O'Riley, as requested in said despatch, by the defendant express company. The telegraph operator who sent the despatch was also the defendants' agent, and upon the arrival of the money he paid it over to the swindler, in good faith, believing him to be the consignee. The court held that the defendants were negligent in not requiring more evidence as to the identity of the swindler, and consequently were liable for the money.

In Duff *v.* Budd, 3 B. & B. 177, a carrier was held liable for a conversion of the goods under the following circumstances. The plaintiffs received an order for goods for Mr. J. Parker, of High St., Oxford. They had never heard of him, but upon inquiry, found that Mr. Parker, of High St., Oxford, was a respectable tradesman. They forwarded the goods by the defendant's wagon, directing the parcel to "*James Parker*, High St., Oxford." The carrier's porter knew William Parker, of High St., Oxford, to whom he had delivered goods before, and after the arrival of the goods informed him of the fact, but learned from him that he had ordered no such parcel, and knew nothing about it. Shortly after this, a person called, to whom the defendant's porter had before delivered goods under the name of Parker, and seeing the parcel said it was his, and he was permitted to take it away without any further or other identification, or that he was the person for whom the goods were intended. The man was an impostor, and the court held that the defendants were liable for a misdelivery of the goods. The rule that the circumstance that the plaintiff was deceived, as well as the carrier, by the person to whom the goods were delivered, does not excuse the carrier, if the person to whom they were delivered was not known by the name in which they were addressed, is illustrated by the case of Winslow *v.* Vermont, &c. R. R. Co., 42 Vt. 700, which was an action against a railroad company to recover damages from them, as carriers, for non-delivery of goods. It appeared that the goods were ordered from the plaintiffs by C., writing under the false name of R. and intending to swindle the plaintiffs. The plaintiffs addressed the goods to R., and forwarded them by defendants' road. C. awaited their arrival, and claimed them under the name of R., which name he assumed for the purpose of getting them; and the defendants

to the care of the defendant, who was a carrier, and who promised to deliver it at a milliner's, in Newcastle-under-Lyme.

delivered them without requiring identification, or taking any other precaution to make sure that the person receiving them was R. It was held that they were liable for a misdelivery. They were chargeable with negligence. They should have required the claimant to identify himself as R., and, on his failure to do so, should have held the goods for the consignors. *The fact that the plaintiffs had been led by fraud to address the goods in a fictitious name did not operate to mislead the company, nor was the error in the name any reason why they should have delivered the goods without inquiry as to the identity of the person claiming them with the one named in the address.* "What," says the court, "should be the effect upon the measure of the defendants' responsibility, of the plaintiff's error in directing the goods to a fictitious address? This might be an important question if the error had misled the defendants, and occasioned them to deliver the goods to the wrong party after they had used that care and precaution which would be reasonable in such matters. But this error in the direction could not excuse the defendants from the exercise of at least ordinary care in the delivery of the property. They did not exercise such care. They were guilty of actual negligence. They delivered the goods to an employee of a truckman upon his mere statement that Roberts sent for them. Any other man in Boston could have obtained them just as easily. The swindler, Collins, was not known as Roberts, and if he had been required to identify himself as Roberts, might never have attempted it; and if he had, it would have been likely to have led to the detection of the fraud." Where the goods actually are delivered to the person who ordered them, the carrier is not excused, if the goods were shipped in a fictitious name, and the person to whom they were delivered was not known by that name, and no reasonable inquiries are instituted by the carrier to ascertain the identity of the consignee as the person to whom they are addressed. The carrier is liable for the loss of the goods. The reason for this rule is, that the carrier must use reasonable diligence in delivering the goods to the party to whom they are addressed, and if they are professedly addressed in a fictitious name, this circumstance of itself puts the carrier upon inquiry, and calls for the exercise by him of increased vigilance in ascertaining whether a person known by a different name is in fact entitled to them, because, as stated in the Vermont case before referred to, such inquiry and vigilance would be calculated to discover the fraud, if any; and if in fact there was no fraud, the parties cannot complain of any delay or inconvenience which their own acts have occasioned. In Price *v.* Oswego & Syracuse R. R. Co., 50 N. Y. 213, this rule was well illustrated. In that case, in an action by a consignor against the defendant as a carrier, to recover for goods claimed to have been wrongly delivered, it appeared that a person addressed a letter to the plaintiff, ordering a quantity of goods to be shipped in the name of a fictitious firm. The plaintiff, without making any inquiry as to the existence or solvency of such a firm, but relying upon the order as having been given by the firm name, and as being *bonâ fide* and honest, shipped the goods to the address named, by the defendant

It also appeared that the plaintiff had eloped from home with the assistance of an attorney's clerk, whose acquaintance with

carrier. The goods reached their destination, and the defendants, not knowing any such firm, and without instituting any inquiries relative thereto, or to ascertain whether there was in fact any such firm, delivered the goods to a stranger who called for them and paid the charges thereon. He was the same person who gave the order for the goods, and his evident purpose was to obtain the goods by falsely assuming to be the party to whom, by his order, they were consigned. The defendant was held liable, the court holding that where a common carrier, without requiring evidence of identity, delivers goods to a stranger, which have been fraudulently ordered by him in the name of a fictitious person or firm, which have been shipped in compliance with the order, directed to the fictitious person or firm, he is liable to the consignor for their value. Not only is the carrier bound to deliver the goods to the consignee or owner, but he is also bound to deliver them *at the place* to which they are shipped; and if, upon the faith of a forged order, he delivers them to a person other than the owner, *although to a person of the same name*, he is liable for the goods Thus in Houston, &c. R. R. Co. *v.* Adams, 49 Tex. 748, 30 Am. Rep. 116, the plaintiff, at Columbus, Ga., delivered his household goods marked "R. Adams," to the defendant, a common carrier, to be transported. He accompanied them as far as New Orleans, and there directed the defendant's agent to forward them to *Bremond*, Tex. By mistake, the agent shipped them to *Brenham*, Tex. There, on the authority of a letter written from *Burton*, Tex., signed "R Adams," they were forwarded to *Burton* and there delivered to a man calling himself Robert Adams, a single man and day-laborer, who had no bill of lading or receipt for them, and was not the *R. Adams* who shipped and owned the goods. The court held that the defendant was liable for the loss of the goods, irrespective of the question whether he was to be treated as a common carrier or warehouseman.

"Admitting," says MOORE, A. J., "that the mistake in freighting the goods to Brenham, instead of Bremond, cannot be imputed to defendant, still it cannot be denied that defendant was bound as a common carrier to deliver the goods in Brenham to the real consignee to whom they in fact belonged, and that the delivery of them to any one else was a violation of the contract, which entitled the owner to an action for their value. The case of Winslow *v.* Vermont & Massachusetts R. R. Co., 42 Vt. 700; s. c. 1 Am. Rep. 365, is strictly in point, and fully sustains this proposition. It is there said: 'It has been urged that the defendants cannot, even as carriers, be held liable for delivering the goods to the wrong party, if they deliver them in the customary manner and in the usual course of business. We think no such exception to the common-law rule can be made. The carrier is under the same contract, obligation, or duty to deliver the goods safely that he is to carry them safely. The law fixes these duties upon the carrier, and he cannot relieve himself from them by proving his usage. It is true, as urged, that it is not as customary for other carriers, as it is for express companies, to oblige themselves to look up the owner and consignee, and deliver the goods to him at his residence or place of

the plaintiff (who was under age) her mother disapproved of. The mother, while in pursuit of the plaintiff, overtook

business. But all classes of common carriers are responsible, and equally responsible, for a loss of the goods by delivery to the wrong person.' And, says the court in McEntee v. New Jersey Steamboat Co., 45 N. Y. 34, 6 Am. Rep. 28: 'Common carriers deliver property at their peril, and must take care that it is delivered to the right person; for if the delivery be to the wrong person, either by an innocent mistake or through fraud of third persons, as upon a forged order, they will be responsible, and the wrongful delivery will be treated as a conversion.' Numerous other cases to the like effect might be easily cited, but it is unnecessary. The proposition is too elementary to require it. Story on Bail. §§ 540, 543, 545 *b*. It certainly follows, if the carrier is guilty of a conversion of the goods by delivering them to the wrong person, though he has acted in good faith and with due caution, he is equally so when he forwards them from their point of destination elsewhere on the order of any one but the party to whom they should have been delivered. Stephenson v. Hart, 4 Bing. 476. The consignee is entitled to receive his goods at the place where the carrier undertook and bound himself to deliver them, and is under no obligation to seek or demand them elsewhere. Nor can he be held bound by, or be supposed to have consented to, their improper shipment or delivery by the carrier, merely by following them to the point to which they have been improperly forwarded, or by demanding them from the party to whom they were wrongfully delivered.

"But the plaintiff in error maintains that its liability to defendant in error as common carrier, in respect to these goods, had ceased even before they were forwarded to Burton; and if not, it certainly had before they were delivered at Burton to Robert Adams. In order to determine whether plaintiff in error incurred any liability to the owner by forwarding the goods to Burton and delivering them after their arrival there to said Robert Adams, it is maintained that recourse must be had to the law applicable to warehousemen, and not to that to which carriers are held subject. But let us see if it is true that defendant's liability as carrier for the delivery of these goods had ended before they were delivered to the pretended owner at Burton, or would when they were forwarded from Brenham. When the course of business of the carrier is such as will not ordinarily admit of a personal delivery of the goods to the consignee, there seems to be some conflict in the adjudged cases as to the precise time and circumstances when the liability of the carrier as such ceases and that of warehouseman begins; but whatever difficulty may be found in determining this point at common law, or in reconciling the different decisions regarding it, is eliminated in this State by statute, by which it is clearly and definitely determined.

"But if the defendant's liability was merely that of warehouseman, would the facts shown in the record have justified the forwarding of the goods from Brenham, or the subsequent delivery of them to a party in whom the evidence fails to show anything more than a mere pretence of right to them? While a warehouseman may no doubt be fully justified in many instances in delivering freight to well-known and

the defendant's cart, who, upon hearing the circumstances of the elopement, gave up the box to her. The case, upon the

responsible business men residing in the immediate vicinity of the place to which goods are sent, we think there can be no hesitancy in saying that it was gross negligence to deliver goods of the description and value of these, to a man without family, or settled place of residence, or permanent occupation, who held no receipt or bill of lading for them; and this, too, in the absence of facts or circumstances of any kind tending to show either that he owned or had any connection with them, except his statement before the arrival of this particular freight, that a lot of freight belonging to him had been shipped to Brenham and that he had ordered it forwarded to Burton, and the bare fact of the similarity of his surname with that of the consignee; and certainly nothing whatever is shown to have warranted the defendant in forwarding the goods to Burton. It does not appear that the defendant's agent knew, or even had ever heard, prior to the receipt of the letter, that such a person as 'R. Adams' was residing there or could rightfully lay any claim to these goods." See to same effect, Price *v.* Oswego, &c. R. R. Co., 50 N. Y. 213. This case, in some of its features, resembles that of Stephenson *v.* Hart, 4 Bing. 476, in which a swindler procured the plaintiff to send a box of goods directed to "J. West, Great Winchester St., London." The carrier found that no such person lived there, and took the box back. Some days afterwards he received a letter purporting to have been written and signed by "J. West," stating that a box had been sent to him, addressed by mistake to Great Winchester St., and asking that it be forwarded to him at another designated place. The carrier sent the box according to such directions, and the swindler obtained it; and the carrier was held liable for a conversion of the goods, upon the ground that he was guilty of negligence in forwarding the goods upon the faith of the letter, when no such person as the consignee was to be found at the place to which the goods were directed. "That circumstance," says BURROUGHS, J., "ought to have awakened the suspicions of the defendants, and they were guilty of gross negligence in parting with them without further inquiry. In the result, they have the goods of the plaintiff in their possession, and they are liable to him if they deliver them wrongfully." GASLEE, J., was of the opinion, however, that the defendants were not liable, because the goods had been in fact delivered to the person for whom they were intended.

The liability of the carrier as to delivery depends upon the question whether or not, in making the delivery to the wrong person, he acted with a proper degree of care and prudence in ascertaining the right of the person to whom the delivery was made, to have the goods, or was, in that respect, guilty of negligence; and there is a class of cases, especially in England, and in some of the States of this country, where a rule apparently contrary to that adopted in the cases already cited is held. Thus, in Western Union Telegraph Co. *v.* Meyer, 61 Ala. 158, 32 Am. Rep. 1, an impostor at Cincinnati sent a despatch to Joseph Meyer, the plaintiff, at Selma, Alabama, in the name of Max Reis, requesting the plaintiff to send him a telegraphic money-order for forty

suggestion of PARK, J., was compromised, but that judge remarked, "that he was decidedly of opinion that in any case

dollars, immediately. The plaintiff received the despatch, and, supposing it to be from his nephew of that name, who was then on his way from New York to Selma, paid the money to the defendants, and received from them a receipt as follows: "Received from Joseph Meyer forty dollars to be paid to Max Reis at Cincinnati, Ohio." On the same day the defendant handed over the money to the person who sent the despatch to the plaintiff, who was not known to the company's agent, or identified as a person whose name was Max Reis, and who, in fact, was an impostor, and not the plaintiff's nephew. The plaintiff had judgment in the court below, but upon appeal the judgment was set aside upon the ground that, as there were no suspicious circumstances to put the company upon further inquiry as to the identity of the impostor, the company could not be charged with negligence in that respect, and therefore were not liable for the money. MANNING, J., who delivered the opinion of the court, and evidently dissented from the opinion of a majority of the court, after a line of reasoning which seems to establish negligence on the part of the company, says: "My brothers think that, where there is nothing to create suspicion in the minds of the company's agents, it is for the person on whom the demand is made to ascertain for himself whether he who makes it is the person he professes to be, and that the company has no right to refuse payment of the money to him in reply to whose message the order to pay it is sent. I was strongly inclined to the other conclusion. But the case is a new one, and I defer to their opinion." But in a New York case, Elwood *v.* The Western Union Telegraph Co., 45 N. Y. 549, a rule adverse to that adopted in this case was held. In that case a telegraph operator at T. received a message dated at E. and addressed to bankers at P., which read as follows: "Keystone Bank will pay the check of T. F. McCarthy to the amount of twenty thousand dollars ($20,000). J. J. TOWN, Cashier of Keystone Bank." The person presenting the message was known to the operator by the name of McCarthy, but no authority from the cashier was shown. The message was transmitted, and proved to be fraudulent. It was held that the operator was guilty of gross negligence, for which the telegraph company was liable.

In a case before the United States Circuit Court, Norwalk Bank *v.* The Adams Express Co., 4 Blatchf. (U. S. C. C) 455, a doctrine in harmony with that of the Ohio case was adopted. In that case a party who had fraudulently obtained possession of a note which he altered as to the time of payment, in order to procure it to be discounted more readily, sent it, in the name of another person, by the defendant company, to be presented to the bank for discount. The bank discounted the note, and the proceeds were paid over to the defendant, to be returned, as was understood, to the person to whom the note belonged. The company returned the money, and turned it over to the person from whom they received the note, believing him to be the person entitled to it. Under this state of facts the court held that the defendants were not liable for the money, as there was nothing in the circumstances calcu-

where a female under age attempted an elopement with a person disapproved of by those under whose guardianship she

lated to excite suspicion, or put them upon inquiry as to the right of such person to have the money. In a Massachusetts case, Dunbar *v.* Boston & Providence R. R. Co, 110 Mass. 26, a similar doctrine was held in a case where a person (an impostor) had bought goods, representing himself as another person who resided in P. The goods were marked C. D., and shipped over the defendants' road to him at P. The impostor, who was known to the defendants' agent at P. by his real name, applied for them as agent for C. D., who was not known to the agent. The goods had been stored for two weeks or so before they were applied for. The goods were delivered to the impostor without the production of the bill of lading by him, and he signed a receipt for them in his true name. When the fraud was discovered the plaintiff brought an action against the company for the goods. The court held that, under the circumstances, the defendant was not liable for the goods as for a misdelivery, inasmuch as the goods had been delivered to the person who really ordered them, and for whom they were intended. The person of whom they were purchased, and who consigned them, sold them to the impostor personally. He knew to whom he was selling them, although he did not know him by his correct name; and the very person to whom he sold them received them from the carrier; and if the plaintiff had been called upon to identify the consignee personally, the person who received the goods must have been the one whom he would have identified as purchaser and consignee. If the goods are ordered in a fictitious name, with an intent to defraud, and are directed to be sent to the address given at a certain street and number, and the goods are so sent, and the carrier takes such steps as he is required to take to deliver them there, he cannot be held chargeable as for a misdelivery, although there is no such person or firm doing business at that place. Thus, in an English case, McKean *v.* McIvor, L. R. 6 Exch. 36, goods were ordered by an impostor named Heddell, and addressed to a fictitious firm at a given number and street; upon the arrival of the goods at their place of destination, the carrier addressed a notice to the consignee at such street and number, and Heddell indorsed the name of the fictitious firm upon it, and obtained the goods. In an action by the consignor against the carrier for the loss of the goods, it was held that he was not liable; MARTIN, B., saying: "When the plaintiff thought fit to act upon the order which Heddell had given in the false name of C. Tait & Co., and gave directions to the defendants to deliver the goods to C. Tait & Co., at 71 *George St., Glasgow*, I think that they affirmed that there were such persons as C. Tait & Co. at that place. That they were led into that belief by the fraud of Heddell makes no matter; they did so state, in fact, and the carriers had the right to assume that this statement was correct, and have a right now to say that the person to whom they delivered the goods was, as he was in fact, the person who represented himself to be C. Tait & Co. But if the carrier delivers at the place indicated, or does what is equivalent to a delivery, he does all that he is bound to do. *He obeys the sender's*

properly was, they (the guardians) would be perfectly justified in preventing such elopement; and it was equally clear to him

orders, and is guilty of no wrong. To make him liable there must be some fault. It is a question of fact, whether there has been any such negligence as makes him liable for the conversion of the goods; and where he has carried out the directions of the sender, the mere fact that he has delivered them to some person to whom the sender did not intend delivery to be made, is not sufficient to support the allegation that he has converted them."

In Heugh *v.* London, &c. Railway Co., L. R. 5 Exch. 50, cited by the author in the preceding note, goods were obtained from the plaintiff by means of a fraudulent letter written in the name of a company which had ceased to do business, by a former employee. The goods were taken to the company's place of business, and were refused, and, according to the usual course of business, an advice note was sent to the company at the place designated for delivery. Some days after, the person who had forged the order upon which the goods were obtained appeared at the carrier's office, with an order for the goods signed with the company's name, but which was forged, directing the carrier to deliver the goods to him, and they were so delivered. In an action by the consignor against the carrier to recover for the conversion of the goods on the ground of misdelivery, it was held that the carrier was not liable, as, after having tendered the goods at the appointed place, and having sent the notice referred to, they ceased to be common carriers, and were only bound to act with reasonable caution; KELLY, C. B., saying: "The plaintiffs contend that this was a misdelivery, on the part of the defendant, amounting to a conversion; but no sufficient authority has been cited in support of this position. It is true that a misdelivery by a carrier has been held to amount to a conversion, but their character as carriers had ceased, and whatever character they filled, it was not that. Their position has been not inaptly described as that of involuntary bailees. Without their own default they found these goods in their hands, under circumstances in which the character of carriers, under which they received them, had ceased. Did they then, as involuntary bailees, become subject to an absolute duty to deliver to the proper person, so as to be liable for misdelivery, though without negligence? The only authorities in the courts of this country cited in support of that proposition, are Stephenson *v.* Hart, and Duff *v.* Budd; but in neither case was it held, or even contended, that the misdelivery amounted, as a matter of law, to a conversion; but in both cases it was admitted to be a question for the jury, *and the question was, in fact, left to them, whether, under all the circumstances, the defendant had acted with reasonable care.* It is plain, then, on the authority of those cases, that misdelivery under such circumstanees is not, as a matter of law, a conversion, and that it is a question of fact for the jury, whether the defendants have exercised reasonable and proper eare and caution. The jury have answered this question in the affirmative, and they are therefore entitled to keep their verdict."

It is important, in the decision of questions of this character to ascertain whether, at the time of the alleged

that they would be justified in stopping her clothes. Being of that opinion, he must have held, if the present case had not

misdelivery, the defendant occupied the relation of carrier, or only that of a warehouseman to the goods; because, as is said in some of the cases, the carrier, as such, is under the same obligation or duty to *deliver* the goods safely that he is to carry them. Winslow *v.* Vermont & Massachusetts R. R. Co., 42 Vt. 700. They deliver property at their peril, and must take care that it is delivered to the right party; for if the delivery be to the wrong person, either by an innocent mistake or through the fraud of third persons, as upon a forged order, they will be responsible, and the wrongful delivery will be treated as a conversion. McEntee *v.* New Jersey Steamboat Co., 45 N. Y. 34. But if they hold the goods only as warehousemen, the authorities are all agreed that he is only responsible where he fails to act with ordinary care and prudence in reference to the keeping or delivery of the goods; and it will be noticed that in some of the cases, the gist of which has been given in this note, more especially in the English cases, this distinction is drawn. In some of the States, as we have seen, especially in Massachusetts, the relation of carrier is held to cease with the arrival of the goods at their place of destination, and in others when they are unloaded and properly stored, and in others in a reasonable time after notice is sent to the consignee of the arrival of the goods, and he has had a reasonable time in which to remove them; and the rule adopted in a given State upon this point will necessarily have an important bearing upon the question of liability for misdelivery. Of course, the determination of this question in all the States depends upon the circumstance whether the carrier is a carrier by rail or water, or whether he belongs to that class, as express companies, who are bound to deliver to the consignee personally, as in the case of carriers by rail and water the liability of the carrier as such may, in any event, be determined by a notice to the consignee of the arrival of the goods and the lapse of a reasonable time for him to act upon the notice; while, as to the other species of carriers there must have been either a tender of delivery, or at least an attempt to deliver, or he must show that he has made due and reasonable inquiry and has been unable to find the consignee. Witbeck *v.* Holland, 46 N. Y. 13. When these conditions exist, the consignor, in order to charge the carrier with liability for the loss of the goods, must show that he has acted negligently in respect to the matter producing the loss; or perhaps it should be said that the carrier may show, to protect himself from liability, that his relation to the goods as carrier had ceased, and that the loss ensued without his fault or negligence. Neal *v.* R. R. Co., 8 Jones (N. C.), L. 482; Fenner *v.* R. R. Co., *ante;* Fisk *v.* Newton, 1 Den. (N. Y.) 45; Weed *v.* Barney, *ante;* Kremer *v.* Southern Express Co., 6 Coldw. (Tenn.) 356; Hudson *v.* Baxendale, 2 H. &. N. 575. In determining whether a carrier who is bound to make a personal delivery has made such reasonable inquiry to find the consignee, so that his liability as a carrier has ceased, depends upon the circumstances of each case; and in determining this question it is competent to show whether or not the consignee was well known at the place to which the goods were consigned. In

been compromised, that the carrier was guilty of no tortious conversion in delivering up the plaintiff's clothes to her mother."

Witbeck *v.* Holland, 45 N. Y. 13, this question was considered under the following circumstances: The plaintiff delivered to the Adams Express Co., at Hart's Island, N. Y., the sum of $320, addressed and to be delivered to "Martin Witbeck, Schenectady, N. Y." The agent of the Express Co. gave a receipt for the package, "upon the special acceptance and agreement that this company is to forward the same to its agent nearest or most convenient to destination only, and there to deliver the same to other parties to complete the transportation, such delivery to terminate all liability of this company for such package." The package was delivered on the 5th of December by the Adams Express Company to the defendant company at its office in New York, the latter giving the following receipt to the former company: —

Received, New York, December 5, 1864, of Adams Express Company (per bills), in good order, the following articles set opposite our respective names:

ARTICLES.	Dollars.	Cents.	Consignee.	Where from.	Destination.	Amount Charged.	By whom received.
Pck.	$320.	•	Martin Witbeck.	H. I.	Schenectady, N. Y.	$1.75.	Myers.

Myers was the authorized agent of the defendant company. The package was transported to Schenectady in due time, and the local agent of defendant company, with a view to making delivery, looked into the directory, but did not find the name Martin Witbeck, although said Witbeck was a resident of Schenectady at that time and for some time afterward. The efforts of the agent were then directed to finding the consignee, but it appears that his inquiries were for Martin Whitbeck instead of Martin Witbeck. The package was deposited in the company's safe a few days afterward, where it remained until January 17, 1865, when the safe was burglarized and the package stolen. The referee found, further, that defendant company was bound to make delivery of the package to Martin Witbeck personally, or at his place of business or residence; that defendant company did not make due effort to make such delivery; and that plaintiff should recover the amount of the package, with interest. Judgment was entered on the report, from which the defendant appealed to the general term, where it was affirmed. An appeal was then taken to the Court of Appeals.

Grover, J., in delivering the opinion of the court, said: "The facts found by the referee showed beyond question that the defendant was a common carrier, and responsible, as such, for property delivered to it for transportation. This finding was warranted by the evidence. It was engaged in transacting a general express business. It is insisted by the counsel for the defendant that its liability was restricted by the contract, proved by the receipt given by the Adams Express Company to the plaintiff, upon the receipt of the money from him by it at Hart's Island. From this receipt it appears that the

SEC. 265. **Proof of Non-delivery.** — Still, where the duty is not dispensed with by circumstances such as those just de-

latter company undertook to forward the package to its agent nearest to its destination, there to deliver it to other parties to complete the transportation, such delivery to terminate all liability of that company for its passage. There is nothing in this or any other restriction at all affecting the liability of the defendant as a common carrier; all the restrictions fonnd in the receipt are by the language limited to the liability of the Adams Company. Indeed, were they applicable to the defendant, they would not affect the liability of the defendant in the action, as they do not inclnde the cause of the loss, unless they relieve the carrier from the dnty of delivery to the consignee. The first inqniry is, whether it was the duty of the carrier so to deliver the package in the absence of any restriction. Carriers by land are bound to deliver or tender the goods to the consignee at his residence or place of business, and until this is done they are not relieved from responsibility as carriers. 2 Kent's Com. 605; Angell on Carriers, § 295; Gibson *v.* Culver, 17 Wend. 305; Fisk *v.* Newton, 1 Den. (N. Y.) 45. But when goods are safely conveyed to the place of destination, and the consignee cannot, after reasonable effort, be found, the carrier may discharge himself from further responsibility by depositing the property in a suitable place for the owner. Fisk *v.* Newton, *supra*. Carriers by vessels, boats, and railways are exempt from the duty of personal delivery. Redfield on Railways, § 127; Thomas *v.* Boston R. R. Co., 10 Met. (Mass.) 472. Such carriers discharge themselves from responsibility, as such, by transporting the goods to their nearest business station to the residence or place of business of the consignee, and notifying the consignee of their readiness to deliver the goods at such station, after the lapse of a reasonable time for him to receive them. But this exemption does not extend to express companies, although availing themselves of carriage by rail. Redfield on Railways, § 127. These were established for the purpose of extending to the public the advantages of personal delivery enjoyed in all cases of land carriage prior to the introduction of transportation by rail.

"It appeared in the present case that the defendant had its vehicles by which they carried articles to the consignees in the city of Schenectady, which had arrived there by rail under contracts with the company for the transportation. This is the usual course of transacting business by such companies; were it otherwise the business done by these companies would be greatly diminished, as it would be equally advantageous in many cases to have the property transported by the railroad company. When the defendant received the package from the Adams Company at New York, consigned to Martin Witbeck, Schenectady, it became liable as carrier for its carriage to Schenectady and its delivery to Witbeck there, if with reasonable diligence he could be found. The performance of this entire service was contracted for by its receipt so addressed, and had the defendant received it from the plaintiff at New York and given him a receipt for its transportation, the obligation to make personal delivery at Schenectady would have been incurred. The only remaining question arises upon the exception taken to the finding by the referee, as

scribed, or by other circumstances, which we shall have occasion to consider, it must be performed strictly; and it has been

a fact, that the defendant did not make due effort, nor use due diligence to find said Martin Witbeck, the consignee of said package. It is insisted by the counsel for the appellant, that the question, what is reasonable diligence, is one of law. That may be so when there is no conflict in the evidence of controversy as to the facts to be inferred therefrom. But that is not this case, nor will most cases of this class be of that description. In most, if not all, the questions will be mixed, both of fact and law. In the present case the finding of the referee was clearly correct. The diligence which the law required of the defendant was such as a prudent man would have used in an important business affair of his own. The evidence shows that the defendant was so inattentive as to mistake the surname of the consignee. Although the package was addressed Witbeck, all its inquiries were made for Whitbeck. This may have prevented their finding him. It further appeared that its inquiries were confined to a few persons in the vicinity of its place of business, and that by these it obtained information of other persons of a like surname, one of whom was the father of the consignee. Surely inquiry should have been made of these persons; and had it been so made, delivery would have been made, and the loss would never have occurred. There is nothing in the point that the negligence of the plaintiff in not giving further information as to the residence of the consignee contributed to the loss. The defendant accepted the package, addressed as it was, and failed in the performance of the duty imposed thereby. For such failure it is responsible, irrespective of the right of the plaintiff to give additional information. I have examined the various exceptions taken by the appellant to the rulings of the referee as to the competency of evidence. The question whether the consignee was well known in Schenectady was proper. The plaintiff had the right to prove this fact if he could. But the testimony given in answer was not material. None of the testimony excepted to could have prejudiced the defendant. The judgment appealed from must be affirmed."

If a carrier takes goods through mistake for transportation over its line which were intended for transportation over another line, and for which no compensation could be charged, it is nevertheless bound to the same degree of diligence, and subject to the same duties and liabilities in reference to its transportation and delivery, as though it had been regularly shipped over such line. This rule is illustrated in Fairfax *v.* New York Central R. R. Co., 73 N. Y. 167, 29 Am. Rep. 119. The plaintiff purchased at Montreal, of the Grand Trunk R. R. Co., a ticket for the city of New York by way of rail to Troy or Albany and thence by steamboat to New York. His portmanteau was checked by the same route. At Troy a railroad agent delivered the portmanteau to the defendant, and the latter carried it to New York on its railway, and put it in its baggage-room. Three days afterwards, as soon as the plaintiff had reason to believe that the defendant had it, he demanded it, but it could not be found. It contained thirty-nine sovereigns and some partly worn clothing. The court held that the defendant, having taken the portman-

sufficient to prove non-delivery, that the consignor should state that he gave the goods to the carrier's servant, properly

teau without the plaintiff's knowledge or assent, was responsible for its contents without regard to their character. EARL, J., said: "The delivery of the baggage to the defendant was the wrongful act of the agent of the Rensselaer & Saratoga R. R. Co. He was not the agent of the plaintiff. The various railroad companies which had contracted to carry him were not his agents. They were contractors with him, and owed him the duty of carrying him and his baggage as they had agreed. Their employees were not his agents in any sense that would enable them to bind him by their acts. The defendant had no right to take and carry this baggage. It was bound to know by the marks on the checks that it was to be carried by another route. But it took the baggage for transportation to New York, and was therefore bound to carry it safely, and when it reached New York was bound to deliver it to the plaintiff upon demand. It there placed the baggage in its baggage-room on the afternoon of October 9th, and it remained there until the morning of the 12th. Between eight and twelve o'clock of that day the plaintiff demanded his baggage, and it could not be found.

"As was decided, when this case was here upon the prior appeal, the defendant incurred at least the responsibility of a warehouseman. Fairfax v. New York Central & Hudson River R. R. Co., 67 N. Y. 11. That responsibility required of it ordinary care in the keeping and delivery of the baggage; and it was before decided upon the facts, as they then appeared, that it was a question of fact for the jury whether the defendant took such care. The facts upon the second trial were not materially changed. They were at least not so far changed that the court could, as matter of law, say that the defendant was not guilty of culpable negligence. The plaintiff demanded his baggage, and that cast upon the defendant the burden of accounting for it in some way. It was bound to show that it had disappeared from its baggage-room without its fault. This it attempted to do, but it failed to show clearly what became of it. It was either stolen or misdelivered. It was under all the circumstances for the jury to determine which. If it was misdelivered, then the defendant became liable for it. The plaintiff cannot be charged with any negligence in not claiming his baggage sooner. As soon as he reached New York, and had reason to believe that his baggage had been carried over defendant's road, he called for it, and demanded it. He thus certainly discharged any duty he owed the defendant, which had taken and carried his baggage and placed it in its baggage-room without his knowledge or assent. The general charge of the court to the jury was as favorable to the defendant as the law required. But several exceptions to the charges, and refusals to charge, were taken, which must be briefly noticed:

"First. The court refused to charge that the relation of carrier to a passenger and his baggage did not exist between plaintiff and defendant. This refusal was proper. The matter was wholly immaterial. I am inclined to think that the defendant, in taking and conveying this baggage, without the knowledge or assent of the plaintiff, might be treated as having voluntarily assumed the responsibility of a common carrier. And whether it might

addressed to the consignee, and that the consignee's servant should state that he did not know of the delivery, and believed that the parcel could not be delivered without his knowledge.[1] And evidence that the weight or amount of goods delivered to the consignee is less than the weight or amount

or not, it is sufficient for this action that it assumed at least the responsibility of a warehouseman, and that imposed upon it the duty of ordinary care; and hence, also, the court did not err in refusing to charge that the defendant was liable only for loss caused by gross negligence.

"Second. The court charged the jury that the defendant was not liable for the loss of the baggage, if it exercised ordinary care, whether such loss was from theft or a misdelivery, and hence all the charge requested in reference to a reasonable time for the plaintiff to claim the baggage was wholly immaterial. The defendant had this baggage without plaintiff's knowledge or assent, and he claimed it as soon as he knew where it was, and he could not, therefore, be charged with any delay or default.

"Third. In the plaintiff's portmanteau were thirty-nine English sovereigns, worth $218.40, and the court charged the jury that they should allow the value of the sovereigns, if they found that the amount of them was a proper, reasonable, and necessary amount for the plaintiff to carry with him in his portmanteau for his journey; and in deciding this point that they should take into consideration the position and circumstances of the plaintiff, the length and character of his journey, the contingencies and accidents that might naturally arise, and the fact that he was in a foreign country. The defendant excepted to this, and asked the court to charge that it was not liable for the sovereigns. The charge, as made, was at least as favorable to defendant as the law required. The plaintiff did not deliver this portmanteau to the defendant for carriage, and in no way practised upon the defendant any fraud as to its contents. He had no opportunity to inform defendant of the contents. It took the portmanteau without his knowledge or assent, and was bound to care for it, and its contents, no matter what they were.

"Fourth. The court did not err in charging the jury that the plaintiff was entitled to recover the full value of clothing for use to him, in New York, and not merely what it could be sold for in money. The clothing was made to fit plaintiff, and had been partly worn. It would sell for but little, if put into market to be sold for second-hand clothing, and it would be a wholly inadequate and unjust rule of compensation to give plaintiff, in such a case, the value of the clothing thus ascertained. The rule must be the value of the clothing for use by the plaintiff. No other rule would give him a compensation for his damages. This rule must be adopted, because such clothing cannot be said to have any market price, and it would not sell for what it was really worth. We do not mean to say that the defendant incurred no greater responsibility than that of a warehouseman. It may be that it was absolutely liable for this baggage upon the theory that its interference therewith was wholly unauthorized and wrongful."

[1] Griffiths v. Lee, 1 C. & P. 110.

of goods delivered to the carrier is sufficient *primâ facie* evidence to charge the latter for the deficiency, or to call on him to show that it did not arise from his negligence.[1] In another case, which was tried at Exeter in 1862, before CHANNELL, B., the question as to what constitutes proof of delivery was considered. The learned judge left it to the jury to say whether there had been a delivery or not, and upon a motion for a new trial, it was held that there had been no misdirection, and that in proving the delivery of goods by a carrier, it is necessary to show an actual delivery into the possession of the consignee or his servants, although it may not be necessary to give evidence of delivery into their hands.[2]

SEC. 266. **When Non-delivery excused.** — Having considered the duty of delivery, what will constitute such a delivery as will discharge a carrier from his liability for the goods, and also as to the proof of delivery or non-delivery, we are now in a position to consider under what circumstances non-delivery of the goods consigned will be excused or justified. With regard to the excuses which will exonerate a carrier, whether he be a common carrier, a carrier for hire who is not a common carrier, or a gratuitous carrier, — in cases where, in the first, the loss arises from an act of God or from the interference of enemies, where, in the second, the loss arises from no want of ordinary diligence, and where, in the third, the loss arises when it cannot be ascribed to his gross negligence, the reader must be referred to a former chapter.[3] And as to those cases where, owing to the limitation of the responsibility of a common carrier by statute or by special contract, the circumstances under which non-delivery will be excused, the reader must also have recourse to a portion of this work already written.[4]

SEC. 267. **Countermand by Consignor, when it may be made.** — It is, of course, within the power of the owner to alter his mind with regard to the destination of his own goods. It

[1] Hawkes *v.* Smith, C. & M. 72. See also Gilbert *v.* Dale, 5 Ad. & El. 543.

[2] Evans *v.* Bristol & Exeter Rail. Co., 10 W. R. 359.

[3] *Ante*, pp. 16, 30, 42.

[4] Chapter vii.

was he who gave them a destination in the hands of the carrier, and he may, if he chooses, countermand his first order. Such a countermand will, of course, justify a non-delivery upon the part of the carrier, and it has been expressly decided that such a countermand may be given at any time during the transit.

SEC. 268. **Carrier's Compliance with Request to return. — Contract to carry according to Owner's Directions.** — The consignor may, therefore, demand back his goods; but when he does so he must be prepared to pay the carriage. This request must be complied with, except where the unpacking and redelivery would be productive of much inconvenience to the carrier.[1] Where, therefore, a package containing goods, and marked "Scotthorn and Co., to the East India Docks, passenger ship, Melbourne, Australia," was sent by the plaintiffs to the Great Bridge Station of the defendants, the South Staffordshire Railway Company, to be taken to London for hire, and the practice of the South Staffordshire Company was, that goods delivered at that station for London were conveyed by their line as far as Birmingham, and thence by the London and North-Western Railway, and it appeared that before the goods in question arrived in London, one of the plaintiffs delivered to a clerk at the Euston Station of the London and North-Western Railway a written order, directing that they should be sent to Ratcliffe Highway, and this order was not complied with, it was held that the plaintiffs were entitled to countermand the directions originally given by them, — that the clerk at the Euston Station was an agent of the defendants having authority to receive the countermand, — and that the defendants were liable for a loss occasioned by their non-compliance with the second order. ALDERSON, B., in giving judgment, stated that the whole question was, "What was the contract between the parties?" "That," he said, "actually amounts to a question of fact. Now there is abundant evidence to show that the contract was, as stated in the declaration, to carry according to the directions of the plaintiffs. It

[1] Scotthorn *v.* South Staffordshire Rail. Co., 8 Exch. 341; 22 L. J. Exch. 121; 7 Rail. Cas. 810.

is very true that originally, when the defendants were put in possession of the goods, the orders were to take them to the East India Docks, but before their arrival in London, the plaintiffs, having changed their intentions, communicated that change to the agents of the defendants in London, who had authority to deliver the goods. The altered directions were: 'Do not send the things to the place marked on the outside of the packages, but transmit them elsewhere.' The question is not whether the clerk had power to make a new contract on behalf of the defendants, — it is enough that he was told not to send them according to the written directions. By some neglect, the instructions were not obeyed, — the articles are sent to Australia, and lost. Then, have the defendants performed their contract? I think there is ample evidence to go to the jury to show that they have not, and that the verdict is therefore right." PLATT, B., concurred. He said: "The declaration states that the defendants received the goods to be delivered according to the plaintiff's directions; that means that they were to have some control over them, and might stop them in any part of their transit. . . . If a carrier undertakes to carry goods from A to B, he does so subject to a right in the owner to countermand the direction at any point of the journey, and, though he may be bound to pay the carrier for his trouble, yet the latter has no right to carry them further against the will of the owner of the goods."[1]

SEC. 269. **Delivery at Place appointed by Consignee.** — But while the consignor has the right to alter the destination of the goods, a similar power is vested in the consignee. And a delivery at any place appointed by the consignee will discharge the carrier from his liability, even although it should not be the place appointed by the owner or shipper thereof.[2] Thus the plaintiff, having sold wheat by sample, to be delivered to the purchaser at his mill, sent it by the defendants' railway. On the arrival of the wheat at a station two miles from the

[1] Scotthorn *v.* South Staffordshire Rail. Co., 8 Exch. 341; 22 L. J. Exch. 121; 7 Rail. Cas. 810. See also Lewis *v.* Galena, &c. R. R. Co., 40 Ill. 281.

[2] London & North-Western Rail. Co. *v.* Bartlett, 7 H. & N. 400; 8 Jur. N. S. 58; 31 L. J. Exch. 92; 10 W. R. 109; 5 L. T. N. S. 399.

mill, the defendants kept it there in consequence of instructions given to them by the consignee, that wheat arriving for him at the station should not be forwarded to the mill without his written order. The plaintiff had no knowledge of these instructions. The consignee examined the wheat at the station, but refused to accept it, and while it remained there it became deteriorated in quality and value.

SEC. 270. **Non-delivery by Order of Consignee.** — In the case last cited it was held that the consignor had no action against the defendants for not delivering the wheat at the mill, as the non-delivery was by the order of the consignee. Therefore we see that the order of the consignee can change the place at which a good and reasonable delivery, discharging the carrier from his liability, can be made. POLLOCK, C. B., said in this case: "It is, I think, quite clear that the consignee of goods may receive at any stage of the journey; and I think that if the consignor directs goods to be delivered at a particular place, it is no contract to deliver the goods at that place, and not elsewhere. The contract is to deliver the goods there, unless the consignee shall require them to be delivered at some other place." BRAMWELL, B., also remarked: "I think it would probably create a laugh anywhere, except in a court of law, if it was said a carrier could not deliver to the consignee short of the particular place specified by the consignor. The goods are intended to reach the consignee, and provided they reach him to his satisfaction, it is immaterial where that place may be; and the consignor cares very little whether it be at one place or another. The obvious meaning of the contract is to deliver to the consignee at the place mentioned, unless the consignee chooses, and the carrier is willing, that they should be delivered somewhere else." [1]

SEC. 271. **Duty discharged by Payment of Damages.** — But there are many other possible circumstances, concerning which a question might arise, as to whether they could be regarded as equivalent to delivery. Thus it would seem that if the

[1] London & North-Western Rail. Co. v. Bartlett, 7 H. & N. 400; 31 L. J. Exch. 92; 10 W. R. 109; 8 Jur. N. S. 58. See also, with regard to this subject, Pollard v. London & South-Western Rail. Co., 22 L. T. N. S. 551.

carrier, believing the goods to have been lost, paid damages to the owner, and he subsequently discovered that the goods were safe, he would not then be bound to deliver them.

SEC. 272. **Claim of Ownership.** — Most difficulty has arisen in cases where, while the goods were still in the hands of the carrier, they have been claimed by some one not the bailor, who asserted his ownership. If the carrier, under such circumstances, delivered the goods to their actual owner, would that terminate his liability to the bailor, which, under ordinary circumstances, is only discharged by delivery to the consignee? In the case of Crouch *v.* Great Western Railway Company,[1] MAULE, J., said: "An agent must account to his principal, and cannot set up the *jus tertii* in an action by his principal against him."

SEC. 273. **Carrier cannot dispute Bailor's Title.** — It follows from this that a carrier cannot, any more than an ordinary bailee, dispute his bailor's title. This is especially clear in cases where the adverse claim is not asserted by the real owner, but is asserted by the carrier, of his own mere motion.[2] He holds for his employer, and if a third party sets up a claim, he will admit it at his peril. In the case of Ogle *v.* Atkinson,[3] however, it was held that a warehouseman, who has received goods from a consignee, who has had actual possession of them, to be kept for his use, may nevertheless refuse to deliver them if they are the property of another. This decision, however, seems bad, both in the light of reason and in the light of some more recent cases.

SEC. 274. **General Rule.** — The general rule, that an agent has no right to set up an adverse title against that of his principal, and that it is the duty of the bailee to redeliver the goods to the person who intrusted them to him, is well established.[4] On the other hand, the bailee must not give up the goods which actually belong to a third person, if he have

[1] 26 L. J. 420 Exch.

[2] See Shelbury *v.* Scotsford, Yelv. 23; Wilson *v.* Anderton, 1 B. & Ad. 450.

[3] 5 Taunt. 759.

[4] Laclough *v.* Towle, 3 Esp. 115; Kieran *v.* Sandars, 6 Ad. & El. 515; Gosling *v.* Birnie, 7 Bing. 339; Holl *v.* Griffin, 10 Bing. 246; Burroughs *v.* Bayne, 29 L. J. 185 Exch. See also Story on Agency, § 217, and Story on Bailm. §§ 450, 582.

notice of the fact, to the person who bailed them to him. And if he does so, and the actual owner brings an action against the carrier, he will be liable if the bailor had no title.[1]

SEC. 275. **Bailee's Situation.** — In the case of Wilson *v.* Anderton,[2] which was a case in which the captain of a ship, who had taken goods on freight, and claimed to have a lien upon them, delivered them to a bailee, and where, upon the real owner demanding them from the latter, and upon his refusing to deliver them without the direction of the bailor, it was held that, the bailor not having any lien upon the goods, the refusal by the bailee was sufficient evidence of conversion. LORD TENTERDEN, C. J., said: "A bailee can never be in a better situation than the bailor. If the bailor has no title, the bailee can have none, for the bailor can give no better title than he has. The right to the property may therefore be tried in an action against the bailee, and a refusal like that stated in the case has always been considered evidence of conversion. The situation of a bailee is not without remedy. He is not bound to ascertain who has the right. He may file a bill of interpleader in a Court of Equity.[3] But a bailee who forbears to adopt that mode of proceeding, and makes himself a party by retaining the goods for the bailor, must stand or fall by his [the bailor's] title." The questions involved in this subject were fully discussed in Sheridan *v.* The New Quay Company.[4] In that case a person who was resident in Manchester contracted to buy of Messrs. George & James Donaldson, of Corsack, near Dumfries, a quantity of oak-bark, to be shipped "for delivery at Liverpool." Messrs. George & James Donaldson accordingly shipped the bark to be delivered at Liverpool to the defendants, who were wharfingers and carriers there, to be by them forwarded to the person who gave the order in Manchester. The bark was to be paid for in cash, and Messrs. G. & J. Donaldson sent a bill

[1] If goods are taken from the bailee by the authority of the law, that will excuse delivery, and be a defence to an action brought against him by the bailor for non-delivery. Bliven *v.* Hudson River R. R. Co., 35 Barb. (N. Y.) 188; Van Winkle *v.* U. S. Mail Steamship Co., 37 Barb. (N. Y.) 122.

[2] 1 B. & Ad. 450.

[3] See, however, 1 & 2 Will. IV. c. 58.

[4] 4 C. B. N. S. 618.

of lading, making it deliverable to Cooper (the person sending the order), or his assigns, together with a bill of exchange, payable on demand, through his bankers, to the Manchester and Salford Bank, with instructions to present the bill for acceptance. The bank at Manchester were unable to find Sheridan, and accordingly they returned the bill of lading and the draft to Messrs. G. & J. Donaldson. Before the bill of lading had been so returned, Messrs. Donaldson, who were at Liverpool when the bark arrived there, believing, from the representations of an agent of the plaintiff (who had bought the bark of Cooper), that the bill of lading had been duly handed over to Cooper, assented to the bark being delivered to the defendants, for the purpose of its being carried to Manchester for the plaintiff, but upon subsequently discovering that Cooper had not got the bill of lading, or paid for the bark, Messrs. Donaldson claimed and received it from the defendants. It was held in this case that the property in the bark never passed to Cooper, and consequently that Messrs. Donaldson had a right to countermand the delivery, and that it was competent to the defendants, although they had received the bark to be carried for the plaintiff, to set up the title of Messrs. Donaldson in an action brought against them by the plaintiff.

SEC. 276. **Bonâ fide Delivery of Goods not belonging to Bailor.** — Where a carrier has received goods from a wrongful owner, and has done his duty by the goods, and delivered them to the consignee before he is made aware that the bailor was not the rightful owner, he cannot, of course, be held liable to the latter. Any such liability, if it existed, would be an intolerable hardship upon the carrier. But further, it would appear that even notice of the real ownership will not necessitate the carrier to retain the goods in his possession for the real owner. He does not, by any actual or constructive knowledge of the right of a third party, thereby become a trustee for that third party, as against the consignee; and it appears that even under such circumstances, and with such information, he will not be liable if he delivers the goods to the consignee, unless he does so under circumstances of fraud.

SEC. 277. **Rule in White v. Bartlett.**—Thus, in a case where the defendant, an auctioneer, employed a person named Catling, who was in embarrassed circumstances, to sell his property, and the defendant sold and paid the proceeds to Catling's order, Catling having shortly afterwards been declared insolvent, it was held that the defendant was not liable to White, the assignee of Catling, although the defendant, when he sold the property, was aware of Catling's embarrassment.[1] And in a case which is reported in a foot-note to that just referred to, a similar decision was given.[2] The defendant in that case was employed to sell, as auctioneer, certain goods then in the plaintiff's possession. Before the sale, a notice was given to the defendants, by the assignees of an insolvent, that the goods were their property as such assignees, and that they had been fraudulently removed by collusion between the plaintiff and the insolvent. The defendant, after that notice, sold the property, and rendered an account of the sale to the plaintiff. At the trial, the jury affirmed the right of the assignees, and found that the plaintiff obtained possession of the goods by fraud between him and the insolvent, and, upon that state of the facts, were directed by PATTESON, J., to find a verdict for the defendant, with liberty to the plaintiff to move to enter a verdict for the amount of the sale in case the court should be of opinion that it was not competent for the defendant, in the peculiar situation in which he stood to the plaintiff, to set up the right of the assignees upon the present occasion. It was accordingly moved to enter a verdict for the plaintiff, on the ground that an agent must account to his principal, and cannot set up the *jus tertii* in an action by his principal against him.[3]

In giving judgment, ALDERSON, B., said: "We think the

[1] White v. Bartlett, 9 Bing. 378.

[2] Hardman v. Willcock, 9 Bing. 382. This case was argued in the Common Pleas at Lancaster before ALDERSON and PATTESON, JJ.

[3] He relied on Nicolson v. Knowles, 5 Mad. 47; Meyler v. Fitzpatrick, 6 Mad. 360; Stonard v. Dunkin, 2 Camp. 344; Dixon v. Hamond, 2 B. & Ald. 310; Roberts v. Ogilby, 9 Price, 269; Gosling v. Bernie, 7 Bing. 339. But see Taylor v. Plumer, 3 M. & S. 562. See also American cases, King v. Richards, 6 Whart. (Penn.) 418; Bates v. Stanton, 1 Duer (N. Y.), 79.

direction of the judge right, and that the verdict ought to stand. There are many authorities which were cited for the plaintiff, which establish, no doubt, that an agent must account to his principal, and cannot set up the *jus tertii* in an action by his principal against him. . . . But we think that all these cases are distinguishable from the present upon the ground that here the jury have found that the plaintiff's possession of the goods arose out of fraud, concerted between him and the insolvent. . . . And we think that the plaintiff, who takes the goods by a fraud between him and the insolvent, can be in no better situation than the insolvent himself. . . . We are, therefore, glad that this case can be thus decided consistently with the general rules of law, as it is obviously in conformity to the substantial justice of the particular case."

SEC. 278. **Carrier's Position. — Interpleader Act.** — The position of the carrier, therefore, in cases where the title to the goods in his possession is disputed, is not altogether satisfactory. In a case where a dispute as to ownership arises, the bailee will be held liable, both to the bailor and to the actual owner. In an action by the latter, he cannot set up the bailment from the wrongful bailor, and in an action by the former, he cannot set up an ownership in a third person. However, there is safety for the carrier if he will avail himself of the Interpleader Act.[1] That is an act entitled "An Act to enable Courts of Law to give relief against adverse claims made upon persons having no interest in the subject of such claims." And by the 1st section of that act it is provided that, "upon application made by or on behalf of any defendant sued in any of Her Majesty's courts of law at Westminster, or in the Court of Common Pleas in the County Palatine of Lancaster, or the Court of Pleas of the County Palatine of Durham, in any action of assumpsit, debt, detinue or trover, such application being made after declaration, and before plea, by affidavit or otherwise, showing that such defendant does not claim any interest in the subject-matter of the suit, but that the right thereto is claimed or supposed to

[1] 1 & 2 Will. IV. c. 58.

belong to some third party, who has sued, or is expected to sue, for the same, and that such defendant does not in any manner collude with such third party, but is ready to bring into court, or to pay or dispose of the subject-matter of the action in such manner as the court (or any judge thereof) may order or direct, it shall be lawful for the court, or any judge thereof, to make rules and orders, calling upon such third party to appear, and to state the nature and particulars of his claim, and maintain or relinquish his claim, and, upon such rule or order, to hear the allegations, as well of such third party as of the plaintiff, and in the meantime to stay the proceedings in such actions, and finally to order such third party to make himself defendant in the same or some other action, or to proceed to trial on one or more feigned issue or issues, and also to direct which of the parties shall be plaintiff or defendant on such trial, or, with the consent of the plaintiff and such third party, their counsel or attorneys, to dispose of the merits of their claims, and determine the same in a summary manner, and to make such other rules and orders therein as to costs and all other matters as may appear to be just and reasonable."

SEC. 279. **1 & 2 Vict. c. 58.** — And a more recent enactment makes it lawful for the court or judge to whom an application is made under the above-quoted section of the 1 & 2 Will. IV. c. 58, to exercise the powers and authorities given to them by that act, "though the titles of the claimants to the money, goods, or chattels in question, or to the proceeds or value thereof, have not a common origin, but are adverse to and independent of one another."[1] With reference to these enactments, however, it has been decided that the sheriff cannot apply to the court under the Interpleader Act unless the goods or money in dispute are actually in his hands.[2] And in Allen *v.* Gilby,[3] it was decided that where an auctioneer had one action brought against him in the Common Pleas and another in the King's Bench by different claimants for the

[1] 23 & 24 Vict. c. 126, § 12. See also §§ 14, 15, 16.

[2] Scott *v.* Lewis, 2 Cromp. M. & R. 289.

[3] 3 Dowl. P. C. 143.

same property, he must, to relieve himself under the Interpleader Act, obtain rules in both courts; and that if a part of a sum claimed by the parties has been paid to one of them before the adverse claim was made, the adverse claimant has a right to have the whole sum he claims paid into court on the holder applying for relief under the Interpleader Act.[1]

SEC. 280. **Stoppage in Transitu, what it is. — What terminates Journey.** — But other circumstances may put an end to the temporary possession of the carrier which will excuse him from the duty of delivery, and discharge him from further liability with reference to the goods. Thus the exercise of the right of *stoppage in transitu* affords a justification of non-delivery. This right is that which is vested in an unpaid vendor of goods, to stop them while they are on their way to the vendee, and before they have actually come into his possession. "Stoppage *in transitu*, as its name imports, can only take place while the goods are on the way; if they once arrive at the termination of their journey, and come into the actual or constructive possession of the consignee, there is an end to the vendor's right over them. And, therefore, in most of the cases the dispute has been whether the goods had or had not arrived at the termination of their journey. The rule to be collected from all the cases is, that goods are *in transitu* as long as they are in the hands of the carrier, as such, whether he was or was not appointed by the consignee, and also so long as they remain in any place of deposit connected with their transmission;[2] but that if, after their arrival at their place of destination, they be warehoused with the carrier, whose store the vendee uses as his own, or even if they be warehoused with the vendor himself and rent be paid to him for them, that puts an end to the right to stop *in transitu*. In the case of Lickbarrow *v.* Mason,[3] which is the leading au-

[1] The jurisdiction of the court extends to a count in case. Lawrence *v.* Matthews, 5 Dowl. P. C. 149.

[2] See, as to this subject, Winslow *v.* Vermont R. R. Co., 42 Vt. 700; Solomon *v.* Philadelphia, &c. Steamboat Co., 2 Daly (N. Y.), 104; Hedges *v.* Hudson River R. R. Co., 6 Rob. (N. Y.) 119. But see Jeffersonville R. R. Co. *v.* Cleveland, 2 Bush (Ky.), 468.

[3] Lickbarrow *v.* Mason, 1 Smith, L. Cas, 6th ed., p. 699; 2 T. R. 63; Nicholls *v.* Lefeuvre, 2 Bing. N. C. 83; James *v.* Griffin, 1 M. & W. 20; Ed-

thority on this subject, it appeared that Turning & Son, merchants at Middlebourg, in the province of Zealand, had shipped goods for Liverpool, by the order and direction, and on the account of Freeman, of Rotterdam, and had drawn bills of exchange on him for the price, and taken from the master three bills of lading for delivery of the goods to order or assigns, two of which were indorsed in blank, and transmitted them, together with the invoice, to Freeman, who sent them and the invoice to the plaintiffs at Liverpool, in the same state in which he received them, in order that the goods might be taken possession of, and sold on his account, and he drew bills of exchange upon them to nearly the amount at which the goods were valued. Freeman and the plaintiffs accepted the bills of exchange drawn upon them respectively. Before the arrival of the ship at Liverpool, and before the bills of exchange fell due, Freeman became bankrupt. Turning & Son, having heard of the bankruptcy, indorsed the bill of lading, which had been retained by them specially, to the defendants, who thereupon received delivery of the goods from the master. Turning & Son paid the bills of exchange drawn by them upon Freeman, and the plaintiffs paid those which had been drawn upon them by Freeman.

SEC. 281. **Right of Stoppage in Transitu.** — The Court of King's Bench decided that, by an assignment made by the consignee for a valuable consideration, and without notice to the assignee that the goods were not paid for, the property was absolutely transferred to the assignee, and that he was by such assignment deprived of the right to stop the goods *in transitu*, which, as against the original consignees, he might have exercised. The Court of Exchequer Chamber reversed the judgment of the King's Bench, holding that a bill of lading is merely the evidence of a contract for the carriage and delivery of goods, and that the assignment gave the assignee

wards *v.* Brewer, 2 M. & W. 375; Hurry *v.* Mangles, 1 Camp. 452; Stoveld *v.* Hughes, 14 East, 308; per LORD CAMPBELL in Nicholson *v.* Bower, 1 E. & E. 172. See also Cates *v.* Railton, 6 B. & C. 427, per BAYLEY, J.; Leeds *v.* Wright, 3 B. & P. 320; Dickson *v.* Baldwin, 5 East, 175; Ellis *v.* Hunt, 3 T. R. 469, per BULLER, J.; Smith *v.* Goss, 1 Camp. 282; Dodson *v.* Wentworth, 5 Scott, N. R. 833.

no other right or title than that which the consignee himself possessed, and consequently that the consignor had a right to stop the goods and prevent their delivery to the assignee. The judgment was brought before the House of Lords, and a *venire de novo* awarded. The Court of King's Bench adhered to their former decision, and in order that the question might be again taken before the House of Lords, the writ of error was brought, but was subsequently abandoned.

SEC. 282. **To whom Notice must be given.** — The case of Whitehead *v.* Anderson is important in this connection.[1] There it was decided that a notice of stoppage *in transitu*, to be effectual, must be given either to the person who has the immediate custody of the goods, or to the principal whose servant has the custody, at such a time and under such circumstances as that he may, by the exercise of reasonable diligence, communicate it to his servants in time to prevent the delivery to the consignee. In this case timber was sent from Quebec to be delivered at Port Fleetwood, in Lancashire. A notice of stoppage given to the shipowner, at Montrose, while the goods were on their voyage, whereupon he sent a letter to await the arrival of the captain at Fleetwood, directing him to deliver the cargo to the agents of the vendor, was held not to be a sufficient notice of stoppage *in transitu*. In delivering the judgment of the court, PARKE, B., said: "The law is clearly settled that the unpaid vendor has a right to retake the goods before they have arrived at the destination originally contemplated by the purchaser, unless in the meantime they have come into the actual or constructive possession of the vendee. If the vendee take the goods out of the possession of the carrier into his own before their arrival, with or without the consent of the carrier, there seems to be no doubt that the transit would be at an end, though, in case of the absence of the carrier's consent, it may be a wrong to him, for which he would have a right of action." This is a case of actual possession which certainly did not occur in the present instance.

SEC. 283. **Constructive Possession.** — A case of construc-

[1] 9 M. & W. 518.

tive possession is where the carrier enters expressly, or by implication, into a new agreement, distinct from the original contract for carriage, to hold the goods for the consignee as his agent, not for the purpose of expediting them to the place of original destination, pursuant to that contract, but in a new character, for the purpose of custody on his account, and subject to some new or further order to be given by him.

SEC. 284. **Possession by marking or taking Samples.** — It appears to us very doubtful whether an act of marking or taking samples or the like, without any removal from the possession of the carrier, done with the intention to take possession, would amount to a constructive possession, unless accompanied with such circumstances as to denote that the carrier was instructed to keep, and assented to keep in the nature of an agent for custody.[1]

SEC. 285. **Action against Carrier for refusing to give up Goods.** — When this right of stoppage *in transitu* exists, and has been exercised, the carrier, if, after tender of freight upon the part of the consignor, he should refuse to deliver up the goods to him, will be subject to an action; and if, in spite of the notice, the carrier should deliver the goods to the consignee, who, becoming bankrupt, transfers them to his assignees, they will still be subject to an action of trover at the suit of the consignor.[2] We may repeat shortly that the right, to be exercised effectually, must be exercised before actual or constructive delivery has taken place. We have seen under what circumstances the *transitus* will be held to have come constructively to an end; and it is to be remembered that it is in connection with cases in which the goods have not actually come into the possession of the consignee, that the greatest doubt and difficulty arises. Wherever a man may bear two

[1] See Foster *v.* Frampton, 6 B. & C. 107; 9 D. & R. 108; Ellis *v.* Hunt, 3 T. R. 464; Dixon *v.* Yates, 5 B. & Ad. 313; per LORD ABINGER in Gibson *v.* Carruthers, 8 M. & W. 341; Tanner *v.* Scovell, 14 M. & W. 28.

[2] Litt *v.* Cowley, 7 Taunt. 169; Stokes *v.* La Riviere, cited in Bothlingk *v.* Inglis, 3 East, 397; Syeds *v.* Hay, 4 T. R. 260.

different relations to the same transaction, and in connection with the same goods, questions as to which of the two characters he bore at a certain time are likely to be raised, and are sometimes not easy to answer. Thus the carrier, who was the agent of the bailor, may, by the operation of some act, which gives the consignee constructive possession, at once become his agent, and be bound to hold for him. So wharfingers or packers, who under one condition of things may still be the agents of the consignor, and it may be their duty to deliver to the consignee, may, under a different set of circumstances, be the agents of the consignee, and it may be their duty to receive from the consignor.[1]

SEC. 286. **Completed Delivery ends Right to stop in Transitu.** — If the transit be at an end, and the delivery is complete, the right to stop *in transitu* has ceased,[2] but as in very few cases the goods actually come to the corporeal touch of the vendee, — which would, of course, oust the right of stoppage *in transitu*,[3] — and, as in most cases, delivery takes place to a person other than the consignee, the question which has to be decided in all these cases is, whether the party into whose possession they actually come be an agent of the consignee in such a sense as to make the delivery to him as full, effectual, and final a delivery as if it had been made to the principal himself.

SEC. 287. **Possession of Goods by Consignee ends Right to stop in Transitu.** — In one case the opinion was expressed that, in order to defeat the right to stop *in transitu*, or the right to

[1] Mills *v.* Ball, 2 B. & P. 457; Holst *v.* Pownal, 1 Esp. 240; Northey *v.* Field, 2 Esp. 613; Hodgson *v.* Loy, 7 T. R. 440; Rowe *v.* Pickford, 8 Taunt. 83; Cooper *v.* Bill, 3 H. & C. 722; 34 L. J. Exch. 161; Wentworth *v.* Outhwaite, 10 M. & W. 436; Dodson *v.* Wentworth, 5 Scott, N. R. 821; 4 M. & Gr. 1080; Bolton *v.* Lancashire & Yorkshire Rail. Co., 35 L. J. C. P. 137; 1 L. R. C. P. 431; Valpy *v.* Gibson, 4 C. B. 837; Browne *v.* Hare, 3 H. & N. 484; affirmed on error, 4 H. & N. 822.

[2] A mere commencement of delivery, not so far completed as to allow the consignee to take actual possession, cannot be construed into a determination of the transit. Crawshay *v.* Eades, 1 B. & C. 181; 2 D. & R. 288. See also Houston on Stoppage in Transitu, p. 119 *et seq.*

[3] Ellis *v.* Hunt, 3 T. R. 464.

seize the goods on non-payment of the price, and the insolvency of the vendee, the completion was necessary,[1] and that the vendee could not anticipate the natural determination of the right, — as, for instance, by going to meet the goods at sea. In the case of Mills *v.* Ball,[2] however, this doctrine was repudiated, and the presiding judge said: "If, in the course of the conveyance of goods from the vendor to the vendee, the latter is allowed to exercise any act of ownership over them, he thereby reduces the goods into his possession, and puts an end to the vendor's right to stop them. So, though it has been said that the right of stoppage continues until the goods have arrived at their journey's end, yet if the vendee meet them upon the road, and take them into his own possession, the goods will then have arrived at their journey's end with reference to the right of stoppage."[3] What has been said concerning this important question of the right of stoppage *in transitu*, although far from covering the whole field of fact and from contemplating the very various circumstances which may arise in connection with the exercise of this right, will yet be sufficient to enable the reader to ascertain the general principles which govern the exercise of the right on the one hand, and which govern the cases and circumstances which may oust that right on the other. In this place it would have been incongruous to dwell more at length upon this subject, as it was only introduced with the view of discovering under what circumstances the liability of the carrier for the non-delivery of goods intrusted to him would be discharged. We have done that. It is almost unnecessary to add, that when the right of stoppage *in transitu* has been exercised, the act is

[1] Per LORD KENYON, in Holst *v.* Pownal, 1 Esp. 240.

[2] 2 B. & P. 461.

[3] See also Oppenheim *v.* Russell, 3 B. & P. 54; Foster *v.* Frampton, 6 B. & C. 107; and Whitehead *v.* Anderson, 9 M. & W. 518, where, as we have seen, it was laid down as indisputable that, if the vendee take the goods out of the possession of the carrier into his own before their arrival, the right to stop *in transitu* is at an end; though if he were to take them without the consent of the carrier, it might be a wrong to him for which he would have a right of action. See also London & North-Western Rail. Co. *v.* Bartlett, 7 H. & N. 400.

in the nature of a claim to lien, and not an absolute resumption of ownership.[1]

[1] See Houston on Stoppage in Transitu; Benjamin's Sale of Personal Property, London, 1868, p. 625; Howe *v.* Stewart, 40 Vt. 145; Schmertz *v.* Dwyer, 53 Penn. St. 335; Wenger *v.* Barnhart, 55 Penn. St. 300; Thompson *v.* Baltimore, &c. R. R. Co., 28 Md. 396; Blum *v.* Marks, 21 La. Ann. 268.

CHAPTER IX.

RESTRICTIONS UPON CARRIERS.

SEC. 288. **The Progress of Law.** — All systems of jurisprudence must be progressive. The most perfect code of laws for one century will be defective for the next. So long as the environment of men is capable of change, so long as men's thoughts and actions are liable to modification by the actual facts of a period, and so long as there is a gradual progress of humanity from one state of being to another, so long must any excellent system of rules or laws be liable to changes and modifications, if it would still retain its character for excellence. These are very evident truths; and even if they were not palpable, the history of the law of carriers would afford a not inappropriate illustration and proof of these propositions. The many changes which have been incident to the last century have rendered many modifications of the laws relating to carriers necessary. We have already had occasion to allude to this fact; but in the present chapter it becomes a more imperative duty to point out some of the changes in the law which the progress of mankind has rendered expedient.

SEC. 289. **Modifications in the Law of Carriers.** — The introduction of railways into this country necessarily modified the conditions of the transit of goods and persons, and the modification of these conditions rendered many changes in the law a matter of necessity. The fact that the speed of convey ance by means of steam was incomparably more rapid than that by means of any of the pre-existing conveyances, gave railway companies a monopoly of the carriage of all goods which had to be conveyed to great distances, at the same time that it facilitated the transmission of goods to places which, but for some such means of carriage, they could never have reached. The impetus that the establishment of this system gave to trade was incalculable. So, just at the time when the calling of a carrier was likely to become exceedingly lucrative, it was monopolized by railway companies. The condition of the existence of such a company made Acts of Parliament necessary for its incorporation. In order to be enabled to make a railway from one place to another, it was found necessary that a company, willing to construct it, must be endowed with certain powers of purchase and the like, and the acts which incorporated the company generally contained clauses regulative of the management of the particular railway. The law of carriers, then, as it applies to railway companies who carry for hire, must depend upon the private acts of incorporation, or upon the public acts of consolidation, which have from time to time been passed. In the case of most railways, the special acts of their incorporation, and in the case of some, the Railways Clauses Consolidation Act, empowers the company to become common carriers.[1] If there are such clauses in their special act, or if, under the other act, they have undertaken the trade of common carriers, they are presumed to be so. The public profession in this case has been equivalent to the public profession of a certain kind of business in the case of a common carrier.[2] It is, however, admissible for railway carriers to act either in the capacity of common carriers or of special carriers for hire; and, as we have seen, the exercise of the functions proper to the former class implies a warranty of the safety of the goods upon the part of the carrier, or, in other words, the insurance of the articles carried. And, as we have also seen in the preceding chapter, a common carrier may so limit his responsibility by means of special contract — may so denude himself of one of the aspects of his character as a common carrier — as to become a special carrier for hire. In the case of railway carriers, there is one restriction upon this power to limit their liability, and that is a statutory exception to the ordinary rule as stated above. They cannot, even by express contract, exempt themselves from liability for gross negligence.

SEC. 290. **Duties of Railway Carriers.** — Where, however, a railway company has assumed the character of a common carrier, it is, for the most part, in the same position, possessed of the same rights, bound to do the same duties as an ordinary common carrier.[3] As the life of an organism is determined entirely by its past experiences, so the life of any institution, which is a kind of organism too, is determined in the same

[1] With regard to canal companies, see 8 & 9 Vict. c. 42.

[2] Per PARKE, B., Palmer v. Grand Junction Railway, 4 M. & W. 768.

[3] 8 & 9 Vict. c. 20, § 89.

way. The company, no more than any other carrier, is not bound to transcend its professed habits. What it has been in the habit of doing determines the duty which it will be bound to perform. Thus railway companies are only bound to carry such goods as they have been in the habit of carrying. They are only bound to carry goods to such places as their public profession has connected their trade with.[1] They are justified in refusing to carry if they have not conveyances, or, after having professed to carry any particular kind of goods, they may discontinue the business.[2]

SEC. 291. **Restrictions.** — Although that is so, railway carriers are subject to certain restrictions, and it is of some importance that these should be pointed out.[3] Any duty that is imposed on one class of carriers, which is not at the same time imposed upon all classes, is a restriction upon the former. Every new duty is an extra penalty on carrying on the trade. What these are it is necessary to inquire.

SEC. 292. **Conveyance of Mails, Troops, &c.** — An act passed at the very beginning of the present reign[4] empowers the Postmaster-General to require all railways to convey the public mails for a reasonable rate of charge. By other acts, railways may be required to convey troops and military stores, at prices to be fixed by the Secretary of State.[5] Such pro-

[1] Oxlade v. North-Eastern Rail. Co., 9 W. R. 272; 3 L. T. Rep. N. S. 671; M'Manus v. Lancashire & Yorkshire Rail. Co., 28 L. J. 354 Exch.

[2] Johnson v. Midland Rail. Co., 4 Exch. 367; 18 L. J. 366 Exch.

[3] It is of importance to remember that any railway company incorporated since the 8th May, 1845, is subject to the 8 Vict. c. 20 (Railways Clauses Consolidation Act), the first section of which declares that the clauses and provisions therein contained are incorporated with the railway's special act, except in so far as they are expressly varied or excepted by such act. Wherever, therefore, it becomes necessary to know the exact extent of the rights and duties, the privileges and disabilities, of railway carriers, it will be necessary to consult not only the act just referred to, but to inspect the copy of the special act, which is kept for public inspection at the principal business office of the company (8 Vict. c. 20, § 162). The acts are to be construed strictly against the company.

[4] 1 & 2 Vict. c. 98. See also 7 & 8 Vict. c. 85, § 11.

[5] 5 & 6 Vict. c. 55, § 20. See also 7 & 8 Vict. c. 85, § 112, and 10 & 11 Vict. c. 85. By a case decided in Ireland, "public baggage, stores, and arms," &c., sent by railway, in charge of any of her Majesty's forces, specified in 7 & 8 Vict. c. 85, § 12, is

visions are obviously restrictions upon the common carrier's "option as to the method in which he will conduct his business,"[1] which option is ordinarily only restricted by the conditions which he holds out to the public.

SEC. 293. **Government Inspection and Control.** — The dangers associated with railway travelling have suggested the necessity of Government inspection and control. The principle which regulates ordinary business affairs, and which allows the vendor of anything, whether it be conveyance or not, to do anything he chooses, so long as the vendee does not object, only goes a very little way, and will not do for a guiding principle in all legislative questions. Wherever, owing to any peculiar circumstances in the condition or position of the vendee, he is placed at a disadvantage in regard to the freedom of his choice relatively to the vendor, the legislature steps in to endeavor to readjust these matters, and to mitigate the evils of this disadvantageous position of the person dealing as against the person dealt with. Now, the practical monopoly which is in the hands of railway carriers, owing to the circumstances of their construction, and the like, places the sender of goods, or the traveller, at a disadvantage; and to remedy this a general supervision of all railways is given to the Board of Trade, who may call for returns of the aggregate traffic in passengers, cattle, and goods, as well as of all accidents attended with personal injury on the railway, and also for tables of tolls, rates, and charges levied from time to time on such traffic.[2] The Board of Trade is, by the same act, empowered to appoint persons to inspect the railway, and all works and engines connected with it, at all reasonable times.[3] No by-laws are, since the passing of that act, valid

"their baggage," no matter what may be the disproportion between the amount of baggage and the number of the forces in charge of it, and must be carried by a railway company at the rates imposed by that section. Attorney-General *v.* Great Southern & Western Rail. Co., 14 Ir. C. L. R. 447 Exch.

[1] Per ERLE, C. J., Oxlade *v.* North-Eastern Rail. Co., 9 W. R. 272; 3 L. T. R. N. S. 671.

[2] 3 & 4 Vict. c. 97, § 1; 14 & 15 Vict. c. 64.

[3] 3 & 4 Vict. c. 97, § 5; 7 & 8 Vict. c. 85, § 15.

till two calendar months after they have been laid before the Board of Trade; and it is in the power of the Board to disallow any such by-laws, before or after they have come into operation.[1] The 11th section provides that, whenever it shall appear to the Board of Trade that any of the provisions of the Railway Acts have not been complied with on the part of the companies, or their officers, and that it would be for the advantage of the public that such provisions should be enforced, the Board of Trade shall certify the same to Her Majesty's Attorney-General for England or Ireland, or to the Lord Advocate for Scotland, as the case may require, and that thereupon the Attorney-General or the Lord Advocate[2] shall, by information, or by action, bill, plaint, suit at law or in equity, or other legal proceedings, as the case may require, proceed to recover such penalties and forfeitures, or otherwise to enforce the due performance of the said provisions, by such means as any person aggrieved by such non-compliance, or otherwise authorized to sue for such penalties, might employ under the provisions of the said acts.

SEC. 294. **Notice of Certificate.** — Notice of such certificate must be given by the Board to the company at least twenty-one days before.[3]

SEC. 295. **Punishment of Servants. — Other Provisions.** — There are provisions for the apprehension and punishment of servants of the company who may be found drunk on duty, or who commit any offence against any of the by-laws, rules, or regulations of the company.[4] It is not lawful to open any railway, or any portion of a railway, for public conveyance, until after one calendar month's notice in writing to the Board of Trade, of the company's intention so to open it, nor until after ten days' notice to the Board of the time when the railway will be complete and fit for inspection.[5] And it is in the power of the Board to postpone the opening of the line, after such inspection, if they think it right to do so.[6] The

[1] 3 & 4 Vict. c. 97, §§ 8 and 9.
[2] See 7 & 8 Vict. c. 85, § 17.
[3] 3 & 4 Vict. c. 97, § 11.
[4] 3 & 4 Vict. c. 97, § 13; 5 & 6 Vict. c. 35, § 17.
[5] 5 & 6 Vict. c. 55, § 4.
[6] *Ibid.* § 6.

same act provides for notices to the Board of all accidents,[1] for the keeping of gates at each end of a road which is crossed by a line of rail,[2] for the speed of trains when approaching such crossings,[3] and for the decision, by the Board, of all questions which affect the public safety, and which arise between companies with a common terminus or line of rails.[4] The weight of the carriages to be used is referred to in the 16th section of the act; and in another section it is enacted, that no railway shall be considered a passenger railway if two thirds or more of the gross annual revenue shall be derived from the carriage thereon of coals, iron-stone, or other metals or minerals.[5] All these provisions, and many others which we shall mention, restrict the freedom of railway companies, acting as common carriers; but such restrictions are necessary for the safety of the public, and are justified on the ground of public policy.[6]

SEC. 296. **Railway Companies as Common Carriers.** — Notwithstanding these restrictions, and others which we shall have occasion to mention when we come to speak of the conveyance of passengers, we shall see that a railway company is not compelled to become a common carrier, and that even when they have taken upon themselves the duties and liabilities attaching to that calling, they are, for the most part, in precisely the same position as an ordinary common carrier. Thus the Railways Clauses Consolidation Act enacts that "It shall be lawful for the company to use and employ locomotive engines, or other moving power, and carriages and wagons to be drawn or propelled thereby, and to carry upon the railway

[1] 5 & 6 Vict. c. 55, § 7.

[2] *Ibid.* § 9; Marfell *v.* South-Western Rail. Co., 29 L. J. 315 C. P.

[3] 8 & 9 Vict. c. 20, § 48.

[4] *Ibid.* § 11.

[5] 5 & 6 Vict. c. 55, § 12. This is of importance in connection with 9 & 10 Vict. c. 57, § 1, which enacts that the gauge of a railway for the conveyance of passengers is not to be less than four feet eight inches in England, and five feet three inches in Ireland.

[6] By 7 & 8 Vict. c. 85, § 13, all railway companies are bound to allow any person authorized by the Board of Trade to enter on the lands of the railway for the purpose of laying down and working a line of electric telegraph, of which the railway company is to have the full benefit, subject to the prior claims of her Majesty and of the proprietors of the telegraph. But see Telegraph Act.

all such passengers and goods as shall be offered to them for that purpose, and to make such reasonable charges in respect thereof as they may from time to time determine upon, not exceeding the tolls by the special act authorized to be taken by them."[1] And also that "Nothing in this or the special act contained shall extend to charge or make liable the company further or in any other case than where, according to the laws of the realm, stage-coach proprietors and common carriers would be liable, nor shall extend in any degree to deprive the company of any protection or privilege which common carriers or stage-coach proprietors may be entitled to, but, on the contrary, the company shall at all times be entitled to the benefit of every such protection and privilege."[2]

SEC. 297. **Dangerous Goods.** — Besides these provisions, the act contains another which exempts the company from the common-law duty to carry goods, if those goods are of a dangerous nature, unless the nature is marked on the outside of the package, and giving them a power to open parcels suspected of containing dangerous goods, with a view of ascertaining whether they do contain such goods or not.[3] It is a question whether the subject of by-laws should be treated in this chapter, under the head of restrictions (for the power which is given to a railway company to make by-laws is subject to the provisions and restrictions of the Railways Clauses Act and of the special act),[4] or not. We prefer, however, to regard them in the former light, and set forth in this place the various clauses bearing upon this subject.

SEC. 297 *a*. **By-laws: their Purposes.** — The 108th section of the Railways Clauses Act enacts that "It shall be lawful for the company, from time to time, subject to the provisions and restrictions in this and the special act contained, to make regulations for the following purposes (that is to say):

"For regulating the mode by which, and the speed at which, carriages using the railway are to be moved or propelled:

[1] 8 & 9 Vict. c. 20, § 86.

[2] 8 & 9 Vict. c. 20, § 89.

[3] 8 & 9 Vict. c. 20, § 105. See *ante*, p. 279 *et seq.* See also 29 & 30 Vict. c. 69.

[4] 8 & 9 Vict. c. 20, § 108.

"For regulating the times of arrival and departure of any such carriages:

"For regulating the loading or unloading of such carriages, and the weights which they are respectively to carry:

"For regulating the receipt and delivery of goods, and other things which are to be conveyed upon such carriages:

"For preventing the smoking of tobacco, and the commission of any other nuisance, in or upon such carriages, or in any of the stations or premises occupied by the company:[1]

"And, generally, for regulating the travelling upon, and using and working upon the railway:

"But no such regulation shall authorize the closing of the railway, or prevent the passage of engines or carriages on the railway at reasonable times, except at any time when, in consequence of any of the works being out of repair, or from any other sufficient cause it shall be necessary to close the railway or any part thereof."[2]

SEC. 298. **Further Provision with regard to By-laws.**—Other acts have, however, dealt with the subject of by-laws: thus, by 8 & 9 Vict. c. 16, the company is empowered from time to time to make by-laws for the purpose of regulating the conduct of the officers and servants of the company, in all respects whatsoever, provided such by-laws are not repugnant to the laws of that part of the United Kingdom where they are to have effect, or to the provisions of that or the special act, and such by-laws are to be reduced to writing, to which the company's common seal is to be affixed, and a copy of these by-laws is to be given to every officer and servant of the company affected thereby.[3] There are also provisions which point out under what circumstances penalties are exigible from the company's servants.[4] There are one or two provisions in the latter of the two acts above referred to, which it will be neces-

[1] But see recent regulations, *post*.

[2] See PARKE, B., 18 L. J. 369 Exch.

[3] 8 & 9 Vict. c. 16, § 124.

[4] *Ibid.* §§ 125, 126, 127, 145, 160.

sary to quote in this place, as the non-compliance with the statutory provisions will result in restrictions of the railway carrier's freedom as a common carrier.

Section 109 (of 8 & 9 Vict. c. 20) enacts that, "For better enforcing the observance of all or any of such regulations, it shall be lawful for the company, subject to the provisions of an act passed in the fourth year of the reign of her present Majesty, intituled 'An Act for Regulating Railways,'[1] to make by-laws, and from time to time to repeal or alter such by-laws and make others, provided that such by-laws be not repugnant to the laws of that part of the United Kingdom where the same are to have effect, or to the provisions of this or the special act, and such by-laws shall be reduced to writing, and shall have affixed thereto the common seal of the company; and any person offending against any such by-law shall forfeit for such offence any sum not exceeding five pounds, to be imposed by the company in such by-laws as a penalty for any such offence; and if the infraction or non-observance of any such by-law, or other such regulation as aforesaid, be attended with danger or annoyance to the public, or hindrance to the company, in the lawful use of the railway, it shall be lawful for the company summarily to interfere to obviate or remove such danger, annoyance, or hindrance, and that without prejudice to any penalty incurred by the infraction of any such by-law."

SEC. 299. **Publication of By-laws.** — Section 110. "The substance of such last-mentioned by-laws, where confirmed or allowed according to the provisions of any act in force regulating the allowance or confirmation of the same, shall be painted on boards, and hung up and affixed, and continued on the front or other conspicuous part of every wharf or station belonging to the company, according to the nature or subject-matter of such by-laws respectively, and so as to give public notice thereof to the parties interested therein or affected thereby, and such boards shall from time to time be renewed as often as the by-laws are obliterated or destroyed, and no

[1] 3 & 4 Vict. c. 97. See also with regard to canal companies, 8 & 9 Vict. c. 42, § 2.

penalty enforced by any such by-law shall be recoverable unless the same shall have been published and kept published in manner aforesaid."

SEC. 300. **Proof of Publication.** — Section 111. "Such by-laws, when so confirmed, published, and affixed, shall be binding upon, and be observed by, all parties, and shall be sufficient to justify all persons acting under the same; and for proof of the publication of any such by-laws, it shall be sufficient to prove that a printed copy, or painted board containing a copy of such by-laws, was affixed and continued in manner by the act directed, and in case of its being afterwards displaced or damaged, then that such paper or board was replaced as soon as conveniently might be."

These clauses contain the statement of duties which devolve, under the act, upon carriers who carry on their trade by means of railways; and as these duties do not devolve upon other common carriers, these must be regarded as, in some sort, special restrictions. When, however, these duties have been performed, — when the by-laws can be pronounced neither unreasonable nor repugnant to the common law, nor to any statutory provision, — when they have been approved of by the Board of Trade, or other authority nominated by the special act, — when they have been published and affixed in a place where they can be seen and read by the public, — they are binding upon all persons.

SEC. 301. **Nature of these Provisions.** — Some cases in which this subject has come under the consideration of the courts are worthy of being considered. With reference to the above requisites to which by-laws must conform, it may be said that the reasonableness of the law must necessarily be an imperative requisite;[1] and that the by-law should in no way be opposed either to the common or statute law is a condition which is evidently, in its very nature, of the most binding

[1] Waite *v.* Garston Local Board of Health, 37 L. J. M. C. 19 Q. B.; Angell & Ames, C. 10; 2 Kent, Com. 296; Davis *v.* Meeting-House in Lowell, 8 Met. 321; Sayre *v.* Louisville Union Benevolent Association, 1 Duvall, 143; Day *v.* Owen, 5 Mich. 520; and see Redfield's Law of Railways, 3d ed., vol. i. p. 88 *et seq.*

character. Any such opposition will, of course, render the by-law inoperative. The question whether it has been confirmed or not has no bearing upon this result.

SEC. 302. **Construction of Power to make By-laws.** — The power to make by-laws is to be strictly construed; and if a particular power is given to a company to make by-laws for the management of one thing, they cannot make by-laws for the carrying on of projects foreign to that thing.[1] Thus a railway company was empowered to make by-laws for the good government of the affairs of the company, and for the management of the undertaking, and of the officers and servants of the company in all respects whatever, and to impose and inflict reasonable fines and forfeitures upon persons offending against the same not exceeding 5*l.* for any one offence, to be levied and recovered as any penalty might by the act be levied and recovered, such by-laws to be binding upon and to be observed by all parties, provided that they were not repugnant to the laws of England or the directions of the act. It was also enacted that it should be lawful for the company to make orders and regulations for regulating the travelling upon, and the use of the railway, and for or relating to travellers upon the line, such orders and regulations to be binding upon travellers and passengers passing on the railway upon pain of forfeiture, and the payment of a sum not exceeding 5*l.* Penalties and forfeitures imposed by the act, of which there were several, or by any by-law, might be recovered in a summary way by the adjudication of justices,—half the penalty to go to the informer, and half to the company. And it should be lawful for any officer or agent of the company to seize any person whose name and residence should be unknown to such officer or agent, who should commit any offence against that act, and to convey him before a justice, without any warrant or other authority than that act. The company made a by-law, whereby a passenger not producing

[1] Child *v.* Hudson Bay Company, 2 P. Wms. 207; and see Meliorucchi *v.* Royal Exchange Assurance Company, 1 Eq. Abr. 8, pl. 8; Rex *v.* Spencer, 3 Burr. 1827; Rex *v.* Ginever, 6 T. R. 732; Rex *v.* Tappenden, 3 East, 186.

or delivering up his ticket was to be required to pay the fare from the place from which the train originally started; and it was held that this was not a by-law imposing a penalty or forfeiture, and that the arrest of a passenger not producing his ticket, and refusing to pay his fare from the place where the train originally started, was illegal.[1] It would, however, it seems, have been competent for the company, under such powers, to make a by-law subjecting any passenger to a fine of 40*s*. if he entered the train without having previously paid his fare, or subjecting him to a similar fine for refusing to show his ticket when required.[2]

SEC. 303. **What By-laws can be made.** — Again, where one section of an act which incorporated a railway company enacted, "That without extra charge it shall be lawful for every passenger travelling upon the railway to take with him articles of clothing not exceeding forty pounds in weight and four cubic feet in dimensions; and that the company shall in no case be responsible for anything whatsoever carried upon the railway with any passenger, other than such passenger's articles of clothing not exceeding the weight and dimensions aforesaid; provided that nothing herein contained shall extend to make liable the company further than where, according to law, stage-coach proprietors and common carriers would be liable." Another section empowered the company to make by-laws for the good government of the affairs of the company, and for the management of the undertaking. The company made a by-law, that every first-class passenger should be allowed to carry 112 pounds of luggage free of charge, but that the company would not be responsible for its care unless booked and the carriage paid for. Under these circumstances it was held that the company had no power to make the by-law, since it was in contravention of the 1st section.[3] The following case will still further illustrate the way

[1] Chilton *v.* London & Croydon Rail. Co., 5 Rail. Cas. 4; 16 M. & W. 212; 11 Jur. 149. But see American law on this subject: Redfield on the Law of Railways, vol. i. p. 89, 3d ed.

[2] Rex *v.* Frere, 24 L. J. 68 M. C. See also Barker *v.* Midland Rail. Co., 25 L. J. 184 C. P.; Beadle *v.* Eastern Counties Rail. Co., 26 L. J. 250 C. P.

[3] Williams *v.* Great Western Rail. Co., 10 Exch. 15; cf. Great Western Rail. Co. *v.* Goodman, 12 C. B. 13.

in which the statutory powers given to company-carriers to make by-laws must be exercised in order to render these by-laws, when made, of any validity and binding upon the public.

SEC. 304. **Way in which Statutory Powers must be exercised.** — By a local act (6 Geo. IV. c. 71) the company of proprietors of a public navigation were empowered to make by-laws for the good government of the company, and for the good and orderly using the navigation, and also for the well-governing of the bargemen, watermen, and boatmen, who should carry any goods, wares, or merchandise upon any part of the said navigation, and to impose and inflict such reasonable fines and forfeitures upon all persons offending against the same, as to the major part of the company should seem meet, not exceeding *5l.* The company made a by-law that the canal should be closed on every Sunday throughout the year, and that no business should be transacted thereon during such time (works of necessity only excepted); nor should any person, during such time, navigate any boat, &c., nor should any boat, &c., pass along any part of the said navigation on any Sunday, except for a reasonable distance, for the purpose of mooring the same, and except on some extraordinary necessity, or for the purpose of going to or returning from any place of divine worship, under a penalty of *5l.* It was held that the act did not authorize the company to make any such by-law, and that it was illegal and void.[1]

SEC. 305. **Sufficient Publication of Notice or By-law.** — Doubt and difficulty always seem to arise with regard to what shall be sufficient publication of a notice or a by-law which is to be binding upon the public. We have already seen how much doubt upon this subject influenced the law with regard to the limitation of the carrier's responsibility, and we shall find that with regard to the publication of by-laws, which are, to some extent, of a nature similar to these notices, like diffi-

[1] The Calder & Hebble Navigation Co. *v.* Pilling, 14 M. & W. 76. See also The Masters, &c. of Gunmakers *v.* Tell, Willis, 389; Bosworth *v.* Herne, Aldey *v.* Reeves, 2 M. & Selw. 53; Dodwell *v.* The University of Oxford, 2 Ventr. 3334.

culties have been felt.[1] It will be remembered that the 8 & 9 Vict. c. 20, § 110, provided that the substance of such by-laws as were made in pursuance of that statute should be painted on boards, &c., and affixed on the front of every wharf or station belonging to the company making them, according to the nature and subject-matter of such by-laws, and that with a view of giving public notice to the parties interested therein or affected thereby. It further provided that no penalty which might be imposed by any such by-law should be recoverable unless the same should have been published, &c., as aforesaid. The following section provided that evidence that a copy of such by-laws was affixed as the act directed, was sufficient proof of their publication. In the case of Motteram *v.* The Eastern Counties Railway Company,[2] the exact meaning of the act, as to the affixing of such notice, was discussed, and the question was decided. This was a case, upon an information before justices, charging a passenger with an infraction of a by-law (prohibiting passengers from quitting a carriage while the train was in motion), and it was proved that a copy of the by-laws was affixed in the manner directed by the act, at the two stations, respectively, at which the passenger entered and quitted the carriage. This was held to be sufficient proof of publication, and that it was not necessary to prove further that copies were affixed at every other station on the line.

This case further decided that the by-laws of a railway company, made pursuant to the Railways Clauses Consolidation Act, sections 108 and 109, are documents of a public nature, and provable as such.

Sufficient has, however, been said to enable the reader to understand the subject of by-laws as modifying the relation of a certain class of carriers to the public, and to appreciate the force of the conditions, which must be complied with in the framing of an operative by-law. These are, as we have said above: 1st. That it should be reasonable, and in no way repugnant, to the common or statute law;[3] 2d. That it should

[1] Great Western Rail. Co. *v.* Goodman, 12 C. B. 13; 21 L. J. 197 C. P.

[2] 29 L. J. 57 M. C.

[3] The old rule of law which says

be confirmed by the Board of Trade, or other authority nominated by the special act; 3d. That it should be duly published and affixed. When these conditions have been complied with, the by-law becomes a kind of agent-law for the principal (the special act), and has such authority as it derives from that act or from the Railways Clauses Act, and it is only valid, as we have seen, when acting within the scope of that authority.

SEC. 306. **Restriction of Preferences.** — We come now to a much larger subject than that which has fallen under consideration in the earlier part of this chapter, and it is to this portion of the subject that this chapter principally owes its name. We shall find that the 17 & 18 Vict. c. 31, was enacted with a view to restraining a system of preferences upon the part of railway carriers, which had every chance of being established. Such a system might doubtless have been for the pecuniary advantages of the carriers, but it would have been detrimental to the interests of the community at large.

SEC. 307. **Railway Monopoly, Effect of.** — We have pointed out that the existence of railways produced a practical monopoly in favor of their proprietors. But the effects of a monopoly are not confined to the branch of trade to which it originally appertains. Indeed, in any country in which the social and mercantile relations are complicated, a possibility of injustice in one department of the social or commercial organism tends to become a possibility in other departments. As the monopoly which was placed in the hands of railway companies had the effect of abolishing the ordinary trade of private carriers, and as all the carriage of goods which was to be effected between X and Y fell into the hands of a single carrying company, it was in their power to make the price of carriage of unequal amount to different individuals. The inevitable effect of such a proceeding would be to place in the

that a by-law bad in part is bad in the whole, is qualified to this extent, — that if the good part be independent of and unconnected with the bad, the good part would be valid and binding. See Blackpool Board of Health *v.* Bennett, 4 H. & N. 127.

hands of railway companies a power of regulating trade. For if A can have his goods transmitted to a certain place for half the amount that his rival dealer B can have his goods transmitted to the same place, it is evident that the latter trader cannot compete in the same market with the former. The monopoly also encouraged railway companies to give preferences to certain individuals as to the time of forwarding their goods, and any such preference thrown into the scales of trade in favor of one individual had the effect of crippling the other in the race of competition, which it has been the object of recent legislation to facilitate, and not to retard. These practices had been indulged in,[1] and with a view to putting an end to them, the 17 & 18 Vict. c. 31, was passed.

SEC. 308. **17 & 18 Vict. c. 31.** — That act is entitled "An Act for the Better Regulation of the Traffic on Railways and Canals," and it enacts, in section 2, that "every railway company, canal company, and railway and canal company, shall, according to their respective powers, afford all reasonable facilities for the receiving and forwarding and delivering

[1] See Parker *v.* Great Western Rail. Co., 7 M. & G. 253. The Railways Consolidation Act, 8 & 9 Vict. c. 20, § 90, had forbidden such practices. That act empowered all railway companies formed since the 8th May, 1845, to take tolls. After reciting that "Whereas it is expedient that the company should be enabled to vary the tolls upon the railway, so as to accommodate them to the purposes of the traffic, but that such power of varying should not be used for the purpose of prejudicing or favoring particular parties, or for the purpose of collusively and unfairly creating a monopoly, either in the hands of the company or of particular parties," it goes on to enact that "It shall be lawful for the company, subject to the provisions and limitations herein and in the special act contained, from time to time to alter or vary the tolls by the special act authorized to be taken, either upon the whole or on any portions of the railway, as they shall think fit, provided that all such tolls shall be charged equally to all persons, and after the same rate, whether per ton, per mile, or otherwise, in respect of all passengers and of all goods and carriages of the same description, and conveyed or propelled by a like carriage or engine passing only over the same portion of the same line of railway under the same circumstances; and no reduction or advance in any such tolls shall be made, either directly or indirectly, in favor of or against any particular company or person travelling upon or using the railway." See Rex *v.* Grand Junction Canal Co., 3 Rail. Cas. 14. See also 8 & 9 Vict. c. 28, which gives a similar power to canal companies and to the commissioners of navigable rivers.

of traffic upon and from the several railways and canals belonging to or worked by such companies, and for the return of carriages, trucks, boats, and other vehicles, and no such company shall make or give any undue or unreasonable preference or advantage to or in favor of any particular person or company, or any particular description of traffic in any respect whatsoever, nor shall any such company subject any particular person or company to any undue or unreasonable prejudice or disadvantage in any respect whatsoever, and every railway company and canal company, and railway and canal company, having or working railways and canals, which form part of a continuous line of railway or canal, or railway and canal communication, or which have the terminus, station, or wharf of the one near the terminus, station, or wharf of the other, shall afford all due and reasonable facilities for receiving and forwarding all the traffic arriving by one of such railways or canals by the other without any unreasonable delay, and without any preference or advantage, or prejudice or disadvantage, as aforesaid, and so that no obstruction may be offered to the public desirous of using such railways or canals, or railways and canals, as a continuous line of communication, and so that all reasonable accommodation may, by means of the railways and canals of the several companies, be at all times afforded to the public in that behalf."

SEC. 309. **Near Stations, "Traffic," "Railway," "Canal," "Railway Company," &c.** — The 1st section of the same act enacts that "a station, terminus, or wharf shall be deemed to be near another station, terminus, or wharf, when the distance between such stations, termini, or wharves shall not exceed one mile, such stations not being situate within five miles from St. Paul's Church in London. 'Traffic' includes, not only passengers and their luggage, and goods, animals, and other things conveyed by any railway company, or railway and canal company, but also carriages, wagons, trucks, boats, and vehicles of every description adapted for running or passing on the railway or canal of any such company. 'Railway' includes every station of or belonging to such railway, used for the purposes of public traffic. 'Canal' includes any navigation[1] whereon tolls are levied by authority of Parliament, and also the wharves and landing places of and belonging to the canal or navigation, and used for the purposes of public traffic. The expression 'railway company,' 'canal company,' or 'railway and canal company,' includes any person being the owner or lessee of, or any contractor working any railway or canal or navigation constructed or carried on under the powers of any Act of Parliament."

SEC. 310. **Application to the Court of Common Pleas. — Direction of Prosecution. — Issue of Writ. — Penalty. — Costs.** — The 3d section provides that "it shall be lawful for any company or person complaining against any such companies or company of anything done, or of any omission made in violation or contravention of the act, to apply in a summary way by motion or summons to the Court of Common Pleas,[2] or to a judge thereof; and upon the certificate to the Attorney-General alleging any such violation or contravention of the act by any such companies or company, it shall be lawful for the Attorney-General to apply to the said court or judge to hear and determine the matter of such complaint, and for that purpose, if the court or judge shall think fit, to direct and prosecute, in such mode and by such engineers, barristers, or other persons as they shall think proper, who, when directed, shall be empowered to receive evidence on oath, and to administer an oath, relating to the matter of such inquiries as may be deemed necessary, to enable the court or judge to form a just judgment on the matter of such complaint; and if it be made to appear to the court or judge on such hearing, or on the report of any such persons, that anything has been done, or omission made, in violation or contravention of the act, by such companies or company, it shall be lawful for the court or a judge to issue a writ of injunction restraining the company from further continuing such violation or contravention of the act, and enjoining obedience to the same; and, in case of disobedience, it shall be lawful for the court or judge to order

[1] See Bennett *v.* Manchester, Sheffield, & Lincolnshire Rail. Co., 6 C. B. N. S. 715.

[2] To the Court of Session in Scotland, and to any of the superior courts in Dublin.

that a writ or writs of attachment shall issue against any one or more of the directors of any company, or against any owner, lessee, contractor, or other person failing to obey the writ, and the court or judge may also, if the court or judge thinks proper, make an order directing the payment, by any one or more of such companies, of such sum of money as the court or judge may determine, not exceeding for each company 200*l.* for every day, after a day to be named in the order, that such companies or company shall fail to obey the injunction. Such moneys shall be payable as the court or judge may direct, either to the party complaining or into court, to abide the ultimate decision of the court, or to her Majesty; and payment may, without prejudice to any other mode of recovering the same, be enforced by attachment, or order, in the nature of a writ of execution, and in any such proceeding the court or judge may order and determine that all or any of the costs thereof or therein incurred, shall and may be paid by or to the one party or the other, as the court or judge thinks fit."

SEC. 311. **Power to rescind or vary Order.** — We come now to the 5th section, which provides that, "upon the application of any party aggrieved by the order made upon motion or summons, it shall be lawful for the court or judge by whom the order was made, to direct, if the court or judge thinks fit to do so, such motion or application, on summons, to be reheard before the court or judge, and, upon such rehearing, to rescind or vary such order." By the 6th section it is enacted that "no proceeding shall be taken for any violation or contravention of the above enactment, except in the manner provided; but nothing therein contained shall take away or diminish any rights, remedies, or privileges of any person or company, against any railway or canal, or railway and canal company, under the existing laws."

SEC. 312. **The Regulations issued by the Court of Common Pleas.** — In pursuance of the 4th section of the act, the Court of Common Pleas promulgated forms and directions for proceeding under the act, which are to the following effect: —

SEC. 313. **Application for Rule. — By Summons.** — 1. Every application made to the court shall be for a rule calling upon the company or companies complained of to show cause why a writ of injunction should not issue against such companies or company, enjoining them to do, or to desist from doing, the thing required to be done, or the thing the doing of which is complained of by the company or person making such application; and every application to a judge at chambers shall be by summons, calling upon the company or companies complained of to show cause in like manner, which summons shall be granted only upon affidavit, and upon a statement made to the judge in like manner as upon an application to the court for a rule to show cause.[1]

SEC. 314. **Order.** — 2. If, on the hearing of the rule or summons, the court or judge shall think fit to direct and prosecute into the matter thereof, under section 3, an order for that purpose is given, the rule or summons being enlarged in the meanwhile.[2]

SEC. 315. **Copies of Affidavits to be furnished.** — 3. Office copies of all affidavits filed by either party, on the hearing of such rule or summons, shall, at the expense of such party, be furnished to the person appointed to make such inquiries, within three days after the making of such order as aforesaid.[3]

SEC. 316. **Fresh Affidavits.** — 4. The parties shall be entitled to be again heard by the judge upon the said report, but no fresh affidavits shall be allowed on such hearing, unless by leave of the court or a judge.[4]

SEC. 317. **Common-law Rights and Remedies of Persons dealing with Carriers.** — It is to be understood that nothing contained in the act above referred to takes away or diminishes the common-law rights or remedies of any person against the company;[5] and it is of the utmost importance clearly to appreciate the effect of the provisions of the above statute, as many of the questions arising in relation to carriers

[1] Reg. Gen. C. P. H. T. 18 Vict. 1855, 15 C. B. 473, R. 1.

[2] R. 2.

[3] R. 3.

[4] R. 4. The form of the writ of injunction is given in the fifth rule, and that of the order directing the payment of money by the company or companies complained of in the sixth.

[5] 17 & 18 Vict. c. 31, § 6.

and their duties must be decided with reference to its provisions.

SEC. 318. **Difficulty of Decisions under this Statute.** — The powers which were by this act placed in the hands of the judges of the Court of Common Pleas necessarily implied the performance of a difficult duty. The determination of what description of traffic afforded unreasonable advantages to particular persons or companies, the determination of what constituted reasonable facilities for receiving and forwarding goods, and of what might fairly be called unreasonable delay, was a matter of considerable difficulty. This was the more felt, because the statute afforded no guidance as to the decision of any one of these matters, its language being explicitly vague and comprehensive. Many complaints have been made against this statute by common-law judges and lawyers, and the reason of these censures is very obvious. Common-law lawyers have been taught to depend exclusively upon the foredone work of the legislator and the judge. Their duty has been, if we may compare great things to small, like that of a tailor, who knows the fashion, and measures his customer; he was not called upon to consider the appropriate use of a certain garment to a certain shape. It was because of the narrowness of the principle involved in this practice that the necessity of an equity jurisprudence came to be felt. And from the very first inauguration of the system to the present time common-law lawyers have felt themselves in an attitude of defence against the encroachments of the principles of equity.[1] This attitude was natural. Nature soon makes whatever we do easy, and the things we do not do difficult. And it was this difficulty which led to the continued separation of the two systems, and which also led to the censure of the large powers which were given to the judges of the Court of Common Pleas by the act under consideration. Instead of being asked to shape a garment, such as he had been in the habit of making, to his customer, the tailor was asked to find out new fashions. His whole past had unfitted him to do so, and consequently we

[1] Story's Equity Jurisprudence, vol. ii. § 874, 10th ed.

find learned judges using language to the following effect, that the questions involved in such an application, under 17 & 18 Vict. c. 31, "assume a very difficult and complicated character, and are such as we feel but little qualified to decide. Nevertheless, as the legislature has thought fit to impose on the judges of this court the duty of dealing with such questions, we must do so to the best of our abilities, whenever it becomes necessary."[1]

SEC. 319. **Question considered.** — For our part, we cannot see that the difficulty of the performance of the duties imposed upon the judges of the Court of Common Pleas in reference to this matter is at all greater than that which devolves upon the judges of the Court of Equity, when they are applied to for a writ of injunction to stay proceedings at law, to restrain vexatious suits, to restrain the alienation of property, to restrain waste, to restrain trespasses, or to prevent other irreparable mischiefs. The ascertainment of what are undue and unreasonable preferences upon the part of a railway company does not seem to us to be more difficult than the ascertainment of what will constitute "extravagant humorous waste" upon the part of a tenant for life without impeachment for waste, which a court of equity has a right to restrain.[2] And the complaint of the absence from the act of some canon of construction seems unreasonable, when we remember the admirable system of jurisprudence which has been constructed by our equity judges. The common lawyer has been taught to look upon a reference to general principles of law as a last resort, instead of allowing such principles to have a concurrent jurisdiction, so to speak, with the common law. Had such been the case, the powers placed in the hands of common-law judges by this act would not, it seems to us, have been complained of. We will now, however, proceed to consider the various cases which have been decided under this statute, and that will enable us to quote some of the most important dicta with reference to these statutory restrictions upon carriers.

[1] Per CRESSWELL, J., in Rausome, *In re*, *v.* Eastern Counties Rail. Co., 1 C. B. N. S. 452; 3 Jur. N. S. 217; 26 L. J. C. P. 91.

[2] Lord Barnard's Case, Prec. Ch. 454; 2 Vern. 738; Aston *v.* Aston, 1 Ves. 265; Abraham *v.* Budd, 2 Freem. Chy. 53.

SEC. 320. **Extent and Application of Statute.**—One or two cases which bear upon the extent and application of the statute may be quoted before we consider under what circumstances injunctions have been granted, and attempt to deduce some conclusion as to what the court regards as due and reasonable preferences, and what it regards as improper and unreasonable. In the case of the Attorney-General *v.* The Great Northern Railway,[1] which was an information by the Attorney-General against the company, which alleged that the company dealt largely in coals, and prayed that they might be restrained from so employing their funds, on the ground that under the acts of their incorporation they were not justified in doing so, it was alleged for the company that 7 & 8 Vict. c. 85, §§ 16 and 17, prescribes a particular remedy in such a case, and that the Attorney-General cannot take proceedings otherwise than in accordance with the terms of that provision. And it was further alleged that, by virtue of 17 & 18 Vict. c. 31, the proper remedy in the case was by application to the Court of Common Pleas. The Vice-Chancellor, in disposing of these objections, said, with regard to the first: "This objection, in truth, involves the contention that this court has no jurisdiction to entertain the suit by the Attorney-General, unless it is instituted under the circumstances mentioned in those sections.[2] The effect of these statutes is not to take away either the right of the Attorney-General to file such an information at his discretion, although there is no certificate of the Board of Trade, or the jurisdiction of the court, to entertain such a suit. The only effect is, that if the Board of Trade has certified the Attorney-General, he is *bound* to act, and compel the railway company to abstain from doing that which is in violation of the law; in that particular case he can exercise no discretion, he must sue; and not only is the discretion of the Attorney-General taken away in that case, but if the judge finds that the acts are not authorized by the law, *his* discretion also is taken away, and he is bound to grant the injunction." In reference to the latter allegation, his Honor said: "On

[1] 1 Drew. & S. 154.

[2] §§ 16 and 17 of 7 & 8 Vict. c. 85.

reading that Act of Parliament[1] it appears to me that it applies to cases of a very different nature from the present. That act applies to cases in which railway companies, acting as common carriers, have favored certain individuals, and given greater advantages or facilities to some persons than to others. The illegal acts sought to be restrained by the present suit are of a different nature." In the year previous to that case, a case was decided in the Court of Common Pleas, in which it was held that the 17 & 18 Vict. c. 31 (The Railway and Canal Traffic Act, 1854), was designed to afford a remedy against an undue preference or undue prejudice to a particular individual or class in respect of the traffic on the railway or canal, and was not intended to apply to the case of a breach or neglect by the company of a public duty, which was already susceptible of redress by mandamus or by indictment. There the Manchester, Sheffield, and Lincolnshire Railway Company were the proprietors of Grimsby Old Dock, and also of another dock, called Grimsby New Dock, communicating with their railway. By Act of Parliament, the company was authorized and required to maintain the Old Dock and the approach thereto, of a given depth. In conformity with the above principle, it was held that the failure to perform this duty, so that the dock and its approach became filled up, and the depth of the water therein became insufficient for vessels to get to the wharf adjoining, was not a subject of redress under this act, although it was suggested that the company were desirous to discourage the traffic to the old dock, and to convert it to the new one.[2]

SEC. 321. **Jurisdiction of the Court of Chancery not abridged by this Statute.** — One other point of importance is to be noted in connection with this part of our subject, and that is, that although the Railway and Canal Traffic Act, 1854, gives to the Court of Common Pleas the power to grant the preventive remedy — an injunction — it does not, by giving a concurrent jurisdiction to that court, in any way abridge the jurisdiction

[1] 17 & 18 Vict. c. 31.

[2] Bennett *v.* Manchester, Sheffield, & Lincolnshire Rail. Co., 6 C. B. N. S. 707.

of the Court of Chancery. That, evidently, was not the intention of the legislature.[1]

SEC. 322. **Railway Company not prohibited under all Circumstances from carrying Similar Goods of Different Owners at Different Rates.** — One of the earliest cases which was heard after the act came into force, decided that a railway company was not, under all circumstances, prohibited from carrying similar goods, for one person or one company, at a less rate than they carried them for another person or company. It never had been doubted that different descriptions of goods could only be carried at different rates; and, in the case referred to, the decision was given upon a principle of common sense, founded upon the acknowledged fact, that if it cost a railway company less to carry the goods of one customer than it did to carry the goods of another, they were entitled to make a reduction in favor of the former.[2] But as the case is one of considerable importance, and involves other points than the one stated above, it may be well to state it more fully.

SEC. 323. **Proceedings and Doctrine adopted in Oxlade v. North-Eastern Railway Co.** — A rule had been obtained, on behalf of William Oxlade, calling upon the company to show cause "why a writ of injunction should not issue against them, enjoining them, first, to carry upon their said railway, for the said William Oxlade, such coal and coke as may be offered to them by the said William Oxlade for that purpose; secondly, to charge for the carriage thereof respectively tolls not higher than the tolls charged by the company for carrying coal and coke respectively to persons for whom the same coal or coke respectively are also carried on the Great Northern Railway, and tolls not higher than the tolls charged by the

[1] Baxendale *v.* West Midland Rail. Co., 3 Giff. 650; affirmed on appeal, 7 L. T. N. S. 297.

[2] Oxlade *v.* North-Eastern Rail. Co., 1 C. B. N. S. 454; 3 Jur. N. S. 637; 26 L. J. C. P. 129. We shall have occasion to refer to the recent case of West *v.* London & North-Western Rail. Co., L. Rep. 6 C. P. 622, in which two of the judges of the Court of Common Pleas held that, as the act relates to facilities for the receiving, forwarding, and delivering of traffic only, it had no jurisdiction to interfere with matters relating to the facilities for storing coal after it had been delivered to the consignee.

said company to persons with whom the said company have private agreements for the carriage of coal or coke; thirdly, to provide for the said William Oxlade depots for depositing and receiving his coal and coke on the stations of the said railway, similar to those provided at such stations for persons with whom they have private agreements for the carriage of coals along the said railway, and similar to those provided at such stations for persons who consign their coal and coke to the said company; fourthly, to afford to the said William Oxlade the same facilities for the receiving and forwarding and delivering of his coals and coke upon and from the said railway, as the said company afford to persons who consign their coal or coke, and for forwarding the same upon the said railway; and why the said North-Eastern Railway Company should not pay to the said William Oxlade, or to his attorney, his costs of, and occasioned by, this application."[1] Affidavits were filed in support of the rule and against it, and upon cause being shown, it was referred to the Masters to inquire and report upon the following questions: First, whether any and what accommodation and facilities are provided or afforded at any and what stations on the line of the said company's railway for the unloading of coal and coke, and for what persons, and under what circumstances. Secondly, whether the said company carry coal and coke for persons other than the said William Oxlade, on any and what terms different from the terms on which the said company have carried or have offered to carry coals and coke for the said William Oxlade. Thirdly, whether there is any and what difference between the circumstances under which the said company have so carried coals and coke for such other persons, and the circumstances under which the said company have carried or have offered to carry coals and coke for the

[1] Subsequent to the reference to the Master, the rule was amended by adding the following: "Sixthly, to afford to the said William Oxlade all reasonable and proper facilities and accommodation for the unloading of his coals and coke at the various stations of the said railway, and to afford to the said William Oxlade at the said stations the same facilities and accommodations for the unloading of his coals and coke as the said company afford to colliery owners or lessees of collieries, or to any other person."

said William Oxlade. Fourthly, whether and in what manner and how the company are enabled, by reason of such difference of circumstances, so to carry such coals and coke for such persons at a cost to the said company less than the cost to the said company of carrying coals and coke for the said William Oxlade.

Upon the first point the Master reported as to the accommodation afforded by the company for unloading coals and coke at the different stations; that they ascertained as nearly as possible the consumption in the neighborhood of each station, and the sort of coal required, and entered into terms with collieries having the particular description of coal, to supply the required quantity, and they appointed a depot agent to manage the sale of the coal so supplied, through whom the orders were transmitted to the colliery, and who accounted to the colliery owners for the proceeds; that all depots were allotted to such agent; that all coal dealers were treated alike; and that this course was adopted by the company for the purpose of preventing any obstruction of the general traffic of the railway. Upon the second point, he found that the company charged for *through rates* $\frac{3}{4}$*d.* per ton per mile for coal and coke going south, unless their wagons were used, in which case they charged one eighth of a penny per ton per mile more for the first hundred miles, and one sixteenth for any distance beyond, and 3*s.* per day for demurrage on every wagon detained more than four days off the line, and there was no variation made in the charge to any one, except in the case of coals carried by the North-Eastern Railway Company in conjunction with the Great Northern Railway Company through from the collieries to London, the North-Eastern Railway Company's haulage ceasing at York, where their railway joined the Great Northern, such coal being made up into full trains, and the wagons for the entire distance being provided by the Great Northern Railway Company, for which the charge was $\frac{1}{2}$*d.* per ton per mile for the whole distance, the circumstances of the coals so carried being carried in entire trains, and at regular times, and without stoppages, enabling them to carry them at such lower rate. The Master also found that a similar arrangement was made with the Midland Railway Company, but not under the same circumstances,— the inducement on the part of the company being a *desire to introduce the northern coke into Staffordshire.*

SEC. 324. **Decision.** — After an argument upon this report, it was held:—

1. That the transaction described in the first portion of the Master's report was not giving an undue or unreasonable preference or advantage to or in favor of any particular person or company, or subjecting any particular person or company, or any particular description of traffic, to any undue or unreasonable prejudice or disadvantage.

2. With reference to the second part of the Master's report, it was decided that it was sufficiently made out that the circumstances stated enabled the company to carry such coals at a cost less to them than the cost of carrying coals and coke for the complainant, and that by carrying them, under the circumstances stated, at such lower rate, no undue or unreasonable preference was given, or any undue and unreasonable disadvantage imposed.

3. As to the third portion of the report, it was held that lowering the rates, for the purpose of introducing the northern coke into Staffordshire, was giving an undue preference to that particular traffic, there being no special circumstances affecting the pecuniary interests of the company to justify the course pursued.[1]

SEC. 325. **Ransome v. Eastern Counties Railway Co.** — In a case which came before the court only the day before that last considered, in the course of which it appeared that a railway company had made an agreement with Messrs. E. & A. Prior & Co. to carry for them a large quantity of coals during three years from Peterborough to various places on their lines of railway at certain rates, and that the complainant, a coal merchant in Ipswich, sent coals (which had been brought to that port by sea) to various places on the same lines of railway, and that the company charged him a much larger sum per ton

[1] Oxlade *v.* North-Eastern Rail. Co., 1 C. P. N. S. 454; 3 Jur. N. S. 637; 26 L. J. C. P. 129.

in proportion to the distance over which his coals were carried than they charged Messrs. E. & A. Prior & Co., the professed object of the difference being to enable Messrs. E. & A. Prior & Co. (whose coal came to Peterborough by railway) to compete in the coal trade of the district with the complainant, who had the advantage of having his coals brought to Ipswich by sea. And this was held to be giving an "undue preference" to Messrs. E. & A. Prior & Co.

SEC. 326. **Meaning of "Undue and Unreasonable Preference," &c.** — In giving judgment in the last-named case, CRESSWELL, J., said: "The first thing to be ascertained is the meaning of the expressions 'undue or unreasonable preference or advantage,' and 'undue or unreasonable prejudice or disadvantage.' Are these words to be construed with reference to the interests of persons using the railway only? or may the interests of the railway owners be taken in any manner into consideration? *Ex. gr.*, if one thousand tons can be carried for a lower sum per ton per mile than one hundred tons, yielding an equal profit per ton to the railway company, may they so regulate the charges as to derive such equal profit? Would the lower rate charged for the larger quantity give an undue preference?[1] Or if goods can be carried one hundred miles at a lower rate than ten, and yield an equal profit per ton per mile, may the company charge less per mile for those carried one hundred miles without giving an undue or unreasonable preference? If that *may* be done without giving what the statute calls an undue or unreasonable preference, may not the company in fixing the rates consider the whole profit, and not the mere profit per mile, and, in order to induce people to carry more on their line, and for longer distances, agree to make a reduction in such a case? It is true that the sender of smaller quantities for a shorter distance will pay more per mile and more per ton in respective cases; but will that be an undue or unreasonable disadvantage?" He put another case thus: "If two railways start from the same terminus, and arrive at the same terminus by different routes, must they charge for the

[1] See Oxlade *v.* North-Eastern Rail. Co., *ante*, p. 381 *et seq.*

whole line at the same rate as from intermediate stations to either terminus? *Ex. gr.*, the London and South-Western *viâ* Bishopstoke and Winchester, and the London, Brighton, and South Coast, by Brighton: must they charge as much *per mile* for passengers and goods from Portsmouth to London as from Winchester or Brighton to London? Or may they carry at a lower rate the whole distance in order to compete with each other without being subjected to the charge of imposing on the Winchester and Brighton traffic an undue or unreasonable disadvantage?" and his Lordship added, that the court was of opinion that the fair interests of the railway ought to be taken into account in the decision of such cases.[1]

SEC. 327. **Object of Legislature.** — The object of the legislature was certainly for the protection of trade, which might, as we before said, be materially injured by the existence of an unregulated monopoly. That such a contingency was likely to arise — nay, that such an event was inevitable — had been proved by the facts adduced in the two last quoted cases. In the one, a railway company was endeavoring to direct a trade into a certain place; and in the other, a railway company was proved to be endeavoring to favor the competition of a certain firm in a place, and under circumstances which, but for the interference of the company, that firm would never have attempted to maintain. The evils which would have resulted from such a system would have been incalculable, and it was upon that account that the legislature interfered. But it was not with the view of disturbing the ordinary self-adjustive requirements of trade that this Act of Parliament was passed; and the circumstances under which a railway company carry, and the possible expense which they may incur in the transit of different quantities of goods, stand precisely upon the same ground, as to the consideration and determination of the rate at which they shall be carried, as the circumstances which attend the conveyance of different kinds of goods, or similar goods for different distances.

SEC. 328. **Principles of Inequality.** — No man could com-

[1] Ransome, *In re*, *v.* Eastern Counties Rail. Co., 1 C. B. N. S. 437; 3 Jur. N. S. 217; 26 L. J. C. P. 91.

plain that he was charged a different rate for the conveyance of his ton of coals than that which was charged to his neighbor for the conveyance of his ton weight of live-stock. Nor could a man demand that there should be a uniform rate of carriage for a ton of coals, whatever the distance of the transit. If such demands be unreasonable and absurd, the prohibition of them would be just and reasonable. And to interfere in the case of the cheaper conveyance of larger quantities, or of similar quantities for longer distances, would be as ridiculous and ill-advised a step as either of those above indicated. In this particular the intention of the legislature has been carried out to the fullest extent by the decisions referred to above.

SEC. 329. **Circumstances which will warrant an Injunction.** — It would have been a perilous thing to allow railway companies to deprive individuals of the advantages which they had with reference to the supply of a particular market, and would ultimately have done irreparable injury to the railway companies themselves by limiting and injuring the trade, on the healthy condition of which railway companies must depend for their prosperity. So it would have been an error to allow a railway company to endeavor to make up to an individual for the natural disadvantages of the position of his colliery in relation to their line, by allowing him reduced charges in consequence of the expense he had been put to in connecting his colliery with their line of railway. Such a proceeding upon the part of the railway company would have been an unwarrantable deprivation of the advantages which any colliery proprietor had a right to on account of the comparative proximity of his colliery to their line, and was a proper case for an injunction.[1]

SEC. 330. **Threat of New Railway not a good Ground for Reduction of Rates. — Private Bargains.** — In the case in which that doctrine was expressed, there was also a point of much importance decided, and that was, that a threat upon the part of any customer of a railway company that the customer would construct a railway which would deprive them of his

[1] Harris *v.* Cockermouth & Workington Rail. Co., 3 C. B. N. S. 693; 4 Jur. N. S. 239; 27 L. J. C. P. 162.

traffic, was not a good ground for the reduction of a rate of carriage, and that if, in consequence of such a threat being used, such a reduction was made, it would be held an undue preference. In commenting upon the question as to whether such a threat was a sufficient reason for or justification of the difference in charges, COCKBURN, C. J., said: "In my opinion, that is not a sufficient ground for the preference so given. The company are bound to regulate their charges so as to be equally applicable to all persons similarly circumstanced. If we were to take into consideration the circumstances upon which the company rely for their justification, there is no case in which we might not be called upon to consider the circumstances which might influence a party to send his goods by a particular railway; every man would be making his own bargain; and it would always be a question how far the company were justified in the particular case in departing from the general rule. I do not think it was the intention or the policy of the legislature to permit railway companies to make private bargains to give advantages to individuals, which must be attended with corresponding disadvantages to others. The obvious intention was, that there should be an equal rate of charge in respect of the carriage of all goods under the like circumstances; and that, although the company may be justified in laying down special rules applicable to particular cases, provided that they *bonâ fide* act with reference to their own interests and the interests of the public, they are not at liberty to make special bargains with individuals, whereby one is benefited to the prejudice of another." [1]

SEC. 331. **Preference to Persons who consign to Company's Agents.** — These principles would have been contravened had the North Devon Railway Company been allowed to give the preference which it promised to those persons who, in sending goods, consigned them to their agents. That company, being possessed of a line of railway, advertised to convey goods in conjunction with another railway company to a place beyond the limits of their own line at the rate of 50*s.* per ton, "pro-

[1] Harris *v.* Cockermouth & Workington Rail. Co., 3 C. B. N. S. 712.

vided they were consigned by and to their own agents at these respective places;" but if the goods were consigned through any one else, the company were to charge 2*s.* 6*d.* per ton more. This was held to be a ground for injunction under 17 & 18 Vict. c. 31.[1]

SEC. 332. **Circumstances of General and Local Character to be considered. — Small Parcels. — Additional Trouble.** — Another case, in which the question of what circumstances would justify a difference of charge, and in which additional strength was given to the intimations (if not absolute decisions) in Ransome's Case[2] and Oxlade's Case,[3] that a railway company is entitled, in determining the rate of tolls they will impose upon any particular traffic, to take into consideration any circumstances, either of a general or local character, which may enable them to charge less in one case than in others, came before the court. There it appeared that a railway company had power by their act to charge any rate they thought proper for parcels under one hundredweight, while by another section they were to charge rates and tolls equally, and to make advances and reductions of rates without partiality. The company (the defendants) charged the plaintiffs, the only common carriers on their line, certain rates for parcels under one hundredweight, but if there were various small parcels of the same article, though loose, delivered at one time and directed to the same person, amounting to more than one hundredweight, they weighed and entered them in the bulk and charged the lower or tonnage rate; but if the parcels, although delivered at the same time, were directed to different persons, they weighed and entered them separately, and charged the higher or small parcels' rate, even although the whole were to be delivered to the plaintiffs at the end of the

[1] Baxendale *v.* North Devon Rail. Co., 3 C. B. N. S. 324. See also, with reference to this subject, two more recent cases, Palmer *v.* London, Brighton & South Coast Rail. Co., 6 L. R. C. P. 194; 40 L. J. C. P. 133; 19 W. R. 627; Parkinson *v.* Great Western Rail. Co., 6 L. R. C. P. 554; 40 L. J. C. P. 222; 24 L. J. N. S. 830. But see a Scotch case in which a different doctrine seems to have been laid down, Pickford *v.* Caledonian Rail. Co., 31 May, 1866, 4 Macph. 755; 38 Jur. 399.

[2] *Ante*, p. 384; 1 C. B. N. S. 437.

[3] *Ante*, p. 381; 1 C. B. N. S. 454.

journey. If among many parcels there were several directed to one person, exceeding together one hundredweight, they were lumped and charged at the tonnage rate. It was held in this case that there was nothing to induce the court to infer that the charges so made were unreasonable, regard being had to the additional trouble of the company; for it appeared that the directed parcels, even although they were all to be delivered to the plaintiffs, caused considerable additional labor to the defendants in their collection for delivery to the consignee, and therefore, for that additional labor, they were entitled to additional remuneration, and hence arose a perfectly just and reasonable distinction between two sets of charges.[1] So, where a railway company (the London and South-Western Railway Company), which had been in the habit of unloading goods conveyed by them on their railway, by taking them out of the trucks and placing them in or adjacent to the wagons of the consignees, established a new system, under which they declined to allow their servants to unload the goods of the complainant (Mr. Cooper) from their trucks without extra charge, at the same time they continued to unload the goods of Messrs. Pickford & Co., as these, from the smallness of their quantity, were not carried, like the goods of the complainant, in separate trucks, but were mixed with the company's own traffic, and it was, therefore, for the company's own convenience that they unloaded them from the trucks, the court refused to make absolute a rule for an injunction under the Railway Traffic Act, 1854, enjoining the company to unload the trucks containing the complainant's goods, and to deliver such goods to the complainant by placing the same in or adjacent to his wagons; but the court intimated that if Mr. Cooper's complaint had been confined to the company's giving an advantage to Messrs. Pickford & Co. in the unloading of their goods, which they withheld from him, he might have been entitled to relief.[2] There can be little doubt that upon this second point the court would — had the

[1] Baxendale *v.* Eastern Counties Rail. Co., 4 C. B. N. S. 63; 27 L. J. C. P. 137.

[2] Cooper *v.* South-Western Rail. Co., 4 C. B. 738; 27 L. J. C. P. 324.

circumstances of the case permitted it — have done well to interfere. But there can be as little doubt that it would have erroneously exercised its power in compelling the company to continue to the complainant a privilege which he had once enjoyed.

SEC. 333. **Where System of Conveyance is dictated by Company's Convenience.** — In Ransome *v.* Eastern Counties Railway Company,[1] it was proved that the defendant railway company had established a system of carrying coals according to assigned districts comprising certain places on their lines and branch lines, — carrying them within those districts at certain lower rates, for quantities not less than a train load of 200 tons. By reason of this arrangement the complainants, who were coal merchants, carrying on their trade at Ipswich and several other places (eight in all) on the branch lines of the company, found that their places of business were distributed among those of the company's districts, so that, to enable them to take advantage of the reduced rates, they would have had to send from Ipswich to their outlying places of business three trains with loads of not less than 200 tons each, or one train to each of the districts in which their places of business were situated. This would have been an amount too large for the trade. On the other hand, the dealers at Peterborough, by reason of the fact that one of the company's districts embraced seven of the eight places at which the complainants dealt, were enabled to send their coals in such quantities as to avail themselves of the reduced rates. As, however, it was sworn, upon the part of the company, that these districts were adjusted, not with a view to give an undue preference to the one set of dealers over the other, but solely with a regard to their own convenience, and their conception of the requirements of the neighborhood, it was held that it was not a case for interference, as the complainants had not shown that they were unduly subjected to this disadvantage, or that it was caused by undue preference.

SEC. 334. **Policy of the Law.** — It is clear that the object of the act was not to relieve any person or company from the

[1] 4 C. B. N. S. 135; 27 L. J. C. P. 166; 4 Jur. N. S. 284.

possible prejudice or disadvantage of any arrangement which might be made by a railway company, even although that arrangement might indirectly favor some other person, if the arrangement was for the advantage of the public at large, for the reasonable increase of the prosperity of the company, and had not been entered into with a view to the advantage or preference of the one party, or the disadvantage or prejudice of the other. But, as in the case to which we have just referred, it appeared that the company had made a scale of charges for the carriage of coals from Peterborough and Ipswich respectively, to various places, which practically diminished the distance of Peterborough from those places, by diminishing the expense of conveyance comparatively with the expense of conveyance from Ipswich to the same places, and consequently diminished the natural advantage which the latter place had by reason of its proximity to these places, and upon this ground it was held that the company had given an undue preference to the dealers in Peterborough.[1]

SEC. 335. **Where Arrangements Beneficial to Individuals may be made.** — Such a decision does not, however, militate against the principles stated above, and, in a case which came before the court, it was expressly decided that it is competent to a railway company to enter into special arrangements and agreements, whereby advantages may be secured to individuals, in the carriage of goods upon the railway, where it is made clearly to appear that in entering into such agreements the company has only the interests of the proprietors and the legitimate increase of the profits of the company in view, and the consideration given to the company in return for the advantages afforded by them is adequate, and the company is willing to afford the same facilities to all others upon the same terms.[2]

SEC. 336. **Where Large Quantities are guaranteed.** — And it

[1] Ransome *v.* Eastern Counties Rail. Co., 4 C. B. N. S. 135; 4 Jur. N. S. 284; 27 L. J. C. P. 166. The principle involved is the same as that in the case of Harris *v.* Cockermouth & Workington Rail. Co., 3 C. B. N. S. 693; 4 Jur. N. S. 239.

[2] Nicholson *v.* Great Western Rail. Co., 4 C. B. N. S. 366; 28 L. J. C. P. 89; 4 Jur. N. S. 1187.

was also held that the 2d section of 17 & 18 Vict. c. 31, was not contravened by a railway company carrying at a lower rate in consideration of a guarantee of large quantities, and full train loads, at regular periods, provided the real object of the company is to obtain thereby a greater remunerative profit by the diminished cost of carriage, although the effect may be to exclude from the lower rate those persons who cannot give such a guarantee.[1] It is not within the province, if it is within the power, of Acts of Parliament to do away with the inevitable advantages which large capital must have in the competition with small capital, and one of the legitimate advantages it possesses is the possibility of making better terms. Large transactions can, of course, be done cheaper than small. The transacting costs money. And it is because it is so that goods bought wholesale are cheaper than those bought retail. So it is that a railway company can carry large quantities of goods at a cheaper rate per ton per mile than small quantities.

SEC. 337. **Reduction on account of Cheapness not an Undue Preference.** — That being an undoubted fact, we have seen that if a company does reduce its charge on account of the cheapness with which it can do the work expected of it, it does not thereby give an undue preference. So in the case where large quantities are not sent at one time, but at stated intervals, the fact in reference to the cheapness with which the railway company can transmit these being the same, it is only a very slight extension of the principle above alluded to, which enables a company to carry these at a lower rate without incurring the possibility of being restrained from so doing under this act.

SEC. 338. **Agreement to employ other Lines of Company "Undue" Ground of Reduction.** — It was imagined that it would only be another slight extension of the same rule which would enable a railway company to give a preference to a customer who engaged to employ other lines of the company for traffic, which lines were, however, distinct from and unconnected with that in respect of which such preference was given.[2] But

[1] Nicholson *v.* Great Western Rail. Co., 4 C. B. N. S. 366.

[2] Baxendale *v.* Great Western Rail. Co., 5 C. B. N. S. 309; 28 L. J. C. P. 69; 4 Jur. N. S. 1241.

it has been decided that such a preference would be an undue one, and upon the obvious ground that another principle was involved in the case from that which was involved in the case of Nicholson *v.* The Great Western Railway.[1]

SEC. 339. **Principle involved.** — Where the transactions are totally distinct, and the lines of rail are not the same, any such agreement tends to place a restriction upon trade, and the preference which is given upon this understanding is apt to bring the carrying company and the trader into such a relation that they will be in a position to combine against the public; and it was exactly this evil that the Railway and Canal Traffic Act, 1854, was introduced to prevent.

SEC. 340. **The Company's Rates must not operate to Disadvantage of Third Parties.** — We have seen that where special agreements are entered into between railway companies and individuals to secure to the latter advantages in regard to the goods sent by them on the company's railway, it must appear that such agreement has only the interest of the proprietors, and the legitimate increase of the profits of the railway in view, otherwise it would be held to be an undue preference. But this doctrine must be still further limited to be clearly understood; for if the company fixes a rate of tolls to be taken on the railway with a view to the promotion of their own interests, but which subjects others to unreasonable disadvantages, or operates to their disadvantage by giving undue preference to third parties, the court will interfere. Thus, where a railway company formerly charged a uniform rate of 3*s.* 6*d.* per ton on all goods conveyed on their line between two places — Reading and Paddington — and the goods were collected and delivered, both by the company and the complainants, at a charge of 4*s.* 10*d.* per ton, it appeared that the company, who had power under their act to impose their own rates of charge for carrying, but no power to impose tolls for collecting and delivering, raised the charge for carrying to 8*s.* 4*d.*, being the aggregate of the above two charges, with an intimation to the public that they would collect and deliver goods free of all charge. The obvious purpose of the arrangement

[1] 4 C. B. N. S. 366; 28 L. J. C. P. 89.

and announcement was to compel persons desiring to have their goods conveyed by the railway, to employ the company to collect and deliver such goods, and thus to secure this business and the profits upon it to the company, as well as to exclude the complainants from competing with them in this department of business. That being so, it was held that this arrangement was an undue preference to the company in their separate capacity of carriers, other than on the line of railway, and also an undue prejudice to the complainants.[1] There is much in the judgment of the Chief Justice which bears on the principles involved in many cases which may arise in practice, and we follow the example of another writer on this subject,[2] by availing ourselves of his admirable statement of the law. He said: "It is abundantly clear from the statutory enactments, which enjoin on railway companies the obligation to afford accommodation on equal and reasonable terms, and from the provisions of the statute, by which jurisdiction is given to this court, against the affording of undue preference or disadvantage, that it was not the intention of the legislature to leave to railway companies the unfettered exercise of their rights as proprietors of their respective lines; but in return for the great power which it has conceded to them, and the monopoly of the carrying business of the country, which in a great degree they have been enabled to acquire, it has imposed upon them the obligation of affording accommodation on equal terms to the whole of the public."

SEC. 341. **Separate Interests vested in same Company.** — With reference to the question of separate interests being vested in the same company, he went on to remark: "It may be convenient in the first place to advert to a distinction, not always kept in sight in argument, between cases in which the interest of the company sought to be promoted by the regulation or act complained of is one which arises with reference to the railway itself as to which the question occurs, and those in which the benefit sought to be obtained by the company is one which has reference to interests distinct from those of the

[1] Baxendale *v.* Great Western Rail. Co., 5 C. B. N. S. 336; 28 L. J. C. P. 81; 4 Jur. N. S. 1279.

[2] Powell on Carriers.

particular railway; as where, for example, the company are proprietors of another railway, or carry on some other business.

SEC. 342. **Position of the Company in relation to Separate Interests.** — "In the latter class of cases it appears to us clear that the company must be taken to be, *quoad* the particular railway, in the position of third parties, and that they cannot, with a view to such separate interests, give an undue preference, or impose an unreasonable disadvantage, any more than they could do so to promote the interests of any other party. Thus, if a railway company, being proprietors of one line from A to B, and of another line from C to D, were, in order to obtain the custom of a particular individual on the first of those lines, on which they might be subject to competition from a rival line, to agree to convey his goods on the line from C to D at a cheaper rate than those of another person using only the latter line; or if a railway company, carrying on, in addition to its business as carriers on the line, that of carriers to and from the termini of the railway, were, with a view to obtain additional custom in the latter, to carry on the railway for those who employed them as carriers to and from the railway at a lower rate than for those who did not; — in both these cases we should have no difficulty in holding that the company must be considered, as regards those separate interests, in the light of third parties, and that they cannot promote these at the expense of the right of the public to that equality on the particular railway which it was the intention of the Act of Parliament to secure.

SEC. 343. **Where the Company seeks to promote its own Interests without Regard to the Interest of Others.** — "Greater difficulty and uncertainty arise in dealing with cases in which the purpose and effect of the thing complained of is the benefit of the company in their character of proprietors of a particular railway. In these cases the court might feel a greater reluctance to interpose, partly from an unwillingness to interfere with the parties in the management of their own affairs for their own advantage, partly from a disposition to give companies credit for acting on an enlightened view of their own interests, as identified with those of the public; yet if the court became clearly satisfied that the company were seeking to promote its own advantage by establishing an inequality, which was unreasonable under the circumstances, and operated unfairly and injuriously upon particular individuals, or that it was affording to one person, or set of persons, an advantage which it would not afford to another under similar circumstances, this court would not hesitate to interfere to prevent such a result, although by so doing they might prevent the company from securing all the profit that it might otherwise derive from the use of its property. Thus, where the complaint made was that a railway company, as between two intermediate stations, charged a higher rate than was due to the intermediate space in proportion to the charge made on the entire line of railway, this court, if it were made to appear that the disproportion was not justified by the circumstances of the traffic, — in other words, was an undue prejudice or unreasonable disadvantage to those using the part of the railway in question, — would interfere to set aside such an arrangement.[1]

SEC. 344. **The Advantage must be given to all Persons similarly Circumstanced.** — "So, again, if an arrangement were made by a railway company, whereby persons bringing a larger amount of traffic to the railway should have their goods carried on more favorable terms than those bringing a less quantity, although the court might uphold such an arrangement as an ordinary incident of commercial economy, provided the same advantage were extended to all persons under the like circumstances; yet it would assuredly insist on the latter condition, and would interfere in the case of any special agreement, by which the company had secured to a particular individual the benefit of such an agreement to the exclusion of others; or even where an attempt had been made by keeping the agreement secret, to make it operate unduly to the prejudice of third parties.

SEC. 345. **Where the Interest of the Company causes Unreasonable Disadvantage.** — "This reasoning appears to us effectually to dispose of the argument that the court cannot inter-

[1] See *In re* Jones and the Eastern Counties Rail. Co., 3 C. B. N. S. 718.

fere to prevent a railway company from fixing the rate of tolls to be taken on its railways, in such a manner as shall best promote its own interests in cases where, by so doing, the company subject others to unreasonable disadvantages, or operates to their prejudice by giving undue preference to third parties." It was argued by the defendants that, as they had the power to raise their rates of charges for carrying on their line, and as they had done so equally with regard to all customers, they were not within the statutory prohibition against undue prejudice, by performing other duties than those which their character of railway carriers made necessary. As to this, the Chief Justice said: "We think this argument rests upon two obvious fallacies, — first, that if, supposing that the whole charge in question is one made by the company in reference to their character and interests with respect to the railway, whereas, in reality, the charge is made by them in a character and interest independent of the railway, *viz.* as carriers to and from the termini of the railway; secondly, that the company can convert that which is in reality a charge for collecting and delivering as well as for carrying, into one for carrying only, by affixing to it the latter denomination in their table of rates. It is true, no doubt, that the company's acts give them the power to impose their own rates of charge for the carriage of this description of traffic: but these acts give them no power to impose tolls or charges for collecting and delivery; and it is palpably an abuse of their powers, if, under the name of a charge for carrying on their line, they impose, otherwise than with the assent of the parties concerned, a charge for a totally different thing. Again, although the legislature has conferred the power of imposing rates of charge, it has annexed to this power the obligation of imposing such rates equally; and the company cannot be permitted to evade this obligation by colorably pretending that that which is in fact a charge for other things as well is a charge for carriage only.

SEC. 346. **The Court will prevent what is, in Effect, an Injustice.** — "The court is bound to look at the transaction in its true light, and cannot suffer itself to be diverted from its duty of interfering to prevent what, in effect, is such an injustice as it was the purpose of the legislature to prevent, because the transaction is attempted to be covered over by a transparent disguise. Looking, then, at the alteration in the rates in its true light, we are of opinion that the arrangement is objectionable, both as an undue preference given on the one hand, and as an unreasonable disadvantage imposed on the other. It is an undue preference to the company in their separate capacity of carriers other than on the line of railway, inasmuch as they thereby practically secure to themselves the entire monopoly of the last-mentioned traffic, to the entire exclusion of the complainants and all others. It is an undue prejudice and an unreasonable disadvantage imposed on the complainants, inasmuch as it is plain that their goods and those of all persons employing them, as, indeed, the goods of all persons other than those who employ the company to collect and deliver, must be subjected, as compared with the goods of the latter, twice over, to the expense attendant on collection and delivery, if they employ others to collect and deliver for them, or to an unnecessary charge if they require no such accommodation."[1]

It was upon these grounds that the court felt it to be their duty to interfere.

SEC. 347. **The Principles of the Decision.** — The principles laid down in the above judgment cannot be called in question. It would not be for the advantage of the public that a railway company, which happened to carry on some other branch of trade besides that of carrying upon their line, should have the power to prefer itself in the latter capacity to others who prosecuted the same calling, in so far as the conveyance of goods was concerned. One obvious result of such a practice would be, that the railway company could distance all competition in the supply of the particular commodity in which it dealt; but when one of the parties competing distances all the others, it ceases to be competition; and in this particular

[1] See also Parkinson *v.* Great Western Rail. Co., 6 L. R. C. P. 554; 40 L. J. C. P. 222; 24 L. T. N. S. 830. But see Pickford *v.* Caledonian Rail. Co., 31 May, 1866, 4 Macph. 755.

case all the rivals of the railway company would inevitably be driven out of the field whenever that undesirable result was produced. The company carrier and trader would sell its goods at a monopoly price, without the least fear of having to lower its prices on the ground of competition, as it could again lower its rates for a time, and so drive competition again out of the field.

SEC. 348. **The Railway Company's two Capacities.** — Now there was in this case an evident distinction between the two capacities in which the railway company worked. It carried goods as a railway carrier, and it also carried goods as a collector and deliverer to the railway company. In the first capacity it gave an undue preference to itself in its second capacity, and the allegation that it received nothing for collection and delivery was disproved by the circumstances of the case. A railway company cannot afford to collect goods, unless it is remunerated for so doing. It will not undertake outlay without a certainty of reimbursement. And it matters not whether it is called charge for carriage by rail, or whether the company professes to collect free of cost, the fact is the same, that they are being remunerated for the collection, as well as for the carriage; and by making the charge for goods which they do not collect, the same as that for goods which they do collect, they are obviously, in the matter of charge for the carriage of the goods, giving an advantage to themselves as collectors and deliverers. The result would have been the ruin of the complainants and others, who were engaged in the trade of collecting and delivering, and the interference of the court was imperatively called for. The principle upon which the decision in Garton *v.* The Great Western Railway Company [1] was founded, was precisely similar to that involved in the case just alluded to.

SEC. 349. **Other Preferences considered. — Collection and Delivery. — The Time of Closing Station. — Price of Carriage.** — In another case, in which this subject was brought before the court, the grounds of complaint against the company were three: "First, that the charge made by the railway company

[1] 5 C. B. N. S. 669; 28 L. J. C. P. 158.

to the complainants for forwarding packages by the van and passenger trains from station to station was the same as the public were charged for so forwarding from station to station, and for collection and delivery; secondly, that the Bristol Goods Station of the company was closed against the reception of goods from the complainants at an hour in the evening after which the company received goods brought there by their agent, Mr. Wall; and, thirdly, that the complainants were charged on all goods from Bristol to Bridgewater and Bridgewater to Bristol at the rate of 6*s.* 8*d.* per ton for the first-class goods, 8*s.* 4*d.* per ton for the second-class goods, 12*s.* 6*d.* for third-class goods, and 16*s.* 8*d.* for fourth-class goods, whilst certain persons at Bridgewater were charged only at the rate of 6*s.* per ton for goods of all classes. With regard to the first of these complaints there can, after what has been said above, be no doubt as to the answer which the court gave to it. As to the second, it appeared that the respondent company closed its goods station at Bristol at 5.15 against all persons except its agent, Mr. Wall, who had a receiving-house about a mile distant from the station, and from whom the company received goods up to 8 P. M. It also appeared that, for the conveyance of goods from the receiving-house to the station, the agent, Wall, charged 1*s.* 8*d.* per ton on all goods above 3 cwt., and 3*d.* for each package below that weight. Although it appeared, upon the oath of the company, that the goods brought to the station by their agent were properly classified, weighed, and prepared for loading, it was held that the company, by so doing, was imposing an undue prejudice upon the complainant.[1]

SEC. 350. **Special Contract for Diminished Rate must be justified by Special Circumstances.** — The third point was, that there was an undue preference of certain parties in so far as the charge for the conveyance of goods from Bridgewater to Bristol was concerned. It appeared that the company had special contracts with certain grocers and ironmongers at

[1] See also Palmer *v.* London, L. R. C. P. 194; 40 L. J. C. P. 133; Brighton, & South Coast Rail. Co., 6 24 L. T. N. S. 135.

Bridgewater, under which they agreed to carry all their ironmongery and grocery goods at a uniform rate of 6*s*. per ton, including delivery. But this was held an undue preference in relation to the general rate of charge for the carriage of goods from Bristol to Bridgewater, and *vice versâ*, which was correctly set out by the complainant, as it did not appear that this diminished charge was justified by any special circumstances of advantage to the company, or to meet competition for another railway or any other mode of carriage.[1]

SEC. 351. **Legitimate Competition with another Railway Company. — Legitimate Increase of Profits.** — Had the railway company entered into an agreement of the nature set out above, *viz.* to carry all or certain individuals' goods at a rate considerably lower than that which was their general charge for the conveyance of goods, with a view to legitimate competition with another railway company which carried goods from the same places and to the same places as the company making the agreement, or could it have shown that the reduction in charges so made did not in any way reduce the profits of the company by reason of the fact of the increased traffic secured compensating for the diminished rates on particular transactions, the case would not have fallen within the statute, as it was evidently not the object of the legislature to interfere with a proper competition on the part of railway companies, which can only tend, in the long run, to the public advantage; nor was it an object of the legislature to meddle with such reductions as were intended, legitimately, — that is, within the scope of that particular branch of business, — to increase the profits of the railway company, it being certain that no such reductions, undertaken honestly with a view to that result, could, in the end, be detrimental to the interests of those who were the objects of the care of the legislature, — the public generally.

SEC. 352. **What will not be held an Unreasonable Prejudice.** — In a case where the complainant and respondent were

[1] Garton *v.* Bristol & Exeter Rail. Co., 6 C. B. N. S. 639; 28 L. J. C. P. 306; 4 Jur. N. S. 1313.

the same as in one of the cases alluded to above, it appeared that, by their scale or tariff, the respondent railway company divided the places through which their line passed into districts, and charged at a reduced rate per ton for coals carried a given distance from Peterborough or Ipswich respectively, when consigned in full train-loads of 200 tons, or 35 trucks. The advantage of this reduced rate was given to persons consigning coals from Peterborough to one of these districts in full train-loads, though, on their arrival at Cambridge, the company, for their own convenience, thought fit to break up the train and carry about one third of it forward by the ordinary goods trains, — the whole consignment, however, ultimately finding its way into the district to which it was addressed by the consignor. Under these circumstances it was held that this was not giving any undue preference to the Peterborough coal dealers, or imposing any undue prejudice on the Ipswich dealers, although the latter were unable to avail themselves of the lower rate of charge for coals consigned by them to the same district, by reason of the insufficiency of the demand for sea-borne coals at the places comprised therein.[1]

SEC. 353. **As to Agent's Receiving-houses.** — Where a railway company permitted a carrier (who also acted as superintendent of their goods traffic) to hold himself out as agent for the receipt of goods to be carried on their line, and his office as the receiving-office of the company, the goods were received by him at that place without requiring the senders to sign conditions which the company required all other carriers who brought goods to their stations to do. The question in the case was, whether the carrier who thus received the goods was agent of the company for receiving and forwarding on their line, — whether persons delivering goods at his office, or receiving-house for that purpose, had the security of the company's liability, or only that of Wall (the carrier). It was held that Wall's office was, as to third persons, to all intents and purposes, the office of the company, and that the effect of the arrangement was to give Wall an advantage over the com-

[1] Ransome *v.* Eastern Counties Rail. Co., 8 C. B. N. S. 709; 7 Jur. N. S. 99; 29 L. J. C. P. 329; 8 W. R. 527; 2 L. T. N. S. 376.

plainants, as to the carriage of goods, which the law did not warrant.[1]

The principles which have guided the Court of Common Pleas in the decision of cases in which injunctions were applied for, in relation to railway companies' traffic in goods, under the 17 & 18 Vict. c. 31, must now be somewhat obvious; and as the same general rules have guided them in other applications made under this act with regard to the stational arrangements, and the conveyance of passengers, these principles will be further explicated by a consideration of some of these cases.[2]

SEC. 354. **Stational Arrangements.** — In the case of Barker *v.* Midland Railway Company,[3] it was decided that an action would not lie against a railway company for refusing to admit a carrier of passengers and goods within the precincts of their station, to which they admitted the public generally; but it was suggested that if there had been sufficient evidence of a dedication to the public, which there was not in this case, it would have been different. The inference is, that if an action would not lie, an injunction would not be granted.

SEC. 355. **Arrangement with other Carrier of Passengers, Undue Preference.** — Where, however, a railway company made arrangements at one of their stations with A., the proprietor of an omnibus running between their station and K., to provide omnibus accommodation for all passengers by any of their trains to and from K., and allowed A. the exclusive privilege of driving his vehicle into the station-yard for the purpose of taking up and setting down passengers at the door of the booking-office, it was held that, in the absence of special circumstances showing it to be reasonable, the granting of such exclusive privilege to one proprietor and refusing to grant the like facilities to another, who also brought passengers from K., as well as from other places beyond, was a breach of the pro-

[1] Baxendale, *In re*, and Bristol & Exeter Rail. Co., 11 C. B. N. S. 787.

[2] Two Scotch cases may be consulted with reference to the construction to be placed upon this statute. Scottish Central Rail. Co. *v.* Ferguson & Co., 27 Feb. 1864, 2 Macph. 781; Wannan *v.* Scottish Central Rail. Co., 19 July, 1864, 2 Macph. 1373.

[3] 18 C. B. 46; 25 L. J. 184 C. P.

hibition against the granting of undue and unreasonable preferences.[1] Had the carrier of passengers paid to the railway company a certain sum of money for the exclusive right of occupying the station-yard with his vehicle, and had it been proved that his supply of vehicles was sufficient for the wants of the public, it seems that an injunction would not have been granted.[2]

SEC. 356. **A Legitimate Arrangement. — A Proof of Substantial Inconvenience necessary to support Injunction.** — So, where a railway company granted exclusive permission to a limited number of fly proprietors to ply for hire within their station, the court refused to grant an injunction against the company under this act, at the instance of a fly proprietor who was excluded from participation in this advantage, although it was sworn by the complainant, and by several other fly proprietors who were likewise excluded, that occasional delay and inconvenience to the public resulted from the course pursued.[3] But the only ground upon which, under such circumstances, an injunction will be granted, is a proof of undoubted and substantial inconvenience or injury arising to the public from such an arrangement,[4] the presumption, founded upon experience, being that, as the company is empowered to take precautions for the ordering and good management of its affairs, such arrangements are, when *bonâ fide*, for the advantage of the public, and do not conduce to the prejudice of any individuals.

SEC. 357. **Time of Closing Goods Station.** — A railway company required other carriers to bring their goods to the railway station at or before 6.30 P. M., while they removed goods at their station at a later time, when those goods were collected by themselves. An injunction was asked for to restrain this practice, which evidently fell within the prohibitory rule laid

[1] Marriott, *In re*, 1 C. B. N. S. 499; 3 Jur. N. S. 493; 26 L. J. C. P. 154.

[2] Beadell *v.* Eastern Counties Rail. Co., 26 L. J. C. P. 250; 2 C. B. N. S. 509.

[3] Painter, *Ex parte*, 2 C. B. N. S. 702.

[4] See, also, per COCKBURN, C. J., in Barrett *v.* Great Northern & Midland Rail. Co., 1 C. B. N. S. 423; 28 L. J. 306 C. P.

down in Garton *v.* Bristol and Exeter Railway,[1] and was granted.[2]

SEC. 358. **Application of Act as to Facilities for Storing Coals. — Arrangements. — Complaint. — Court will look to True Character and Effect of Arrangements.** — In a recent case it appeared that a railway company, having land adjoining one of their stations, let the whole of it to Perkins, a coal merchant, for the purpose of storing coals brought by their line, and that Perkins did not require, or actually use, the whole of the land for this purpose. West, another coal merchant, applied to the company to provide him, on similar terms, with land for storing coals, or to let him the part of the land not actually used by Perkins. The company refused to do so, and West applied to the court, under the Railway and Canal Traffic Act, 1854, § 3, for an order compelling the company to desist from allowing Perkins to store coals on the land, or to give similar facilities to him. As, on the hearing, the court was equally divided, BOVILL, C. J., and KEATING, J., holding an opinion that the rule which had been obtained in favor of West should be made absolute, while MONTAGUE SMITH and BRETT, JJ., held that it should be discharged, it may be well to quote some portions from the judgments which were delivered. BOVILL, C. J., in delivering the judgment of himself and KEATING, said: "From the nature of the inland coal trade, the wharf or depot accommodation is almost essential to its being carried on profitably to the merchant. It also promotes the traffic of carrying coals upon the railways, and the practice of the companies providing such accommodation is very general upon most of the railways. . . . The refusal to allow the complainants any wharf accommodation at Lubenham, which, however, is, for all commercial purposes (as it appears to have been considered by both parties), virtually preventing the coal being sent by the complainants to that station. . . . They complain that, by the arrangements in question, an undue preference and advantage

[1] 6 C. B. N. S. 639; 28 L. J. C. P. 306.

[2] Baxendale *v.* London & South-Western Railway Co., *In re*, 12 C. B. N. S. 758. See also Palmer *v.* London, Brighton, & South Coast Rail. Co., *In re*, 6 L. R. C. P. 194; 40 L. J. C. P. 133; 24 L. J. N. S. 135.

is given by the company to Mr. Perkins, and that they are subjected to undue prejudice and disadvantage, and there can be no doubt that the effect of what has been done by the company is to exclude the complainants from any share of the facilities for the coal traffic which exists at the station, and that it does practically exclude them from sending coal to Lubenham station for the purposes of their trade, and thus creates a monopoly of the trade in favor of Mr. Perkins, and to the prejudice, not only of the complainants, but of the public. . . . It seems to us that the space of ground used for the deposit of coals at Lubenham station must be considered a part of the railway within the meaning of the Railway Traffic Act, and that the wharf accommodation to coal dealers is not only a usual and ordinary and reasonable accommodation for the coal traffic coming to the railway, but that it is in fact so necessary, that without it the trade in coal and the traffic of coal on the railway cannot practically and commercially be carried on. . . . In most of the decided cases, the question has arisen upon a difference in the amounts charged for carriage to particular persons; but the court has always considered that the Act of 1854 prohibited any difference being made in the *accommodation*, also, that was afforded to different persons; and the court will always look at the true character and effect of the arrangements which are complained of. I cannot bring my mind to doubt that what was done in this case was distinctly what the legislature intended to prevent. It gives a direct advantage to Mr. Perkins at the expense of the complainants, and is a direct prejudice to the complainants to the benefit of Mr. Perkins. There is no sufficient reason shown for giving this preference to Mr. Perkins; and there are no circumstances, not even the benefit of the public, to excuse or justify it. Indeed, the public, if such monopolies could be created by railway companies at this and other stations, would suffer most materially; and it seems to me that there is nothing to make the arrangement in question otherwise than undue and unreasonable within the meaning of the statute."

SEC. 359. **As to the Court's Jurisdiction under the Act.** —

The Complaint must relate to the Receiving, Forwarding, or Delivering of Goods. — MONTAGUE SMITH, J., in giving judgment for himself and BRETT, J., said: "The question arises whether the court has jurisdiction, under the Railway and Canal Traffic Act, to carry out this object, and it seems to us it has not. It strikes one at the outset that what the applicants want from the company has nothing whatever to do with the conveyance and transport of coal, or with any facilities or accommodation relating to conveyance and transport. They really want the company to provide them with a wharf or store, where they may sell their coal when and as they please. . . . [He then referred to 17 & 18 Vict. c. 31.] These being the enactments of the statute, it seems to us that this court has no jurisdiction under it to deal with the complaint in question. That complaint does not relate to the conveyance of the coal, or to the receiving, forwarding, or delivering of it. The coal is received at the place whence it is consigned, and it is forwarded to Lubenham, and, when it is there, handed over to such a consignee as Mr. Perkins is, in order that he may stack it and keep it, and sell it at his pleasure to a purchaser. We think it is delivered within the meaning of the statute. We think that the complaint relates to matters wholly distinct from the receiving, forwarding, and delivering of the coal. It relates to a matter foreign to all these things, and, arising after all that concerns the conveyance and delivery of the coal, is absolutely and entirely at an end. It is said that the company, by letting their wharf to Mr. Perkins for the above purposes, give him an advantage in the sale of his coals over the applicants. But this is not an advantage in the conveyance or transport of the coal; and if it is not one of the advantages within the act, the fact that it is an advantage to him and a disadvantage to others becomes immaterial, and cannot give the court jurisdiction. It seems to us that if we were to extend our jurisdiction to things beyond those which relate to the conveyance of traffic, and the matters incidental to its transport, we should exceed the authority conferred on us by the act, and might then be asked to extend our interference to various matters not at all contemplated by it, such as the arrangements respecting refreshment-rooms, book-stalls, and other like matters."[1]

We should have imagined that such a difference of opinion need not necessarily exist in this case, but such are the facts of the decision.

SEC. 360. **Question of Method.** — A question of method arises in this place, and that is, whether the restrictions which have been imposed upon railway companies in relation to the conveyance of passengers, their fares, and the trains by which they are conveyed, should be treated of in this chapter, or would find a more fitting place, having regard to logical sequence, in that portion of this work which is devoted to the consideration of the law in relation to passenger traffic in all its bearings. We would, however, deal, at least, with those cases which fall directly under the above statute, as the whole subject of injunction is more apt to be thoroughly understood if treated of in its entirety; and when we come to that part of our subject where the questions arising in connection with this subject have an equally good right to be alluded to, we would refer the reader to this part of our work. Such a course will, it seems to us, fulfil the logical requirements of the subject, and will avoid a repetition which would be unnecessary in any other point of view.

SEC. 361. **Fares, Passengers, and Trains. — The Convenience of the Public.** — Throughout this chapter we have endeavored to make it clearly understood that the restrictions here alluded to are imposed upon railway companies for the benefit of the public. It was the prejudice which arose to the public from the preference of certain individuals that indicated the necessity of some such measure as that which was introduced, and, in the various decisions which have been made under this statute, this principle has been kept in view. Thus the court will not interfere with a railway company's practice in reference to the running of through trains on a continuous line of railway,

[1] West *v.* London & North-Western Rail. Co., 5 L. R. C. P. 622; 29 L. J. C. P. 282; 23 L. T. N. S. 371; 18 W. R. 1028. See, also, a Scotch case, Napier *v.* Glasgow & South-Western Rail. Co., 25 Nov. 1865; 4 Macph. 87; 38 Jur. 55.

unless it be convinced that the demand for such through train is reasonable, and also that such through train is necessary to the convenience of the public. Where there was such an application at the instance of an individual, the court refused to interfere, on the ground that there was a continuous line by which through tickets might be obtained, though by a somewhat longer route, that no additional cost or serious loss of time had been thereby incurred, and no substantial inconvenience thereby occasioned to the public, and that no complaint had been made of the inadequacy of the existing accommodation.[1]

SEC. 362. **The Granting of Season Tickets.** — Where a railway company granted season tickets to passengers upon their line between Harwich and London, upon certain terms, and an injunction was applied for to compel the company to grant season tickets to passengers between Colchester and London, and there was a suggestion that it was an unreasonable preference upon the part of the railway company to grant season tickets between the former places at a lower rate (the distance being considerably greater) than between the latter places, the court refused to interfere, on the ground that these facts did not constitute a case of undue preference under the act.[2]

SEC. 363. **To induce Interference with Branch Lines, Existing Arrangements must be shown to be Inconvenient to Public. — Reasonableness, how to be judged of. — Shelter at Junction.** — In the case of the Caterham Railway Company[3] one or two important points were raised, and one of the decisions bore on the subject under consideration. That decision was to the effect that, in order to induce the court to interfere on behalf of the proprietors of a branch line with a view to compelling the stoppage of a greater number of the trains running on the main line at the junction, or with a view to altering the times of the stoppage of trains, it must be shown that the existing

[1] Barret, *In re*, 1 C. B. N. S. 423; 26 L. J. C. P. 83.

[2] Jones *v.* Eastern Counties Rail. Co., 3 C. B. N. S. 718. See, also, Hozier *v.* Caledonian Rail. Co., Scotch Session Cases, vol. xvii. N. S. p. 302.

[3] 1 C. B. N. S. 410; 26 L. J. C. P. 161.

arrangement is not of such a nature as to meet the requirements of the public. It was also held that the reasonableness of the accommodation with regard to travelling on one branch line must be looked at in relation to the accommodation afforded to the public on other branch lines. Thus the fact that the company working the main line refuses to grant third-class return tickets to the branch line, is not a good ground for complaint, unless it can be shown that it does grant such tickets to another branch line similarly situated to that concerning which the complaint is made, — in which case the court would grant an injunction. On the other hand, if there is no shelter provided at the junction for the passengers on the branch line who are waiting the arrival of trains, this will be held to be an unreasonable prejudice to these passengers, upon the ground that the public is entitled in this respect to reasonable accommodation.

SEC. 364. **Unequal Charges.** — With reference to the first point raised in this case, CRESSWELL, J., said: "The first ground of complaint is, that the companies against whom the application is directed make unequal charges to persons travelling along the lines to the Caterham branch. It does not, however, appear that there is any inequality as compared with the rates charged on another line. The words of the 2d section are, that 'no such company shall make or give any undue or unreasonable preference or advantage to or in favor of any particular person or company, or any particular description of traffic in any respect whatsoever, nor shall any such company subject any particular person or company or any particular description of traffic to any undue or unreasonable prejudice or disadvantage in any respect whatsoever.' I apprehend that it cannot be said that because persons may travel between London and Epsom at a less rate than they can between London and Caterham, any undue or unreasonable preference or advantage is given, or any undue or unreasonable prejudice or disadvantage imposed. All persons, it appears, who come from London to Caterham, are charged alike."[1] Consequently

[1] 1 C. B. N. S. 419.

only where there is an inequality of charge for travelling over the same line or portion of a line will the court interfere.

SEC. 365. **Practice on Remedy.** — Some statement of the practice on remedy may be necessary in this place. A rule calling upon a railway company to show cause why they should not act in compliance with the Railway Traffic Act is too vague.[1] It ought to be remembered, in connection with this subject, that the complainant ought, before coming to the court, to represent his grievance to the company, and only make application for injunction in case of their refusal to grant him the redress he seeks.[2]

SEC. 366. **Affidavit.** — In reference to the affidavit, it ought to set out, without vagueness, a public as well as a private inconvenience, as the actual or possible result of the grievance;[3] and although in some cases the court may be inclined to grant an injunction where a public inconvenience cannot be shown to be the direct and necessary result of the grievance complained of,[4] it is always better, if such grievance can be shown in any way, directly or indirectly, to arise from the conduct of the company, to set it forth. The affidavit of complaint must disclose a grievance, which is strictly in accordance with the facts, and a mistake or misdescription of the ground upon which relief is sought, or of the circumstances complained of, will, even where a substantial grievance of an analogous nature is disclosed on the argument, be fatal.[5] Where, however, a real ground of grievance is stated, the court will probably mould the rule so as to give the redress really required, even

[1] Marriott, *In re*, *v.* London & Southwestern Rail. Co., 26 L. J. C. P. 154; 3 Jur. N. S. 154.

[2] Cooper *v.* London & South-Western Rail. Co., 4 Jur. N. S. 762 C. P.

[3] *Re* Marriott *v.* London & South-Western Rail. Co., 26 L. J. C. P. 155; Caterham Rail. Co., *In re*, 1 C. B. N. S. 410; 26 L. J. C. P. 161; *Ex parte* Painter, 2 C. B. N. S. 705; Ransome *v.* Eastern Counties Rail. Co., 27 L. J. C. P. 166.

[4] Nicholson *v.* Great Western Rail. Co., 28 L. J. C. P. 89; BYLES, J., in Garton *v.* Bristol & Exeter Rail. Co., 28 L. J. C. P. 310.

[5] Cooper *v.* London & South-Western Rail. Co., 27 L. J. C. P. 324; Ransome *v.* Eastern Counties Rail. Co., 27 L. J. C. P. 166; cf. Crickmar *v.* Eastern Counties Rail. Co., 26 L. T. Rep. 220; Baxendale *v.* Great Western Rail. Co., 28 L. J. C. P. 72.

while they refuse to grant the whole amount of relief which is prayed for.

It has been decided that, where a rule to show cause has been obtained upon affidavits, the complainant will not be allowed to file additional affidavits to strengthen the rule, even although the other side have not filed affidavits in reply, or done anything except give notice of their opposition to the rule. But if the court thinks fit, it may allow the complainant to abandon the rule and move a new one, and will suspend the costs of the rule so abandoned until after the new one has been disposed of.[1] Where the affidavits disclose circumstances of a special nature, which are essentially matters of calculation, and such as cannot be conveniently dealt with by the court, it will refer the case to the master, who will take the evidence and report thereon to the court. On the report the court will act with due regard to the conflicting rights and interests of the public and the company.[2] The court will not, when a rule has been disposed of, allow it to be reopened on affidavits of new facts, although they have the power to do so if they think fit.[3]

SEC. 367. **Attachments.** — The court refused to grant an attachment against a railway company for disobedience to a writ enjoining them to desist from giving an undue preference in respect of the carriage of coals from a certain place, P., or other places to or towards certain other places mentioned in the order, the affidavits on the part of the company showing a *bonâ fide* endeavor to conform to the order of the court, although it appeared that the reformed scale of charges still operated, in some other respects, injuriously to the interests of the complainants, and advantageously to the parties.[4]

SEC. 368. **Costs.** — Where costs are not asked for, they will not be given,[5] although in one case, where an application was

[1] Ransome *v.* Eastern Counties Rail. Co., 2 L. T. N. S. 237.

[2] Nicholson *v.* Great Western Rail. Co., 2 L. T. N. S. 234; 28 L. J. C. P. 89.

[3] Baxendale *v.* Great Western Rail. Co., 32 L. T. 257; 28 L. J. C. P. 85 n.

[4] Ransome *v.* Eastern Counties Rail. Co., 4 C. B. N. S. 159; 4 Jur. N. S. 859; and see De la Rue *v.* Fortescue, 2 H. & N. 324; 26 L. J. Exch. 339.

[5] Marriott, *In re*, 3 Jur. N. S. 493; 26 L. J. C. P. 154.

made under 17 & 18 Vict. c. 31, and the rule was moved without mention of costs, it was made absolute with costs.[1] When the rule is moved with costs, it will either be made absolute with costs[2] or discharged with costs.[3] Where a complainant asked for a rule more than he was entitled to, and the company was proved to have been partially in the wrong, the court refused to allow costs to either.[4] Where a railway company has so acted as to render it necessary and proper for any person to come to the court for redress under the Railway and Canal Traffic Act, the court will, as a general rule, make the rule absolute with costs.[5] Where a judge at chambers, in the exercise of his discretion, had refused to allow costs upon the unsuccessful application for an injunction under this act, the court refused to review his decision.[6]

SEC. 369. **Restrictions Independent of 17 & 18 Vict. c. 31, § 2.** — But, besides those restrictions which are placed upon the trade of a carrier by the statute, the provisions of which we have just considered, other restrictions have been placed on the free exercise of the trade of carriers, who carry by rail, either by the special acts under which they were incorporated or by the courts of law, with a regard to the rights of the public and the necessary conditions of a healthy commerce. Many cases which do not fall under the Railway and Canal Traffic Act, 1854, have come before our courts, and from the decisions in these it may be gathered that the charges for the carriage of like goods under similar circumstances must be the same; that where there is additional risk incurred by the carrier he is entitled to charge an additional premium; that a mere difference of packing, which has been effected with a view to the convenience of the sender, will not justify an increase of charge; but that a difference in bulk, quality, or

[1] Ransome *v.* Eastern Counties Rail. Co., 26 L. J. C. P. 154.

[2] Baxendale *v.* Great Western Rail. Co., 28 L. J. C. P. 69.

[3] Nicholson *v.* Great Western Rail. Co., 28 L. J. C. P. 86.

[4] Oxlade *v.* North-Eastern Rail. Co., 1 C. B. N. S. 454.

[5] Baxendale, *In re*, *v.* London & South-Western Rail. Co., 12 C. B. N. S. 758.

[6] Ilfracombe Public Conveyance Co. *v.* London & South-Western Rail. Co., 4 L. R. C. P. 151.

weight may be a ground for difference in the price of the carriage of goods. It will, however, be better to consider these principles in connection with the cases in the course of which they have been enunciated, both on the ground of brevity and clearness.

SEC. 370. **Railway Company's Power to impose Tolls and Charges.** — We have seen that it is usual to empower a railway company to impose certain tolls and charges for the carriage of goods on their line, and a case came before the court in which the extent of the applicability of such a power was discussed. There a company had under its original act this power conferred upon it. But subsequently it obtained certain other acts, and, among them, one which empowered the company to make a junction and branch railways, incorporating the Lands' and Railways' Clauses Acts, and including a number of enactments, in which the words "the railway" were used in some places so as to be applicable only to the junction and branch lines, but in others, which had the effect of introducing a new system of tolls and charges, implying that "the railway" meant the whole system belonging to the company. This was a question of construction, and it was held that the term "the railway" must, in the light of all the statutes of the company, and under all the circumstances, mean the whole system of railway belonging to the company, and that it was over it that the tolls and charges were intended to extend, and not over the junction and branch line only.[1]

SEC. 371. **"Manufactured Goods," what they are.** — Another case, which decided a principle which may be regarded as preliminary to those involved in the questions of equality of charges for similar articles, may be taken cognizance of in this place. There a railway company was entitled to charge a certain rate "for all cotton and other wools, drugs, and manufactured goods;" and it was held that this meant not all goods "upon which human skill was employed, but those articles made in what are in popular language called manufactories."[2]

[1] Bristol & Exeter Rail. Co. *v.* Garton, 4 H. & N. 33; 28 L. J. Exch. 169 Exch. Ch.

[2] Parker *v.* Western Rail. Co., 6 El. & Bl. 77; 25 L. J. Q. B. 209.

SEC. 372. **Construction of Special Acts.** — Before considering the general principles which have regulated the framing of the special acts of railway companies, in so far as these acts empower the companies to exact tolls and charges according to certain definite principles, it is well to remember that each act must be read with due reference to its special language and application, but that at the same time a certain unity of principle is to be found in all these acts, and in all the cases which have come before courts of law in which the construction of these acts was in question. The cases which have been examined will illustrate this statement.

SEC. 373. **Inequality of Charge.** — The Grand Junction Railway Company became carriers on the London and Birmingham lines, and published a list of charges for the carriage of goods from Manchester to London. They were by their special acts empowered to carry on a fixed scale of reasonable and equal charges. Among the items in the published list, the carriage of "Manchester packs," from the former of these two places to the latter, was charged 3*s.* 3*d.* per cwt., or 65*s.* per ton. At the foot of this list there was a notice that goods were brought to the station at Camden Town, without extra charge, and that there was no charge for delivery in London. The company made an agreement with Messrs. Chaplin and Horne, that the latter should carry from the station, and deliver in London all such goods carried by the railway, and for so doing should receive 10*s.* per ton out of the entire charge of 65*s.* per ton. At the same time, the company charged 65*s.* per ton, even when the goods were received by the persons to whom they were sent, or by their agents at Camden Town; and the court held this to be both an unreasonable and unequal charge upon the part of the company.[1]

SEC. 374. **Packed Parcels.** — Another question arose in the course of this case, and that was whether, on a scale which fixes a lower rate of charge for goods above a specified weight, and a higher charge under that weight, can a parcel above the

[1] Pickford *v.* Grand Junction Rail. Co., 10 M. &. W. 399; 3 Rail. Cas. 193. See, also, Parker *v.* Great Western Rail. Co., 17 M. & G. 253; 7 Scott, N. R. 855.

specified weight consigned to one person, but in reality composed of different packages for different consignees, each of which parcels is under the specified weight, be charged on the higher scale, either as an entire package, or as if each of such parcels had been sent separately? In deciding in the negative, PARKE, B., said: "The charge is no doubt to be varied according to the trouble, expense, and responsibility attending the receipt, carriage, and delivery of different articles; and for small parcels more ought to be paid than a proportionate part, according to weight, of the price of larger parcels of the same commodity, by reason of the greater trouble in receiving, despatching, and delivering them, and their exposure to much greater risk of abstraction or loss. But if all the small parcels are united in one large package, and delivered to a carrier in that package consigned to one person, the trouble and responsibility are apparently reduced precisely to the same degree as if all the articles contained in the package were the property of the same owner, and intended to be delivered to him. There would seem, therefore, to be no right to charge for such package of distinct parcels, belonging to different owners, more than if they belonged to the same."[1]

SEC. 375. **How Equality of Charge is to be estimated.** — The question, then, as to whether the charges are equal and alike in two cases must be decided by a consideration of the circumstances of the case; for if any circumstance renders the carriage of the goods of one person a greater trouble, a greater expense, or a greater responsibility[2] to the carrier than the carriage of the similar goods of another, he is entitled to charge more to the former than the latter, and that without inequality, upon the Spartan principle of calling that equal which is just, and not calling that just which is equal.

SEC. 376. **Extortion under Company's Special Act.** — The London and North-Western Railway Company was empowered to take rates and tolls from all persons alike under the same and similar circumstances. Their ordinary price for

[1] 10 M. & W. 422.

[2] See Baxendale *v.* Eastern Counties Rail. Co., 4 C. B. N. S. 63; 27 L. J. C. P. 137; Branly *v.* South-Eastern Rail. Co., 12 C. B. N. S. 74; 31 L. J. C. P. 286.

carrying a parcel from L. to B. was ½*d.* per pound. They refused to carry the plaintiff's parcel from L. to B. unless he paid 1*d* per pound; and, the plaintiff having done so, it was held that the charge was an extortion under the company's special act, and that the plaintiff was entitled to recover back the excess of his payment over the ordinary rate.[1]

SEC. 377. **Reduction in Favor of some Carriers for Loading, &c.** — A railway company (the Great Western) was authorized by its act to make rates and tolls for goods and passengers conveyed by others than the company along the railway which should be reasonable and equal to all persons. And by a subsequent act the charges for the carriage of any passengers, goods, &c., to be conveyed by the company, or for the use of any power supplied to them, should be, at all times, charged equally to all persons, and after the same rate per mile, or per ton per mile, in respect of all passengers, and of all goods of the like description to be conveyed by a like carriage on the same portion of the line, and no reduction or advance in any charge for conveyance, or for the use of any locomotive power to be supplied by the company, should be made either directly or indirectly in favor of or against any particular company or persons travelling upon, or using the same portions of the railway. Upon a case stated for the opinion of the court, it appeared that the company had always charged the public for the carriage of goods at the rates specified in certain printed bills, and a scale-book annexed to the case, and that for such charge they performed the loading, unloading, and reloading of the goods, as explained in the case, and also the weighing, but that by a general arrangement with carriers the latter had performed all these duties, and, in addition, had made out what they called ticking-off notes and carriers' declaration tickets, and had been allowed by the company a deduction of 10 per cent from the charges made to the public at large, — the performance of these duties being stated in the case to be a reasonable equivalent for the allowance of 10 per cent. The question was whether the company was justified in withholding the allowance from the

[1] Crouch *v.* London & North-Western Rail. Co., 2 C. & K. 789.

plaintiff, a carrier who was willing to discharge, and in fact did discharge, the duties, for the performance of which such allowance was made. And it was decided that they were not, and that the proof that the company were ready and willing to perform all the things which formed the consideration for the allowance was immaterial.[1]

SEC. 378. **Aggregate Weight, and Separate Parcels charged for. — Disclosure of Name of Consignor and Consignee.** — In the same case it appeared that if any of the public (not being a carrier), as a consignor, brought several packages of goods addressed to different consignees and paid the charge, or if several of the public brought several packages addressed to one consignee (not being a carrier), who paid the carriage, the company had been in the habit of charging upon the aggregate weight only. If, on the other hand, a carrier, under the same circumstances, acted as a consignor or consignee of goods, the company had been in the habit of charging separately for each package. From the principles already enunciated, the decision on this point was "that the company are bound to treat the plaintiff as consignor and consignee for all purposes, including the mode of charging in the aggregate, and that they have no right to make a distinction in that respect between him and any other individual member of the public." The learned judge, TINDAL, C. J., went on to remark: "Of the sum constituting this third head of claim it appears that a small portion, *17l. 5s. 5d.*, would not have been discharged had he disclosed the names of the consignors and consignees of the goods; but we find nothing in the statute requiring him to make such a disclosure, and the company had no right to withhold from him, in consequence of his refusal to make it, any allowance to which he would have been otherwise entitled."

SEC. 379. **Principles.** — Each of the points raised in that case was decided according to the principles which we have so repeatedly alluded to: That even the indirect favor which a railway company has it in its power to show to certain indi-

[1] Parker *v.* Great Western Rail. Co., 7 Scott, N. R. 835; 7 M. & G. 253; 13 L. J. C. P. 105.

viduals of the public, or certain individuals of a class, has the effect of directly prejudicing the public. It cannot be doubted that had the company been allowed to persist in its refusal to allow the plaintiff the reduction of 10*l.* per cent on the charges made to the public, and to grant that reduction to other carriers, the result would have in the first instance been prejudicial to the plaintiff, but it would indirectly have prejudiced the undoubted rights of the public. Again, the fact that a consignor is a common carrier is not a reason why he should be charged more than a consignor who does not carry on that trade. The existence of a class of persons who devote themselves to that particular kind of work is a decided advantage to the public. To charge them more than is charged to individuals who are not carriers, would, of course, compel them to carry on their trade at a disadvantage, or might compel them to abandon it in favor of one in which the restrictions, which it is in the power of a monopolist to impose, cannot militate against their reasonable profits. Thus it would come about that the public would be injured by this provision of the company, that a useful trade would be abolished, and that the company would, in all probability, become the collectors and deliverers of goods to be forwarded by rail at a monopoly charge, — hence the necessity of interference in the case just alluded to; and, in another, in which the company was empowered by its special act, and by the 8 & 9 Vict. c. 20, § 90 (The Railways Clauses Consolidation Act, 1845), which was incorporated with its special act, to charge what sum it thought fit for the carriage of parcels, and had the power of changing and varying its tolls and charges, but that always under the proviso that they were to be charged equally to all persons, and to advantage none and prejudice none. In that case the company charged more to a common carrier than they did to the rest of the public, and it was held that such overcharging upon the part of the company was not justified. And, at the same time, it was very properly admitted that the company might charge more for packed parcels than for an ordinary package.[1]

[1] Crouch *v.* Great Northern Rail. Co., 9 Exch. 556; 7 Rail. Cas. 787; 23 L. J. Exch. 148.

SEC. 380. **All the Provisions of Special Act to be considered.** — A class of cases, which, at first sight, resembles the above, is to be distinguished from it. The case of Parker *v.* The Great Western Railway Company [1] will illustrate the distinction. It was proved that the company had entered into an agreement with agents to collect and deliver goods for them. The agents charged the public a small sum for so doing, and at the same time received an additional allowance out of the receipts of the company. It appeared that by their act the company, while it was bound to charge all persons equally for conveyance, was, nevertheless, entitled to make agreements as to the collection and delivery of merchandise. At the same time there was a proviso that any one prejudiced by any such arrangement upon the part of the company giving special facilities to others might appeal to sessions against such an arrangement. It also appeared that the plaintiff, a carrier, who collected and delivered his own parcels, was charged as highly as the rest of the public. Consequently the effect of the arrangement above alluded to was to cause him to carry at a disadvantage, as, in reality, the goods sent by him were charged more for than the goods which were sent by the railway company's agent. As, however, the plaintiff had not appealed to the sessions against the agreement between the company and the agents, the agreement must be held to be without prejudice to the interests of the plaintiff, and, consequently, it did not render the charges of the company an overcharge. The distinction between these two cases is very obvious.

SEC. 381. **Proviso for Collection and Delivery of Goods.** — Where a company had the ordinary powers to charge what they thought fit, to vary such charges, always under the proviso that the charges were to be made equally to all persons, they had, as in the last case referred to, a power to enter into or make arrangements for the collection and delivery of goods. By a subsequent act some modification was made in the powers of the company. By it they were enabled to demand for the carriage of small parcels, *i. e.* parcels not exceeding 500

[1] 6 El. & Bl. 77; 2 Jur. N. S. 325; 25 L. J. Q. B. 209.

lbs. weight each, any sum which they thought fit. They had been in the habit of allowing a rebate in their charge for the conveyance of goods along their line when the goods were brought to or received at their stations. They, with a view to changing their practice in this respect, issued a notice, that for parcels under 500 lbs. weight, they would no longer make the usual allowance, and they then charged the through rate, as if goods had been collected and delivered by themselves. It was held that the company was not entitled to charge parties who brought their goods to, and received them at, the different stations the same rate that was charged to others not so bringing and receiving their goods, and that the plaintiff was entitled to recover back from the company the amount of the rebate in an action for money had and received.[1] This decision was affirmed on appeal.[2]

SEC. 382. **Change of Practice.** — There is nothing unreasonable in a company changing its practice, in so far as, instead of carrying bulky commodities at certain rates per ton, giving notice that in the future it will only carry such articles on certain terms other than those, *viz.* at a certain minimum rate per truck (capable of carrying three tons), whether filled or not, the rate per ton being far less than the ordinary rate. And where a case of this character came before the court, and it was proved that although the plaintiff objected to the terms, yet without any departure of the company therefrom he continued to send such commodities, sometimes in quantities less than three tons, the court held that he was not entitled to be charged, as he claimed, at the minimum rate per ton, and was bound to pay at the rate per truck. The court also decided that there was nothing unreasonable in such a rate of charge, and that even if there were, the proper remedy was under 17 and 18 Vict. c. 31.[3]

SEC. 383. **Strictness of Construction of Special Acts.** — Some strictness is to be used in the construction to be placed

[1] Baxendale *v.* Great Western Rail. Co., 14 C. B. N. S. 1; 32 L. J. C. P. 225; 9 Jur. N. S. 1174; 8 L. J. N. S. 833.

[2] 16 C. B. N. S. 137; 33 L. J. C. P. 197; 10 Jur. N. S. 496; 12 W. R. 602; 9 L. T. N. S. 814 Exch. Ch.

[3] Great Western Rail. Co. *v.* Toorner, 11 W. R. 464 Q. B.

upon the special Acts of Parliament under which railway companies operate. And, as we have seen, the rule for construing such acts is to regard them unfavorably to the parties procuring them, and favorably — after a comprehensive view of their whole bearings — to the public; for it must be remembered that these acts are passed not with the direct view of aggrandizing a company, but of benefiting the community. Thus, where a railway company were required by their special act to carry as common carriers for hire, and to afford to all persons conveying or sending goods upon their railway every reasonable convenience and facility for loading and unloading goods, and the act also authorized the company to demand a toll not exceeding 3*d.* per ton per mile, it was held that the company were not entitled to charge an additional sum for services performed, accommodation afforded, and expense and risk incurred in and about the receiving, loading, unloading, and delivering (terminal charges) the goods.[1]

SEC. 384. **Terminal Charges in relation to Special Act.** — The services in that case were the unloading of 100 sacks of flour from the carts in which the plaintiff conveyed the flour to the defendants' station, wheeling it to the platform, and there reloading it upon the defendants' trucks. And it was thought by the court that the defendants had as much right to charge for the expense of making the railway as for the performance of these services. The remuneration for both of these things, to which the defendants were undoubtedly entitled, was covered by the sum allowed to be charged by the statute. Regard being had to the obligations of common carriers, which are these, — that persons holding themselves out to the world as common carriers are under an obligation to act as such (1) in relation to goods they profess to carry (2) and have accommodation for, (3) provided that the goods are tendered to them with a reasonable remuneration, and (4) without subjecting the owner of the goods to any unreasonable condition,— it was, evidently, an unwarrantable exercise of the functions of a railway company to refuse to carry the goods of

[1] Pegler *v.* Monmouthshire Rail. Co., 6 H. & N. 644; 39 L. J. Exch. 249; 9 W. R. 597.

a certain individual, unless he signed certain unjust and unreasonable conditions. In the case in which that was decided, it appeared that the Bristol and Exeter Railway Company had, in addition to the charges for the carriage of goods from place to place, charged for collection and delivery where, in fact, they had not collected, and did not deliver the goods. Under these circumstances the plaintiff, having paid such charges, was entitled to recover.[1] So, by its first act, it was empowered to charge for the carriage of parcels, but, by a subsequent act, which amended the former act, the company was authorized to carry at so much per ton per mile, and it was decided that the latter provision overrode the former so far as concerned parcels exceeding 500 lbs. in weight, but not as to parcels below that weight, and that if there had been an excess paid upon parcels exceeding 500 lbs. in weight, it might be recovered back.[1] Besides that, where sometimes by mistake, and sometimes intentionally, the company had charged the sender a heavier rate than was set out in the bills published by them, the difference or excess might be recovered.[1] Where, however, the charges had been unequal, not *inter se* as regards the individual himself, but unequal as looked at in comparison with those demanded of others, the plaintiff could not recover the sum in which the former was in excess of the latter.[1] Inequality in the amount of trouble or expense incurred by the railway company is a good ground for inequality in the charges made by them for the conveyance of goods. But such an inequality will require to be clearly made out. Thus in Baxendale *v.* London and South-Western Railway Company[2] the company was proved to be bound to take the same rates and charges from all persons alike under the same or similar circumstances. They were in the habit of charging a tonnage rate upon goods over one hundredweight, and a higher rate for articles under that weight; when several parcels, each under one hundredweight, were delivered at one and the same time to the company by one person in a single consignment, and

[1] Garton *v.* Bristol & Exeter Rail. Co., 1 B. & S. 112; 30 L. J. Q. B. 273; 9 W. R. 734.

[2] 4 H. & C. 130; 35 L. J. Exch. 108; 1 L. R. Exch. 137; 14 W. R. 458; 12 Jur. N. S. 274.

addressed to one and the same consignee, the company charged a tonnage rate upon the aggregate weight. Common carriers (the plaintiffs in the action) used the company's railway for transmitting large consignments of goods directed to themselves as consignees, each of such consignments consisting of several parcels, many of them bearing the names and addresses of the persons to whom they were to be conveyed by the plaintiffs. The company charged the plaintiffs for each parcel contained in each consignment, according to the weight of the package, and such charge was, as compared with that made to other persons, held to be an inequality, and it was also held that the plaintiffs were entitled to recover back the excess.[1]

SEC. 385. **Charges for Packed Parcels.** — Of course it is unreasonable to make different charges to different persons for the same packed parcels. There may be additional risk attendant upon the conveyance of packed parcels, and some extra charge might not be unreasonable upon that ground, although MARTIN, B., was inclined to lay down the general rule "that no extra charge should be made for such parcels;" but it is evidently an unreasonable inequality to charge 50 per cent, in addition to the usual rate for the highest charged description of goods, for such parcels when they are sent by carriers, such a charge not being exacted when packed parcels are sent by any other individual.[2]

SEC. 386. **Rules of Construction.** — One rule of construction must be noticed, and that is, that where a company has an absolute power given to it by an Act of Parliament to fix charges for railway carriage, such power is not rendered conditional by a subsequent clause, requiring that all the charges made shall be made equally on like goods carried under like circumstances for all persons, the court holding, in the case of The Great Western Railway Company *v.* Sutton, that the condition only attaches after the power has been exercised.[3]

[1] See also Garton *v.* Bristol & Exeter Rail. Co., 1 B. & S. 112; 30 L. J. Q. B. 273; 7 Jur. N. S. 1234.

[2] Garton *v.* Bristol & Exeter Rail. Co., 4 H. & N. 33; 28 L. J. 169 Exch Ch. We shall have another opportunity of considering the subject of packed parcels.

[3] 4 L. R. H. L. Cas. 226; 38 L. J. Exch. 177; 18 W. R. 92.

Another point which is of importance in connection with the construction not only of special acts but of the Railway Clauses Act and other public statutes, is the question as to the precise meaning of the equality clause when it speaks of things of the "like description" conveyed under the "like circumstances."

SEC. 387. **Meaning of "Like Description" and "Like Circumstances.** — In his answer to the question proposed to the judges by the Lord Chancellor (CAIRNS) in the case last referred to, WILLES, J., said: "The question as to the meaning of that clause ought, I think, to be answered by saying that things are of a 'like description' when — although their component parts are 'not identical,' which would be expressed by 'the same description,' and not 'like description' — they are like in those qualities which affect the risk and expense of carriage, and that they are conveyed under like circumstances where the labor of risk and expense are, in the opinion of the jury, the same; otherwise not. For instance, bags of red wheat and bags of white wheat are in the nature of things of a like description. Bags of cotton and bags of jute, of like weight and value, are of the like description, if there is no other dissevering circumstance proved; but if it were superadded that one was more risky or troublesome to carry than the other, the jury would hold that the goods were of different descriptions; and bags of silk may be suggested as an instance in which the jury were sure so to hold. I think 'like description' is exhausted upon the goods, and 'like circumstances' upon the carriage, and that neither can be extended to the personal qualities of the individual who sends the goods." And these opinions were indorsed by LORD CHELMSFORD in giving the judgment of the House of Lords.[1]

SEC. 388. **As to Packed Parcels and Inequality of Charge. — Grounds of Warrantable Inequality. — Principles considered.** — The question as to the meaning of the equality clause naturally leads us to the consideration of a class of cases in which the question as to whether the packing of the parcel sent is to be allowed to warrant an inequality in the charge, has come

[1] Great Western Rail. Co. *v.* Sutton, 38 L. J. Exch. 184.

before the courts of law; and we are of opinion that the above excerpt from the answer of MR. JUSTICE WILLES contains the principle which must regulate the decision of all such cases. Wherever there is such a difference in the nature, either of the goods themselves, or of the way in which they are sent, as will cause a greater amount of trouble, expense, or risk to the railway company, they are entitled to make an additional charge, but the addition to the ordinary charge for the conveyance of goods must be reasonable. It is evident that a freedom to increase charges under any other circumstances or conditions might be productive of incalculable evil, directly to the public, and indirectly to the railway company. The monopoly of railways has, as yet, only extended to the carriage of goods of large amounts, or for long distances, and there is still a class of carriers who undertake the conveyance of small parcels, or who carry for short distances in our towns. If a railway company confines itself to the transmission of goods between its own stations, such a business almost necessarily implies the existence of other carriers who will undertake the conveyance of the goods, to be despatched by rail, from the house of the consignor to the company's station, and who will, after the goods have been transmitted, convey them from the destination station of the company to the house of the consignee. Such a trade for the collection and delivery of goods may be extensive and lucrative; and, in many instances, firms have been able, through their branch establishments, to perform the double duty of collecting and delivering the same goods. Under such circumstances the expediency of the consignor making a payment which would cover the whole expenses of the collection, transmission by rail, and delivery to the carrier with whom he was brought into immediate contact, suggested itself. That being the case, the railway company would carry for the carrier, as consignor to the carrier's agents, as consignee, and the names and directions of the ultimate consignees on the parcels would be a matter of trouble and labor to the carrier's agent, but not to the railway company, if there was, through the legibility of the direction, no doubt about the destination of the parcels, in so far as their own duty in connection with them went. Therefore, as the number or addresses of the parcels did not increase the risk, trouble, or expense of the company, or make it greater than what it would have been if they had not been so directed and packed, there could be no reason for a larger charge, in consequence of the fact of their being so addressed to different consignees. That such a course, if pursued, would have some object, is obvious; and that, had it been permitted, it would have had an effect, is equally clear.

SEC. 389. **The Probable Result of such a System.** — The result of the imposition of such extra charge would have been the annihilation of the system we have described above. The carriers would no longer have been able to carry on the work they had been able to perform at the same rate, and either the work that was effected by one transaction would have had to be done by means of two or more such bargains or transactions, or the railway company would, either itself or by its agents, have extended its monopoly to the collection and delivery of goods. Thus a system which the convenience of the public had suggested, and the success of which had been confirmed, would have been broken up, and inconvenience to the public and injury to trade would have been the result; but such a charge under such circumstances was held to be unreasonable.[1]

SEC. 390. **Company's Power to prevent Carriers entering into Competition with it considered.** — The case of Piddington *v.* The South-Eastern Railway Company[2] illustrates what we have said. In that case the defendants, by their Act of Incorporation, were empowered to fix the sum to be charged by them in respect of the carriage of small parcels (not exceeding 100 lbs. each), "as to them should seem proper," but there was a proviso that this power was not to extend to "articles, matters, or things sent in large aggregate quantities, although

[1] Pickford *v.* Grand Junction Rail. Co., 10 M. & W. 399; 3 Rail. Cas. 193; S. P. Edwards *v.* Great Western Rail. Co., 11. C. B. 588; 21 L. J. C. P. 21; Crouch *v.* Great Northern Rail. Co., 11 Exch. 742; 25 L. J. Exch. 137.

[2] 5 C. B. N. S. 111; 27 L. J. C. P. 295; 4 Jur. N. S. 953.

made up of separate and distinct parcels, such as bags of sugar, coffee, meal, and the like, but only to single parcels unconnected with parcels of a like nature, which might be sent upon the railway at the same time." By a subsequent act it was provided, "that the charges by that act authorized to be made for the carriage of goods, &c. by the company, should be at all times charged equally to all persons, and after the same rate in respect of all goods of a like description, and conveyed on the same portion of the line, and that no reduction or advance should be made, either directly or indirectly, in favor of or against any particular company or person." The defendant company had charged double the ordinary rate for packed parcels. And the jury having found that the alleged increased risk from the carriage of packed parcels was altogether illusory, it was decided that the company were wholly unjustified in doubling their charge, and WILLES, J., in his judgment, said: "The first circumstance of the goods being packed or tied together does not make them cease to be goods of a like description. . . . It is clear upon the whole facts of the case that the increased charge is made for the purpose of preventing people who are likely to send packages of the description in question, *viz.* carriers, from entering into competition with the company in the conveyance of goods, — a thing which it has over and over again been decided that these companies cannot be permitted to do." In the case of Sutton *v.* Great Western Railway Company, and Sutton *v.* South-Eastern Railway Company,[1] which was tried before MARTIN, B., in London, in July, 1864, it was proved that the plaintiff was a carrier, and that his business was to collect parcels from different tradesmen, to put the parcels into one package, and to send it by railway, that the company issued a tariff of carriage rates, and that the carrier was charged under it for "packed parcels." Evidence was given that four wholesale houses in London were in the habit of sending packages containing their own goods, and also the goods of other tradesmen, and that they were never charged for packed parcels but at a less rate. These

[1] 3 H. & C. 800; 11 Jur. N. S. 879; 35 L. J. Exch. 18; 13 W. R. 1091; 13 L. T. N. S. 221 Exch. Ch.

houses were never asked to state the contents of the packages sent by them, and it did not appear that the company had any direct information on the point. It also appeared in evidence, that at an arbitration, held in London in 1849, it had been proved, in the presence of the company's solicitor, that it was the practice of the London houses to send packed parcels without charge, and the question, "Has this practice of packing parcels been notorious?" having been allowed, it was answered that for the last forty years it had been so general as to be notorious among carriers. The learned judge directed the jury that there was evidence upon which they might find that parcels had been carried by the company for other persons containing goods of a like description, and under like circumstances, at a less rate; and that there was evidence upon which they might find that the company knowingly charged the carrier more than they did other persons; and he left it to them, if they believed that the company knowingly and purposely charged him a higher rate upon a packed parcel than other persons, to find a verdict for the plaintiff. In this case it was held that the evidence was properly received, and that the direction of the judge was correct.[1]

SEC. 391. **Charge for "Smalls."** — In the same case it was held that although the company was entitled, under 10 & 11 Vict. c. 224, § 53, to charge what they think fit for "smalls," it was a power which they must exercise subject to the equality clause (§ 50) of 7 & 8 Vict. c. 3.

SEC. 392. **Every Special Act is to be specially considered.** — While these principles must be a guide in the construction of the special acts under which railway companies operate, and have been had regard to in the framing of these acts, each statute must be carefully considered in all its particular bearings, which may materially alter and vary the general rules as stated above. Thus, in one case, by a special act, a railway company was entitled to charge for goods carried on their line at rates not exceeding certain rates per ton. They were permitted to charge a higher rate for small parcels, not exceeding

[1] Sutton *v.* Great Western Rail. Co., 3 H. &. C. 800; 35 L. J. Exch. 18; and Sutton *v.* South-Eastern Rail. Co., 11 Jur. N. S. 879.

500 lbs. weight, provided that "articles sent in large aggregate quantities, although made up of separate parcels, such as bags of sugar, coffee, meal, and the like, shall not be deemed small parcels; but such term shall apply only to single parcels in separate packages. The plaintiff, a carrier, sent to the company at once many packages, all consigned to one consignee, each parcel being less than 500 lbs. weight, of articles of similar classes, but not being separate packages of one article. That being so, the company charged for them as separate parcels, and it was held that they were justified in so doing, as the proviso applied only to articles that were of such a nature that a large quantity was generally made up in separate packages.[1]

SEC. 393. **Where Equality Clause does not operate.** — In this case, of course, owing to the very definite wording of the statute, the equality clause did not operate, and therefore there was no call for the introduction of those principles which have been enunciated above. A higher charge for small parcels, in proportion to weight, than for large parcels, is reasonable and just. In connection with these, the company does undertake more responsibility, seeing that from the very fact of their size they are more apt to be lost or stolen. Such a provision clearly is in conformity with the necessities of the trade, and with the best opinions expressed upon the obligations of railway carriers. Again, that the higher rate for small parcels should not be charged, if they are merely separate parcels of an aggregate quantity, — say of sugar, — is just, as we have seen that the more trade a company has, the more cheaply can it perform its duties in relation to it; and it is just and reasonable to make reductions in favor of customers who purchase largely or employ you much. In this case, then, and under these circumstances, there was nothing in the conduct of the company which was calculated to prevent carriers entering into competition with the company in the conveyance of goods, and it was, therefore, distinguishable upon the broadest principles from those cases to which we have already alluded.

[1] Parker *v.* Great Western Rail. Co., 6 El. & Bl. 77; 2 Jur. N. S. 325; 25 L. J. Q. B. 209.

SEC. 394. **Separate Parcels.** — The second point which was raised in this case, and which was also given in favor of the company, admirably contrasts with that stated above, so as to mark the distinction we have insisted upon. It appeared that the plaintiff had sent a parcel of coffee less than 500 lbs. weight, and afterwards, although upon the same day, another parcel of coffee, both consigned to himself, and for the same train. When the first was left, notice was given that the plaintiff would probably send more, but it was not received on any special terms. The company charged for these as separate parcels, and were justified in so doing.[1]

SEC. 395. **Where the Contract has been made in a Foreign Country.** — One other case which is to be distinguished, in so far as the principles which led to its decision are concerned, from those above referred to, or rather which confirms those principles by reason of the exceptional nature of the facts, deserves some attention. That is the case of Branley *v.* The South-Eastern Railway Company.[2] That company was incorporated for the conveyance of passengers and goods from London to Folkestone, under acts of Parliament which prohibited them making unequal charges. They obtained another act, enabling them to establish a communication by steam-vessels with Boulogne, which contained no provision as to equality of rates for the carriage of goods. It appeared that there was nothing in the law of France which precluded the company as public carriers from making such contracts for that purpose as they might think most for their own interest. The company, by their tariff, charged certain rates for small parcels, with a double charge for "packed parcels;" and it was held that, so far as regarded the contract for the carriage of such parcels *from Boulogne to London*, there was nothing illegal in this increased charge. This was, of course, decided upon the principle that the legality of a contract is to be determined by the *lex loci contractus*.

SEC. 396. **31 & 32 Vict. c. 119.** — Before quitting this subject, the Regulation of Railways Act, 1868,[3] remains to be

[1] Parker *v.* Great Western Rail. Co., 6 El. & Bl. 77; 25 L. J. Q. B. 209.

[2] 12 C. B. N. S. 63; 31 L. J. C. P. 286; 6 L. T. N. S. 458.

[3] 31 & 32 Vict. c. 119.

mentioned. That act contains provisions of fairs at stations for securing equality of treatment where a railway company works steam-vessels, for securing the public against extortion when two railways are worked by one company, and for the furnishing of particulars of charges for goods, which, as they may be regarded as restrictions upon the railway company, may with advantage be set out in this place.

SEC. 397. **Provision for securing Equality of Treatment where Railway Company works Steam-vessels.**—The 16th section enacts that "where a company is authorized to build, or buy, or hire, and to use, maintain, and work, or to enter into arrangements for using, maintaining, or working steam-vessels, for the purpose of carrying on a communication between towns and ports, and to take tolls in respect of such steam-vessels, then, and in every such case, tolls shall be at all times charged to all persons equally, and after the same rate in respect to passengers conveyed in a like vessel passing between the same places under like circumstances; no reduction or advance in the tolls shall be made in favor of or against any person using the steam-vessel in consequence of his having travelled, or being about to travel, on the whole or any part of the company's railway, or not having travelled, or not being about to travel, on any part thereof, or in favor of or against any person using the railway in consequence of his having used, or being about to use, or his not having used, or not being about to use, the steam-vessels, and where an aggregate sum is charged by the company for the conveyance of a passenger by a steam-vessel and on the railway, the ticket shall have the amount of toll charged for conveyance by the steam-vessel distinguished from the amount charged for conveyance on the railway.

SEC. 398. **Company bound to furnish Particulars of Charges for Goods.**—"The provisions of the Railway and Canal Traffic Act, 1856,[1] so far as the same are applicable, shall extend to the steam-vessels and to the traffic carried on thereby." The 17th section enacts that "where any charge shall have been made by a company in respect of the conveyance of goods over their railway, on application in writing within one week

[1] 17 & 18 Vict. c. 31.

after payment of the said charge made to the secretary of the company by the person by whom or on whose account the same has been paid, the company shall within fourteen days render an account to the person so applying for the same, distinguishing how much of the said charge is for the conveyance of the said goods on the railway, including therein tolls for the use of the railway, for the use of carriages, and for locomotive power, and how much of such charge is for loading and unloading, covering, collection, delivery, and for other expenses, but without particularizing the several items, of which the last-mentioned portion of the charge may consist."

SEC. 399. **Charges where two Railways are worked by one Company.** — The 18th section provides that "where two railways are worked by one company, then, on the calculation of tolls and charges for any distance in respect of traffic (whether passengers, animals, goods, carriages, or vehicles) conveyed on both railways, the distances traversed shall be reckoned continuously on such railways as if they were one railway."

SEC. 400. **Mileage.** — A question arises in this connection, which is of some importance. It is this: Is a railway company, which by its act is empowered to charge a mileage rate for the carriage of goods, and which has an option of conveying the goods by either route, one of which is considerably longer than the other, and has actually conveyed them by the longer route, entitled to charge the mileage rate for the route actually taken? And it was decided that it was so entitled,[1] if such deviation was reasonable. WILLES, J., said: "A carrier is not bound to carry goods by the shortest route, but only by the route by which he generally carries them, and which he professes to go. In the old coach days two coaches often travelled between the same two towns by different routes, one longer than the other, and I apprehend that if the act now under discussion had applied to such coaches, they would each have been entitled to charge for the distance they actually went. So the South-Eastern Railway Company, who have

[1] London & South-Western Rail. Co. *v.* Myres, 21 L. T. N. S. 460; 18 W. R. 69; 5 L. R. C. P. 1.

made a new and shorter line through Sevenoaks, might keep that for passenger traffic and use their old line for the carriage of goods, and might charge for the longer distance which they would thus actually carry them." That is undoubtedly true; but if a company had two such lines to the same place, and one of these was not exclusively used for passenger traffic, but was used, like the other, for both kinds of traffic, it would undoubtedly be a prejudice to one party, of which he would have a right to complain to the court, that while his goods were always sent by the longer route, a rival tradesman's goods were invariably sent by the shorter, by reason of which the latter was advantaged in his trade to the prejudice of the former. And it seems to us that under such circumstances the court would interfere if it could be shown that the company so acted systematically.

SEC. 401. **Recovery of Over-Charges. — The Allowance of Interest. — Amount Recoverable.** — In the case of Edwards *v.* The Great Western Railway Company,[1] which was tried before the 7 & 8 Vict. c. 3, came into operation, it appeared that the company were obliged by 2 & 3 Vict. c. 27, § 24, to charge for carriage to all persons equally, but that they charged Parker, a carrier, more than they did the public. This, as we have seen,[2] had already been decided to be an over-charge, and in this case it was decided that the over-charge was recoverable as money received to the carrier's use. Another point of some importance in connection with this subject was raised in this case. The question was as to whether the arbitrator was authorized, if he thought fit, to give interest. The answer to this question depended on the construction of a statute at that time recent, and on the answer to the question, Was that a sum certain? The plaintiff contended that he had been paying from the commencement a sum certain in excess of every charge. There was a demand in writing of the debt, and a demand of interest under the Act of Parliament, and consequently the court held that there was a sum certain, in respect of which the demand had been made for principal and interest,

[1] 21 L. J. C. P. 72; 11 C. B. 545.

[2] *Ante*, p. 427, and Parker *v.* Great Western Rail. Co., 6 El. & Bl. 77; 2 Jur. N. S. 325; 25 L. J. Q. B. 209.

and that the arbitrator might, if he thought fit, give interest. Where a carrier sent goods by the Bristol and Exeter Railway Company to be carried on their line, as also on that of the Great Western, a continuous line, he objected to the charges as excessive, but paid the amount claimed under protest, making no tender of any sum as a reasonable charge; it was held that he was entitled to recover back the amount paid above what was a fair and reasonable charge in an action for money had and received, and that the whole sum so overpaid was recoverable against the defendants, though a portion of it was received by them as agents for the Great Western Railway Company.[1] In that case it was held that the court was governed by the decision in Ashmole *v.* Wainwright.[2]

SEC. 402. **Where Money was paid to obtain Possession of Goods.** — In that case carriers refused to redeliver the plaintiff's goods, which they had carried for him, except upon payment of *5l. 5s.* charges. He insisted that he was not liable to pay anything; but, ultimately, the carriers, having said that they would take nothing less than the whole sum, he paid the whole to regain his goods, at the same time protesting that he was not liable to pay anything, and that, if he was liable, the charge made by the defendants was exorbitant. He had not tendered or named any smaller sum. The facts, therefore, in this and in the last case were very similar. Afterwards the plaintiff, without having demanded the return of any surplus, brought an action for money had and received, claiming by his particulars the whole sum as having been paid, in order to obtain possession of his goods, under protest that he was not liable to pay the same, or any part thereof; or, if he was liable to pay some part, that the sum was exorbitant. The jury found that the carriers were entitled to 1*l.* 10*s.* 6*d.*, and the court held, upon these facts, that the plaintiff was entitled to recover the difference in this form of action, and that it was not necessary to his right of recovery that he should have

[1] Parker *v.* Great Western Rail. Co., 6 Rail. Cas. 776; 6 Exch. 702. See also Snowden *v.* Davis, 1 Taunt. 359.

[2] 2 Q. B. 837; 2 P. & D. 217; 6 Jur. 729.

tendered any specific sum. Two other points of law may be noticed, shortly, in connection with the question of when money is paid in excess of the amount which a railway company has, under its special acts or under some public statute, a right to charge, and these are, first, that the 17 & 18 Vict. c. 31, does not in any way interfere with the right of a party aggrieved by over-charges to maintain an action to recover back the sums paid in excess.[1] Consequently, where a company has, in contravention of the equality clauses, exacted a larger sum from an individual than it was entitled to charge, the amount of that excess can be recovered back as money had and received.[2]

SEC. 403. **Restrictions upon Carriers other than Railway Carriers.**—We come now to the consideration of the restrictions which are incident to other branches of the trade, and these also are statutory restrictions. As considerable attention and space have been devoted to the consideration of the questions which occur in the event of the carrier being a carrier by rail, it will scarcely be necessary to devote so much time to the restrictions which are imposed upon inland carriers by water, or upon carriers by sea. We have already seen, and the general plan of our work has sufficiently indicated, that there is no distinction in principle between the law relating to one of these classes and the law relating to the other.[3] Independently of certain statutes, already alluded to,[4] the liabilities and duties

[1] Baxendale *v.* Eastern Counties Rail. Co., 4 C. B. N. S. 63; 27 L. J. C. P. 137.

[2] The Great Western Railway *v.* Sutton, 4 L. R. H. L. Cas. 226; 38 L. J. Exch. 177; 18 W. R. 92. Some modifications with regard to inspection of railways, the company's return of accidents to the Board of Trade, &c., were made by the Railway Regulation Amendment Act, 34 & 35 Vict. c. 78, §§ 3, 4, 5, 6, 7, 8.

[3] Per BULLER, J., Trent Navigation Co. *v.* Wood, 3 Esp. 132; Wardell *v.* Mourillyan, 2 Esp. 693; Dale *v.* Hall, 1 Wils. 281; Richardson *v.* Sewell, per LORD ELLENBOROUGH, 2 Sm. 205; Morse *v.* Slue, 1 Vent. 190, 238; Sutton *v.* Mitchell, 1 T. R. 18. See also Story on Bailm. § 496, 5th ed., and Angell on Carriers, 4th ed., § 88.

[4] See 7 Geo. II. c. 15, which enacts that the proprietor of a vessel shall not be liable beyond the amount of the value of the ship and freight for the loss by theft, &c. of certain things, such as gold, silver, &c.; and 26 Geo. III. c. 86, § 2, which exempts the owner of a ship from liability for loss by fire. See also Hunter *v.* M'Gown, 1 Bligh, 573; cf. Morewood *v.* Pollock, 1 El. & Bl. 743; 22 L. J. Q. B. 251.

of carriers on inland waters, or on outland waters, or the sea, are the same as those which affect common carriers on land. Wherever there was ground for distinction between these classes, we have pointed out what that distinction was, and generally upon what principles the distinction had been made.

SEC. 404. **Assimilation of Railway and Canal Traffic Law.** — But when the traffic upon lines of railway was regulated by statutory enactments, the anomalous character of laws which left free canal and navigation companies similarly circumstanced with the railway companies, for which they had legislated, struck the Houses of Parliament, and several acts, which to some extent assimilated the law of canals to that of railways, were introduced and passed.[1] And more recently certain provisions have been made for those carriers who undertake external traffic as well as those who act as carriers within the confines of the realm. We have already pointed out that by the 8 & 9 Vict. c. 28, the power which is given to canal companies and to the commissioners of navigable rivers to vary their tolls, rates, and charges on different parts of their navigation, is restricted by a similar provision to that which is in force in relation to railway companies, — that the tolls shall be charged equally to all persons under like circumstances. We will now quote some of the provisions of another act of the same year, which brought the law which bears upon canal companies still more nearly into conformity or parallelism with that which regulates traffic on lines of railway.[2] It begins by reciting that "whereas by divers Acts of Parliament railway companies have been empowered to convey upon their railways all such goods, wares, merchandise, articles, matters, and things, as may be offered to them for that purpose, and to make such reasonable charges for such conveyance as they may from time to time determine upon, and whereas greater competition for the public advantage would be obtained if

[1] See 3 & 4 Vict. c. 50, and 8 & 9 Vict. c. 28. See also Whitehouse v. Birmingham Canal Co., 27 L. J. Exch. 25; Manley v. St. Helen's Canal Co., 27 L. J. Exch. 159; Cowley v. Mayor of Sunderland, 30 L. J. Exch. 127.

[2] 8 & 9 Vict. c. 42.

similar powers were granted to canal and navigation companies which have from time to time been incorporated or established under the authority of Parliament: Be it therefore enacted: That from and after the passing of this act it shall be lawful for the company of proprietors, trustees, or the undertakers of any canal, river, or navigation, or their respective committees, directors, or managers, or their superintendents, or other agents, by them duly authorized to carry as common carriers, for their own profit, upon their respective canals, rivers, or navigations, or upon any railways or tramways belonging thereto, and constructed under the powers of their respective Acts of Parliament, or upon any other canals, rivers, or navigations communicating therewith, either directly or by means of any intermediate canal, river, or navigation, all such goods, wares, merchandise, articles, matters, and things, as may be intrusted to them for that purpose; and for the better enabling them to do so to purchase, hire, and construct, and to use and employ any number of boats, barges, vessels, rafts, carts, wagons, carriages, and other conveniences, and also to establish and furnish such haulage, truckage, or other means of drawing or propelling the same, either by steam, animal, or other power, or for the purpose of collecting, carrying, conveying, warehousing, and delivering such goods, wares, merchandise, articles, matters, and things, as to any such company or undertakers shall seem fit, and to make such reasonable charges for such conveyance, warehousing, collecting, and delivery as they may respectively from time to time determine upon, in addition to the several tolls or dues which any such company or undertakers are now authorized to take for the use of the said canals, navigations, or railways."

SEC. 405. **Company to be subject to By-laws of any other Company upon whose Canal they may act as Carriers.** — The 2d section provides that "Any such company, commissioners, trustees, or undertakers, using or employing any steam-power for propelling by means of paddle-wheels, boats, barges, vessels, or rafts, upon any canal, river, or navigation (other than the respective canals, rivers, and navigations), shall use and employ the same, subject to such by-laws, rules, and regulations, touching the construction, dimensions, power, rate of speed, and otherwise, of such boats, barges, vessels, or rafts, so propelled by steam as aforesaid, as the directors, commissioners, or undertakers of the canals, rivers, and navigations, respectively, on which such last-mentioned boats, barges, vessels, or rafts shall be used and employed, shall see fit to make and publish in that behalf; and they are hereby authorized and empowered to make and publish such by-laws, rules, and regulations, and from time to time to add to or amend the same as need may require, but it is hereby expressly provided and enacted that any by-laws, rules, and regulations so to be made and published shall be made equally applicable and binding on all companies and persons so using such last-mentioned boats, barges, or other vessels."

SEC. 406. **Powers of such Company, Trustees, &c.** — By section 3, "It shall be lawful for any such company, trustees, or undertakers to purchase or provide and use boats and other vessels, and also horses, steam, or other power, and machinery for hauling, tracking, and towing upon their own canals, rivers, or navigations, or upon any other canals, rivers, or navigations communicating therewith, either directly or by means of any intermediate canal, river, or navigation, and to employ a sufficient number of competent persons for those purposes, and to demand and receive for the use of such boats, and for such hauling, tracking, or towing, such reasonable hire or remuneration as shall be fixed by the respective committees, directors, or managers of such canals or navigations, or as shall be agreed upon between them and any person desiring the use of any such boats or vessels, or requiring such hauling, tracking, or towing."

SEC. 407. **Tolls to be charged equally to all Persons.** — Section 4, however, provides that "All charges to be made by any such companies for the carriage of any such goods or wares, merchandise, articles, or things, or for the use of their boats and other vessels, or for the supply of haulage, trackage, or other power, shall be at all times charged equally to all persons, and after the same rate whether per mile or per ton per mile, or otherwise, in respect of all goods, wares, merchandise, articles, or things of a like description, and conveyed or propelled in a like boat or vessel, at the same rate of speed, and passing along the same portion of any such canal or navigation, under the like circumstances, and no reduction or advance in any of such charges shall be made either directly or indirectly in favor of or against any particular company or person passing along or using, or sending goods, wares, merchandise, articles, or things, along the same portion of any such canal or navigation, under the like circumstances."

SEC. 408. **Liability of such Company.** — And the 6th section of the same act enacts that "Nothing herein contained shall, in any case, extend to charge or make liable any such company further or in any other case than where, according to the laws of this realm, for the time being, common carriers would be liable, nor shall anything herein contained extend to deprive such company of any protection or privilege which either now or at any time hereafter common carriers have or may be entitled to, but such company shall from time to time and at all times have and be entitled to the benefit of every such protection and privilege."

It is, it seems to us, unnecessary to consider this enactment at any considerable length. It is of importance that the writers of text-books should endeavor to make clear the principles which have regulated legislative action with regard to any particular subject, and, at the same time, to make equally clear the principles which have influenced the decisions of our courts of law. But where two enactments are the same in principle, and differ only in their application to facts and circumstances, their duty is performed if they give their readers an opportunity of judging for themselves of the similarity of the principles involved, and allow them to adapt those principles to the varying circumstances of individual cases. It is, however, necessary to state that the 17 & 18 Vict. c. 31, is an act which regulates the traffic and tolls on canals, as well as on railways, as we have seen by the quotations made from it in an earlier part of this chapter, and that the remedies given to the public in the event of preferences given or prejudices imposed by a canal company are the same as those which are bestowed upon individuals complaining of a contravention of the provisions of that act. It is unnecessary, therefore, in this place, as the rules and forms of proceeding against canal companies violating the provisions of this statute[1] were given in the same place, to do more than to refer the reader to what we then said,[2] and to pass on to the consideration of one or two cases which will indicate the similarity of the principles involved in all these cases. This briefly.

SEC. 409. **Light Goods and Heavy Goods.** — Where a canal act gave a higher tonnage for light goods than for heavy goods. If a jury find that certain goods were heavy goods when the act passed, ten years' subsequent consent of the country to consider the same species of goods light goods will not entitle the canal company to demand for these the toll on light goods.[3] By a canal act a toll of one shilling per ton was imposed on all coal, &c. (in addition to the ordinary toll), navigated on any part of the canal from a particular specified place, or from any place within two miles thereof. In a case in which this provision had to be interpreted, it was held that this only applied to voyages commencing within the specified limits, and that no such additional toll was payable for coal loaded at a place more than two miles from the spot specified, although conveyed upon a part of the canal within two miles of that spot.[4] Under a canal act imposing a toll "on coals, lime, timber, bricks, stone, and all other goods, wares, or merchandise whatsoever," gravel, and materials for the repair of turnpike roads are liable to toll.[5]

SEC. 410. **The Rules of Construction applicable to such Acts.** — These and other cases[6] indicate that the rules of construction applied to the special acts of canal companies are the

[1] See Reg. Gen. C. P. H. T. 18 Vict.; 15 C. B. 473, 476.

[2] *Ante*, p. 250 *et seq.*

[3] Staffordshire & Worcestershire Canal Co. *v.* Trent & Mersey Canal Co., 6 Taunt. 151.

[4] Brittain *v.* Cromford Canal Co., 3 B. & Ald. 139.

[5] Coulton *v.* Ambler, 3 Rail. Cas. 724 n.; 13 M. & W. 403.

[6] Fisher *v.* Lee, 12 A. & E. 622; 4 P. & D. 447; Grantham Canal Navigation *v.* Hall, 3 Rail. Cas. 710; 13 M. & W. 114; 13 L. J. Exch. 283; affirmed, 14 M. & W. 880.

same as those which apply to railway companies' acts. This principle will be more clearly understood by a perusal of the under-noted cases, which refer to the amount of tolls so taken on canals, and the circumstances under which these are exigible.[1] With reference to the special subject of this chapter, the restrictions which are imposed upon monopolist companies for the benefit of the public, little need be said. The following cases will illustrate the correctness of the statements made above.

SEC. 411. **Rule in Lees v. Manchester Canal Co.** — In Lees v. The Manchester Canal Company,[2] it appeared that the defendants were empowered to take such rates as should be fixed at a general assembly of the proprietors, not exceeding 1*d.* per ton per mile upon coal, and to reduce the rates at a general assembly held on certain notice, but no such reduction was to be made without the consent of the major part in value of the proprietors. A contract was made by individuals with the company, but not at such general meeting; by which agreement, in consideration that those individuals would make a navigable cut to convey water from their collieries, through land not within the statutable line of the canal, into the canal, and convey the same to the company, the latter should permit them to carry their coals through the cut and along the canal for 1*s.* 3*d.* per ton, the company paying back 6*d.* per ton. This agreement was held to be illegal and void: "1st, as a speculation by which the company might gain more or less than the legislature intended they should take under similar circumstances from the public in general; 2dly, as extending in effect the power of the company to purchase land beyond the limits assigned by the act; 3dly, as enabling them to raise more capital than they were entitled by the act to do, by means of paying for land or works by a total or partial sale of their tolls, which tolls are made security for the money sub-

[1] Tamar Navigation Co. *v.* Wagstaff, 9 Jur. N. S. 1324; 4 B. & S. 288; 32 L. J. Q. B. 295; Same *v.* Grand Junction Canal Co., 11 Exch. 786; 25 L. J. Exch. 222; Reg. *v.* Leicester & Northamptonshire Union Canal Co., 3 Rail. Cas. 780 Exch. Ch.; Leeds & Liverpool Canal Navigation Co. *v.* Hustler, 2 D. & R. 556; 1 B. & C. 424.

[2] 11 East, 645.

scribed or taken on mortgage; and 4thly, because the tolls could, in no instance, be reduced but at a general assembly, and that this, in fact, operated as a reduction of the tolls *pro tanto*."

SEC. 412. **Equality Clause in a Canal Act. — Competition.** — By an Act of Parliament, the Swansea Canal Company was entitled to demand a fixed sum for goods carried upon any part of the canal, which rates should be equal throughout the whole length of the intended canal. By 8 & 9 Vict. c. 28, subsequently passed, proprietors of canals were empowered from time to time to alter, or vary, the tolls granted to them, either upon the whole, or on any particular portion or portions of such canals, according to local circumstances, or the quantity of traffic or otherwise, as they should think fit, with a proviso that such tolls were to be charged equally to all persons, and after the same rate, whether per mile, or per ton per mile, in respect of all goods of the like description conveyed, or propelled, in a like boat passing along, or using, the same portion of the canal under the like circumstances. In this case it was held incompetent to the company to take a proportionally less toll per ton per mile for goods carried a given distance (5 miles) along any portion of the canal than for goods carried less than that distance.[1] In the same case it was held that it was competent to the company to agree to carry at a lower rate for a particular individual in consideration of a large guaranteed minimum toll, in order to enable the company to enter into competition with a rival line of railway.[1]

SEC. 413. **Restrictions on Carriers by Water.** — One reason has induced us to dwell with less minuteness upon all the details incident to the carriage of goods by sea, and that is, that the subject is so carefully considered and so admirably expounded in various works upon shipping. It would almost seem supererogatory to do more than refer to these works for all the accurate and minute information that may be required,

[1] Strick *v.* Swansea Canal Co., 16 C. B. N. S. 245; 12 W. R. 711; 10 L. T. N. S. 460. See also Rex *v.* Tone Conservators, 1 B. & Ad. 561; Goody *v.* Penny, 9 M. & W. 687.

while we, at the same time, point out those general principles which regulate the traffic upon the waters other than canals and navigable rivers. With regard to the subject under consideration, in so far as it refers to ships, and the transit of goods by sea, it may be said that our limits do not permit of our dealing with it in this place. In one light the whole of the statutory provisions with reference to the registration of ships[1] might be looked upon as restrictions upon the common carrier's right to trade under the ordinary obligations imposed upon him by the common law. So also might the statutory regulations with regard to the wages and disbursements,[2] the penalties imposed upon masters of ships for refusing to employ a pilot,[3] and the like, be regarded as restrictions upon the freedom of such a carrier, but these subjects evidently could not be considered in this treatise, and are done ample justice to in works devoted to the law of shipping, and to the consideration of the Merchant Shipping Acts.

SEC. 414. **Inapplicability of some Restrictions to Ship-owners.** — As the same statutory restrictions which have been imposed upon railway and canal companies, with a view of preventing the injury of trade, and the prejudice of the public which would arise, through the spread of monopoly from the trade of conveying to the trade of sale, do not apply, for very obvious reasons, to carriers by sea, and as the statutory regulations which are in force with regard to passenger ships will fall under our notice in a subsequent part of this work, we need in this place do nothing more than end the chapter.

[1] 17 & 18 Vict. c. 104; 18 & 19 Vict. c. 91; 17 & 18 Vict. c. 120, repealing 3 & 4 Will. IV. c. 55; 8 & 9 Vict. c. 89; 12 & 13 Vict. c. 29, and 16 & 17 Vict. c. 131; and as to Certificate of Registry, 17 & 18 Vict. c. 104, § 44, &c.

[2] 17 & 18 Vict. c. 104, pt. iii. § 191; 24 & 25 Vict. c. 10, § 10.

[3] 17 & 18 Vict. c. 104, § 353.

CHAPTER X.

THE RIGHTS OF CARRIERS.

SEC. 415. **Relations of Right and Duty considered.** — Up to the present time we have been, for the most part, occupied in the consideration of the duties of carriers. The right of one man is connected with the duty of another. A right to *a thing* cannot exist. If we can enjoy the uses of a thing, then what we call our right to it is a right to the non-intervention of our neighbors, whose interference might prevent the enjoyment of the uses which the article subserves. This is evidently a right to a duty. Right is a mental fact, and it can only have for its correlative another mental fact, — duty. Now the duties of a carrier are the rights of the public. The duty to carry is a right of the public to have its goods carried. The duty to deliver is a right of those individuals who have intrusted their goods to the carrier for conveyance, to have those goods delivered to the person and at the place to which they were directed and sent. This scarcely requires explanation. It is, however, equally evident that where there are two parties to a transaction, and all the rights are upon one side, and all the duties upon the other, the affair is apt to merit the name of injustice. Of course, where men enter voluntarily into an agreement, it is incumbent upon them to see that they get fair play. As a rule, they are in the habit of effecting this object. And while to a mere spectator there may be seeming injustice in some transaction, there may, nevertheless, be a perfect equilibrium of rights and duties. Such things as generosity and gratitude are facts in human nature, and a man has a perfect right to exercise these mental qualities. Thus a man who is intolerant of a ledger which will not balance to the eighth of a farthing will undertake a great deal of work, or sign a check (which is equivalent to past work) for a charity. Such a transaction, so long as it is voluntarily undertaken, cannot be said to be unjust. In many aspects it is excellent. A man knows best what his rights and duties are. But law has not left all matters to a man's free will. Law has become aware of the fact that, under certain circumstances, a will apparently free is apt to be put really in chains, and the excuse for the interference of legislative enactments with rights is the protection of those who are not in a position to exercise their wills with freedom, and to bring about that equilibrium between rights and duties in every transaction which ought to exist, and which would exist between two men in any case in which they started from equality in rights and in strength with regard to exaction. In every transaction both parties ought to have some advantage. Otherwise transactions would cease. Now the object of all law is, that the advantage gained by each of the parties to any transaction should be as nearly of equal value as it is possible it should be. This is to be brought about by an equilibrium of duties and rights. And as that cannot be effected by simple voluntary acts, the law has interfered to bring it about. Not without much thought have the correlative rights and duties of the carriers and the public been laid down and established. We have already, at some length, considered the rights of the public as connected with the duties of carriers, in so far as the carriage of goods is concerned. We will now consider the rights of the carrier as connected with the duties of the public.

SEC. 416. **Carriers' Right to retain Goods bailed to Them. — Special Property.** — Of course carriers have a right to retain the possession of the goods bailed to them, otherwise they would be unable to do that on account of which the goods were intrusted. Indeed, possession is of the very essence of the lien,[1] and cannot exist except where possession accompanies it.[2] The necessities of law have caused this quasi-right to be designated a *special property*, and, consequently, if the carrier's possession is disturbed, or if injury is done to the goods while they are still in his possession, he can maintain an action by reason of his special property in the goods.[3] The idea connected with the phrase "special property" is, that the property is to be regarded as his (the carrier's) for a special purpose. In a philosophical sense, all property is only a man's for one or two purposes. Absolute proprietorship is impossible. The rights of property are limited in relation to

[1] Jordan *v.* James, 5 Ohio St. 88.

[2] M'Farland *v.* Wheeler, 26 Wend. (N. Y.) 467.

[3] Bac. Abr. Contract, C; Jones on Bailm. 80.

every sense, and they wear out in time. On this subject STORY, J., in his work upon Bailments, has well remarked: "Every bailee ought to have a general right of action against mere wrong-doers to the property while in his possession, whether he has a special property therein or not, for (as it has been well said[1]) a man ought not to be charged with an injury to another without being able to resort to the original cause of that injury, and in amends thereof to do himself right."[2]

* SEC. 417. **Carriers have an Insurable Interest in Goods.** — Carriers have also an insurable interest in the goods in their keeping, and can secure an indemnity against such accidents to the goods in their possession as will render them liable to the consignor.[3] But they have also an insurable interest as against the assurers to the full value of the goods, and not simply to the extent of their own particular interest as carriers in the goods.[4] The rule is that, where by statute, the common law, or by contract, a person is liable to another for an injury to or loss or destruction of property temporarily in his care, he may protect himself against such contingent liability by insurance, as an innkeeper,[5] a lighterman,[6] railroad companies,[7] carriers of every description,[8] warehousemen or wharfingers,[9] or indeed any person having the care or custody of goods for another for any person, who is liable for their

[1] Bac. Abr. Bailments, D. See also The Propeller Commerce, 1 Black (U. S.), 574; Merrick *v.* Brainard, 38 Barb. (N. Y.) 574; Steamboat Co. *v.* Atkins, 22 Penn. St. 522; Dulop *v.* Thorne, 1 Rich. (S. C.) 213; Morgan *v.* Cougdon, 4 N. Y. 551; Bailey *v.* Shaw, 24 N. H. 297; White *v.* Vann, 6 Humph. (Tenn.) 70; Little *v.* Fossett, 34 Me. 545; Ely *v.* Ehle, 3 N. Y. 506; Hagerstown Bank *v.* Adams Express Co., 45 Penn. St. 419.

[2] Story on Bailm. § 93 f.

[3] Crowley *v.* Cohen, 3 B. & Ad. 478; Wolf *v.* Horncastle, 1 B. & P. 316; Carruthers *v.* Shelden, 6 Taunt. 14.

[4] Waters *v.* The Monarch Insurance Co., 5 E. & B. 870; London & North-Western Rail. Co. *v.* Glyn, 1 E. & E. 652.

[5] Wood on Insurance, 527.

[6] Achard *v.* King, Q. B. Dec. 19, 1874.

[7] Eastern R. R. Co. *v.* Relief Ins. Co., 105 Mass. 84; Monadnock R. R. Co. *v.* Manufacturers' Ins. Co., 113 Mass. 74.

[8] Chase *v.* Washington Ins. Co., 12 Barb. (N. Y.) 595; Schackell *v.* West, 6 Jur. N. S. 95; Morewood *v.* Pollok, 1 E. & E. 743.

[9] Getchell *v.* Ætna Ins. Co., 14 Allen (Mass.), 325.

safe keeping.[1] But the important questions in connection with the rights of carriers fall under two heads: 1. Lien; and 2. Remuneration. It will be necessary to consider these with some minuteness. First of Lien.

SEC. 418. **Lien.** — We have already seen that if goods are offered to the carrier along with a reasonable reward for his trouble and expense, he is bound to carry them.[2] That obligation, however, does not arise if he is, from the fulness of his vehicle or conveyance, unable to carry the goods. The law which necessitated impossibilities would be bad; nor does it arise if the goods are not of a nature that he is in the habit of conveying. It would be unfair to ask the proprietor of a stage-coach to carry a cow or a hogshead of molasses. We have, however, already examined this subject at some length, and we know that if the obligation has arisen an action will lie for the breach of this common-law duty of the carrier. Frequently, however, goods are carried by carriers without the reasonable reward to which they are entitled having been paid. It is sometimes much more convenient that the carrier should be remunerated at the end of the journey, or when the goods are delivered, than at the beginning of the journey, when the goods are received. And as the carrier has the goods in his hand, which must almost inevitably be of more value than the amount which is due to the carrier for conveying them, or otherwise they would not be sent, he would in all cases be sure of his remuneration if the law allowed him to retain the possession of the goods at the end of the journey until he had received the reasonable reward which is his due. This is what the law does allow the carrier to do, and the right to do so is the carrier's lien.[3]

SEC. 419. **Property in Goods still in the Consignee.** — The carrier's right of lien is, of course, only a right of possession. The property in the goods is still in the consignee. In many

[1] Chase *v.* Ins. Co., *ante;* Getchell *v.* Ins. Co., *ante.*

[2] Jackson *v.* Rogers, 2 Show. 327; Lane *v.* Cotton, 1 Ld. Raym. 646; Edward *v.* Sherratt, 1 East, 604; Riley *v.* Horne, 5 Bing. 217; Batson *v.* Donovan, 4 B. & Ad. 21, &c.

[3] Wilson *v.* Grand Trunk Rail. Co., 56 Me. 60.

respects the right to lien is like the right to stoppage *in transitu.* The remarks of BULLER, J., in Lickbarrow *v.* Mason,[1] on the right of stopping goods *in transitu*, and on the nature and principles of liens, are directly in point. "Neither of them," he says, "is founded on property, but they necessarily suppose the property to be in some other person, and not in him who sets up either of these rights.[2]

SEC. 420. **Lien a Qualified Right. — How long he can retain Goods.** — "They are qualified rights, but in given cases may be exercised over the property of another; and it is a contradiction in terms to say a man has a lien upon his own goods, or a right to stop his own goods *in transitu.* If the goods be his, he has a right to the possession of them, whether they be *in transitu* or not, he has a right to sell or dispose of them as he pleases without the option of any other person: but he who has a lien only on goods has no right so to do; he can only retain them until the original price be paid, and therefore, if goods are sold for 500*l.*, and by a change in the market before they are delivered they become next day worth 1,000*l.*, the vendor can only retain them till the 500*l.* be paid, unless the bargain be absolutely rescinded by the vendee's refusing to pay the 500*l.*

SEC. 421. **When Liens at Law exist, and when they terminate.** — "Liens at law exist only in cases where the party entitled to them has the possession of the goods, and if he once parts with the possession after the lien attaches, the lien is gone;[3] it is known, and unquestionable law, that if a carrier, a farrier, a tailor, or an innkeeper deliver up goods, his lien is gone."

SEC. 422. **Two Kinds of Liens, Particular and General.** — Liens are of two kinds. They are either particular or general. Particular liens, perhaps more frequently called specific liens, attach only to specific chattels, for the unpaid price or carriage, or for work done on or in connection with

[1] 1 Smith Lead. Cas. p. 736, 6th ed.; 2 T. R. 63.

[2] See opinion of BAYLEY, J., in Bloxam *v.* Sandars, 4 B. & C. 948; 7 D. & R. 396; and that of LORD KENYON, in Hodgson *v.* Loy, 7 T. R. 445.

[3] See Levy *v.* Barnard, 8 Taunt. 149.

them. A general lien attaches to all goods in the possession of the individual in whom the right is vested, and that for claims or demands which need not necessarily arise in relation to the goods retained, but for general claims upon transactions of a nature analogous to that which brought the specific goods retained into the possession of the person exercising the right.

SEC. 423. **Question as to the Expediency of a General Lien.** — Doubt as to the excellence and expediency of the existence of a specific lien in many cases has never, so far as we are aware, existed, but grave doubts have been entertained as to the advisability of the existence of a general lien, and it has been regarded with much jealousy by courts of law.[1] "They" (general liens), observed LORD ELLENBOROUGH, "are encroachments on the common laws.[2] If they are encouraged, the practice will be continually extending to other traders and other matters. . . . It is not for the convenience of the public that these liens should be extended further than they are already established at law. But if any particular inconvenience arise in the course of trade, the parties may stipulate with their customers for the introduction of such a lien into their dealings."

SEC. 424. **Courts discourage General Liens.** — Therefore, where there is no general usage affecting the custom of the realm, where there is no express agreement between the parties, and no evidence to show that they had been in the habit of dealing in the same way on previous occasions, the courts, in accordance with the above opinion, discourage further extension of such liens, and a jury is warranted in negativing any right beyond the specific lien to which parties are entitled at common law.

SEC. 425. **General Usage. — Carrier's Lien. — Effect of General Notices. — The Rule applicable to Carriers.** — A carrier's lien, however, is a particular lien, and where he does set up a claim to a general lien for his general balance, it is not favored unless arising from an implied agreement to be inferred from the general usage of trade, which must be proved by clear and satisfactory instances, "sufficiently numerous and

[1] See Cross on Lien, p. 14.

[2] Rushforth v. Hadfield, 7 East, 229.

general to warrant so extensive a conclusion affecting the custom of the realm; and a few recent instances of such usage amongst the body are insufficient to establish the requisite proof of it."[1] Where, therefore, the common carriers, who carried on their trade in a particular district, proved that such a general right had been exercised by them for ten or twelve, and even in one case for thirty years, it was held insufficient, and, the jury having upon such evidence negatived the general usage, the court refused to grant a rule for a new trial.[2] It would, however, be against all the policy of the law if carriers were prevented from securing such a general lien by a special agreement with those who trust them with goods to be conveyed. The customer, if he clearly understands the whole terms of the agreement, would certainly not have entered into it unless he still, granting this concession, had some advantage from the particular service of the carrier. This is a reasonable presumption, and upon this presumption the carrier is allowed to secure such a general lien in the way mentioned. Difficulty has arisen with reference to this question, as it did in connection with the limitation of the common-law liability of carriers, as to the effect of general notices. In one case, where the defendant was a bleacher, in the county of Lancashire, and one of a great body of persons there, who, having found that losses to a considerable amount were incurred by them from their not being entitled to retain goods put into their hands for a general balance, came to an agreement that they would not receive the goods of any person who would not consent that they should be retained for any general balance that might happen to be due to them. This agreement, which was published and came to the plaintiff's knowledge, was held to be binding upon him; but, as LORD KENYON remarked, it was in the option of those persons who promulgated this general notice to work for this or for that person if they chose,

[1] Rushforth *v.* Hadfield, 6 East, 518; 2 Smith, 624; Whiteheart *v.* Vaughan, 2 Smith, 523 n.; Holderness *v.* Collinson, 7 B. & C. 212; 1 Man. & Ry. 406. See also Aspinall *v.* Pickford, 3 B. & P. 44 n. See also Leonard *v.* Winslow, 2 Grant's Cas. 139; Baggs *v.* Linseed, 1 Black. 108.

[2] Rushforth *v.* Hadfield, 7 East, 224; 3 Smith, 221.

and therefore the rule which applied to them could not apply to innkeepers or carriers. With regard to the latter, he said: "The case of a carrier has been mentioned, but it is not like this. They have no right to say they will not receive any goods but on their own terms. I believe there is an Act of Parliament[1] giving power to the justices at the Quarter Sessions to regulate the price of the carriage of goods."[2]

SEC. 426. **Creation of General Lien by Notice, and by Contract. — Knowledge of Party.** — It has been said that there is an implication in the case of Rushforth *v.* Hadfield,[3] that the common carrier can create a general lien by means of notice;[4] and the words of LORD ELLENBOROUGH would seem to bear out this assertion; while GORSE, J., says: "I take it to be sound law that no such lien can exist except by the contract of the parties expressed or implied." LORD ELLENBOROUGH seemed to think that the knowledge of the party who dealt with the carrier of his intention to create such a lien would warrant the jury in finding that a usage of an extended or general lien existed. But still the words are far from definite, and another construction is not by any means impossible.

SEC. 427. **Proposed Restriction on this Right.** — From the way in which these kinds of lien were spoken of in that case, it seems to the writer of this, that it would be well to restrict the effect of notices with regard to them, as the law has already restricted their effect with regard to the limitation of the carriers' liability. In many cases the detention of goods would be a matter of serious importance to a consignee; and as there was always difficulty in bringing home the knowledge of the notice with regard to limitation of liability to the person sending the goods, the same difficulty would arise in these cases and lead to needless and unnecessary litigation. The circumstances of the case of Kirkman *v.* Shawcross, *ante*, were, as the learned judge remarked, different from those in which a common carrier attempts to create a general lien by means of a notice.

[1] *Vide* 3 W. & M. c. 12; and 21 Geo. II. c. 28. See also Jackson *v.* Rogers, 2 Show. 327.

[2] Kirkman *v.* Shawcross, 6 T. R. 14.

[3] 7 East, 224.

[4] See also, per BAYLEY, J., in Wright *v.* Snell, 5 B. & Ald. 353.

SEC. 428. **Distinction between Duties.** — Where the law imposes no duty upon a man to deal with everybody who chooses to tender him remuneration, and he may deal with whom he pleases, it is incumbent upon each man who wishes to enter into business relations with him to find out the mode in which he is in the habit of dealing. But where the law imposes a duty upon a man to deal with all, and to deal in a certain way, it is the duty of the person so bound to force any difference in his method of dealing upon the notice of those who would be his customers.

SEC. 429. **Restriction of the Right to create Liens.** — As that is the case, and as the whole of the principle of general liens is an encroachment upon the common law,[1] it seems to us well that the right to create such liens should be restricted, and that the doctrine as to the carrier's right to create a lien for a general balance of accounts should stand upon the same footing as the doctrine as to the carrier's right to limit his common-law liability.[2] Such a parallelism would be according to the spirit of the policy of law. Such an assimilation of branches of law would be an exegesis of both.

SEC. 430. **Right of Carrier to retain Goods does not affect Consignor's Right to stop in Transitu.** — In the case of Wright *v.* Snell,[3] a carrier had given notice that all goods would be subject to lien, not only for the freight of the particular goods, but also for any general balance due from their respective owners. Goods having been sent by the carrier, addressed to the order of E. Robinson, who was a mill factor, it was held that the carrier had not, as against the real owner, any lien for the balance due from the factor, E. Robinson.[4] In the

[1] Bock *v.* Gorrissen, 30 L. J. 42 Ch.

[2] *Ante*, p. 252.

[3] 5 B. & Ald. 350. The case of George *v.* Claggett, 7 T. R. 359, differs materially from that quoted above.

[4] MR. CROSS, in his work on Lien (pp. 283, 284), has stated that doubts have been entertained how far the decision in the case of Wright *v.* Snell might have been affected had the notice been more comprehensive in its terms, and included the goods, not only of the respective owners, but of every person to whomsoever addressed; and whether, if that had been so, the carrier would not have been entitled to a general right of lien against all parties. He goes on to remark: "With a view to enable such an enlargement of power, MR. CHITTY, in his Practice of the Law (vol. i. p. 493), has suggested the expediency of introducing

case of Oppenheim *v.* Russell,[1] it was expressly decided that a usage for carriers to retain goods as a lien for a general balance of account between them and the consignees does not affect the right of the consignor to stop the goods *in transitu.*

SEC. 431. **Carrier's Lien a Specific Lien at Common Law. — Applies to Passenger's Luggage.** — At common law, then, a carrier has a specific lien,[2] and is thereby authorized to retain the goods until the price of the carriage, due upon those particular goods, is paid.[3] This rule is, as we should have ex-

words to the effect 'that the goods of all persons dealing with the party in his trade, and whether belonging to the customer *or to any other person or persons, or in which he is in any respect interested,* whether for a lien or otherwise, or which may be in the possession of the advertiser, or whether going from or to his manufactory or premises, must be understood to be, and shall be, subject to a general lien for all moneys due to the advertiser, as well from the customer, as from any person or persons entitled to, or interested in such goods.' Yet, to grant the validity of so extensive a claim would be to allow, by special agreement, a power against third parties, not recognized by the courts, even though sanctioned by immemorial custom (Leuckhart *v.* Cooper, 3 Bing. N. C. 90; 2 Hodges, 150); for, to give validity and effect to usage, it has been decided that it must be reasonable, as well as ancient; and it can scarcely be contended that the detention of the goods of the consignor for the debt of the consignee is either just or reasonable (Leuckhart *v.* Cooper, 3 Bing. N. C. 90). The principle of such decision should, therefore, and probably would regulate the judgment, were the question suggested to come before the court. The precautionary measures proposed in the form of notice may, at least, be pursued *majori cautela;* but to permit the annexation of terms so inconsistent with the general principle, that carriers are compellable to carry the goods of all customers for reasonable reward, would at once be an abrogation of the rule, and a permissive power vested in carriers, which immemorial custom has not been able to establish in others. 'I should doubt,' observed BEST, J. (Wright *v.* Snell, 5 B. & Ald. 355), 'if any form of words would be able to establish a liability of such kind. It is, however, sufficient, in the case before the court, to say that the plaintiff is the owner of the goods, and, there being nothing due from him to the carrier, the modes of the notice do not impose any liability upon him. If any question should arise falling within the terms of the notice last given (see *ante*, p. 336), *it would be very fit to consider whether a carrier can make so unjust a regulation as is there attempted.*"

[1] 3 Bos. & P. 43.

[2] Butler *v.* Woolcott, 2 N. R. 64.

[3] Skinner *v.* Upshaw, 2 Ld. Raym. 752; Rushforth *v.* Hadfield, 6 East, 518; 7 East, 224; Gisbourn *v.* Hurst, 1 Salk. 249; Middleton *v.* Fowler, 1 Salk. 282. A postmaster-general is not, as we have seen (*ante*, pp. 74, 143; Lane *v.* Cotton, 1 Ld. Raym. 646; Whitfield *v.* Lord Le Despencer, Cowp. 744), a common carrier, within the custom of the realm; and, consequently, the above rule is not applicable to him.

pected from what we have already ascertained with regard to the law as it bears upon the luggage of passengers, applicable to such goods as an individual may take with him, who is being carried by means of a public conveyance. Thus it was decided that where a person goes to a coach-office, and directs that a place be booked for him by a particular coach, and in conformity with his request that is done, if he has left his portmanteau (as was the fact in the case under consideration), the coach proprietor has a lien on the portmanteau for something, but not for the full amount of the coach fare; if, on the other hand, the portmanteau has been left during the time that the proprietor has been making inquiries as to whether there is an earlier coach, the carrier will have no lien at all.[1]

[1] Higgins *v.* Bretherton, 5 C. & P. 2. A common carrier has a lien upon goods transported by him, for the freight, and neither the consignee, owner, nor any officer of the law, can take them from him until such freight is paid. Rucker *v.* Donovan, 18 Kan. 231; Langworthy *v.* New York & Hudson River R. R. Co., 2 E. D. S. (N. Y. C. P.) 195; Hunt *v.* Haskell, 24 Me. 339; Sullivan *v.* Park, 33 Me. 438; Goodman *v.* Stewart, Wright (Ohio), 216; Bowman *v.* Hilton, 11 Ohio, 303; Clarkson *v.* Edes, 4 Cow. (N. Y.) 470; Barker *v.* Havens, 17 Johns. (N. Y.) 234. Nor can the owner who stops the goods *in transitu*, on account of the insolvency of the consignee who purchased them of him on credit, take the goods until he has paid the carrier his freight, or tendered it to him. Chandler *v.* Belden, 18 Johns. (N. Y.) 157; Raymond *v.* Tyson, 17 How. (U. S.) 53; The Eddy, 5 Wall. (U. S.) 481; The Schooner Volunteer, 1 Sum. (U. S.) 551. Upon the general proposition, see Cowing *v.* Snow, 11 Mass. 415; Lewis *v.* Hancock, 11 Mass. 72; Lane *v.* Penniman, 4 Mass. 92. But this lien may be waived by the carrier, and, if he delivers the freight to the owner without insisting upon prepayment of the freight, or expressly retaining his lien, he is treated as having waived it. But there must be a complete and unconditional delivery. So long as the goods remain upon his premises, or any part of them, although the owner may have set them apart and put them by themselves with the consent of the carrier, or even sold and taken away a part of them, the lien remains. Thus, in Lane *v.* Old Colony R. R. Co., 14 Gray (Mass.) 143, several cargoes of coal, delivered by their owner upon the wharf of a railroad company, were successively carried over their railroad, and at the place of destination unladen, assorted, and deposited by the owner's servants in bins on the land belonging to the railroad, adjoining the owner's land, and portions carried away and delivered by the owner to purchasers from time to time, until he became insolvent, when the company forbid the taking away of any more coal until the unpaid freight and wharfage had been paid. The court held that the company had a lien upon the coal which remained upon their land for the unpaid wharfage and freight of

SEC. 432. **Where Consignor is Wrongful Owner.** — The right of the carrier to retain the goods for the price of their convey-

all the cargoes. This is in accord with the generally accepted doctrine, that the lien of the carrier is not lost as to goods carried by him so long as any of the goods remain in his possession, although he has delivered a part, as to the part still retained by him. Of course, as to the part actually delivered, his lien is gone, but he may enforce his lien for the *whole* freight upon the part retained by him. Fuller *v.* Bradley, 25 Penn. St. 120; Briggs *v.* Martin, 13 B. Mon. (Ky.) 239. But the owner or consignee cannot insist upon an apportionment of the freight, and its delivery in parcels upon the payment of the freight upon each parcel. The carrier may insist that the whole freight shall be paid before any part of the goods are taken. Brittain *v.* Barnaby, 21 How. (U. S.) 527; and, according to the case last cited, neither can the carrier insist upon a delivery by parcels, and the payment of the freight upon each parcel as delivered, although a contrary doctrine has been held in England. Paynter *v.* James, L. R. 2 C. P. 348. If goods are obtained from a carrier without payment of the freight, by trick or fraud, the lien is not lost, as the carrier's right to the possession still remains, and he may replevy them from the hands of the consignee. Thus, in Bigelow *v.* Heaton, 6 Hill (N. Y.), 43, a carrier delivered goods to a consignee under a fraudulent and false promise that he would pay the freight immediately on receipt. He failed to do so, and it was held that the carrier had not lost his lien for freight, but might disaffirm and sue the consignee in replevin for the goods. Hays *v.* Riddle, 1 Sandf. (N. Y. Superior Ct.) 248. This lien being a personal right, and one which the carrier alone can insist upon or enforce, Ames *v.* Palmer, 42 Me. 197; Everett *v.* Saltus, 15 Wend. (N. Y.) 474; Alden *v.* Carver, 13 Iowa, 253, it follows that he may waive the right, and such waiver may be express or implied; and where the carrier enters into a contract for the transportation of goods by which a credit for freight is given which extends beyond the time when the property transported is to be delivered and placed out of the carrier's control, a waiver of the lien will be inferred, because its existence is inconsistent with the contract. Thus in Pinney *v.* Wells, 10 Conn. 104, a manufacturer, and B, a common carrier, on the 1st of May, 1833, entered into a contract, wherein it was stipulated that B should transport 1,500 tons of anthracite coal, belonging to A, from Philadelphia, and deliver it at Collinsville in this State, between the date of the contract and the 1st of March, 1834; that he should deliver some of the coal at Collinsville by the 15th of June, 1833, and continue to deliver it there so fast that A should not have less than 50 tons on hand at any time between the 1st of June and the completion of the contract; that the coal delivered at Collinsville should be shovelled, by B's men, into the coal-house of A; that in case of any breach of or detention on the canal, B should get the coal along as soon as possible after the breach should be repaired; and in case of such a breach or continued breaches on the canal as should utterly prevent B from getting on the coal, he should be excused from getting it on that season, but should do it the ensuing season, unless A

ance is the same whether the consignor was a wrongful owner or not; and he can retain them until such time as his reason-

should choose to get it round by Connecticut River, which he should have the privilege of doing; that A should pay B for the transportation of the coal from Philadelphia to Collinsville, \$4.37½ per ton; that at the settlement, an interest computation should be made, in which the freight to Avon [a few miles short of Collinsville], and from that place to Collinsville, should be considered as cash, whenever 100 tons should arrive at those places respectively; but that A should have the privilege of giving his notes, payable at the Hartford Bank, instead of paying the cash; all notes so given previous to the 1st of August, 1833, to be payable in four months, and all given after that time to be payable in three months, from the dates thereof. B immediately commenced the transportation of the coal under the contract, and before the 10th of September, 1833, had transported from Philadelphia to New Haven, 1,276 tons, of which he had transported 753 tons from New Haven to Avon, and 653 tons from Avon to Collinsville, when A failed, and made a general assignment of his property, including the coal at New Haven and Avon, in a course of transportation, in the possession of B; and A, at different times between the 28th of June and the 9th of September, 1833, gave B his notes pursuant to the contract, to the amount of \$3,450, which were outstanding at the time of A's failure, and remain unpaid: it was held that this was substantially a contract upon which B gave A a credit, and that B thereby waived the benefit of a lien on the coal in his possession, either for the transportation of the whole, or of the parcels not delivered. See also The Bird of Paradise, 5 Wall. (U. S.) 545; Pickman *v.* Wells, 6 Pick. (Mass.) 248; Tamvaco *v.* Simpson, 19 C. B. N. S. 453; Raymond *v.* Tyson, 17 How. (U. S.) 53; Schooner Volunteer, 1 Sum. (U. S.) 551; Chandler *v.* Belden, 18 Johns. (N. Y.) 157. But it will be seen that in *all* the cases no waiver will be inferred unless the existence of the lien is inconsistent with the contract, which is never the case unless by the terms of the contract it is evident that delivery is to precede the payment of the freight, Howard *v.* Macondray, 7 Gray (Mass.), 516; Clarkson *v.* Edes, 4 Cow. (N. Y.) 470; Drinkwater *v.* Brig Spartan, 1 Ware (U. S. C. C.), 145, or that the freighter is to give security for the freight money, or do some other act, which he fails to do, in which case the lien remains, because the condition precedent to its relinquishment has not been performed. Tate *v.* Meek, 8 Taunt. 280. Nor will the lien be treated as lost, although a credit is agreed on, unless the contract clearly shows that the freight was to be delivered *before* the term of credit expires. Thus, if it is agreed that the freight shall be paid within *five*, or any other number of days after the *discharge* of the cargo, the contract will not be construed as requiring a delivery of the freight within that time, so as to defeat the carrier's lien. Logs of Mahogany, 2 Sum. (U. S.) 589; The Kimball, 3 Wall. (U. S.) 37. The carrier's lien extends only to his charges for freight, Steamboat Virginia *v.* Knaft, 25 Mo. 76; and, where they came to him over connecting lines, such charge for back freight as he has had to pay thereon. Briggs *v.* Boston, &c. R. R. Co., 6 Allen (Mass.), 246; Galena, &c. R. R. Co.

able demand is paid, even where the actual proprietor claims his own.[1] This doctrine is founded upon the reasonableness

v. Rae, 18 Ill. 488; White *v.* Vann, 6 Humph. (Tenn.) 70; Wells *v.* Thomas, 27 Mo. 17; Travis *v.* Thompson, 37 Barb. (N. Y.) 236. But a lien for back freight which he has paid to preceding carriers, who were paid in advance, does not exist, Nordemeyer *v.* Loescher, 1 Hilt. (N. Y.) 499, unless the consignee or owner has been guilty of negligence or bad faith in respect thereto; and it seems that if the bill of lading contains no mention of such part-payment, the carrier may hold the goods for the back freight as well as his own. Travis *v* Thompson, *ante.* The carrier has no lien for charges except such as are clearly connected with the transportation of the goods, and are within the contemplation of the parties. Cromelin *v.* R. R. Co., 4 Keyes (N. Y.), 90; Faith *v.* East India Co., 4 B. & Ald. 630. Thus, where a carrier, by rail or water, whose duty is ended by the arrival of the goods at his wharf or storehouse, sends the goods to the consignee at his place of business, he has no lien for the additional expense of transportation, unless he was authorized to send the goods in that way, either by the consignor or consignee. Richardson *v.* Rich, 104 Mass. 156. It seems that a carrier by rail has a right to a lien as warehouseman upon freight, for the detention of his cars which the consignee is bound to unload, if he gives the consignee explicit notice that he shall charge a certain sum per day for each car which is not unloaded within a certain time. Miller *v.* Mansfield, 112 Mass. 260. In England it is held that the carrier, being obliged to receive all goods offered to him for carriage, has a lien upon them against the real owner, whether they were intrusted to him by a wrong-doer or not, and even though they were stolen, and intrusted to him by the thief. Exeter's Carrier Case, cited 2 Ld. Raym. 867. But in this country the current of authority is the other way, and the carrier is held not to acquire a lien upon the goods against the real owner, where he received them from a wrong-doer, however innocently he may have received them. Robinson *v.* Baker, 5 Cush. (Mass.) 137; Stevens *v.* Boston, &c. R. R. Co., 8 Gray (Mass.), 262; Clark *v.* Lowell, &c. R. R. Co., 9 Gray (Mass.), 231; Gilson *v.* Gwinn, 102 Mass. 126; Fitch *v.* Newberry, 1 Mich. 1; Collman *v.* Collins, 2 Hall (N. Y.), 369; Buskirk *v.* Purrinton, 2 Hall (N. Y.), 561; Travis *v.* Thompson, *ante.* The carrier's lien only gives him the right to hold the goods for the payment of the freight, and gives him no right to use or sell them. Chandler *v.* Belden, *ante;* Fox *v.* McGregor, 11 Barb. (N. Y.) 41; Briggs *v.* Boston & Lowell R. R. Co.,

[1] Yorke *v.* Greenaugh, 2 Ld. Raym. 867; Butler *v.* Woolcott, 2 N. R. 64. But see Turrell *v.* Crawley, 13 Q. B. 197; Johnson *v.* Hill, 3 Stark, 172; Binns *v.* Pigot, 9 C. & P. 208. This doctrine has been disputed in this country. Fitch *v.* Newberry, 1 Mich. 1; Robinson *v.* Baker, 5 Cush. (Mass.) 137; Everett *v.* Saltus, 15 Wend. (N. Y.) 474; Clark *v.* Lowell, &c. R. R. Co., 75 Mass. 231; Stevens *v.* Boston, &c. R. R. Co., 8 Gray (Mass.), 262; Buskirk *v.* Purington, 2 Hall (N. Y.), 561; Collman *v.* Collins, 2 Hall (N. Y.), 569. But see King *v.* Richards, 6 Whart. (Penn.) 418.

that those who are bound by law to receive should be paid for carrying. But while the doctrine seems to be well settled in England, as stated in the text, yet a contrary rule seems to prevail in this country, and the carrier is held not to be entitled to a lien for freight where the consignor is a wrong-doer as to the goods.[1] From the very nature of this right, as it has been explained above, it follows that this right of retention, which the carrier has at common law, only extends to the amount which is owing for the carriage of the goods. He cannot set up this right in order to recover incidental outlays, such as for booking or warehouse-room.[2] Thus, where a railway company were carriers of goods on their line of railway from their B. station, having also an establishment at D., where they made and repaired their own locomotive engines, and also occasionally repaired those belonging to colliery proprietors, whose works were connected with the main line of the railway, a colliery company carried on business as coal merchants and coal proprietors about two miles from the B. station, at which latter their works were connected, by a tramway of

ante; Grace *v.* Palmer, 8 Wheat. (U. S.) 605; Rankin *v.* Packet Co., 9 Heisk. (Tenn.) 564; Hunt *v.* Haskell, 24 Me. 339. He must enforce his lien by action for the freight and a levy upon the goods, unless the statute has given him another remedy.

[1] Travis *v.* Thompson, 37 Barb. (N. Y.) 236; Gilson *v.* Gwinn, 107 Mass. 126; Clark *v.* Boston, &c. R. R. Co., 9 Gray (Mass.), 231. But in King *v.* Richards, *ante*, it seems to be conceded that a lien does exist under such circumstances, and it would certainly seem that the English rule has more foundation in reason than ours.

[2] Lambert *v.* Robinson, 1 Esp. 119. See Rice *v.* Humphrey, M'Clel. & Y. 173. The rule may be said to be that a consignee of goods, who is ready to pay freight on having the goods delivered to him, may maintain trover against the carriers or their agents, who, having no legal claim on the goods for anything besides the freight, refuse to deliver them unless a further sum is first paid; the consignee, in such a case, is not bound to make any tender to those in possession of the goods, and their refusal to deliver the goods is evidence of a conversion. Adams *v.* Clark, 9 Cush. (Mass.) 215. A carrier who has received goods from a wharfinger, with whom they have been deposited by their owner without authority to forward them, has no lien on them for freight against the owner. Clark *v.* Lowell, &c. R. R. Co., 9 Gray (Mass.), 231. If the freight is paid in advance, a carrier who receives it from another carrier has no lien therefor. Nordemeyer *v.* Loescher, 1 Hilt. (N. Y. C. P.) 499, as the last carrier, in such cases, may be said to be the agent of the first. Travis *v.* Thompson, 37 Barb. (N. Y.) 237.

their own, with the main line of the railway company, and in June, 1864, the railway company opened a monthly credit account with the colliery company for the carriage of their goods by the railway from the B. station, upon written conditions, the 6th of which provided that if the monthly accounts were not paid in accordance with the specified conditions, the railway company was "to have the right, at any time, to detain any goods or wagons in their possession, by way of lien, to secure the general balance owing to them." In July, 1864, a locomotive engine of the colliery company, used by them for taking coals and goods from their works to the lines at B., being out of repair, it was sent by agreement to the railway company's establishment, at D., to be repaired by them, and was drawn by the railway company from B. to D. for that purpose, attached to one of their ordinary luggage trains, and a sum of *2l.* *18s.* for such haulage was charged by the railway company to the colliery company in the monthly carriage account for July, and was not disputed by the latter before their bankruptcy. Upon the subsequent adjudication of the colliery company as bankrupts, the railway company claimed to hold the locomotive engine, which was then in their establishment at D., undergoing repairs, as a security, not only for the cost of such repairs and the charge for haulage, but also for a general balance due to them for the carriage of coals for the colliery company. It was held in this case that the terms of the 6th condition of the agreement between the railway company and the colliery company, which was intended merely to enlarge the rights of the railway company as carriers, and to give them as such a right of lien beyond what they would have at common law, applied only to coals and such like goods to be carried in the ordinary way, and not to the engine in question, which was delivered to the railway company, not under any contract to carry, but under an agreement to repair, to which the charge of haulage was incidental, and, therefore, that the right of general lien, claimed by the railway company, did not attach;[1] and by a recent case the law upon this subject has been made still more definite. In

[1] Kinnear *v.* Midland Rail. Co., 19 L. T. N. S. 307 Exch.

that case it was decided that the 8 & 9 Vict. c. 20, § 97, gives no lien upon goods for tolls or charges due to the company for other goods previously conveyed by them as carriers, but only for tolls previously due for the use of the line by persons conveying goods in their own carriages.[1]

SEC. 433. **Custom of Trade in Case of Wharfinger and Warehouseman.** — In the case of warehouseman and wharfinger, the custom of their trade gives a lien on goods in their possession for a general balance between them and the owners of the goods;[2] but where the carrier wishes to have a lien for such work, and such storage, he must expressly contract for it.

[1] Wallis *v.* London & South-Western Rail. Co., 5 L. R. Exch. 62; 39 L. J. Exch. 57; 18 W. R. 347; 21 L. T. N. S. 675.

8 Vict. c. 20, § 92. "It shall not be lawful for the company, at any time, to demand or take a greater amount of toll, or make any greater charge for the carriage of passengers or goods, than they are by this and the special act authorized to demand; and upon payment of the tolls, from time to time demandable, all companies and persons shall be entitled to use the railway with engines and carriages properly constructed," &c.

Sections 93 and 94 provide for the publication on boards of a list of all the tolls authorized by the special act to be taken, and for maintaining milestones along the line.

Sec. 95. "No tolls shall be demanded or taken by the company for the use of the railway during any time at which the toll boards are not exhibited.

Sec. 96. "The tolls are to be paid upon or near to the railway as the company shall, by notice to be annexed to the lists of tolls, appoint.

Sec. 97. "*If, on demand, any person fail to pay the tolls due in respect of any carriage or goods, it shall be lawful for the company to detain and sell such carriage, or all, or any part of such goods, or,* if the same shall have been removed from the premises of the company, *to detain and sell any other carriages or goods* within such premises belonging to the party liable to pay such tolls, and out of the money arising from such sale to retain the toll payable as aforesaid, and all charges and expenses of such detention and sale . . . or it shall be lawful for the company to recover any such tolls by action at law."

Section 98 provides that an account in writing of the goods transmitted be given.

Section 3 (interpretation clause). "The word 'toll' shall include any rate, or charge, or other payment payable under the special act for any passenger, animal, carriage, goods, merchandise, articles, matters, or things conveyed on the railway."

[2] Naylor *v.* Mangles, 1 Esp. N. P. Cas. 109; Spears *v.* Hartley, 3 Esp. 81; Bock *v.* Gorrissen, 30 L. J. 39 Ch. But, in order to be entitled to a lien, the person must be a warehouseman; and a person merely receiving the goods of another for storage is not a warehouseman, and consequently not entitled to a lien for the storage. Alt *v.* Weidenberg, 6 Bosw. (N. Y.) 176.

Special usage is not only to be effective in protecting the carrier by extension of the privilege of lien; it will also limit that right under circumstances which would be held to justify the inference of the existence of such a usage. Thus, if by the custom of a particular trade a carrier is to be paid for the carriage of the goods by the consignor, he has no right to detain them against the consignee, who has paid the price for them, on account of the carriage of other goods of a similar sort sent by the consignor.[1]

SEC. 434. **Limitation or Cessor of Right of Lien by Contract.** — It need scarcely be added that a special contract can limit or do away with the lien. If the carrier parts with his rights he has doubtless some reason for doing so. Many men prefer the chance of much to the certainty of little. But as the carrier has the right of lien at common law, where the special agreement between the customer and carrier as to the terms on which the goods are to be carried docs not expressly destroy the carrier's right to lien by its inconsistency therewith, that right will continue.

SEC. 435. **Where Charges not to be paid until Future Date. — Receipt of Goods by Mistake.** — Where, however, the charges are not to be paid until a future date, that negatives the possibility of the continuance of the right of lien in the meantime.[2] One other case remains to be mentioned, and that is the case of delivery of goods to a carrier who receives them by mistake, or the delivery to a carrier who is not bound to receive and carry such goods. Here it is evident that even after such delivery he will be bound to redeliver them to the owner if he tenders payment of all reasonable charges, but until the tender, or payment, of such charges the carrier will have a lien on the goods.[3]

SEC. 436. **Over what Goods Lien extends.** — The contract must be the guide in saying over what goods a lien extends. If there is a separate contract for the carriage of each of a number of parcels, a separate lien will attach to each, and such

[1] Butler *v.* Woolcott, 2 N. R. 64.

[2] Crawshay *v.* Homfray, 4 B. & Ald. 50.

[3] Rooke *v.* Midland Rail. Co., 16 Jur. 1069.

lien will only be in respect of charges due on the carriage of that one package.

SEC. 437. **Where Contracts are not Separate.** — Where, however, no such separate contract exists in respect of each package, but the goods conveyed are delivered to the carrier in separate parcels, he will doubtless have a lien on the whole of the packages so delivered, which will attach in respect to any charges incurred in the carriage of the whole or any one or more of the parcels.[1]

SEC. 438. **Lien lost with Loss of Possession.** — We have already seen that a right of lien is limited in its duration to the time that the goods are in the possession of the carrier, and it will be understood that, that being so, if he has once parted with the possession, or otherwise waived his lien, it will not be revived by a resumption of the possession, nor does it give him any right to stop the goods *in transitu*.[2]

SEC. 439. **Lien of Ship-owner. — Whether Ship Chartered or General Ship. — Resumption of Possession. — Why a Question of Importance in this Connection.** — It is almost unnecessary to state, what has been for the most part assumed throughout, that as the duties of the owners and masters of ships are almost identical with those of common carriers by land, their rights will be identical.[3] We have seen that the owners or masters of general[4] ships and vessels carrying goods for hire on the high seas, or on navigable rivers and canals, as hoymen and lightermen, are common carriers by the custom of the realm.[5] They are, therefore, entitled by the common law to a particular lien of the same nature as that described above, which attaches to goods delivered to them in the course of their trade for the price of their carriage.[6] This right has

[1] Chase *v.* Westmore, 5 M. & S. 180; Stevenson *v.* Blakelock, 1 M. & S. 535.

[2] Sweet *v.* Pym, 1 East, 4, per BULLER, J.; Lickbarrow *v.* Mason, *supra;* Coombs *v.* Bristol & Exeter Rail. Co., 27 L. J. 401 Exch.; Artaza *v.* Smallpiece, 1 Esp. 23.

[3] Coggs *v.* Barnard, 2 Ld. Raym. 918; Jones on Bailm. 106; Abbott, p. 249.

[4] As to the meaning of the term "general ship," see Abbott on Ship. pp. 112, 215; Kirchner *v.* Venus, 12 Moore, P. C. C. 361; 7 W. R. 455.

[5] *Ante*, p. 74.

[6] Kirchner *v.* Venus, 12 Moore, P. C. C. 361.

been recognized in almost every other country in Europe.[1] And the same principle is regulative whether the ship be a chartered or a general ship. In neither case is the master bound to part with the possession of any part of his cargo until the freight and other charges due in respect of such part be paid.[2] We have just seen that no resumption of possession, after it has once been parted with, will make the right of lien reattach, and the question naturally arises as to what constitutes such a parting with possession as will terminate the carrier's lien.[3] It is really a question of more importance in relation to carriers by water than with regard to carriers by land, or may be so, for cargoes generally take a considerable time to disembark and deliver, and the difficulty is to say whether a delivery of a part will terminate the lien as to the part which is still actually in the possession of the master of the ship. In one case the master of a ship was allowed a lien on a part of a cargo which had been removed into a lighter sent by the vendee alongside of the ship, but which the captain afterwards fastened to the ship's side to prevent its final removal.[4] Thus any part of the merchandise may be detained for the freight of all that is conveyed to the same person.

SEC. 440. **Express Stipulations.** — Where, however, the time and manner of payment of the freight are agreed upon and regulated by express stipulations in the charter-party, and

[1] Abbott on Ship., 11th ed., p. 237.

[2] Artaza *v.* Smallpiece, 1 Esp. 23; Anon. Cases, 12 Mod. 447, 511. See Moeller *v.* Young, 5 E. & B. 755; 24 L. J. Q. B. 257, Exch. Ch.

[3] Baggs *v.* Linseed, 1 Black (U. S.), 108; Sears *v.* Allen, 212; One hundred and fifty-one Tons of Coal, 4 Blatchf. (U. S. C. C.) 368. See also The Nestor, 1 Sum. (U. S.) 73; Eads *v.* The H. D. Bacon, 1 Newb. (U. S.) 274.

[4] Sodergren *v.* Flight, cited in Hanson *v.* Meyer, 6 East, 622. In the Court of Admiralty, where a lien exists upon freight for damage by collision, it has been held that part of the cargo may be detained for the whole freight, the other part having been given up to the consignee before the arrest of the vessel and her cargo. The Roecliffe, L. R. 2 Adm. & Ecc. 363; 3 Mar. Law Cas. o. s. 243. But the lien for the whole freight on part of a cargo only attaches where the goods are consigned to one consignee to be delivered at the same time, and at the same place, and if there are different contracts, and different places of delivery, a lien only exists on each set of goods. Bernal *v.* Pim, 1 Gale, 17.

this is very frequently the case, of course no such right attaches, and the only way of compelling payment is by proceeding on the charter-party.[1] And, in a case above cited, it has been decided that the power to retain in possession goods which have been carried, with the view of enforcing the payment of the charges incurred in the conveyance, does not permit a master to detain the goods on board ship, as, if that were the case, the consignee would have no opportunity of inspecting the goods with a view to ascertaining their condition.[2]

SEC. 441. **Modifications introduced by Revenue Regulations.** — The laws of a trade of the revenue regulations may modify the customs of a trade, and will to that extent modify the rights incident thereto. Thus, if a master, in obedience to some such revenue regulations, lands goods at a particular wharf, he does not by so doing lose his lien on them for the freight. In a case in point, it was held that the ship-owners' lien for freight continued after the landing of the cargo at the West India Docks, although they did not give notice to the company to retain the cargo until payment of the freight.[3] The possession of the carrier may be constructively extended so as to lengthen the duration of the lien. Thus, where no contract exists as to the landing of goods at a particular wharf, and the practice is to land them at a public wharf, and direct the wharfinger not to part with them until the charges upon them have been paid, the wharfinger becomes the agent of the ship-master, and the goods therefore remain in his possession constructively.[4]

SEC. 442. **Termination of Lien.** — The termination of the lien with the termination of the possession is, as we have had

[1] Abbott on Ship., 11th ed., p. 246.

[2] Abbott on Ship., 11th ed., p. 375. But see Artaza *v.* Smallpiece, 1 Esp. 23.

[3] Wilson *v.* Rymer, 1 Maule & S. 157; Faith *v.* East India Co., 4 B. & Ald. 630; Horncastle *v.* Farran, 3 B. & Ald. 497; and see East India Company's Act, 54 Geo. III. c. 228, § 18. The Loudon Dock Act, 45 Geo. III. c. 58, § 15, expressly reserves the lien for freight; and by 6 Geo. IV. c. 107, § 134, if goods are landed and sold by the officers of the customs, the freight not having been paid, the produce of the sale is applicable, in the first instance, to its liquidation. See Abbott on Ship., pt. iv. c. 11, 11th ed., p. 256.

[4] Abbott on Ship., pt. vi. c. 4, 11th ed., p. 618 *et seq.*

occasion to observe, the invariable rule of the common law. Where, however, the possession is terminated by the fraud of the person to whom the goods are delivered, or where the delivery is made to the consignee, in consequence of his false or fraudulent promise that he will pay the freight as soon as the goods are received, this will not deprive the carrier of his lien, and a carrier who is deprived of his possession by such means may sue the consignee in replevin.[1] A common-law lien may be lost where the parties enter into an express agreement for a lien of a greater or less extent, such contract being treated as a waiver of the lien arising from the operation of law;[2] but a mere change in the *form* of indebtedness does not defeat a lien unless there is an agreement to that effect, or it is apparent that such was the intention of the parties.[3] The lien can only be defeated by some act of the party which operates as a waiver;[4] and whether he has done so or not, is a question for the jury.[5] If he attaches the property upon a debt against the owner, the lien is waived;[6] but their attachment at the suit of a third person does not defeat the lien.[7]

SEC. 443. **Lien upon Passenger's Luggage.** — It is necessary to remember that the right of lien extends to the luggage of a

[1] Neither, of course, can a lien be created by reason of a fraudulent possession of a chattel; as, in the words of McKINLEY, J., "To create a lien on a chattel, the party claiming it must show the just possession of the thing claimed; and no person can acquire a lien founded upon his own illegal or fraudulent act or breach of duty; nor can a lien arise where, from the nature of the contract between the parties, it would be inconsistent with the express terms or the clear intent of the contract." Randel *v.* Brown, 2 How. (U. S.) 406. See also Cranston *v.* The Philadelphia Insurance Co., 5 Binn. (Penn.) 538; Turno *v.* Bethune, 2 Desau. (S. C.) 285; Jarvis *v.* Rogers, 15 Mass. 389, 395; Gray *v.* Wilson, 9 Watts (Penn.), 512; and see, further, Weymouth *v.* Bowyer, 1 Ves. Jun. 416; Taylor *v.* Robinson, 8 Taunt. 648; Madden *v.* Kempster, 1 Camp. 12; Johnson *v.* Hill, 3 Stark. 172; Binns *v.* Pigot, 9 C. & P. 208; King *v.* Indian Orchard Canal Co., 11 Cush. (Mass.) 231; The Bolivar Olc (U. S. C. C.) 474.

[2] Brown *v.* Gillam, 4 Wheat. (U. S.) 255; Schanck *v.* Arrowsmith, 9 N. J. Eq. 314.

[3] Clark *v.* Draper, 19 N. H. 419; Lewis *v.* Starke, 18 Miss. 120; Muir *v.* Cross, 10 B. Mon. (Ky.) 277; Succession of Kercheval, 14 La. Ann. 457.

[4] Parker *v.* Kelly, 18 Miss. 143.

[5] Buckley *v.* Handy, 2 Miles (Penn.), 449.

[6] Legg *v.* Willard, 17 Pick. (Mass.) 140.

[7] Outcolt *v.* Darling, 25 N. J. L. 443.

passenger, for the recovery of the money due by him for his conveyance, and therefore in such a case the lien extends to goods for charges not actually incurred in carriage. Of course, the master has no lien on the traveller himself, nor has he a lien upon the clothes worn by the traveller when about to leave the vessel.[1]

SEC. 444. **Rule as to a Number of Parcels.** — A similar rule is applicable to the lien upon merchandise carried by sea, as that which was stated above with reference to merchandise conveyed by land carriers, where the parcels are many. From what has been said above, it will be understood that where several packages of goods belonging to the same owner are carried the same voyage, a delivery of some of these packages will not defeat the lien on those packages which have not been delivered.[2]

SEC. 445. **Where there are two Contracts.** — If, however, there be two contracts to carry with different *termini* to the voyage in each contract, no lien attaches for freight under the one contract upon goods shipped under the other and improperly detained on board by the carrier;[3] for in this, as in all other cases, no lien can be acquired by wrongful possession. No lien, therefore, attaches, if the goods which are directed to one place are improperly carried to another.[4]

SEC. 446. **Where Carrier is Charterer of Ship.** — A difficulty arises in the case where the carrier is not the actual owner, but only the charterer of the ship, because the right of lien only arises where the carrier has possession of the goods, and

[1] Wolf *v.* Summers, 2 Camp. 631. Formerly it was held that an innkeeper possessed not only a right of lien on the property of his guest, but that this right gave him the power to detain the person of his guest until satisfaction of his claim. See Newton *v.* Tring, per EYRE, J., 1 Show. 269. This doctrine has since been overruled. Sunbolf *v.* Alford, 3 M. & W. 248; 1 H. & H. 13. This case also decided another point — that the goods of a guest are liable to such lien only when in the actual possession of the innkeeper. Hence the clothes he wears are not seizable, and a basket or bundle in his hand is protected against the lien of the innkeeper. See Cross on Lien, p. 343. See a Scotch case, M'Kichen *v.* Muir, 1 J. Shaw, 223.

[2] Boggs *v.* Martin, 13 B. Mon. (Ky.) 239; Fuller *v.* Bradley, 25 Penn. St. 120; Lane *v.* Old Colony R. R. Co., 12 Gray (Mass.), 143.

[3] Bernal *v.* Pim, 1 Gale, 17.

[4] Cross on Lien, p. 290.

a vessel freighted under a charter-party is not necessarily transferred from the possession of the owner to that of the freighter. In such a case the owner of a ship, retaining the possession of it, has a lien on the cargo for the hire of a ship under a charter-party.[1] The question as to whether the possession remains properly and legally in the owner can be answered by a construction of the charter-party.

SEC. 447. **Who has Legal Possession of Ship.** — Under the stipulations contained in some charter-parties, the owner must be held to retain such a control over the ship as to be considered in legal possession of the ship and goods during the voyage through, or by means of, the master and crew as his agents or servants. Consequently, when the goods arrive at their destination, the owner has, in such a case, a lien over them for the stipulated hire of the ship. In other cases the construction of the charter-party will lead to the conclusion that the owner's possession of the ship does not continue, and that, therefore, no such lien attaches to the goods on board. The question to be answered, then, is, when the possession in the ship passes from the owner to the freighter. "The broad principle," says MR. CROSS, "formerly maintained, that, in the case of a chartered ship, the charterer, during the existence of the charter-party, was, to all intents and purposes, the owner of the ship, and that, therefore, when goods were put on board by him in that character, the owner had no right to resume possession of the ship until the goods were unloaded, and had, consequently, no right to detain the goods, has been much narrowed and qualified by subsequent decisions."[2] Where, by a charter-party, it was covenanted that the owner should receive on board, in London, all such goods as the freighter thought fit to load, and should proceed therewith to Madras, and there, after delivering her outward cargo, receive from the freighter's agents a homeward cargo, and deliver the same in

[1] Saville *v.* Campion, 2 B. & Ald. 503; Tate *v.* Meek, 8 Taunt. 280; and see also Trinity House *v.* Clark, 4 M. & S. 288.

[2] Cross on Lien, p. 301. See Hutton *v.* Bragg, 7 Taunt. 14; 2 Marsh, 339; since overruled. See Saville *v.* Campion, 2 B. & Ald. 503; and Christie *v.* Lewis, 2 B. & B. 410; 5 Moore, 211. See also Lane *v.* Penniman, 4 Mass. 91; Portland Bank *v.* Stubbs, 6 Mass. 422.

London; and that all the cabins but one, which was reserved for the use of the captain, should be at the disposal of the freighter, who was to appoint a supercargo to superintend the stowage of the goods, while the freight was to be paid at so much per ton on the registered tonnage of the ship; the captain and crew were employed and paid by the owner: it was held that, there being no express words of demise of the ship itself in the charter-party, the freighter did not thereby become the owner for the voyage, but that the possession continued in the owner, and that he, therefore, had a lien upon the cargo for his freight.[1] Such a case differs from that in which the charterer takes the vessel into his own service, and agrees to pay a certain freight for *the use and hire* of her.

SEC. 448. **There can be no Lien where there is neither Actual nor Constructive Possession. — Construction.** — The effect, then, of the charter-party is to be considered in each case, and the question to be decided is, whether the owner continues in possession, or is divested of possession; the invariable rule being that there can be no lien where there is neither an actual nor a constructive possession of the cargo. In such a construction the intention of the parties is to be had regard to, rather than any technical sense of the terms used.[2] Thus, where the owner of a ship had entered into a charter-party with a freighter, by which the former "granted, and to freight *let*," and the latter "*hired*, and to freight took," for a voyage out and home, it was held that, taking the whole charter-party into consideration, the possession of the ship did not pass to the freighter, but remained in the owner, notwithstanding the words of grant used in its commencement, and that the mere circumstances of his having entered into an agreement with the charterer as to the mode by which he should be paid for freight, did not divest him of his lien on the cargo, and it made no difference that he had delivered the homeward cargo to the consignees, and received the freight due upon the bills of lading, which was different from that due on the charter-party.[3]

[1] Saville *v.* Campion, 2 B. & Ald 503. See also Campion *v.* Colvin, 3 Bing. N. C. 17; 2 Hodges, 116.

[2] Fowler *v.* Kymer, 3 East, 396.

[3] Christie *v.* Lewis, 2 B. & B. 410.

SEC. 449. **Stipulations equivalent to Actual Demise.**—On the other hand, though the charter-party contain no words of actual demise, there may be stipulations equivalent in their effect to an actual parting with the ship, *pro hâc vice.* Thus, it was held that where the owners of a ship by deed appointed one Betham to the command of their ship, on a voyage from London to Calcutta and back, the latter loading her out and home, and guaranteeing to the owners a certain amount of freight, to be paid monthly, and secured by the freight bills—which were to be made payable to certain trustees for the owners and Betham, and transmitted to England—but retaining the surplus, or making good the deficiency, and the owners, placing an agent on board to superintend the management of the stores, with power to displace Betham and appoint another commander, in case of his breaking the agreement on his part; it yet amounted as an appointment of the freighter to the legal ownership of the ship *pro tempore*, and he alone was entitled to receive the freight for the carriage of the goods.[1] The grounds upon which it was attempted to establish the possession of the owners were, first, that the freighter was appointed to the command of the ship by them; secondly, that an agent was put on board by the owners, with powers inconsistent with Betham's ownership; and, thirdly, that the owners virtually received the benefit of the homeward freight, by the transmission of the freight bills to England.

CHIEF JUSTICE TINDAL, in delivering judgment, said: "With respect to the objection, it is almost the invariable practice and usage that the owners of a ship, although they let it out upon freight to a charterer, do themselves appoint the captain and the crew,—the chartering of the ship not being so much the chartering of the hull as of the ship in a state fit for the purposes of mercantile adventure.

"The second objection is answered by the fact that the authority of the agent was limited to the superintendence of the acts of Betham, as captain, and not as freighter, the utmost authority given to the agent being that of displacing

[1] Newberry *v.* Colvin, 1 Cromp. & J. 192; 7 Bing. 190, overruling s. c. nom. Colvin *v.* Newberry, 8 B. & C. 166; 2 M. & R. 47.

the master and appointing another, in case Betham should be guilty of a breach of any of the covenants or agreements on his part. But if Betham ceased to be master, he continued, nevertheless, by the terms of the charter-party, to be the freighter of the ship, possessing the same power to take goods on board, and liable to the same responsibilities on the one hand to the owners, for the time-freight for which he had contracted; on the other hand, to the shippers of goods for the safe conveyance of the goods shipped.

"As to the third objection, the charter-party gave the owners a security on freight-bills received by the freighter, but gave them no direct or immediate interest in the freight earned, the whole of the surplus of which belonged to Betham. If Betham had obtained no homeward cargo from Calcutta, so that no freight-bills could have been transmitted, the owners would still have been entitled to their time-freight. The freight earned by Betham on the intermediate voyage was not a security to the owners; and even in the homeward voyage, if the ship had been lost, there might have been no freight payable to the freighter, but still he must have made good his liability to a monthly freight for the use and hire of the vessel." [1]

SEC. 450. **How the Question of Ownership is to be decided.** — The judgment in this case indicates how the question of ownership is to be tested, under such circumstances, with the view of ascertaining whether the owner has still the possession of the ship, and consequently a lien upon the cargo. Any words contained in the charter-party which clearly indicate the intention of the one party to give up, and the other to take and hold possession of, the ship for a certain time will deprive the owner of that possession which was his, and consequently of the right of lien under consideration.

[1] The question of the *pro hâc vice* ownership of vessels has often been considered in cases of collision and salvage. See Fenton *v.* The Dublin Steam Packet Co., 8 Ad. & El. 835; Quarman *v.* Bennet, 6 M. & W. 499; Martin *v.* Timperley, 4 Q. B. 429; M'Laughlin *v.* Prior, 4 M. & G. 48; Schuster *v.* M'Kellar, 7 E. & B. 704; 26 L. J. N. S. Q. B. 281; Scott *v.* Scott, 2 Starkie, 348; The Alfen, Swab. 189; The Waterloo, 2 Dods. 433; The Maria Jane, 14 Jur. 859; The Collier, L. R. 1 Adm. & Ecc. 83; 2 Mar. Law Cas. O. S. 473; The Scout, 1 Asp. Mar. Law Cas. 1.

SEC. 451. **Owner's Power to reserve his Right of Lien.** — It is to be remembered that, notwithstanding the correctness of the above statement of the law, it is in the power of the owner of the ship to reserve to himself, by a "full and unequivocal declaration of intention" in the charter-party, his right of lien upon the cargo of the vessel, and that although a construction of the charter-party might result in showing that the owner had divested himself of his possession of the ship in favor of the freighter. Thus, where a lien on the lading of a ship had been expressly reserved to the owner by a charter-party, it was held that goods which the charterer purchased and put on board, and thence transferred with a stipulation to convey them to their destination, for a certain amount of freight, were, even as against an indorsee of a bill of lading, subject not only to that freight but to the ship-owner's lien for a balance due to him under the charter-party, whether the possession of the ship was by the charter-party completely out of the ship-owner and vested in the charterer or not.[1] And where, by a charter-party which was negotiated by A, as agent of B, the charterer (B) engaged to pay a lump-freight of 735*l.* for a voyage to the coast of Africa and back to London, payable in cash on correct delivery of the return cargo, and the charter-party contained the following clause: "The master to sign bills of lading at any rate of freight without prejudice to this charter," B, the charterer, shipped certain oil on his own account for London, for which the master signed a bill of lading, making the oil deliverable to A or assigns, "he or they paying freight for the said goods as usual." This bill of lading B indorsed to A, in part payment of advances made by him on the purchase of the outward cargo. It was held, in this case, that, A having notice of the terms of the charter-party, the owner was entitled to a lien on the oil for the entire chartered freight.[2]

[1] Small *v.* Moales, 9 Bing. 574; 2 M. & Scott, 674.

[2] Kern *v.* Deslandes, 10 C. B. N. S. 205. See also Gledstancs *v.* Allen, 12 C. B. 202. See also Campion *v.* Colvin, 3 Bing. N. C. 17; 2 Hodges, 116; Gilkison *v.* Middleton, 2 C. B. N. S. 134; Pearson *v.* Göschen, 17 C. B. N. S. 352; 33 L. J. C. P. 265.

SEC. 452. **Where no Lien exists.** — No lien exists in respect of unliquidated damages. Where the freighter of a ship covenanted that if she should not be fully laden, he would not only pay for the goods on board, but also for so much in addition as the ship would have carried, for which he had before stipulated to pay freight, according to different rates for three descriptions of goods; it was held that the ship-owner had no lien upon the goods actually on board for the amount of the *dead freight*, in other words, for the compensation in damages, which he was entitled to for the freighter's breach of contract in not putting full loading on board; which damages were unliquidated, and, there being no lien in such a case, either by the usage of trade or the express contract of the parties.[1]

SEC. 453. **Lien for Port Charges.** — Still pursuing our investigation as to when and how the right of lien arises to the owner of a ship, we shall find that a special provision in the charter-party that the charterer shall pay the port charges will not entitle the owner to any lien in respect of the payment of them (for they are not of the nature of freight[2]), unless it be specially stipulated in the charter-party that the owner shall exercise such right if the charges be not paid on the delivery of the goods. Another point deserves notice in this place, and the law upon it follows necessarily from what has already been said of the indefeasibility of a contract for lien under a charter-party by the sale of the cargo; and that is, that sub-freighters are subject to the lien of the ship-owner under the contract of the original freighter to the extent of their freight, though the ship be freighted by the latter as a general ship.[3] It was argued, in Faith *v.* East India Company,[4] that if the sub-

[1] Phillips *v.* Rodie, 15 East, 547. A mutual obligation in a penal sum on the parties, the ship, the tackle, or the merchandise consigned will not alter the rights of the owner in this respect, so as to entitle him to a right of lien on the breach of the covenant therein contained. Birley *v.* Gladstone, 3 M. & S. 205; see also Gray *v.* Carr, 6 L. R. Q. B. 522 Exch. Ch.; and M'Lean *v.* Fleming, 2 L R. H. of L., 128; 1 Asp. Mar. Law Cas. 160 H. of L.

[2] Faith *v.* East India Co., 4 B. & Ald. 630.

[3] Faith *v.* East India Co., 4 B. & Ald. 630; Mitchell *v.* Scaife, 4 Camp. 298; Paul *v.* Birch, 2 Atk. 261.

[4] 4 B. & Ald. 630.

freighters had paid the freight in advance they would not have been bound to have paid it over again, and that therefore the owner could not in that case have insisted on his lien. ABBOTT, C. J., in giving judgment, observed: "It is not necessary to decide what effect the payment of the freight, if paid before the goods were laden on board in the East Indies, would have had. If such an event had happened, which, however, is not very probable, perhaps the owner's lien for freight might have been thereby defeated." We have been unable to discover any case since that of Faith *v.* East India Company, in which this point has been raised, and, therefore, in so far as our courts of law go it is still unsettled. The best opinion, however, seems to be that as the ante-payment of freight is unusual, it would require the clearest proof of the *boná fide* nature of such payment before it could be allowed to defeat the owner's lien. As such a thing "is," in LORD TENTERDEN'S words, "not very probable," the fact of it having been done would suggest the probability of a fraud, and a satisfactory proof that no fraudulent intention dictated the departure from the ordinary usage of the trade should be demanded.

SEC. 454. **Payment of Freight at Lading of Ship or on Delivery.** — Lien attaches whether the payment of the freight is to precede or be concomitant with the delivery of the lading of the ship. Thus, in the case of Yates *v.* Railston,[1] the owner of a vessel was proved to have covenanted by charter-party to let the vessel on freight, and to deliver the cargo in good condition, and the freighters covenanted to pay the freight on delivery of the cargo, — part in money, and the remainder by bills at four months. On these facts it was decided that the owner might detain the cargo until payment of the freight, the delivery of the cargo and the payment of the freight being concomitant acts. And if the owner covenanted to deliver the cargo agreeably to the bills of lading, and the freighters covenanted to pay one third in cash on arrival

[1] 8 Taunt. 293; 2 Moore, 294. See also Shepherd *v.* De Bernales, 13 East, 565; Crozier *v.* Smith, 1 Scott, N. R. 338; Tate *v.* Meek, 2 Moore, 278; Alsager *v.* St. Katherine's Dock Co., 14 M. & W. 794; 15 L. J. Exch. 34.

and the remainder on delivery of the cargo by good bills of exchange at four months' date, and the captain land the goods in his own name, and offer them to the freighter at one delivery on receiving the stipulated freight, it was held that the owner has a lien upon them until such bills of exchange are produced by the freighter.[1]

SEC. 455. **Payment at certain Subsequent Date.** — From what has been already said in reference to this matter,[2] it is evident that if by the bill of lading the freight is made payable according to the terms of a charter-party, which stipulates for the payment at a certain date subsequent to delivery, no lien attaches to the freight.[3] The negotiation of bills, given in payment of the freight according to the terms of the charter-party, by the owner, amounts to an approval of the bill, and a relinquishment of his lien on the goods.[4]

SEC. 456. **Revival of Lien.** — If, however, the bills be dishonored before the possession of the goods, or of some part of them, has been given up, the owner's lien revives either upon the whole or on such as remain undelivered, as the case may be.[5] It is now definitely established, although doubt was once thrown upon the principle, that the existence of a special contract between a common carrier and his employer, which has reference to the rights and duties of each, does not deprive the carrier of his lien, unless there is something in the contract inconsistent with the existence of such lien.[6]

[1] Yates *v.* Mennell, 2 Moore, 297. See also Tate *v.* Meek, 2 Moore, 278; Brown *v.* Tanner, 37 L. J. Ch. 923; 3 L. R. Ch. 597; Black *v.* Rose, 2 Moore, P. C. C. N. S. 277; 10 Jur. N. S. 1009; Tamvaco *v.* Simpson, 19 C. B. N. S. 453; 11 Jur. N. S. 926; 34 L. J. C. P. 268; affirmed on appeal, 1 L. R. C. P. 363, Exch. Ch.

[2] *Ante*, p. 465.

[3] Lucas *v.* Nockells (in error), 4 Bing. 729; 1 M. & P. 783; 2 You. & J. 304.

[4] Horncastle *v.* Farran, 3 B. & Ald. 497.

[5] Marsh *v.* Pedder, 4 Camp. 257; Smith *v.* Terraud, 7 B. & C. 19; 9 D. & R. 803; Robinson *v* Read, 9 B. & C. 449; Strong *v.* Hart, 6 B. & C. 160; 9 D. & R. 189. If a freighter is, through mistake, given a receipt in full for freight charges, or expressing that the charges are "paid through," when in fact only the charges of the first carrier have been paid, the connecting carrier is entitled to a lien for his charges. Wolf *v.* Hough, 22 Kan. 260.

[6] Chase *v.* Westmore (per LORD ELLENBOROUGH), 5 M. & S. 180. With regard to what is inconsistent, see Raitt *v.* Mitchell, 4 Camp. 149. As

SEC. 457. **Remuneration.** — In considering the rights of carriers, that which he has to remuneration must not be overlooked. Before he receives goods to be carried, he is entitled to demand payment of a reasonable amount for the carriage; and if the owner of the goods does not pay such reasonable amount upon the demand being made, the carrier may refuse to carry.[1] But where a carrier has undertaken the carriage of goods without such demand, and without payment being made,[2] he not only has the right to retain the goods in his possession until his reasonable demands have been satisfied, as we have just seen; but should he have parted with the possession of the goods without a settlement of his just claims, he may resort to an action at law to recover compensation for his services.[3]

SEC. 458. **Freight. — Express Agreement.** — With regard to this branch of our subject, we can with some confidence assert that a very detailed account of the law does not seem necessary. But still some mention must be made of it, and what we shall say, although bearing chiefly upon questions connected with shipping, will be applicable to carriers generally. The compensation which the carrier has a right to recover is generally called "freight." [4] In order to entitle the carrier to recover in such an action, it must be made clear that the goods were conveyed by the consent of the owner, or, to put it negatively, that they were not conveyed against his will;[5] and it has been decided that in the event of the death of an animal (and the same thing is true of passengers) during the journey or voyage, without any fault or negligence upon the part of the carriers, freight will, in the absence of an express agree-

to waiver of lien, see Cargo of the Anna Kimball, 2 Sprague (U. S. C. C.), 33; Spartali *v.* Beneke, 10 C. B. 212; 19 L. J. 293. See also Benjamin on the Sale of Personal Property, p. 598 *et seq.*

[1] Per BEST, C. J., in Batson *v.* Donovan, 4 B. & Ald. 28; PARKE, B., in Wyld *v.* Pickford, 8 M. & W. 448.

[2] See Wilson *v.* Grand Trunk Rail. Co., 56 Me. 60.

[3] Bastard *v.* Bastard, 2 Show. 81.

[4] Kirchner *v.* Venus, 12 Moore, P. C. C. 361. See also Willis *v.* Palmer, 7 C. B. N. S. 340; Jackson *v.* Isaacson, 3 H. & N. 405; Seeger *v.* Duthie, 8 C. B. N. S. 45; 29 L. J. C. P. 253.

[5] The voyage must also be legal to entitle the carrier to freight. Blanck *v.* Solly, 1 Moore, 531; Holt, 554.

ment as to whether the freight is to be paid for the lading or transporting of the animals, be payable just as if the animal had reached its destination alive. If such express agreement does exist, and shows that the payment of freight was to be for the lading of the cattle, it is clear that the death of any of the cattle subsequent to the lading, through natural causes, cannot deprive the carrier of his right to freight. If, on the other hand, the agreement is for the payment of freight for transporting the cattle, no freight is due for those that die during the voyage, upon the ground that as to them the contract is not performed.[1]

SEC. 459. **When Owner is to be regarded as a Carrier. — Terms of Contract.** — Where, under a charter-party, there is no actual demise of the ship from the owners to the freighters, but where the legal possession of the ship remains in the owner, the owner is to be looked upon as a carrier, and is subject to the liabilities of a person professing that trade. Under such a charter-party freight would be due, but the right of recovery of such freight must, of course, depend upon the terms of the contract; and with regard to the construction of such documents, we have already seen[2] that it should be liberal, agreeable to the intentions of the parties, and conformable to the general and particular usages of trade. If a charter-party provides that the goods shall be delivered in accordance with bills of lading to be signed by the master, and the master does, upon receiving the goods, sign bills of lading for delivery upon payment of freight, and this right has not been insisted upon by the master, the merchant charterer is answerable for the freight.[3] If the consignee or indorsee of a bill of

[1] Abbott on Ship. 409 *et seq.*; Dig., 14, 2, 10. See Andrew *v.* Moorhouse, 5 Taunt. 435; 1 Marsh, 122; Osgood *v.* Groning, 2 Camp. 466; Cook *v.* Jennings, 7 T. R. 381; Mashiter *v.* Buller, 1 Camp. 81; S. P. Clark *v.* Druisina, 1 Marsh, 123; Blakeley *v.* Dixon, 2 B. & P. 321; Cargo *ex* Galam, 2 Moore, P. C. C. N. S. 216; 33 L. J. Adm. 97; Vlierboom *v.* Chapman, 13 M. & W. 230; Hunter *v.* Prinsep, 10 East, 378; Swett *v.* Black, 2 Sprague (U. S. C. C.), 49; The Excelsior, 2 Ben. (U. S. C. C.) 434; Seers *v.* Linseed, 1 Cliff. (U. S. C. C.) 68; Donahoe *v.* Kettell, 1 Cliff. (U. S. C. C.) 135; Hart *v.* Shaw, 1 Cliff. (U. S. C. C.) 358.

[2] *Ante*, p. 472.

[3] Fox *v.* Nott, 6 H. & N. 630. See also Shepherd *v.* De Bernales, 13 East, 567; Penrose *v.* Wilks, Abbott on Ship. 415; Tapley *v.* Martin, 8 T. R. 445; Christie *v.* Rowe, 1 Taunt. 300.

lading containing the goods deliverable to him on payment of freight, accepts the consignment, there is either a legal presumption that he contracted to pay the freight,[1] or evidence from which the jury would be justified in finding a contract by the consignee to pay the freight.[2]

SEC. 460. **When Freight is due.** — As freight is the price of *carriage*, and not of *receiving goods* to be carried,[3] it follows that no freight becomes due or recoverable until the voyage is completely performed. The contract is indivisible, and the carrier can recover for no portion of the voyage that has been made until the whole is finished and the goods delivered.[4] Still the intention of the parties will guide the decision of the court. Thus, in a case where a ship is hired to sail to a certain port, and then to make a return voyage still in the same service, it might be difficult to say whether this constituted one entire voyage or two distinct voyages. In such a case the intention of the parties will assist in the determination.[5] It is, however, in the power of the consignees to accept goods short of their destination, when the whole of the contract of the carrier will have been virtually performed.

SEC. 461. **Where Right commences.** — While the law is careful to give each person a remedy who has a right, it is not careful — and it is well it should not be so — to lay remedies thick upon one another; so the right to an action for freight

[1] Scaife *v.* Tobin, 3 B. & Ad. 523; Dougal *v.* Kemble, 3 Bing. 383; Cork *v.* Taylor, 13 East, 399; Jesson *v.* Solly, 4 Taunt. 53.

[2] Sanders *v.* Vanzeller, 4 Q. B. 260; Kemp *v.* Clark, 12 Q. B. 647; Zwilchenbart *v.* Henderson, 9 Exch. 722; Moller *v.* Young, 5 E. & B. 755. See also Cock *v.* Taylor, 13 East, 399; Tobin *v.* Crawford, 5 M. & W. 235; 9 M. & W. 716; Dougal *v.* Kemble, 3 Bing. 383; and see the Bills of Lading Act, 18 & 19 Vict. c. 111; Smurthwaite *v.* Wilkins, 11 C. B. N. S. 847; Lewis *v.* M'Kee, L. R. 2 Exch. 37. See as to right to recover freight, Duthie *v.* Hilton, 4 L. R. C. P. 138; 38 L. J. C. P. 93; Brown *v.* Tanner, 37 L. J. Ch. 933; 3 L. R. Ch. 597; Paynter *v.* James, 16 W. R. 768.

[3] Per LORD LOUGHBOROUGH, in Mason *v.* Lickbarrow, 1 H. Bl. 359.

[4] Osgood *v.* Groning, 2 Camp. 466.

[5] See Smith, Merc. Law. 299; Andrew *v.* Moorhouse, 5 Taunt. 435; Blakely *v.* Dickson, 2 B. & P. 321; Mashiter *v.* Buller, 1 Camp. 84; Crozier *v.* Smith, 1 M. & G. 407; Cargo *ex* Galam, 2 Moore, P. C. C. N. S. 216; 33 L. J. Adm. 97; Vlierboom *v.* Chapman, 13 M. & W. 230; Hunter *v.* Prinsep, 10 East, 378; and see Morris *v.* Robinson, 5 D. & R. 35; 3 B. & C. 196.

does not arise until the delivery of the goods, when, as we have seen, the right of lien ceases.[1]

SEC. 462. **Arrangements for Conveyance. — Application of Law to Circumstances. — Payment by Tons. — Part Delivery.** — Questions of some nicety arise in connection with this subject, and these are due to the variety of modes in which contracts for carriage by sea are formed, and the uncertainty which often exists at the time that the contract is entered into as to the species of goods that are to be conveyed. It is common to arrange for such conveyance in one of two ways, — either to hire the entire ship at a specific price, or to load the cargo at a settled price per ton. Under either of such set of circumstances the application of the law is not difficult. If under a contract of the former nature the owner of the goods only fills part of the ship, he is, of course, still liable for the whole sum agreed upon. In a case where the covenant was to pay for hides at so much per pound net weight at the scales, and it happened that the packages were wrapped in hides of an inferior quality which are generally somewhat damaged, and the evidence varied as to whether freight was paid for them or not, and whether they paid duty, it was held that they must pay both freight and duty.[2] Where an entire ship, of a certain specified burden, is hired, and the charterer agrees to pay a certain sum for every ton of goods which he shall put on board, but does not agree to supply a full cargo, he is only liable for the actual amount carried.[3] If part of the cargo has been delivered to, and received by, the consignees, freight is payable upon it, even though the rest has not been delivered, and though it has not been landed at the port named in the charter-party, but at some other port to which the consignee directed the captain to come.[4]

[1] Blakely v. Dickson, 2 Bos. & P. 321; Andrews v. Moorhouse, 5 Taunt. 435; Mashiter v. Buller, 1 Camp. 84; Crozier v. Smith, 1 Man. & G. 407; Smith's Merc. Law, 299. With regard to transshipment, see Shipton v. Thornton, 9 A. & E. 314; Rosetto v. Gurney, 11 C. B. 176.

[2] Moorson v. Page, 4 Camp. 103.

[3] James (Lady) v. East India Co., Abbott on Ship. 412; and see Hunter v. Fry, 2 B. & A. 421; Thomas v. Clarke, 2 Stark. 457.

[4] Christie v. Rowe, 1 Taunt. 300.

SEC. 463. **Mode of calculating Freight which has been fixed for Articles that are not carried.** — A question of some interest in reference to freight has more than once been raised, and that is, where the rate of freight has been fixed with a view to certain articles, and either none or only some of these have been actually carried, what freight is payable on the remaining articles?[1] A definite answer, however, has been given to it, to the following effect: "Where a charter-party provides for the carriage of various classes of goods at specified rates, and gives no permission for the substitution of other goods; or permits, but does not provide, a scale of payment for such substituted goods, — in either case the freight payable in respect of them is calculated upon an average of what would have been earned by carrying a similar amount of all the enumerated articles in equal quantities."[2]

SEC. 464. **Capture. — Recapture. — Transshipment.** — If the ship is captured, the owners lose their freight, and the merchant loses his goods; the contract is suspended, but the right of freight will revive upon the recapture of the ship, and its arrival at its original destination.[3] Again, if a ship be disabled before completing the voyage, and is in such a condition that the voyage cannot be completed, the goods may be transshipped to their destination, and such a transshipment will be in furtherance of the original purpose, and entitle the carrier to his freight.[4] It is clear that it is a paramount duty to send

[1] As to how it ought to be calculated, see Geraldes *v.* Denison, Holt, N. P. 346; Moller *v.* Living, 4 Taunt. 102.

[2] Capper *v.* Foster, 3 B. N. C. 938; Cockburn *v.* Alexander, 6 C. B. 791.

[3] Beale *v.* Thompson, 3 B. & P. 420, 431; The Race-Horse, 3 Rob. A. 101. See also Curling *v.* Long, 1 B. & P. 634.

[4] Shipton *v.* Thornton, 9 A. & E. 314. In that case the court said: "It may be taken to be either the *duty* or the *right* of owner to transship. If it be the former, it must be so in virtue of his original contract; and it should seem to result from a performance by him of that contract that he will be entitled to the full consideration for which it was entered into, without respect to the particular circumstances attending the fulfilment. If it is the latter, a right to the full freight seems to be implied. The master is at liberty to transship; but for what purpose, except for earning his full freight at the rate agreed on?" See also Mathews *v.* Gibbs, 7 Jur. N. S. 186; 30 L. J. Q. B. 55. The master is allowed a reasonable time to transship, so as to earn his freight. The Soblomstein, 1 L. R. Adm. 293; 36 L. J. Adm. 5.

on the cargo to its destination, when, in the opinion of a prudent man, that will be most for the benefit of all concerned.[1]

SEC. 465. **Apportionment of Freight.** — Where the master of a ship, having put into a port short of the destination of the cargo, does not hire another ship to complete his contract, and so entitle himself to the whole freight, the ship-owner is still entitled to be paid a proportionate part of the freight, according to the part of the voyage performed.[2] If the merchant, his consignee, or agent, is willing to dispense with the performance of the whole voyage, and voluntarily accepts the goods before the whole of the duty, imposed by the original contract, has been performed, a proportionate amount of freight will be due *pro ratâ itineris*.[3] But it seems to be clearly established, as a principle of law, that under no other circumstances than these will any proportion of the freight be due. Consequently, if the master of a ship by any means — such as refusing to repair his ship when it is in such a condition that the goods of the shipper would run the risk of being lost if it put to sea — compels the owner to accept his cargo, that will not be such an acceptance as will entitle the ship-owner to *pro ratâ* freight.

SEC. 466. **When Performance of Voyage is Impossible.** — A very difficult question has been raised in a very recent case as to how far a court of equity will presume an implied contract on the part of the consignee to accept goods short of their destination, where the circumstances are such that delivery at the agreed port has become impossible, through no fault of the ship-owner or master. In the case of The Teu-

[1] Smith, Merc. Law, 180; Liddard *v.* Lopes, 10 East, 526; Wilson *v.* Millar, 2 Stark. 1; Manning *v.* Newman, 2 Camp. 624. A sale is seldom advisable. Freeman *v.* East India Co., 5 B. & Ald. 617; Wilson *v.* Dickson, 2 B. & Ald. 2.

[2] Abbott on Ship., 11th ed., p. 385; Maclachlan on Ship. See also Xenos *v.* Fox, L. R. 4 C. P. 65; 38 L. J. C. P. 351; Greeves *v.* West Indian Pacific Steam Co., 20 L. T. Rep. N. S. 912.

[3] The Newport, Swabey, 335; Abbott on Ship., pt. iv. c. 9, p. 385, 11th ed. See also, per STORY, J., in The Nathaniel Hooper, 2 Sum. (U. S.) 542. See also The Mohawk, 8 Wall. (U. S.) 153; Cook *v.* Gowan, 81 Mass. 237; M'Kibbin *v.* Peck, 39 N. Y. 262.

tonia,[1] it appeared that a Prussian ship, carrying an English cargo, was chartered to proceed to Falmouth, for orders which were to be given within three days after arrival there, for one safe port in Great Britain, or on the Continent between Havre and Hamburgh, both included, and thence to proceed to that port to deliver her cargo. The vessel duly called at Falmouth, on July 10th, 1870, and on July 11th received orders for Dunkirk, a French port, for which she at once sailed. On July 16th, off Dunkirk, the master was informed by a French pilot, in official uniform, that war had been declared between France and Prussia, and he immediately put back to the Downs, to make inquiries, and arrived there on the 17th, but could get no information. On the 18th he was again told war had broken out, and on the 19th he put into Dover. On the 19th war was actually declared. Under these circumstances the contract to deliver at Dunkirk became illegal for the Prussian ship, and the master declined to proceed, and he further refused to deliver the cargo at Dover, except on payment of freight. The consignees sued the ship in the Admiralty Court, for breach of the charter-party in not delivering the goods at Dunkirk; and SIR R. PHILLIMORE, after a learned exposition of the law both of England and of America, as well as of the opinions of Continental jurists, held that the master was not bound to deliver except on the payment of a *pro ratâ* freight. On this the consignees appealed to the Privy Council, and although the decision was there practically upheld, the Judicial Committee avoided the difficulty by holding[2] that, as the master was entitled to be sent to a safe port, and on the outbreak of war the consignees were bound to give another order, and that, as they demanded their goods at Dover, the master was not bound to deliver there, it being a port within the meaning of the charter, except on payment of full freight, and that the master by delivering at Dover would substantially perform his contract. In delivering the judgment, MELLISH, L. J., said:

[1] L. R. 3 Adm. & Ecc. 24 L. T. Rep. N. S. 521; 1 Asp. Mar. Law Cas. 32.

[2] The Teutonia, 1 Asp. Mar. Law Cas. 214. Almost all the cases on the subject will be found there cited in the arguments.

"Their Lordships having come to the conclusion that the ship-owner has still a lien for the full freight, it becomes unnecessary to consider whether, if Dunkirk had been the only port of discharge, the ship-owner would have been entitled either to freight *pro ratâ itineris* or to a sum by way of compensation for the carriage of the goods from Pisagua to Dover, and they wish to be understood as giving no opinion on these questions, which no doubt are questions of great difficulty and importance;" thus leaving the above question untouched. Another case, somewhat similar, was that of Osgood *v.* Groning.[1]

SEC. 467. **Probable Holding of Courts of Equity.** — It is difficult to see, however, how a court of equity could imply a contract under such circumstances, as the only ground upon which they could proceed to force a consignee to pay would be, that delivery at the intermediate port was in some degree as advantageous to the consignee as the fulfilment of the contract, which would be barely the case in contracts of affreightment. Moreover a court of equity would probably hold that, as a charter-party was a written contract, the parties were bound by its terms, and that, if they had wished to provide against the contingency of the contract becoming illegal, they were bound to have made some provision in their contract so as to meet the emergency, and that having neglected to do so the law could not be expected to help them. Still it is to be remarked that, according to the report of the case of Osgood *v.* Groning in Abbott, the Lord Chancellor "ordered the merchant to admit that he had accepted the goods in the port of London, if it should appear that the master could not reasonably have been required to proceed on the voyage; considering that, if the master could not reasonably have been required, the merchant ought to have accepted the goods, and his refusal to accept them was an act against conscience and a proper subject for the jurisdiction of a court of equity, which, on many occasions, places parties in the situation in which they would stand if that which ought to have been had

[1] 2 Camp. 466; Abbott on Ship., 11th ed., pp. 401, 402.

actually been done."[1] This, however, is the only case in which such a thing seems to have been done.

SEC. 468. **Abandonment of Cargo by Owner.** — Doubt has been felt concerning another incident of freight, and no decision has been arrived at in reference to the point.[2] It is this: Suppose that upon the arrival of the ship at its port of destination, the merchant or his agent chooses to abandon the goods, and leave them in the hands of the master, has he thereby discharged himself from the liability to pay freight? In the case above referred to, LORD ELLENBOROUGH intimated that if the merchant refused to receive the goods on the ground of damages occasioned by the default of the master or mariners, the point would admit of some doubt; and LORD TENTERDEN adds, "In such a case the merchant would derive no benefit whatever from the conveyance, nor would the master have fulfilled his engagement according to the terms of the lading; *quære*, therefore, whether the master could oblige the merchant to pay freight."[3] This *quære* has, however, been answered in the case of Dakin *v*. Oxley, where it was held that a plea that the goods were so damaged by the default of the master as to be of less value than the freight, and that thereupon the owner abandoned them for the said freight to the master, was no answer to a declaration for freight, under a charter-party, and that the owner was bound to pay freight, and could not set off his damage, but had his remedy by way of cross-action. It necessarily results from this case that under no circumstances can the owner abandon his goods in lieu of paying freight, where the master or ship-owner refuses to receive them. The whole law, American, English, and Continental, was there elaborately reviewed by WILLES, J.[4]

[1] Abbott on Ship., 11th ed., pp. 401, 402. See also Ordinance de la Marine de Louis XIV., lib. iii. tit. 3, art. 15; Valin, Emerigon Traité des Assurances et des Contrats à la grosse; par Boulay-Paty, tit. 1, ch. 12, sect. 31, § i.; Pothier, tom. ii.; Des Charteparties, tit. 2, no. 69; Boulay-Paty, tit. 8, sect. 10, tom. ii.; Morgan *v*. Insurance Co. of North America, 4 Dall. (U. S.) 421.

[2] Miles *v*. Bainbridge, cited in Abbott on Ship., 11th ed., p. 380, n.

[3] Abbott on Ship., 11th ed., p. 380, n.; and see Basten *v*. Butler, 7 East, 479.

[4] Dakin *v*. Oxley, 15 C. B. N. S. 646;

SEC. 469. **Legality of Voyage.** — The voyage must be legal to entitle a ship-owner to freight, for freight is the reward which the law allows a person to recover for bringing goods lawfully upon a legal voyage.[1] Where a vessel was freighted from Dantzic to London, and was, on her arrival, and after part of her cargo had been delivered, seized by the revenue officers, on suspicion that she was Prussian built, the treasury, on petition, ordered the ship to be restored on condition that the cargo should be exported, and on payment of 50*l.* as satisfaction to the seizing officers; and it was held that this of itself was sufficient to show that the voyage was illegal, without condemnation, and that, although the freighters accepted and exported the cargo according to the terms of the order, the master was precluded from recovering freight.[2]

SEC. 470. **Right to Cargo.** — There is another right which a carrier has, which must be mentioned, and that is to have the cargo which has been contracted for supplied. If the merchant shipper fails to do so, an action brought by the ship-owner will lie, and the damages will be measured by the difference between what the plaintiff would have earned if the contract had been fulfilled, and that which he has earned, notwithstanding the breach;[3] but supposing he is unable to earn anything, he will be entitled to a sum equivalent to the freight under the contract, less the expenses he would have incurred in earning that freight. But a ship-owner, whose charterer fails to supply a cargo, is bound to use due diligence in endeavoring to procure another; he is not entitled by reason of the failure to lie idle, and to claim his full freight.

SEC. 471. **8 & 9 Vict. c. 20, § 97.** — Another right of carriers requires to be mentioned in this place. Looked at in one aspect, it might be called a special right, as it is bestowed by Act of Parliament upon a certain class of carriers. As it is so, and as there can be very little doubt as to the exact meaning of

2 Mar. Law Cas. o. s. 6; Abbott on Ship., 11th ed., pt. iv. c. 9, § 7, p. 379.

[1] See Muller *v.* Gernon, 3 Taunt. 394. See also Blanck *v.* Solly, Holt, 554.

[2] Blanck *v.* Solly, 1 Moore, 531; Holt, 554. See also Hatchwell *v.* Cooke, 6 Taunt. 577.

[3] Hunter *v.* Fry, 2 B. & A. 421, 424 *et seq.*; Cockburn *v.* Alexander, 6 C. B. 814; Harriss *v.* Edmonds, 1 C. & K. 686.

the statute, a very few words will suffice. By the 8 & 9 Vict. c. 20, § 97, it is provided that, "if on demand any person fail to pay the tolls due in respect of any carriage or goods, it shall be lawful for the company to detain and sell such carriage, or all or any part of such goods, or, if the same shall have been moved from the premises of the company, to detain or sell any other carriages or goods within such premises belonging to the party liable to pay such tolls, and out of the moneys arising from such sale to detain the tolls payable as aforesaid, and all charges and expenses of such detention and sale, rendering the overplus, if any, of the moneys arising by such sale, and such of the carriages and goods as shall remain unsold to the person entitled thereto." In the case of Field *v.* Newport, Abergavenny, and Hereford Railway Company,[1] it was decided that a demand of the sum actually due for tolls is a condition precedent to the right to sell. In that case the circumstances were these: The company was by its act empowered to take tolls for the use of its railway in respect of tonnage of articles conveyed upon the railway, certain sums per ton, and a further sum if the goods were conveyed in the carriages of the company, together with tolls for the use of engines. There was fixed a maximum rate of charge, including the charges for the use of the carriages, wagons, or trucks, and for locomotive power, and all other charges incident to such conveyance. The company was also entitled to take increased charges for the conveyance of goods, by agreement with the owners of the goods, by reason of any special service. The company, having for a considerable time carried on their line coals, in carriages belonging to the plaintiff, from Pontypool Junction to Hereford, made a demand of a gross sum equal to the amount of the tonnage rates for coals and use of engines; and also of a sum claimed by them for sending back the plaintiff empty carriages from Hereford to Pontypool. They gave no explanation of the items making up the gross sum claimed. The plaintiff, having omitted to pay the amount claimed, the company sold the plaintiff's carriages and goods to satisfy the amount due.

[1] 3 H. & N. 409; 27 L. J. Exch. 396.

SEC. 472. **Construction of Statute.** — But it was held by the court that the sum claimed by the company for sending back the return wagons was not toll, and that, the company having demanded a larger sum than that due for tolls, the sale was unlawful. These statutory powers must be complied with in all strictness. That is evident from the case just quoted, and still more clearly so from another case, in which it appeared that the railway company under its act was entitled to seize and sell goods for which tolls due to the company have not been paid; but at the same time it provided that the persons seizing the goods should have their names annexed to the list of tolls, and that a demand should, previous to such seizure, have been made; and that, on refusal to satisfy the demand, the goods have been appraised. In the case under consideration, it appeared that goods were seized by the company, who had been in the habit of carrying goods belonging to the plaintiff, and to whom arrears of tolls were due, without the goods having been appraised, and the only evidence of a demand, in conformity with the statute, was the presenting of a bill of the plaintiff for the amount of the tolls, which was dishonored. Under these circumstances the company had no right to seize the goods.[1]

[1] North *v.* London & North-Western Rail. Co., 14 C. B. N. S. 132; 9 Jur. N. S. 869; 32 L. J. C. P. 156; 11 W. R. 624.

CHAPTER XI.

CARRIERS OF PASSENGERS.

SEC. 473. **The Importance of the Subject.** — There are few subjects, the thorough knowledge of which is of more importance to the lawyer than that to which we must now turn our attention. Its importance at the present time is infinitely greater than it ever was before. Owing to the facilities of communication which have been produced and perfected in recent years, the number of persons travelling is now infinitely greater than it ever was at any previous period. In bygone times populations were sedentary. The difficulties and disagreeables of a journey, the slowness of all the modes of conveyance, and the time necessarily occupied in even the shortest journey deterred many from ever leaving the town or county in which they were born. Now, these conditions being reversed, the result is as much an extreme in the other direction. Everybody travels in our days, and hence the increased importance of the law which has to do with their mutual relations to the individuals or companies who undertake to carry them as passengers; for the importance of a law is in the direct proportion to the number of persons it directly or indirectly affects.

SEC. 474. **Difference between Duties of Carriers of Goods and Passengers.** — As the traffic in passengers has been of rapid growth, so has this department of law been of rapid development. The first case in which damages were recovered for injury done to a person seems to have been tried in the end of the last century.[1] There LORD KENYON said that when the proprietors of mail-coaches "carried passengers, they were bound to carry safely and properly."[2] There can be no doubt, whether these words "to carry safely and properly" contain the whole duty of a carrier of passengers or not, that the duty which devolves upon a common carrier of persons, as passengers, and a common carrier of goods, must differ from one another in a variety of important ways. The fact that goods are not endowed with intelligence, and cannot be supposed to exercise any care or caution with a view to their own safety, evidently makes an important distinction between them and persons who can exercise such a care, in so far as their conveyance by a carrier is concerned. If a carrier knows that he carries gold and silver, he is bound to be more diligent than if he were carrying stone or lime. Reason points out the probability of the former running much greater risk of being stolen than the latter. So, even with regard to the same kind of goods, the carrier's care and diligence must vary from time to time in degree, as there is greater danger at night than during the day, and as some places are known, from their lonely nature or disreputable character, to be more lawless than others; so in distinguishing between the duties

[1] White *v.* Boulton, Peake's Cases, 81.

[2] The rule adopted in this country has been repeatedly held to be that a stage proprietor is bound to furnish good coaches, gentle and well-broken horses, and a prudent and skilful driver, and that a recovery may be had for an injury resulting to a passenger from any fault in these respects. McKinney *v.* Niel, 1 McLean (U. S.), 540; Farish *v.* Reigle, 11 Gratt. (Va.) 697; Peck *v.* Neil, 3 McLean (U. S), 22; Hanley *v.* Harlem R. R. Co., 1 Edm. (N. Y.) Sel. Cas. 359; Sales *v.* Western Stage Co., 4 Iowa, 547; Ingalls *v.* Bills, 9 Met. (Mass.) 1. But he is not liable for a mere accident. McKinney *v.* Niel, *ante;* McLane *v.* Sharp, 2 Harr. (Del.) 481.

appertaining to these two kinds of traffic — goods traffic and passenger traffic — reason must be brought to bear; and it will show that the intelligence of persons carried as passengers, their immunity from theft, their capacity to avoid dangers, and their liability through their own want of care to incur risks which are not incident to bales and boxes, must draw a broad distinction between the duties and liabilities which devolve upon and are incurred by carriers who undertake these dissimilar branches of the same trade.

SEC. 475. **Carrier of Passengers not an Insurer.** — The intelligence and volition of the persons carried makes such a material difference in all possible calculations, that it precludes the carrier from assuming the duty of the insurer with regard to them, and the law has not felt it necessary to impose this duty upon him.[1] Had the law done so, one result would inevitably have followed, and that would have been either the refusal of carriers to undertake passenger traffic, or their refusal of it, except upon special contracts affecting every individual case. They must necessarily by one means or another have brought down their liability to that of special carriers for hire, or have increased their charges to such an extent as to cover all possible losses, not only from unavoidable accidents, but from voluntary fraud or personal negligence. But the law has not done so, and the carrier of passengers — although he is called a common carrier [2] — does not insure or warrant the safety of his passengers; he contracts only to use reasonable skill and prudence in carrying, and he is consequently liable only for actual or culpable negligence.[3] This distinction was made by PARKE, J., in the case of Crofts *v.*

[1] The duty of a carrier of passengers must bear some relation to the capability of the individual to take care of him or her self; just as the duty of a common carrier of goods is modified in relation to the nature and value of the goods intrusted to him. Thus it would behoove a carrier to be more careful of the very young or the very aged and infirm, than he is of persons in the prime of life. Sheridan *v.* Brooklyn, &c. R. R. Co., 36 N. Y. 39; Sawyer *v.* Dulany, 30 Tex. 479.

[2] But see Aston *v.* Heaven, 2 Esp. 533; Sharp *v.* Grey, 9 Bing. 460; Bennett *v.* Peninsular Steamboat Co., 6 C. B. 775; 18 L. J. 85.

[3] Redhead *v.* Midland Rail. Co., 2 L. R. Q. B. 412; and in Exch. Ch. 4 L. R. Q. B. 379.

Waterhouse.[1] "There is a wide distinction," he said, "between contracts for the conveyance of passengers and those for the conveyance of goods. In the latter case the parties are liable at all events, except the goods be destroyed or damaged by the act of God or the king's enemies; whilst in the former case they are only responsible to their passengers in case of express negligence."

SEC. 476. **Duty of a Carrier of Passengers.** — Now the latter is just the duty that a special carrier for hire is bound to perform, and if he does not do it he is responsible to the owner. Consequently the duty and liability of a common carrier of passengers are similar to the duty and liability of a special carrier of goods for hire. It is at the same time evident that the liability of a carrier is not a constant quantity (so to speak), even although he is only a special carrier for hire, and he is bound to bestow that amount of care that the thing or person requires; and as the circumstances may vary, so may his duty, and consequently, in the event of injury, his liability.[2] The policy of the law made common carriers insurers of the goods they carried, with a view to preventing fraudulent combinations, which, if the law had been less strict in this particular, would doubtless have arisen between the carrier and the robber; and the policy of the law continues that extensive responsibility in the persons of the carriers of passengers with regard to the luggage which the passengers carry with them.[3] But to hold that a similar rule was necessary with regard to those carriers who conveyed passengers was to shut one's eyes to the reason of its introduction in the other case. Consequently a carrier of this nature is not liable for an injury to a passenger which cannot be ascribed to any want of due care, diligence,

[1] 11 Moore, 138; cf. Lovett *v.* Hobbs, 2 Shaw. 428. See also Christie *v.* Griggs, 2 Camp. 79, per SIR JAMES MANSFIELD.

[2] Stokes *v.* Saltonstall, 13 Pet. (U. S.) 150; Boyce *v.* Anderson, 2 Pet. (U. S.) 150; The New World *v.* King, 16 How. (U. S.) 469; Brockway *v.* Lascala, 1 Edm. (N. Y.) Sel. Cas. 135; Maverick *v.* Eighth Avenue R. R. Co., 36 N. Y. 378; Johnson *v.* Winona, &c. R. R. Co., 11 Minn. 296; Wheaton *v.* North Beach, &c. R. R. Co., 36 Cal. 590; Fuller *v.* Naugatuck R. R Co., 21 Conn. 563, 576; Hall *v.* Connecticut River Steamboat Co., 13 Conn. 326.

[3] *Ante*, pp. 112, 113.

or skill upon his part. But the highest degree of care must be exercised to preserve the safety of passengers, and it has been held that the mere circumstance that a passenger is injured, in the absence of circumstances repelling it, raises a presumption of negligence;[1] and this is undoubtedly the rule when the circumstances are such as to fairly warrant the presumption,[2] but not otherwise.[3] He is not liable to a passenger as a common carrier, nor as an insurer of his safety, because, being himself a rational being, it is presumed that the passenger will look after his own safety, — as a reasonable being naturally would, — except in so far as he must necessarily depend upon the carrier.[4]

SEC. 477. **What is Due Care, Skill, and Diligence in Carrier of Passengers.** —What will amount to such a culpable want of skill, care, or diligence has already been indicated; but with a view to making the matter clear, we may allude to one or two decisions which indicate the true scope of the duty. Thus, in the case of Toomey *v.* The London, Brighton, and South Coast Railway,[5] it appeared that on the platform of one of the com-

[1] Sullivan *v.* Philadelphia, &c. R. R. Co., 30 Penn. St. 234; Baltimore, &c. R. R. Co. *v.* Worthington, 21 Md. 275.

[2] Feital *v.* Middlesex R. R. Co., 109 Mass. 398; Iron R. R. Co. *v.* Mowery, 26 Ohio St. 418; Delaware, &c. R. R. Co. *v.* Napheys, 90 Penn. St. 135; Dougherty *v.* Missouri, &c. R. R. Co., 9 Mo. App. 478.

[3] Holbrook *v.* Utica, &c. R. R. Co., 12 N. Y. 236.

[4] Redman's Law of Railway Carriers, 5.

[5] 3 C. B. N. S. 146. See also Botch *v.* Smith, 7 H. & N. 736. The rule laid down by MANSFIELD, C. J., in Christie *v.* Griggs, 2 Camp. 79, that while a carrier does not warrant the safety of a passenger, yet he is bound to provide for his safe conveyance, *so far as human care and foresight will go*, is generally adopted in this country. Indianapolis, &c. R. R. Co. *v.* Horst, 93 U. S. 291; New Jersey R. R. Co. *v.* Kennard, 21 Penn. St. 203; Meir *v.* Pennsylvania R. R. Co., 64 Penn. St. 225; Laing *v.* Calder, 8 Penn. St. 479; The Oriflamme, 3 Sawyer (U. S. C. C.), 397; Philadelphia, &c. R. R. Co. *v.* Derby, 14 How. (U. S.) 468; Tuller *v.* Talbot, 23 Ill. 357. Thus, while a railroad company is not liable for an injury resulting from a latent defect in an axle or wheel, which is not discoverable by the ordinary tests, Meir *v.* Pennsylvania R. R. Co., *ante*, yet it is liable for an injury resulting from a defect not externally discoverable, when it has made no effort to detect such defects. Scott *v.* Ohio, &c. R. R. Co. (Penn.), 13 Leg. Int. 336. In reference to the safety of the vehicles employed to carry passengers, the question as to whether the carrier is liable for injuries resulting from imperfections therein, depends upon the circumstance as to whether he has been guilty of negligence in reference

pany's stations there were two doors in close proximity to each other; the one for necessary purposes had painted over it the words "For Gentlemen," the other had over it the words "Lamp Room." The plaintiff, having occasion to go to the urinal, inquired of a stranger where he should find it, and, having received a direction, by mistake opened the door of the "lamp room," and fell down some steps and was injured. In an action against the railway company it was held that, in the absence of evidence that the place was more than ordinarily dangerous, the judge was justified in nonsuiting the plaintiff, on the ground that there was no evidence of negligence upon the part of the railway company. In that case, WILLIAMS, J., stated a rule which has been adopted by judges in subsequent cases, which is to the following effect: "It is not enough to say that there was *some* evidence. A scintilla of evidence or a mere surmise that there may have been negligence on the

to them, and this largely involves the question as to whether skilful workmen were employed for their construction, and proper diligence was used to ascertain whether suitable materials were used, or there were imperfections therein arising from any cause; and if the injury arose from any hidden defect which could not be discovered by the utmost vigilance, the carrier cannot be held responsible for injuries resulting therefrom, because he has not been guilty of negligence in respect thereto. M'Elroy *v.* Nashua & Lowell R. R. Co., 4 Cush. (Mass.) 400. In Ingalls *v.* Bills, 9 Met. (Mass.) 1, a passenger in a stage-coach was injured by the breaking of one of the iron axletrees, in which there was a small flaw, entirely surrounded by sound iron one fourth of an inch thick, and which could not be discovered by the most careful examination, and the court held that the stage proprietors could not be held chargeable for the injury thus received. The rule adopted in this case, and which is generally recognized, is that carriers of passengers for hire are bound to use the utmost care and diligence in providing safe, sufficient, and suitable coaches, harnesses, horses, and coachmen, in order to prevent those injuries which human care and foresight can guard against, and that if an accident happens from a defect in a coach, which might have been discovered and remedied upon the most careful and thorough examination of the coach, such accident must be ascribed to negligence, for which the owner is liable; but that, on the other hand, if the accident arises from a hidden and internal defect, which the most thorough examination would not disclose, and which could not be guarded against by the exercise of a sound judgment and the most vigilant oversight, the owner of the coach cannot be held answerable therefor. The same rule has been applied to railroad companies, not only as to their cars, tracks, structures, &c., but also in the management of their trains. M'Elroy *v.* Nashua & Lowell R. R. Co., *ante.*

part of the defendants clearly would not justify the judge in leaving the case to the jury; there must be evidence on which they might reasonably and properly conclude that there was negligence."[1]

SEC. 478. **Implications.** — Necessarily much uncertainty has been felt as to what circumstances will render a carrier liable to a passenger in case of injury occurring during the journey, and as to what the carrier does actually undertake to do for an individual who becomes a passenger by his conveyance. No human transaction is fully explicated at the time it is entered upon. Much is in most cases left unexpressed, but is not the less an important part of the transaction with regard to the rights and duties of the parties, although it is introduced only by implication. Some things are so obvious that it does not seem necessary to point them out, and some incidents to a bargain are so absolutely necessary to the objects with a view to which it is entered upon that the statement of them at the time would seem a redundancy. Where that is the case, the law makes the necessary implication as much a part of the contract as the actual expression. Thus, where a person sells a piece of land in the centre of his own property, it might not occur to the buyer to stipulate for the right to pass over the vendor's property to reach his purchase. It seems so obvious that no one would purchase property in such a position without some such condition that the vendee is entitled to conclude that no one would think of selling the thing without at the same time disposing of this incident right. Hence upon these grounds the implication would be regarded as a part of the contract. So in all questions with regard to the carriage of passengers. The contract which is expressly entered upon is that of conveyance, but conveyance without a considerable certainty of safety would not be entered upon; so, with a view of securing that, the law has thought it best to impose a duty of

[1] Where a train runs off the track, Feital *v.* Middlesex, &c. R. R. Co., 109 Mass. 398, or is overturned, Pittsburg, &c. R. R. Co. *v.* Thompson, 56 Ill. 138; Yonge *v.* Kinney, 28 Ga. 111, or is submerged by reason of the washing away of an embankment, this is *primâ facie* evidence of negligence. Brehm *v.* Great Western R. R. Co., 34 Barb. (N. Y.) 256.

carrying with a certain amount of care upon the carrier, for a breach of which an action will lie. The express contract is to carry, but there is an understanding that the business of carrying will be undertaken and accomplished with care and caution. And it is because this is an almost necessary result of human nature, under the circumstances it has become law; and we find that a carrier must use due care and diligence, and that in case these are not used, and injury is done to a passenger, which is directly ascribable to his neglect, he will be liable to that passenger for the injury done. We have considered these broad principles which lie at the foundation of this matter, and we have examined some of the cases which bear principally upon stational arrangements and the like; but we may turn for a time to the consideration of those cases in which negligence in carrying has been the ground of action, for, although the principles involved in all these are the same, it is sometimes more convenient for a reader to have actual illustrations than to be possessed of the grounds upon which individual cases were actually decided.

SEC. 479. **Evidence of Negligence.** — Thus, in one case, where a passenger by an excursion train was injured in an accident which occurred upon the line of the London, Brighton, and South Coast Railway Company, owing to the excursion train which had been hired by a society from the company, — the tickets for which had been sold and distributed, not by a servant of the company, but by the secretary of the society that hired the train, — running in the dark against another train which was standing still at an intermediate station, and where the declaration alleged that the plaintiff had at the request of the company become a passenger for hire in one of their trains, and that in consequence of the carelessness, negligence, and want of skill of the company and their servants, the plaintiff was injured, it was held that the mere fact of the accident having occurred was *primâ facie* evidence of negligence on the part of the company, and also that there was evidence to go to the jury in support of the allegation that the plaintiff became a passenger for hire with the company.[1]

[1] Skinner *v.* London, Brighton, & South Coast Rail. Co., 5 Exch. 787; 15 Jur. 299; Zemp *v.* Wilmington, &c. R. R. Co., 9 Rich. (S. C.) 84;

SEC. 480. **Rule in Carpue v. London, &c. Railway Co.** — In Carpue *v.* London and Brighton Railway Company,[1] it appeared that the defendants were empowered to make a railway, which all persons were to have the liberty of using, with carriages, on payment of tolls, regulated by the act. The company was also empowered to provide locomotive engines and charge for their use, and to use locomotive engines and carriages for the conveyance of passengers, and to charge for such conveyance in addition to the tolls, within a limited amount. It was enacted that no action should be prosecuted against any person for anything done, or omitted to be done, in pursuance of the act, or in the execution of the powers given by it without twenty days' notice in writing. A declaration against the company charged, that they were owners of the railway and of carriages used for the conveyance of passengers along it for reward, that the plaintiff became a passenger in one of the carriages for reward to them, and it became their duty to use due care in conveying him; breach, that they did not use due care in conveying him, but so negligently conducted themselves in carrying him, and managing the carriage in which he was a passenger, the train to which it was attached, and the engine whereby it was drawn upon the railway, that the carriage was thrown off the rails and the plaintiff injured. In this case it was held that no notice of action was necessary, the company being sued in their capacity of carriers, and not for anything done or omitted under the act. The duty to carry, with due and proper care and skill, was held to arise in relation to a person who accompanied letters carried on a railway pursuant to 1 & 2 Vict. c. 28.[2]

SEC. 481. **Rule in Cornman v. The Eastern Counties Railway Co.** — In Cornman *v.* The Eastern Counties Railway Company,[3] the defendants, a railway company, had on their platform, standing against a pillar which passengers passed

Sullivan *v.* Philadelphia, &c. R. R. Co., 30 Penn. St. 234; New Orleans, &c. Co., 38 Miss. 242.

[1] 5 Q. B. 747; D. & M. 608; 3 Rail. Cas. 692; 13 L. J. Q. B. 138.

[2] Collet *v.* London & North-Western Rail. Co., 11 Jur. 1053; 20 L. J. Q. B. 411; 16 Q. B. 984.

[3] 4 H. & N. 781; 29 L. J. Exch. 94.

going to and from the trains, a portable weighing-machine, which was used for weighing passengers' luggage, and the foot of which projected about six inches above the level of the platform. It was unfenced, and had stood in the same position without any accident having occurred to persons passing it for about five years. The plaintiff, being at the station on Christmas Day inquiring for a parcel, was driven by the crowd against the machine, caught his foot in it, and fell over it. It was held that there was no evidence of negligence to go to the jury, the machine being in a situation in which it might have been seen, and the accident not being shown to be one which could have been reasonably anticipated. BRAMWELL, B., said: "In such a case it is always a question whether the mischief could have been reasonably foreseen. Nothing is so easy as being wise after the event. Here the evidence was that the company might reasonably have anticipated that no mischief could occur, since no mischief had resulted from keeping the machine in the position in which it stood for so long a period."[1]

SEC. 482. **Stational Arrangements.** Another case which bears on the duty of a carrier in so far as stational arrangements are concerned, and one which is nicely distinguished from those just referred to, is the case of Longmore *v.* The Great Western Railway Company.[2] There the defendant company, with a view to the more convenient access of passengers between the two platforms of a station, erected across the line a wooden bridge, which the jury found to be dangerous, and it was held that the defendants were liable for the death of a passenger through the faulty construction of the bridge, although there was a safer one about one hundred yards further round, which the deceased might have used.[3] If their premises are reasonably and ordinarily fit for safe use, and an accident happens, it is no valid argument that

[1] See also, per ERLE, C. J., in Marfell *v.* South Wales Rail. Co., 8 C. B. N. S. 525, 534; Rigg *v.* Manchester, &c. Rail. Co., 14 W. R. 834.

[2] 19 C. B. N. S. 183.

[3] See also Martin *v.* Great Northern Rail. Co., 16 C. B. 179; and Leishman *v.* London, Brighton, & South Coast Rail. Co., 19 W. R. 106.

the best possible precautions had not been used. Where the defendants had a staircase at one of their stations for the use of passengers — it led from the arrival platform to the street, was about six feet wide, had walls on either side, and had wooden steps nosed with brass, which had become smooth from use — and the plaintiff who, together with a large number of others, had used these stairs without accident for months, on ascending them slipped on the brass nosing and hurt himself, brought an action, and relied on the evidence of a builder, who said that brass nosings were improper on such a staircase, that lead would be the proper material to use, and that there should be hand-rails, it was held that there was no evidence to go to the jury.[1]

SEC. 483. **Invitation to alight. — Rule in Praeger v. The Bristol, &c. Railway Co.** — In the case of Praeger *v.* The Bristol and Exeter Railway Company,[2] it appeared that the plaintiff had been travelling as a second-class passenger from Clevedon to Bristol by the defendants' line of railway, and occupied the last compartment of the hindmost carriage of the train, which consisted of an engine and tender and two composite carriages. The journey from Clevedon is performed on a branch line, as far as Yatton, at which place there are separate platforms for the branch and main lines. The branch platform at Yatton is about 130 feet long, and for about 100 feet of its length, from the inner, or Yatton, end of it, runs quite straight or parallel with the branch line rails, and for that distance the space between it and the carriages is about ten inches wide. The further or outer end of the platform is, for the purposes of the traffic, curved or bevelled off from the line of rails, so that at that part of it the space between it and the carriages is about eighteen inches wide. There is, however, attached to each carriage, immediately outside the door, an iron step, ten inches wide, so that the space between the platform and

[1] Crafter *v.* Metropolitan Rail. Co., L. R. 1 C. P. 300; 35 L. J. C. P. 132. See also Blackman *v.* London, Brighton, & South Coast Rail. Co., 14 W. R. 769. See also Leishman *v.* London, Brighton, & South Coast Rail. Co., 22 L. T. N. S. 712.

[2] 23 L. T. N. S. 366; and 24 L. J. N. S. 105 Exch. Ch.

the carriages is thereby bridged over by the step, and reduced thereby to the width of eight inches. Upon the day in question it appeared that the train in which the plaintiff was travelling drew up at the branch platform, and was stopped about twenty feet short of the extreme end of it, where stationary buffers, or "dead ends," are fixed, and the compartment of the carriage in which the plaintiff was sitting was, when the train stopped, immediately opposite the curved or bevelled-off part of the platform described above. The name of the station was called out, and the door of the carriage was opened, and several of the plaintiff's fellow-passengers got out and alighted in safety on the platform. The plaintiff then proceeded to follow them, and stepped out of the carriage, as he had always before been in the habit of doing, without using the iron step, expecting to step as usual upon the platform, instead of which he stepped into the eighteen-inch vacant space between the carriage and the platform, and falling through received the injury for which he sought compensation in the action alluded to. It was admitted that he had often travelled by the same line before, and knew the nature of the platform, but he had never before travelled in the last compartment of the hindmost carriage, and was not aware that he had stopped opposite the curved part of the platform. There were paraffin oil lamps on the platform, and one in the carriage itself, but it did not appear that the lights, whatever and wherever they were, were such as to enable a passenger clearly to distinguish the vacant space from the solid platform. Negligence was charged by the plaintiff and denied by the defendants, and the defendants charged the plaintiff with contributory negligence. The jury found for the plaintiff for 1,600*l.* damages. Upon a rule it was held by KELLY, C. B., and PIGOTT, B. (MARTIN, B., *dissentiente*), that there was no evidence to go to the jury of negligence upon the part of the defendants. This decision was reversed in the Court of Exchequer Chambers, where it was held that there was evidence of the negligence of the defendants to go to the jury, inasmuch as there was a clear invitation to the plaintiff to alight and no warning given, although in consequence of the insufficiency of light the danger was not apparent.

SEC. 484. **With regard to Stational Arrangements.** — In an action against a railway company, it was proved that the plaintiff was bitten by a stray dog at a railway station belonging to the defendants while waiting for a train. It was also proved that at 9 P. M. the dog flew at and tore the dress of another female on the platform; that at 10.30 he attacked a cat in the signal-box near the station, when the porter there kicked him out and saw no more of him, and that he made his appearance again at 10.40 on the platform, where he bit the plaintiff. In this case it was held that there was no evidence to warrant a jury in finding that the company had been guilty of any negligence in keeping the station reasonably safe for passengers.[1] Another duty of the common carriers, in so far as they are possessors of stational accommodation, which they erect with

[1] Smith *v.* Great Western Rail. Co., 2 L. R. C. P. 4. See also Hammack *v.* White, 11 C. B. N. S. 588; 31 L. J. C. P. 129; Byrne *v.* Boadle, 2 H. & C. 722; 33 L. J. Exch. 13; Scott *v.* London Dock Co., 3 H. & C. 596; 34 L. J. Exch. 220. See also Daniel *v.* Directors of the Metropolitan Rail. Co., 6 L. R. H. of L. 45; 40 L. J. C. P. 121. In this case the plaintiff, while travelling by the defendant railway, was injured by the fall of an iron girder which was being placed over part of the railway with the knowledge of the defendants, and in the construction of works which were to be partly executed to their satisfaction, but were not under the control of the defendant company. It was proved that the work was extremely dangerous, although this was the first occasion upon which a girder had fallen. It also appeared that when work of such a nature was being carried on over a railway, the company had posted a signalman either to warn the work-people of the approach of a train, and to stop them if they were under the control of the railway company, or to warn the driver of the train so as to stop the train before incurring any danger, and that upon this occasion this precaution had not been adopted. By consent a verdict had been entered for the plaintiff, with leave reserved to defendants to set it aside, on the ground that there was not sufficient evidence of the defendants' negligence, the court to be at liberty to draw inferences of fact, and to adjudge upon the evidence. The result of the decision in this case was to establish the principle, that where the execution of work, which, if carefully and properly done, need not result in accident to passers-by, is intrusted to skilled and proper workmen, there is no obligation on a railway company, whose line adjoins the work, to take special precautions to avert from their passengers a danger which can only be apprehended on the supposition that the workmen engaged will do their work negligently, — at all events, if the company have no control over the workmen, and are otherwise not responsible for their acts; and LORD WESTBURY held that it would not affect the doctrine if those proper and skilled workmen were employed directly by the company.

the purpose of conveniencing the passengers who come to them to be carried, was discussed in the case of Foy *v.* London, Brighton, and South Coast Railway Company.[1]

SEC. 485. **Platform Accommodation.** — On the arrival of a train of the defendant company at the railway terminus, there not being room for all the carriages to be drawn up to the platform, some of the passengers were required to alight upon the line beyond it, the depth from the carriage to the ground being about three feet. In so alighting, a lady, the wife of the plaintiff, instead of availing herself of the two steps, with the assistance of a gentleman, jumped from the first step to the ground, and sustained a spinal injury from the concussion. The jury having found that the company were guilty of negligence in not providing reasonable means of alighting, and that the lady had not by any misconduct on her part contributed to the injury, and having awarded her 500*l.*, the court held that there was evidence to warrant their finding, and declined to interfere with the amount of damages. So, in Bridges *v.* The North London Railway Company,[2] an

[1] 18 C. B. N. S. 225; affirmed Exch. Ch. L. R. 4 Exch. 117; 38 L. J. Exch. 67. See also Harrold *v.* Great Western Rail. Co., 14 L. T. Rep. 440; Adams *v.* Lancashire & Yorkshire Rail. Co., 38 L. J. C. P. 277; Plant *v.* Midland Rail. Co., 21 L. T. Rep. 836.

[2] L. R. 5 C. P. 459 n. It is an invariable rule that railroad companies must provide reasonable accommodations for passengers at their stations, and the safety of passengers must be consulted in those respects as well as in respect to their cars and machinery. McDonald *v.* Chicago, &c. R. R. Co., 26 Iowa, 124. And it has been held gross negligence to leave a hole in the depot floor, Liscomb *v.* New Jersey, &c. R. R. Co., 6 Lans. (N. Y.) 75, or not to provide suitable lights to enable a passenger to see to get on and off the train. Patten *v.* Chicago, &c. R. R. Co., 32 Wis. 524. Upon the duty of a railway company in this respect, see Caswell *v.* Boston, &c. R. R. Co., 98 Mass. 194; Memphis, &c. R. R. Co. *v.* Whitfield, 44 Miss. 466; Stewart *v.* International R. R. Co., 53 Tex. 289. This liability is not strictly to passengers, but exists as well in favor of all persons who are lawfully at the station upon business. Thus in Tobin *v.* Portland, &c. R. R. Co., 59 Me. 183, the defendant was held liable to a hackman for an injury received by him while carrying a passenger to the depot for transportation, by stepping into a cavity in the platform, and occasioned solely by such unsafe condition of the platform.

But where the company has provided safe platforms, &c., it is not liable for injuries resulting to a passenger by voluntarily alighting at some other point. Pennsylvania R. R. Co. *v.* Zebe, 33 Penn. St. 318; Forsyth *v.* Boston & Albany R. R. Co., 103 Mass. 510.

action was brought by a widow to recover compensation for the death of her husband through the defendants' negligence. The facts of the case were, that a train of the defendants' drew up at the Highbury Station, the last carriage, in which the deceased was sitting, being in a tunnel, which terminated at the station, and not at the platform. The name of the station was called out by a porter, and the deceased immediately got out and fell on the rails and was killed. The jury expressed a strong opinion that, the train having stopped and the name of the station having been called out, the passengers had a right to presume that they might get out. BLACKBURN, J., however, nonsuited the plaintiff, with leave to the plaintiff to enter a verdict for 1,200*l*. Upon motion, the Court of Queen's Bench held that the calling out of the name of the station did not necessarily entitle the passengers to get out, and that, under all the circumstances of the case, the deceased was not justified in doing so.[1]

SEC. 486. **Invitation to alight.** — The result of these cases as bearing upon the question of the liability of railway companies for accidents occurring at stations in consequence of the drawing up of a train in such a way as to lead passengers to suppose that they are invited by the railway company's servants to alight, seems to be this, that there must be sufficient evidence to induce a reasonable man to believe that the train is actually at the alighting platform, and that the passengers are invited to alight, and at the same time there must be the exercise of such care upon the part of the passenger as will free him from the imputation of having contributed to the accident of which he complains.[2] In one case, although the train had drawn up at the platform, the name of the station had not been called out, and some of the judges of the Court of Common Pleas held that without some such announcement a passenger was not justified in getting out of the carriage,

[1] See also Petty *v.* Great Western Rail. Co., 5 L. R. C. P. 461 n. Other cases have come before the court since this one in the Queen's Bench. See also Siner *v.* Great Western Rail. Co., 4 L. R. Exch. 117.

[2] St. Louis, &c. R. R. Co. *v.* Cantrell, 37 Ark. 519; 40 Am. Rep. 105; Commonwealth *v.* Boston & Maine R. R. Co., 129 Mass. 500; 37 Am. Rep. 382; also reporter's note, 384.

and that, having got out at a place where the platform was some feet from the carriage, and having fallen and been injured, she had been guilty of contributory negligence, which relieved the railway company from the responsibility of its servant the engine-driver.[1] In another case, however, where a long train of the defendant company's was stopped at a platform, so that part of it was alongside the parapet of a bridge, and in the dark, the plaintiff, after the train had stopped and the defendants' servants had called out the name of the station, stepped upon the parapet, believing it was the platform, and fell over, it was held by the same court that, in an action brought to recover damages for the injuries sustained by the fall, the judge was right in leaving it to the jury to determine whether the circumstances amounted to an invitation to the plaintiff to alight; and further, that there was evidence of negligence on the defendants' part to justify the verdict which the jury found for the plaintiff.[2]

SEC. 487. **What will entitle Passenger to alight.** — The mere calling out of the name of the station would not of itself entitle a passenger to alight if there were other circumstances which led him to believe that the carriage was not at the platform. Nor would the absence of all proof that the name of the station had been publicly announced free a railway company from liability for the consequences of an accident occurring through some defect in their platform arrangements, if there had been other indications of an invitation, upon the part of the defendants' servants, to the passengers to leave their carriages, as, for instance, the opening of the carriage

[1] Cockle *v.* London & South-Western Rail. Co., 5 L. R. C. P. 457; 39 L. J. C. P. 226. In Forsyth *v.* Boston & Albany R. R. Co., 103 Mass. 510, a passenger alighted from the train, on a dark night, at a station of the defendant, on one of two platforms extending along each side of the track to a highway which, as the plaintiff knew, crossed the railroad, and having a step at the end next to the highway. Instead of keeping on the platform he voluntarily stepped from it to cross the track to the highway, and in doing so stepped into a cavity dug across the track for a cattle-guard, and was injured. The court held that the company was not liable, as he was not at the time in the exercise of due care.

[2] Whittaker *v.* Manchester, Sheffield, & Lincolnshire Rail. Co., 22 L. T. N. S. 545.

doors without the intimation that it was for the inspection of tickets, or the removal by any such servant of part of the passengers' luggage or the like. But the question of what circumstances amount to an invitation to alight is clearly one for a jury; and although there seems to have been difficulty felt in time past by some of our judges in reference to this point of law, it seems impossible that any further doubt should exist.[1]

SEC. 488. **Latent Defects.** — One case of much importance in the decision of all questions relating to the responsibility of a carrier for an injury caused to a passenger, has been somewhat recently decided. The question in that case was as to the effect of a latent defect upon the common-law duty devolving upon the carrier of passengers to exercise care and diligence and skill.[2] There the casualty occurred through the breaking of the tire of a wheel, owing to a flaw in the welding caused by an air-bubble. There was evidence to the effect that such a defect would sometimes occur in spite of the greatest care on the part of the manufacturer; that it was impossible to discover it in the process of manufacture, or afterwards, either by inspection or by experiment. LUSH, J., who tried the case, left it to the jury, directing them that if the accident was occasioned by any neglect upon the part of the defendants, they were to find for the plaintiff, but that if it was occasioned by a latent defect in the wheel, such that no care or skill on the part of the defendants could detect it, the verdict should be for the defendants. The jury gave a verdict for the defendants, and subsequently the direction of the judge was held to be right by the Court of Queen's Bench,[3]

[1] Southern, &c. R. R. Co. *v.* Kendrick, 40 Miss. 374; Jeffersonville, &c. R. R. Co. *v.* Hendrick's Adm'r, 26 Ind. 228; Imhoff *v.* Chicago, &c. R. R. Co., 20 Wis. 344; Evansville, &c. R. R. Co. *v.* Duncan, 28 Ind. 441; Fairmount, &c. R. R. Co. *v.* Stutlev, 54 Penn. St. 375; Fuller *v.* Naugatuck R. R. Co., 21 Conn. 576.

[2] Cockle *v.* London & South-Eastern Rail. Co., 5 L. R. C. P. 457; Whitaker *v.* Manchester, &c. Rail. Co., 22 L. J. N. S. 545; Reynolds *v.* South-Western Rail. Co., C. P. 16 Nov. 1870; Praeger *v.* Bristol & Exeter Rail. Co., 23 L. T. N. S. 366 Exch.; Plant *v.* Midland Rail. Co., 21 L. T. N. S. 836; Harrold *v.* Great Western Rail. Co., 14 L. T. N. S. 440.

[3] Redhead *v.* Midland Rail. Co., 2 L. R. Q. B. 412.

and their judgment was affirmed by the Court of Exchequer Chamber.[1] But in giving his judgment, BLACKBURN, J., expressed his opinion that, although carriers of passengers were not insurers, like common carriers of goods, they were bound, at their peril, to supply carriages reasonably fit for the journey, and that it was not enough that they made every reasonable effort to secure that result, if the carriage was, in fact, not sufficient.[2]

SEC. 489. **The Degree and Kind of Care Necessary in Carrier of Passengers.** — In the Exchequer Chamber, however, the judges were unanimously of opinion that there is no contract, either of general warranty or insurance, such as exists between the carrier of goods and their owner, or of a limited warranty, as to the vehicle being sufficient, entered into by the carrier of passengers, and that the contract of such a carrier, and the obligation which is imposed upon him, is to take *due care* to carry a passenger. As we have seen, however, the words "due care" have been held to imply the exercise of reasonable skill and foresight. The above case does a good deal to indicate the degree and kind of negligence which will render a carrier liable, in case of an injury to his

[1] 4 L. R. Q. B. 379; Caldwell *v.* New Jersey Steamboat Co., 56 Barb. (N. Y.) 425.

[2] See upon this question, Pittsburg, &c. R. R. Co. *v.* Thompson, 56 Ill. 138; Hegeman *v.* Western R. R. Co., 13 N. Y. 9; but see McPadden *v.* N. Y. Central R. R. Co., 44 N. Y. 478, where a different rule was adopted, and it was held that the company could not be held chargeable for an injury *resulting from a defect not discoverable by human prudence and caution.* See also, to same effect, Crogan *v.* New York & Harlem R. R. Co., 18 Alb. L. J. 70. But he is bound to exercise the highest degree of care in the selection of his vehicles and appliances, and to properly inspect them and apply such tests to ascertain their soundness as are usually applied by men of the highest prudence and caution, and those skilled in such matters. Nashville, &c. R. R. Co. *v.* Jones, 9 Heisk. (Tenn.) 27. And if the manufacturer was guilty of negligence in the selection of materials for or in their construction, the decided weight of authority sustains the position that the carrier will be liable the same as though he had himself manufactured them. McPadden *v.* New York, &c. R. R. Co., 44 N. Y. 478; Illinois Central R. R. Co. *v.* Phillips, 49 Ill. 234; Bissell *v.* New York, &c. R. R. Co., 25 N. Y. 442; Meir *v.* Pennsylvania R. R. Co., 64 Penn. St. 225; Pittsburg, &c. R. R. Co. *v.* Nelson, 51 Ind. 150. As to the Scotch law, see Bell's Com., 6th ed., p. 153.

passengers, and the case of Francis *v.* Cockerell[1] will make this subject still clearer. In that case, which was an action brought by the plaintiff against the defendant, who had been admitted, on payment of money, to a building erected by the defendant as a grand stand at a race meeting, and where, in consequence of negligence and impropriety of the construction of the stand it fell, and the plaintiff was injured, HANNEN, J., in delivering the judgment of the court said: "The nearest analogy to this case is afforded by that of carriers of passengers. The carrier is paid for providing the means of transporting the passenger from place to place. The defendant received payment for providing the means of supporting the spectator at a particular place. This distinction does not appear to give rise to any difference in principle between the contract to be implied in the one case and the other, as to the safety of the means for carriage or support. In the present case it is not found that the defendant was himself wanting in due care, and no power to draw inferences of fact is given to the court; and if it were, we should not be able to draw the inference that the defendant was personally guilty of any want of care. He employed competent and proper persons, who had efficiently executed similar work on previous occasions. The circumstances that the defendant did not himself survey, or employ any one to survey, the stand after it was erected, does not in itself establish the charge of negligence, for it does not appear that the defect was such as could have been discovered on inspection; and even if it had been, it cannot be laid down as necessarily a want of care not to inspect, although it would, in some circumstances, be evidence from which a jury might properly find that due care had not been taken. It becomes necessary, therefore, for us to consider whether the contract by the defendant, to be implied from the relation which existed between him and the plaintiff, was, that due care had been used, not only by the defendant and his servants, but by the persons whom he employed as independent contractors to erect the stand. . . . Unless, therefore," he went on to remark, "the presumed intention of the parties be

[1] 5 L. R. Q. B. 184 Exch. Ch. 501.

that the passenger should, in the event of his being injured by the breach of the manufacturer's contract, of which he has no knowledge, be without remedy, the only way in which effect can be given to a different intention is, by supposing that the carrier is to be responsible to the passenger, and to look for his indemnity to the person whom he selected, and whose breach of contract caused the mischief. But not only do we think that, when the reasons of justice and convenience on the one side and on the other are weighed, the balance inclines in favor of the plaintiff, but we are also of opinion that the weight of authority is on the plaintiff's side."[1]

SEC. 490. **The most Exact Diligence required of Carrier of Passengers.**—Hence the law seems to be that the carrier is bound to use the most exact diligence, and is answerable for any negligence, however slight. And this is true, not only of a default which is due to the carrier himself, but of any default of those employed by him, or of those from whom he has purchased anything which he uses in the conveyance of passengers, and which, from a want of skill in its construction, may cause injury to any of the carrier's passengers.[2] Consequently a railway company which carries passengers is as responsible for the state of the rails, the condition of the points, and the like, as it is for the safe construction of the carriages.[3] And where an accident happens to a passenger upon the line, by reason of the carriage breaking down or running off the rails,[4] or by mismanagement in driving, so that the train is run against the permanent buffers at a terminus,[5] there is *primâ facie* evi-

[1] See Christie *v.* Griggs, per SIR JAMES MANSFIELD, 2 Camp. at p. 81; Crofts *v.* Waterhouse, per BEST, C. J., 3 Bing. at p. 321; Sharp *v.* Grey, per ALDERSON, B., at p. 459; Grote *v.* Chester & Holyhead Rail. Co., 2 Exch. 251; Brazier *v.* Polytechnic Institution, 1 F. & F., per WIGHTMAN, J., at p. 508.

[2] Daniel *v.* Metropolitan Rail. Co., 3 L. R. C. P. 216, 591; Philadelphia & Reading R. R. Co. *v.* Derby, 14 How. (U. S.) 468; M'Guire *v.* The Golden Gate, 1 M'All. (U. S.) 104.

[3] Pym *v.* Great Northern Rail. Co., 2 F. & F. 619; Great Western Railway of Canada, 1 Moore, P. C. N. S. 106; Grote *v.* Chester & Holyhead Rail. Co., 2 Exch. 251.

[4] Dawson *v.* Manchester, Sheffield, & Lincolnshire Rail. Co., 5 L. T. N. S. 682.

[5] Burke *v.* Manchester, Sheffield, & Lincolnshire Rail. Co., 22 L. T. Rep. 442.

dence from which a jury may infer negligence upon the part of the railway company.

SEC. 491. **Liability for Servants and Agents.** — This doctrine as to the liability of a carrier for the want of due skill and diligence upon the part of those who are employed by him has been held to extend so as to make a railway company answerable to a passenger for the negligence of another company, over whose line they have contracted to carry him; and that is true, whether there is an agreement between the two companies, by which the passenger traffic of the one is forwarded by the other, which would make the latter the agent of the former for that purpose, or whether the one company has only running powers over the other's line.[1] In action against a carrier for negligently carrying the plaintiff from Milford Haven to Liverpool, it appeared that the defendant had agreed to carry the plaintiff from the former to the latter of these two places, and that the mode of transit provided was that the plaintiff should come on to a hulk lying in the harbor of Milford Haven, and wait till a steamer came and took him to Liverpool. On the hulk, close to a ladder down which the plaintiff had to pass to reach the steamer, was a large hatchway, which was negligently left unguarded and improperly lighted, and the plaintiff fell through this hatchway and was injured. The hulk belonged to a third party, and the defendant had only acquired a right to use it for the purpose of embarking passengers on his steamer. It was held in this case that the defendant was answerable for all injury occurring through the means of transit being improper, whether it arose from the negligence of his own servants or other parties who helped to provide the means of transit; and the court even went further, and intimated that the defendant, having invited the plaintiff on to the hulk, was bound to protect him from concealed dangers, and was liable for injury he sustained

[1] Great Western Rail. Co. *v.* Blake, 7 H. & N. 987; 31 L. J. Exch. 346; Buxton *v.* North-Eastern Rail. Co., 3 L. R. Q. B. 549; Thomas *v.* Rhymney Rail. Co., 5 L. R. Q. B. 226; Philadelphia & Reading R. R. Co. *v.* Derby, 14 How. (U. S.) 468; Knight *v.* Portland, &c. R. R. Co., 56 Me. 234; Railroad Co. *v.* Barrow, 5 Wall. (U. S.) 90; Wheeler *v.* San Francisco, &c. R. R. Co., 31 Cal. 46. See Wood's Law of Master and Servant, chap. xiii.

through the condition of the hatchway, even though it was under the care of others and not his own servants.[1]

SEC. 492. **Contributory Negligence.—Concurrent Negligence.**—The circumstances connected with the conveyance of passengers are in many respects of such a nature as to alter the relation of the carrier to the person with whom he contracts. Not only may the carrier's negligence conduce to the injury of a passenger, but a passenger's own negligence or foolhardihood may bring him into such jeopardy that he may be seriously injured or possibly lose his life. Where, through his own negligence, a passenger is injured, there of course can be no responsibility upon the part of the carrier. It is not a carrier's duty to restrain his passengers from injuring themselves. But nice questions arise when both the carrier and the passenger have made default in that diligence and care which are necessary to prevent accident, and when, in consequence of such a combination of heedlessness, accident has actually happened, and injury to the passenger has actually been done. Where such a case occurs the passenger cannot recover damages, for it would be wrong in principle to allow him to complain to a court of law of an injury which his own negligence has contributed to cause.[2] Although that is a correct statement, the principle requires modification to be accurately true. Thus, if, although there has been negligence upon the part of a passenger, the negligence upon the part of the carrier is of such a nature that the person injured could not, by the exercise of ordinary care, have avoided the consequences, the carrier will still be liable.[3] And it might be

[1] John *v.* Bacon, 5 L. R. C. P. 437; 22 L. T. N. S. 477; and see Thomas *v.* Rhymney Rail. Co., 39 L. J. Q. B. 141; 22 L. T. N. S. 297; Knight *v.* Portland, &c. R. R. Co., 56 Me. 234.

[2] Waite *v.* North-Eastern Rail. Co., El. Bl. & El. 719; 28 L. J. Q. B. 258; Tuff *v.* Warman, 2 C. B. N. S. 740; 27 L. J. C. P. 322, Exch. Ch.; Flower *v.* Adam, 2 Taunt. 314.

[3] Bridge *v.* Grand Junction Rail. Co., 3 M. & W. 244. See also Jones *v.* Boyce, 1 Stark. 204, where LORD ELLENBOROUGH said: "If I place a man in such a situation that he must adopt a perilous alternative, I am responsible for the consequences." The American law on this subject is precisely similar to the English. Eckert *v.* Long Island R. R. Co., 57 Barb. (N. Y.) 555, at p. 560; Stokes *v.* Saltonstall, 13 Pet. (U. S.) 181; Eldridge *v.* Long Island Rail. Co., 1 Sandf. (N. Y.) 89; Buel *v.* N. Y. Central R. R. Co., 31 N. Y. 314; Ingalls *v.* Bills, 9 Met. (Mass.) 1; Galena R. R. Co. *v.*

held in such a case that the passenger's negligence had not really brought about the injury. Only then where the plaintiff's negligence is, as it were, an attribute of the injury and not an accident, using these words in their logical sense, can his negligence be regarded as excusing that of the defendant.[1]

Again, if, even after the negligence upon the part of the passenger, the carrier could by the exercise of care have avoided the consequences of such negligence, and he does not use that care, and an accident and injury ensues, the negligence of the former will not, under such circumstances, excuse the negligence of the latter.[2] Where, therefore, the drivers of two rival omnibuses were competing for passengers, the one endeavoring to get before the other, and both driving at great speed and trying to avoid a cart which got in their way, and the wheel of the defendant's omnibus came in contact with the projecting step of the omnibus on which the plaintiff was riding, and caused it to swing against a lamp-post, and the plaintiff to be thrown off and injured, it was held that he was not disentitled to recover damages from the proprietor of the rival omnibus by reason of the misconduct of his own driver.[3] So, where the plaintiff in a steamboat was injured by the fall of an anchor on it, caused by the collision with the steamboat of the defendant, it was held that it was no defence to say that the anchor may have been improperly stowed in the steamboat, or that the plaintiff was standing on a part of the deck where he ought not to have been.[4]

SEC. 493. **Duties which devolve and Rights which accrue to Passenger Carriers.** — Having distinguished between common carriers of goods and carriers of passengers, and, as far as is

Yarwood, 15 Ill. 488; South-Western R. R. Co. *v.* Paulk, 24 Ga. 356; Fairmount, &c. R. R. Co. *v.* Stutlev, 54 Penn. St. 375.

[1] Butterfield *v.* Forrester, 11 East, 60; Clayards *v.* Dethick, 12 Q. B. 446; Singleton *v.* Eastern Counties Rail. Co., 7 C. B. N. S. 287.

[2] Davis *v.* Mann, 10 M. & W. 549; and see, per COLERIDGE, J., in Sells *v.* Brown, 9 C. & P. 601.

[3] Rigby *v.* Hewit, 5 Exch. 240; Greenland *v.* Chaplin, 5 Exch. 247; Thorogood *v.* Bryan, 8 C. B. 115; 18 L. J. C. P. 336.

[4] Greenland *v.* Chaplin, 5 Exch. 243. See Vennell *v.* Garner, 1 Cr. & M. 21. With reference to this subject, see Kent *v.* Elstob, 3 East, 18; Vanderplank *v.* Miller, 1 Moody & M. 21; Lack *v.* Seward, 4 C. & P. 106.

necessary, alluded to the circumstances which will render the latter liable in case of injury occurring to his passengers, it will now be necessary to consider the various duties which devolve, and rights which belong, to the carriers of passengers. For greater convenience, we will in this place distinguish between certain classes of carriers, and. found our distinction upon the kind of conveyance used by them, as we shall see that this circumstance has been the cause of considerable modification in their respective rights and duties. It will only be necessary to distinguish between five such classes, and these are: (1) coach proprietors; (2) railway carriers; (3) hackney-coach or cab proprietors; (4) tramway carriers; and (5) by means of ships.

SEC. 494. **Duty to receive Passengers.** — It is the duty of any common carrier of passengers, as distinguished from a private or special carrier of the same for hire, to receive all persons who apply to him to be carried. In this respect there is no difference between the principles which apply to a common carrier of goods and a common carrier of passengers.[1] The reasons which have led to the imposition of this duty are the same in each case, *viz.* the injury which would arise to the public if a person were allowed publicly to profess to carry goods for all persons, and then refused the goods of certain individuals. The same hardship would arise in the case of passengers, and hence the duty imposed on each is similar. At the same time it is limited in the same way: first, by the condition that the carrier has room in his coach; and, second, that the passenger has tendered his fare.[2] It is, of course, within the province of carriers of passengers to limit their liability by express contract. The principles which are applicable to such contracts are, in the main, the same as those which have been considered in relation to carriers of goods.[3]

SEC. 495. **Rule in Masiter v. Cooper.** — The case of Masiter

[1] East Tennessee, &c. R. R. Co. *v.* Nelson, 1 Coldw. (Tenn.) 272.

[2] See Bretherton *v.* Wood, 3 B. & B. 54; Austin *v.* Great Western Rail. Co., 2 Q. B. 442.

[3] See *ante*, p. 75 *et seq.*; and see Welles *v.* New York Central R. R. Co., 26 Barb. (N. Y.) 641.

v. Cooper[1] is in point. There the declaration stated that the defendant, being the owner of a chaise for hire, undertook to carry the plaintiff, and it appeared that the plaintiff's luggage had been tied on, and he had himself got into the chaise, when the owner insisted on a previous payment of the hire, which was charged exorbitantly. The plaintiff tendered him the regular fare, and the sum which had at first been agreed upon to be taken, but afterwards refused. LORD ELLENBOROUGH held that, although the owner might make his own regulations, or any special contract, and insist upon his own established mode of dealing, yet after the person was in the chaise and had tendered the money, it was too late to refuse to complete the journey; the owner of the chaise was bound to proceed, and if the jury found the tender the plaintiff was entitled to recover. In an American case in which this duty of a common carrier of passengers to receive the applicant was considered, STORY, J., said: "There is no doubt that this steamboat is a common carrier of passengers for hire, and therefore the defendant, as commander, was bound to take the plaintiff as a passenger on board, if he had suitable accommodations, and there was no reasonable objection to the character or conduct of the plaintiff. The question then really resolves itself into the mere consideration whether there was, in the present case, upon the facts, a reasonable ground for the refusal. The right of passengers to a passage on board of a steamboat is not an unlimited right. But it is subject to such reasonable regulations as the proprietors may prescribe for the due accommodation of passengers, and for the due arrangement of their business. The proprietors have not only this right, but the further right to consult and provide for their own interests in the management of such boats, as a common incident of their right of property. They are not bound to admit passengers on board who refuse to obey the reasonable regulations of the boat, or who are guilty of gross and vulgar habits of conduct, or who make disturbances on board, or whose characters are doubtful or dissolute or suspicious, and *à fortiori*, whose characters are unequivocally bad. Nor are

[1] 4 Esp. 260.

they bound to admit passengers on board whose object is to interfere with the interests or patronage of the proprietors, so as to make the business less lucrative to them."[1]

SEC. 496. **When Refusal to carry is a Ground of Action.** — But where the duty undoubtedly exists in relation to a particular person, and is not performed by the carrier, it is a ground for action, and the individual is entitled to recover damages. Thus, in Hamlin *v.* Great Northern Railway Company,[2] a person in business travelling to meet his customers, booked himself by railway as a passenger from London to Hull by a train which the company advertised to arrive at Hull the same night. On reaching Grimsby, where the company's line ended, it was found that the Hull train had left; and although the plaintiff might have reached Hull that night by taking a special conveyance, and hiring a boat to cross the Humber, he remained at Grimsby and proceeded by train the next morning, but he was too late to reach Driffield and other places by the hour he had previously appointed for meeting his customers, and in consequence he was obliged to hire conveyances to see some of his customers elsewhere, and was detained several days waiting for the market days to see others. He brought an action against the company for a breach of the contract to carry him to Hull, and it was decided that he was entitled to recover the amount of his hotel expenses at Grimsby, and the railway fare next day to Hull, but was not entitled to recover for any damage occasioned by his not reaching Driffield and other places at the time he might have reached them if the company had performed their contract. In Buckmaster *v.* Eastern Counties Railway Company,[3] however, the plaintiff recovered a reasonable sum for loss of market in consequence of the failure of the company to perform the duty imposed upon them of carrying, and the contract to carry at a certain time.

SEC. 497. **Statutory Regulations.** — This duty to receive,

[1] Jencks *v.* Coleman, 2 Sum. (U. S.) 224, 225; quoted in Story on Bailm. § 591*a*. See also Bennett *v.* Dutton, 10 N. H. 481; Markham *v.* Brown, 8 N. H. 523; Commonwealth *v.* Power, 7 Met. (Mass.) 596; Day *v.* Owen, 5 Mich. 520; Ansell *v.* Waterhouse, 2 Chitty, 1; Tarbell *v.* Central Pacific R. R. Co., 34 Cal. 616.

[2] 5 H. & N. 408; 2 Jur. N. S. 1122; 26 L. J. Exch. 20.

[3] 23 L. T. N. S. 471.

limited as it is, is incumbent upon all carriers of passengers; but there are certain statutory regulations with regard to different classes of carriers of passengers, which we cannot do more than refer to in this place. The 2 & 3 Will. IV. c. 120, which consolidated and amended the laws relating to stage carriages, the number of passengers to be carried, the amount of luggage, &c., was repealed by the 2 & 3 Vict. c. 66, which substituted other duties for those imposed by the repealed act; but all the regulations and penalties respecting the duties imposed by the former act are to apply to the duties imposed by the latter. The second section of 2 & 3 Vict. c. 66, makes a penalty exigible from any proprietor who marks upon his stage carriage any inscription differing from the license as to the number of passengers authorized to be carried thereby. And those who wish to know more about the duties that are payable by virtue of that act, and the regulations and penalties which are made for the better regulation of passenger traffic under that and the 2 & 3 Will. IV. c. 120, must have recourse to the statute in question, as the limits of our work do not permit of a more detailed account of these enactments.[1] Several points, however, must be noted, par ticularly in relation to stage-coach proprietors, before we proceed to a consideration of the duties which are common to all those who carry persons, or to a consideration of the special duties incident to railway conveyance, which is possibly the most important branch of our present subject.

SEC. 498. **Modification of Duties by Contract.** — We have seen that, although a carrier has common-law duties, he may modify these by contract, and it is only when no such contract exists that we must have recourse to common law, with a view to ascertaining his duties. In a case, then, in which the declaration stated that the defendant, being the owner of a stage-coach, undertook to carry the plaintiff, her children, and servants, together, in and by a stage-coach, and where evidence was given that the whole inside of the coach was taken for the plaintiff and her three daughters, and two outside places for her servants, it was held that such evidence sup-

[1] See also Metropolitan Public Carriage Act, 1869, 32 & 33 Vict. c. 115.

ported the declaration. It appeared that the defendant sent a double-bodied coach, and refused to take the plaintiff and her daughters unless one of them would travel in one body and the others in the other body. And this was held to be a breach of the defendant's agreement.[1] Where a passenger has paid his fare, he has evidently a right to his seat, and he does no injustice to the carrier if, instead of taking his seat at the place of departure of the coach, having paid the fare for the whole distance, he takes it at a stage or two nearer its destination. Indeed, the advantage is on the side of the carrier, as his horses have less to carry. He has, therefore, no right to fill up the place for which the fare has been paid merely because it is not occupied at the place from which the coach departs, or, at all events, he must be prepared to supply the passenger with the seat when he demands it. This is, however, not the case if the passenger, instead of paying the whole fare, has only paid a deposit, or a sum for booking; for in that case the coach might, through the refusal of the carrier to take other passengers, travel empty from place to place, and the carrier thereby lose the full fares, and only secure the deposits.[2]

SEC. 499. **Duty of Carrier of Passengers limited by his Ordinary Trade and Custom. — Other Conditions.** — As a common carrier's duty is limited by the profession he has made, so it is in the case of those who conduct passenger traffic. Therefore the time and place at which the carrier is bound to receive passengers is to be judged of in relation to his ordinary custom. That some such limitation as this is absolutely necessary to the continuance of the trade is beyond doubt; and as its continuance is a public convenience, the public must be content to suffer such a modification of their right to be received. Besides these, as we have seen, there are other conditions which are precedent to the duty to receive, and these are, that the person applying is a fit person and in a fit condition [3] to be received, and that he will conform to the reasonable regulations of the carrier, which have been made for the

[1] Long *v.* Horne, 1 C. & P. 610.

[2] Kerr *v.* Mountain, 1 Esp. 27.

[3] See as to hackney carriages and small-pox patients, *post.*

purpose of procuring the greater convenience and comfort of his passengers. All these conditions are exactly analogous to those which exist in the case of common carriers of goods. Thus the common carrier is only bound to receive such goods as he has been in the habit of carrying. He is not bound to receive goods packed in such a way that they will necessarily cause damage to the other goods of which he is the bailee, and he can make regulations as to booking, statement of value, and the like. So a passenger may be refused if he is not a fit person to be carried, — if he is in such a state that he will insult or inconvenience other passengers, or if he refuses to book himself, or take a ticket, or comply with reasonable regulations.[1]

We have already touched somewhat amply on the duties associated with the performance of the contract in speaking of negligence, but it will not be out of place to mention some of the cases on this subject which particularly apply to stage-coaches. Thus, in one case, it was held that every stage-coach proprietor undertakes that his coach shall be sufficiently secure to perform the journeys it undertakes, and that he ought to examine its sufficiency before each journey, and that, if he neglects to do so, and by the insecurity of the coach a passenger is injured, an action is maintainable against the coach proprietor for negligence. And this rule was held to apply in a case in which the coach had been examined previously to the second journey before the accident, and though it had been repaired at the coach-maker's only three or four days before.[2] It was decided also, in a case we have already had occasion to refer to, that if the accident happens from a defect in the original construction, although the defect is out of sight, and not discoverable upon ordinary examination, the proprietor was liable.[3] In Mayor *v.* Humphries,[4] which was

[1] See Tarbell *v.* Central Pacific R. R. Co., 40 Vt. 88.

[2] Bremner *v.* Williams, 1 C. & P. 414; McKinney *v.* Neil, 1 McLean (U. S.), 540; Peck *v.* Neil, 3 McLean (U. S.), 22; Hanley *v.* Harlem R. R. Co., 40 Vt. 88; McPadden *v.* New York, &c. R. R. Co., 47 Barb. (N. Y.) 247; affirmed, 44 N. Y. 478.

[3] Sharp *v.* Grey, 9 Bing. 457; 2 M. & S. 621. See also Francis *v.* Cockerell, L. R. 5 Q. B. 184; 39 L. J. Q. B. 113.

[4] 1 C. & P. 251.

an action against a coach proprietor by a passenger for injury done to him in consequence of the overturning of the coach, the declaration stated that the defendant negligently "drove, conducted, and managed the coach;" and it was held that, as the negligence of the defendant was in sending out an insufficient coach, the plaintiff was not entitled to recover.

SEC. 500. **Evidence of Negligence in Case of Accident.** — Where a passenger pays his fare, he is entitled to expect reasonable accommodation, and, as in the case of stage-coaches the number of passengers to be carried is, as we have seen, regulated by statute, the courts have, of course, discouraged any breach of this statutory duty, and the way they have done this is by deciding what shall be evidence of negligence in case of accident. Christie *v.* Griggs[1] decided that it is *primâ facie* enough to prove negligence, if evidence is given of the coach having broken down; but if evidence is given that at the time of the accident there were more passengers in the coach than the statute allows, it is conclusive proof of negligence upon the part of the proprietor.[2] But not only will the proprietor be responsible for his own negligence, but he has been held responsible for the negligence or misconduct of his driver.[3]

SEC. 501. **Duty in Circumstances of Danger.** — Where danger is inevitable, not from such misconduct, but from the nature of the road, or any other circumstance which may cause an accident and consequent injuries to the passengers, without any fault upon the part of the driver, he still has a duty to perform if he would protect his master from liabilities in case the accident should happen. His clear duty is to warn the passengers of the risk they run, and of the nature of the danger to be incurred before it is incurred; and if he proceeds without giving them this information, and therefore without giving them the opportunity of taking such means as they may think fit to avoid it, the proprietor will be liable for any injury that they may suffer in consequence of an accident aris-

[1] 2 Camp. 79.

[2] Israel *v.* Clark, 4 Esp. 259.

[3] White *v.* Boulton, Peake, 81; Dudley *v.* Smith, 1 Camp. 167. But see Aston *v.* Heaven, 2 Esp. 533, S. P.; Christie *v.* Griggs, 2 Camp. 79; Crofts *v.* Waterhouse, 11 Moore, 133.

ing from the anticipated quarter.[1] So in a case where, through the default of the coach proprietor in neglecting to provide proper harness, the coupling-rein broke, and, one of the leaders becoming ungovernable whilst the coach was on a descent, the coachman drew the coach to one side of the road, where it came in contact with some piles, one of which it broke, it appeared that the plaintiff, imagining himself in imminent peril, jumped off the coach and broke his leg. LORD ELLENBOROUGH, in addressing the jury, left two questions to them: 1st. Whether the proprietor was guilty of any default in omitting to provide the safe and proper means of conveyance; and, 2d. Whether that fault was conducive to the injury, "for," he said, "if it was not so far conducive as to create such a reasonable degree of alarm and apprehension in the mind of the plaintiff as rendered it necessary for him to jump down from the coach in order to avoid immediate danger, the action is not maintainable." The jury found for the plaintiff.[2]

SEC. 502.. **Possible Avoidance of Accident may render Carrier Responsible.** — Besides these circumstances, another may be mentioned where, although the accident is not conduced or caused by the negligence of the driver, yet, where but for his negligence or want of skill, even when it was occurring, the injury and result might have been avoided. Here, then, if the driver does not, when in peril, take the safest course, the owner will be responsible for the mischief which ensues, for in such a case the driver's negligence contributed to the injury.[3]

SEC. 503. **Rule in Crofts v. Waterhouse.** — In Crofts *v.* Waterhouse,[4] which was an action against a coach proprietor for having by negligence overturned his coach and injured the defendant while travelling by it, it was proved at the trial that the defendant's coachman, in turning the corner on the right-hand side of the road, had driven so near to the side as to

[1] Dudley *v.* Smith, 1 Camp. 167. See also Brockway *v.* Lascala, 1 Edm. (N. Y.) Sel. Cas. 135.

[2] Jones *v.* Boyce, 1 Stark. 493.

[3] Jackson *v.* Tollit, 2 Stark. 37; Mayhew *v.* Boyce, 1 Stark. 423; Card *v.* New York, &c. R. R. Co., 50 Barb. (N. Y.) 39.

[4] 3 Bing. 319.

gather a bank, by which the coach was overturned; that, though it was between two and three in the morning, there was a full moon, and light enough to distinguish objects of all kinds; that the road was twenty-four feet wide, and, at the time, clear of all obstructions, so that there was nothing to prevent the coachman from keeping to the middle or even to the left side of the road. The defence set up was, that between the time of the disaster and the time when the coachman had last passed the place where it happened (about twelve hours before), the first of two cottages which stood close to the corner in question had been pulled down, and the rubbish left by the side of the road; that the coachman, mistaking the second cottage for the first, and wishing to save his horses by going as close to the corner as possible, drove out of the road over the rubbish of the demolished cottage. The judge who tried the cause (LITTLEDALE, J.) told the jury that, as there was no obstruction on the road, the coachman ought to have kept within the limits of it, and that, the accident having been occasioned by his deviation, the plaintiff was entitled to a verdict. And in this case the court granted a new trial, on the ground that the jury should have been directed to consider whether or not the deviation was the effect of negligence. Again, in an action against a coach proprietor for negligence, it appeared that the plaintiff became an outside passenger, and that there was luggage on the roof of the coach, and no iron railing between the luggage and passenger; and that the plaintiff, being seated with her back to the luggage, was, by a sudden jolt, thrown from the coach, and her leg was broken. The judge directed the jury to find for the plaintiff, if they were of opinion that the injury sustained was occasioned by the negligence of the defendant. The jury found for the plaintiff, and stated that they so found, on account of the improper construction of the coach, and of the luggage being on the seat. Held, that the case was properly submitted to the jury, and that the facts found specially by them amounted to negligence.[1]

[1] Curtis *v.* Drinkwater, 2 B. & Ad. 169. See also Thorogood *v.* Bryan, 8 C. B. 115; 18 L. J. C. P. 336; Harris *v.* Costar, 1 C. & P. 636.

SEC. 504. **Duties of Carriers as to Sufficiency of Conveyance.**—These cases not only indicate when the carrier will be liable for injuries sustained by his passengers, but they also show what his duties as to conveyance are, and how these must be performed. For the decision, as in Dudley *v.* Smith,[1] as to when, and until when, he is liable for injuries occurring to his passenger, also indicates the duration of his duty and the circumstances which will be held to absolve him from further performance; for, as it is a question of much importance, in relation to goods, when delivery has taken place, and what constitutes delivery, so, in relation to persons, it is of importance to ascertain when carriers have discharged all the duties of their contract to the passenger. The custom of the carrier must be regarded as ruling this in many cases; but, of course, the custom can be abrogated in any individual case by special agreement. But it may be taken as a general rule, that without any special agreement every passenger is understood to contract for the usual reasonable accommodation.[2] We have, in another place, considered the liability of a carrier of passengers for the luggage of the persons he carries, as in relation to that luggage the duties of the carrier are those of a common carrier; although, in relation to the person of his passenger this extensive duty and liability has been limited, as we have already seen. We may refer the reader to that earlier chapter, and only allude by reference to some of the more important decided cases.[3]

SEC. 505. **Railways.—Statutory Provisions.**—We have already forestalled something of what we feel bound to say concerning railway carriers of passengers. Still the subject is a large one, and a good deal remains to be said. We have seen that a general supervision of railways is given to the

[1] 1 Camp. 167.

[2] Story on Bailm., 8th ed., § 597.

[3] *Ante*, p. 67, chap. iv. See also Shepherd *v.* Great Northern Rail. Co., 8 Exch. 30; 7 Rail. Cas. 310; Beauchamp *v.* Pawley, 1 M. & Rob. 38; Brooke *v.* Pickwick, 4 Bing. 218; 12 Moore, 447; Powles *v.* Hider, 6 El. & Bl. 207; 25 L. J. Q. B. 331; Hudson *v.* Midland Rail. Co., 10 B. & S. 504; Becher *v.* Great Eastern Rail. Co., 22 L. T. N. S. 299; 18 W. R. 627; Great Western Rail. Co. *v.* Talley, 19 W. R. 154; 23 L. T. N. S. 413 C. P.; Tunz *v.* South-Eastern Rail. Co., 4 L. R. Q. B. 539.

Board of Trade, who are entitled to call for returns of the aggregate traffic in passengers as well as in goods and cattle, and who may demand particulars of all accidents attended with personal injury on the railways, and also for tables of all tolls, rates, and charges levied from time to time on such traffic.[1] Besides these powers the Board has power to appoint inspectors,[2] to disallow by-laws submitted to them for their approval and confirmation,[3] and by certificate to direct prosecutions against railway companies for offences against any of the Railway Acts.[4] Besides this, there is an important provision that any officer or agent of the railway company may "seize and detain any engine-driver, guard, porter, or other servant in the employ of the company, who shall be found drunk when employed upon the railway, or commit any offence against any of the by-laws, rules, or regulations of the company, or who shall wilfully, maliciously, or negligently do, or omit to do, any act whereby the life or limb of any person passing along, or being upon the railway, or the works thereof, shall be, or might be, injured or endangered, or whereby the passage of any of the engines, carriages, or trains, shall be, or might be, obstructed or impeded." [5]

SEC. 506. **Penal Provisions. — Servants. — Against other Persons.** — The same act provides that any person so apprehended may be taken before a justice of the peace, without warrant, and may be imprisoned, with or without hard labor, for not more than two calendar months, or be fined not more than 10*l.* and be imprisoned, with or without hard labor, in default of payment.[6] The 15th section enacts that any person doing, or causing to be done, anything to obstruct any engine or carriage, or to endanger the safety of persons conveyed in the same, or who shall aid therein, is guilty of a misdemeanor, and, on conviction, may be imprisoned, with or without hard labor, for two years.

[1] 3 & 4 Vict. c. 97, § 1; 14 & 15 Vict. c. 64.

[2] 3 & 4 Vict. c. 97, § 5; 7 & 8 Vict. c. 85, § 15.

[3] 3 & 4 Vict. c. 97, §§ 8, 9.

[4] 3 & 4 Vict. c. 97, § 11.

[5] 3 & 4 Vict. c. 97, § 13; 5 & 6 Vict. c. 53, § 17.

[6] 3 & 4 Vict. c. 97, § 13. The magistrate may, if he chooses, send the case to quarter sessions — § 14.

SEC. 507. **Provision for Inspection of every Railway.** — By another statute no railway, nor portion of any railway, may be opened for public conveyance until after one calendar month's notice, in writing, to the Board of Trade, of the company's intention to open the railway, nor until after ten days' notice to the Board of the time when the railway will be complete and fit for inspection.[1] And, after such inspection, the Board may, if they think fit, postpone the opening.[2] Other provisions for notices of accident, in case there has been serious personal injury,[3] for gates at level crossings over highways, turnpikes, and statute labor roads, for the closing of such gates,[4] and for the speed of trains before arriving at such crossings,[5] are contained in the same act.

SEC. 508. **What is a "Passenger Railway."** — It is further provided that, if two thirds or more of the gross annual revenue of a railway shall be derived from the carriage thereon of coals, ironstone, or other metals or minerals, it shall not be considered a passenger railway.[6] By another act it is not lawful, and has not been lawful since the 18th August, 1846 (with a few exceptions), to construct any railway for the conveyance of passengers on any gauge other than four feet eight inches and a half in Great Britain, and five feet three inches in Ireland;[7] and now, by 5 & 6 Vict. c. 55, § 16, carriages of a greater weight than four tons may be used.

SEC. 509. **Necessity for Regulations.** — Before going further we may remark that, if certain regulations, external to those made by a railway company for its own convenience, are necessary, where the company was only a carrier of goods, such or similar regulations are more urgently required where the railway company undertakes the conveyance of passengers. In every country, and in every code, life has always been regarded as the first object; property after life. Hence the criminal laws have generally reached considerable maturity

[1] 5 & 6 Vict. c. 55, § 4. See also 34 & 35 Vict. c. 78.

[2] *Ibid.* § 6.

[3] *Ibid.* § 7.

[4] *Ibid.* § 9; Marfell *v.* The South-Western Rail. Co., 29 L. J. C. B. 315.

[5] 8 & 9 Vict. c. 20, § 48.

[6] 5 & 6 Vict. c. 55, § 12.

[7] 9 & 10 Vict c. 57, § 1.

before the civil laws were upon the fair way to perfection. Now railway companies are not only, as carriers, intrusted with the care of goods, but they become, as it were, the bailees of hundreds of lives. That being the case, and it being true that, owing to the speed of travelling, the smallest amount of negligence is apt to lead to disastrous consequences, it became necessary that there should be some other control than that which they exercised over themselves,—as some apparently praiseworthy attempt upon the part of directors to increase the profits, and to raise the dividends, might lead to a catastrophe which, while it caused infinite loss and sorrow to many, might not produce a commensurate injury to the company,—and that control was supplied by statutory enactments, some of which were to be rules for the safe conduct of such companies, and others providing a vicarious authority which had better means of administering a remedy and protecting the public. Some of these we have already considered, but it behooves us to dwell with more minuteness upon some of the most important provisions which apply to passenger traffic which are made by other acts.

SEC. 510. **7 & 8 Vict. c. 85.**—The 6th section of the 7 & 8 Vict. c. 85, after reciting that, "whereas it is expedient to secure to the poorer class of travellers the means of travelling by railway at moderate fares, and in carriages in which they may be protected from the weather," enacts, "That on and after the several days hereinafter specified, all passenger railway companies which shall have been incorporated by any act of the present session, or which shall be hereafter incorporated, or which, by any act of the present or any future session, have obtained or shall obtain, directly or indirectly, any extension or amendment of the powers conferred upon them respectively by their previous acts, or have been or shall be authorized to do any act unauthorized by the provisions of such previous acts, shall, by means of one train at the least to travel along their railway from one end to the other of each trunk or branch or junction line belonging to or leased by them, so long as they shall continue to carry other passengers over such trunk, branch, or junction line, once at the least each way on every week-day except *Christmas Day* and *Good Friday* (such exceptions not to extend to *Scotland*), provide for the conveyance of third-class passengers to and from the terminal and other ordinary passenger stations of the railway, under the obligations contained in the several Acts of Parliament, and with the immunities applicable by law to carriers of passengers by railways, and also under the following conditions (that is to say): —

"Such train shall start at an hour to be from time to time fixed by the directors, subject to the approval of the Lords of the Committee of Privy Council for Trade and Plantations.

"Such train shall travel at an average rate of speed not less than twelve miles an hour for the whole distance travelled on the railway, including stoppages.

"Such train shall, if required, take up and set down passengers at every passenger station which it shall pass on the line.

"The carriages in which the passengers shall be conveyed by such train shall be provided with seats, and shall be protected from the weather, in a manner satisfactory to the Lords of the said Committee.

"The fare or charge for each third-class passenger by such train shall not exceed one penny for each mile travelled.[1]

"Each passenger by such train shall be allowed to take with him half a hundredweight of luggage, not being merchandise or other articles carried for

[1] If the distance is a portion of a mile, and does not amount to one mile, the fare for such portion of a mile may be one penny; or when such distance amounts to one mile, or two or more miles, and a portion of another mile, the fare or charge for such portion of, if the same amounts to or exceeds one-half mile, may be one halfpenny. And no fare shall be deemed excessive if the same shall not exceed the rate of one farthing for each entire quarter of a mile travelled. 21 & 22 Vict. c. 71, §§ 1 & 2; made perpetual by 23 & 24 Vict. c. 41. See Rice *v.* Dublin & Wicklow Rail. Co., 8 Ir. C. L. R. 160 C. P.

hire or profit, without extra charge, and any excess of luggage shall be charged by weight at a rate not exceeding the lowest rate of charge for passengers' luggage by other trains.

"Children under three years of age accompanying passengers by such train shall be taken without any charge; and children of three years and upwards, but under twelve years of age, at half the charge of an adult passenger."

SEC. 511. **The Effect of these Provisions considered.** — The effect of a portion of this section was considered in the case of The Great Northern Railway Company *v.* Shepherd.[1] This was an action to recover damages amounting to 40*l.* 3*s.* 2*d.*, and it appeared that Shepherd, the plaintiff, in County Court of Yorkshire, at Sheffield, had taken a third-class ticket of the defendants at the Great Northern Railway Station at Sheffield, to go to London and return to Sheffield for the sum of 5*s.* During his stay in London he purchased a quantity of ivory handles for table-knives. During his return journey to Sheffield, a collision took place. The plaintiff and his wife were both hurt, and the former, upon being assisted into another train which was to convey them to Sheffield, spoke to one of the railway porters about the luggage, who told him not to make himself uneasy, it would be all right. It did not turn out to be so, however; for although some portions of his luggage were afterwards forwarded to him, a bag containing the ivory handles never reached him. The act above quoted allows a passenger to carry luggage of 56 lbs. in weight, if it is not merchandise, and it was held that under the act the plaintiff and his wife, when travelling together, were entitled to 112 lbs. of personal luggage. The train in which they travelled, however, was an excursion train, and did not seem to be subject to the regulations in force as to third-class trains; consequently it was held that the company were not liable as at common law for the loss of the goods, that the fare for passengers included only personal luggage, and that, as the goods had been delivered and carried ostensibly as lug-

[1] 10 Exch. 30; 24 L. J. Exch. 286.

gage, when actually they were merchandise, the carrier was not liable. PARKE, B., said: "The provision of the Act of Parliament is equivalent to notice that the company will carry with each passenger 56 lbs. of luggage, but *not merchandise.* It is necessary to ascertain whether or no the company were, with respect to persons travelling by the excursion train, entirely released from the conditions imposed by the statute upon third-class passengers. If they were, they might, nevertheless, contract to carry under the obligations relating to parliamentary trains, in which case it is clear the plaintiff could not recover. But if the matter was left at large, the defendants were under the ordinary obligations of carriers at common law." The question as to what constitutes personal luggage need not be again referred to in this place.[1]

SEC. 512. **7 & 8 Vict. c. 85, § 10.** — The 10th section of the same act[2] provides, "that whenever any railway company, subject to the hereinbefore-mentioned obligation of running cheap trains, shall, from and after the days hereinbefore specified on which the said obligation is to accrue, run any train or trains on Sundays for the conveyance of passengers, it shall, under the obligations contained in its Act or Acts of Parliament, and with the immunities applicable by law to carriers of passengers by railway, by such train each way, on every Sunday, as shall stop at the greatest number of stations, provide sufficient carriages for the conveyance of third-class passengers at the terminal and other stations at which such Sunday train may ordinarily stop, and the fare or charge for each third-class passenger by such train shall not exceed one penny for each mile travelled."[3] By the 8 & 9 Vict. c. 20, § 86, under the head, "with respect to the carrying of passengers and goods upon the railway, and the tolls to be taken thereon," it is enacted that "it shall be lawful for the company to use and employ locomotive engines, or other moving

[1] But see Mytton *v.* Midland Rail. Co., 28 L. J. Exch. 385; Harrison *v.* London & Brighton Rail. Co., 29 L. J. Q. B. 209.

[2] 7 & 8 Vict. c. 85.

[3] Almost all railway companies now provide carriages for the convenience of third-class passengers in connection with all their trains.

34

power, and carriages and wagons to be drawn or propelled thereby, and to carry and convey upon the railway all such passengers and goods as shall be offered to them for that purpose, and to make such reasonable charges in respect thereof as they may from time to time determine upon, not exceeding the tolls by the special act authorized to be taken by them." And the 89th section provides, as we have seen above, that "nothing in this or the special act contained shall extend to charge or make liable the company further or in any other case than where, according to the laws of the realm, stage-coach proprietors and common carriers would be liable, nor shall extend in any degree to deprive the company of any protection or privilege which common carriers or stage-coach proprietors may be entitled to; but, on the contrary, the company shall at all times be entitled to the benefit of every such protection and privilege."

SEC. 513. **Travelling without having paid Fare.** — By the 103d section, it is provided that, "if any person travel or attempt to travel in any carriage of the company, or of any other company or party using the railway, without having previously paid his fare, and with the intent to avoid payment thereof, or if any person, having paid his fare for a certain distance, knowingly and wilfully proceed in any such carriage beyond such distance, without previously paying the additional fare for the additional distance, and with the intent to avoid payment thereof, or if any person knowingly and wilfully refuse or neglect, on arriving at the point to which he has paid his fare, to quit such carriage, every such person shall for every such offence forfeit to the company a sum not exceeding 40*s*."

SEC. 514. **Apprehension and Detention of Offender.** — The 104th section enacts that, "if any person be discovered either in or after committing or attempting to commit any such offence as in the preceding enactment mentioned, all officers and servants and other persons on behalf of the company, or such other company or party as aforesaid, and all the constables, jailers, and peace officers may lawfully apprehend and detain any such person until he can be conveniently taken before some justice, or until he be otherwise discharged by due course of law." Those provisions have to some extent been made more exact in their application to circumstances, by certain cases which have come before the courts since these acts were passed, and we may say that that is almost the invariable result of the decision of cases following upon a statute.

SEC. 515. **Payment of Fare for Longer Distance.** — Thus, under these acts it has been decided that, if a passenger pays the fare demanded of him for a longer distance, he cannot be apprehended for the non-payment of the fare for a shorter distance, although the latter may be higher than the former, and although he was aware of this difference between the charges.[1] As the acts are to be interpreted strictly as against the company, they will not — under a by-law, which gives them the power to recover the fare, should it be refused, or should the passenger refuse to deliver up his ticket, by proceeding before a magistrate — be entitled to apprehend a passenger on such refusal.[2] We shall have a subsequent opportunity of speaking more fully of the passenger's duty with regard to the delivery of his ticket and other matters, but in this place it may be said generally, that, if the fare has been paid, the company will, if they apprehend a passenger merely on the ground that he refuses, or omits, or is unable to give up his ticket when it is demanded of him by the company or their servants, be liable to an action of false imprisonment.[3] And in such cases an action either for false imprisonment,[4] for assault and battery,[5] or for any negligent or malicious wrong,[6] according to the circumstances, but not for malicious prosecution,[7] will lie against a railway company, if there be evidence

[1] Rex *v.* Frere, 24 L. J. M. C. 68.

[2] Tollemache *v.* London & South-Western Rail. Co., 26 L. T. 222.

[3] Eastern Counties Rail. Co. *v.* Broom, 6 Exch. 314; 20 L. J. Exch. 196; Goff *v.* Great Northern Rail. Co., 30 L. J. Q. B. 148. See also Chilton *v.* London & Croydon Rail. Co., 16 M. & W. 212.

[4] Roe *v.* Birkenhead Rail. Co., 7 Exch. 36; 21 L. J. Exch. 9.

[5] Eastern Counties Rail. Co. *v.* Broom, 6 Exch. 314; 20 L. J. Exch. 196.

[6] Green *v.* London General Omnibus Co., 24 L. J. C. P. 13.

[7] Stevens *v.* Midland Rail. Co., 10 Exch. 352; 23 L. J. Exch. 328.

that the servant was acting under the express or implied authority of the railway company,[1] or that the company subsequently approved or ratified his act.[2] Some of the provisions of the Regulations of Railways Act, 1868,[3] still remain to be noticed.

SEC. 516. **Provisions for Safety of Passengers.— Communication with Guard.** — The 22d section of that act makes it necessary, with a view to the safety of the passengers, after the 1st of April, 1869, for every company to provide and maintain in working order, in every passenger train that travels more than twenty miles without stopping, "such efficient means of communication between the passengers and the servants of the company in charge of the train, as the Board of Trade may approve." And it also enacts that "any passenger who makes use of the said means of communication without reasonable and sufficient cause, shall be liable for each offence to a penalty not exceeding five pounds." It also contains other provisions for the safety of passengers, for preventing trespasses on lines,[4] and for the removal of trees which are in danger of falling.[5] Besides the safety, the convenience of the passengers is had regard to; for this act makes it necessary for all railway companies — except the Metropolitan Railway Company — to provide smoking compartments for each class of passengers in every passenger train, unless they are exempted by the Board of Trade.[6]

SEC. 517. **The Necessity for Exceptional Legislation for Railway Companies.** — The necessity of many of these regulations must have struck every one who had become aware of their existence. The length of the journey taken, the isolation of a passenger in one compartment of a railway carriage, owing to the rapidity of motion and the noise caused by the train, the tendency of companies to neglect the comparatively unre-

[1] Goff *v.* Great Northern Rail. Co., 30 L. J. Q. B. 148; Roe *v.* Birkenhead Rail. Co., 7 Exch. 36; 21 L. J. Exch. 9.

[2] Eastern Counties Rail. Co. *v.* Broom, *supra.*

[3] 31 & 32 Vict. c. 119. See also 34 & 35 Vict. c. 78.

[4] *Ibid.* § 23.

[5] *Ibid.* § 24.

[6] *Ibid.* § 20.

munerative passenger traffic which takes place between small centres and requires cheap conveyance, the liability which railway companies are under to be fraudulently dealt with, and the many occasions which render such dealing easy upon the part of passengers, — all these drew attention to the necessity of exceptional legislation for railway companies as to many of the incidents of passenger traffic. At the same time it has been the desire of the legislature to interfere as little as possible with the rights and privileges of railway companies, and the exceptional legislation which has taken place has been carefully limited by a consciousness of the danger which arises in connection with it, of overdoing it. And, as we have seen, the 8 & 9 Vict. c. 20, § 89 (Railway Clauses Act, 1854), expressly retains in favor of railway carriers all protection and privileges which common carriers or stage-coach proprietors are entitled to.[1]

It now becomes incumbent upon us to consider some of the cases which relate to the rights and duties of the carriers of passengers, when they carry by rail, at least in so far as these differ from the ordinary common-law duties and privileges already described.

SEC. 518. **Contract.** — First. *With regard to the Contract.* — In a case in which it appeared that the plaintiff took a ticket at Cardiff, to be carried by the Great Eastern Railway Company to Newcastle-upon-Tyne, *viâ* the Midland Railway, and the complaint was, that the train from Milford, by which he was to proceed on that journey, instead of arriving at Cardiff so as to start at its accustomed time, 4.34 P. M., did not reach Cardiff until 6 o'clock, and in consequence passengers wishing to go through to Newcastle missed the corresponding train at Gloucester, and could not be carried on until the evening of the next day. The gravamen, therefore, was, that the company were guilty of a breach of duty or a breach of contract,

[1] As in the case of carriers of goods, questions relating to carriers of passengers by railway must be decided in connection with and by reference to the special acts of the company. The importance of this will be seen from the case of Kent *v.* Great Western Rail. Co., 4 Rail. Cas. 699; Garton *v.* Great Western Rail. Co., 31 L. T. Rep. 233.

because the Milford train arrived at Cardiff an hour and a half behind its usual time.

SEC. 519. **What amounts to a Contract.** — In giving judgment, ERLE, C. J., said: "I am of opinion that the mere taking of a ticket does not amount to a contract upon the part of the railway company, or impose upon them a duty, to have a train ready to start at the time at which the passenger is led to expect it; and in order to maintain an action it is incumbent on the plaintiff to show either a breach of contract or a breach of some legal duty. If there were any such contract here, it would appear from the time-bills published by the company, and if the plaintiff (whose duty it was to do so) had put in the time-bill, we should have seen what the real contract was, *viz.* that the company do not warrant that their trains shall arrive with punctuality at the different stations. There clearly was nothing like a special contract in the talk with the officials on the platform at Cardiff. A mere casual conversation with a person whose duty it is to open and shut the carriage doors, or the like, cannot amount to evidence of a special contract with a company. It is perfectly consistent with all the evidence here that the company have done all they contracted to do."[1]

SEC. 520. **Civil Wrong and Pure Wrong.** — Again, where a servant took a ticket and travelled on the defendants' railway, and was injured during the journey through the negligence of the defendants, and his master brought an action against the company for the loss of the servant's services through the defendants' negligence, it appearing that there was no contract between the railway company and the plaintiff, it was held that, inasmuch as the servant was injured, not by a simple wrong, but by a wrong arising out of a breach of duty, imposed upon the railway company by their contract with the servant, the action was founded on contract, and consequently would not lie.[2] What distinguished this case from the many in which masters have recovered for the loss of services of a

[1] Hurst *v.* Great Western Rail. Co., 19 C. B. N. S. 310; 11 Jur. N. S. 730; 34 L. J. C. P. 264.

[2] Alton *v.* Midland Rail. Co., 19 C. B. N. S. 213; 34 L. J. C. P. 292; 13 W. R. 918.

servant,[1] was the fact that this was a civil wrong which was complained of, and not a pure wrong. These cases indicate the nature of the transaction which must take place before a railway company can be held to have contracted to carry an individual, and before an action will lie for its breach. The first of these established the rule that a passenger taking a ticket from a railway company is not such an act as will amount to a contract with the company so as to impose the duty to have a train ready to start at the time the passenger was led to expect; but the case of Denton *v.* The Great Northern Railway Company[2] is pertinent to this subject, and indicates, from the distinction which is to be drawn between it and that of Hurst *v.* The Great Western Railway Company,[3] as precisely as could well be, the law upon this particular point. In that case, which was an action brought by the plaintiff against the defendant company for not running a train according to their time-tables, it appeared that the time-tables published by the company stated that a train would leave Peterborough, for Hull, at 7.20 P. M. It also appeared that the whole line, from the former to the latter of these places, was not the property of the company, and that the part from Milford Junction to Hull belonged to the North-Eastern Railway Company. It was proved that on the 27th of February (1855), prior to the publication and affixing up at the stations of the company's time-tables for the month of March, but after the same had been printed and issued, the latter railway company gave the company sued notice of their intention to cease running the train from Milford to Hull which carried on the passengers who arrived at Milford by the train leaving Peterborough at 7.20. The time-table contained the following notice: "The companies make every exertion that the trains shall be punctual, but the arrival and departure at the times stated will not be guaranteed, nor will the companies hold themselves respon-

[1] Hall *v.* Hollander, 4 B. & C. 660; 7 D. R. 133; Martinez *v.* Gerber, 3 M. & G. 88; 3 Scott, N. R. 386; Gough *v.* Brian, 2 M. & W. 770; Hodsoll *v.* Stallebrass, 11 Ad. & E. 301; 3 P. & D. 200; 8 Dowl. P. C. 482; Gilbert *v.* Schwenck, 14 M. & W. 488.

[2] 5 El. & Bl. 860; 25 L. J. Q. B. 129; 2 Jur. N. S. 185.

[3] 19 C. B. N. S. 310; 34 L. J. C. P. 264.

sible for delay, or any consequence arising therefrom." LORD CAMPBELL, C. J., in giving judgment in this case, said: "It seems to me that the representations made by railway companies in their time-tables cannot be treated as mere waste-paper, and in the present case I think the plaintiff is entitled to recover on the ground that there was a contract with him, and also on the ground that there was a false representation by the company. It seems to me that if the company promised to give tickets for a train running at a particular hour, to a particular place, to any one who would come to the station and tender the price of the ticket, it is a good contract with any one who so comes. I take it to be clear that the issuing of the time-tables in this way amounts, in fact, to such a promise; any one who reads them would so understand them. Then, is it a good contract in law? The consideration is one which is a prejudice to the person who makes his arrangements with a view to the fulfilment of the contract, and comes to the station on the faith of it." WIGHTMAN, J., agreed that the publication of these time-tables amounted to a promise to any one of the public who would come to the station and pay for a ticket that he should have one by a train at a particular hour. And he held that the provision appended to the time-tables did not protect the company under the circumstances; and he said: "But whether there be a contract or not, the defendants are liable, as having induced the plaintiff, by a continued knowingly false representation, to believe that there was a train at seven to Hull, which he, believing, acted upon to his prejudice. All essentials for an action for false representation are here. The representation is untrue; it is known by the person making it to be untrue; it is calculated to induce the plaintiff to act, and he, believing it, is induced to act accordingly." CROMPTON, J., agreed that there was ground for an action for deceit, but held that there was no contract, although the company were liable for a breach of their public duty as carriers.

SEC. 521. **How Terms of Contract to be ascertained.** — It will be remembered that in the other case referred to the plaintiff neglected to put in the company's time-tables, and that ERLE, C. J., said: "If the plaintiff had put in the time-bill we should have seen what the real contract was, — *viz.* that the company do not warrant that their trains shall arrive with punctuality at the times indicated at the different stations." It appears, then, that in all the contracts made between railway companies and persons who are to be carried by them as passengers, reference will be made to the company's time-tables, with a view to ascertaining the exact terms of the contract, and it is evident that these time-tables are a part of the public profession of the railway carriers, which, as we have repeatedly seen, indicates the extent and character of their business. There seems to be no reason for distinguishing in this respect between railway carriers and others, and where there is no ground for distinction, any arbitrary modification of the rights and duties of either class would be impolitic and unjust. But such modification has not been made, and the law upon this matter is somewhat precise.

SEC. 522. **Rule in The Great Northern Railway Company v. Harrison.** — In the case of The Great Northern Railway Company *v.* Harrison,[1] it appeared that the defendants were in the practice of allowing the reporters of a London newspaper ("Bell's Life" newspaper), when going to country races on the defendants' line, for the purposes of framing their reports, to travel on the defendants' line carriage free. The reporter was for such purpose supplied with a ticket by the company, which had written upon it the name of a person in the reporting department. The ticket also purported on the face of it to be not transferable, and there was also a memorandum on it to the effect that any party other than the person named in it using the pass would be liable to the penalty which a passenger incurs by travelling without having paid his fare, or that he should be liable to pay the fare; but it did not distinctly appear which of these two liabilities was stated in the memorandum, and, if the former, it did not appear what the penalties were which were alluded to. The plaintiff acting *bonâ fide*, and going on the business of the journal, and entitled by the usage to have the benefit of a ticket with his name on it, went

[1] 10 Exch. 376; 2 C. L. R. 1136; 23 L. J. Exch. 308.

to the station with a ticket such as that described. His name, however, was not upon it, but there was the name of another person who, however, was a reporter, and in the same department with himself. The plaintiff showed this ticket to the porter at the station, whose business it was to examine passengers' tickets, who said that it was all right, and placed the plaintiff in a carriage. There was no distinct evidence, however, that the porter knew personally who the plaintiff was. It appeared that the plaintiff and other reporters had, on several previous occasions, travelled with similar tickets not bearing the names on them of those who used them, and there was evidence that the persons whose names were on the tickets were personally known to some of the officers and servants at the station. In an action by the plaintiff against the company for an injury received on their line whilst travelling in one of the company's carriages, in which the declaration alleged that "the plaintiff then lawfully was," and which allegation was denied by the plea, the question having been left to the jury, and a verdict having been found for the plaintiff, it was held on error, on a bill of exceptions, that there was evidence for the jury in support of the issue, and that the question was rightly left to them.

SEC. 523. **Railway Companies do not warrant Carriages Road-worthy.** — We have already, in speaking of the question of negligence, alluded to some of the incidents of the contract which is entered into between a railway company and a passenger, and have seen that, according to the doctrine laid down in Redhead *v.* Midland Railway Company,[1] railway companies, as common carriers of passengers by land for hire, do not, by their contract to carry, impliedly warrant that their carriages are road-worthy; and though they are liable for negligence, yet they are not liable to a passenger for an injury to him caused by a hidden defect in their carriage, which no amount of care or skill, either in the manufacture, purchase, or use, could have discovered. And we also saw, from the case of Francis *v.* Cockerell,[2] that it was a positive duty of the

[1] 36 L. J. Q. B. 181; 2 L. R. Q. B. 412; 15 W. R. 831.

[2] 5 L. R. Q. B. 184, 501, Exch. Ch.

carrier to use due care and skill in everything connected with the carriage of passengers, and that the employment of an independent contractor, being a competent person, to do some particular thing, would not exonerate the carrier, if the due care and skill had not been adhibited, even although the defect was of such a nature that it could not have been discovered by inspection made subsequently to the completion of the contractor's work.[1] The distinction between these two cases is so nice that upon this particular incident to the contract the law may be said to be perfectly definite, for in proportion to the closeness of two distinguishable cases is the definiteness of the principle which is the reason of the distinction.

SEC. 524. **Responsibility for Delay and Ordinary Stipulation. — Loss of Market. — Accident or other Causes.** — Before quitting the subject of the contract which is entered into between railway companies and passengers, which may be for a single journey, a double journey, or for any length of time, as a month, or a season, we may mention the case of Buckmaster *v.* The Great Eastern Railway,[2] in which the ordinary stipulation on railway tickets, that the company shall not be liable for any delay in the starting or arrival of trains arising from "accident or other cause," received a more definite connotation. In that case it appeared that the plaintiff went to the terminus of a branch line of the Great Eastern Railway, intending to travel to London by a certain train, that he might attend a corn market. The train was at the station, but the engine which had to draw it had not sufficient steam up, in conse-

[1] See also Daniel *v.* Metropolitan Rail. Co., L. R. 3 C. P. 216, 591, and other cases cited above. See also Alden *v.* New York Central R. R. Co., 26 N. Y. 102; Hanley *v.* Harlem R. R. Co., 1 Edm. (N. Y.) Sel. Cas. 359; M'Padden *v.* New York, &c. R. R. Co., 47 Barb. (N. Y.) 247.

[2] 23 L. T. N. S. 471. The publication of a time-table, in common form, is held to impose upon a railroad company the duty to use due care and skill to have its trains arrive and depart at the precise time specified in the tables, but does not make the company responsible for delays not occasioned by its negligence. Gordon *v.* Manchester, &c. R. R. Co., 52 N. H. 596. And it seems that it is not a defence that the conductor wilfully delayed the train. Weed *v.* Panama R. R. Co., 17 N. Y. 362. See, upon this point, Benson *v.* New Jersey R. R. & Transportation Co. 9 Bos. (N. Y.) 412.

quence of the fireman having neglected to light the fire in time, and the train could not go. The plaintiff was compelled to take a special train, and suffered loss in his business through his late arrival at market. It was held that the cause of the non-starting of the ordinary train was not accident, but an act of negligence on the part of a servant of the company, and that the plaintiff was entitled to recover from the company the sum he had paid for a special train, and likewise a reasonable sum for his loss of market. In summing up, MARTIN, B., said: "Now the first question to be tried is, whether this non-starting of the train arose from 'accident or other causes.' The words 'other causes,' as used in the condition on the ticket, mean 'other causes, of accidental kind,' and 'not any cause whatever.' The delay in the present case arose, very likely, through the fact of the man whose duty it was to light the engine fires not getting up early enough in the morning. That cause was not accident or anything like it, but an act of negligence on the part of a servant of the company. This line was only a branch of the main line of railway, and if the engine had blown up, or had met with any of the various mishaps to which engines are liable, the defendants might perhaps be excused, but doubtless you will be of opinion that this case was not one of accident of any kind."

SEC. 525. **Negligence in not starting Train. — Reasonable Restrictions.** — And it consequently appears that a railway company cannot absolve itself from the results of negligence in not starting a train by stating on the time-tables that the company will not "hold itself responsible for delay or any consequences arising therefrom." Any such restrictions or limitations must be reasonable, or they will not be held to be warrantable in a court of law. Further, in relation to the contract it must be noted, that where, by the traffic arrangement between two railway companies, passengers are booked through, the contract is one entire contract between the passenger and the company issuing the ticket. Where, therefore, a traffic arrangement for booking passengers through existed between the South Wales Railway Company and the Midland Railway Company, and the fares paid were divided between the companies according to the mileage, and the former issued a through ticket to a passenger from Newport to Birmingham, the words "*viâ* Midland from Gloucester" were printed on the ticket, the passenger having lost his portmanteau on the Midland line between Gloucester and Birmingham, it was held that he had no cause of action against the Midland Railway Company, the contract entered into by him being with the South Wales Company for the whole distance, which latter company was protected by its act, which provided that a passenger's ordinary luggage should be conveyed at his own risk.[1]

SEC. 526. **Contract to carry Passengers further considered.** — Another case which bears upon the subject of the contract of railway companies to carry passengers may be alluded to in this place. The plaintiff, intending to go to London and back by the defendants' railway, paid for and received from them the following ticket at Barnsley, and went to London with it: "Barnsley to King's Cross and back — excursion ticket. To return by the trains advertised for that purpose on any day not beyond fourteen days after date thereof." Morning and evening return excursion trains were advertised for the Saturdays, but they were not advertised to go to Barnsley. On a Saturday morning within the fourteen days the plaintiff presented himself at King's Cross Station in time for the morning return train. It became full, so that the plaintiff could not find room in it, and it would have been dangerous to add other carriages to it. The company refused to let him go by an ordinary train, but kept him waiting until the evening return train, in which he found a place. That train took him only to Doncaster, where it arrived on Sunday morning. No trains ran from Doncaster to Barnsley on Sundays. The line from Doncaster to Barnsley belonged not to the defendants, but to another company, and the plaintiff hired a carriage to take him from the former to the latter of these places, and brought an action to recover the expense from the defendants. Under these circumstances it was held that, by the terms of the excursion ticket and advertisement, the defendants contracted to carry the plaintiff back to Barnsley on any day within the

[1] Mytton *v.* Midland Rail. Co., 4 H. & N. 615; 28 L. J. Exch. 385.

fourteen days which he might choose, and by any of the advertised trains that he might select, that not sending him by the morning train was a breach of contract, and that taking him only to Doncaster instead of to Barnsley without previous notice was a second breach, and that consequently the action was maintainable.[1]

SEC. 527. **Rule in Le Conteur v. South-Western Railway Co.** — The case of Le Conteur *v.* The South-Western Railway Company[2] decided the point that a common carrier who enters into a contract with a passenger to convey him from one place to another, part of the journey to be performed by land in England, and the rest by sea, is entitled to the protection of the Carriers' Act, 11 Geo. IV. and 1 Will. IV. c. 68.

SEC. 528. **Fares.** — We have quoted certain provisions of the 21 & 22 Vict. c. 75, which was made perpetual by the 23 & 24 Vict. c. 41, with reference to the rate which railway companies are to charge for the conveyance of third-class passengers, and have dwelt upon the reasons of these provisions as being discoverable in a rational politics, which must consider the right of all to the advantages which progress places within the power of a few. As we may now bestow some more minute attention upon the duty of the passengers, although that has been, to some extent, indirectly explicated in treating of the duties of those with whom they contract in case those are railway carriers, we may mention a case which has reference to the question, what will be held an evasion of these statutes upon the part of a passenger. In that case a by-law of a company made it necessary that every passenger should pay his fare previously to entering a carriage of the company, and provided that upon such payment being made the passenger would be furnished with a ticket specifying the class of carriage and distance for which the fare was paid, and that any passenger who entered a carriage without having paid his fare should be subject to a penalty; and it appeared that an individual intending to go from Colchester to Diss

[1] Great Northern Rail. Co. *v.* Hawcroft, 21 L. J. Q. B. 178; 16 Jur. 196, C. C. A.

[2] 6 B. & S. 961.

(Diss being an intermediate station between Colchester and Norwich) took a ticket for Norwich, and upon his arrival at Diss left the carriage. The fare from Colchester to Diss was 7*s.*, while the fare from Colchester to Norwich was only 5*s.* At Diss the difference between these two fares was demanded from the passenger, but he refused to pay it. Upon these facts the borough justices of Colchester convicted him, under the by-law, of having unlawfully and wilfully entered the carriage of the company for the purpose of travelling upon the railway from Colchester to Diss, not having previously paid his fare for so travelling. On an appeal against this conviction it was held that the borough justices had jurisdiction over the alleged offence, but that the conviction could not be sustained, as the appellant had paid his fare within the meaning of the by-law.[1]

SEC. 529. **Principle of Interpretation.**—The principle, which is one simply of interpretation, is the same in another case more recently decided in Ireland. There one of the by-laws of the company provided that "no passenger will be allowed to enter any carriage without having first paid his fare and obtained a ticket, which ticket such passenger is to show whenever required." "Any passenger not producing his ticket will be required to pay the fare from the place whence any part of the train originally started, or, in default of payment, shall forfeit and pay a sum not exceeding 40*s.*" Notwithstanding this by-law, a passenger, who had taken a return ticket from H. to D., and upon his out-journey alighted at D., on his return journey, instead of getting in at D., went to S., the next station upon the line, but further from H. than D. was. Before entering the train, he was told that he would not be allowed to travel without getting a ticket from S. to D.; but he showed his return ticket, and offered to pay the fare from S. to D. The servants of the company refused to receive the difference of fare, and removed him forcibly from the carriage, and it was decided in the Exchequer Chamber (Ir.) that they were entitled to do so.[2]

[1] Reg. *v.* Frere, 4 El. & Bl. 598; 1 Jur. N. S. 700; 24 L. J. M. C. 68. See also Gelen *v.* Hall, 2 H. & N. 379.

[2] M'Carthy *v.* Dublin, Wicklow, & Wexford Rail. Co., 18 W. R. 762 Ir. Exch. Ch.

SEC. 530. **Passengers' Duty to show and deliver up Ticket.**— This naturally leads us to the consideration of the duty which is imposed upon passengers of showing and delivering up their tickets, and the consequences of a failure to do so. The imposition of this duty is to be defended upon the ground of expediency; and so long as expediency is judged of in reference to the public good, the ground is a good one. But to some it has seemed a hardship that the passenger should be compelled, as it were, to do a part of the book-keeping of the railway carrier, and that an efficient system might be devised by which this inconvenience might be abrogated. However that may be, the duty has been somewhat carefully circumscribed by the law, so that unavoidable failure to comply with the requisites of such by-laws, or to perform this duty, does not subject the traveller to disagreeable consequences, in case he is free from all intention to defraud.[1]

SEC. 531. **Correlative Duty upon the Part of the Company.**— One rule is to be remembered, and that is that a railway company, in order to enforce a by-law, as to the production of tickets, must bring themselves strictly within its terms.[2] Thus, where a master took tickets for himself and three servants, keeping the tickets in his own care, and told the guard he had the servants' tickets, and the servants were allowed to enter the train, without each having or showing his own ticket, it was held that by so doing the company was estopped from pleading, as a defence to an action by the master against the company, for afterwards expelling the servants from the train, and refusing to carry them, the by-law, "No passenger will be allowed to enter any carriage, or travel therein, without having paid his fare and obtained a ticket, which ticket such passenger is to show when required, and to deliver up before leaving the company's premises."

SEC. 532. **Rule of Construction of By-laws.**—It is evidently

[1] The Railway Clauses Act (8 & 9 Vict. c. 20, § 103) has only reference to persons travelling without a ticket and with fraudulent intent. Dearden *v.* Townsend, 12 Jur. N. S. 120; 25 L. J. M. C. 50; 14 W. R. 52.

[2] Jennings *v.* The Great Northern Rail. Co., 35 L. J. Q. B. 15; 1 L. R. Q. B. 7; 12 Jur. N. S. 331; 44 W. R. 28.

the only safe rule of construction applicable to by-laws, that the company, who have the making of them for the direct convenience of the management of their lines, should be strictly bound by them, and that where two constructions are possible, that which is in favor of the public and in prejudice of the company should be adopted. But where by-laws exist and are explicit, this simple rule of construction is not to be erected into a rule of law, to over-rule the clear provisions of by-laws, which, although made primarily for the advantage of the company, are secondarily, as we have shown, beneficial to the public. Thus, under a by-law of a railway company, which provided that "each passenger, booking his place, will be furnished with a ticket, which he is to show and deliver up, when required, to the guard," and that "each passenger, not producing or delivering up his ticket when required, is hereby subjected to a penalty not exceeding 40*s*.," it was held that the holders of annual tickets for travelling on the line were bound to produce their tickets to the railway officers as much as ordinary passengers.[1]

SEC. 533. **Fraudulent Intention.**—The meaning of the 103d section of the 8 & 9 Vict. c. 20, which enacts "that, if any person travel in any carriage of the company without having paid his fare, with intent to avoid payment thereof, or if any person, having paid his fare for a certain distance, knowingly and wilfully proceed in any such carriage beyond such distance without previously paying the additional fare for the additional distance, and with intent to avoid payment thereof, he shall forfeit, &c.," came under the consideration of the Court of Queen's Bench in the case of Dearden *v.* Townsend.[2] In that case it appeared that the Lancashire and Yorkshire Railway Company had made amongst other by-laws one which provided that "no passenger will be allowed to enter any carriage used on the railway or to travel therein upon the railway without having first paid his fare and obtained a ticket, or (as the case may be) without having paid for and

[1] Woodward *v.* Eastern Counties Rail. Co., 7 Jur. N. S. 971; 30 L. J. M. C. 126; 9 W. R. 660.

[2] Dearden *v.* Townsend, 35 L. J. M. C. 50; 12 Jur. N. S. 120; 14 W. R. 52.

obtained a contract or season ticket, giving him authority to travel during a stipulated period of time. Each passenger, on payment of his fare or the price of his contract or season ticket, will be furnished with a ticket, specifying the class of carriage and the distance for which, or places for travelling between which, the payment has been made, which ticket (whether a contract or season ticket or otherwise) such passenger is to show, whenever required by the guard in charge of the train, or some other servant of the company, and which ticket (if other than contract or season ticket) such passenger is also to deliver up before leaving the company's premises, upon demand, to the guard or other servant of the company authorized to collect tickets. Any passenger not producing his ticket as aforesaid (whether it be a contract or season ticket or otherwise), or any passenger not delivering up his ticket as aforesaid (if it be other than a contract or season ticket), will be required to pay the fare from the place whence the train started, and in default of payment thereof shall forfeit and pay a sum not exceeding 40*s*." The respondent in this case took at Ewood Bridge, a station on the appellant's line, a return ticket of the first class, thence to Salford (another station on the company's line), and back. He travelled to Salford and back again to Ewood Bridge, but, instead of alighting at the latter place, he travelled without taking another ticket to New Church. On the arrival of the train at New Church, the respondent produced and delivered up to the authorized servant of the company his return ticket from Ewood to Salford, and then tendered to him in addition the full local fare charged by the company for the conveyance of a first-class passenger between the two stations, Ewood Bridge and New Church, but it was refused. And the company's officer demanded payment of the full fare from Salford to New Church, which the respondent refused to pay. There was no intention on the part of the respondent to defraud the company, nor was any such intention charged in the information. Upon these facts it was held the respondent was not liable to be convicted, under such a by-law, for not producing and delivering up a ticket to New Church, or for not paying the fare from Salford to New Church, in the absence of any intention to defraud.

SEC. 534. **Intention to defraud Ingredient of the Offence.** — And COCKBURN, C. J., in giving judgment, said: "The intention of the person offending is therefore made by the statute an essential ingredient in the offence. But if the company, by a by-law, were to constitute the same state of facts an offence, and omit the element of intention, I think they would then not be making a by-law subject to the general act, but legislating in a sense repugnant to its provisions. I am of opinion, however, that the construction which the appellant would put upon this by-law is not the true one, and that it is meant to apply to persons who have taken a ticket and have it in their possession, but who will not produce it when required. No doubt, if a person travelling on this railway will not produce his ticket when demanded by the guard or other authorized person, the company would be right in assuming that he had a ticket and would not produce it, and in requiring him to pay the fare from the place whence the train originally started, but here the respondent produces his ticket, such as had been given him by the company, when demanded. . . . But the offence is provided for by statute, and therefore the question of intention becomes material. The company cannot apply this by-law to such a state of facts as the present."

SEC. 535. **Construction of By-law.** — In a case already referred to, a similar construction was placed upon a similar by-law in Ireland. In that case the wording of the by-law was as follows: "No passenger will be allowed to enter any carriage without having first paid his fare and obtained a ticket, which ticket such passenger is to show whenever required by the guard in charge of the train, or some other servant of the company. Any passenger not producing his ticket as aforesaid, will be required to pay the fare from the place whence any part of the train originally started, or in default of payment thereof shall forfeit, &c." This was held by WHITESIDE, C. J., only to apply to the case of a person having a ticket and refusing to show it.[1]

[1] M'Carthy *v.* Dublin, Wicklow, & Wexford Rail. Co., 3 Ir. R. C. L. 511; 17 W. R. 1101 Q. B. See also 18 W. R. 762 Ir. Exch. Ch.

SEC. 536. **Restrictions on Preference.** — But sufficient, it seems to us, has been said to indicate in what way and for what reasons the law, as it relates to the carriage of passengers by railways, differs from the legislative rules which regulate the rights and duties of the carriers of passengers by other modes of conveyance. In the course of our inquiry we have had opportunities of pointing out some of the principles which have guided legislative and executive action in relation to this branch of the law, which were not peculiar to railway carriers of passengers, but which, for many reasons, found more adequate illustration and convenient expression in that context. Before quitting this subject it may be expedient to refer the reader to what has already been said of the restrictions which are imposed upon the carriers of passengers by railway, in so far as the prevention of undue and unreasonable preference goes, under the 17 & 18 Vict. c. 31 (the Railway and Canal Traffic Act, 1854). This subject has been treated somewhat fully in another chapter, upon the ground that the principle which led to the prevention of undue and unreasonable preference in the case of goods was the same as that which led to the prevention of the same practices in connection with passenger traffic, and that was the protection of the interests of the public against the practical effects of the monopoly which circumstances had placed in the hands of railway companies. This branch of the law of carriers will be found to some extent explicated in the chapter upon the restrictions imposed upon carriers.[1]

SEC. 537. **Tramways, Object of Statutory Enactments.** — We come now to a consideration of the law which is applicable to street railways, or tramways. From what has been already said, it will be evident that when the existence of a practical monopoly, in so far as carriage went, necessitated stringent legislative measures, the existence of an actual monopoly of use will make some such legislative interference and regulation absolutely necessary in the case of street railways.[2] In the latter case, however, the legislative interfer-

[1] *Ante*, p. 357 *et seq.*

[2] Maverick *v.* Eighth Avenue R. R. Co., 36 N. Y. 378; Vinton *v.* Middlesex R. R. Co., 11 Allen (Mass.), 304.

ence will be more peculiarly of a kind to protect other persons than those who have become passengers; while in the former, it will be entered upon more particularly with the view of protecting those individuals who have contracted with the carrier to be conveyed, for the obvious reasons that railways run over ground belonging to the company, and on which, except at level crossings — for which special regulations exist, as we have seen — no person has a right to be, while tramways are upon the public streets and roads, where every person has a right to be. But, further, there is another reason why, in the case of tramways, the legislative provisions should be directed more to secure the safety of the public who are not passengers, than that of the public who are; and that is, that, owing to the speed with which railways travel, and the comparative slowness with which tramway omnibuses convey, the danger in the one case to passengers is small, when compared with the possible danger in the other. Therefore, if the legislature would interfere with excellent effect, it must interfere so as to produce extra care where there is additional danger, and must constantly endeavor to leave each carrier as free as a rational regard for the interests and safety of the public will permit. There were several attempts at legislation upon the matter of tramways, the greater convenience of that mode of conveyance having been proved in America before its introduction into this country. And besides the 24 & 25 Vict. c. 152, which was an act to facilitate internal communication in Ireland by means of tramways,[1] the 24 & 25 Vict. c. 69, which was an act providing for the formation of tramways on turnpike and statute labor roads in Scotland, and the 28 & 29 Vict. c. 74, which enabled the Secretary of State for the War Department to lay down and use a tramway across certain public roads in the county of Devon, several private and local acts have been passed enabling companies to lay down and use tramways in various places in England. But on the 9th of August, 1870,[2] an act was passed to facilitate the construction,

[1] Amended by 24 & 25 Vict. c. 102; 25 & 26 Vict. c. 67, § 7.

[2] The Tramways Act, 1870, 33 & 34 Vict. c. 78; and see the Metropolitan Tramways Provisional Orders Suspension Act, 1871, 34 & 35 Vict. c. 69.

and regulate the working of these street railways, or tramways, some of the provisions of which must be alluded to in this place.

SEC. 538. **Provision for Application to Board of Trade. — Confirmation of Provisional Order.** — By this act, and with a view to carrying out these purposes, provision is made for application to the Board of Trade, with the consent of the local or road authority of the district in which the proposed tramway is to be constructed, by the promoters, and for the making of a provisional order by the Board of Trade, if they think fit. The Board of Trade, in granting such application, may do so with or without modification, or subject, or not subject, to any restriction or condition.[1] The same section also enacts that "every such provisional order shall empower the promoters therein specified to make the tramway upon the gauge and in the manner therein described, and shall contain such provisions as (subject to the requirements of this act) the Board of Trade, according to the nature of the application, and the facts and circumstances of each case, think fit to submit to Parliament for confirmation, in manner provided by this act, but so that any such provisional order shall not contain any provision for empowering the promoters, or any other person, to acquire any lands, even by agreement, except to an extent therein limited, or to construct a tramway elsewhere than along or across a road, or upon land taken by agreement." The 9th section provides that "every tramway in a town, which is hereafter authorized by provisional order, shall be constructed and maintained, as nearly as may be, in the middle of the road, and no tramway shall be authorized by any provisional order to be so laid that for a distance of thirty feet or upwards a less space than nine feet and six inches shall intervene between the outside of the footpath on either side of the road and the nearest rail of the tramway, if one third of the owners or one third of the occupiers of the houses, shops, or warehouses abutting upon the part of the road where such less space shall intervene as aforesaid, shall,

[1] Sec. 8.

in the prescribed manner, and at the prescribed time, express their dissent from any tramway being so laid."

SEC. 539. **Specification of Nature of Traffic.** — The 10th section enacts that "every such provisional order shall specify the nature of the traffic for which such tramway is to be used, and the tolls or charges which may be demanded and taken by the promoters in respect of the same, and shall contain such regulations relating to such traffic, and such tolls and charges as the Board of Trade shall deem necessary and proper."

SEC. 540. **Publication and Confirmation of Order. — Powers of Board of Trade.** — The 13th section provides for the publication, and the 14th for the confirmation by Parliament, of the provisional order.[1] By the 16th section the Board of Trade has power to revoke, amend, extend, or vary any provisional order. There are also provisions for the cesser of the powers given by any provisional order at the expiration of the prescribed time,[2] for the way in which tramways shall be constructed,[3] for the breaking up of streets, with a view to such construction,[4] for the repair of the roads where the tramway is laid,[5] as to gas and water companies, and the protection of sewers.[6]

SEC. 541. **Tolls, &c. — By-laws by Local Authority.** — The third part of the act, under the head General Provisions, gives authority to the promoters to use the tramways, with flange-wheeled carriages,[7] and provides for the granting of licenses to use the tramway, to third parties by the Board of Trade.[8] And the 45th section of the act provides that "the promoters or lessees of a tramway authorized by special act may demand and take, in respect of such tramway, tolls and charges not exceeding the sum specified in such special act, subject and according to the regulations therein specified. A list of all the tolls and charges authorized to be taken shall be exhibited in a conspicuous place inside and outside each of the carriages used upon the tramways." The 46th section enacts that,

[1] The Act of Parliament confirming a provisional order is to be deemed a Public General Act, § 14.

[2] Sec. 18.

[3] Sec. 25.

[4] Sec. 26.

[5] Sec. 28.

[6] Secs. 30 & 31.

[7] 33 & 34 Vict. c. 78, § 34.

[8] *Ibid.* § 35.

"subject to the provisions of the special act authorizing any tramway and this act, the local authority[1] of any district, in which the same is laid down, may from time to time make regulations as to the following matters: —

"The rate of speed to be observed in travelling upon the tramway;

"The distances at which carriages using the tramway shall be allowed to follow one after the other;

"The stopping of carriages using the tramway;

"The traffic on the road in which the tramway is laid.

"The promoters of any tramway and their lessees may from time to time make regulations, —

"For preventing the commission of any nuisance in or upon any carriage, or in or against any premises belonging to them;

"For regulating the travelling in or upon any carriage belonging to them."

And the section goes on to provide for the alteration of any such by-laws, for publication of notice of the making of such by-laws, and for the nullity of any such by-law which shall be disallowed by the Board of Trade.

SEC. 542. **Powers for enforcing Rules, &c.** — Another section enacts that reasonable penalties may be imposed by such by-laws, not exceeding 40*s.* for each offence.[2] And another gives to the local authority like powers of making and enforcing rules and regulations, and of granting licenses with respect to all carriages using the tramways, and to all drivers, conductors, and other persons having charge of, or using the same, and to standings for the same, as they are for the time being entitled to make, enforce, and grant with respect to hackney carriages, and the drivers and other persons having charge thereof, and to the standings for the same in the streets and district of or under the control of the local authority.[3]

By the 50th section of the said act, it is provided that, "If any person without lawful excuse (the proof whereof shall lie on him) wilfully does any of the following things, *viz.* —

[1] For the meaning of the term "local authority," see 33 & 34 Vict. c. 78, § 3.

[2] 33 & 34 Vict. c. 78, § 47.

[3] *Ibid.* § 48.

"Interferes with, removes, or alters any part of the tramway, or of the works connected therewith, places or throws any stones, dirt, wood, refuse, or other material on any part of a tramway;

"Does, or causes to be done, anything in such manner as to obstruct any carriage using a tramway, or to endanger the lives of persons therein or thereon;

"Or knowingly aids or assists in the doing of any such thing, —

he shall for every such offence be liable (in addition to any proceedings by way of indictment or otherwise, to which he may be subject) to a penalty not exceeding *5l.*"

SEC. 543. **Other Penalties.** — Further, there are provisions for the infliction of penalties on passengers practising frauds upon the promoters,[1] for bringing dangerous goods on the tramway,[2] and on persons using the tramways with carriages with flange wheels;[3] and it is provided that "the promoters or lessees, as the case may be, shall be answerable for all accidents, damages, and injuries happening through their act or default, or through the act or default of any person in their employment, by reason or in consequence of any of their works or carriages, and shall save harmless all road and other authorities, companies, or bodies collectively and individually, and their officers and servants, from all damages and costs in respect of such accidents, damages, and injuries;"[4] and again, that nothing in that act, or in any by-law made under it, should take away or abridge the right of the public "to pass along, or cross, every or any part of any road along or across which any tramway is laid, whether on or off the tramway, with carriages not having flange wheels, or wheels suitable only to run on the rail of the tramway."[5]

[1] 33 & 34 Vict. c. 78, § 51.

[2] *Ibid.* § 53.

[3] *Ibid.* § 54.

[4] *Ibid.* § 55.

[5] *Ibid.* § 62. There has been an injunction granted, by MALINS, V. C., against an omnibus company for altering its wheels to the gauge of the tramway. A street railway track is treated as private property, and cannot be used by others by having the wheels of their carriages adapted thereto Jersey City, &c. R. R. Co. *v.* Jersey City, &c. R. R. Co., 20 N. J. Eq. 61; Brooklyn Central R. R. Co. *v.* Brooklyn City R. R. Co., 32 Barb. (N. Y.) 358; Metropolitan R. R. Co. *v.* Quincy R. R. Co., 12 Allen (Mass.), 262.

SEC. 544. **Analogy between Street and other Railway Carriers.** — These, then, and other provisions to which it is unnecessary to allude in this place, indicate the rights and the duties of those carriers of passengers who carry by means of street railways or tramways, and it will be perceived that many of the provisions thus made are, in many respects, analogous to those which exist in the case of railways. Wherever there is no reason for difference, there are many reasons for similarity, and much of the case law which has been accumulated in relation to railway cases, in so far as they are carriers of passengers, is applicable, it seems to us, to carriers by means of tramway omnibuses. The differences which exist in the statute law applicable to these two classes of carriers are merely differences in matters of detail, and the principles which dictate the provisions as to restrictions, by-laws, and the like, are the same in both cases. As that is the case, and as we have described with considerable minuteness the law as it relates to railway carriers of passengers, it is unnecessary to dwell at greater length in this place upon that class of carriers who convey passengers in or by means of tramways.

SEC. 545. **Hackney Carriages.** — There is another class of carriers of passengers who are distinguished from those already alluded to by the kind of conveyance which they use for the purposes of carriage. All the differences in law depend upon differences in fact. The law is something which has arisen out of dead facts, as the phœnix is supposed to rise out of dead ashes. Now the circumstances connected with conveyance of passengers by means of hackney carriages, or cabs, are sufficiently unlike those connected with the conveyance of passengers by any other vehicle, as to make some distinction in the law applicable to these necessary. Such necessity is dictated by a reasonable desire upon the part of the legislature to secure the convenience of the public, and from a consciousness that the more general the attainment of this end is, the more wisely are they performing their functions, and the more successfully arriving at the very object of their existence.

SEC. 546. **History of Legislation.** — The history of legislation in reference to this matter is somewhat long, and we will content ourselves by referring the reader to some of the statutes which have, from time to time, been passed. The first important act which was passed was the 1 & 2 Will. IV. c. 22,[1] which had to do with the collection and management of the duties on vehicles of this description, and placed them under the Commissioners of Stamps.[2] But the acts which, up to the 32 & 33 of Victoria, were the most important in this connection, in so far at least as metropolitan cabs were concerned,[3] were the 16 & 17 Vict. c. 33, and the 16 & 17 Vict. c. 127.[2] These acts were passed with the view of regulating metropolitan stage and hackney carriages, of reducing the duties payable in respect of such carriages, and also of amending the law relating to the granting of licenses and payment of duties in respect of such carriages, and, at the same time, of making provision as to the charge for their hire in certain cases. The actual provisions of these acts need not be more specifically referred to in this place.[4] In 1869, however, another act was passed, for the purpose of amending the law relating to cabs within the metropolitan police district.[5] This act places the power of licensing, or withholding a license to such vehicle, in the hands of one of Her Majesty's principal Secretaries of State,[6] provides for the infliction of penalties for the use of unlicensed carriages,[7] for the licensing of drivers,[8] and, by its 9th section, that the said "Secretary of State may, from time to time, by order, make regulations for all or any of the following purposes; that is to say, —

"1. For regulating the number of persons to be carried by any hackney or stage carriage, and in what manner

[1] See also 1 & 2 Vict. c. 79; 16 & 17 Vict. c. 86; 22 & 23 Vict. c. 115.

[2] See also 6 & 7 Vict. c. 86, and 13 & 14 Vict. c. 7. See Frost *v.* Williams, 7 A. & E. 773; 2 N. & P. 475.

[3] As to provincial hackney carriages, see 10 & 11 Vict. c. 89, § 37.

[4] See also 30 & 31 Vict. c. 134, 31 & 32 Vict. c. 5, and 32 & 33 Vict. c. 14.

[5] The Metropolitan Public Carriage Act, 1869, 32 & 33 Vict. c. 115.

[6] 32 & 33 Vict. c. 115, § 6.

[7] *Ibid.* § 7.

[8] *Ibid.* § 8.

such number is to be shown on such carriage, and how such hackney carriages are to be furnished and fitted;

"2. For fixing the stands of hackney carriages, and the distances to which they may be compelled to take passengers, and the persons to attend at such stands;

"3. For fixing the rates of fares, as well for time as distance, to be paid for hackney carriages, and for securing the due publication of such fares; provided that it shall not be made compulsory on the driver of any hackney carriage to take passengers at a less fare than the fare payable at the time of the passing of this act;

"4. For forming, in the case of hackney carriages, a table of distances, as evidence for the purpose of any fare to be charged by distance, by the preparation of a book, map, or plan, or any combination of a book, map, or plan;

"5. For securing the safe custody and redelivery of any property accidentally left in hackney or stage carriages, and fixing the charges to be paid in respect thereof, with power to cause such property to be sold, or to be given to the finder, in the event of its not being claimed within a certain time.

"Subject to the following restrictions:—

"1. In fixing the stands for hackney carriages within the city of London, and the liberties thereof, the consent of the Court of the Lord Mayor and Aldermen shall be required to any stand appointed by the Secretary of State;

"2. No hackney carriage shall be compelled to take any passenger a greater distance, for any one drive, than six miles;

"3. During such portions of time between sunset and sunrise as is from time to time prescribed, no driver shall ply for hire unless the hackney carriage under his charge be provided with a lamp, properly trimmed and lighted, and fixed outside the carriage in such manner as is prescribed." [1]

Other provisions occur in this act, to which, however, it is unnecessary for us to refer.[2] The above quotation shows in what way the law has been modified, and in whose hands the power of regulating this description of passenger traffic is at present placed. Before alluding to some of the cases which have been decided since the passing of this act, it may be well to refer to one or two previous decisions upon this subject.[3] This, however, must be done briefly.

SEC. 547. **With regard to Licensing.** — Where a conviction alleged that a coach-master, not being licensed, did drive and let to hire a certain coach and two coach-horses, being within the bills of mortality, and within and upon the streets of London and Westminster, and in the information on which the conviction was founded, it was stated that the defendant did drive to hire a certain coach and two coach-horses within and upon such paved streets, and that the driver conveyed a person in the coach for hire within the limits aforesaid, it was held that such a conviction could not be supported under any of the statutes by which hackney coaches were licensed or regulated, as it was not alleged to be a hackney coach within 9 Anne, c. 23, nor was it "driving for hire with a coach" within 1 Geo. I. c. 57.[4]

In another case it was decided that, notwithstanding the terms of 6 & 7 Vict. c. 86, § 8, a commissioner of police may exercise a discretion in granting licenses to metropolitan omnibus drivers and conductors, and may propose such questions to them with relation to their application for such licenses as he may think proper, and is not bound to renew such licenses upon the bare production of a certificate of the good conduct

[1] This clause does not repeal 5 & 6 Vict. c. 79, § 13, so far as regards existing carriages, or any which may be built within one year after the passing of the recited act.

[2] See further on this subject, 29 & 30 Vict. c. 64, § 10, and 29 & 30 Vict. c. 36, § 1.

[3] The act relating to hackney carriages is expressly limited from extending to steam carriages. 3 & 4 Will. IV. c. 48.

[4] Cloud *v.* Turfery, 9 Moore, 595; 2 Bing. 318.

and fitness of the applicant.[1] And it was decided that a license for hackney carriages, granted by the Commissioners of Stamps under 2 & 3 Will. IV. c. 120, does not dispense with the necessity of a license under the Towns Police Clauses Act, 1847,[2] the first being required for the purposes of revenue, the second for the purposes of police.[3]

SEC. 548. **Standing and Plying.** — In a case where it appeared that a Paving Act authorized the commissioners to direct and regulate the hackney-coach stands within their district, it was held that they might remove a hackney-coach stand altogether if it obstructed the public street.[4] We refer to these cases because, although legislative alterations have been made in the authority which is to regulate this kind of traffic, the principles which are to govern the exercise of that authority are the same as those which are to be found explicated in the cases referred to.[5] One other case, which has still importance in this connection, may be quoted, — that is the case of The Blackpool Board of Health *v.* Bennett.[6] By an order in council the entire area, places, and parts of places comprised within the boundary of a township were constituted a district, for the purposes of the 11 & 12 Vict. c. 63. An Improvement Act empowered the local board from time to time to make by-laws for regulating the conduct of the drivers of hackney carriages plying within the district, and for fixing the stands of such hackney carriages. The local board made the following by-law: "That the several places in the district where painted boards shall from time to time be placed by the local board to distinguish them as stands, shall be the stands for such number of carriages, horses, asses, mules, &c., as shall be mentioned on such boards, and no driver of any such carriage, &c., shall place the same on any other than one of such

[1] Metcham, *Ex parte*, 10 Jur. N. S. 1254; 5 B. & S. 585; S. C. nom. Reg. *v.* Commissioners of Metropolitan Police, 12 W. R. 983; 33 L. J. Q. B. 325.

[2] 10 & 11 Vict. c. 89, § 37.

[3] Buckle *v.* Wrightson, 13 W. R. 92; 11 L. T. N. S. 341; 34 L. J. M. C. 43; 5 B. & S. 854.

[4] Rex *v.* Rawlinson, 9 D. & R. 7; 6 B. & C. 23.

[5] See also Duck *v.* Addington, 4 T. R. 447.

[6] 4 H. & N. 127; 28 L. J. M. C. 203; 7 W. R. 382.

stands, or shall ply for hire in any of the streets or places within the district (except on one of such stands), under a penalty not exceeding 40*s*." In this case it appeared that a licensed driver had been convicted of plying for hire off a stand, and on appeal the justices stated that it was proved to their satisfaction that he was driving a licensed carriage on the beach within the district, that he got off, spoke to some people, and took them up, having then passed a stand. It was held that, although the by-law did not state on the face of it the exact localities where the stands were to be, it was valid, that the sea-shore between high and low water mark was within the district, and that the driver was properly convicted of plying for hire off a stand.

SEC. 549. **Provisions as to Extra Payments. — Number of Persons. — Children.** — One of the sections of one of the acts above alluded to[1] provides that, when more than two persons shall be carried inside any hackney carriage or cab drawn by one horse only, a sum of 6*d.* for each person shall be paid for the whole hiring in addition to the fare directed to be paid for two persons under 16 & 17 Vict. c. 33, and that two children under ten years of age shall be considered as one adult person. It was held that if two children under ten years of age are carried in excess of two persons, they shall be counted and paid for as one adult; but that if one child only be so conveyed in excess, he shall still be considered as an extra person within the meaning of the act, and paid for accordingly.[2] We come now to the consideration of one or two cases which have come before the courts of law since the passing of the Metropolitan Public Carriage Act, 1869. In one of these, which came before the Court of Queen's Bench, it was decided that a carriage, whilst on the premises of a railway company, under a contract with them to await the arrival of their trains, for the conveyance of any passenger by railway who chooses to

[1] 16 & 17 Vict. c. 127, § 14.

[2] Norton *v.* Jones, 11 W. R. 573; 8 L. T. N. S. 241 Q. B. In reference to defacing a license, forbidden under 6 & 7 Vict. c. 86, see Hurrell *v.* Ellis, 2 C. B. 265; 9 Jur. 1013; Rogers *v.* Macnamara, 14 C. B. 27; 23 L. J. C. P. 1; Heathe *v.* Brewer, 15 C. B. N. S. 803; 9 L. T. N. S. 653.

hire it, is plying for hire within the meaning of the act, is therefore a hackney carriage, and must be licensed.[1]

SEC. 550. **Power of Home Secretary to license Cabs. — Specification in Application.** — We have seen that the act under consideration empowers the Home Secretary to license hackney carriages in such manner and in such form, and subject to such conditions, as he may by order prescribe, and also to make regulations for (amongst other things) fixing the rates of fares, and for securing the due publication thereof. In pursuance of the power thus conferred upon him, the Home Secretary made an order prescribing a form of license which was to contain the rate to be charged for the hire of each carriage per mile and per hour. The order further required that the application for a license should specify the sums which the applicant desired to have inserted in the license as the rates at which the carriage should ply for hire; that the carriage should be inspected prior to the license being issued; and that, before plying for hire, the proprietor should affix to the top of the carriage a metal flag with the rates to be charged in accordance with his license. As we have seen, penalties were imposed by the act for breach of the order. Upon a summons against the proprietor of a hackney carriage for non-compliance with the order in respect of the affixing of a flag with the fares, the magistrate refused to convict the defendant on the ground that the order was not a sufficient compliance with the act, inasmuch as the Secretary of State had no power to authorize an indefinite number of scales of charges for hackney carriages, but only one scale, binding upon all hirers and all proprietors. This decision was reversed in the Court of Common Pleas. "The objection to this order," remarked WILLES, J., in delivering his judgment, "seems to be, that the Secretary of State has not fixed the fares so as to be in compliance with the statute. It might, possibly, have been more convenient to divide the licensed hackney carriages into classes, and to have allowed a fixed rate, say, 1*s.* 6*d.*, 1*s.*, and 6*d.* per mile, respectively. Instead of doing so, the order provides

1 Clarke *v.* Stanford, 6 L. R. Q. B. 357. See Case *v.* Storey, 4 L. R. Exch. 319. See also Allen *v.* Tunbridge, 6 L. R. C. P. 481.

that, when a license is applied for, the carriage shall be inspected by the proper officer, that the application for the license shall specify the sums which the applicant desires to have inserted in the license as the rates at which the carriage shall ply for hire by distance and by time respectively, and that the license, when granted, shall state that charge. . . . The course which the Secretary of State has by this order adopted, seems to me to determine sufficiently the scale of fares, and the mode of making such scale, in each case, known to the public. The result will be that carriages will be provided at the accustomed fares, or a better class of conveyance for a higher charge. The inspector will take care that the order is properly carried out in this respect."[1]

SEC. 551. **Sanitary Precautions.** — One other subject in connection with that which is at present under consideration may be noticed in this place. The advance of science has made us more thoroughly acquainted with the conditions of health and disease, and has consequently enabled us to take such precautions as will tend to secure to some extent the former, and to avoid to some extent the latter. At best, our knowledge is very scanty, and it therefore the more behooves us to act with the greatest caution in all sanitary matters, and at the same time to neglect no means which may tend to the maintenance of the public health as being second — if second — only to the public order and peace. With this view much has recently been done to attain these ends, yet much, even in the present state of scientific knowledge, remains to be done. The more thorough knowledge alluded to brought to light the fact that there were other dangers to be feared in connection with conveyance of persons from place to place than those which met the eye, or were to be placed under the head of accidents, and treated by surgical appliances. It became familiar to all that there were dangers which did not meet the eye, dangers which were more perilous than those which may arise from latent defects of construction in the carriage, and dangers from which the public could only be protected by strict statutory enactments. These dangers were those which arise from the

[1] Bocking *v.* Jones, 6 L. R. C. P. 29.

peculiar nature of the propagability of disease; and, to avoid the evils which might arise from healthy persons being carried in vehicles in which persons suffering from infectious diseases had been conveyed, the legislature introduced several measures. The first of these, 18 & 19 Vict. c. 116, is applicable to Scotland, and the most recent of these, the 29 & 30 Vict. c. 90, contains the following provisions:[1] "It shall be lawful at all times for the nuisance authority to provide and maintain a carriage or carriages suitable for the conveyance of persons suffering under any contagious or infectious disease, and to pay the expense of conveying any person therein to a hospital or place for the reception of sick, or to his own house."[2] "If any person suffering from any dangerous infectious disorder shall enter any public conveyance without previously notifying to the owner or driver thereof that he is so suffering, he shall, on conviction thereof before any justice, be liable to a penalty not exceeding 5*l.*, and shall also be ordered by the justice to pay to such owner and driver all losses and expenses they may suffer in carrying into effect the provisions of this act; and no owner or driver of any public conveyance shall be required to convey any person so suffering until they shall have been first paid a sum sufficient to cover all such losses and expenses."[3]

SEC. 552. **Passengers by Water.**—Another subject of much importance remains for consideration in connection with the conveyance of persons, and that is the law relating to the carriage of passengers on water by means of ships. Several circumstances combine to make this subject one of great importance, but all these circumstances are reducible to their effects upon human minds, for the purposes of a work of this nature. The dangers which are incident to sea transits, the skill and experience which are requisite on the part of those to whom the conduct of a ship is trusted, the unforeseen circumstances which may arise, and the promptitude which is required upon the part of those who manage the ship in dealing with emergencies, and little opportunities out of which gigan-

[1] See also 21 & 22 Vict. c. 97, 22 & 23 Vict. c. 3, on the subject generally.

[2] 29 & 30 Vict. c. 90, § 24.

[3] *Ibid.* § 25. Similar provisions have been made in some of the American statutes.

tic events may be hatched,— all these circumstances which imperil human life and happiness, all these circumstances which are associated with the exercise of skill and judgment, and which, but for the exercise of these, may result in catastrophe, are important only in their relation to the human mind and the human heart. Those events which are fraught with much emotion we call important, and it is in relation to important events that law is important, and not otherwise. Laws may be looked upon as the precautions which the head takes for the convenience of the heart.

SEC. 553. **The Reason of the Importance of this Subject. — Authority on board Ship. — Its Scope. — Defence. — Power to leave the Ship.** — The extent of this kind of traffic, the nomadic condition of men at the present time, the growing necessity for emigration, and the leading of workers to work instead of leaving them to starvation, — these circumstances show how many hopes and fears must be connected with the safety of the conveyance of passengers by means of ships, and hence indicate the necessity of a definite rule of law and careful legislative provisions. But the circumstances alluded to necessarily impose other duties upon passengers than those which devolve upon individuals travelling by land-carriage, for it is evident that the dangers of the sea make it necessary that the person to whose skill and conduct life and property are intrusted, should be endowed with an almost unlimited authority at the time of peril. There is no time to vote what shall be done in a storm. Therefore it is a passenger's obvious duty to obey this authority in all matters which are within its scope.[1] That scope may be defined as whatever is for the security of the vessel, the discipline of the crew, and the safety of all on board.[2] With regard to this duty of obedience, which, owing to the circumstances of the case, is almost peculiar to the carriage of passengers by means of ship, several decisions indicate in what directions it primarily lies. Thus a passenger on board a ship in time of danger is bound to do works of necessity in defence of the ship if attacked, and

[1] Boyce *v.* Bayliffe, 1 Camp. 57.
[2] King *v.* Franklin, 1 F. & F. 360; Aldworth *v.* Stewart, 14 L. T. N. S. 862; 4 F. & F. 957.

for the preservation of those on board, if required to do so;[1] but it was decided in the same case that he might, if he chose —except under peculiar circumstances — depart the ship; and that, if he remained voluntarily, and risked his personal safety to succor her in her distress, he might be entitled to remuneration, in the nature of salvage, for his assistance.[2] In the case of Boyce *v.* Bayliffe,[3] which was an action for false imprisonment on board an East Indiaman on a voyage from Bombay to London, it appeared in evidence that the plaintiff was a passenger in the gunner's mess, and that the defendant was captain of the ship. Near the Cape of Good Hope two strange sail were descried in the offing supposed to be enemies. The defendant immediately mustered all hands on deck, and assigned to every one his station. The plaintiff, with the other passengers, he ordered on the poop, where they were to fight with small-arms. This order all readily obeyed except the plaintiff, who, conceiving that he had been ill-used by the defendant some time before in being forbidden to walk on the poop, positively refused to go there, but offered to fight in any other part of the ship with his messmates. The defendant, for this contumacy, ordered him to be carried upon the poop, and there kept him in irons during the whole night. Next morning no enemy appeared, and the ship reached St. Helena in safety. There the plaintiff quitted her. LORD ELLENBOROUGH said, after the case opened, "that he did not know, till he should hear all the facts, whether the defendant might not be justified. A captain of a ship had authority to do what was necessary for the safety of those on board. On the approach of an enemy he had a right to assign them all a station, which it was their duty to accept. As the plaintiff had refused to obey the orders given him, perhaps his confinement might be necessary to the discipline of the crew and the security of the vessel; and, if so, would be justifiable in law." However, when it came out that the plaintiff had been kept

[1] Newman *v.* Walters, 3 B. & P. 612.

[2] Newman *v.* Walters, 3 B. & P. 612. See also The Two Friends, 1 Rob. Rep. 285; The Beaver, 3 Rob. Rep. 292; The Joseph Harray, 1 Rob. Rep. 306.

[3] 1 Camp. 57.

all night in irons on the poop, his Lordship held that the defendant had clearly exceeded the limits of his authority.[1]

SEC. 554. **Duties of Passenger Carriers.** — Having spoken of this preliminary matter, we are now in a position to consider the questions as to rights and duties of carriers by water, which are more analogous to those incident to the same trade, when carried on by land carriage. It is quite evident that they are, like the carriers of passengers by land, bound to use the utmost care and diligence, and are responsible for any want of like care and diligence upon the part of their servants. They are likewise responsible for the sufficiency of the water craft, or the seaworthiness of the ships in which they convey passengers. Again, it is the duty of the owners and masters of vessels, who hold themselves out as carriers of passengers, to receive all persons who apply for a passage, but in this case, as in the case of professed carriers of passengers by land, the duty is subject to modifications, on account of the amount of accommodation, the character of the person, the tender of payment, and the like. In this respect there is no difference between carriage of passengers by water from place to place in the same country, and carriers of passengers beyond the seas.

SEC. 555. **Within and beyond the Realm.** — In the case of Bennett *v.* The Peninsular Steamboat Company,[2] the question arose whether a man could be a common carrier of passengers from a place that is within to a place that is without the realm — that is, whether or not the defendants were common carriers of passengers for hire from Southampton to Gibraltar. It appeared on the trial, before WILDE, C. J., that the defendants were the proprietors of certain steam-vessels, one of which was advertised by circulars issued by the defendants to sail every ten days from Southampton for Corunna, Riga, Oporto, Lisbon, Cadiz, and Gibraltar, the circulars gave the times of starting, and the terms upon which the passengers and goods were to be conveyed to those places respectively, if there was room for them. It appeared that the plaintiff went

[1] See also Aldworth *v.* Stewart, 14 L. T. N. S. 862; 4 F. & F. 957.

[2] 6 C. B. 775.

to Southampton for the purpose of taking his passage by "The Montrose," one of the defendants' vessels; but that in consequence of some communication which had been made to the defendants by the Portuguese consul, their agent refused to allow him to take a passage, although it was admitted that there was plenty of room. It was submitted, on the part of the defendants, that the common-law liability of carriers did not extend to carriers of passengers, or to extra-territorial carriers; and that the company's circulars imported a limited, and not a general undertaking to carry passengers. The learned judge left it to the jury to decide whether or not there was evidence to induce them to believe that the defendants carried on the business of common carriers for hire, and the jury found in the affirmative. Upon leave being given to the defendants to move to enter a verdict for them, if the court should be of opinion that this was not the fair legal inference from the evidence, it was held that the question was properly left to the jury; and that the declaration of the plaintiff, when it calls the defendants "common carriers of passengers," did not mean to allege that they were carriers within the realm, and according to the custom of the realm, but that they were persons who were in the habit of conveying passengers for hire from England to certain places beyond the seas. And every person taking passage is presumed to contract in respect to accommodations, &c., during the voyage (in the absence of special agreement) in reference to the usage of the particular voyage. In all cases of commercial usage, the law presumes that the parties contracting did not mean to commit to writing the whole of their contract, by which they intended to be bound, but that they contracted on the understanding that the established usage should explain what is left doubtful.

SEC. 556. **Statutes.** — Wherever it is possible to compel the performance of duties which are imposed for the safety and convenience of the public without recourse to actual legislative enactment, it is expedient to forego legislative interference. Wherever individuals can secure their rights by the remedies which are within their reach in the civil courts of this country, it may be well not to set in motion that other system of compulsion which has recourse to pains and penalties for its efficient working, for it seems to us that the perfection of laws would be *a law*, and that when remedies and penalties are multiplied in number, they are, in many cases, diminished in their efficiency. But it was found that the remedies by civil process were not sufficient to secure that care and skill upon the part of ship-owners and masters which was so necessary to the safety and welfare of the passengers they carried,[1] and consequently several acts were passed with the view of securing the seaworthiness of ships, a due proportion between the tonnage of ships and the number of passengers they carried, the preservation of the health of the passengers during the voyage, an adequate supply of water and provisions for their use, and at the same time to maintain a due regard for the interests of those who undertook the important duty of transporting passengers by water. In the reign of George III. an act[2] was passed which, after reciting that in various parts of the United Kingdom several persons had been seduced to leave their native country under false representations, and had suffered great hardships on shipboard for want of water and provisions and other necessaries, and of proper accommodation on their passage, proceeded to make general regulations for the carriage of passengers to foreign parts. All former statutes were repealed by the 4 Geo. IV. c. 84, which was an act "for regulating the carriage of passengers from the United Kingdom to foreign parts," and that in its turn was repealed by an act two years later, and another act "for regulating vessels carrying passengers to foreign parts"[3] was substituted

[1] During 1834, no fewer than seventeen ships, with passengers on board bound for Quebec, were wrecked on the passage, — seven hundred and thirty-one emigrants losing their lives in consequence, while many more lost part of their property and were reduced to the greatest distress. Emigrants to Quebec are mostly taken out in ships engaged in the timber trade, and it is well known that, speaking generally, these are a very inferior class, it being the usual practice to turn worn-out ships, unfit to carry dry cargoes, into this department Most part of the catastrophes alluded to may, we are assured, be ascribed to this circumstance, and to the misconduct of the master and crews. M'Culloch's Dic. of Com. Sup. tit. "Emigrants;" Abbott on Ship.

[2] 43 Geo. III. c 56 See also 53 Geo. III. c. 36; 56 Geo. III. c. 83; 56 Geo. III. c. 114; 57 Geo. III. c. 10.

[3] 6 Geo. IV. c. 116.

for it. Since that time various acts have been passed and superseded;[1] but the 18 & 19 Vict. c. 119 (the Passengers' Act, 1855), together with some of the provisions of 16 & 17 Vict. c. 84, relative to the passage of natives of Asia or Africa, and passages between the Island of Ceylon and certain parts of the East Indies, and as amended by the 26 & 27 Vict. c. 51, may be regarded as the law upon this subject.

This act came into operation on the 1st of October, 1855, and it applies to every passenger ship proceeding on any voyage from the United Kingdom to any place out of Europe, and not within the Mediterranean Sea, and on every colonial voyage such as it describes,[2] and it is to be carried into effect by the Colonial Lands Emigration Commissioners.[3] By the third section, the expression "passenger" is to signify all passengers except cabin-passengers, and except laborers under indenture to the Hudson's Bay Company and their families, conveyed in ships the property of and chartered by the said company, and no persons shall be deemed cabin-passengers unless the space allotted to their exclusive use shall be in the proportion of at least thirty-six clear superficial feet to each statute adult, nor unless they shall be messed together throughout the voyage at the same table with the master or first officer of the ship, nor unless the fare contracted to be paid by them respectively shall be in the proportion of at least 30*s.* for every week of the length of the voyage, as computed under the provisions of the act for sailing vessels proceeding from the United Kingdom to any place south of the equator, and of 20*s.* for each vessel proceeding to any place north of the equator, nor unless they shall be furnished with a duly signed contract ticket in a prescribed form.

SEC. 557. **Statutory Provisions.** — The act contains numerous provisions, by tonnage check and space check, for determining the number of passengers to be carried by any ship,[4]

[1] 9 Geo IV. c. 21; 5 & 6 Will. IV. c. 56; 5 & 6 Vict. c. 107; 8 & 9 Vict. c. 14; 10 & 11 Vict. c. 103; 11 & 12 Vict. c. 6; 12 & 13 Vict. c. 33; 14 Vict. c. 1; 15 & 16 Vict. c. 44.

[2] 18 & 19 Vict. c. 119, § 4.

[3] *Ibid.* § 6. See Steel *v.* Schomberg, 4 E. & B. 623; 24 L. J. Q. B. 87.

[4] 18 & 19 Vict. c. 119, § 14.

for the signature of passengers' lists,[1] for the examination or survey of all such ships before clearing-out,[2] for the construction of the beams and decks,[3] the arrangement and size and occupancy of the berths,[4] for the construction of privies,[5] for the securing of light,[6] ventilation,[7] boats,[8] life-buoys,[9] anchors,[9] fire-engines,[9] for efficient crew,[10] for sufficient ballast,[10] for the supply of water,[11] and good provisions,[12] for a sufficient dietary,[13] for the provision of cooks,[14] medical men,[15] stewards,[16] medicine and medical appliances.[17] Besides these, there are further provisions which relate to the sickness of passengers and the purifying of the vessel,[18] to the return of passage-money to passengers re-landed on account of sickness,[19] for the compensation of passengers where passages are not provided for them according to contract,[20] to the putting back of ships for provisions,[21] to the transshipment of passengers in case of wreck or damage,[22] to the remuneration of the owners of ships which shall pick up or take off from a wreck passengers at sea,[23] to penalties for the breach of any of these duties, or for the wrongful landing of passengers.[24]

SEC. 558. **Rules and Regulations prescribed by Order in Council.** — The 59th section of the act provides that "it shall be lawful for Her Majesty, by an order in council, to prescribe such rules and regulations as to Her Majesty may seem fit, for the following purposes (that is to say): —

"1st. For preserving order, promoting health, and securing cleanliness and ventilation on board of 'passenger ships,' proceeding from the United Kingdom to any port or place in Her Majesty's possessions abroad.

[1] 18 & 19 Vict. c. 119, § 16.
[2] *Ibid.* § 19.
[3] *Ibid.* § 20.
[4] *Ibid.* § 21 *et seq.*
[5] *Ibid.* § 25.
[6] *Ibid.* § 26.
[7] See also Dobson *v.* Hudson, 1 C. B. N. S. 652; 26 L. J. C. P. 153.
[8] 18 & 19 Vict. c. 119, § 27.
[9] *Ibid.* § 27.
[10] *Ibid.* § 29.
[11] *Ibid.* §§ 31, 33, 34.
[12] *Ibid.* § 32.
[13] *Ibid.* § 35.
[14] *Ibid.* § 29.
[15] *Ibid.* §§ 41, 42.
[16] *Ibid.* § 38.
[17] *Ibid.* § 43.
[18] *Ibid.* § 45.
[19] *Ibid.* § 46.
[20] *Ibid.* § 48.
[21] *Ibid.* § 50.
[22] *Ibid.* § 51.
[23] *Ibid.* § 52.
[24] *Ibid.* § 56, &c.

"2d. For permitting the use on board of 'passenger ships' of an apparatus for distilling water, and for defining, in such case, the quantity of fresh water to be carried in tanks and casks for the passengers.

"3d. For prohibiting emigration from any port or ports at any time when choleraic or any epidemic disease may be generally prevalent in the United Kingdom or any part thereof, or for reducing the number of passengers allowed to be carried in passenger ships generally, or from any particular port under the provisions of this act.

"4th. For requiring duly qualified medical practitioners to be carried in passenger ships in cases where they would not be required under the provisions of this act."

SEC. 559. **Licensing Passage Brokers, making By-laws, &c. — Definition of "Passenger Ship."** — There are other provisions for the licensing of passage brokers, for the making of by-laws by the trustees of docks, regulating the landing and embarkation of intending emigrants, and for licensing emigrant porters, for the approval of such by-laws by the Secretary of State, and others which it is unnecessary that we should allude to in this place.

This act was, as we said above, amended by the "Passengers' Act Amendment Act, 1863,"[1] in several particulars. Amongst these, the definition of a "passenger ship" given in the 3d section of the act, just alluded to, was repealed; and it was enacted that the term "passenger ship" should signify every description of sea-going vessel, whether British or foreign, carrying, upon any voyage to which the provisions of the said "Passengers' Act, 1855," shall extend, more than fifty passengers, or a greater number of passengers than in proportion of one statute adult to every thirty-three tons of the registered tonnage of such ships, if propelled by sails, or than one statute adult to every twenty tons, if propelled by steam.[2] This act

[1] 26 & 27 Vict. c. 51.

[2] It is evident, then, that the term "passengers" includes all passengers except cabin passengers, as defined by 18 & 19 Vict. c. 119, § 3. With regard to such, it has been held that persons who are in every respect cabin passengers within the meaning of the

also repeals the prohibition contained in the "Passengers' Act, 1855," against carrying horses and cattle, or cargo in "passenger ships," under certain conditions;[1] the provisions respecting passengers landed on account of sickness are extended to cabin passengers,[2] those which relate to providing a passage and maintenance, for the passenger, in case of wreck or damage to the passenger ship, before or after the commencement of the voyage, or when taken, or brought back on account of such damage, to a port of the United Kingdom;[3] and those which provide for the forwarding to his destination of any passenger, or cabin passenger, from any colonial or foreign port or place, other than that in which he had contracted to land,[4] are also amended by this act.

SEC. 560. **Expense of forwarding Passengers, &c.** — There are other provisions contained in the Passengers' Act Amendment Act, 1863, with regard to the expenses incurred in forwarding passengers under the sections alluded to being debts to the Crown, and as to such passengers not being entitled to the return of their passage-money; but for a more thorough and accurate knowledge of those provisions, the reader must be referred to the statutes themselves.

SEC. 561. **The Merchant Shipping Act, 1854.** — Besides these acts, the Merchant Shipping Act, 1854,[5] contains provisions as to the build, equipment, inspection, survey and certificates of passenger steamships (that is, all British ships carrying passengers between any place or places in the United Kingdom, except steam ferry-boats or "bridges" working in chains), — the number of passengers they are entitled to carry, their engines, boats, life-boats, life-buoys, and provisions to prevent the danger of collision, and the like.[6]

SEC. 562. **Penalties. — Payment of Fare. — Refusal to re-**

third section, except that they have not been furnished with contract tickets, according to the form (K) of that Act of 1855, are not to be counted as passengers, so as to make a ship a passenger ship, which would not otherwise be a passenger ship within the meaning of the act. Ellis *v.* Pearce, E. B. & E. 431; 27 L. J. M. C. 257.

[1] 26 & 27 Vict. c. 51, § 8.

[2] *Ibid.* § 11.

[3] *Ibid.* § 14.

[4] *Ibid.* § 15.

[5] 17 & 18 Vict. c. 104.

[6] *Ibid.* §§ 291–329.

ceive Passenger. — One or two of the provisions of the last-mentioned act may be quoted. The 322d section enacts that "the following offenders, that is to say: —

"(1.) Any person who, after having been refused admission into any steamer by the owner or person in charge thereof, or any person in the employ of the owner thereof, on account of such steamer being full, and after having had the full amount of his fare (if he paid the same) returned or tendered to him, nevertheless persists in attempting to enter the same; and

"(2.) Any person, having got on board any steamer, who upon being requested, on the like account, by the owner or person in charge thereof, or by any person in the employ of the owner, to leave such steamer before the same has quitted the place at which such person got on board, and upon having the full amount of his fare (if he has paid the same) returned or tendered to him, refuses to comply with such request,

shall for each such offence incur a penalty not exceeding forty shillings, to be paid to the said owner." The 323d section enacts that the following offenders, that is to say: —

"(1.) Any person who travels, or attempts to travel, in any passenger steamer which has been duly surveyed in conformity with the provisions of this act, without having previously paid his fare, and with the intent to avoid payment thereof; and

"(2.) Any person who, having paid his fare for a certain distance, knowingly and wilfully proceeds in any such steamer beyond such distance, without previously paying the additional fare for the additional distance, and with the intent to avoid payment thereof; and

"(3.) Any person who knowingly and wilfully refuses or neglects, on arriving at the point to which he has paid his fare, to quit any such steamer,

shall for every such offence incur a penalty not exceeding five shillings, in addition to the fares payable by him, such penalty being payable to the owner of such steamer."

The 324th section enacts that "the master of any home

trade passenger steamship may refuse to receive on board thereof any person who by reason of drunkenness, or otherwise, is in such a state, or misconducts himself in such a manner, as to cause annoyance to other passengers on board, or, if such person is on board, may put him on shore at any convenient place; and no person so refused admittance, or put on shore, shall be entitled to the return of any fare he may have paid."[1] A master is not bound to receive or carry in any ship goods of a dangerous nature, or parcels which he suspects to contain goods of a dangerous nature, and may cause such parcels to be opened to ascertain the fact, and any person who carries or sends by any ship any such goods without distinctly marking their nature outside the package, or giving notice to the master or owner, is liable to a penalty of 100*l.*[2]

SEC. 563. **Report of Accident to the Board of Trade.** — Three other sections are of importance to us here. The first of these provides that the owner or master of any steamship which has sustained or caused any accident occasioning loss of life or serious personal injury, or has been damaged in such a way as to affect her seaworthiness, must, within twenty-four hours after the accident, or as soon thereafter as possible, report in writing to the Board of Trade, under a penalty of 50*l.*[3]

SEC. 564. **Report in Case of Supposed Loss.** — The second of these enacts that the owner of a steamship which from its non-appearance he has reason to believe is lost, must within a reasonable time send notice of the fact to the Board of Trade, under a like penalty.[4]

SEC. 565. **Entry of Circumstances of Collision in Log-book.** — The third provides that in case of any collision, in which it is practicable to do so, the master is required to enter, immediately after the occurrence, a statement thereof and its circumstances in the official log-book (if any), to be signed by himself and the mate, or one of the crew, under a penalty of 20*l.*[5]

[1] See also 25 & 26 Vict. c. 63, § 35. See also Jenks *v.* Coleman, 2 Sumn. 221; Pearson *v.* Duane, 4 Wall. 605.

[2] 17 & 18 Vict. c. 104, § 329.

[3] *Ibid.* § 326.

[4] *Ibid.* § 327.

[5] *Ibid.* § 328. Besides these acts, the 18 & 19 Vict. c. 104, regulates

SEC. 566. **Contracts for the Conveyance of Passengers.** — In speaking of contracts for carriage, and the implications which were incident to them, we had occasion to point out that the whole of the contract was scarcely ever fully expressed, and that much which obviously and necessarily followed from what was said, was to be held in certain cases as forming a part of the transaction, and consequently modifying the contract as expressed. Under some circumstances the existence of a usage will have the effect of introducing terms into a contract which were not expressly stipulated for.[1] At the same time it is to be understood that an express exclusion of the usage, or its exclusion by express stipulations incompatible with it, is competent to the person who contracts. It is of importance to consider some of the cases in which the incidents of a contract between a passenger and the owner or master of a ship have been brought before courts of law, and to understand the influence of an existing usage upon a contract which may be made under such circumstances.

SEC. 567. **Accommodation and Provisions.** — In the case of Corbin *v.* Leader,[2] the defendant, the master of an East Indiaman about to sail from Calcutta on a voyage to London, by an agreement under seal, granted and let to the plaintiff the whole of the cabins and accommodations fitted up for the reception, convenience, and conveyance of passengers on board the ship; and the defendant covenanted to promote, as far as in him lay, the comfort and convenience of the plaintiff, and such persons as he should engage and contract with, and who should be received as passengers in and on board the said ship, in consideration whereof the plaintiff covenanted with the defendant, among other things, to pay the defendant the sum therein agreed on, and that he would in every respect

ships employed in the conveyance of Chinese emigrants in the Chinese seas; and 24 & 25 Vict. c. 52, empowers the governors of the Australian colonies to regulate the number of passengers to be carried in vessels plying between the Australian ports. The American acts relating to the carriage of passengers in steamboats in the United States will be found in Angell on Carriers, Appendix, pp. 309–348.

[1] See judgment of PARKE, B., in Hutton *v.* Warren, 1 M. & W. 474.

[2] 6 C. & P. 32; 10 Bing. 275.

support and uphold the authority and command of the defendant, and in no way interfere with the management or navigation of the ship, or with the affairs thereof. The plaintiff further covenanted that if, in the progress of the voyage, it should be necessary for the convenience, and at the request, of the plaintiff, to touch at St. Helena, he would bear and pay all port and other necessary charges, which might be incurred thereby. The court held that this stipulation, as to the payment of the charges of touching at an intermediate port, thus interwoven with the covenant of the defendant, clearly showed that stopping in the course of the voyage was a thing contemplated by the parties as conducive to the convenience of the passengers, and that the defendant was bound so to stop at the request of the plaintiff, unless it would have interfered with the safety of the vessel.

SEC. 568. **Deficiency of Water.** — In the same case it was held that a covenant to keep up a supply of the necessary and usual quantity of water for the use of the passengers is not broken by a deficiency for a short time, occasioned by the unusual length of the voyage. In an action against a captain of a ship for not furnishing good and fresh provisions to a passenger on a voyage, LORD DENMAN, in summing up, said: "I think the result of the evidence is, that the captain did not supply so large a quantity of good and fresh provisions as is usual under such circumstances. But there is no real ground of complaint, no right of action, unless the plaintiff has really been a sufferer; for it is not because a man does not get so good a dinner as he might have had, that he is therefore to have a right of action against the captain who does not provide all that he ought; you must be satisfied that there was a real grievance sustained by the plaintiff."[1]

SEC. 569. **Time of Sailing.** — Two cases bear upon the question as to what will be regarded as a breach of the contract entered into between the passenger and the ship-owner, in case of a delay arising in the sailing of the ship. In the first of these, the case of Yates *v.* Duff,[2] the plaintiff, the master

[1] Young *v.* Fewson, 8 C. & P. 55. Thompson, 3 M. & W. 456; Sansom
[2] 5 C. & P. 369. See also Ellis *v.* *v.* Rhodes, 8 Scott, 544.

of a vessel, sought to recover damages from the defendant for the breach of a verbal agreement, by which the defendant had engaged two cabins on a voyage from England to Madras, and agreed to pay a certain sum for them. He had refused to go because the vessel, which was advertised to leave the docks on a certain day, did not do so. At the trial it was proved to be the rule of the East Indian trade that, when a passenger refused to go in consequence of a delay in the sailing of a vessel, he was to forfeit half the amount of the passage-money agreed for. The ship, it appeared, did not leave the docks until the 21st of October. CHIEF JUSTICE TINDAL directed the jury to find for the plaintiff, with half the passage-money as damages, if they thought that the time of sailing was matter of representation, but not an essential part of the contract, and that, under the circumstances, the ship had sailed within reasonable time.

SEC. 570. **What amounts to Warranty.** — The other case is that of Cranston *v.* Marshall.[1] In that case the plaintiff, who was resident in Ireland, having applied to certain emigration agents in London, respecting a passage for himself and family on board their ships to Australia, received in answer a letter in which they agreed to convey him and his family for a certain sum of money. This letter was written on the fly-sheet of a circular, headed "Emigration to Australia," and which stated that ships "will be despatched on the appointed days (wind and weather permitting), for which written guarantees will be given." Then followed a list of ships, amongst which the "Asiatic" was named as to sail from London on the 15th of August, and from Plymouth on the 25th. In another part of the circular it was stated: "Passengers from Ireland can readily join at Plymouth. A deposit of one half the passage-money to be paid at the time the berths are engaged, the balance to be paid prior to granting the embarkation order." The plaintiff engaged a berth on board the "Asiatic," and paid the agents a deposit; but no written guarantee was given. The "Asiatic" did not arrive at Plymouth until the 3d of

[1] 5 Exch. 395; 19 L. J. Exch. 340. (U. S. C. C.) 524, affirming s. c. 10 See also Cobb *v.* Howard, 3 Blatchf. N. Y. Leg. Obs. 353.

September, although not prevented by wind or weather. The berth was kept vacant from London to Plymouth. The court held that the statement in the circular was not a mere representation, but a warranty, that the "Asiatic" would sail on the days appointed, and that, as she did not, the plaintiff was justified in taking a passage on board another vessel, and was entitled to recover from the emigration agents the amount of the deposit, and the expenses he had been put to by the delay at Plymouth.

SEC. 571. **Conveyance.** — In the case of Coppen *v.* Braithwaite,[1] the declaration, which was on an agreement to carry the plaintiff in a ship to a particular place, and alleged, as a breach, that the defendants by their agent caused him to be disembarked at an intermediate point, and by their agent caused the disembarkation to be conducted in a scandalous and disgraceful manner, whereby, and also by contemptuous usage and insulting language addressed to the plaintiff by the agent in effecting the disembarkation, the plaintiff sustained damage, was held good. In that case the judge had received evidence of the language of the captain in putting the plaintiff on shore, in which he described him as being a pickpocket, and belonging to the swell mob; and on the motion for a rule, that evidence was held to have been rightly received. And it was further held that the direction of the judge, that the defendants were responsible for any injury naturally resulting from the acts of the captain, when acting as their servant, and that the plaintiff was entitled to fair compensation for the injury done to him in being put on shore at the intermediate place, so far as injury arose from the act of the captain in putting him on shore, was correct. And in the case of Corbin *v.* Leader,[2] the particulars of which are stated above, it was held that the captain was bound to put into port for the convenience, and at the request and expense, of the plaintiff,

[1] 8 Jur. 875. See also Flint *v.* Norwich, &c. Transp. Co., 6 Blatchf. 158; 34 Conn. 554. But see Abbott *v.* Bradstreet, 55 Me. 530.

[2] 10 Bing. 275; M. & Scott, 751; 6 C. & P. 32. See also Denison *v.* Wataga, 1 Phil. xi, 7; Sunday *v.* Gordon, Blatchf. & How. 569; Howland *v.* The Lavinia, 1 Pet. Adm. 123.

unless he could show that putting in would be dangerous. That circumstance will of course modify many express contracts, whether in respect of provisions, time, or conveyance.

SEC. 572. **Duty of Captain to secure Safety of Passengers.** — It is the duty of the captain to fulfil his contract in all these particulars, but there is a more imperative duty, and that is the care of the safety of the lives of those on board. The performance of the latter duty will in many cases excuse and justify a breach in the former. Were it not so, the captain would be tempted to run all sorts of risks, which his experience told him it would be well to avoid, in order to free himself from the legal consequences which might follow the smallest deviation from the terms of the contract. Such risks would result in catastrophe, and these would bring about a change in the laws. Laws have a way of making themselves. If you made murder legal, your Act of Parliament would be nonsense. There is a law in the human heart which legalizes our legislation, and which in time repeals all useless statutes. It is with the view of securing the safety of all that the person to whose care and skill the lives of those on board the ship are intrusted is endowed in the time of need with such absolute authority.[1] And the convenience of other passengers will, in many cases, warrant a breach of a contract which has been made with one; thus, conduct unbecoming a gentleman in the strict sense of the word will justify a captain of a ship excluding a passenger from the cuddy table, although he has engaged by contract to provide for him there. But "it is difficult to say," according to TINDAL, C. J., "in what degree want of polish would in point of law warrant a captain in excluding a passenger from the cuddy;" but he went on to remark that "a man who had threatened the commanding officer of the ship with personal violence would not be a fit person to remain at the table at which he presided." [2]

[1] King *v.* Franklin, 1 F. & F. 360; Aldworth *v.* Stewart, 14 L. T. N. S 862; 4 F. & F. 957; Boyce *v.* Bayliffe, 1 Camp. 57; Newman *v.* Walters, 3 B. & P. 612.

[2] Prendergast *v.* Compton, 8 C. & P. 454.

SEC. 573. **Passage-money, Recovery of.** — But there are still other incidents of the contract entered into by a passenger with a ship-owner. One of these has to do with the passage-money, and one or two cases will indicate the principal rules of law upon this subject. The case of Gellan *v.* Simpkin[1] was an action for money had and received, to recover passage-money paid to the defendant as master of a ship in which he had agreed to carry the plaintiff as a passenger to Antigua. The plaintiff, who had paid the money before the commencement of the voyage, had intended to have gone on board at Portsmouth, but the luggage was shipped in the river Thames, and in proceeding round from thence to Portsmouth, the ship was lost. It appeared in evidence that it is usual for the passage-money to be paid in London, and that the stores for the use of passengers were always put on board in the river. CHIEF JUSTICE GIBBS, in his direction to the jury, said: "If the money had been to be paid at the end of the voyage, the defendant could not have recovered any part of it, there being an entire contract to carry the plaintiff from London to Antigua. But if the voyage was commenced, and the ship was prevented from completing it by perils of navigation, the captain may be entitled to retain the passage-money previously paid to him. The contract for this purpose may either be express, or may be evidenced by established usage. Here it is proved that in West India voyages the passage-money is paid before the voyage commences, and it does not appear to be returned, although the voyage is defeated. On the other hand, if the ship were lost before the commencement of the voyage for which these parties had contracted, the money paid by anticipation must be returned."[2]

SEC. 574. **Obligation to repay.** — Where the executors of an East India captain, who had died in the East Indies before the commencement of the homeward voyage, brought an action against the chief mate of his ship, on whom the command had devolved, to recover the amount of the sum he had received from the passengers brought home in the ship, for their

[1] 4 Camp. 241.

[2] See also Leeman *v.* Gordon, 8 C. & P. 392; Denison *v.* Wataga, 1 Phil. xi, 7.

passage and entertainment during the voyage, it was contended for the plaintiff that the passage-money must belong to the representatives of the captain; for the defendant, that he was entitled to the whole because he had the actual command during the voyage. "If," said BAYLEY, J., "there be no usage on the subject, I think the law is, that where the captain has contracted to carry passengers, and dies, his representatives are entitled to the benefit of the contract, and may maintain an action for the passage-money. If the mate lays out money in purchasing stores for such passengers, he is the agent of the representatives for that purpose, and may oblige them to repay him. But where, after the death of the captain, the mate contracts to carry passengers on the homeward voyage, he is himself entitled to the benefit of the contract, and may retain the whole of the passage-money. If for the entertainment of such passengers he has any part of the stores laid in by the captain, for so much he must account to the captain's representatives."[1] So, where the plaintiff contracted to carry the defendant, his family, and luggage from Demerara to Flushing, and in the course of the voyage, within four days' sail of Flushing, the ship was captured by an English ship of war and brought to England, and the ship and cargo libelled for prize in the Court of Admiralty, and the cargo condemned, and proceedings still pending against the ship; but the defendant and his family were liberated, and their luggage in fact restored to their possession: it was held by the court, that, however the question might be as to the plaintiff's right to recover passage-money upon an implied assumpsit *pro ratâ itineris*, if the ship was restored, yet pending the proceedings against the ship, as prize in the Admiralty Court, no such action could be maintained, for *non constat* but that the ship might be condemned and the freight decreed to the captors.[2] Again, in an action to recover passage-money brought by a mortgagee of a ship against a mortgagor, which passage-money had been recovered by the mortgagor as part of the earnings of the ship, before the ship

[1] Siordet v. Brodie, 8 Camp. 253.

[2] Muloy v. Backer, 5 East, 316; 1 Smith, 447.

was taken possession of by the mortgagee, it was decided that the mortgagee could not recover.[1]

SEC. 575. **Insurance by the Owners.** — In another case, in which a policy of insurance was effected upon the passage-money of emigrants upon a voyage from Liverpool to Boston against the perils of the sea, at the end of the policy there was the following memorandum: "on passage-money of emigrants, subject to pay a loss *pro ratâ*, and subject to the clauses and conditions under sections 47 to 51 of the 15 & 16 Vict. c. 44, and against these risks only." Held, that the policy extended to any expense occasioned by the perils insured against, which were thrown upon the ship-owners by any of the enumerated sections; but not to the expense of maintaining the passengers during the detention of the ship at a foreign port for the purpose of repairs, the ship afterwards completing the voyage with the passengers on board, such expense being cast on the owners by section 32.[2] In the case of Gibson *v.* Bradford,[3] which was referred to in the last-mentioned case, it was held that a policy of insurance by the owners against all liabilities to which they might become by perils of the sea liable under sections 49 and 50 of the 15 & 16 Vict. c. 44, covered a liability for expenses incurred by the captain in forwarding, without the intervention of the governor, and before the lapse of six weeks, passengers who were in a colony to which they were not ultimately destined, in consequence of the loss of the ship in which they sailed.

SEC. 576. **Lien on Passenger's Luggage.** — Before quitting this question of passage-money, it may be expedient to state that the law with regard to lien on the passenger's luggage for his passage-money is the same in relation to carriers by water as it is in relation to carriers by land. The master has consequently no lien on the passenger himself, or upon the clothes which he is actually wearing when about to leave the vessel.[4] And it may not be supererogatory to state that in a

[1] Willis *v.* Palmer, 7 C. B. N. S. 340; 6 Jur. N. S. 732; 29 L. J. C. P. 194; 8 W. R. 295.

[2] Willis *v.* Cooke, 5 El. & Bl. 641; 1 Jur. N. S. 1164; 25 L. J. Q. B. 16.

[3] 4 El. & Bl. 586; 1 Jur. N. S. 520; 24 L. J. Q. B. 159.

[4] Wolf *v.* Summers, 2 Camp. 631.

case in which a passenger in a steamer from America paid for and received a passenger-ticket from the agents of the owners, containing a condition exempting the owners from liability in case of loss or detention of the ship by accidents of navigation, or perils of the sea, and from responsibility for luggage, goods, or other description of property, unless bills of lading had been signed therefor, it was held that, the latter condition not having been observed by the passenger, he could not recover for the loss of his luggage, though the loss was caused by the ship having been wrecked, owing to the negligence of the captain.[1]

SEC. 577. **Collisions.** — The many questions which arise in connection with collisions between vessels, and the relation of these questions to that of negligence, would open up a wide field of legal speculation and research. The decisions, some of which are noted below,[2] have been very many upon this

[1] Wilton *v.* Royal Atlantic Mail Steam Navigation Co., 10 C. B. N. S. 453; 8 Jur. N. S. 232; 30 L. J. C. P. 369; 9 W. R. 748.

[2] Buller *v.* Fisher, 1 Esp. 67; Smith *v.* Scott, 4 Taunt. 125; Sells *v.* Brown, 9 C. & P. 601; Raisin *v.* Mitchell, 9 C. & P. 613. See Abbott on Ship., 11th ed., pt. iv. ch. 6, p. 341 *et seq.*; Hay *v.* Le Neve, 2 Shaw's Scotch Appeal Cases, 395; Kent *v.* Elstob, 3 East, 18; Dowell *v.* Gen. Steam Nav. Co., 5 E. & B. 195; Gen. Steam Nav. Co. *v.* Mann, 14 C. B. 127; Vanderplank *v.* Miller, 1 M. & M. 21; Lack *v.* Seward, 4 C. & P. 106; Vennal *v.* Garner, 1 Cro. & Mee. 21; Cattlin *v.* Hills, 8 C.B. 123; Thorogood *v.* Bryan, 8 C. B. 115: Rigby *v.* Hewitt, 5 Ex. 240; The China, 7 Wall. (U. S.) 53; Camp *v.* The Marcellus, 1 Cliff. (U. S. C. C.) 481; The Alabama *v.* The Gamecock, 1 Ben. (U. S. D. C.) 471; The Siren, 7 Wall. (U. S.) 152; The Grace Girdler, 7 Wall. (U. S.) 196; The Nichols, 7 Wall. (U. S.) 656; The Bella, 1 Ben. (U. S. D. C.) 317; Baker *v.* Steamship City of New York, 1 Cliff. (U. S. C. C.) 75; The Illinois, 5 Blatchf. (U. S. C. C.) 256; The Scranton and Wm. F. Burden, 5 Blatchf. (U. S. C. C.) 400; The Island City, 5 Blatchf. (U. S. C. C.) 264; The Parkersburgh, 5 Blatchf. (U. S. C. C.) 247; Wakefield *v.* The Governor, 1 Cliff. (U. S. C. C.) 93; The Wings of the Morning, 5 Blatchf. (U. S. C. C.) 15; The Bedford, 5 Blatchf. (U. S. C. C.) 200; The Scotia, 5 Blatchf. (U. S. C. C.) 227; The Nellie, 5 Blatchf. (U. S. C. C.) 245; Pope *v.* The R. B. Forbes, 1 Cliff. (U. S. C. C.) 331; Amoskegg, &c. Co. *v.* The John Adams, 1 Cliff. (U. S. C. C.) 404; The Chesapeake, 5 Blatchf. (U. S. C. C.) 411; The Ocean Queen, 5 Blatchf. (U. S. C. C.) 493; Meegs *v.* The Northerner, 1 Wash. Terr. 91; Philadelphia, &c. R. R. Co., 25 Md. 521; The Favorita, 1 Ben. (U. S. D. C.) 23; The Empire State, 1 Ben. (U. S. D. C.) 57; The Brideport, 1 Ben. (U. S. D. C.) 65; Wright *v.* Norwich, &c. Transp. Co., 1 Ben.

question, and upon those which are connected with it; but as the principles which will be discovered to be the foundation of these are identical with those which have ruled the decisions in the case of land carriage, and as the subject is too extensive to be dealt with efficiently within the limits at our disposal, we must be content to do no more than mention it in this connection, and refer the reader to the works and cases whence he can derive fuller information as to matters of detail. The extent of the subject will be understood from the words of LORD STOWELL in the case of The Woodrop Sims,[1] with regard to the possibilities under which a collision may occur. "In the first place," he said, "it may happen without blame being imputed to either party; as where the loss is occasioned by a storm, or any other *vis major*. In that case the misfortune must be borne by the party on whom it happens to light, the other not being responsible to him in any degree.[2] Secondly, a misfortune of this kind may arise where both parties are to blame, or where there has been want of due diligence or of skill upon both sides; in such case the rule of law is that the loss must be apportioned between them as having been occasioned by the fault of both of them. Thirdly, it may happen by the misconduct of the suffering party only, and then the rule is that the sufferer must bear his own burden. Fourthly, it may have been the fault of the ship which ran the other down, and in this case the innocent party would be entitled to an entire compensation from the other." Other questions as to anchorage, the sufficiency of the mooring, the

(U. S. D. C.) 156; The Cayuga, 1 Ben. (U. S. D. C.) 171; The City of Paris, 1 Ben. (U. S. D. C.) 174; The Scranton, 2 Ben. (U. S. D. C.) 25; The Baltic, 2 Ben. (U. S. D. C.) 98; The Beaver, 2 Ben. (U. S. D. C.) 118; The Alhambra, 2 Ben. (U. S. D. C.) 158; The D. S. Gregory, 2 Ben. (U. S. D. C.) 166; The St. John, 2 Ben. (U. S. D. C.) 192; The Elizabeth English, 2 Ben. (U. S. D. C.) 365; The Louisiana, 2 Ben. (U. S. D. C.) 371; The Baltic, 2 Ben. (U. S. D. C.) 396; The Western Metropolis, 2 Ben. (U. S. D. C.) 399; The Emilie, 2 Ben. (U. S. D. C.) 419; The Thornton, 2 Ben. (U. S. D. C.) 429; The Baltic, 2 Ben. (U. S. D. C.) 452; The America, 2 Ben. (U. S. D. C.) 475; The Warren, 2 Ben. (U. S. D. C.) 498; The Queen, 2 Ben. (U. S. D. C.) 533; The Brooklyn, 2 Ben. (U. S. D. C.) 547.

[1] 2 Dods. 83.

[2] See Story on Bailm. § 608.

duty of ships in motion avoiding ships at rest, the necessity of placing a buoy over a ship sunk by inevitable accident in a navigable river, of removing wreck, of bearing a light when anchored in a navigable river, the rule of the road, and the like,[1] do not fall really within the scope of our subject, any more than the system of points and signals is in connection with the law applicable to railway travellers. Some writers upon the law of carriers have thought it necessary to enter upon this complicated branch of the law of shipping as administered in the Court of Admiralty and in the common-law courts; but to us it seems unnecessary, in speaking of the carriers of passengers by water, to do more than refer to the subject.[2]

1 See Holt's Rule of the Road.

2 See further, on the subject of passenger carriers, Maclachlan's Law of Shipping, ch. 7, p. 290.

CHAPTER XII.

ACTIONS AGAINST AND BY CARRIERS.

SEC. 578. **Logical Arrangement of the Subject.** — We are now in a position to consider the legal remedies which belong to carriers, or those who deal with them, and the processes by which the machinery of the law can be put in motion. The logical arrangements of our subject made it necessary that this portion of the law of carriers should be placed after the consideration of the rules of law which actually apply to cases of this nature, and which will actually be put in force by legal tribunals. The method of a text-book is to be to some extent determined by the actual sequence of events in the practice of a lawyer, and in all cases the lawyer has to come to some definite opinion as to the merits of the case, and the possibility or non-possibility of obtaining a legal remedy, before he is called upon to consider the form of the action, the pleadings in the case, or the evidence necessary to support it. Indeed, a case only comes into court when two lawyers have given different opinions concerning the law applicable to the facts, so that a judicial decision is an arbitration between these two diverse opinions.

SEC. 579. **Remedy for not Carrying. — Form of Action.** — We have already seen that it is the duty of a carrier to receive all goods that may be brought to him to be carried, if he can carry them, if reasonable compensation is offered, and if the nature of his trade has advertised him to the public as a carrier of that particular kind of goods; and that, if he refuses to perform this duty, he is liable to an action at law.[1] The form of action under these circumstances is case, and it is necessary to aver in the declaration that the plaintiff was *willing and ready* to pay the defendant the amount which the defendant was legally entitled to receive for the receipt of carriage of them, though it is not necessary that it should aver an absolute *tender*.

SEC. 580. **Absolute Tender not necessary.** — In Pickford *v.* Grand Junction Railway Company,[2] the declaration stated, "That whereas the defendants, before and at the time hereinafter mentioned, to wit, on the 24th of November, 1840, were

[1] See Parker *v.* Bristol & Exeter Rail. Co., 17 L. T. 202.

[2] 8 M. & W. 372; 9 D. P. C. 766; 6 Rail. Cas. 592; 5 Jur. 731. It appears that a carrier may be *indicted* for a breach of his common-law duty, on the same principle that an innkeeper may be indicted for refusing to receive a guest. Per PATTESON, J., Pozzi *v.* Shipton, 1 P. & D. 12; Rex *v.* Ivens, 7 C. & P. 213; 4 Bl. Com. 167.

common carriers of goods and chattels for hire, from Birmingham, in the county of Warwick, to Manchester, in the county of Lancaster, and from Manchester aforesaid to Birmingham aforesaid, and thereupon heretofore, to wit, on the 24th of November, 1840, the plaintiff caused to be tendered to the defendants, they being such common carriers as aforesaid, to wit, at a certain place in Birmingham aforesaid, being the place by them then used in the way of their said business, as common carriers for the receipt of parcels and goods to be by them carried and conveyed as such common carriers as aforesaid, a certain parcel of goods of the plaintiff's, to wit, a hamper containing divers goods then of great value, to wit, of the value of 100*l.*; and then requested the defendants to receive and to carry and convey the same from Birmingham aforesaid to Manchester aforesaid, and the defendants then had ample convenience for receiving and carrying and conveying the same according to the said requirements of the plaintiffs in that behalf, and the plaintiffs were then *ready and willing, and then offered to pay to the defendants such sum of money as the defendants were legally entitled to receive*, for the receipt and carriage and conveyance of the said parcel, and all other charges whatsoever which the defendants were then authorized, or in any wise entitled to make or receive for the receipt, carriage, and conveyance of the said parcel from Birmingham aforesaid to Manchester aforesaid, to wit, the sum of 2*l.*; and the defendants then had notice of the premises; yet the defendants, not regarding their duty as such common carriers as aforesaid, but contriving and wrongfully and unjustly intending to injure the plaintiffs, though they did receive as aforesaid and carry and convey the goods of divers other persons from Birmingham aforesaid to Manchester aforesaid, did not, nor would, at the said time when they were so requested or at any time afterwards, receive the said parcel, or carry or convey the same from Birmingham aforesaid to Manchester aforesaid, but wholly neglected and refused so to do, though they might, and could, and ought, as such carriers, to have received and carried and conveyed the same as aforesaid, whereby the plaintiffs were then forced and obliged to carry and convey the said parcel from Birmingham aforesaid to Manchester aforesaid with great labor, cost, and inconvenience, and were put to great expense, &c., in and about the carriage and conveyance of the said parcel, &c., and were and are otherwise greatly annoyed, injured, inconvenienced, and damaged." To this declaration there was a special demurrer, assigning for cause that the declaration *did not aver a tender* to the defendants of the money which they were entitled to receive for the carriage of the goods. In this case it was held that the averment was sufficient, and that it was not necessary to aver an actual tender of money for the carriage. BARON PARKE, who delivered the judgment, said: "The court think that this is not like the case of a strictly legal tender, a term which is only applicable where an absolute duty, such as the payment of an antecedent debt, is imposed on the party making it, in which case the tender stands in the place of payment, and is in fact payment, so far as it is in the power of the party tendering it to make one, but which remains incomplete, only because the party to whom the money is offered refuses to accept it. Such a tender we consider to be altogether unnecessary in the present case, the acts to be done by both parties, *viz.* the receipt of the goods, and the payment of a reasonable sum for their carriage, being contemporaneous acts, the carrier being bound to receive the goods on the money being paid or tendered, and the bailor to pay the reasonable amount demanded on the carrier's taking charge of the goods. The case of Rawson *v.* Johnson [1] clearly shows that, whenever a duty is cast on a party in consequence of a contemporaneous act of payment to be done by another, it is sufficient, if the latter pay or be ready to pay the money when the other is ready to undertake the duty. Here the acts to be done by the plaintiffs and defendants are altogether contemporaneous. The money is not required to be paid down by the plaintiffs until the carrier receives the goods which he is bound to carry. Our judgment, therefore, must be for the plaintiffs.[2]

[1] 1 East, 203.

[2] See also Ashmole *v.* Wainwright, 2 Q. B. 837.

SEC. 581. **Where Action will lie.** — Having stated this much, we think it well, before considering these forms of action and the incidents of each in connection with actions against carriers, to consider the preliminary question as to where actions lie. In this connection there are some statutory provisions which must be noted.

SEC. 582. **Statutory Provisions.** — By the 5th section of an act already more than once referred to (the 11 Geo. IV. and 1 Will. IV. c. 68) it is enacted that "any one or more of mail contractors, stage-coach proprietors, or common carriers shall be liable to be sued by his or her or their name or names only, and no action or suit commenced to recover damages for loss or injury of any parcel, package, or person, shall abate for the want of joining any co-proprietor or co-partner in such mail, stage-coach, or other public conveyance by land for hire."

The 7th section provides that, "where any parcel or package which has been delivered, and, the value being declared, the increased rate of charges paid, has been lost or damaged, the party entitled to recover damages in respect of such loss or damage shall also be entitled to recover back the increased charges so paid in addition to the value." By the 9th section it is provided that "carriers are not to be concluded by the declared value, but are only to be liable to such damages as are proved, not exceeding the declared value, together with the increased charges." And section 10 provides that "money may be paid into court in all actions for loss or injury."

SEC. 583. **Notice of Action to Railway Companies.** — We have seen that in certain cases railway companies are entitled under Act of Parliament to notice of action before it is brought, and, where that is the case, such notice is a necessary preliminary to any legal proceedings; it is therefore necessary to consider this subject before proceeding to the other questions to which it is proposed this chapter should supply some answer. Thus the Great Western Railway Company were by their act entitled to notice of action before any action should be brought against them for anything done or omitted to be done in pursuance of their act. An action was commenced against the company for money received by them to the plaintiff's use and on account stated. The company pleaded that no notice of action had been given, but failed to allege that the money was received or the accounts stated in pursuance of their act; consequently their plea was held to be bad, as the court could not presume, even after verdict, that the receipt of money, or the stating of accounts, was a thing done in pursuance of their act.[1] By 8 & 9 Vict. c. 20, § 138, any notice, writ, or other proceeding at law or in equity, may be served by being left at, or transmitted through, the post directed to the principal office of the company, or one of their principal offices, where there shall be more than one. It appeared that a notice of action against the company for an overcharge for the carriage of goods from Bristol to London was served by the plaintiff upon the superintendent of the Bristol Station; but this was held insufficient, inasmuch as the secretary was in London, and the control of the railway was carried on, and the ordinary meetings of the directors were held there.[2]

SEC. 584. **Rule of Construction.** — These cases indicate the application of the rules of construction which our courts of law will enforce in relation to these Acts of Parliament, and they throw light upon it in a different connection and in a new direction. These rules were, as we have seen, strictness of interpretation, and, in case of doubt, a construction favorable to the public and unfavorable to the company.[3] So, in a case against the Great Western Railway Company, which was an action brought to recover sums extorted by the company in excess of the charges which they were entitled to make by their act, it was held that, in virtue of the provision mentioned above, the company was entitled to notice of the action.[4]

Again, where a railway company was entitled by Act of Parliament to carry goods and passengers on the railway,

[1] Garton *v.* Great Western Rail. Co., El. Bl. & El. 837; 5 Jur. N. S. 1244; 28 L. J. Q. B. 321 Exch. Ch.

[2] Garton *v.* Great Western Rail. Co., 4 Jur. N. S. 1036; 27 L. J. Q. B. 375.

[3] See Smith *v.* Shaw, 10 B. & C. 284, per BAYLEY, J.; Graves *v.* Arnold, 3 Camp. 242; Smith *v.* Hopper, 9 Q. B. 1005.

[4] Kent *v.* Great Western Rail. Co., 3 C. B. 714; 16 L. J. C. P. 72.

and to keep in repair the fences of the same, and the same act contained a clause that no action should be brought against the company for anything done or omitted to be done, in pursuance of the act, unless fourteen days' previous notice of action was given of such intention, and where the company, having undertaken to carry some horses for the plaintiff, failed to do so in consequence of an accident to the train, caused by the fences by the railway having been broken down, in which the horses were being conveyed, and by which they were killed, it was held that the company, being sued in their capacity of carriers, was not entitled to notice of action.[1] The distinction between this case and those already quoted is fine, but easily appreciated.

SEC. 585. **Remedy in Case of Loss, Damage, or Non-delivery of Goods.** — Enough has been said of the action which lies on a breach of the carrier's duty to receive and carry; and the next subject which falls under our consideration is the duty which the common law imposes on a common carrier of insuring the safety of goods intrusted to him, and the action which will lie against him in case of their loss or damage.

SEC. 586. **The Form of Action in such a Case. — Arising ex Contractu or ex Delicto.** — In reference to this matter, some difficulty existed in the minds of pleaders as to the proper form of action in such a case. Considering the occupation of carriers as a public duty, the breach of it would be a *tort*, for which they were liable to an *action on the case* at common law. But, as we have seen, the doctrine of the existence of a contract in such a case came to be admitted, and carriers, therefore, became liable to an action of *assumpsit* on their undertaking. Thus it comes about that the case may be looked at either as arising *ex contractu* or *ex delicto*, according as the neglect of duty or breach of promise is to be relied upon as the cause of injury.[2]

[1] Palmer *v.* Great Junction Rail. Co., 4 M. & W. 749; 7 D. P. C. 232; s. P. Carpue *v.* London and Brighton Rail. Co., 5 Q. B. 747; 13 L. J. Q. B. 138.

[2] Coggs *v.* Barnard, 1 Sm. L. Ca. note, p. 177, per DENISON, J., in Dale *v.* Hall, 1 Wils. 282; per LORD KENYON, in Buddle *v.* Wilson, 6 T. R. 373. See also Tattan *v.* Great Western Railway, 2 El. & El. 844; Govett *v.* Radnidge, 3 East, 63; Ross *v.*

SEC. 587. **Rule in Brotherton v. Wood and other Cases.** — One or two of the decisions in the under-noted cases which bear upon the question of the form and nature of the action, may be referred to as proving the truth of the above assertion. In the case of Brotherton *v.* Wood,[1] it was decided that proof of contract is not necessary to support an action against common carriers; they may be sued in an action on the case for an injury as arising *ex delicto*, and such an action, it was held, is not necessarily to be considered *quasi ex contractu*, or founded on contract. In the case of Pozzi *v.* Shipton[2] the declaration stated that the plaintiff delivered to the defendants, and they accepted, a package to be taken care of and carried from L. to B., and there delivered to A., for reasonable reward, and thereupon it became their duty to take due care in the conveyance of the package. At the trial the jury found a verdict for one of the defendants and against the other. It was held that the declaration might be read as charging the defendants in tort on the general custom of the realm and not on contract, and the court was bound so to read it after verdict, and to support the finding, though against one only. In the more recent case of Tattan *v.* The Great Western Railway Company,[3] which was an action against the company as a common carrier, for the breach of his duty to carry safely goods delivered to him as such to be carried for hire, whereby the goods were lost, it was held that that was an action, not of contract but of tort, in substance as well as in form, the duty being imposed upon him by the custom of the realm, and being distinct from and independent of his obligation under the contract of carriage, in respect of which latter he may also be sued in an action of contract; and it was consequently held that a plaintiff in an action against a common carrier for the breach of the duty in question, brought in a superior court

Johnson, 5 Burr. 2825; Dickon *v.* Clifton, 2 Wils. 319; Powell *v.* Layton, 2 B. & P. 365; Brotherton *v.* Wood, 3 B. & B. 54; Pozzi *v.* Shipton, 8 A. & E. 963; 1 P. & D. 4; 1 W. W. & H. 624; Ansel *v.* Waterhouse, 2 Chitt. 1.

[1] 6 Moore, 141; 9 Price, 408; 3 B. & B. 54.

[2] 8 A. & E. 963; 1 W. W. & H. 624.

[3] 2 El. & El. 844; 6 Jur. N. S. 800; 29 L. J. Q. B. 184; 8 W. R. 606.

to recover the sum of *20l.*, is not deprived of his costs by 19 & 20 Vict. c. 108, § 30, if the defendant suffers judgment by default, for that the action is not one of contract within that section.[1]

SEC. 588. **Rule in Woodward v. Booth.** — In the case of Woodward *v.* Booth,[2] it was held that, in an action against a carrier for a loss of a trunk, the *terminus in quo* is immaterial, as the gist of the action is the non-delivery at the place it ought to have gone to.[3]

SEC. 589. **Advantages of each Mode of Declaring.** — In relation to this subject it may be well to note that each of these modes of declaring has advantages and inconveniences incident to it, and it is the duty of a skilful practitioner to adopt that mode in any individual case which may be best suited to the requirements of the circumstances. Thus, as a general rule, it is to be remembered that, where there is any doubt as to the defendants, it is advisable, if it be possible, to declare in tort rather than *ex contractu,* because the consequences of a misjoinder, or non-joinder, of parties are less serious in the former than in the latter. Thus, in the case of Brotherton *v.* Wood,[4] there were too many defendants. This case was in the Exchequer Chamber. At the trial, which was an action on the case against ten defendants, as proprietors of a coach, for injuries sustained by the plaintiff in consequence of negligent driving, the jury found a verdict against *eight* of the defendants, and in favor of the other two. DALLAS, C. J., who delivered the judgment of the court, said: "This action is on the case against a common carrier, upon whom a duty is imposed by the custom of the realm, in other words, by the common law, to carry and convey their goods and passengers

[1] See Legge *v.* Tucker, 1 H. & N. 500; 2 Jur. N. S. 1235; 26 L. J. Exch. 71.

[2] 7 B. & C. 301. See also Clark *v.* Richards, 1 Conn. 59; Orange Bank *v.* Brown, 3 Wend. (N. Y.) 158.

[3] Tucker *v.* Cracklin, 2 Stark. 385. See also Boson *v.* Sandford, 2 Show. 478; Dale *v.* Hall, 1 Wils. 281; Mitchell *v.* Tarbutt, 5 T. R. 649; Budle *v.* Wilson, 6 T. R. 369; Govett *v.* Radnidge, 3 East, 62; Hambly *v.* Trott, Cowp. 375; Powell *v.* Layton, 5 B. & P. 365; Max *v.* Roberts, 12 East, 89.

[4] 3 B. & B. 54; 6 Moore, 141; 9 Price, 408.

safely and securely, so that, by their negligence or default, no injury or damage happen. A breach of this duty is a breach of the law, and for this breach an action lies founded on the common law, which action wants not the aid of a contract to support it. It appears by the different books of entries (Brownlow Redivivus, 11; Clift. 38, 39; Mod. Ent. 145) that this form of action is a very ancient use. Nor is it material whether redress might or might not have been had in an action of *assumpsit.* That must depend on the circumstances, of which this court has no knowledge; but whether the action of *assumpsit* might or might not have been maintained, still *this action on the case* may be maintained. The action of *assumpsit*, as applied to cases of this kind, is of modern use. If the action be not founded on contract, but on a breach of duty depending on the common law, on a tort or misfeasance, it cannot be contended that the judgment is erroneous; for, from the nature of the case, and the form of the action, it is several and not joint, and may be maintained against *some only* of those against whom it is brought."[1]

SEC. 590. **Non-joinder of Partners.** — It has been decided that, if a carrier in partnership is sued singly in an action arising *ex delicto*, he cannot plead the non-joinder of others in abatement or in bar, or give it in evidence under the general issue; for a plea in abatement can only be adopted in those cases where regularly all the parties *must* be joined, and not where the plaintiff may join them or not at his election.[2] Therefore, to an action on the case against the defendants, part-owners of a ship, for the negligence of their servants in running down a ship laden with sugar belonging to the plaintiff, whereby the sugar was lost, the defendants, it was decided, could not plead in abatement that there were other part-owners not joined in the suit, because the action being *ex delicto* the trespass was several.[3] There is another advantage gained by declaring in tort, where the plaintiff has an option

[1] Allen *v.* Sewall, 2 Wend. (N. Y.) 338; Weed *v.* Schenectady R. R. Co., 19 Wend. (N. Y.) 534; Tell *v.* Arnold, 2 Penn. 292; Cook *v.* Chaplain Trans. Co., 1 Den. (N. Y.) 91.

[2] Child *v.* Sands, Carth. 294, quoted in Gow on Part. p. 201.

[3] Mitchell *v.* Tarbutt, 5 T. R. 649.

which form of action he will choose, and that is, that when that is done, it is not necessary to state the undertaking with as much form as is requisite in an action of *assumpsit*.[1]

SEC. 591. **Count in Trover may be joined in Action on Case. — Where this can be done.** — Another incident of the action on the case makes it, under many circumstances, more convenient than an action founded on contract, and that is, that where an action is brought against a common carrier for breach of duty, a count in trover may be joined with the other counts. "I own," said WILMOT, C. J., in the case of Dickon *v.* Clifton,[2] "that, in many books, it is reported that trover and a count against a common carrier cannot be joined, but common experience and practice is now to the contrary. The true test to try whether two counts can be joined in the same declaration is, to consider and see whether there is the same judgment in both, and not whether they both require the same plea; and wherever there is the same judgment in both, I think they may well be joined."[3] But it is to be borne in mind that a count in trover is to be maintained on only in the case of misfeasance, as it implies a conversion,[4] by the defendant, of the goods of the plaintiff. LORD MANSFIELD described this action as being in *form* a fiction, in *substance* a remedy to recover the value of personal chattels wrongfully converted by another to his own use.[5] Two things are necessary to be proved to entitle the plaintiff to recover in this kind of action, — 1st. Property in the plaintiff, and 2d. A wrongful conversion by the defendant.[6]

[1] Per PARKE, B., in Wyld *v.* Pickford, 8 M. & W. 443. See also Govett *v.* Radnidge, 3 East, 62; Morrow *v.* Belcher, 4 B. & C. 704.

[2] 2 Wils. 319.

[3] M'Cahan *v.* Hirst, 7 Watts (Penn.), 175; Dwight *v.* Brewster, 1 Pick. (Mass.) 50; Emery *v.* Fanning, 9 Barb. (N. Y.) 176; Packard *v.* Edman, 4 Wend. (N. Y.) 613; Moses *v.* Norris, 4 N. H. 304.

[4] See Burroughes *v.* Bayne, 5 H. & N. 296, 301; Chinnery *v.* Veale, 8 H. & N. 288; Giles *v.* Taff Vale Rail. Co., 2 E. & B. 822; Simmons *v.* Lillywhite, 8 Exch. 431; Glover *v.* London and North-Western Rail. Co., 5 Exch. 60; Powell *v.* Holyland, 6 Exch. 67; Mayhew *v.* Herrick, 7 C. B. 229. See also Buckland *v.* Johnson, 15 C. B. 145; Meyerstein *v.* Barber, L. R. 2 C. P. 38, 661; Towne *v.* Lewis, 7 C. B. 600.

[5] Cooper *v.* Chitty, 1 Burr. 31.

[6] See Jefferies *v.* Great Western Rail. Co., 5 E. & B. 802; Walker *v.* Clyde, 10 C. B. N. S. 381.

SEC. 592. **Conversion, what it is.** — "The very assuming," says LORD HOLT, "to one's self the right to dispose of another man's goods is a conversion."[1] So, where a carrier drew out a part of a vessel, and filled it up with water, it was held to be a conversion of all the liquor.[2] The delivery of the goods, either by the carrier or by his servant, to a wrong person, will support a count in trover, even although it be proved that the misdelivery occurred by mistake,[3] and even although the misdelivery has been brought about, not by the carelessness of the carrier, but by the deceit of the person receiving the goods.[4] In a recent case it was decided that a carrier must commit some fault or wrongful act with respect to the goods in order to render himself liable for an action for wrongful conversion; and where he strictly pursues the directions of the consignors, the mere fact of delivering the goods to a person who was not intended by the consignors to get possession of them does not amount to such conduct, on the carrier's part, as renders him responsible for misdelivery and conversion.[5] Where the facts are such as have been indicated by the above cases, it is clear that conversion has taken place, but a difficulty might arise as to whether the simple non-delivery of the goods would constitute such a conversion as would support a count in trover, or, indeed, whether it could be regarded as a conversion at all. A mere neglect to deliver would not then be a conversion; but if the goods have been demanded by the consignee or owner,

[1] Baldwin *v.* Cole, 6 Mod. 212. See M'Combie *v.* Davies, 6 East, 538; Cooper *v.* Willomatt, 1 C. B. 672. Of course simple failure to deliver goods will render the carrier liable, and is to be regarded as a conversion. See Jeffersonville R. R. Co. *v.* White, 6 Bush (Ky.), 251.

[2] Richardson *v.* Atkinson, 1 Stra. 576.

[3] Devereux *v.* Barclay, 3 B. & Ald. 702; Hawkins *v.* Hoffman, 6 Hill (N. Y.), 588; Clark *v.* Spruce, 10 Watts (Penn.), 335; Willard *v.* Bridge, 4 Barb. (N. Y.) 361; Scovill *v.* Griffith, 14 N. Y. 509; Caflin *v.* Boston R. R. Co., 7 Allen (Mass.), 341; Alden *v.* Pearson, 3 Gray (Mass.), 342; Bowlin *v.* Nye, 64 Mass. 419; Robinson *v.* Amos Austin, 68 Mass. 564; Hoffman *v.* Carow, 22 Wend. (N. Y.) 284; Schroeppell *v.* Corning, 5 Den. (N. Y.) 240; Koch *v.* Branch, 44 Mo. 542; Delaware Bank *v.* Smith, 1 Edm. (N. Y.) Sel. Cas. 351.

[4] Per PARKE, B., in Wyld *v.* Pickford, 8 M. & W. 443; Youl *v.* Harbottle, Peake, N. P. Cas. 49; Lubbock *v.* Inglis, 1 Stark. 104.

[5] Per MARTIN, B., in M'Kean *v.* M'Iver, 24 L. T. N. S. 559; 6 L. R. Exch. 36.

and the carrier still neglects or refuses to deliver them, these facts will be held ample evidence of conversion.[1] Still, although these circumstances are evidence of conversion, they are liable to be rebutted by evidence that the goods have passed out of the carrier's keeping by negligence, or have been stolen.[2] Therefore a count in trover would not be supported in such a case. On this subject LORD ELLENBOROUGH remarked, "that what begins in contract, a non-performance of what the party undertakes to do, or a bare non-delivery of what he undertook to deliver, is not to be considered as of itself amounting to a *tortious* conversion. The principle was recognized some time ago in the King's Bench, in an action against a carrier for not delivering goods. If the carrier says he has the goods in his warehouse, and refuses to deliver them, that will be evidence of conversion, and trover may be maintained, but not for a bare non-delivery without any such refusal." [3]

SEC. 593. **Assumpsit.** — The action of assumpsit is founded on a promise express or implied, or upon a contract or agreement not under seal.[4] We have seen that the very nature of a carrier's employment is the undertaking of a trust and duty, and consequently in the contemplation of law the implication of a promise upon his part to perform the various duties incident to the nature of the bailment with integrity, diligence, and skill. The reasons for this have already been considered. But if he should fail to perform the contract

[1] It has been decided in this country that a consignee of goods, who is ready to pay freight on having the goods delivered to him, may maintain trover against the carriers or their agents, who, having no legal claim on the goods for anything besides freight, refuse to deliver them unless a further sum be paid. The consignee, in such a case, is not bound to make any tender to those in possession of the goods, and their refusal to deliver the goods is evidence of conversion. Adams *v.* Clark, 7 Cush. (Mass.) 215; Bullard *v.* Young, 3 Stew. (Ala.) 46; Packard *v.* Getman, 6 Cow. (N.Y.) 747; Johnson *v.* Strader, 3 Mo. 359.

[2] Anon. 2 Salk. 655; Owen *v.* Lewyn, 1 Vent. 223.

[3] Anon. 4 Esp. 157; and see Attersol *v.* Bryant, 1 Camp. 409; and opinion of LORD KENYON in Youl *v.* Harbottle, Peake, N. P. Cas. 49; Bromley *v.* Coxwell, 2 B. & P. 438; Rose *v.* Johnson, 5 Burr. 2825.

[4] See, as to the nature of this action, Slade's Case, 4 Rep. 94. See also Chitt. Pl., 7th ed., vol. i. pp. 111, 122.

which he has by implication entered into, if in any of these three particulars of integrity, diligence, or skill, he should fall short of the requirements which the common sense, guided by the ordinary experience of mankind, makes necessary, the party who suffers loss of or injury to his goods by reason of such dishonesty or negligence may, in most cases, have his remedy for such breach of contract by action of assumpsit, as well as by action on the case. This doctrine is not peculiar to the law of carriers. Thus gross and culpable negligence upon the part of an attorney causing injury to the interests of his client exposes him to an action of assumpsit, or upon the case, at the instance of his client. For all the purposes of an action the implied contract is as good as an express promise, and in the declaration the promise is stated exactly as the law implies it.[1] At the same time the implication must be obvious, and any express promise different from that which is implied, which has a consideration to support it, may be stated in the declaration.

SEC. 594. **Advantages of adopting Action of Assumpsit.** — As we considered the various advantages to be derived from the adoption of the action on the case, it is expedient to state some of the countervailing advantages which attach to the action of assumpsit. By adopting it the plaintiff has the advantage of joining the common money counts, if he has other causes of action to which they are applicable. Again the action of assumpsit survives against the defendant's executor while the action on the case against a common carrier will not be against his executor or administrator, as it is in tort.[2] These advantages, however, have to be set against the disadvantages indirectly alluded to while speaking of the action on the case. Thus the plaintiff is bound to sue all the parties jointly liable, and must prove that all the defendants in the action are liable, and he is precluded from joining a count in trover, because counts upon promise and upon tort cannot be joined.[3] At the same time assumpsit is sometimes main-

[1] See Appendix.

[2] Chitt. Pl., 7th ed., p. 116; per LORD MANSFIELD in Hambly *v.* Trott, Cowp. 375.

[3] See Corbett *v.* Packington, 6 B. & C. 268; 1 Chitt. Pl., 7th ed., p. 156.

tainable where trover will not lie. This is the case if a carrier, instead of conveying the parcel according to his directions, transfers it to another carrier for that purpose, whereby the parcel is lost.[1]

SEC. 595. **Who may sue.** — Another matter in some sense preliminary to the action and preliminary to the pleadings remains for consideration, and that has reference to the parties to an action or the parties to sue and be sued. Of the former, first. It is evident that there are two parties interested in the safe custody of the goods by the carrier. The very fact that there exists in the consignor the right of stoppage *in transitu* for the unpaid price, proves that he has an interest in their safe custody; and as the goods are to be delivered to the consignee, who may be the vendee or who is at least in some way interested in them, there might seem to be a difficulty as to whether it was in the consignor or consignee to maintain the action in case of the loss or damage of the goods while they were in the custody of the carrier. The carrier must be liable to one party or the other; and if the wrong party were to recover against him, he would be liable to be harassed again.[2] Hence the importance of coming to some definite understanding as to the rights of each; for it has been held that where the property in goods has passed to a consignee it is no defence to an action by him against the carrier for the loss that the consignor has claimed, and that the carrier has *bonâ fide* paid him the amount of the loss.[3]

SEC. 596. **Vendee or Consignee generally Proper Person to sue.** — The introduction of the principle or doctrine that delivery of the goods to the carrier vests the ownership *primâ facie* in the consignee, makes the carrier presumptively the agent of the consignee,[4] and therefore, in an action against a

[1] Sleat *v.* Fagg, 5 B. & Ald. 349.

[2] Per WILLIAMS, J., in Coats *v.* Chaplain, 3 Q. B. 489.

[3] Coombs *v.* Bristol & Exeter Rail. Co., 3 H. & N. 1; 27 L. J. Exch. 269; W. & A. Railroad *v.* Kelly, 1 Head (Tenn.), 158.

[4] Dawes *v.* Peck, 8 L. R. 330; Dutton *v.* Solomonson, 3 B. & P. 582. See Smith's Mercantile Law, p. 291; Richardson *v.* Dunn, 2 Q. B. 224; Vale *v.* Bayle, Cowp. 294; Godfrey *v.* Furzo, 3 P. Wms. 186; Joseph *v.* Knox, 3 Camp. 320; Brown *v.* Hodgson, 2 Camp. 36; King *v.* Meredith, 2 Camp. 639; Griffin *v.* Langfield, 3 Camp. 254; Fragano *v.* Long, 4 D. & R. 283.

carrier for such loss or damage, the vendee or consignee is generally the proper plaintiff.

SEC. 597. **Consignor may sue.** — Although the statement that the delivery of goods to a carrier generally vests the ownership of the goods in the consignee is true, it is not necessarily so. This principle was discussed in a case in the House of Lords,[1] in which the Lord Chancellor said: "It is no doubt true, as a general rule, that the delivery by the consignor to the carrier is a delivery to the consignee, and that the risk is after such delivery the risk of the consignee. That is so if, without designating the particular carrier, the consignee directs that the goods shall be sent by the ordinary conveyance; the delivery to the ordinary carrier is then a delivery to the consignee, and the consignee incurs all risk of the carriage. And it is still more strongly so if the goods are sent by a carrier, specially pointed out by the consignee himself; for such carrier then becomes his special agent. But though the authorities all establish the general inference, as I have stated, yet that general inference is capable of being varied by the circumstances of any special arrangement between the parties, or of any particular mode of dealing between them. If a particular contract be proved between the consignor and the consignee, — and the circumstance of the payment of freight and insurance is not alone conclusive evidence of ownership, — as where the party undertaking to consign undertakes to deliver at a particular place, the property, till it reaches that place and is delivered according to the terms of the contract, is at the risk of the consignor. And again, though in general the following the directions of the consignee and the delivering the goods to a particular carrier will relieve the consignor from the risk, he may make such a special contract that, though delivering the goods to the carrier specially intimated by the consignee, the risk may remain with him, and the consignor may by a contract with the carrier make the carrier liable to himself. In an infinite variety of circumstances the ordinary rule may turn out not to be that which regulates the liabilities of the parties." In the light of this case,

[1] Dunlop *v.* Lambert, 6 Cl. & F. 600.

then, where the consignor has specially contracted with the carrier or otherwise retains the ownership of the goods, he will be the proper plaintiff. And in case it is doubtful whether goods were delivered to the carrier at the risk of the consignor or at the risk of the consignee, the question is one which must be left to the jury.[1]

SEC. 598. **The Principle involved.** — This principle is in conformity with the general rule of law in respect to all questions, and that is that the action should be brought in the name of the person whose legal right has been affected. Now the question as to whether the consignor or the consignee is to take the risk is the question which is calculated to decide the point as to who is in fact the proprietor of the goods which are bailed to the carrier.[2] It is a very patent fact that under all circumstances it is the party who is injured in his rights who has most need of the remedy, and who is most likely to put it in force directly for his own advantage, and indirectly for the advantage of his neighbors. For every man that goes to law is to some extent practically philanthropic.

SEC. 599. **General Rule.** — It follows then, from what has been said, that, as a general rule, a mere servant or agent with whom a contract is made on behalf of another, and who has no direct beneficial interest in the transaction, cannot support an action thereon;[3] if, however, the agent or servant have a beneficial interest in the performance of the contract, or a special property or interest in the subject-matter of the agreement, he is entitled to support an action in his own name upon the contract.

[1] Dunlop *v.* Lambert, 6 Cl. & F. 600; 1 Sm. L. Ca. 103 *b.* See also Davis *v.* James, 5 Burr. 2689; Moore *v.* Wilson, 1 T. R. 659; Hunter *v.* Westbrook, 2 C. & P. 578. These were cases in which there was an express agreement between consignor and carrier, by which the latter agreed to be responsible to the former for goods on consideration of the former guaranteeing the latter his hire. See Mayall *v.* Boston & Maine R. R. Co., 19 N. H. 122; Elkins *v.* Boston & Maine R. R. Co., 19 N. H. 337.

[2] Goods may be sent to consignee, on approval, when of course the property is still in the consignor. Swain *v.* Shepherd, 1 M. & Rob. 224. See also Stevenson *v.* Hart, 4 Bing. 476; 1 M. & P. 357; Duff *v.* Budd, 3 B. & B. 177; Norman *v.* Phillips, 14 M. & W. 277.

[3] Sargent *v.* Morris, 3 B. & A. 277.

SEC. 600. **Factor, Carrier, &c., may maintain an Action for Goods intrusted to them.** — Thus, a factor, a broker, a warehouseman, a carrier, and a captain of a ship [1] are sufficiently interested in goods which do not belong to them to maintain an action for goods which have been intrusted to them; or, in the case of a captain of a ship, to maintain an action for freight. In the case of Freeman *v.* Birch,[2] which was an action on the case against a carrier for negligence, it appeared at the trial that the plaintiff, a laundress at Hammersmith, was in the habit of sending linen to and from London by the defendant's cart, which travelled from Chiswick to London; it further appeared that on one occasion a basket of linen belonging to a person of the name of Spinks was sent by the defendant's cart, and on its way to London part of the contents were either lost or stolen. Spinks did not pay the carriage of the linen, and it was objected upon the part of the defendant that the present action was misconceived, and that the action ought to have been brought by the owner of the linen. The learned judge, PATERSON, J., overruled the objection, and a verdict was found for the plaintiff. Subsequently a motion was made for a new trial, on the ground of misdirection, which the Court of Queen's Bench refused, on the ground that under the circumstances the bailee must be taken to retain a special property in the goods sufficient to support the action.

SEC. 601. **Rule in Metcalfe v. London, &c. Railway Co.** — In the case of Metcalfe *v.* The London, Brighton, and South Coast Railway Company,[3] the facts that appeared in evidence were as follows: The plaintiffs were brothers, and were both acting as agents of a Mr. Hollingham, of Worthing, in the sale of an article used for agricultural purposes, called English guano. They both lodged in Mr. Hollingham's house in Augusta Place,

[1] Shields *v.* Davis, 6 Taunt. 65; Brown *v.* Hodgson, 4 Taunt. 189. See also Joseph *v.* Knox, 3 Camp. 320; White *v.* Bascom, 28 Vt. 268.

[2] 2 Q. B. 492; 1 Nev. & M. 420; Nichols *v.* Bastard, 2 Cro. M. & R.; Sims *v.* Bond, 5 B. & Ad. 389; Steamboat Farmer *v.* M'Craw, 26 Ala. 189; and see 12 N. Y. 243; Everett *v.* Saltus, 15 Wend. (N. Y.) 474; Law *v.* Hatcher, 4 Blatchf. (U. S. C. C.) 364. See also Moran *v.* Portland S. P. Co., 35 Me. 55.

[3] 4 C. B. N. S. 318; 4 Jur. N. S. 487; 27 L. J. C. P. 333.

Worthing. On a certain day they left that place for the purpose of proceeding to London by the 2.40 P. M. train, accompanied by a man named Oliver, a servant of Mr. Hollingham, who carried their carpet-bags. On their arrival at the station it was discovered that a deal box which they had intended to take to London with them had been left behind, and accordingly they sent Oliver back to Augusta Place for it, with instructions to forward it to "The Queen's Head Inn," Borough, by the next train. On his return to Augusta Place, Oliver received the box from Mr. Hollingham with a direction on it to "J. T. Metcalfe, 'Queen's Head,' Borough," and delivered it to the porter at the station at Worthing, in time for the 4.20 train. The box when delivered by Oliver was secured by a padlock, and had in it, amongst other things, the articles enumerated in the declaration enclosed in the box, *some of the articles being the property of each of the brothers.* On the morning of the following day the box was delivered at the "Queen's Head" by a porter belonging to the company, to whom a receipt was given for it by John Thomas Metcalfe, who paid for the carriage. The box was immediately carried upstairs to a bedroom, and opened by George Metcalfe, when it was found that the box had been opened and its contents had been abstracted. For the defence it was submitted that there was no evidence of a joint bailment by the plaintiffs who brought the action, but the court held that there was; COCKBURN, C. J., remarking: "I think there was abundant evidence of a joint contract. The box appears to have contained property belonging separately to each of the plaintiffs, but none in which they had a joint ownership. The question is whether there was a delivery to the company to be carried on behalf of the two jointly. I am of opinion that there was. The delivery was not by the hand of either of the plaintiffs, but by a third person with whom the company contracted, as with the agent of an unknown principal. Having so contracted with him, it turns out that he was agent, not for one of the plaintiffs only, but for both. If so, the contract was with the two jointly." And WILLES, J., said: "It is certainly a very strange question for the company to raise, inasmuch as the only effect of holding the contract to have been with each separately would be that the company must be harassed by two actions, when the whole merits might be disposed of in one. The remedy would be by striking out the name of George Metcalfe, to whom the box was not addressed, and who did not pay the carriage of it, pursuant to the leave reserved at the trial. But it appears to me that the point is disposed of by saying that there was some evidence that the box, with its contents, was delivered to the company upon a joint contract, to be carried for the two plaintiffs, because it was delivered by a person who might reasonably be considered to have been at the time the servant of both."

SEC. 602. **When Reward to be paid by Plaintiff need not be stated.** — Another case of some importance in this connection, and also illustrating the importance of choosing rightly the form in which the action is to be brought, may be shortly referred to in this place. In that case a person of the name of Marshall was the plaintiff, and the York, Newcastle, and Berwick Railway Company were the defendants. The declaration in case against the company for the loss of a passenger's luggage stated that the defendants received the passenger, to be safely carried, together with his luggage, "for reward to the defendants in that behalf;" it then alleged that it was the defendants' duty safely and securely to carry the plaintiff and his luggage, and averred a breach of that duty, whereby the luggage was lost. It was held that, the action being founded on the breach of duty and not on contract, it was not necessary to allege or to prove that the reward was to be paid by the plaintiff, but that the plaintiff was entitled to recover, although it appeared that the fare had been paid by the plaintiff's master, with whom he was travelling at the time.[1] In case of negligence of servants, it has been held that one of two joint proprietors, who has been sued separately, may recover contribution against his co-proprietor, if the former was not present when the accident occurred;[2] but no action can be maintained by the personal representative of a person

[1] Marshall *v.* York, Newcastle, & Berwick Rail. Co., 11 C. B. 655; 12 Jur. 124; 21 L. J. C. P. 34.

[2] Woolley *v.* Batte, 2 Car. & P. 417.

killed by accident, if such person contributed to such accident by his own negligence.[1] These cases indicate the relationship which must exist between the party injured or damnified and the carrier, as well as the relationship which must exist between a person complaining of an injury and the goods damaged, in order to support an action. It has been held that an individual to whom goods are sent for inspection has not thereby acquired such an interest in them as to maintain an action upon account of damage done to them.[2] So that between these positive and negative cases there can be little doubt of the accuracy of the rule stated above.

SEC. 603. **Who can sue. — Master may sue for Injury to Servant when.** — Another case bearing upon this subject, which exemplified the doctrine that one who is no party to a contract cannot sue in respect of the breach of duty arising out of the contract, is not unworthy of attention. This was an action brought against a railway company by two brewers for the loss of services of a traveller in their employ through the defendants' negligence. The declaration was to the effect that one Charles Thomas Baxter was, before and at the time of the accident, complained of in the employment of the plaintiffs; that the defendants were carriers of passengers upon the Midland Railway from Trent to Nottingham for hire; that the said Baxter became a passenger by the defendants' railway, to be then safely and securely carried from the former to the latter of the above-mentioned places; that thereupon it became and was the *duty* of the defendants to use due and proper care and diligence in and about the carriage and conveyance of the said C. T. Baxter; yet the defendants did not safely and securely carry the said C. T. Baxter, and did not use due and proper care and diligence in and about the carriage and conveyance of the said C. T. Baxter, and by their servants so negligently, unskilfully, carelessly, and improperly behaved and conducted themselves in that behalf, that the said C. T. Baxter was thereby, and by reason of the negligence, carelessness, unskilfulness, and improper conduct of the defendants and their servants, wounded and injured, and became

[1] Tucker v. Chaplin, 2 C. & K. 730; cf. Simon v. Ward, 28 L. J. Q. B. 139.

[2] Swain v. Shepherd, 1 M. & R. 224.

and was sick and disabled, and unable to attend to the necessary business of the plaintiffs, about which he was employed at the time of the injuries complained of, and so remained for nineteen weeks, during which time the plaintiffs lost the services of the said C. T. Baxter in their business, and that the said business thereby suffered injury, and the plaintiffs were, by reason of the premises, and of the wrongful and improper conduct of the defendants, otherwise injured and damnified. To this declaration the defendants pleaded that they contracted with the said C. T. Baxter to carry him as such passenger, as in the declaration mentioned, on the said journey; and that they received him, as in the declaration mentioned, under and by virtue of that contract, and they did not contract with the plaintiffs to carry the said C. T. Baxter; and that the matter complained of in the declaration was not a breach of any contract between the defendants and the plaintiffs, but was a breach of the said contract between the defendants and the said C. T. Baxter. The defendants also demurred to the declaration, the ground of demurrer stated in the margin being, "that the defendants are not liable to third persons for breach of the contract between their passengers and themselves." In giving his judgment, Erle, C. J., said: "The demurrer to the plea admits that the relation between the defendants and Baxter was created by contract. The plaintiffs, therefore, are seeking to recover consequential damages by reason of the breach of a contract between the defendants and a third person. I take the law to be clear, that where a servant is injured by matter *ex delicto*, and his master in consequence loses the benefit of his services, the master may have an action against the wrong-doer for that consequential damage. The distinction upon which I rely is, that in all the cases where the master has recovered damages in such an action, the injury has been occasioned to the servant by the tortious act of the defendant. I find none where the damage has arisen by means of a breach of a contract. I do not go into the origin of the master's right to sue for the wrong done to his servant, or inquire whether, as Mr. Smith puts it,[1] it may have

[1] Master and Servant, p. 86.

originated at a time when the master claimed a property in the services of his servant. I take the law as I find it; and I find no case where an action has been sustained by the master for consequential damages for an injury done to his servant, when the injury arose from the breach of a contract between the servant and the defendant. Hall *v.* Hollander,[1] Martinez *v.* Gerber,[2] and Gough *v.* Brian,[3] were all cases of direct wrong done to the servant. Upon that general view I found my opinion that for the consequential damages on the present occasion the plaintiffs cannot sue."[4]

SEC. 604. **Principal and Agent.** — One important legal doctrine must not be overlooked in connection with this branch of our subject, and that is, that if it is not expressed that an agent contracts in behalf of another, and the name of the principal is not disclosed by him, a suit may be maintained in the name of the principal. Thus, in the case of Sims *v.* Bond,[5] LORD DENMAN, in delivering the judgment of the court, said: "It is a well-established rule of law that where a contract, not under seal, is made with an agent, in his own name, for an undisclosed principal, either the agent or the principal may sue upon it, the defendant, in the latter case, being entitled to be placed in the same situation, at the time of the disclosure of the real principal, as if the agent had been the contracting party. This rule is most frequently acted upon in sales by factors' agents or partners, in which cases either the nominal or real contractor may sue, but it may be equally applied to other cases, and we do not say that where a person lends money nominally on his own account, but really on account of and as a loan of another, the real lender may not sue for the money."[6] A case is mentioned by ANGELL,[7] in which this doc-

[1] 4 B. & C. 660; 7 D. & R. 133.

[2] 3 M. & G. 88; 3 Scott, N. R. 386.

[3] 2 M. & W. 770.

[4] Alton *v.* Midland Rail. Co., 19 C. B. N. S. 213; 11 Jur. N. S. 672; 34 L. J. C. P. 292.

[5] 5 B. & Ad. 389.

[6] See also Higgins *v.* Senior, 8 M. & W. 834. See also Beebe *v.* Robert, 12 Wend. (N. Y.) 413; Tainton *v.* Prendergast, 3 Hill (N. Y.), 72; Elkins *v.* Boston, &c. R. R. Co., 19 N. H. 337; Sanderson *v.* Lamberton, 6 Binn. (Penn.) 129; Lapham *v.* Green, 9 Vt. 407; Davis *v.* M'Kinney, 6 Coldw. (Tenn.) 15. Compare Fulver *v.* Burke, 56 Barb. (N. Y.) 390.

[7] On Carriers, § 494, 4th ed.

trine was acknowledged and applied in the case of a common carrier. It occurred in Pennsylvania.[1] "It was also," he says, "recently applied by the Supreme Court of the United States in an important case on appeal in the Admiralty, in which the respondents were common carriers by sea. The case referred to originated in the loss of the steamboat 'Lexington,' with the cargo on board, by fire, in Long Island Sound, in the month of January, 1840, but the decision was not made until the December term of that court, 1847. The property in question (a large amount of *specie*) was delivered to one H., an 'express' forwarder, for transportation, and by him delivered for that purpose to the New Jersey Steam Navigation Company, who, with other steamboats, ran the 'Lexington' to and from New York and Stonington. It was held that, notwithstanding the contract of affreightment was made by H. with the company personally, and without disclosing the name of the libellants, who were the owners of the specie lost, the suit by them against the company should be sustained." [2]

SEC. 605. **Statute of Frauds.** — Again, where the case is within the Statute of Frauds, it is of importance, in determining the question of ownership, with a view of ascertaining who may properly sue a carrier for the loss or injury of goods intrusted to him, to discover whether, according to the requirements of that statute, the contract of sale is complete. Thus, where A.'s traveller ordered goods from the plaintiff above the value of 10*l.* for A.; nothing was said as to the mode of transmitting them to A., and no contract was signed, but the plaintiff transmitted the invoice to the person for whom the goods were purchased: it was held that there was no acceptance of the goods by A., no complete contract with A., and therefore, that the plaintiff, as consignor, was the person to sue for the loss on the transit.[3]

[1] Sanderson *v.* Lamberton, 6 Binn. (Penn.) 129.

[2] New Jersey Steam Nav. Co. *v.* Merchants' Bank, 6 How. (U. S.) 344.

[3] Coats *v.* Chaplin, 3 Q. B. 483; cf. Frango *v.* Long, 4 B. & C. 219. See also Duff *v.* Budd, 6 Moore, 469; and Stevenson *v.* Hart, 4 Bing. 476.

SEC. 606. **General Rule. — Incomplete Contract.** — We have seen that, as a general rule, the following the directions of the consignee, and the delivery of the goods to a particular carrier named by him, will relieve the consignor from risk, yet, if the contract is incomplete within the Statute of Frauds, the vendor is the proper person to sue in case of the loss of the goods; and it further appears that, in order to render such a contract complete by constructive acceptance, it is necessary that the consignee should have an opportunity of examining and rejecting the goods before acceptance. Thus, in Coombs *v.* The Bristol and Exeter Railway Company,[1] it appeared that the plaintiff, an umbrella-maker at Bristol, bought of one Avery, a dealer in whalebone at Exeter, a parcel of whalebone (which he sent *per* rail to Bristol), and also agreed with Avery to take all the whalebone he might be able to supply, at 2*s*. 7*d*. a pound, to be sent by the defendants' railway, the plaintiff to pay for the carriage. According to this arrangement, Avery afterwards from time to time sent whalebone to the plaintiff in that manner. Upon one occasion Avery wrote to the plaintiff that about one hundredweight of whalebone, such as the plaintiff had ordered, had been sent to him *per* the Bristol and Exeter Railway Company Office at Exeter. Soon afterwards the plaintiff wrote to Avery, "I have not received *your* bone," and again, "I will send the draft as soon as the bone is received." Subsequently Avery wrote: "Have the railway company settled for the missing whalebone? Let me know if you have taken the responsibility upon yourself." The whalebone turned out to be lost, and after the action the defendants settled with Avery. It further appeared that the parcel was directed to the plaintiff in the usual and proper way, but that he had received no invoice of it beyond the letter above stated, and it was objected that he had no right to sue. WATSON, B., held that the special plea was not strictly proved, as a bad plea must be, but on the general issue reserved the question as to the right of action. When the case came before the Court of Exchequer, POLLOCK, C. B., said: "The question is whether the property had passed; if so, then the consignee

[1] 27 L. J. Exch. 401.

was the proper person to sue; if not, then the vendee. For it would be very inconvenient to hold the liability of a carrier to be ambulatory or dependent upon some act to be done by the consignee, subsequent to the loss, perhaps, with the very bringing of the action itself, for to that extent the argument was pressed on the part of the plaintiff. The question really came, therefore, to this — whether the property had passed. And that depends upon this — whether a delivery to the particular carrier named by the vendee is a delivery to and acceptance by the vendee. The only way in which that could be made out, was by arguing that the adoption of the contract is equivalent to the previous consent. But that cannot be, for, if so, then in all the cases the consignee might have entitled himself to sue by an express adoption of the contract. In all cases, however, it seems to have been assumed that the property must have passed at the time of the loss. And Hunt *v.* Hechts[1] decided that it was not sufficient to satisfy the statute, for that the vendee should have an opportunity of rejecting the goods. The statute requires not only delivery, but acceptance. And it seems to me that in this case there was no acceptance nor anything else to take the case out of the operation of the 17th section of the Statute of Frauds, and therefore we cannot allow the contract of sale to have been valid, and, if not, then any other contract dependent upon it must also fail."[2]

SEC. 607. **Where the Consignee, even when the Property has not passed, may sue.** — So, where B., a miller in Suffolk, sold flour to the plaintiff, and, according to the usual course of business between them, consigned it to him in Kent, paying the carriage by the Great Eastern Railway to London, and, the Great Eastern Railway Company having delivered it to the South-Eastern Railway Company, the latter forwarded it to the plaintiff in Kent, and charged him for the carriage by their line, it was held that, although the property in the flour might not have passed to the plaintiff under the Statute of

[1] 8 Exch. 814; 22 L. J. Exch. 293.

[2] See also Meredith *v.* Meegh, 22 L. J. Q. B. 401. The case of Hart *v.* Sattley, 3 Camp. 528, must be held to be overruled.

Frauds, he was — as he had contracted with the latter railway company for the carriage — entitled to sue them for damage done to it in the transit over their line.[1]

SEC. 608. **Property in Goods.** — Again, in the case of Sheridan *v.* The New Quay Company,[2] the substantial question related to the passage of property from one person to another, and, consequently, it bears upon the subject under consideration. There C., who resided at M., ordered goods of D., to be shipped to the port of L., and to be paid for in cash against the bill of lading. C. never obtained the bill of lading, or paid for the goods, but he sold the latter to the plaintiff. The goods arrived at the port of L., but were not to be delivered except on payment of the freight. At an interview between the captain and B. (the plaintiff's agent at L.), at which D. was present, the captain said, in answer to B.'s question where the bill of lading was, that D. had passed it on to C., which was true, the bill having, in fact, been sent to D.'s agent at M. for that purpose, but C. not paying for the goods the bill was returned to D. after this interview. No arrangement was then come to, but shortly afterwards B., as plaintiff's agent, paid the freight on receiving from the captain a document given to him by D. when the bill of lading was signed, by which D. requested C.'s agent at L. to pay the captain his freight. The defendants, who were common carriers, were then employed by B. to forward the goods to the plaintiff. It was held that the plaintiff had acquired no right to take possession of the goods as buyer, either by the purchase from C. or by the conduct of D. at the interview between the captain and B., coupled with the document requesting payment of freight, and the payment of freight thereon.[3]

[1] Mead *v.* South-Eastern Rail. Co., 18 W. R. 735.

[2] 28 L. J. C. P. 58; Sanquer *v.* London & South-Western Rail. Co., 16 C. B. 163.

[3] See 18 & 19 Vict. c. 11, § 1, which enacts "that every consignee of goods named in a bill of lading, and every indorsee of a bill of lading to whom the property in the goods therein mentioned shall pass upon or by reason of such consignment or indorsement, shall have transferred to and vested in him all rights of suit, and be subject to the same liabilities in respect of such goods, as if the contract contained in the bill of lading had been made with himself." See also, per BRAMWELL, B., in Foster

SEC. 609. **"Bill of Lading" defined.** — In connection with this case, a clause of "The Customs Tariff Amendment Act, 1860," may be alluded to, by which the term "bill of lading" "is construed to mean any bill of lading, or other instrument equivalent thereto, or used in the place thereof, for the consignment or forwarding of any goods to foreign parts, or which shall or may be used by any shipper, carrier, forwarder, or consignee, broker, or other person, as and for, or to serve the purpose of, a bill of lading, for the exportation of goods, whether shipped direct from port of shipment or forwarded by railway, canal, or other mode of transit or carriage, to any port or place for shipment."[1]

SEC. 610. **"Carrier" defined.** — By the same act, the term "carrier" or "forwarder" is defined to mean "any public carrier or other person undertaking the through carriage, by land or sea, of any goods to foreign parts, or the carriage of any goods to any port or place of shipment, to be there shipped and exported to foreign parts," and the term "goods" means only wares and merchandise exported in this way, and does not apply to small parcels or articles for which shipping bills are not required.[2]

SEC. 611. **Where Delivery to Carrier operates as Delivery to Purchaser. — Vendor may stop in Transitu. — Person employing Carrier must bring Action. — Special Agreement.** — It may then be laid down, as we have seen, as a general rule, "that if a tradesman order goods to be sent by a carrier, though he does not name any particular one, the moment the goods are delivered to the carrier it operates as a delivery to the purchaser; the whole property immediately vests in him, he alone can bring an action for any injury done to the goods, and if any accident happen to them it is at his risk. The only exception to the purchaser's right over the goods is that the vendor, in case of the former becoming insolvent, may stop them *in transitu*."[3] And when a deviation has to be

v. Colby, 28 L. J. Exch. 81, 88; Shand *v.* Sanderson, 28 L. J. Exch. 778, where declaration was based on statute.

[1] 23 Vict. c. 22, § 21.

[2] *Ibid.* § 24. See Maclachlan on Ship. p. 341.

[3] Per LORD ALVANLEY in Dutton *v.* Solomonson, 3 B. & P. 584; see also Jacobs *v.* Nelson, 3 Taunt. 423; Richardson *v.* Dunn, 2 Q. B. 224.

made from that rule it must be in conformity not with the rule laid down by LORD KENYON in Dawes *v.* Peck,[1] that the question whether the consignor or the consignee is the party to sue must be governed by the answer to the question in whom the right of property is vested, but in conformity with the ruling of PARKE, J., in Freeman *v.* Birch,[2] which was that the person employing the carrier must bring the action. In that case the circumstance of the legal right being vested in one of the parties may be evidence of the employment of the carrier by that person. It is, however, important in all cases to discover, in the first instance, whether there is any special agreement; for if there exists any such agreement between one of the parties and the carrier, for the carriage and conveyance of the goods, it is indubitably the proper duty of the person who entered into the agreement to sue upon its breach, and if another party did sue upon the agreement the action would not lie. Where the consignor has made himself personally responsible for the hire of the carriage, then he will be the proper party to sue for the loss of the goods.[3] In Joseph *v.* Knox,[4] the plaintiff, the consignor having received goods from Amsterdam to be transmitted to the consignee in Surinam, shipped them on board the defendant's vessel upon a bill of lading which stated that the goods were shipped by the plaintiff, that they were to be delivered in Surinam to the consignee or his assigns, and that the freight was to be paid by the plaintiff in London; it was held by LORD ELLENBOROUGH that the defendant after having signed such a bill of lading could not bring the ownership of the goods in question;

[1] 8 T. R. 322. See also Snee *v.* Prescott, 1 Ld. Raym. 271; Evans *v.* Martlett, 6 East, 22; Newson *v.* Thornton, 4 East, 211; Cox *v.* Harden, 7 T. R. 440; Hodgson *v.* Loy, 8 T. R. 330; Davis *v.* James, 5 Burr. 2680; Moore *v.* Wilson, 1 D. & E. 659; Dutton *v.* Solomonson, 3 B. & P. 582; Potter *v.* Laming, 1 John. (N. Y.) 217; Lyle *v.* Barker, 5 Binn. (Penn.) 457; Sanderson *v.* Lamberton, 6 Binn. (Penn.) 129; Griffiths *v.* Ingledew, 6 S. & R. (Penn.) 428; Chandler *v.* Sprague, 5 Met. (Mass.) 306; Conard *v.* Atlantic Ins. Co., 1 Pet. (U. S.) 386.

[2] 1 Nev. & M. 420.

[3] Davis *v.* James, 5 Burr. 2680; Sargent *v.* Morris, 3 B. & Ald. 277; Moore *v.* Wilson, 1 T. R. 659; Robinson *v.* Dunmore, 2 B. & P. 416. But see Griffiths *v.* Ingledew, 6 S. & R. (Penn.) 429.

[4] 3 Camp. 320.

the consideration upon which the contract was founded moved from the plaintiff, the undertaking was made to him, and he was therefore entitled to maintain the action to recover the value of the goods, and would hold the sum recovered as trustee for the real owner. BURROUGHS, J., in delivering his judgment in the case of Stevenson *v.* Hart,[1] which was a case in which the duty of the carrier to deliver goods at the address to which they were directed was considered, said: "The defendants were directed to deliver the box at No. 27 Great Winchester Street, and on its being taken there, according to the direction, the defendants' porter found that the house was untenanted, and that no such person as West (to whom the box was addressed) ever lived there, nor was there any person of that name in the street. The defendants had performed their contract when they took the box to the house to which it was directed, and it afterwards remained in their hands as the property of the sender. A new contract then arose between the plaintiff (the consignor) and the defendants as carriers, and they ought to have taken care of the box for him." This places the subject in a new and not unimportant light.

SEC. 612. **Where Consignee cannot be found.** — Where no consignee can be found the property in the goods cannot be said to be vested in him; but because no consignee can be found the carrier's duties in relation to the goods which were intrusted to him have not thereby come to an end. He may have done all that he was paid to do, with the exception of performing that part of his duty which would determine his responsibility, namely, delivering the goods at the place to which they were addressed, and that duty may have been unperformed through the interposition of inevitable circumstances, and not through any neglect upon his part.

SEC. 613. **Carrier's Duty. — Consignor's Remedy.** — Still until delivery, or something equivalent, has taken place, the carrier is not discharged, and his duty is to hold them for, and upon payment of all fair and reasonable charges to return them to, the consignor. If he should fail to do so, it is clear that the consignor who bailed the goods to him, might main-

[1] 1 Moore & P. 357.

tain an action against him ; and if while they were in the hands of the carrier they were lost, the consignor would be the proper person under these circumstances to sue.

SEC. 614. **In Case of Carriers by Water, Bill of Lading to be referred to.** — We have seen that, in all cases, it is of importance first to ascertain whether there is any special contract between the parties, as to the carriage of the goods, before coming to a decision as to the proper party to sue. Now, although the general principles stated above are applicable both to land carriers and water carriers, still, in the case of the latter, the bill of lading should always be referred to as indicating the intention of the parties, and as showing for whose use the contract was entered into, which latter point is of some importance in determining the parties to an action of this nature, when the right of action arises on a simple contract. "If goods by bill of lading are consigned to A., A. is the owner, and must bring the action against the master of the ship if they are lost, but if the bill be special, to be delivered to A. to the use of B., B. ought to bring the action; if, however, the bill be general to A., and the invoice only shows that they are upon the account of B., A. ought always to bring the action, for the property is in him, and B. has only a trust."[1] Where, however, bills of lading constructively of the same import, and for the same goods, are in the hands of different holders, whose equities are equal, possession is determined in favor of him who has the legal title. Where, therefore, a Jamaica planter procured bills of lading to be signed by the master, one making the goods deliverable to his agent in this country, and two deliverable to the shipper himself, and he indorsed the latter two to A. B. in this country, forwarding also the remaining one to his agent, who was informed of the indorsement of the others, and who, nevertheless, indorsed the bill of lading sent to him over to C. D., it was held, first, that the agent being, for the purposes of law, identical with his principal, all the bills of lading were constructively deliverable to the shipper; and, secondly, that the

[1] Sargent *v.* Morris, 3 B. & Ald. 612; Evans *v.* Martlett, 1 Ld. Raym. 277. See Pinder *v.* Wilks, 5 Taunt. 271.

first legal title rested in A. B. by indorsement of the bills of lading to him, and he was therefore entitled to possession of the cargo, although C. D. had been the first to claim it.[1]

SEC. 615. **Bill of Lading, Evidence of what.** — It is to be remembered that a bill of lading is evidence of a contract safely to carry the goods whereof bailment is acknowledged, and to deliver the same at the destined port to the person mentioned or his assigns, and upon the terms mentioned.[2] Except where the bill of lading introduces special circumstances as modifying the contract, the law is the same as that applicable to any other kind of bailment for conveyance. Where a consignee at Liverpool, on receipt of a bill of lading, by which goods actually laden at Longford were made deliverable to certain persons in Dublin, "in care for and to be shipped to" him, accepted on the faith of the consignment a bill of exchange, it was held that the bill of lading was evidence of an intention on the part of the consignor at the time of the lading to vest in the consignee the property in the specific chattels laden, and that he might bring an action in trover for them against a person to whom they had been delivered under a subsequent order of the consignor. But the statute quoted above in reference to this matter operates a transfer of the contract with its rights and liabilities, on condition of the vesting of the property, and that fact is, as we have seen, difficult, in many cases, of detection, being always dependent upon the evidence of intention in respect of it.[3] The mere possession of goods by a carrier as a bailee entitles him to maintain an action against any one for loss of or damage caused to them while they are in his hands.[4]

SEC. 616. **Parties to be sued.** — Sufficient has been said concerning this subject in this place,[5] and we turn to the con-

[1] Caldwell *v.* Ball, 1 T. R. 205.

[2] Caldwell *v.* Ball, per BULLER, J., 1 T. R. 205, 216. Per BRAMWELL, B., in Foster *v.* Colby, 28 L. J. Exch. 81, 85.

[3] Reyans *v.* Wise, 4 M. & W. 775; Van Casteel *v.* Booker, 2 Exch. 69; Anderson *v.* Clarke, 2 Bing. 20. See Brown *v.* Hare, 3 H. & N. 484.

[4] Jefferies *v.* Great Western Rail. Co., 5 El. & Bl. 508; 25 L. J. Q. B. 107.

[5] See further on this subject, Abbott on Ship., pt. iv. ch. 4, p. 284, 11th ed.; Maclachlan on Ship., ch. viii. p. 338, &c.

sideration of the question, Who may be sued? It is as important to answer this question correctly as to come to a satisfactory conclusion in reference to that just discussed. At first sight it might seem to be a question as to whether, when a master carrier employed a large number of servants, and the accident which caused the loss or injury to the goods had occurred through the negligence of one of these, it was the injured parties' duty to sue the servant or his employer. But the whole of the principles of law point to the master as the proper person to be sued, and an action will not lie against the servant. The principal and not the agent is responsible for accidents occurring through the negligence of the latter, and the only way in which a master can protect himself from consequences for which he is not directly responsible is to exercise care in the choice of those he engages to do his work. There is no great hardship in this. Human nature can be relied upon. Men habitually careful will be careful in time to come. If a man builds a house with timber which is rotten, he is responsible for the fall of the house; so, if he employs an individual concerning whose skill and caution he has no knowledge, he is responsible for any mishap which may arise from a want or absence of these qualities, the presence of which he was not at pains to ascertain.

SEC. 617. **Latent Defects in Men.**—One question which has not, so far as we know, been considered in a court of law, has relation to latent defects which may exist in men, just as they exist in railway tires or axles. A latent defect in the making of a manufactured article is one which no care can avoid and which no inspection could have discovered. It seems to us that under such circumstances an accident arising from such a defect might with justice be considered as due to the act of God, and therefore one of those casualties against which the carrier does not insure. The fact that it arises from the inside, as from a flaw in welding of a wheel tire caused by an air bubble,[1] instead of from the outside, as from a storm of wind, a flash of lightning, or the attack of overwhelming

[1] Redhead *v.* Midland Rail. Co., L. R. Q. B. 412; 4 L. R. Q. B. 379, Exch. Ch.

enemies, seems to us to make no manner of difference. It is the inevitability and the unavoidability which is the point to be considered. If no human care or ability could in the present condition of knowledge have averted the catastrophe, it would be absurd upon every ground to hold the person responsible. If, then, a man may select a wheel with a defect in it, which may cause an accident for which he will not be held responsible, so it seems to us may a master select a servant with a latent defect, concerning which he can know nothing and can procure no information — as, for instance, a hereditary tendency to insanity, a liability of epileptic or cataleptic seizures — through which, if an accident occurred, he could not with justice be regarded as in any way responsible. To our knowledge the doctrine of latent defects has not as yet been acknowledged as applicable to this branch of the law of carriers, and the general principle which is to guide the practitioner is that an action for negligence is to be brought against the master and not against the servant.

SEC. 618. **Action to be brought against Master for Injury caused by Servant. — The Scope of Authority to be considered.** — Still this general principle requires to be more minutely considered. Thus there are some servants of carriers, who do a little business on their own account. The driver of a coal-cart, whose master only undertakes to carry coal, and who is therefore only a common carrier in relation to that mineral, may be intrusted with a hand-parcel, to convey from one place to another. In such a case the master would not be responsible for the loss of the parcel.[1] But wherever the undertaking is clearly within the scope of the servant's authority, the master will be regarded as the proper person against whom the action may be brought. In Williams *v.* Cranston,[2] it appeared that a watch had been delivered to the driver of a stage-coach, to be delivered, and LORD ELLENBOROUGH held that the master, and not the servant, was liable for the loss, and that, as the plaintiff had brought his action against the servant only, he must be nonsuited. He remarked: "I

[1] Beauchamp *v.* Powley, 1 M. & R. 38.

[2] 8 Stark. 82.

accede to the proposition, that if the defendant could be considered as having taken the watch to be carried on his own account, for reward to be paid to him, he would be liable, although he acted in fraud of his master. If it could be shown that he had been in the habit of conveying parcels for hire, the case would certainly be altered, but, being the mere servant, it cannot be inferred that he took the parcel to be carried for hire and reward without further proof. The only fact is, that he was the driver of the coach; no contract has been proved; there is nothing to indicate that the defendant received the parcel otherwise than in the character of a servant. I should have been glad if the case could have been carried further. At present, the loss appears to have resulted from the negligence of the master, through the negligence of his servant." The law on that point is clear.

SEC. 619. **The Agent's Authority.** — In all such cases the scope of the authority of the agent is to be considered. Of course, in no case can an accident be said to be strictly within the scope of the authority of the agent, but that is not what is meant by the above statement. It is not the authorization by the principal in reference to a particular act which will make him responsible for his servant's negligence. The question to be decided is, whether, when the act of negligence occurred, the servant was acting within the scope of his general authority. Thus a proprietor of stage-coaches may have a man-servant, who, with a view of enjoying a holiday, hires or borrows a vehicle, and drives himself out into the country.

SEC. 620. **Action to be brought against Servant when.** — If upon such an excursion the servant, through reckless driving, injures any one, the injured party must bring his action against the servant, and not against the master, for at the time the accident occurred the servant was not, *quoad* that particular conveyance, the servant of his master. Where, too, the servant conducts himself in direct contravention of the express authority of his master, or exceeds such authority in an unreasonable way, the master will not be held liable for injury arising therefrom. Another rule is of importance, and that is that a man may become a principal after the fact by adopting the acts of a person who at the time of the commission of the act pretended, without any ground for so doing, to be his agent. Unless, however, the person at the time held himself out as the agent, no subsequent ratification of the acts will render the individual so ratifying or confirming liable as principal.[1]

SEC. 621. **Joinder of Parties.** — A question arises here as to when it will be right to join partner-carriers as defendants.[2] It can be answered shortly. 1. Where the action is in *tort*, and is founded on a breach of the common-law duty, it is several in its nature, and is therefore maintainable against some only of those who are joined as defendants. 2. Where the declaration is in assumpsit, and founded in contract, the plaintiff must prove a joint promise, as by proof that all the defendants were proprietors.

SEC. 622. **Distinction in this Particular between Carriers by Land and Water.** — Here, however, it is necessary to distinguish in this particular between carriers by land and carriers by water. The law, as it applies to these two classes, is not, in regard to this matter, the same. The master of a ship is not regarded as a mere servant of the owner. He has large powers, and is to be looked upon as an independent officer. It is perhaps necessary for the safety of all that he should be held, as he is, liable to an action for the loss or injury of the property intrusted to his care, and as personally responsible to the proprietors of the bailed goods.[3]

SEC. 623. **Rule in Blakie v. Stembridge.** — In one case[4] a ship was chartered by the owner to one A. for a voyage with cargo to Port Louis and back, for a stipulated rate of freight per ton

[1] Wilson *v.* Furman, 6 Scott, N. R. 894; and see New Jersey Steam Nav. Co. *v.* Merchants' Bank, *ante;* 6 How. (U. S.) 344. See, generally, as to ratification, Gulick *v.* Grover, 33 N. J. L. 463. See also Drakeley *v.* Grigg, 8 Wall. (U. S.) 242; Vincent *v.* Rather, 31 Tex. 77; Stoddart's Case, 4 Ct. of Cl. (U. S.) 511.

[2] Waland *v.* Elkins, 1 Stark. 272.

[3] See Abbott on Ship., 7th ed., 167, 346; Goff *v.* Chukard, 1 Wils. 288; per HOLT, in Boson *v.* Sandfold, 1 Shaw, 101. See Stone *v.* Ketland, 1 Wash. (U. S. C. C.) 142; Bussey *v.* Donaldson, 4 Dall. (Penn.) 206; Purvrance *v.* Angus, 1 Dall. (Penn.) 180.

[4] Blakie *v.* Stembridge, 28 L. J. C. P. 329; 6 C. B. N. S. 894.

on the homeward cargo — the cargo to be taken to and tendered alongside at the charterer's risk and expense, the ship to be conveyed to charterer's agent at ports of loading and discharge, and a *stevedore for the outward cargo to be appointed by the charterer, but to be paid by and act under the captain's orders.* The charterer put up the ship as a general ship for Port Louis, and appointed a stevedore, who, with his men, went on board for the purpose of stowing the vessel in the usual course of his business. The master gave no orders to, or in any way interfered with, the stevedore, only looking into the hold occasionally to see how the cargo was being stowed, for the safety of the ship. The plaintiff's agents arranged with the broker of the charterer for the freight and carriage to Port Louis of certain sugar pans, and sent them alongside the ship. Whilst the pans were being hoisted on board from the lighter *by the stevedore and his men*, two of them were by their negligence damaged. It was held that under these circumstances the stevedore was not the servant or agent of the master so as to render him responsible. WILLES, J., in the course of his judgment, said: "By the maritime law, in the absence of custom or agreement to the contrary, it is the duty of the master, on the part of the owner, to receive and properly stow on board the goods to be carried; which, ordinarily, are to be delivered to him alongside. For any damage occasioned to the goods by negligence in the performance of such duty the owner is liable to the shipper. If the damage result from misconduct of the master, he is answerable to the owners, and probably also directly to the shipper.

SEC. 624. **Scotch Rule.** — "Where it happened through the misconduct of the mate, or others of the crew, without fault on the part of the master, it was held by the majority of the Court of Session in Petrie's Executors *v.* Aitchison,[1] that the master was not answerable to the owners, though it appears to have been taken for granted, perhaps upon the principle asserted by STORY, J., in the passage cited,[2] that

[1] 15 Faculty Decisions, 493 (6th Feb. 1841).

[2] "There is one important exception to the rule already stated, as to the non-liability of agents to third persons for the negligence and omissions of

the master would in such case have been answerable to the shipper." [1]

SEC. 625. **Option of Plaintiff to sue Master or Owner.** — While the master is thus liable, it is still in the option of the plaintiff, unless there is some special contract with the owners, to sue either the master or his masters; and on the other hand a special contract with the master will equally bind the plaintiff to proceed against him instead of the owners. One other case may be alluded to in this connection. In that case a ship was chartered for a voyage from Oporto to the United Kingdom, to load, from the factors of the affreighter, a full cargo of wine, or other merchandise, at 18*s.* 6*d.* per ton; the captain to sign bills of lading at any rate of freight, without prejudice to the charter; the ship to be addressed to charterer's agent at Oporto on usual terms. The ship was accordingly consigned to the charterer's agents at Oporto, and was

duty of themselves, and of their sub-agents, founded upon the principles of maritime law. In the case of masters of ships, who, although they are the agents or servants of the owners, are also, in many respects, deemed to be responsible as principals to third persons, not only for their own negligences and non-feasances, but also for the negligences, non-feasances, and misfeasances of their subordinate officers, and others employed by and under them. We have already seen that the master of the ship is responsible upon contracts made by him in regard to the usual employment of the ship, and also upon contracts made by him for the repairs and necessaries supplied for the ship, as well as for the wages of the seamen employed in navigating the ship. This liability is founded upon the doctrine of the maritime law, which treats the master not merely as an agent contracting on his own behalf, as well as for the owner; but which upon a broader policy treats him as in some sort a subrogated principal and qualified owner of the ship, possessing authority in the nature of the exercitorial power for the time being. And his liability, founded upon this consideration, extends not merely to his contracts, but to his own negligences and non-feasances and misfeasances, as well as to those of his officers and crew. His responsibility for the officers and crew has this additional reason for its support, that he is thus induced to exercise a superior watchfulness over their acts and conduct; and, if he were not so made liable for their acts and conduct, he might often, by his connivance in their frauds, misfeasances, and negligences or non-feasances, subject the shipper of goods, as well as the owners of the ship to great losses and injuries without their having any adequate redress. The policy of the maritime law has, therefore, indissolubly connected his personal responsibility with that of all the other persons on board who are under his command, and are subject to his authority." Story on Agency, § 314.

[1] See also Sack *v.* Ford, 13 C. B. N. S. 90; 32 L. J. C. P. 12; Newbury *v.* Colvin, 1 Cl. & T. 283.

put up by them as a general ship without any intimation that she was under charter. The plaintiff shipped some casks of wine, and received bills of lading in the common form signed by the master. The wine was stowed by a stevedore, appointed by the charterer's agents, and paid by them, the money being ultimately repaid them by the master. The goods having been damaged, by reason of improper stowage, the plaintiff brought an action against the defendants, as owners of the vessel, and the question which the court had to decide was whether, under the circumstances, they were liable. It was held in the affirmative, and that the action against them lay. In delivering the judgment of the court, COCKBURN, C. J., said:[1] "It is unnecessary to decide whether the charterer would or would not have been liable, if an action had, under the circumstances, been brought against him. Our judgment proceeds on a ground wholly irrespective of the question of the charterer's liability, and not inconsistent with it, namely, that the plaintiffs, having delivered their goods to be carried, in ignorance of the vessel being chartered, and having dealt with the master, as clothed with the ordinary authority of a master, to receive goods, and give bills of lading on behalf of the owners, are entitled to look to the owners as responsible for the safe carriage of the goods. . . . There is here no demise of the ship itself, either express or implied. It amounts to no more than a grant to the charterer of the right to have his cargo brought home in the ship, while the ship itself continues, through the master and crew, in the possession of the owners, the master and crew remaining their servants. It is on this ground that our judgment is founded. We think that so long as the relation of owner and master continues, the latter, as regards parties who ship goods in ignorance of any arrangement, whereby the authority ordinarily incidental to that relation is affected, must be taken to have authority to bind his owner by giving bills of lading. We proceed on the well-known principle that, where a party allows another to appear before the world as an agent in any given capacity, he must be liable to any party who contracts

[1] Sandeman *v.* Scurr, 2 L. R. Q. B. 86, at p. 95.

with such apparent agent in a matter within the scope of such agency. The master of a vessel has by law authority to sign bills of lading on behalf of his owners. A person shipping goods on board a vessel, unaware that the vessel has been chartered to another, is warranted in assuming that the master is acting by virtue of his ordinary authority, and, therefore, acting for his owners in signing bills of lading. It may be that, as between the owner, the master, and the charterer, the authority of the master is to sign bills of lading on behalf of the charterer only, and not of the owner. But, in our judgment, this altered state of the master's authority will not affect the liability of the owner, whose servant the master still remains, clothed with a character to which the authority to bind his owner, by signing bills of lading, attaches by virtue of his office. We think that, until the fact that the master's authority has been put an end to is brought to the knowledge of a shipper of goods, the latter has a right to look to the owner as the principal with whom his contract has been made."[1] With regard to another point raised in the case, his Lordship said: "We attach no weight to the fact that the stevedores, by whom the cargo was loaded, were appointed by the charterer's agents. The stowage of goods, in the absence of any special agreement, forms part of the obligation which the carrier takes upon himself. It is a duty to be discharged by the master and crew. By this charter the intervention of a stevedore is only made necessary in order to ascertain the quantity the ship could carry. There is nothing to release the master and crew from their responsibility in respect of the stowage. The stevedores were probably appointed by the charterer's agent for the convenience of the master, the agents being acquainted with the port, and knowing who were fit persons to be employed. The expense was ultimately defrayed by the master. At all events, the plaintiffs were no parties to the employment of the stevedores, and have a right to look to the owners for the proper stowage and safe conveyance of the goods."[2]

[1] See also, per Dr. Lushington, in The St. Cloud, Brow. & Lush. 4, 15.

[2] See Sack *v.* Ford, 13 C. B. N. S. 90; Swainson *v.* Garrick, 2 L. J. Exch. 225.

SEC. 626. **Objects of the Law.** — This judgment places the law upon this subject clearly before the reader, and indicates the true principles which have guided the legislature in directing persons injured where to look for the remedy which the law allows them, and the definite principles which are to guide lawyers in future in reference to the liability of owners for injuries occurring in their ships, although there may be a charter-party which is not brought to the knowledge of the party intrusting his goods to be carried. Were the law other than it is, it would be an inducement to set up fraudulent charter-parties to protect owners from the merited consequences of their own negligence, just as the protection of owners from the consequences of the negligence of their masters or crew would afford opportunities of fraud and collusion which it is the object of the law to prevent and avoid.

SEC. 627. **The Pleadings.** — One fact has become more recognizable in recent times, and that is that the profession of the law is not an end in itself. It is a tendency of all means to become ends. And the difference between wisdom and folly, between true greatness and indubitable smallness, exists to a large extent in the capacity of recognizing what are instruments and what are objects, — what are means and what are ends. The history of superstition proves the fact that the usefulness of an instrument is apt to raise it out of its position and place it among the gods of a nation. All worship is truly a worship of causes, and hence, when the indispensableness of anything began to be felt, it began silently to assert the necessity of its existence, independent of the attainment of the ends which it was intended to subserve. So it has been with institutions which are the instruments of a country, — the tools of a people. They have not unfrequently ruled the people who in the beginning wielded them! So it was with professions which were useful institutions, and, as Burke says, "The degree of estimation in which any profession is held becomes the standard of the estimation in which the professors hold themselves."[1] For a long time it might have seemed that laws really existed for the sake of lawyers, and

[1] Reflections on French Revolution.

not for the benefit of society. But laws are really like the hoops of a barrel, and lawyers are only the rivets which keep them in their places. Now, however, as we have said above, the fact has become more recognizable, and many of those things which existed more for the sake of the profession than for the direct benefit of the public, have been done away with. Hence our present task is more easy than a few years ago it would have been.

SEC. 628. **The Common-Law Procedure Act, 1852.**—Pleadings are now comparatively simple, and have gradually been becoming more and more so since the Common-Law Procedure Acts of 1852 and 1854. Before speaking of certain incidents of pleading in detail, we may remark that, as the reader is aware, under the Common-Law Procedure Act, 1852, all pleadings, however inartificial, are sufficient if they set out, clearly and intelligibly, the substantial cause or ground of the declaration or other pleadings;[1] that questions of fact, after writ issued, may by consent of the parties and leave of a judge, be raised without any formal pleadings;[2] that questions of law may be raised summarily in a special case for the opinion of the court;[3] that where there are pleadings, they may generally, in any stage of the action, and even at the trial, be amended, and ought to be amended by the court or a judge, in order to raise the substantial issue on the merits of the case between the parties;[4] and that where an adverse party objects to the inartificial nature of a pleading as calculated to "prejudice, embarrass, and delay the fair trial of the action," he cannot, as he once could, demur specially, but, unless he waives the defect, must apply to a judge to strike out the pleading, or to order it to be amended.[5]

SEC. 629. **Declarations.—Statement of Contract or Duty.—In Actions of Tort.—Special Contract.**—Notwithstanding the simplification to which the technical science of pleading has been subjected of late years, there is much care in matters of

[1] See Holt *v.* Inhabitants of Penobscot, 56 Me. 15.

[2] 15 & 16 Vict. c. 76, § 42.

[3] *Ibid.* § 46.

[4] *Ibid.* § 222; cf. 23 & 24 Vict. c. 126, § 36.

[5] *Ibid.* § 51, 52.

minute detail necessary to render an action successful, at least in so far as the professional work of a lawyer is concerned, and it is necessary to consider what will be held fatal to the successful issue of an action. In considering the forms of action which may be adopted by a plaintiff against a carrier, we have, in alluding to the varying advantages of each, considered some of the necessities of the declarations in such cases,[1] but still more remains to be said. First, then, the declaration must correctly state the contract, or the particular duty or consideration from which the liability results, and on which it is founded, and a variance in such statement or description may be as fatal, though in an action *ex delicto*, as in an action *ex contractu*.[2] Care must be taken in stating the inducement in an action *ex delicto*, if, instead of relying on the general statement, the plaintiff enters into particulars. A misdescription in such particulars would be held to be a fatal variance, just as in an action for slander of a physician it is not necessary in general to show that he has regularly taken his degree, yet if the declaration alleges that he had duly taken the degree of Doctor of Physic, it is then necessary to prove it.[3] In actions of tort the plaintiff may prove a part of his charge if the averment be divisible, and there be enough proved to support his case.[4] This, however, is not the case in the statement of a special contract, and a variance between the evidence and the statement will be fatal to the action, because it is entire in its nature, and must be proved as laid.[5]

SEC. 630. **Reward, Carriage for.** — Where the declaration against a carrier for the loss of goods states that he undertook to carry them for a certain reward, or a reason-

[1] For forms of declaration in action on the case, and in the action of assumpsit, see Appendix.

[2] Max *v.* Roberts, 12 East, 89; Govett *v.* Radnidge, 3 East, 7; Brotherton *v.* Wood, 5 B. & B. 54. See also, per BOSANQUET, J., in Ireland *v.* Johnson, 1 Bing. N. C. 162.

[3] Moises *v.* Thornton, 8 T. R. 308; and see Rix *v.* Everett, 8 B. & C. 114.

[4] Figgins *v.* Cogswell, 3 M. & S. 369.

[5] Chitty, Pl., 5th ed., 334; King *v.* Pippit, 1 T. R. 240; and see Indin *v.* Samuel, 6 East, 333; Hughes *v.* Great Western Rail. Co., 14 C. B. 637; York Rail. Co. *v.* Crisp, 14 C. B. 527; Slim *v.* Great Northern Rail. Co., 14 C. B. 647. See also Stone *v.* Kicowlton, 3 Wend. (N. Y.) 374.

able hire and reward, it is not necessary to be more specific, and state the amount or nature of the reward. Thus, in the old case, Dalston *v.* Janson,[1] the allegation in the declaration was that the defendant was to carry "for a reward to be therefor had." In an action against a carrier for losing goods, the contract, as we have seen, should be stated correctly, and not only the contract, but the termini.[2] A variance, however, is amendable, in most cases, at trial.

SEC. 631. **Receipt of Goods and Breach of Contract.** — In relation to such a contract to carry safely and securely for hire, the delivery and receipt of the goods by the defendants must be averred, and the breach must be distinctly assigned in the declaration.[3] In an action of special assumpsit against the defendant as the master of a ship for not safely conveying goods, consigned by the plaintiffs, to a foreign port, evidence that the goods were seized in another port by the Government, together with a letter of the defendant's in which he acknowledged that he was accountable for the goods, is sufficient to warrant the jury in finding for the plaintiffs without any further proof of the cause of seizure. On behalf of the defendant it was objected that there was a variance between the bill of lading and the declaration, and between the undertaking as laid in the first two counts and the breach assigned, the undertaking being laid to deliver for the plaintiffs at the island of Batavia, and the breach being that the defendant did not deliver to the plaintiffs. But ABBOTT, C. J., refused to nonsuit the plaintiffs upon this objection.[4] Again, where the carrier is declared against as a common carrier, the contract may be treated and stated as implied. In other

[1] 1 Ld. Raym. 58. See also Clarke *v.* Gray, 6 East, 564; Hall *v* Cheney, 36 N. H. 26.

[2] Hayman *v.* Raymond, 5 Taunt. 289; Tucker *v.* Cracklin, 2 Stark. 385; Beckford *v.* Crutwell, 5 C. & P. 242; Ditcham *v.* Chivis, 4 Bing. 706; Woodward *v.* Booth, 7 B. & C. 301; Wicks *v.* Gordon, 2 B. & Ald. 335.

[3] Max *v.* Roberts, 12 East, 89; Pianciani *v.* London & South-Western Rail. Co., 18 C. B. 226. See also Myers *v.* Davis, 6 Blatchf. (U. S. C. C.) 77, in which the proper form of declaration in an action of assumpsit is explained.

[4] Cullin *v.* M'Alpine, 2 Stark. 552. See also Samuel *v.* Darch, 2 Stark. 60; Streeter *v.* Horlock, 7 Moore, 283; 1 Bing. 34.

cases an express statement of the contract is absolutely necessary.[1]

SEC. 632. **In Case of Gross Negligence.** — A declaration, stating that goods had been delivered to the defendants, as carriers, to be conveyed by them for a reasonable reward, and that they undertook to carry them safely and securely, and deliver them accordingly, and assigning for breach that they lost the same, was, in the case of Smith *v.* Horne,[2] held to be sufficient to admit proof that they had been guilty of gross negligence. Where the plaintiffs declared against the defendants as common carriers, subject to the terms of a special notice, for the loss of a truss of silk by the gross negligence of the defendants, and the felonious acts of their servants, the allegation of gross negligence and felony was held to be surplusage.[3] An averment of an undertaking to carry goods to R., to be delivered to C. B., to be paid for on delivery, shows with sufficient certainty that the price of the goods was to be paid by C. B., the consignee, to the carrier.[4] In Bracegirdle *v.* Hincks,[5] the declaration stated that the defendant was indebted to the plaintiff for the carriage of goods, and it was held that that statement was not supported by proof that the defendant undertook to carry goods for the plaintiff in consideration that the plaintiff would carry a like quantity for the defendant.

We have of course already, in other parts of this work, dealt with the allegations which are admissible, and the evidence which is necessary to support them in the various actions which may be brought against carriers. One cannot allude to the decision in any case without indirectly alluding to the pleadings and the indirect decision upon them. We, of course, do not in this place propose to deal systematically with the whole question, but purpose to supply such information as may, when taken in conjunction with other

[1] Pozzi *v.* Shipton, 8 Ad. & El. 963; Bowman *v.* Brown, 3 Q. B. 510.

[2] 2 Moore, 18; 8 Taunt. 144; Holt, 643. But see Mayor *v.* Humphries, 1 C. & P. 251.

[3] Butt *v.* Great Western Rail. Co., 11 C. B. 140; 20 L. J. C. P. 241.

[4] Jacobs *v.* Nelson, 3 Taunt. 423.

[5] 9 Exch. 361; 18 Jur. 70; 23 L. J. Exch. 128.

parts of this treatise, form a complete guide in all matters touching the validity of declarations and pleas. One or two cases may be alluded to with this view.

SEC. 633. **Terms in Ticket, Part of Contract.** — In the case of Shaw *v.* The York and North Midland Railway Company,[1] the declaration, which was in case, alleged that the defendants were proprietors of a railway and of carriages for the conveyance of passengers, cattle, goods, &c., for reward; that the plaintiff delivered to them, and they received from him, a horse of plaintiff's, to be "safely and securely" carried by them upon their railway, and to be safely and securely delivered to the plaintiff at a place mentioned, for reward. It averred that thereupon it was their duty "safely and securely" to convey and deliver the horse as aforesaid, yet that defendants did not use due care about its conveyance, but so negligently conducted themselves therein that, by reason of the defective state of the carriage in which the horse was conveyed, it was killed. It appeared at the trial that a receipt was given to the plaintiff for the amount paid at the time the horse was received, at the foot of which receipt was written,— "N.B. This ticket is issued subject to the owner's undertaking all risks of consequence whatsoever, as the company will not be responsible for any injury or damage (however caused) occurring to horses or carriages while travelling, or in loading or unloading." It was held that the terms of the memorandum formed part of the contract for the conveyance of the horse, and that they disproved the alleged duty of the defendants "safely and securely" to carry and convey. In delivering the opinion of the court, LORD DENMAN, C. J., said: "It appears to us to be clear that the terms contained in the ticket given to the plaintiff at the time the horses were received, formed part of the contract for the carriage of the horses between the plaintiff and the defendants, and that the allegation in the declaration that the defendants received the horses *to be safely and securely carried by them*, which would throw the risk of conveyance upon the defendants, is disproved by the memorandum at the foot of the ticket, and the alleged duty of

[1] 13 Q. B. 347; 6 Rail. Cas. 78; 18 L. J. Q. B. 181.

the defendants safely and securely to carry does not arise from such a contract.

"It may be that, notwithstanding the terms of the contract, the plaintiff might have alleged that it was the duty of the defendants to have furnished proper and sufficient carriages, and that the loss happened from a breach of that duty; but the plaintiff has not so declared, but has alleged a duty which does not arise upon the contract as it appeared in evidence."

SEC. 634. **Limitation of Liability always to be considered. — Qualified and Unqualified Contract.** — This decision indicates the importance of considering the whole subject of the limitation of the responsibility of carriers, and the consequent modification of the contract entered into by persons delivering goods to them to be carried, in connection with this branch of the subject. When any such modification of the duty or liability of a common carrier is introduced by contract, it will, as the above case shows, be fatal to declare, as if no such modification had been introduced. Another case which explicates the same doctrine may be mentioned here, — that is the case of Austin *v.* The Manchester, Sheffield, and Lincolnshire Railway Company,[1] already repeatedly referred to. In that case the declaration alleged that the defendants were proprietors of a railway and carriages for the conveyance of passengers, cattle, &c., for hire; that the plaintiff delivered to them and they received horses from the plaintiff, to be carried for the plaintiff in their carriages for reward; and that one of the wheels of a carriage in which some of the horses were being conveyed caught fire from friction; that the plaintiff at the next station requested the defendants to change such carriage, and not to persist further in conveying his horses in the same; that in spite of such request they did so persist; that the wheel afterwards, from want of precaution against friction, and not otherwise, was snapped asunder, whereby the carriage was thrown off the rails, and the horses were injured. It appeared that the plaintiff, at the time of agreeing for the carriage of the horses, was informed by the station-master that he would have to run all risks of carriage, to which he as-

[1] 16 Q. B. 600; 20 L. J. Q. B. 440; 15 Jur. 670.

sented; and he also signed a ticket in a book of the company, which contained a memorandum that the owner of the horses was to be required to see to the efficiency of the carriages; that the company was not to be responsible for any alleged defects in their carriages or trucks, unless complaint was made at the time of booking, or before leaving the station, nor for any damage, however caused, to horses, &c., travelling upon the railway. It was held that, whether the declaration was founded upon the common-law liability of the defendants as carriers, or upon a special contract, there was a variance; in the former case, because there was proof of a special contract; in the latter case, because the declaration alleged an unqualified contract to carry, whereas the contract proved was to carry, the defendants not being answerable for certain risks; that the allegation traversed by the plea was a material allegation, as the extent of the defendant's liability depended upon the nature of the bailment to them; and that an allegation of a delivery to be carried was equivalent to an allegation of a delivery to be safely and securely carried, subject to such exceptions as the law will create.[1]

SEC. 635. **Reasonable Time.** — In an action against a carrier, the declaration alleged that the plaintiff delivered goods to him to be carried for hire from London to Birmingham, and there to be delivered, and that it became his duty safely and securely to carry and deliver the goods at Birmingham, and that a reasonable time for so doing had elapsed, but that he did not safely or securely carry or deliver the same, but so negligently conducted himself that the goods became wholly lost to the plaintiff. TINDAL, C. J., in considering the two questions, — first, as to the defendant's duty, and second, as to the breach of that duty, — said: "It was not denied that if the action had been brought for the total loss of the parcel, and the evidence has shown that it had *never* been delivered, the plaintiff would have been entitled to recover upon the declaration as now framed; and if so, then it necessarily fol-

[1] See also White *v.* Great Western Rail. Co., 2 C. B. N. S. 7; and Simons *v.* Great Western Rail. Co., 2 C. B. N. S. 620; and see *ante*, ch. vii. p. 190; Kimball *v.* Rutland & Burlington R. R. Co., 26 Vt. 247.

lows that the evidence given as to the contract and duty of the defendants would prove the *duty* as laid. Neither could it be denied that if it had been alleged to be the defendant's duty to deliver within a reasonable time, the same evidence would have been sufficient to support the allegation, the duty to deliver within a reasonable time being merely a term engrafted by legal implication upon a promise or duty to deliver generally. No valid objection therefore exists to the proof of the duty as alleged. Whether such allegation would have been good upon special demurrer, if the only breach had been the non-delivery within a reasonable time, is another question, not material to our present inquiry. But it is said no such breach is alleged in this declaration, and yet that is the only breach supported by the evidence. But we think that the breach in this declaration may be read as, in effect, stating that the defendants did not within a reasonable time, or at any time afterwards, deliver the goods to the plaintiff, but that by the defendants' negligence they became wholly lost to the plaintiff. And if the breach had been so in form, it would have been sufficient for the plaintiff to prove so much of the breach as would support his right of action; and as the onus of proving the delivery would rest upon the defendants, unless they proved a delivery within a reasonable time, the plaintiff's right of action, and, consequently, the breach alleged, would be established."[1]

SEC. 636. **Breach of Implied Duty sufficient Declaration.** — In an action against a cab proprietor, the declaration stated that the plaintiff hired the vehicle, and that, in consideration of the premises, and that the plaintiff, with his luggage, would become a passenger, and of certain reward, the defendant promised the plaintiff to carry and convey him and his luggage safely and securely, and alleged a loss of part of the luggage by the negligence of the defendant's servants. Under these circumstances it was held that the declaration was sufficient to charge the defendant for a breach of his implied duty to use an ordinary degree of care, the words "safely

[1] Raphael *v.* Pickford, 5 M. & G. 551; 6 Scott, N. R. 478; 12 L. J. C. P. 176. See Levene *v.* Great Western Rail. Co., 18 L. T. N. S. 295.

and securely" not necessarily importing a more extended liability. In delivering his judgment, TINDAL, C. J., said: "In the present case any express promise is out of the question, from the circumstances out of which this action arose; and we have therefore to consider whether any implied promise, such as is alleged in the declaration, arose out of the contract there stated.

SEC. 637. **The Words "safely and securely."**—"Perhaps, if we look at the words 'safely and securely,' according to their strict meaning they do not state the promise which the defendant has impliedly made; but the question is, whether they may not be modified according to the relation of the parties as it appears in the declaration, and I think they may. First, there is a long series of precedents, where the duty is laid wider than would be proper unless this sense is given to the words; and we must, therefore, suppose that the law has sanctioned this mode of laying the declaration, though it may be wider in its apparent meaning than the actual breach of the duty alleged. Thus, to take an example from the precedents which have been cited, we see that, in an action against a party for not taking care of his fire, the words *salvo et securé* are used, though the law only imposed a duty of properly keeping a fire;[1] so, for improperly craining goods, one cannot suppose that in that case a formal agreement was previously made, and yet the words used are, '*Salvo et securé absque damno proprietarii cranare.*'[2] One can only infer, therefore, from the general observance that we are to look to the words with relation to the parties as they appear before us. In the present case the party was a cabman, and I think the words mean 'safely and securely, with reference to the care which the law imposes upon him liability for.' If the party had been a common carrier, then the words would have been absolute, except the act of God or the king's enemies. If, on the other hand, the party were a gratuitous bailee, then a less degree of care and caution would be required, so that the way in which the words are to be construed is safely and securely, with reference to the duty imposed."[3]

[1] See also Cliff's Entries, p. 39.

[2] Rastall's Entries, 3 *b*.

[3] Rose *v*. Hill, 15 L. J. C. P. 182, 185; 2 C. B. 877; 3 D. & L. 788.

SEC. 638. **Termini to be correctly stated.** — As we remarked above,[1] the termini must be correctly stated in the declaration.[2] But an averment of a contract to carry goods from London to Bath is sufficiently supported by evidence of a contract to carry from Westminster to Bath; for if the evidence as to the termini substantially supports the allegation in the declaration, and is not inconsistent with it, there is no variance, and therefore no fatality. Where a plaintiff alleged that the defendant having agreed to convey her safely by his coach from London to Blackheath, neglected his duty by permitting the horses to move on while she was getting up, whereby she was thrown down and injured, it was held to be no variance that the defendant's coach ran from Charing Cross to Blackheath, and that the plaintiff got up at the Elephant and Castle; though the defendant had inscribed on his coach "London to Blackheath."[3] In another case the declaration stated that the plaintiff delivered a trunk to the defendant to be put into a coach at Chester, in the county of Chester; to wit, at, &c., and safely to be carried to Shrewsbury, and that through the defendant's negligence it was lost. It appeared at the trial that the trunk was delivered to the defendant at the city of Chester, which is a county of itself, separate from the county of Chester at large, but within its ambit; and it was held that that was not a material variance, but that the declaration was supported by the evidence, as no evidence was given of any other place called "Chester."[4]

SEC. 639. **Pleas. — Non assumpsit. — Not Guilty.** — The distinction between an action on the case for tort and an action of assumpsit against a carrier, is made more clear in relation to the pleas, — the general issue in the former case being "not guilty," and in the latter *non assumpsit*. The New Pleading Rules, Hilary Term, 1853, r. 6, determines that "In

See Harris *v.* Costard, 1 C. & P. 636; Beauchamp *v.* Powley, 1 M. & R. 38. See also Dudley *v.* Smith, 1 Camp. 167; Brind *v.* Dale, 8 C. & P. 207; and Cairns *v.* Robins, 8 M. & W. 258; 10 L. J. Exch. 452.

[1] *Ante*, p. 629.

[2] Hayman *v.* Raymond, 5 Taunt. 289; Tucker *v.* Cracklin, 2 Stark. 385.

[3] Ditcham *v.* Chivis, 4 Bing. 706.

[4] Woodward *v.* Booth, 7 B. & C. 301; St. Louis, &c. R. R. Co. *v.* Thomas, 47 Ill. 116.

all actions on simple contract, except as hereinafter excepted, the plea of *non assumpsit*, or a plea traversing the contract or agreement alleged in the declaration, shall operate only as a denial of the express contract, promise, or agreement alleged, or of the matters of fact from which the contract, promise, or agreement alleged may be implied by law; *ex. gr.*: —

"In actions against carriers and other bailees for not delivering, or not keeping goods safe, or not returning them on request, such plea will operate as a denial of any express or implied contract to the effect alleged in the declaration, but not of the breach."[1] The 16th rule declares that "in actions for torts the plea of not guilty shall operate as a denial only of the breach of duty, or wrongful act alleged to have been committed by the defendant, and not of the facts stated by the inducement; and no other defence than such denial shall be admissible under that plea. All other pleas in denial shall take issue on some particular matter of fact alleged in the declaration, *ex. gr.*: —

SEC. 640. **Plea of Not Guilty.** — "In actions against a carrier, the plea of not guilty will operate as a denial of the loss or damage, but not of the receipt of the goods by the defendant as a carrier for hire, or of the purpose for which they were received." In Webb *v.* Page,[2] which was an action for negligence against a carrier, it was held that it was not competent to him, under not guilty, to set up as a defence that the plaintiff misrepresented the weight of the goods which the defendant agreed to carry, the plea operating only as a denial of the loss or damage, and not of the receipt of the goods by the defendant, who ought either to plead the misrepresentation specially, or traverse the acceptance of the goods for the purpose of being carried.

SEC. 641. **Rule in Wyld v. Pickford.** — The holdings in the case of Wyld *v.* Pickford[3] throw some light on this sub-

[1] Reg. Gen. Q. B. C. P. and Exch. T. T. 16 Vict. r. 6; 1 El. & Bl. App. lxxix.; M'Connico *v.* Stallworth, 43 Ala. 389; M'Gavock *v.* Puryear, 6 Coldw. (Tenn.) 34.

[2] 1 Scott, N. R. 971; 6 M. & G. 196; 1 D. & L. 531. See Hoyt *v.* Allen, 2 Hill (N. Y.), 322.

[3] 8 M. & W. 443.

ject. The defendants were carriers, and one of the counts in the declaration stated delivery to them of a case containing maps to be carried, and alleged a receipt by them, whereby it became their duty to take due and proper care, but that they did not take due and proper care of them, whereby the maps were lost. A second count was in trover. Plea, to the first count, that, at the delivery of the case and its contents, the defendants were common carriers for hire, and gave notice to the plaintiff, who had notice and knowledge that they would not be responsible for the loss of or damage done to goods and chattels delivered to them for the purpose of carriage, and maps in packages, or otherwise, unless the same were insured according to their value, and paid for at the time of their delivery; that they received the case and maps to be carried upon the terms and conditions of the notice, and upon no other terms whatsoever, of which the plaintiff at the delivery had notice; and that the maps were not, at the delivery, insured according to their value, or paid for. To the count in trover there was a similar plea, alleging the conversion to have been by a misdelivery through a mistake and inadvertence. It was held, first, that the action being founded on a breach of duty *ex contractu*, the allegation in plea of a special contract was sufficient, and that, as the defendants accepted the goods only on the terms of the notice, a special averment of the plaintiff's consent was unnecessary; secondly, that the plea was not an argumentative traverse of the facts in the declaration, from which the breach of duty was implied; thirdly, that, as the declaration might apply to any kind of negligence, it was not necessary to allege in the plea that the loss was occasioned by such negligence as the defendants were not responsible for; and that, if they had committed negligence for which they were liable, notwithstanding their notice, the plaintiff should have new assigned it; fourthly, that the plea to the count in trover could not be supported, inasmuch as it admitted a conversion by inadvertent delivery, and did not show that the inadvertence was such as was protected by the notice.

SEC. 642. **Common-Law Procedure Act, 1852. — Misleading**

Clause. — As to the general issue it may be well to notice a section of the "Common-Law Procedure Act, 1852,"[1] which, as a learned author remarks, is calculated to mislead.[2]

The 74th section of that act, after reciting that "certain causes of action may be considered to partake of the character both of breaches of contract and of wrongs," that "doubts may arise as to the form of pleas in such actions," and that "it is expedient to preclude such doubts," goes on to enact that "any plea which shall be good in substance shall not be objectionable on the ground of its treating the declaration either as framed for a breach of contract or for a wrong." "It may naturally be inferred from this language," remarks the same writer, "that if an action be brought against a carrier for the loss of a parcel, and the declaration be so framed as not clearly to show whether the plaintiff is complaining of a breach of contract or of a tort, the defendant will be equally safe in pleading *non assumpsit*, or not guilty, and that the pleas, though differing in form, will be regarded as substantially setting up the same defence. The fact, however, is quite otherwise, for while the plea of *non assumpsit* will put in issue the promise and admit the breach, the plea of not guilty will admit the bailment and deny the breach. This is obviously a result never contemplated by the framer of the clause in question."[3]

SEC. 643. **What may be proved under General Issue.** — So we see that, in an action on contract against a carrier for negligence in conveying the goods, the defendant may prove under the general issue that the goods were received by him on an express condition that the plaintiff should accompany them for the purpose of protection, and that he neglected to do so, in consequence of which the goods were lost; because such evidence, showing that the promise was conditional, goes to negative the unqualified promise alleged in the declaration.[4]

[1] 15 & 16 Vict. c. 76, § 74.

[2] Taylor on Evidence, 5th ed., p. 321, vol. i.

[3] *Ibid.* vol. i. § 283.

[4] Brind *v.* Dale, 2 M. & W. 775, recognized by TINDAL, C. J., in Webb *v.* Page, 6 M. & J. 202. See also Mounsey *v.* Perrott, 2 Exch. 522; Nash *v.* Breeze, 11 M. & W. 352; Whitaker *v.* Mason, 2 Bing. N. C. 359; Wade *v.* Simeon, 2 C. B. 548, 561.

Under *non assumpsit* the defendant cannot raise a defence under the Carriers' Act. Thus, in an action against a carrier for the loss of a parcel of more than 10*l.* value, it was held that, in order to avail himself of the want of notice of value, he must plead it specially.[1]

SEC. 644. — **What may amount to General Issue.** — It is, however, to be remembered that a plea which does not consist of matter of excuse may amount to the general issue without the use of the formal words, "not guilty." In Elwell *v.* The Grand Junction Railway Company,[2] the declaration was in case for the loss of goods delivered to the company as common carriers, to be safely and securely carried and conveyed. The defendants pleaded that at the time of such delivery the plaintiff became and was a passenger by the railway, and that the goods were delivered to be conveyed with him as such passenger, and that no part thereof was an article of clothing of the plaintiff. To this plea there was a replication *de injuriâ*. On special demurrer it was held that the replication was ill, as the plea did not consist of matter of excuse, but amounted to the general issue, being an argumentative traverse, that goods were delivered to the defendants as common carriers. Where a declaration alleged that the defendants were common carriers of passengers from Southampton to Gibraltar, a place beyond the seas, a plea that they were not common carriers of passengers only puts in issue the fact of the defendants carrying passengers from Southampton to Gibraltar for hire, and not whether they were common carriers in the strict technical sense of the term, and liable as such accordingly to the custom of England.[3]

SEC. 645. **What amounts to Argumentative Traverse of Bailment.** — Again, where a declaration alleged that the defendants were common carriers of goods for hire, and that the plaintiff delivered to them as such common carriers a package to be

[1] Syms *v.* Chaplin, 5 D. P. C. 429; 5 A. & E. 634. This case was decided prior to Hilary Term 1853; but the new Rules do not alter the law as to carriers. See Levene *v.* Great Western Rail. Co., 18 L. T. N. S. 295.

[2] 5 M. & W. 669; 8 D. P. C. 225.

[3] Bennett *v.* Peninsular & Oriental Steamboat Co., 6 D. & L. 387; 6 C. B. 775; 18 L. J. C. P. 85.

carried by them to the Euston Station, and there to be safely and securely kept by them for the plaintiff, and that it became the duty of the defendants safely and securely to carry and keep the package; breach, that the defendants did not safely and securely carry the same, but that through their negligence it was lost. It was pleaded that the defendants gave notice to the plaintiff that they would not carry any package containing several packages, addressed to and intended for several parties, unless the addresses and contents of the enclosed packages were declared, and that they would not be responsible for such packages unless such declaration were made that each of the packages in question contained several parcels addressed to and intended for different parties, and that the addresses and contents of the enclosed parcels were declared. On demurrer it was held that the plea amounted to an argumentative traverse of the bailment stated in the declaration.[1]

SEC. 646. **Admission of Allegation.**—In Benson *v.* Davison,[2] the declaration was in assumpsit, and stated that the defendants were the owners of a vessel lying in a certain river, and bound to Liverpool; that the plaintiff caused to be shipped on board her a quantity of potatoes, to be safely carried by the defendants, as owners of the said vessel, to Liverpool, and in consideration thereof, and of certain freight, the defendants promised the plaintiff to take proper care of, and safely carry the said goods as aforesaid, with a breach that through the defendants' negligence they were damaged. The defendants pleaded *non assumpserunt*, and it was held that the ownership of the defendants was not admitted by the plea; PARKE, B., remarking: "It is not necessary to say more than this as to the effect of an admission on the record, that, at all events, the taking issue on one fact averred in the declaration is only an admission of the other *material* averments necessary to be proved. Taking it that here there is an admission of the material allegations, there is no admission of the allegation of ownership, because that is perfectly immaterial. The declara-

[1] Crouch *v.* London & North-Western Rail. Co., 7 Exch. 705; 21 L. J. Exch. 207.

[2] 3 M. & W. 179; 1 H. & H. 46.

tion would be good if that, as well as the other allegations, that the defendant received the goods to be safely carried as aforesaid, were struck out; the statement that, in consideration that the defendants had shipped goods on board the vessel, and of the freight, the defendants promised safely to carry them, is quite sufficient, coupled with the allegation that the goods were not safely carried, to make a complete case of liability against the defendants. The admission on the record, then, being only an admission of material averments, not of all immaterial statements which the pleader chooses to introduce, there is no admission here that the defendants were owners, so as to raise the inference that the captain was their agent. The fact in issue upon the plea of *non assumpserunt* is, whether any such contract as alleged was made; and the plaintiff must prove that it was, by showing that the defendants made it themselves, or, if the captain made it, that he was their agent."

To a declaration on a contract by a bill of lading, by a master of a vessel, to convey goods from Dublin to London, and to deliver the same at the port of London, to the plaintiff or his assigns, a plea that, after the arrival of the vessel at London, the defendant caused the goods to be deposited on a wharf, being a place where goods from Dublin were accustomed to be landed, and fit and proper for such purposes, and that before a reasonable time for delivery elapsed they were destroyed by fire, which broke out there by accident, was held ill. The defendants were to be regarded as responsible, both for taking care of the goods at the wharf and for carrying the goods from the wharf; inasmuch as both these duties formed a part of the same express contract, and are paid for by the same reward, and the master, during the whole of the time while the goods are in his possession, is under the obligation of a common carrier. It is, therefore, to be concluded as certain, that such a plea would be no answer to the loss of the goods by fire at the wharf; a common carrier being liable for every loss except those arising from the act of God and the public enemy.[1]

[1] Gatliffe *v.* Bourne, 4 Bing. N. C. 314.

SEC. 647. **Inevitable Accident.** — Where an inevitable accident would be an excuse, and a railway company relies upon it as a defence, all the facts which, in the contention of the company, constitute such inevitable accident, must be brought out.[1] In one case a passenger by a railway, as to which notice had been given that no merchandise would be carried as luggage, but must be paid for, took a box of merchandise with him as luggage, and after a guard had, in the course of the journey, demanded and taken away the box, with the purpose of carrying it separately, from the passenger, but without demanding an extra rate, it was stolen by some of the company's servants. The passenger sued the company, and alleged that the company undertook to carry safely, and that by reason of gross neglect it was lost. The defendants pleaded that the case contained merchandise, and that the passenger had not paid for it as such, though he knew the rule. The replication was, that the box manifestly contained merchandise, and yet was received as luggage. It was held that, assuming the declaration showed a good cause of action in tort, the plea answered it.[2]

SEC. 648. **Replications.** — In the same case the replication which we have set forth above was held to be bad for not averring that the company had notice that the box contained merchandise,[2] which brings us by an easy transition to another matter, which must be considered in connection with the subject of pleading, and concerning which we shall say very little in this place. In the case of Butt *v.* The Great Western Railway Company,[3] which was an action against the defendant company for the loss of a package intrusted to them to carry, subject to the terms of a special notice by the company not to be responsible for articles of certain descriptions, or of a certain value, unless entered and paid for accordingly, the declaration alleging a loss arising from gross negligence of the company, and the felonious acts of their servants, the com-

[1] Burns *v.* Cork & Bandon Rail. Co., 13 Ir. C. L. R. 543 Exch.; Evans *v.* Hutton, 4 M. & G. 954.

[2] Belfast & Ballymena Rail. Co. *v.* Keys, 9 W. R. 793; 4 L. T. N. S. 841; 9 H. L. Cas. 556; 8 Jur. N. S. 367.

[3] 11 C. B. 140; 20 L. J. C. P. 241.

pany pleaded (except as to so much of the declaration as alleged that the loss arose from the gross negligence of the company, and the felonious acts of their servants), that the goods were within the description, and of the value mentioned in the notice, and that their nature and value were not declared at the time of their delivery to the company. The plaintiff newly assigned that he issued his writ and declaration thereupon; for that, while the goods were in the custody and possession of the company as common carriers, they were feloniously stolen by certain servants of the company unknown to the plaintiff. In this case it was held that the new assignment was bad, as applying to a portion of the declaration to which the plea was not addressed, and further, that the replication of felony by the company's servants only, without alleging gross negligence upon the part of the company, would have been bad.

In another case, to a declaration against carriers for the loss of a trunk, containing articles of jewelry and female apparel, they pleaded, as to articles of jewelry, one of the dresses, &c., that the goods consisted of articles and property of the descriptions following, or of some or one of such descriptions, that is to say, gold or silver in a manufactured or unmanufactured state, &c. (enumerating the several articles mentioned in the Carriers' Act, 11 Geo. IV. and 1 Will. IV. c. 68), and that their value exceeded 10*l.*; that, at the time of the receipt of the goods by them, they had only affixed the notice required by section 2; and that the plaintiff gave them no notice of the nature or value of the goods, nor did she pay or tender the increased rate of charge demandable under the act. Upon special demurrer, it was held that the plea was bad for not alleging with certainty that the articles in question were of some one of the descriptions mentioned in the act; WILDE, C. J., remarking that "it was too uncertain," and that "it ought to have been more specific."[1]

SEC. 649. **Evidence.** — Whether the action be founded in tort or assumpsit, it is necessary, in an action against a carrier, to prove three things: 1st. A contract implied or ex-

[1] Smith *v.* London, Brighton, & South Coast Rail. Co., 7 C. B. 782.

pressed; 2d. The delivery of the goods to the carrier; and 3d. The defendant's breach of duty or promise. Of these, then, in their order. So much has already been incidentally said upon this subject, that a full explanation would only be a recapitulation. As that is to be avoided, we may say shortly that, when it appears in evidence that the defendant is a common carrier, the plaintiff will generally rely upon an implied promise; for, as we have seen in the case of common carriers, the law makes the implication perfectly definite and specific by the duties and liabilities it imposes, and the restrictions and limitations it allows.

SEC. 650. **Evidence of Occupation as Common Carrier. — Terms of Contract. — Implied Contract.** — We have already considered what evidence proves a man to be a common carrier, in answering the question who are to be regarded as such.[1] Where, however, the defendant is not a common carrier, it is of course necessary to prove what the terms of the contract by which he undertook to carry were.[2] By that contract his duties and liabilities are to be determined. Even although he may not be a common carrier, the contract may be implied only and not expressed, in which case it is necessary to prove the circumstances from which the implication of the contract arises, and circumstances which will indicate, as nearly as possible, the precise nature of the contract thus understood. Thus, where A., by parol, made arrangement with a railway company to convey cattle for him to K. station, and he, at the same time, without noticing its contents, signed a consignment note, by which the cattle were directed to be

[1] Brind *v.* Dale, 2 M. & Rob. 80; 8 C. & P. 207; Palmer *v.* Grand Junction Rail. Co., 4 M. & W. 744; Ingate *v.* Christie, 3 C. & K. 61; Walker *v.* Jackson, 10 M. & W. 161; Willoughby *v.* Horridge, 12 C. B. 751; Oxlade *v.* North-Eastern Rail. Co., 9 W. R. 272; Ross *v.* Hill, 2 C. B. 877; White *v.* Humphrey, 11 Q. B. 43; Dale *v.* Hall, 1 Wils. 28; Whalley *v.* Wray, 3 Esp. 74; Richardson *v.* Sewell, 2 Smith, 205; Trent Navigation Co. *v.* Wood, 3 Esp. 127; Goff *v.* Clinkard, 1 Wils. 282; Maving *v.* Todd, 1 Stark. 72; Ansell *v.* Waterhouse, 2 Chit. 1; Barton *v.* Hanson, 2 Taunt. 49; Wayland *v.* Elkins, Holt, 227; Smith *v.* Taylor, 2 Chit. 142; Fremont *v.* Coupland, 9 Moore, 319; Helsby *v.* Mears, 8 D. & R. 289; Wooley *v.* Batte, 2 C. & P. 417.

[2] See M'Millan *v.* Michigan Southern Rail. Co., 15 Mich. 79.

taken to E., an intermediate station on the line to K., it was held that the parol evidence was admissible to show that the company agreed to carry on the cattle to K., as it did not contradict, but only supplemented the written contract.[1] In Thompson *v.* Travis,[2] which was an action against the defendant, a carrier, for negligence in the conveyance of goods by water, whereby they were wetted and spoiled, it appeared that the goods were put on board under one entire contract, for their conveyance from Boston to Leeds; one half to be delivered there, the other to be conveyed and delivered at Bradford. At the trial, the plaintiff proved the contract and its execution by oral testimony; but it appeared from the examination of one of the witnesses, that, at the time of the receipt of the goods by the carrier, two notes were delivered by him to the plaintiff (each applying to a moiety of the goods), which ascertained the destination of the goods, and the terms upon which they were to be carried. Only one of these was produced at the trial, and the absence of the other was not satisfactorily accounted for; it was held that that was ground for a nonsuit. It is not, as we have already seen, necessary to aver or prove a readiness to pay the hire unless it be traversed.[3]

SEC. 651. **Of Delivery to Defendant.** — The acceptance of goods by a carrier, for the purpose of forwarding them at once, raises his responsibility with regard to them, and it is not necessary, when the question as to whether he was responsible or not arises, to prove any special agreement as to reward. With regard to this question, also, much has been anticipated. However, we may add in this place that, in an action against a carrier, it will be sufficient to prove delivery to a duly authorized agent; thus, in one case — an action for the loss of a parcel — it was held to be sufficient to bind the

[1] Malpas *v.* London & South-Western Rail. Co., 1 L. R. C. P. 336; 35 L. J. C. P. 166; 1 H. & R. 227.

[2] 8 Scott, 85. See also, as to the evidence of ownership and contract, Barford *v.* Nelson, 1 B. & Ald. 571; Woodward *v.* Booth, 7 B. & C. 301; Detcham *v.* Chivis, 1 M. & P. 735; 4 Bing. 706; Beckford *v.* Crutwell, 1 M. & R. 187; 5 C. & P. 242.

[3] Wyld *v.* Pickford, 8 M. & W. 443.

owner of the coach to prove the delivery of the parcel to the driver.[1]

SEC. 652. **Delivery on Wharf to Officer.** — So a delivery of goods on the wharf to some officer accredited for that purpose, as to the mate, will bind the ship-owner.[2] If the master of a ship receives goods at the quay or beach, or sends his boat for them, the receipt of the goods at once makes the ship-owner responsible.[3] This presumption, however, may be disproved by the proof that the owner of the goods did not intend to trust the owner of the ship with the custody, which will be inferred from the fact that he sent his own servant along with the goods, and placed him in charge of them.[4] In one case the only proof of delivery was that the goods had been left at the yard of the inn at which the defendant and other carriers were in the habit of putting up, and that was held to be insufficient.[5] And in a case somewhat analogous to that just referred to, it appeared in evidence that goods had been left piled up on a wharf amongst other goods, but that no communication had been made to any one; it was held that such evidence was not sufficient to prove constructive delivery to the wharfinger.[6] In an American case already referred to,[7] where it appeared that the goods were delivered to an express forwarder, and that he delivered them over to a steamboat company, who acted as common carriers, to be transported, this evidence was held to support an action brought directly against the latter, with whom the contract was to be deemed to have been made through the agency of the express forwarder, the contract with the steamboat company being ratified by the owner of the goods, by his bringing an action against them.[8]

[1] Williams v. Cranston, 2 Stark. 82; Citizens' Bank v. Nantucket Steamboat Co., 2 Story (U. S. C. C.), 16.

[2] Coblau v. Downe, 5 Esp. 41; British Columbia, &c. Co. v. Nettleship, 3 L. R. C. P. 499.

[3] Abbott on Ship., 10th ed., p. 258; citing Molloy, b. 2, c. 2, § 2.

[4] East India Co. v. Pullen, 1 Stra. 690.

[5] Selway v. Holloway, 1 Ld. Raym. 46.

[6] Buckman v. Levi, 3 Camp. 414.

[7] *Ante*, p. 507.

[8] New Jersey Steam Navigation Co. v. Merchants' Bank, 6 How. (U. S.) 344.

SEC. 653. **Ordinary Course of Business.** — Where the ordinary course of business at a railway office was to accept goods, with a special limitation of liability in writing, and this was known to the plaintiff, who nevertheless caused his goods to be left with a railway porter at the station, without complying with the regular course, and the porter received them and they were lost, it was held that the company was not liable as on contract, the delivery not being in due course, and the porter not being shown to have, or to have professed to have, power to contract with the plaintiff, otherwise than in the ordinary course.[1]

SEC. 654. **Production of Books by Defendants.** — It is scarcely necessary to add, what must be very obvious, that with a view to the proof of delivery, notice should be given to the defendant to produce his book of entries and way-bill, if any; and the circumstances under which the box was delivered, as to the way in which it was packed, secured, and addressed, may, in many cases, be of importance. Much, however, in all such cases, must be left to the didactic nature of the facts of the individual case. They, to any ordinary intelligence, are not without guidance as to the method by which it will be most expedient to deal with them.[2]

SEC. 655. **Proof of Loss.** — In the case of Cullen *v.* M'Alpine,[3] to which we have already had occasion to refer, which was an action against the master of a ship for not safely conveying goods to a foreign port, evidence that the goods were seized in another foreign port by the government, coupled with a letter of the defendant's, in which he acknowledged that he was accountable for the goods, was held sufficient evidence to warrant the jury in finding for the plaintiff without further proof of the cause of seizure. In the case of Mayhew *v.* Nelson,[4] in which the question was whether hat bodies, which are made partly of the soft substance taken from the

[1] Slim *v.* Great Northern Rail. Co., 14 C. B. 647; 23 L. J. C. P. 166.

[2] As to receipts given at the time of delivery, see M'Cotter *v.* Hooker, 8 N. Y. 497; Sandford *v.* Housatonic, 11 Cush. (Mass.) 155.

[3] 2 Stark. 553.

[4] 5 C. & P. 58. See also Tompkins *v.* Saltmarsh, 14 S. & R. (Penn.) 275; Beardslee *v.* Richardson, 11 Wend. (N. Y.) 25.

skin of rabbits and partly from the wool of sheep, came under the description of furs in the Carriers' Act (11 Geo. IV. and 1 Will. IV. c. 68), it was proved that inquiry had been made of the coachman, the servant of the defendants, as to what had become of the parcel, for the loss of which the action was brought, and his reply was that he understood it had been lost. This answer was held by TINDAL, C. J., to be evidence.

SEC. 656. **General Rule as to the Admissibility of Servants' Evidence.** — The general rule as to the admissibility of the evidence of agents and servants is, however, that it should be excluded. Any person who has a direct interest in the event of the suit is apt to be to some extent corrupted by such interest, and *Male verum examinat omnis corruptis judex.* The law upon this matter is clearly stated in MR. STARKIE'S work upon Evidence. "So where," he remarks, after speaking of the right to share or liability to contribute, "the issue involved any breach of duty or default in respect of which the witness would be liable over to the party calling him. Such a witness, for whichever party called, was obviously interested in protecting himself against the consequence of failure by procuring a verdict to pass for the party that called him. Although guilty of misconduct, the record would conclusively show that the party calling him had received no prejudice so far as that cause was concerned. If called for the defendant, he would also be interested in obtaining a verdict for him, and to exclude a record which would be evidence against himself as to the amount of consequential damage in an action afterwards brought against him by his party." Where the party employed was the actual agent who transacted the business of the principal, he was competent on the score of necessity;[1] but although an agent who actually executed the business of the principal was in all cases competent to prove that he acted according to the directions of his principal on the ground of necessity, and because the principal could never maintain an

[1] Adams *v.* Davis, 3 Esp. c. 48; Matthews *v.* Haydon, 2 Esp. c. 509; Spencer *v.* Goulding, Peake's C. 129; Barker *v.* Macrae, 3 Camp. 144; R. N. P. 289; and see Ilderton *v.* Atkinson, 7 T. R. 480; Evans *v.* Williams, 7 T. R. 481, n.; Theobald *v.* Treggott, 11 Mod. 261.

action against his agent for acting according to his own directions, whatever might be the result of the cause,[1] yet, if the cause depended upon the question whether the agent had been guilty of some tortious act, or some negligence in the course of executing the orders of the principal, and in respect of which he would be liable over to the principal if he failed in his action, the agent was not competent without a release.[2]

SEC. 657. **Rule in Hawkins v. Finlayson.** — So in the case of Hawkins *v.* Finlayson,[3] which was an action against the captain and owner of a steam vessel for an injury resulting from the improper management of the vessel, it was decided that if it appear that the pilot had the control, such pilot is not a competent witness for the defendant, although the defendant himself was on board at the time; and in another case, a guard, who was implicated in a like mismanagement of a stage-coach, was held an incompetent witness in an action against the proprietor.[4]

SEC. 658. **Burden of Proof.** — As to the burden of proof, it will, of course, in most cases lie on the plaintiff, although this rule may seem in contravention of that which declares the inexpediency of demanding proof of a negative.[5] This latter rule is founded upon the wisdom of experience, but at the same time it admits of many and great exceptions. Thus, in the case of carriers, where an action is brought for the non-delivery or loss of goods, the plaintiff must give some proof of his allegation.[6] Under some circumstances, however, the law removes the burden of proof from the plaintiff to the defendant by a presumption against the carrier, and in favor of the person who deals with him. Thus, if a public conveyance is overturned or breaks down without apparent cause,

[1] Morish *v.* Foote, 8 Taunt. 454. See the observations of MANSFIELD, C. J., in De Symonds *v.* De la Cour, 2 N. R. 374.

[2] Rother *v.* Elton, Peake's C. 84; Miller *v.* Falconer, 1 Camp. 251; Starkie on Evidence, 4th ed., p. 121.

[3] 3 C. & P. 305. See also Green v. The New River Co., 4 T. R. 589.

[4] Whitamore *v.* Waterhouse, 4 C. & P. 383; and see Morish *v.* Foote, 2 Moore, 508; 8 Taunt. 454; Bailey *v.* Shaw, 24 N. H. 297; The Peytona, 2 Curt. (U. S. C. C.) 21.

[5] Baltimore, &c. R. R. Co. *v.* Schumacher, 29 Md. 168.

[6] Tucker *v.* Cracklin, 2 Stark. 385.

the law implies negligence, and consequently it falls upon the owners to rebut this presumption.[1] A loss, too, by private theft is presumptive evidence of ordinary neglect.[2]

SEC. 659. **In Action against Common Carrier. — Proof in "Assumpsit" and in "Case."** — Where the action is brought against a common carrier, the burden of proof is upon him to show, if he can, that the loss was occasioned by the act of God or of the Queen's enemies.[3] The evidence, where the action is in case, differs from that which is necessary when it is in assumpsit. In the latter it is sufficient to prove delivery,[4] or, at most, a very meagre proof of loss, as proof that the goods were not in the parcel at the time that it was delivered to the consignee,[5] or that he or his agents have heard nothing of them,[6] will suffice; in the former it is necessary to show that the property did not safely reach its destination.

SEC. 660. **Non-delivery within Reasonable Time, Proof of.** — In case the action is in assumpsit, the proof may also be of non-delivery within a reasonable time.[7] In the case of Hawkes *v.* Smith,[8] in which it appeared that 69 tons of bones were put on board the plaintiff's vessel, and that at the end of the voyage there were not 69 tons, but a much smaller weight, ROLFE, B.,

[1] Christie *v.* Griggs, 2 Camp. 79; and see M'Kinney *v.* Neil, 1 M'Lean (U. S.), 540; Stokes *v.* Saltonstall, 13 Pet. (U. S.) 181. See also U. S. Act of July 7, 1838, § 313; 5 Stat. at Large, 306; The New World *v.* King, 16 How. (U. S.) 469; Levering *v.* Union Transportation, &c. Co., 42 Mo. 88.

[2] Jones on Bailm. 38, 40, 66, 77, 109; but see Story on Bailm. § 39; and see Mackenzie *v.* Cox, 9 C. P. 632. See also Mobile, &c. R. R. Co. *v.* Jarvoe, 41 Ala. 644.

[3] The Martha, Olc. (U. S.) 140; Merriman *v.* The May Queen, 1 Newb. (U. S.) 464; Soule *v.* Rodocanachi, 1 Newb. (U. S.) 504; Clark *v.* Barnwell, 12 How. (U. S.) 272; Rich *v.* Lambert, 12 How. (U. S.) 347; Hunt *v.* Cleveland, 1 Newb. (U. S.) 221; Turner *v.* The Black Warrior, 1 M'All. (U. S.) 181; Bearse *v.* Ropes, Sprague (U. S.), 331; The Emma Johnson, Sprague (U. S.), 527; Nelson *v.* Woodruff, 1 Black (U. S.), 156, 160; King *v.* Shepherd, 3 Story (U. S. C. C.), 349.

[4] Tucker *v.* Cracklin, 2 Stark. 385; Day *v.* Ridley, 16 Vt. 48.

[5] Crouch *v.* Loudon & North-Western Rail. Co, 2 C. & K. 789. See Woodbury *v.* Frink, 14 Ill. 279; M'Questen *v.* Sanford, 40 Me. 117.

[6] Griffiths *v.* Lee, 1 C. & P. 110; 1 Sm. L. Ca. 103.

[7] Raphael *v.* Pickford, 5 M. & G. 551; Pickford *v.* Grand Junction Rail. Co., 12 M. & W. 766.

[8] 1 C. & M. 72.

said: "I think this is evidence from which the jury may infer negligence, and that if there is no negligence on the part of the defendant, he should show that." That action was in assumpsit. But in the case of Gilbert *v.* Dale,[1] it was held that, in an action on the case against a booking-office keeper for the loss of a parcel by negligence, it was not sufficient evidence of negligence to show that the parcel was delivered to the defendant, and that it had not reached its destination. In that case PATTESON, J., remarked: "Let us look at what the contract with the defendant is. The defendant is not a carrier; he is the keeper of a booking-office, and his contract with the plaintiff is to take care of those goods left with him, that they may be forwarded to their destination, either by coach or by some carrier; in other words, his contract is to deliver them to some carrier, in order that they may be forwarded. Now the contract of a carrier is to deliver to the consignee, and Griffiths *v.* Lee[2] is very good authority to show that the non-delivery to the consignee is sufficient evidence of negligence against the carrier, for *his* contract is to deliver the goods."

SEC. 661. **Contracts.** — This leads us to remark that there are many cases in which common carriers limit or qualify their liability and responsibility in relation to the goods of their customers by notice, which notice may affect the terms of the contract in various directions, as, for instance, as to non-liability as an insurer, or as to non-liability for articles above a certain value, or as to non-liability unless the contents of packed parcels be made known, and the like. Such notice may reduce the responsibility of the carrier (not a railway or a canal carrier) from that which was imposed upon him by the common law, if it is brought to the knowledge of the person intrusting the goods to him, to that of a private carrier for hire.[3] This point has been amply dwelt upon. When that is the case, then the contract which is entered into is not the same as that entered into in the case of a common

[1] 1 Nev. & P. 22.

[2] 1 C. & P. 110.

[3] Merriman *v.* The May Queen, 1 Newb. (U. S. C. C.) 464; Hunt *v.* Cleveland, 1 Newb. (U. S. C. C.) 221; Turner *v.* The Black Warrior, 1 M'All. (U. S. C. C.) 181.

carrier; and in relation to the evidence which will be necessary to support an action against a carrier thus trading with a limited liability, it becomes necessary to consider, as in the last case quoted, what that contract really is. As we have seen that, in the case of a common carrier for hire, the law does not presume negligence in case of loss of or injury to the goods in his possession, it is evident that, in such a case, the burden of proof will be upon the plaintiff, who would recover.[1] At the same time, several burdens lie upon the defendant, and these are, first, of proving that he had issued such a general notice, and, secondly, that it had come to the knowledge of the plaintiff,—these two with the view of showing that his common carrierhood had been abandoned, by consent, in relation to that individual transaction.

SEC. 662. **As to Value of Lost Goods.** — Presumptions are most valuable things in law. They are as useful in law as hypotheses are in science. In determining the value of the goods lost or damaged, great difficulty might be expected to arise. If an individual sent a box, the contents of which are known only to himself, and that box is lost, it is evident that his evidence, which would be the only direct evidence obtainable on the point, might, in many cases, be most unfairly prejudicial to the carrier, to whom the box had been bailed. The law has to take for granted the existence of dishonest people, and it is obvious that the owner of the box might, feeling himself protected from discovery by the ignorance of the defendants, make a statement as to the value of the contents, far in excess of the fact of value.[2] Such a fraud would do away with all the advantages of the system, as it at present exists, of insurance in connection with carriage, and with the legitimate right which a proprietor of goods has to receive them or their value, if the return of the specific goods is impossible, at the end of the bailment. But the law has protected carriers against this possible injustice by one of its presump-

[1] Merriman *v.* The May Queen, 1 Newb. (U. S. C. C.) 464; Hunt *v.* Cleveland, 1 Newb. (U. S. C. C.) 221; Turner *v.* The Black Warrior, 1 M'All. (U. S. C. C.) 187.

[2] As to evidence of amount of damage, see Eames *v.* Cavarock, 1 Newb. (U. S. C. C.) 528.

tions. It presumes that the owner of the goods will exaggerate their value, and therefore raises the legal probability that he has made a demand in excess of his right, and makes him clearly prove his demand by precise evidence. But, under some circumstances, this might be a hardship to the plaintiff, and if there were not some countervailing presumption, it would inevitably become so. Thus, if the presumption was always against the owner of the goods, dishonest carriers would be tempted to act fraudulently, to profit by the advantage they would gain by paying, on a low estimate, what was, in fact, perhaps worth much more than had been allowed for it. To guard against this, the law has said that this presumption against the owner of the goods shall arise only where there has been perfect good faith upon the part of the carrier. And in case there is any evidence of fraud upon his part, the presumption shall be in favor of the accuracy of the plaintiff's demand.[1] In this way alone can the minimum of injustice be attained in such cases; and that, it seems to us, is all that the laws attempt to attain, or, at least, can possibly arrive at. In the case of Butler *v.* Basing,[2] in which the amount of damages to be paid to a plaintiff as proprietor of a box which had been lost by the defendant, a stage-wagoner, was in question, GARROW, B., in summing up, said: "With regard to the amount of damages in case a verdict passes for the plaintiff, it is right that I should tell you that there is no distinct evidence as to the contents of the box; however, I should recommend you not to pare down the amount of damages, because the articles contained in it cannot be distinctly proved. It very often happens that persons, more especially those in the station in life in which the plaintiff is, pack their own clothes, and in such cases it must be always impossible to give evidence of the precise contents of the boxes or portmanteaus. I should therefore recommend you, if you find for the plaintiff, to give damages proportioned to the value of the articles which, in your judgment, you think the box might and did fairly contain."[3]

[1] See Clunnes *v.* Pezzay, 1 Camp. 8; and Armory *v.* Delamire, 1 Strange, 505. See also Thompson *v.* Traves, 8 Scott, 85. See also Manning *v.* Hoover, Abb. Adm. (U. S.) 188; Bailey *v.* Shaw, 24 N. H. 297.

[2] 2 C. & P. 613.

[3] See also 1 Bell's Commentaries,

SEC. 663. **Disqualification of Witness.** — It has been held that the old rule, that interest in the result of the cause in the *record* as an instrument of evidence would disqualify a person from being a witness in a suit,[1] must from the necessity of the case be excepted to in some cases, such as that which we have just referred to. Indeed, as one writer observes, the rule has become a pure matter of legal history. So that there is no longer any reason to exclude the evidence of the owner as to the contents of a box, if the result is guarded by the presumption to which we have alluded above.[2]

SEC. 664. **Evidence for Carrier in Non Assumpsit.** — We have considered the evidence which is necessary to support a claim against a carrier, but it is of some importance to say what evidence it is necessary for a carrier to produce in *non assumpsit.* Of course, in treating of the evidence which an owner of goods must rely upon in an action against a carrier, we have really at the same time, although indirectly, considered the evidence which will not support his claim, and the evidence which will rebut certain presumptions at law. But it seems expedient to collect one or two of the rules applicable to this subject in one place and under one head. Thus, under *non assumpsit*, the carrier may show that he is not a carrier, that he neither expressly nor impliedly undertook to carry; but it is scarcely necessary to add that he cannot, under that plea, prove delivery to the consignee, or otherwise traverse the breach.[3] Again, where he pleads any defence under the Carriers' Act, or other special matter, he must prove all his substantial averments.[4] He is also entitled to give evidence in reduction of damages.

6th ed., p. 164. See also as to presumption of good condition of goods sent by owner, Terega *v.* Poppe, Abb. Adm. (U. S.) 397; The Columbo, 3 Blatchf. (U. S.) 521. As to proof of condition, see Kerr *v.* The Norman, 1 Newb. (U. S.) 525; Dill *v.* The South Carolina R. R. Co., 7 Rich. (S. C.) 158.

[1] See Starkie on Evid., 4th ed., p. 118; Best's Principles of Evid., 5th ed., p. 199.

[2] 14 & 15 Vict. c. 99, § 2.

[3] Reg. Gen. H. T. 16 Vict.

[4] *Ibid.* r. 8, 17. See Sauquer *v.* London & South-Western Rail. Co., 16 C. B. 163. See Sedgwick on Damages, 4th ed., p. 402. See also Jackson *v.* The Julia Smith, 6 M'Lean (U. S. C. C.), 404: Jackson *v.* The Juliana, 1 Newb. (U. S.) Adm. 61; O'Connor *v.* Foster, 10 Watts (Penn.). 418; Ogden *v.* Marshall, 8 N. Y. 340; Arthur *v.*

SEC. 665. **Under General Issue.** — A carrier, under the general issue of not guilty, may rebut by evidence the loss or damage, but cannot disprove the receipt of the goods.[1] Where negligence is the ground of the plaintiff's action, the defendant may, under the general issue, prove any facts or circumstances which will disprove the negligence.[2] But the justification, by means of proving contributory negligence upon the part of the plaintiff, cannot be shown under the general issue, but must be specially pleaded.[3] Again, under not guilty, a carrier may prove an actual or constructive delivery.[4] In an action against a railway company for negligence in forwarding goods, where they lost a market, the declaration alleged that the defendants were common carriers, and received the goods in question, to be carried by them as such common carriers for hire and reward, and the plea traversed the averment that the defendants received the goods as common carriers; this plea was held to be proved by evidence that the defendants did not receive goods to be carried by them as common carriers, unless the consignor signed a paper of conditions which the court thought reasonable.[5]

SEC. 666. **Damages.** — We come now to the consideration of almost the last subject which it is necessary for us to consider in relation to actions brought against carriers in relation to their traffic in goods, and that is the measure of damages.[6] In all cases it is necessary to find some standard by which the amount of damages to be paid is to be determined, and the most obvious criterion is of course the amount of injury suffered. But although this seems a very obvious conclusion, it cannot be accepted in its entirety without much explanation. Thus, in many cases, it would be difficult or almost impossible to discover the actual amount of the injury sustained, either by reason of a refusal to carry, or by the loss of goods by a

The Schooner Cassius, 2 Story (U. S.), 81; The Flash, 1 Abb. Adm. (U. S.) 119.

[1] Reg. Gen. H. T. 16 Vict.

[2] Carpue *v.* London & Brighton Rail. Co., 5 Q. B. 747.

[3] Webb *v.* Page, 6 M. & G. 196; Great Northern Rail. Co. *v.* Harrison, 10 Exch. 376; 23 L. J. Exch. 308.

[4] Hyde *v.* Trent & Mersey Navigation Co., 5 T. R. 389.

[5] White *v.* Great Western Rail. Co., 2 C. B. N. S. 7; 26 L. J. C. P. 158.

[6] See Pothier, Traité des Obligations, pt. i. c. 2, § 159.

carrier after they have been placed in his care and keeping. But we will speak of the question of damages in relation to these two matters separately.

SEC. 667. **Damages for refusing to carry. — When Nominal.** — If a carrier refuses to carry goods that are brought to him for the purpose of being carried, an action, we have seen, will lie against him at the instance of the owner of the goods, and the damages to be assessed will be regulated by the amount of damages actually and necessarily incurred.[1] If the freighter could not procure any other ship, the damages would be measured by the injury suffered from having his cargo left on his hands. But, as we shall have occasion to see, in connection with the leading case upon this subject, the damages suffered must be such as the contracting parties were led to contemplate.[2] If another ship was procurable, the damages would be measured by the increased rate of freight payable, and if such freight was in fact less than that contracted for, the damages would be merely nominal for breach of contract. In such a case the plaintiff has really little to complain of.

SEC. 668. **Injuries must be Direct Consequences of Breach.** — In all cases, however, it is to be remembered the injuries complained of must be the necessary and immediate consequences of the breach. It is constantly the custom of people to ascribe stupendous results to some very insignificant circumstance. As a long line of kings may come from a puny progenitor, so the loss of a certain market might lead to results which would only terminate in the ruin of a family or a trade. No one can compute the consequences of any one event. The remote consequences of some trivial circumstance may be catastrophic. But, as that is the case, the law has very properly limited the damages done, which are to form the standard of the measure of damages to be paid, to those which necessarily and immediately arise from the breach.[3]

[1] Hunter *v.* Fry, 2 B. & A. 421, 427; Walton *v.* Fothergill, 7 C. & P. 392. See rule, in case of refusal to carry passengers, The Zenobia, Abb. Adm. (U. S.) 80; Porter *v.* Steamboat New England, 17 Mo. 290.

[2] Hadley *v.* Baxendale, 9 Exch. 341.

[3] See Medbury *v.* New York & Erie R. R. Co., 26 Barb. (N. Y.) 564.

Were such not the case, the result would be deplorable. The laws, in attempting to do too much, would do too little,—in attempting to do perfect justice, would fall short of all equity.

SEC. 669. **Illustration.**—The rule of law is that stated above. A case will illustrate this rule. A ship's husband covenanted to load brandy on board a ship and proceed with it to Madeira, and the merchant covenanted to pay for it there, and load it with a full cargo home. The merchant arranged at Madeira to barter the brandy, which he expected, for fruit, which was to form the cargo. The ship's husband sued and recovered against him for not supplying cargo. He then sued the ship's husband for not bringing the brandy, laying as special damage that, by reason of his not doing so, plaintiff had been unable to procure a return cargo, and in this way he claimed to recover the amount paid in the former action and its costs. It was held that such damage was too remote, and TINDAL, C. J., said: "If I contract to transfer stock and do not, the party with whom I contracted has no right to tell me a month afterwards that, if I had transferred the stock, he could have bought an estate with the money. There was a case of a man who brought an action against the keeper of a ferry-boat for refusing to carry him across a river, in consequence of which he sustained a loss by not being able to keep an appointment. But it was held that he could not recover damages on any such ground."[1]

SEC. 670. **Effect of Notice in Cases of Special Damage.**—In all cases of special damage it is of importance to discover whether or not there was any notice upon the part of the owner as to the effect that might result from his breach of contract, to ascertain the exact nature of such notice, and the fact of its having been brought to the knowledge of the carrier or not. In a case where the plaintiff sent goods by rail, which he intended to sell at Bedford market on Saturday, and which ought to have arrived in time for it, but did not give notice that they were sent for that purpose, it appeared that the

[1] Walton *v.* Fothergill, 7 C. & P. 394. See also Watson *v.* Ambergate Rail. Co., 15 Jur. 488.

plaintiff's clerk proceeded to Bedford upon the Saturday, and, owing to the non-delivery of the goods until the Monday following, he removed them to another place for sale; it was held in the action which was brought for the non-delivery of the goods within a reasonable time, that the expenses so incurred — that was, the expense of removal, together with the clerk's wages and expenses while absent on his duty — might be given by the jury as damages.[1] So, where R. sent goods from Manchester by railway to his traveller at Cardiff, and the delivery of the goods was, through the negligence of the company, delayed until the traveller had left Cardiff, and R. in consequence lost the profits which he would have derived from a sale at Cardiff, it was held that, in the absence of notice to the company of the object for which the goods were sent, R. could not recover from the company such profits as damages for the delay.[2]

SEC. 671. **Damages for Loss of or for Injury to Goods.** — As we said above, the rule that the value of the goods lost, or the amount by which the value is diminished by the injury, is to be the measure of damages, requires some explanation.[3] The value of goods varies, and the question at once arises as to whether it is the value of the goods at the time they were consigned to the carrier's custody, or at the time of the loss, or at the time that they ought to have been delivered, which is to be taken as the standard in computing the damages. The very fact that goods are sent from one place to another, the very existence of carriers proves that the value of goods varies from time to time, and in different places, and, at the same time, shows that the value of the goods will be greater at the

[1] Black *v.* Baxendale, 1 Exch. 410; and see Mayne on Damages, p. 154.

[2] Great Western Rail. Co. *v.* Redmayne, 1 L. R. C. P. 329; 35 L. J. C. P. 123. See also Hales *v.* London & North-Western Rail. Co., 4 B. & S. 66; Woodger *v.* Great Western Rail. Co., 2 L. R. C. P. 318; 36 L. J. C. P. 177.

[3] See Ludwig *v.* Mayer, 5 W. & S. (Penn.) 435; Hand *v.* Baynes, 4 Whart. (Penn.) 204; Segura *v.* Reed, 3 La. Ann. 695; Sherman *v.* Wells, 28 Barb. (N. Y.) 403; Hackett *v.* Boston, &c. R. R. Co, 35 N. H. 390; Laurent *v.* Vaughan, 30 Vt. 90; Worthen *v.* Wilmot, 30 Vt. 555; New Orleans, &c. R. R. Co. *v.* Moore, 40 Miss. 39; M'Gregor *v.* Kilgore, 6 Ohio, 358.

end of the transit than at the time they were received by the carrier. Goods are transported from place to place because of the greater requirements of the people in one town or country for particular goods at particular times. There is a greater demand in one place, at one time, for a certain kind of goods, and hence the price of that particular kind of goods is higher in that place at that time than it is in other places. Therefore, if the difference of prices is greater than the amount to be paid for the carriage of the goods between the two places, people will send their goods to the place where they can get the most money for them. Hence the goods have two values,—that of the time of starting, and that of the time of arriving. And it might come to be a question, in case of the loss of the goods during the transit, which of these was to determine the amount to be paid to the owner by the carrier. These facts show the necessity of a more definite rule as to the measure of damages than the one alluded to above, and it seems to be settled that it will be the value of the goods at the time that they were lost which will be the standard to go by, and that is to be looked at in relation to the price of the goods at the destination.[1] In an action against ship-owners for loss of goods, LORD ELLENBOROUGH said that the plaintiffs were entitled to recover the value of the goods on board at the time she was captured, by reason of the deviation. That, in the absence of other evidence as to the profit of the adventure, that value could not be taken at more than the cost price and shipping charges, and that the insurance premium could not be added, as no new value was given to the goods by insuring them.[2] Where the cargo was conveyed to its proper destination, and there handed over to a person who was not entitled to it, it was decided that the value at the port of discharge was the proper measure of damages. In that case PARKE, J., remarked: "The plaintiffs are entitled to be put in the same situation as they would have been if the cargo had been delivered to their order at the time it was delivered to B., and the sum it would have fetched at that time is the amount of

[1] Mercer v. Jones, 3 Camp. 477. [2] Parker v. Jones, 4 Camp. 112.

loss sustained by the non-performance of the defendants' contract." [1]

SEC. 672. **Distinction between Bailment for Carriage and for Safe Keeping.** — There is a distinction to be drawn between the rules of law applicable to bailees when the bailment is for the purpose of carriage, and to bailees when the goods are bailed simply with a view to safe custody. In the latter case the bailee is not answerable for any special or consequential damage arising to the bailor from the loss beyond the value of the goods, unless such a liability has been created in him by express contract. Thus, in the case of Henderson, or Anderson, *v.* North-Eastern Railway Company,[2] where the plaintiff, a commercial traveller, sued the company, as warehouseman, for the loss of a case of patterns, it was held that he was entitled to recover only the value of the case and of the patterns, and was not entitled to recover either salary or the expenses he had incurred while he was waiting for new patterns. In that case POLLOCK, C. B., said: "There is a great difference between a carrier and a warehouseman. Where a carrier is employed, it is known, and must be assumed, that the goods are going for some purpose, and so far it is notice which may render the carrier responsible for damages resulting from loss of the goods beyond their actual value, but the simply depositing a parcel at a warehouseman's till to-morrow, cannot be notice which shall affect the warehouseman in case of the loss of the parcel, beyond the actual value of the article." [3]

[1] Brandt *v.* Bowlby, 2 B. & Ad. 932, 939; Dusar *v.* Murgatroyd, 1 Wash. (U. S. C. C.) 13; The Gold Hunter, Blatchf. & How. (U. S.) 300; The Joshua Barker, Abb. Adm. (U. S.) 215; The Colonel Ledyard, Sprague (U. S.), 530; Spring *v.* Haskell, 4 Allen (Mass.), 112; Dean *v.* Vaccaro, 2 Head (Tenn.), 488; Louis *v.* Steamboat Buckeye, 1 Handy (Ohio), 150; Gillingham *v.* Dempsey, 12 S. & R. (Penn.) 183; Warden *v.* Greer, 6 Watts (Penn.), 424; Nourse *v.* Snow, 6 Me. 208; Sangamon, &c. *v.* Henry, 14 Ill. 146; Ringold *v.* Haven, 1 Cal. 108; Price *v.* The Steamship Uriel, 10 La. Ann. 412; Shaw *v.* South Carolina R. R. Co., 5 Rich. (S. C.) L. R. 462; Nettles *v.* South Carolina R. R. Co. 9 Rich. (S. C.) L. R. 462; Van Winkle *v.* The United States Mail Steamboat Co., 37 Barb. (N. Y.) 122; Bailey *v.* Shaw, 4 N. H. 297. See also two more recent cases, Rice *v.* Ontario Steamboat Co., 56 Barb. (N. Y.) 384; Rome R. R. Co. *v.* Sloan, 39 Ga. 636.

[2] 9 W. R. 519; 4 L. T. N. S. 216.

[3] 4 L. T. N. S. 216. See also Needles *v.* Howard, 1 E. D. S. (N. Y. C. P.) 54.

SEC. 673. **Distinction considered.** — With deference for the opinion of that learned judge we would submit that the distinction is possibly more apparent than real, and that he has been led into a fallacy by the pseudo attractiveness of extreme cases. It is true that, when goods are given to a carrier, he may understand that it is with a purpose that they are given to him, that he is to convey them to a certain place, and so convenience and benefit the sender of the goods. He may understand that the delivery of these goods at their destination will result in profit to the consignor, and, consequently, that he has in his possession, and under his care, goods of a value greater than that which attached to them when they were delivered to him. All this may, and rightly would be, held to be a kind of constructive notice which might, as the Chief Baron holds, render him responsible for the damages resulting to the goods beyond the actual value. But where goods are bailed to a warehouseman, may he not assume that they are so left "for some purpose"? — is that purpose not the convenience and benefit of the bailor? In what way do the cases differ? Warehousemen are not simple bailees who keep a parcel "until to-morrow;" they have the custody of goods for long periods, which are intrusted to them frequently with a view to the ultimate profit of the owner, by a rise in price of the particular kind of goods. As the owner who gives his goods to a carrier sends his supply to "demand" in *space*, so the owner who warehouses his goods is, as it were, sending his goods to "demand" in *time*. The warehouseman, as it were, transports the goods through weeks and months in safety, instead of over miles and leagues. That being the case, the distinction seems to us to be entirely arbitrary. To return, then, to the question of the measure of damages, we may allude to a matter already described, and that is, the presumption which exists in any case where it appears that the goods have been lost by the wrongful act of the carrier, that the goods lost are the best of their kind. In the case of Armory *v.* Delamerie,[1] which was an action in trover for a jewel, PRATT, C. J., directed the jury that, unless the defendant could

[1] 1 Strange, 505; 1 Sm. L. Ca. 256.

disprove that it was of the finest quality, they ought to presume it to be so, and that the measure of damages ought to be the value of such jewel.[1] Where the plaintiff is not himself the owner of the goods, but has only a qualified property in them, he will be entitled to recover their whole value from the carrier, if he is himself liable for their value to the owner, and it is not necessary that he should actually have paid the owner.[2]

SEC. 674. **Under the Carriers' Act.** — Before passing to the other cases which throw light upon the question of the measure of damages, it may be well to notice the law as to the loss of valuable goods under the Carriers' Act,[3] and the proof of value which is made necessary by that enactment. The 9th section of that act provides that "such mail-contractors, stage-coach proprietors, or other common carriers for hire, shall not be concluded as to the value of any such parcel or package by the value so declared as aforesaid, but that he or they shall in all cases be entitled to require from the party suing, in respect of any loss or injury, proof of the actual value of the contents by the ordinary legal evidence, and that the mail-contractors, stage-coach proprietors, or other common carriers as aforesaid, shall be liable to such damages only as shall be so proved as aforesaid, not exceeding the declared value, together with the increased charges as before mentioned." This reference is to the 7th section, which provides "that where any parcel or package shall have been delivered at any such office, and the value and contents declared as aforesaid, and the increased rate of charges been paid, and such parcels or packages shall have been lost or damaged, the party entitled to recover damages shall also be entitled to recover back such increased charges so paid, in addition to the value of such parcel or package."

SEC. 675. **Common-Law Rule.** — But this enactment has to do with a somewhat limited class of cases, and concerning the

[1] See also, per GARROW, B., in Butler *v.* Basing, 2 C. & P. 613.

[2] Crouch *v.* London & North-Western Rail. Co., 2 C. & K. 789; and see Sanquer *v.* London & South Coast Rail. Co., 16 C. B. 163.

[3] 11 Geo. IV. and 1 Will. IV. c. 68.

much larger class to which it does not refer, there is only the rule of law to which we have alluded above, *viz.* that the owner of goods is entitled to recover such damages from a carrier, through whose negligence his goods have been lost, as will compensate him not only for the actual value of the goods at the time when they left his hands, but also for the profits which he might have derived by their sale at their intended destination. At the same time the law will not allow compensation to be given for the consequential damages arising from the breach of contract, in so far as these are simply inconvenience and vexation to the plaintiff;[1] and, as we have seen, the carrier will be held responsible only for injuries which are proximate and direct consequences of the breach, and not for those which are remote and indirect.[2]

SEC. 676. **Consequential Damages.** — The leading case upon this subject is, as we have said, Hadley *v.* Baxendale.[3] The plaintiff in that case claimed damages from the defendant, a carrier, for a delay of several days in the delivery of some broken iron to the engineer who was to repair it. It appeared that the carrier had been informed, at the time the goods were delivered to him, that the pieces of iron formed the broken shaft of the plaintiff's mill, but notice did not appear to have been given that the mill could not be worked until the shaft should be returned. The plaintiff claimed compensation for the loss of the profits which he would have made by this mill if the shaft had been returned at the proper time. At the trial, the judge left the question of damages to the jury without any special direction, but the court above granted a new trial. In delivering the judgment of the court, ALDERSON, B., said: "We think the proper rule in such a case as the present is this: where two parties have made a contract which one of them has broken, the damages which the other party ought to receive in respect of such breach of contract should be such as may fairly and reasonably be considered either arising

[1] Hamlen *v.* Great Western Rail. Co., 1 H. & N. 408; 26 L. J. Exch. 22.

[2] Watson *v.* Ambergate, Nottingham, & Boston Rail. Co., 15 Jur. 448.

[3] 9 Exch. 341; 18 Jur. 358; 23 L. J. Exch. 179.

naturally, *i.e.* according to the usual course of things, from such breach of contract itself, or such as may reasonably be supposed to have been in the contemplation of both parties, at the time they made the contract, as the probable results of the breach of it. Now, if the special circumstances under which the contract was actually made were communicated by the plaintiff to the defendants, and thus known to both parties, the damages resulting from such a breach of contract, which they would reasonably contemplate, would be the amount of injury which would ordinarily follow from a breach of contract under these special circumstances so known and communicated. But, on the other hand, if these special circumstances were wholly unknown to the party breaking the contract, he, at the most, could only be supposed to have had in his contemplation the amount of injury which would arise generally, and, in the great multitude of cases, not affected by any circumstances from such a breach of contract. For had the special circumstances been known, the parties might specially have provided for the breach of contract by special terms as to the damages in that case; and of this advantage it would be very unjust to deprive them."

SEC. 677. **Consequences of Breach of Contract.** — His Lordship went on to point out that, in the case under consideration, the communication that the pieces of iron were the shaft of a mill did not reasonably show to the carrier that the profits of the mill must be stopped by an unreasonable delay in the delivery by the carrier. In conclusion, he remarked: "It follows, therefore, that the loss of profits here cannot be considered such a consequence of the breach of contract as could have been fairly and reasonably contemplated by both the parties when they made this contract. For such loss would neither have flowed naturally from the breach of this contract in the great multitude of such cases occurring under ordinary circumstances, nor were the special circumstances, which perhaps would have made it a reasonable and natural consequence of such breach of contract, communicated to or known by the defendants. The judge ought, therefore, to have told the jury that upon the facts then before them they ought not to take the loss of profits into consideration at all in estimating the damages."[1]

SEC. 678. **Average Percentage on Profits.** — Several cases have come before the courts of law in recent times in which the rule of law as to the measure of damages has been made still clearer. Some judges have thought that it might be fairer to allow an average percentage upon the mercantile profits,[2] or the average profits to be made by the use of the article,[3] as a measure of damages in any case in which goods have been lost by a carrier. But in the very case in which these opinions were expressed it was thought that in an action for non-delivery of a ship the damages were not too high, although they gave the difference between profits which the ship would have made if she had been duly delivered when freights were high, and the profits she earned when delivered some months later when freights were low.[4]

SEC. 679. **More Precise Rule necessary.** — Several of the recent cases are important in this connection, some of them indicating what is not the measure of damages, and others as clearly indicating what will in many cases be regarded as the legal standard or criterion. This is the more important, as it has been held by some of the judges that, "although a very excellent attempt was made in Hadley *v.* Baxendale to lay down a rule of practice, it has been found that the rule will not meet all cases," and that "it will probably be found, when

[1] See also Portman *v.* Middleton, 27 L. J. C. P. 231; Le Peinteur *v.* South-Eastern Rail. Co., 2 L. T. N. S. 170; Randal *v.* Roper, 28 L. J. Q. B. 266; Josling *v.* Irvine, 30 L. J. Exch. 78; Smeed *v.* Foord, 28 L. J. 178; Prior *v.* Wilson, 1 L. T. N. S. 549; Griffen *v.* Colver, 16 N. Y. 489; Hamilton *v.* M'Pherson, 28 N. Y. 72; Shepherd *v.* Milwaukee Gas Light Co., 15 Wis. 318; Hinckley *v.* Beckwith, 13 Wis. 31; Abbott *v.* Gatch, 13 Md. 314; Copper Co. *v.* Copper Mining Co., 33 Vt. 92; Ashe *v.* De Rossett, 5 Jones (N. C.), 299; Meade *v.* Rutledge, 11 Tex. 44; Baldwin *v.* Bennett, 4 Cal. 392; Cunningham *v.* Dorsey, 6 Cal. 19; Page *v.* Ford, 12 Ind. 46; Fessler *v.* Love, 43 Penn. St. 313; Adams Express Co. *v.* Egbert, 36 Penn. St. 360.

[2] JERVIS, C. J., in Fletcher *v.* Tayleur, 17 C. B. 27; 25 L. J. C. P. 66.

[3] WILLES, J., 17 C. B. 29; 25 L. J. C. P. 66.

[4] See also the suggestion of VICE-CHANCELLOR WOOD (LORD HATHERLEY), in De Mattos *v.* Gibson, 30 L. J. Chan. 145.

the matter comes to be more solemnly discussed, that in this, as in many other cases of contract, there is no measure of damages at all, and that we are seeking to find a rule where a rule cannot be made."[1]

SEC. 680. **Consequential Damages where not allowed.** — In the case in which the judicial opinion just quoted was expressed, and which in many respects resembled the case of Hadley *v.* Baxendale, the facts were these: The plaintiffs delivered to the Lancashire and Yorkshire Railway Company ten tons of cotton, to be carried from Liverpool to Oldham. In the usual course the cotton should have been received on the following day, but it did not, in fact, arrive till four days afterwards. In consequence of the delay a new mill of the plaintiffs' was stopped for want of cotton to go on with. It further appeared that at the time of the bailment to the company nothing was said as to the particular consequences likely to result from the delay in forwarding it. But on the day before it was delivered to the company, and repeatedly on each succeeding day until it arrived at Oldham, one of the plaintiffs called to inquire about it, and on each occasion told the manager of the goods department, at the Oldham Station, that the mill was at a stand solely on account of the non-delivery of the cotton. The plaintiffs brought an action against the company for neglect in delivering the cotton, and the plaintiffs proved that they had, during the time the mill was at a stand, paid in wages 7*l.*, and that the profit which would have been made, if the mill had been at work, was 7*l.* 10*s.* The judge of the county court told the jury, that where, by the neglect of a carrier, a man had no material to carry on his business, he had a right to charge as legal damages such loss as immediately and naturally arose from stopping the mill; that the plaintiffs were entitled to the money they had actually paid as wages, 7*l.*; and that the profit which the plaintiffs would have made was a fair subject of calculation, and the jury should therefore give, over and above the 7*l.*, such amount as would be the actual loss and detriment the plaintiffs had suffered by

[1] Per WILDE, B. (agreeing with MARTIN, B.), in Gee *v.* Lancashire & Yorkshire Rail. Co., 6 H. & N. 211; 30 L. J. Exch. 11.

the non-arrival of the cotton in due course. In the Court of Exchequer, however, it was held that this was a misdirection, and that the plaintiffs were not entitled to the amount of wages paid and of the profits lost as legal damages, inasmuch as it assumed that the stoppage of the mill arose entirely from the non-delivery of the cotton, when in fact it arose partly from that and partly from the plaintiffs having no cotton to go on with.[1]

SEC. 681. **Rule in Davis v. North-Western Railway Co.** — In a case where a party delivered, after paying the carriage, to a railway company, goods to be carried from A. to B., and to be delivered to a party at the latter place, part of the transit was effected by another railway company, which refused to deliver up the goods to the consignee without payment of an additional specified sum; but, an action having been threatened against the contracting company, an offer was made to deliver them up without that payment. The action was, however, persevered in, the plaintiffs declaring against the company as carriers with a count in trover for the conversion of the goods, subsequently to which they were given up in a damaged state. In this case it was held that the additional sum demanded for the goods was not the measure of damages.[2]

SEC. 682. **Rule in Simmons v. South-Eastern Railway Co.** — Again, in a case in which the plaintiff having sent a quantity of hops, of more than 10*l.* value, by a railway company, and the consignee refused to receive them on the ground of their not having been delivered in time, and afterwards sent to the plaintiff a signed memorandum of the original contract, it was held that in assessing the damages for negligence the jury was not at liberty to take into account the loss of the bargain between the plaintiff and the consignee.[3] In another analogous case goods were not delivered until after the season for them had passed, and it was held that the measure of damages was the difference between the market value of them at the

[1] See also Great Western Rail. Co. *v.* Redmayne, 1 L. R. C. P. 329.

[2] Davis *v.* North-Western Rail. Co., 4 Jur. N. S. 1303.

[3] Simmons *v.* South-Eastern Rail. Co., 7 Jur. N. S. 849.

time of delivery, and the time when they ought to have been delivered; and that the plaintiff could not include anything for the loss of the profits which he might have made by them if they had been delivered at the proper time and during the season.[1]

SEC. 683. **What will be the Measure of Damages.** — So much for the negative. Some cases, however, have positive indications of what may be regarded as the measure of damages. Thus, where the plaintiff, a hop-grower in Kent, sent by rail to London some pockets of hops, consigned to a purchaser, the railway company kept the hops for some days on their premises in an open van, whereby a small portion was stained by wet, and the purchaser rejected the whole, as he was entitled to do, by the custom of the market. The plaintiff dried the stained hops, and they were rendered as good as ever for actual use, but the staining had depreciated the market value of the bulk. The plaintiff sent the hops to a factor for sale, but at that time the market price of hops had fallen considerably from what it was at the time the hops ought to have been delivered. The company had no notice that the hops were sent to London for sale. It was held, under these circumstances, first, that the plaintiff was entitled to recover as damages the amount of the depreciation in the market value of the hops, and was not confined to the portion actually damaged; secondly, that he was entitled to recover as damages the difference between the market price on the day when the hops were sold and the day when they ought to have been delivered.[2] It is somewhat difficult to distinguish between these cases in the principle of their decision.

SEC. 684. **Where Test is Inapplicable.** — Where goods are intrusted to a carrier for conveyance, and lost by the way, the measure of damages is, as we have said, the market value of the goods at the place of destination at the time they should have been delivered.[3] If, however, this test is inapplicable by

[1] Wilson *v.* Lancashire & Yorkshire Rail. Co., 3 L. T. N. S. 859; 9 C. B. N. S. 632.

[2] Collard *v.* South-Eastern Rail. Co., 7 H. & N. 79; 30 L. J. Exch. 393.

[3] See *ante*, p. 660, and Rice *v.* Baxendale, 7 H. & N. 96; 3 L. J. Exch. 371.

reason of there being no market for goods of the description at the place of delivery, the jury, in assessing the damages, must ascertain the cost price of the goods and the expenses of transit (if paid), and add to these such a sum for importer's profits as may in their discretion appear reasonable.[1]

SEC. 685. **Measure the Amount that will replace.—Reasonable Compensation.**—In the case of The British Columbia Saw-Mill Company *v.* Nettleship,[2] the plaintiffs delivered to the defendant's servants, on a quay at Glasgow, for shipment on board the defendant's vessel, which lay alongside, several cases containing machinery, which was intended for the erection of a saw-mill in Vancouver's Island. The master gave a bill of lading for them, describing the cases as containing "merchandise." The defendant knew generally of what the shipment consisted. On the arrival of the vessel at her destination, one of the cases, which contained machinery without which the mill could not be erected, could not be found on board; and the plaintiffs were obliged to send to England to replace the lost articles. It was held that the measure of damages for the breach of contract was the cost of replacing the lost articles in Vancouver's Island, with interest at 5 per cent upon the amount, until judgment, by way of compensation for delay. BOVILL, C. J., said, "The extent of the carrier's liability is to be governed by the contract he has entered into, and the obligations which the law imposes upon him. He is not to be made liable for damages beyond what may fairly be presumed to have been contemplated by the parties at the time of entering into the contract. It must be something which could have been foreseen and reasonably expected, and to which he has assented expressly or impliedly by entering into the contract. The defendant admits that he was liable for the value of the articles which were lost. Beyond that, I think he is responsible for delay, as a consequence of his breach of duty. In considering the question of delay, and the principle upon which the damages for it are to be

[1] O'Hanlan *v.* Great Western Rail. Co., 6 B. & S. 484; 11 Jur. N. S. 797; 34 L. J. Q. B. 154.

[2] 3 L. R. C. P. 499; 18 L. T. N. S. 604.

assessed, many serious considerations arise. No stronger instance can be put than that of a failure of an engagement to pay acceptances at maturity. The non-payment may cause the destruction of the creditor's trade, and the debtor may know that inevitable ruin will be the result. And yet, what in that case is the measure of damages which the creditor is entitled to recover? Has it ever been held to be the actual amount of the damage sustained? Certainly not. The true measure is a reasonable compensation for the non-performance of the contract."[1]

SEC. 686. **Wider Liability.** — Yet, although there can be little doubt that that is the present rule of law, there have been many decisions in favor of a much wider liability, — a liability which made a defendant, on breach of contract, responsible in damages for the loss not only directly due to the breach, but for damage arising out of the plaintiff's inability to fulfil a contract which, but for the defendant's failure, he would in all probability have fulfilled.[2] This, however, is no longer the rule of law in reference to this matter, and the truth of the assertion can be amply gathered from the cases above.[3]

SEC. 687. **Contributory Damage.** — Two points are to be noted before leaving this subject. The first is, that contributory damage on the part of the plaintiff will discharge the liability of the defendant,[4] and that the plaintiff's claim to

[1] See also, per COCKBURN, C. J., in Corry v. Thames Ironworks Co., 3 L. R. Q. B. 181.

[2] Waters v. Towers, 8 Exch. 401; Dunlop v. Higgins, per LORD COTTENHAM, 1 H. of L. Cas. 403; Josling v. Irvine, 30 L. J. Exch. 78.

[3] See also Caledonian Rail. Co. v. Cole, 3 L. T. N. S. 252; Prior v. Wilson, 8 W. R. 260; Spark v. Heslop, 28 L. J. Q. B. 197; Dingle v. Hare, 29 L. J. C. P. 143; Mastreton v. Mayor of Brooklyn, 7 Hill (N. Y.), 62; New York & Harlem R. R. Co. v. Story, 6 Barb. (N. Y.) 419; Seaton v. Second Municipality, 3 La. Ann. 45; Shepherd v. Milwaukee Gas Light Co., 15 Wis. 318; Hinckley v. Beckwith, 13 Wis. 31; Story v. New York & Harlem R. R. Co., 6 N. Y. 85; Fox v. Harding, 7 Cush. (Mass.) 516; Philadelphia, &c. R. R. Co. v. Howard, 13 How. (U. S.) 307; Cook v. Commissioners of Hamilton, 6 M'Lean (U. S. C. C.), 612; Hay v. Gronoble, 34 Penn. St. 9; Chapin v. Norton, 6 M'Lean (U. S. C. C.), 500; Coweta Falls Manufacturing Co. v. Rogers, 19 Ga. 417.

[4] Davis v. London & North-Western Rail. Co., 7 W. R. 105; Emblen v. Myers, 30 L. J. Exch. 71.

damages will be measured materially by his ability to compensate himself. An omission to do so will reduce the damages; thus, where sold goods were not duly delivered, it was held that the vendee could recover only the difference between the contract price and the market price of them.[1]

SEC. 688. **Where the Damage arises out of Wrong.** — The other point is, that the principle which must guide the assessment of damages issuing out of wrong is not so strict as that which governs the same duty when the damage has arisen out of a breach of contract. It is a rule that for every breach of duty nominal damages, at least, must be given.[2] But as there is no certain measure of damages, the jury must be left to their common sense in the application of the above principle (that in Hadley *v.* Baxendale), and the court will not disturb their verdict.[3]

SEC. 689. **Exemplary and Vindictive Damages.** — Where, however, the wrong is of a malicious character, the jury may award exemplary or vindictive damages. Thus, if a railway company, with a view of obtaining a monopoly, or of injuring a rival company, refuse to carry goods which they are bound by law to carry, the jury will be directed to use their discretion in this matter.[4] The jury is entitled to take into consideration the injury to the party's feelings, and the pain he has experienced, — as, for instance, the amount of violence proved in an action of tort, and the like.[5]

SEC. 690. **Master's Duty with regard to Repair of Ship. — Indemnity.** — It is the master's first duty to convey the cargo to its destination in the same ship, and if the ship be damaged, it is his duty to repair it. To do this he is entitled, in cases of urgent necessity, to sell the cargo. If he does so, it raises an implied contract of indemnity from the owner, for whose

[1] Gainsford *v.* Carroll, 2 B. & C. 524.

[2] CROMPTON, J., Fray *v.* Vowles, 28 L. J. Q. B. 232.

[3] Day *v.* Holloway, 1 Jur. 794; Williams *v.* Currie, 1 C. B. 841.

[4] Crouch *v.* Great Northern Rail. Co., 25 L. J. Exch. 137; Bell *v.* Midland Counties Rail. Co., 4 L. T. N. S. 293. See also Goddard *v.* Grand Trunk Railway, 57 Me. 202.

[5] POLLOCK, C. B., in Hamlen *v.* Great Northern Rail. Co., 26 L. J. Exch. 20; cf. Robin *v.* Steward, 23 L. J. C. P. 148.

benefit the act was done, in favor of the shipper.[1] This implied contract raises the question, How are the goods to be valued for the purpose of this indemnity? Where the ship has arrived, there is no doubt that the owner is entitled to the amount which they would have fetched at the port of destination.[2] A doubt has arisen as to whether, in the event of the goods having been sold for a greater amount than they would have been worth if they had been delivered, the owner can claim the difference or not.[3] Where, however, the ship never reaches its destination, but has been lost since the sale, it seems certain that the goods cannot be taken at their price at a place which they never would have reached. It is a question in such a case whether the owner would be liable at all.[4] Certain Acts of Parliament restrict the liability of ship-owners for damages, and it is necessary that the reader should refer to these, at the same time bearing in mind that the principles applicable to carriers by water differ in no material particular from those already referred to.[5]

SEC. 691. **Actions against Passenger Carriers.** — Concerning this branch of our subject, we shall be enabled to speak with greater brevity than would have been consistent with our duties in relation to the last subject treated. Much that we have already said concerning the carriers of goods is equally applicable to carriers of persons. One or two points in which the law differs in respect to these two modes of traffic, or in respect of which we feel that enough has not been already said, must be referred to here.

SEC. 692. **Parties to sue.** — We have already examined and

[1] Benson *v.* Duncan, 1 Exch. 537; 2 Exch. 644.

[2] Alers *v.* Tobin, Abb. on Ship. 372; Hallet *v.* Wigram, 9 C. B. 580.

[3] Per LORD ELLENBOROUGH, in Campbell *v.* Thompson, 1 Stark. 490; and per HOLROYD, J., in Richardson *v.* Nourse, 3 B. & A. 237.

[4] Atkinson *v.* Stephens, 7 Exch. 567.

[5] 17 & 18 Vict. c. 104, §§ 503, 504. See also Morris *v.* Robinson, 3 B. & C. 196, 205; Abb. on Ship. 400; Wilson *v.* Dickson, 2 B. & A. 2; Brown *v.* Wilkinson, 5 M. & W. 391; *Ex parte* Rayne, 1 Q. B. 982; and see, as to small craft, Hunter *v.* M'Gowan, 1 Bligh, 508. See, as to the liability of ship-owners, 17 & 18 Vict. c. 110, § 388; but see Stuart *v.* Isemonger, 4 Moore, P. C. 11; Hammond *v.* Rogers, 7 Moore, P. C. 170; Rodringues *v.* Melhuish, 24 L. J. Exch. 26.

commented on a case in which a master brought an action against a railway company for the loss of his servant's services through their negligence, and in which it was held that, as the servant was injured, not by simple wrong, the action was founded on contract, and would not lie.

SEC. 693. **7 & 8 Vict. c. 85.** — By the 7 & 8 Vict. c. 85, § 6, as we have seen, railway companies are bound to carry, by certain trains, children under three years of age, without charge, and are entitled to half the fare charged for an adult in respect of all children between three and twelve years of age. The plaintiff's mother, carrying in her arms the plaintiff, a child of three years and two months old, took a ticket for herself by one of these trains on the defendants' railway, but did not take a ticket for the plaintiff.[1] In the course of the journey an accident occurred, through the negligence of the defendants, and the plaintiff was injured. It appeared that at the time the plaintiff's mother took her ticket, no question was asked by the defendants' servants as to the age of the child, and that there was no intention on the part of the mother to defraud the company, and it was held that the plaintiff was entitled to recover against the defendants for the injury he had received.[2]

SEC. 694. **Form of Action. — Advantages of different Forms.** — We have already entered somewhat fully into the question of the duties of the carriers of passengers, and have seen that, although they are not insurers, they are bound to carry all persons as passengers who offer to become such.[3] A non-performance of this duty is a breach of the law, for which an action will lie. In such a case the declaration would be in case. But we have also seen that it is a duty of a carrier, as well as an implied contract upon his part, to carry safely; and if he fails to do so in consequence of negligence or misconduct upon his own part, or upon that of his servants, he will

[1] Alton v. Midland Rail. Co., 19 C. B. N. S. 213; 34 L. J. C. P. 292.

[2] Austin v. Great Western Rail. Co., 3 L. R. Q. B. 442; 8 B. & S. 327; 36 L. J. Q. B. 201. As to who may sue under the Passengers' Act, 1855, see that act (18 & 19 Vict. c. 119, § 84).

[3] *Ante*, p. 507.

be liable to an action at the instance of the person injured, which may either be in assumpsit on the implied contract for safe conveyance, or in case, as for the tort.[1] These, as in the case of an action brought against a carrier of merchandise, have different advantages to recommend their adoption in different cases. Thus, if assumpsit is chosen as the form of action, to entitle the plaintiff to recover he must prove the liability of all the parties to be sued; but in action on the case against the defendants as the proprietors of a coach for injuries sustained by the plaintiff, a passenger, which was due to negligence, the jury found a verdict against eight of the defendants, and in favor of the other two, and judgment was entered accordingly.[2] If, however, although the action is framed in case, it is really founded on contract, such a verdict could not have been given. The plaintiff can, of course, only recover upon the grounds alleged in his declaration, and therefore, in a case already alluded to, in which a passenger brought an action for injury done to him by the overturning of a stage-coach, the declaration stated that the servants of the defendant "negligently drove, conducted, and managed the coach," and it appeared that the accident happened by reason of the insufficiency of the coach, it was held that the plaintiff could not recover.[3]

SEC. 695. **Advantage of Adoption of Assumpsit.** — Another advantage attaching to the adoption of the action in assumpsit in preference to an action on the case is, that it survives against the executor or administrator. The rule of law is, *actio personalis moritur cum personâ*, a personal right of action dies with the person, and this leads us to the legal fact, that all rights of action for injuries merely personal determine upon the death of the person who suffered the injury. The executor or administrator is only the representative of the temporal property of the deceased, but personal wrongs are not represented after death, unless they affect the personal estate in the hands of his representatives.[4] This principle

[1] Knight *v.* Quarles, 2 B. & B. 102.

[2] Brotherton *v.* Wood, 3 B. & B. 541.

[3] Per LITTLEDALE, J., in Mayor *v.* Humphries, 1 C. & P. 251.

[4] Knight *v.* Quarles, 2 B. & B. 102;

was at one time extended to the protection of those persons who, through negligence, caused the death of others, upon the seeming principle that the injury, death, had been suffered during the life of the individual. This rule of law was evidently of a most improper nature, for it subjected carriers and others who, through negligence, caused a temporary injury to any of their passengers, to an action for damages, while, if, through graver negligence, they caused the death of such persons, they were exempt from all legal penalty.[1]

SEC. 696. **Lord Campbell's Act, 9 & 10 Vict. c. 93.** — To remedy this, LORD CAMPBELL'S Act[2] was passed, which, after reciting that "no action at law is now maintainable against a person who, by his wrongful act, neglect, or default, may have caused the death of another person, and it is oftentimes right and expedient that the wrong-doer in such case should be answerable in damages for the injury so caused by him," enacts that, "wherever the death of a person shall be caused by wrongful act, neglect, or default, and the act, neglect, or default is such as would (if death had not ensued) have entitled the party injured to maintain an action and recover damages in respect thereof, then and in every such case the person who would have been liable if death had not ensued, shall be liable for an action for damages, notwithstanding the death of the person injured, and although the death shall have been caused under such circumstances as amount in law to felony."

SEC. 697. **Action to be brought in Executor's Name.** — The 2d section of the act provides that "every such action

Siboni *v.* Kirkman, 1 M. & W. 423; Baker *v.* Bolton, 1 Camp. 493; Hall *v.* Hollander, 4 B. & C. 660; Williams *v.* Holland, 6 C. & P. 23.

[1] In the Supreme Court of the State of Massachusetts, it has been held that no action lies where the death ensued instantaneously on the injury, on the ground that no right of action ever *accrued* to the deceased, and none consequently could survive to his representatives. Kearney *v.* Boston & Worcester R. R. Co., 9 Cush. (Mass.) 108. We should have thought that the time for such distinctions as that had passed away. But some lawyers prefer to make a puzzle of the law, and to make its principles trifling quiddities rather than broad and philosophical rules.

[2] 9 & 10 Vict. c. 93. See Illinois Act of 1853 considered, Conant & Griffin, 48 Ill. 410.

shall be for the benefit of the wife, husband, parent, and child of the person whose death shall have been so caused, and shall be brought by and in the name of the executor or administrator of the person deceased. And in every such action the jury may give such damages as they may think proportioned to the injury resulting from such death to the parties respectively for whom and for whose benefit such action shall be brought. And the amount so recovered, after deducting the costs not recovered from the defendant, shall be divided amongst the before-mentioned parties in such shares as the jury by their verdict shall find and direct."

SEC. 698. **Number of Actions, and Time within which it must be brought.** — The 3d section makes provision that "not more than one action shall lie for and in respect of the same subject-matter of complaint, and that every such action shall be commenced within twelve calendar months after the death of such deceased person."

SEC. 699. **Particulars of Person, &c., on whose Behalf Action is brought. — Interpretation Clause.** — By section 4, it is provided that "in every such action the plaintiff on the record shall be required, together with the declaration, to deliver to the defendant, or his attorney, a full particular of the person or persons for whom and on whose behalf such action shall be brought, and of the nature of the claim in respect of which damages shall be sought to be recovered." The 5th section enacts that "the following words and expressions are intended to have the meanings hereby assigned to them respectively, so far as such meanings are not excluded by the context or by the nature of the subject-matter; that is to say, words denoting the singular number are to be understood to apply also to a plurality of persons and things, and words denoting the masculine gender are to be understood to apply also to persons of the feminine gender; and the word 'person' to bodies politic and corporate, and 'parent' shall include father and mother, and grandfather and grandmother, and stepfather and stepmother, and the word 'child' shall include son and daughter, and grandson and granddaughter, and stepson and stepdaughter."

SEC. 700. **27 & 28 Vict. c. 95.** — This enactment was followed by the 27 & 28 Vict. c. 95, which by its 1st section provides that, "if and so often as it shall happen at any time or times in any of the cases intended and provided for by 9 & 10 Vict. c. 93, that there shall be no executor or administrator of the person deceased, or, there being such executor or administrator, no such action as in the said act mentioned shall, within six calendar months after the death of such deceased person, as therein mentioned, have been brought by and in the name of his or her executor or administrator, then and in every such case such action may be brought by and in the name or names of all or any of the persons (if more than one) for whose benefit such action would have been brought by and in the name of such executor or administrator, and every action so to be brought shall be for the benefit of the same person or persons, and shall be subject to the same regulations and procedure as nearly as may be, as if it were brought by and in the name of such executor or administrator." [1]

SEC. 701. **Payment of Money into Court.** — The 2d section provides that "it shall be sufficient, if the defendant is advised to pay the money into court, that he pay it as a compensation in one sum to all persons entitled under the said act, for his wrongful act, neglect, or default, without specifying the shares into which it is to be divided by the jury, and if the said sum be not accepted, and an issue is taken by the plaintiff as to its sufficiency, and the jury shall think the same sufficient, the defendant shall be entitled to the verdict upon the issue." [2]

[1] Statutes similar to the English act have been passed, and are in force, in many of the American States: Pennsylvania, Act April 26, 1855 (Laws 1555, p. 309); Iowa, R. S. 1860, p. 705, § 4111 (2500); Missouri, Gen. Stat. 1865, c. 147, p. 601; Illinois, Act Feb. 12, 1853; Laws (1862), p. 80; Ohio, R. S. (1860) p. 1139; Connecticut, Gen. Stat. tit. i. §§ 97, 98; Rhode Island, R. S. 1857, c. 176, § 21; Michigan, 2 Comp. Laws, 1857, c. 151; Wisconsin, R. S. 1858, c. 135, § 12.

[2] As to actions under the Passengers' Act, 1855, see that act, 18 & 19 Vict. c. 119, § 2. As to notice of action, venue, and general issue, § 92. See the act passed in Massachusetts (Act of 1840, c. 89). That statute enacts that, "if the life of any person, being a passenger, shall be lost by

In dealing with the answer to the question who may sue, under our present head, in actions against the carriers of passengers it would have been inexcusable to have omitted all mention of these important statutory enactments, and it is equally necessary to allude to some of the cases in which the expressions contained in the above clauses have received a more definite connotation, and, in doing so, we shall not confine ourselves strictly to cases in which carriers were defendants, as the question has not so much to do with the actual employment in connection with which the accident causing death occurred as with the negligence which was the cause of the accident.

SEC. 702. **Rule in Read v. The Great Eastern Railway Company.** — In one case, in which a mother sought reparation for the loss of her son from a master of the works whose default had been the cause of the accident, it was held that, as the mother had a legal claim on her son for support, and as it appeared that he actually was supporting her at the time of his death, her claim was valid.[1] But an illegitimate child is not within the contemplation of the statute, under section 2.[2] In the case of a husband suing for compensation on the death of his wife, occasioned by negligence, it is not necessary to disclose or allege in the declaration any pecuniary damage suffered by him beyond the mere claim of damages.[3] It has been held that in an action by the representatives of a deceased party the declaration need not negative the existence of any relations entitled to compensation other than those for

reason of the negligence or carelessness of the proprietor or proprietors of any railroad, steamboat, stage-coach, or of common carriers of passengers, or by the unfitness or gross negligence or carelessness of their servants or agents in this commonwealth, such proprietor or proprietors and common carriers shall be liable to a fine not exceeding five thousand dollars, nor less than five hundred dollars, to be recovered by indictment to the use of the executor or administrator of the deceased person for the benefit of his widow and heirs, one moiety thereof to go to the widow and the other to the children of the deceased; but if there shall be no children, the whole to the widow; and if no widow, to heirs, according to the law regulating the distribution of intestate personal estate among heirs."

[1] Weems *v.* Mathieson, 4 Macq. H. L. Cas. 215.

[2] Dickinson *v.* North-Eastern Rail. Co., 2 H. & C. 735; 33 L. J. Exch. 91.

[3] Chapman *v.* Rothwell, 27 L. J. Q. B. 315; 4 Jur. N. S. 1180. See Pennsylvania R. R. Co. *v.* Goodman, 62 Penn. St. 329.

whose benefit the action purports to be brought.[1] The case of Read *v.* The Great Eastern Railway Company[2] is of importance in indicating who may and who may not sue. There the declaration was by a widow against a railway company for negligence, whereby her husband, a passenger, was injured, and in consequence died. The company pleaded that in the lifetime of the deceased they had paid him, and he accepted a sum of money in satisfaction and discharge of all claims and causes of action which he had against them; and the court held that the plea was good, as the cause of action was the negligence of the company, which had been satisfied in the deceased's lifetime, and his death did not give a fresh cause of action to his widow.[3]

SEC. 703. **Persons to be sued.** — We have already said almost enough concerning this subject, but a few matters remain to be noted in this place. Some difficulty might be expected to arise in connection with passenger traffic on railway lines where one company has running powers over another company's lines; and the fact that there are decisions on the point proves that doubts must at one time have existed in certain minds as to the law applicable to such cases. Past doubts are paths to present certainties, and now it is clear that where a railway company has contracted with a passenger they are answerable for the negligence of another company over whose lines they have contracted to carry him;[4] and it has been held that, in the absence of evidence to the contrary, trains running over a particular line of railway are to be presumed to be the property of, or at any rate under the control of, the company to whom the line belongs, although other companies have running powers over the part of the line in question.[5]

[1] Barnes *v.* Ward, 9 C. B. 392; 2 C. & K. 661; 19 L. J. C. P. 194.

[2] 3 L. R. Q. B. 555; 16 W. R. 1040; 18 L. T. N. S. 82.

[3] See also Pym *v.* Great Northern Rail. Co., 4 B. & S 396; Franklin *v.* South-Eastern Rail. Co., 3 H. & N. 211; Dalton *v.* South-Eastern Rail. Co., 4 C. B. N. S. 296; Flinn *v.* Perkins, 32 L. J. Q. B. 10; Gellard *v.* Lancashire & Yorkshire Rail. Co., 12 L. T. N. S. 356.

[4] Great Western Rail. Co. *v.* Blake, 7 H. & N. 987; 31 L. J. Exch. 346; Buxton *v.* North-Eastern Rail. Co., 3 L. R. Q. B. 549; Thomas *v.* Rhymney Rail. Co., 5 L. R. Q. B. 226. See also John *v.* Bacon, 5 L. R. C. P. 437.

[5] Ayles *v.* South-Eastern Rail. Co., 37 L. J. Exch. 104; 3 L. R. Exch.

SEC. 704. **Where Action under Lord Campbell's Act maintainable.** — In connection with this subject, the answer to the question where an action under Lord Campbell's Act (9 & 10 Vict. c. 93) is maintainable, is not unimportant. We have seen that the wording of the act is clear in giving the action to the representatives of a person killed by negligence, only when, had he survived, he himself would have been entitled to maintain an action at common law.[1] Consequently, if in an action where death is alleged to have been caused by the negligence of the defendant's servants, it is shown that the deceased, by his own negligence and carelessness, contributed to the accident, the defendant would be entitled to a verdict.[2] In all cases, therefore, where it is proposed to bring an action against a carrier under this act for the death of an individual, which would not have happened but for the negligence of the carrier, it is of the greatest importance to ascertain whether any negligent act upon the part of the deceased was of such a nature as to place him in the position to be injured and killed by the defendant's negligence, for if there was any such act upon his part the action will not lie.[3] This leaves us in a position to consider shortly the subject of contributory or conductive negligence, and the legal principles which are applicable to it, in so far as passenger traffic is concerned. No action will lie for the consequences of a negligent act where the party complaining has, by his own want of due care and caution, been in any degree contributory to the misfortune.[4]

SEC. 705. **Contributory Negligence.** — An action may be brought and damages recovered for an injury sustained by a collision of carriages if the collision is due wholly to the negligence of the driver of the defendant's vehicle. In such a

146. See also Berket *v.* Whitehaven Junction Rail. Co., 4 H. & N. 730; 28 L. J. Exch. 348.

[1] Sec. 1, and Senior *v.* Ward, 5 Jur. N. S. 172; 28 L. J. Q. B. 139.

[2] Tucker *v.* Chaplin, 2 C. & K. 730.

[3] See also Dakin *v.* Brown, 8 C. B. 92; 18 L. J. C. P. 344; and Wigmore *v.* Jay, 5 Exch. 354.

[4] Witherley *v.* Regent's Canal Co., 12 C. B. N. S. 2; 3 F. & F. 61; Coleman *v.* South-Eastern Rail. Co., 4 H. & C. 699; 12 Jur. N. S. 944; Waite *v.* North-Eastern Railway Co., 4 Jur. N. S. 1300; 27 L. J. Q. B. 417; affirmed on appeal, 5 Jur. N. S. 936; 28 L. J. Q. B. 258.

case the action may be in trespass. It matters not whether the act which was the immediate cause of the injury was done intentionally or through negligence, so long as the act complained of is the direct, and not merely the indirect, cause of the injury.[1] In a case in which it appeared that the defendant, while driving on the wrong side of the road, it being dark, drove by accident into the plaintiff's curricle, it was held that the injury which the plaintiff had sustained having been immediate from the act of the driving of the defendant, trespass might be maintained.[2] And in the case of Hopper *v.* Reeve,[3] it was held that it is a direct trespass to injure the person of another by driving a carriage against the carriage wherein such person is sitting, although the last-mentioned carriage is not the property nor in the possession of the person injured. Where, however, the negligence of the defendant's servant, and not the defendant personally, caused the injury, the action must be in case.[4] Thus, if the agent of A. negligently drove the carriage of A. against that of B., the agent would be liable in trespass, and A. would be liable in case for the negligence of his servant.[5] If, on the other hand, the agent of A. wilfully drove A.'s carriage against that of B., without the assent of A., the latter would not be responsible.[6]

SEC. 706. **Evidence.** — Where the plaintiff brings his action against the carrier for refusal to carry, it will be necessary for him to prove that the carrier is a common carrier of passengers, as evidenced by his public profession, advertisements, or the like, and either that there was an express contract, which may be proved by the payment of his fare, the booking of a place, or the fact that he was permitted to take his place in the conveyance by the defendant, or a general invitation to all comers upon the part of the carrier. He should also prove room in the defendant's vehicle, readiness to pay his fare, and

[1] Covell *v.* Laming, 1 Camp. 497.

[2] Leame *v.* Bray, 3 East, 593.

[3] 7 Taunt. 698.

[4] See Moreton *v.* Hardern, 4 B. & C. 223. See also Vose (Admx.) *v.* Lancashire & Yorkshire Rail. Co., 37 L. J. Exch. 249.

[5] Morley *v.* Gainsford, 2 H. Bl. 441.

[6] Macmanus *v.* Crickett, 1 East, 106. See also Croft *v.* Alison, 4 B. & Ald. 590; Gregory *v.* Piper, 9 B. & C. 591.

the fitness of his own condition. In the case of an express contract with the plaintiff, the want of room in his conveyance will not excuse the carrier. The defendant's refusal must be proved, and any special damage which has arisen to the plaintiff by reason of such refusal. The rules applicable in all these cases are precisely similar to those which we have considered in reference to the carriers of goods. Where the plaintiff complains of injuries caused by the negligence of the defendant, he must prove the negligence. It is not incumbent on the carrier to show that he used reasonable care.[1] Where the accident is of such a nature as to afford a presumption of negligence, — as where a railway locomotive ran off the rails,[2] — it will be sufficient to prove the accident; but in many cases negligence will not be presumed from such a casualty, and then it will be necessary to prove the negligence itself. Overloading, causing an accident, is sufficient proof of negligence.[3] Where the accident happened in foggy weather, it was not held to be presumable that the accident was sufficient indication of negligence.[4] As to whether the defendant is the proper person to be made defendant, and the evidence necessary to support it, several cases referred to below will be instructive.[5]

SEC. 707. **In the Case of Carriers by Water.** — As to the evidence in actions against carriers of passengers in ships little need be said. In an action for negligently steering a ship, whereby she was wrecked, and the plaintiff lost his passage in her, it was held that no evidence could be given of a specific act of negligence which is not the foundation of the action, but that evidence that the master had often expressed his conviction that the officer to whom he gave charge of the

[1] Marsh *v.* Horne, 5 B. & C. 327; Israel *v.* Clark, 4 Esp. 259.

[2] Carpue *v.* London & Brighton Rail. Co., 5 Q. B. 747; Christie *v.* Griggs, 2 Camp. 79; Curtis *v.* Drinkwater, 2 B. & Ad. 169.

[3] Israel *v.* Clark, 4 Esp. 259. But see Aston *v.* Heaven, 2 Esp. 533; Wakeman *v.* Robinson, 1 Bing. 319.

[4] Crofts *v.* Waterhouse, 3 Bing. 319.

[5] Barford *v.* Nelson, 1 B. & Ad. 571; Stables *v.* Eley, 1 C. & P. 614; Strother *v.* Willan, 4 Camp. 24; Tucker *v.* Walpole, 14 East, 226; Smith *v.* Fuge, 3 Camp. 406; Fraser *v.* Hopkins, 2 Taunt. 5; Cooper *v.* South, 4 Taunt. 802; Tweed *v.* Martin, 2 Camp. 107; Ditchburn *v.* Spracklin, 5 Esp. 31.

ship was incompetent for his situation was admissible. It was also held to be allowable to call experienced nautical men, and ask them whether in their judgment particular facts which had been proved amounted to gross negligence.[1]

SEC. 708. **Damages.** — We come now to the question of damages. We have already seen[2] that in many cases the jury must be left to their common sense in the application of the principle laid down in Hadley *v.* Baxendale, and if they do so the court will not disturb the verdict.[3] In a railway accident, where the plaintiff's eye was injured by collision, which was due to the negligence of the defendants, and affected with chronic inflammation which was likely to impair the sight permanently, LORD CAMPBELL left it to the jury to say what was the fair amount of damages, and they gave the plaintiff 500*l.*[4] In all such cases it is of course most difficult to com-

[1] Walton *v.* Nesbit, 1 C. & P. 70. But see Sills *v.* Brown, 9 C. & P. 601. As to the statutory provisions, see 17 & 18 Vict. c. 104, § 126; 18 & 19 Vict. c. 119, §§ 54, 89 to 90 and 91.

[2] *Ante*, p. 672.

[3] Day *v.* Holloway, 1 Jur. 794; Williams *v.* Currie, 1 B. & C. 841.

[4] Plant *v.* Oxford & Worcester Rail. Co., "Times," 5 Feb. 1856, quoted in Powell on Carriers. In Grindle *v.* Eastern Express Co., 67 Me. 313, it was held that the carrier could not be charged with the full loss, where the plaintiff might, by reasonable diligence on his own part, have averted such loss in a measure. In that case it appeared that one Wardwell in his lifetime procured an insurance upon his life in the Continental Life Insurance Company, the semi-annual premium on which was about to become due, and Wardwell delivered to the defendant's agent at Castine the sum of $24, to be forwarded to Belfast and there delivered to the agent of the company to pay the premium. The defendant failed to deliver the money, and in consequence thereof, the policy lapsed and became void. The plaintiff, as administrator of Wardwell's estate, Wardwell having died within a year after the lapse of the policy, brought this action to recover the amount of the policy of the defendant, on the ground that the policy was invalidated through its loss. The court held that the company was not liable for the full amount of the policy, but only for its surrender value at the time of the lapse, upon the ground that Wardwell took no steps to have the policy reinstated, and the plaintiff gave no evidence tending to show that there was anything at that time in the state of Wardwell's health or physical condition which would have prevented such reinstatement.

VIRGIN, J., in delivering the opinion of the court, said: "On April 15, 1870, the Continental Life Insurance Company assured the life of the plaintiff's intestate for his sole use, in the sum of one thousand dollars, for the term of sixteen years or until his de-

pute what would be a fair amount to allow to a plaintiff who has suffered a personal injury. Unlike goods, a man has not

cease, in case of his death before that time; and the company, by their policy under seal, of that date, did covenant with the assured, to pay him the sum insured within ninety days after he shall have been insured the term mentioned, or in case he should die before that time, then to his wife Edna, if living, otherwise to the legal representatives of the assured. Being an endowment policy for sixteen years, it was primarily intended to be for the benefit of the assured himself. And being a covenant under seal, no one but the assured or his legal representative could maintain an action upon it, he being the only party in whom the legal interest was vested. Hinkley *v.* Fowler, 15 Me. 285; Flynn *v.* North American Life Insurance Co., 115 Mass. 449. This is not an action against the insurance company for a breach of any covenant contained in the policy; but an action on the case against the defendants as common carriers of goods, for an alleged violation of their duty in failing to seasonably deliver to one Beale, of Belfast, agent of the insurance company, a certain sum of money sent through them by the plaintiff's intestate on May 8, 1873, for the purpose of paying his semi-annual premium due on his policy May 15, 1873.

"The defendants do not deny their receipt of the money in the capacity mentioned. Being such carriers, and their general obligation depending upon their public profession (Johnson *v.* Midland Rail. Co., 4 Exch. 367), they were bound, in the absence of any special agreement, to receive the money and carry and deliver it, within a reasonable time, at whatever place directed within the route which they hold out to the public as theirs, and no further. There their common-law liability ceases. Perkins *v.* Portland, S., & P. R. R. Co., 47 Me. 573, 589; Hales *v.* London & North-Western Rail. Co., 4 B. & S. 66. They might contract to carry further to any point beyond their regular line; or might simply undertake to deliver to a connecting carrier; in which latter event their liability would cease with a safe carriage and prompt delivery; for they would then have done all the law and all their contract required. Perkins *v.* Portland, S., & P. R. R. Co., *supra*; Skinner *v.* Hall, 60 Me. 477; Plantation No. 4 *v.* Hall, 61 Me. 517. The proof of a contract for carriage beyond their route should be clear. Nutting *v.* Connecticut R. R. Co., 1 Gray (Mass.), 502. But it may be express or by implication; by direct or circumstantial evidence; by words, conduct, or usage. Gray *v.* Jackson, 51 N. H. 9, 11; s. c. 12 Am. Rep. 1; Knapp *v.* United States & Canada Express Co., 54 N. H. 348, and cases *supra*. *Receiving goods marked or directed to some point beyond their regular route is not sufficient evidence of an implied contract to carry them to that place.* Pendergast *v.* Adams Express Co., 101 Mass. 120. Where the consignor accepts a special contract, it is no answer that he did not know its terms; for in the absence of fraud, imposition, or deceit, he is conclusively presumed to understand its terms and legal effect. Squire *v.* New York Central R. R. Co., 98 Mass. 239; Grace *v.* Adams, 100 Mass. 505; s. c. 1 Am. Rep. 131; Belger *v.* Dinsmore, 51 N. Y. 166; s. c. 10 Am. Rep. 575; Snider *v.* Adams Express Co., 63 Me. 376.

a cost price and a marketable value, and in many cases the injuries done may be irreparable by any money payment.

"The defendants claim that Belfast is not within their route; that they made no contract, and neither by conduct nor usage created any obligation to deliver the money outside of their route; that Castine is the most convenient point on their line whence public communication is had with Belfast, and that they delivered the money the next day after its receipt to the usual means of conveyance between Castine and Belfast. If these facts appear at the trial, they will constitute a good defence. Any special contract in the premises must be shown by the plaintiff. By the terms of the report, if the action is maintainable on the facts as claimed by the plaintiff, what is the measure of damages against the express company? 'The plaintiff claims that at the time the money was delivered to the defendants' agent, he was informed and knew for what purpose it was sent to Beale.' Upon this hypothesis we are of the opinion that primarily the defendants would be liable for the net value of the policy on May 15, when it lapsed and became void, qualified as hereinafter mentioned. It had a surrender value which the company would have paid. It could have been assigned by the consent of all concerned. Then the assured — for whose sole benefit it was primarily issued — was alive. The wife was no party to it. She simply had an equitable interest therein depending upon the contingency of her husband's decease prior to May 15, 1886, and the seasonable payment of the semi-annual premiums to the date of his death. When the policy lapsed, the contingency of his death had not occurred, and the assured alone was injured. The general rule of damages in an action on the case against a common carrier for the non-delivery of goods is their value when and where they should have been delivered, with interest thereon from that date; and if money be the article transported, the measure of damages is the principal sum with interest. So, where the delivery is negligently delayed, the carrier is liable for the diminution in their market value, which occurred during the delay. Weston *v.* Grand Trunk Rail. Co., 54 Me. 376. Although this rule includes such profits as depend upon market values, it excludes all such uncertain, contingent profits as may result merely from a private or special speculation, especially when they are the subject of some collateral undertaking. Bridges *v.* Stickney, 38 Me. 361. While this is the general rule in the absence of special stipulations, it may be modified by circumstances. The courts in England as well as in this country have adopted substantially the doctrine of the civil law, and applied it alike to breaches of contract and violations of duty. 'When the debtor,' says POTHIER, 'cannot be charged with fraud, and is merely in fault for not performing his obligation, . . he is only liable for the damages and interest which might have been contemplated at the time of the contract; for to such alone the debtor can be considered as having intended to submit. In general, the parties are deemed to have contemplated only the damages and interest which the creditor might suffer from the non-performance of the obligation in respect to the particular thing which is the object of it, and not such as may have been incidentally occasioned by it. . . . Sometimes the debtor is lia-

Can 500*l.* be said to be compensation for the loss of an eye? Or what is the value of a leg?[1]

ble for the damages and interest of the creditor, although extrinsic; as when it appears they were contemplated in the contract, and that the debtor submitted to them either expressly or tacitly, in case of non-performance.' 1 Poth. on Oblig. 161, 162. CHANCELLOR KENT also declared that 'damages for breach of contract are only those which are incidental to, and directly caused by, the breach, and may reasonably be supposed to have entered into the contemplation of the parties.' 2 Kent, Com. (12th ed.) 480, note.

"So in this State WESTON, J., said: 'In general, the delinquent party is holden to make good the loss occasioned by his delinquency. But his liability is limited to direct damages, which, according to the nature of the subject, may be contemplated or presumed to result from his failure. Remote or speculative damages, although susceptible of proof, or deducible from the non-performance, are not allowed.' Miller *v.* Mariners' Church, 7 Me. 51. This was reaffirmed in True *v.* International Telegraph Co., 60 Me. 9, 25; s. c. 11 Am. Rep. 156, 166; Bartlett *v.* Western Union Telegraph Co., 62 Me. 209; s. c. 16 Am. Rep. 437. The leading and famous case upon this subject in England is Hadley *v.* Baxendale, 9 Exch. 353, decided in 1854. In that case ALDERSON, B, said: "Where two parties have made a contract which one of them has broken, the damages which the other party ought to receive in respect of such breach of contract should be such as may fairly and reasonably be considered either arising naturally, *i. e.* according to the natural course of things from such breach of the contract itself, or such as may reasonably be supposed to have been in the contemplation of both parties at the time they made the contract, as the probable result of the breach of it.' The action was against a common carrier for negligent delay in delivery; and the rule here enunciated has been followed in numerous English cases against carriers, and of failure to deliver goods on contract of purchase, or to manufacture and deliver personal property, &c. BLACKBURN, J., in Cory *v.* Thames Iron Works, &c. Co., L. R. 3 Q B. 181, 186, stated the rule in brief, thus: 'Damages are to be what would be the natural consequences of a breach under circumstances which both parties were aware of.' And LORD CAMPBELL said that the rule in Hadley *v.* Baxendale merely affirmed what was to be found in 2 Kent, Com., &c; Smeed *v.* Foord, 1 El. & El. 602.

"The latest English case which has come under observation is Simpson *v.* London & North-Western Rail. Co., Q. B. Div. 24 W. R. 294. The plaintiff attended agricultural fairs with samples of cattle spice, &c., of which he was the manufacturer. The defendants received these samples from the plaintiff's agent on a certain fair-ground to be forwarded, by a certain

[1] The damages for death or injury to passengers by sea-going ships are regulated by Act of Parliament. See 17 & 18 Vict. c. 104, § 510, and 18 & 19 Vict. c. 119, § 73. See also Boyce *v.* Bayliffe, 1 Camp. 58. But these provisions refer only to sea-going ships, and the damages recoverable in other cases are governed by the same rules which apply in ordinary actions.

SEC. 709. **Principle of Measure of Damages. — Illustration. — Recovery for Pain. — Recovery for Loss of Business.** — The prin-

day named on the consignment note, to a certain other fair-ground when and where a cattle-fair was to be held. The goods did not arrive until the fair was closed; and the court held that the plaintiff was entitled to recover the loss of profit he would have gained on the orders received through the exhibition of his samples at the show, and for his loss of time in waiting at the latter place for the arrival of the goods. COCKBURN, C. J., said: 'I think it is now settled that wherever the prospect of loss of profits was either expressly brought to the knowledge of the carrier, or the goods were received under such circumstances that he ought reasonably to have inferred their nature and destination, so that the use of them might be within the contemplation of both parties, then the plaintiff is entitled to recover damages for the loss of profits he would have made if the contract had been duly carried out.' The general rule in Hadley *v.* Baxendale has been recognized and applied by the courts in most, if not all, of the States of this Union. Cutting *v.* Grand Trunk Rail. Co., 13 Allen (Mass.), 381, 384; Scott *v.* Boston & New Orleans Steamship Co., 106 Mass. 468; Griffin *v.* Colver, 16 N. Y. 489; Hamilton *v.* McPherson, 28 N. Y. 72; Booth *v.* S. D. R. M. Co., 69 N. Y. 487, 492, 493. Therefore, while the loss of another's money received for transportation by a carrier, without reasonable knowledge of the purpose for which it is sent, will lay the carrier under obligation merely to refund the principal sum with interest, still, when it is seasonably sent for the specific purpose of paying the sender's premium on his life-policy which will lapse if the money be not paid at the particular time, and the carrier is reasonably informed in relation to the premises, and has a reasonable time to perform the duty undertaken, but negligently fails to perform it, the law will justly hold him primarily, at least, for the net value of the policy which lapsed in consequence of his negligence. From their knowledge of the special circumstances, both parties must be presumed to have contemplated such consequences when the money was deposited with the carrier. We consider Favor *v.* Philbrick, 5 N. H. 358, a parallel case, where, in consequence of the carrier's unreasonable delay in the delivery of the plaintiff's account against a third person, it became barred by the statute of limitations, the carrier was held liable for the amount of the account. So, where an express company received from the plaintiff a promissory note against a third person which they agreed to collect of the maker, but during the company's negligent delay in pressing the collection the maker failed and the note became worthless, the company were held for the amount of the note. Knapp *v.* United States & Canada Express Co., 55 N. H. 348. To the same purport see, also, Parks *v.* Alta California Telegraph Co., 13 Cal. 422; Bryant *v.* American Telegraph Co., 1 Daly, 575.

"But the law makes it incumbent upon a person for whose injury another is responsible to use ordinary care and take all reasonable measures within his knowledge and power to avoid the loss and render the consequences as light as may be; and it will not permit him to recover for such losses as by such care and means might have been prevented. Miller *v.* Mari-

ciple which must govern such decisions is to be brought out of such theoretical considerations and brought to more practical grounds of computation. A man's value in money to himself or others may be said to be what he can earn; and that fact will in many cases be the ground for determining how much his price as a laborer is impaired, and how much is consequently due to him as a compensation for any injury he may have sustained. Some cases will make this clearer. Where the plaintiff had been given into custody on a charge that he had not paid his fare, which proved unfounded, and was taken without delay before a magistrate by whom he was discharged, 50*l.* damages was held liberal but not excessive.[1] On a policy of insurance guaranteeing a certain sum in the event of injury, by a railway accident, the damages are con-

ners' Church, *supra;* True *v.* International Telegraph Co., *supra;* Bartlett *v.* Western Union Telegraph Co., *supra.* The principle is illustrated by SHAW, C. J., in Loker *v.* Damon, 17 Pick. (Mass.) 284, where in trespass for removing a few rods of fence, the cost of repairing it, and not the injury to the following year's crop caused by cattle passing through the gap in the fence, was held to be the measure of damages in favor of the plaintiff who knew the fence was down. So, where the plaintiff's cow was made dangerously sick by eating poisoned hay purchased of the defendant, it was held to be the duty of the plaintiff to employ the best remedies within her reasonable reach, at reasonable trouble and expense, to cure the cow. French *v.* Vining, 102 Mass. 132; s. c. 3 Am. Rep. 440. See, also, Eastman *v.* Sanburn, 3 Allen (Mass.), 594; Sherman *v.* Fall River Iron Works, 2 Allen (Mass.), 524; Scott *v.* Boston & New Orleans Steamship Co., *supra;* Sutherland *v.* Wyer, 67 Me. 69.

"The same doctrine is held in New York, in Hamilton *v.* McPherson, 28 N. Y. 72, 77; Milton *v.* Hudson River Steamboat Co., 37 N. Y. 210; Baldwin *v.* United States Telegraph Co., 45 N. Y. 744, 753; s. c. 6 Am. Rep. 165. And in Iowa, in Mather *v.* Butler County, 28 Iowa, 253; Simpson *v.* City of Keokuk, 34 Iowa, 568.

"Some insurance companies are accustomed to reinstate the assured without expense in case of accidental lapse, especially when the policy, like the one in question, has run but a short time. All will reinsure on payment of a premium based on increased age, if, on re-examination, the health of the assured remains unimpaired. Whether or not the assured made any effort of the kind, during the fifteen months he survived the policy, the case does not find. We think, however, it was incumbent on him to use the care and adopt all reasonable means in the premises known to him. And unless he can show some legal excuse for not doing so, such as want of knowledge, failing health, failing circumstances of the company, &c., he should not recover damage for such loss as he might have prevented."

[1] Goff *v.* Great Northern Rail. Co., 30 L. J. Q. B. 148.

fined to compensation for bodily pain and suffering, and the amount of the medical attendant's bill; and damages for loss of time and profits are not recoverable.[1] In that case, POLLOCK, C. B., remarked that it was "unmanly, though undoubtedly legal, to claim damages for pain or suffering."[2] As in the case of goods, where a carrier must know that they are wanted at a certain time, he is held to have constructive notice of the necessity, and, therefore, to have had in contemplation the possible results, as loss of profit or the like, so must carriers of passengers be aware, in most cases, that the time of the people they carry is of importance to them, as an element of the profit of any trade or profession which they may pursue, and, consequently, they may be held to have constructive notice of that fact, and to have the consequences of a breach of their contract in view at the time they entered upon it; and, therefore, if through an accident such a person, being a passenger, is injured, the jury may consider the profits which he would have derived from his business or occupation, and may give compensation accordingly.[3]

[1] Theobald *v.* Railway Assurance Co., 10 Exch. 45; 23 L. J. Exch. 249; Georgia Bridge Association *v.* Loonies, 20 Ill. 235; Hunt *v.* Hoyt, 20 Ill. 540; Morse *v.* Auburn & Syracuse R. R. Co., 10 Barb. (N. Y.) 621; Ransom *v.* New York & Erie R. R. Co., 15 N. Y. 415; Keys *v.* Devlin, 3 E. D. S. (N. Y. C. P.) 518; West *v.* Forrest, 22 Mo. 344. That physical pain and mental distress are to be had regard to in computing the amount of damages. Seger *v.* Barkhamsted, 22 Conn. 290; Masters *v.* Town of Warren, 27 Conn. 293; Lawrence *v.* Housatonic R. R. Co., 29 Conn. 390; Mason *v.* Inhabitants of Ellsworth, 32 Me. 271; Fairchild *v.* Call Stage Co., 13 Cal. 599. As to the irrecoverability of the possible future profits of a business which may on account of the injury have to be foregone. Ballon *v.* Farnum, 11 Allen, (Mass.) 73; Caldwell *v.* Murphy, 1 Duer (N. Y.), 233; affirmed, 11 N. Y. 416; and see Kimsey *v.* Crocker, 18 Wis. 74.

[2] Where the injury is of a permanent nature, the future must be had regard to in the computation of damages as well as the past. Frink *v.* Schroyer, 18 Ill. 416; Slater *v.* Rink, 18 Ill. 527. The suffering which will follow the trial as well as what has gone before may be proved. Aaron *v.* Second Avenue R. R. Co., 2 Daly (N. Y.), 127.

[3] Per PAGE WOOD, V. C., in De Mattos *v.* Gibson, 30 L. J. Chan. 146. See also Illinois Central R. R. Co. *v.* Barron, 5 Wall. (U. S.) 90. It has been held that, as in actions of tort the quantum of damages is very much within the discretion of the jury, evidence of the nature and extent of the plaintiff's business and the general rate of profit he has realized therefrom, which has been interrupted by the defendant's wrongful act, is prop-

SEC. 710. **Cases under Lord Campbell's Act.** — These principles will be more clearly understood in connection with their application to certain cases which have arisen under the 9 & 10 Vict. c. 93. In an action founded on that act by a wife, husband, parent, or child [1] of a person killed by misfeasance, the jury, in estimating the damages, cannot take into consideration mental suffering or loss of society, but must give compensation for pecuniary loss only. In a case in which this was decided, it was argued that, as the first section states that the newly given action may be maintained, although death has ensued, in those cases where if the party had survived he would have had a right of action; so here the party injured, if he had recovered, would have been entitled to a *solatium* for wounded feelings, pain, and suffering; therefore his representatives were entitled to damages of a similar nature. But COLERIDGE, J., in delivering the judgment of the court, said: "It will be evident that this act does not transfer this right of action to his (the deceased's) representatives, but gives to the representatives a totally new right of action on different principles. . . .

SEC. 711. **Damages not a Solatium.** — "The measure of damages is not the loss or suffering of the deceased, but the injury resulting to his family." [2] In England the injury sustained by the accidental death of a relative must, in order to be compensated by a jury, be of a pecuniary character, and the jury cannot give damages for affliction.[3] In Scotland the

erly received, not on the ground of its furnishing a measure of damages to be adopted by the jury, but to be taken into consideration by them in the exercise of that discretion. New Jersey Express Co. *v.* Nichols, 33 N. J. L. 434. See also Allison *v.* Chandler, 11 Mich. 543; Taylor *v.* Dustin, 43 N. H. 493; Somans *v.* Brown, 5 R. I. 299; Wade *v.* Leroy, 20 How. (U. S.) 34; Lincoln *v.* Saratoga & Schenectady R. R. Co., 23 Wend. (N. Y.) 425. See also Ingram *v.* Lawson, 6 Bing. N. C. 212.

[1] Duckworth *v.* Johnson, 29 L. J. Exch. 25.

[2] Blake *v.* Midland Rail. Co., 18 Q. B. 93, 110. Scotch decisions are only received in England if the law upon which they turn is the same. 9 & 10 Vict. c. 93, does not apply to Scotland.

[3] See, as to American law, Braunberger *v.* Cleis (Penn.), 4 Am. Law Reg. (N. S.) 587; Pennsylvania R. R. Co. *v.* Zebe, 33 Penn. St. 318; Pennsylvania R. R. Co. *v.* Vandever, 36 Penn. St. 298; North Pennsylvania R. R. Co.

jury administers a *solatium* for wounded feelings.[1] In the case of Armsworth *v.* The South-Eastern Railway Company,[2] it was decided that the damages are not to be estimated according to the value of the deceased's life calculated by annuity tables, but that the jury should give what they consider a fair compensation; and it was also decided in that case that a proper question for the jury in such cases is, whether the circumstances are such that if the deceased, instead of meeting his death, had been only wounded in consequence of the conduct of the defendant, he would have been entitled to damages for the injury.

SEC. 712. **Nominal Damages.** — The action cannot be supported to recover nominal damages,[3] and it is clear that damages of a pecuniary nature must be shown, but that the damages are not to be given merely in reference to the loss of a legal right. They should be calculated in reference to a reasonable expectation to pecuniary benefit, as of right or otherwise, from the continuance of the life of the deceased.

SEC. 713. **What gives Right to Recover.** — Thus in an action by a father for the death of his son: the father was an old man, getting infirm, who lived in the lodge of an hospital, and was employed to carry coals round the wards, for which he was paid 3*s.* 6*d.* a week — whether under a contract or by way of gratuity did not appear; the son was a young man, earning good wages, who did not live with his father, but was in the habit of gratuitously assisting him by carrying the coals

v. Robinson, 44 Penn. St. 175; Ohio & Mississippi R. R. Co. *v.* Tindal, 13 Ind. 366; M'Intyre *v.* New York Central R. R. Co., 47 Barb. (N. Y.) 515; Donaldson *v.* Mississippi & Missouri R. R. Co., 18 Iowa, 280; City of Chicago *v.* Major, 18 Ill. 349; Telfer *v.* Northern Rail. Co., 30 N. J. L. 188; State of Maryland to the use of Mary Coughlan *v.* Baltimore & Ohio R. R. Co., 5 Am. Law Reg. (N. S.) 397; Quin *v.* Moore, 15 N. Y. 432; Lehman *v.* Brooklyn, 29 Barb. (N. Y.) 234; Corsant *v.* Griffin, 48 Ill. 410; Pennsylvania R. R. Co. *v.* Goodman, 82 Penn. St. 329.

[1] Paterson *v.* Walace, 1 Macq. H. L. Cas. 748. See as to the latter point, Ersk. Inst. 1074, B. 4, tit. 4, § 105; Black *v.* Caddell, Dict. Decis. vols. 31 and 32, p. 13905; Brown *v.* Macgregor, Fac. Collect, lib. 26, 1813, pp. 232, 233; Children of Forrest *v.* Clerkington, Dict. Decis. vols. 31 and 32, p. 13903, &c.

[2] 11 Jur. 758.

[3] Boulter *v.* Webster, 13 W. R. 289.

round the wards for him, but the father not being in need was not supported by him in any other way: it was held that the father had such a reasonable expectation of pecuniary benefit from the continuance of his son's life as would enable him to maintain the action. But, the jury having found a verdict for him with 75*l.* damages, it was held that the damages were excessive.[1] In another case it was held that legal liability alone is not the test of injury in respect of which damages may be recovered, but that the reasonable expectation of pecuniary advantage by the relation remaining alive may be taken into account by the jury, and damages may be given in respect of that expectation being disappointed, and the probable pecuniary loss thereby occasioned.[2] That case was very similar to the last in all particulars, and the judgment of POLLOCK, C. B., in that case is applicable to both. "The statute does not," he remarked, "in terms say on what principle the action it gives is to be maintainable, nor on what principle the damages are to be assessed, and the only way to ascertain what it *does*, is to show what it *does not*, mean. Now it is clear that damage must be shown, for the jury are to 'give such damages as they think proportioned to the injury.' It has been held that the damages are not to be given as a *solatium*, but are to be given in reference to a pecuniary loss. That was so decided in Blake *v.* The Midland Railway Company (18 Q. B. 93).

SEC. 714. **The Principle of Damages allowed to Relatives. — Funeral Expenses.** — "It is also clear that the damages are not to be given merely in reference to the loss of a legal right, for they are to be distributed among relations only,[3] and not to all individuals sustaining such a loss; and accordingly the practice

[1] Franklin *v.* South-Eastern Rail. Co., 3 H. & N. 211; 4 Jur. N. S. 565.

[2] Dalton *v.* South-Eastern Rail. Co., 4 C. B. N. S. 296; 4 Jur. N. S. 711; 27 L. J. C. P. 227; Condon *v.* Great Southern & Western R. R. Co., 16 Ir. L. R. N. S. 415. See also Tilley *v.* Hudson R. R. Co., 29 N. Y. 252; Oldfield *v.* New York & Harlem R. R. Co., 14 N. Y. 310; Pennsylvania R. R. Co. *v.* M'Closkey's Adm'r, 23 Penn. St. 526. In another case it was decided that if the services of the deceased *might have been* of some value to the next of kin, a nonsuit should not be directed. M'Intyre *v.* New York Central R. R. Co., 43 Barb. (N. Y.) 552.

[3] See also Dickins *v.* New York Central R. R. Co., 23 N. Y. 158; and Illinois Central R. R. Co. *v.* Barron, 5 Wall. (U. S.) 90.

has not been to ascertain what benefit could have been enforced by the claimants had the deceased lived, and give damages limited thereby. If then the damages are not to be calculated on either of these principles, nothing remains except that they should be calculated in reference to a reasonable expectation of pecuniary benefit, as of right, or otherwise, from the continuance of the life." In the case of Dalton *v.* The South-Eastern Railway Company,[1] WILLES, J., approved of the decision just quoted, and with regard to a point which did not arise in the former case, he remarked: "As to the expenses of the funeral and mourning, however, we think they ought not to be allowed. The subject-matter of the statute is compensation for injuries by reason of the relative not being alive, and there is no language in the statute referring to the cost of the ceremonial of respect paid to the memory of the deceased in his funeral, or in putting on mourning for his loss."

SEC. 715. **How Damage must have accrued.**—Besides these points, it is important to note that actual damage must have accrued from the death of the deceased. In one case it was held that proof of death and of the relationship of the parties does not give a right to nominal damages. In that case an action was brought by a father for injury resulting from the death of his son. It appeared that the father was a working mason, and that the son was a boy of fourteen, who had earned four shillings a week for about a year or two, but at the time of his death was without employment. There was no evidence of the cost of boarding and clothing the boy. The judge left it to the jury to say whether the father had sustained any pecuniary loss by the death of his son, and they found a verdict for him, with 50*l.* damages. It was held in the Court of Exchequer that as there was evidence for the jury the father was entitled to retain the verdict for the amount.[2] Where a person, possessed of an income of 4,000*l.* a year, met his death while travelling upon a railway, through the negligence of the

[1] 4 C. B. N. S. 296, at 306; 27 L. J. C. P. 227.

[2] Duckworth *v.* Johnson, 4 H. & N. 653; 5 Jur. N. S. 630; 29 L. J. Exch. 25.

company's servants, and it appeared in evidence that the bulk of his property was settled upon his eldest son, a smaller portion being reserved for the benefit of his wife and younger children, it was held that his representatives might maintain an action for the benefit of the wife and younger children in respect of the injury arising to them from a pecuniary loss occasioned by the death, although that pecuniary loss would not have resulted from the accident to the deceased had he lived.[1] In such a case as this it is evident that, from the nature of the settlement, the widow and younger children sustained a greater loss by the death than they might have done had the circumstances been different, and, therefore, it is for the jury to regard the damage which has been suffered by the respective members of the family, in so far as their reasonable expectations of pecuniary benefit, in case the death had not occurred, goes, notwithstanding the fact that the estate of the deceased survived for the benefit of his family in general.[2] In the case just referred to it was further held that in the case of a widow and younger children of a deceased person (who was seised in fee-tail of landed estates, passing at his death to his eldest son), the damages arising from the loss of education, and the comforts and conveniences of life, are not too remote, but may be the subject of pecuniary estimate, and are consequently within the statute.[3] Again, in an action for negligence, whereby the plaintiff's wife was killed, LORD ELLENBOROUGH said: "The jury could only take into consid eration the bruises which the plaintiff had himself sustained, and the loss of his wife's society, and the distress he had suffered on her account from the time of the accident till the moment of her dissolution." And he added, "In a civil court, the death of a human being could not be complained

[1] Pym *v.* Great Northern Rail. Co., 8 Jur. N. S. 819; 31 L. J. Q. B. 249; affirmed on appeal, 4 B. & S. 396; 32 L. J. Q. B. 377.

[2] Baker *v.* Bolton, 1 Camp. 493; and see Kramer *v.* Waymark, 1 L. R. Exch. 241; 4 H. & C. 427; 35 L. J. Exch. 148.

[3] It is evident that in estimating damages it is of the utmost importance that the jury should consider the exact situation, annual earnings, health, habits, family, and estate of the deceased. Chicago, &c. R. R. Co. *v.* Morris, 26 Ill. 400.

of as an injury, and in this case the damages, as to the plaintiff's wife, must stop with the period of her existence."

SEC. 716. **Jurisdiction of Court of Admiralty.** — The 24 Vict. c. 10, § 7, enacts that "the High Court of Admiralty shall have jurisdiction over any claim for damage done by any ship." In a recent case it was held that the word "damage" does not include loss of life and personal injury, and that consequently the above section confers no jurisdiction upon the High Court of Admiralty to entertain a suit under Lord Campbell's Act (9 & 10 Vict. c. 93), from damages resulting from negligence in the management of a vessel which has caused personal injury and death.[1] The law which is applicable to the recovery of damages for loss of life or personal injuries to passengers in ships is not the same as that which is applicable in the case of carriers by land. No person can bring an action for compensation until the Board of Trade has instituted and completed an inquiry or has refused to do so.[2] The mode of procedure at such an inquiry, if the Board of Trade thinks fit to institute it,[3] is set forth at length in other sections of the act.[4] The summoning of witnesses and impanelling of the jury are to be enforced in the manner provided for by the Lands Clauses Consolidation Act, 1845.[5] At the same time, the Passengers' Act, 1855, provides that the remedy for breach of contract for not carrying, or for loss of or non-delivery of luggage, will be the same as in the case of carriers by land.[6]

SEC. 717. **31 & 32 Vict. c. 119.** — Before quitting the subject of damages, and at the same time going out of the front door of our subject, which is opened by the last page, it is necessary to mention a provision of a recent statute with reference to this subject. By 31 & 32 Vict. c. 119, § 25,[7] it is enacted "that where a person has been injured or killed by an acci-

[1] Smith *v.* Brown, Asp. Mar. Law Cas., vol. i. pt. ii. p. 56. See also The George and Richard, 24 L. T. Rep. N. S. 717, and Asp. Mar. Law Cas., vol. i. pt. ii. p. 50.

[2] 17 & 18 Vict. c. 104, § 512.

[3] *Ibid.* § 507.

[4] *Ibid.* §§ 507, 508.

[5] 8 Vict. c. 18.

[6] 18 & 19 Vict. c. 119, § 58. See also § 73.

[7] See also § 26.

dent on a railway, the Board of Trade, upon application in writing, made jointly by the company from whom compensation is claimed, and the person, if he is injured, or his representatives, if he is killed, may, if they think fit, appoint an arbitrator, who shall determine the compensation, if any, to be paid by the company."

APPENDIX.

[As the forms of pleading given in this Appendix by the author are of practical value in most of the States, becauee they embody the substantial grounds essential to be stated to uphold or defeat an action, they are given entire.]

INTRODUCTION TO PLEADING.

THE present system of pleading is founded upon that which has existed for many centuries; but so great have been the alterations effected by the Common-Law Procedure Act, 1852, that the practical working of pleadings has undergone a considerable change.

The result of these alterations is, that every declaration and subsequent pleading, which clearly and distinctly states all such facts as are necessary to sustain the action, plea, or replication, will suffice; and it is unnecessary that the facts of the case should be stated technically and formally, so long as they are in conformity with the statutes and rules. In accordance with this principle, all statements which need not be proved, such as the statements of time, quantity, quality, and value, where they are immaterial, the statement of losing and finding, and bailment, in actions for goods or their value, the statement of acts of trespass having been committed with force and arms, and against the peace of our Lady the Queen, the statement of promises which need not be proved, as promises in *indebitatus* counts, and mutual promises to perform agreements, and all statements of a like kind, are now to be omitted.

By section 52 of the above statute it is enacted, that if any pleading be so framed as to prejudice, embarrass, or delay the fair trial of the action, the opposite party may obtain an order from the court or a judge to have it struck out or amended.

The *declaration* is the first step in the pleadings; in this the plaintiff states his cause of action, and he is not confined to the statement of one cause only, for the declaration may consist of several *counts*, and each of these may state a separate and distinct cause of action, with this exception: that *ejectment* and *replevin* cannot be joined together, or with any other form of action.

The principal parts of the *declaration* are the title, venue, and body, — setting forth the cause of action, and the conclusion stating the redress sought. The title of every pleading consists of the name of the court in which the action is brought, and of the day of the month and year when the same is pleaded.

The venue is inserted in the margin, — thus, London to wit, *or*, London. In the county named in the margin the action will be tried, unless an order is made, by consent or otherwise, to change it. The venue is either *transitory* or *local*, — it is transitory where the cause of action might have happened anywhere, in which case the plaintiff may lay his venue wherever he chooses. In an action upon a contract, the venue would be of this description. Local venue is when the cause of action could have happened in one place only, — as in trespass to land, and the venue must be laid in the county where the close is situated. To ascertain under what circumstances the venue can be changed, reference may be made to the several works on pleading.

The body of the declaration sets out the cause of action. Some ordinary forms are given in the schedule to the Common Law Procedure Act, 1852. The declaration concludes with a statement of the sum sought to be recovered, and, if required, the claim for a writ of mandamus or injunction. The claim should be sufficient to include the largest amount of debt or damages likely to be recovered, for the jury cannot give more than the amount thus claimed; should the jury *assess* the damages at a greater amount, the plaintiff may move for a new trial, and for leave to amend the declaration, which might be granted on payment of costs.

The plea is the defendant's answer to the declaration, and

is either *in abatement* or *in bar*. The former does not contain any substantial answer to the declaration, but shows that some informality has been committed, and points out the right mode of procedure. These pleas must be verified by affidavit, which must be delivered with the pleas; and they must be delivered within four days after the receipt of the declaration. This defence is not often resorted to, as it is discouraged by the courts, as tending to throw technical difficulties in the plaintiff's way. If the plea be for non-joinder of a person also liable, it must be accompanied by a statement that he is resident within the jurisdiction, and an affidavit must be made, stating his place of residence. A plea in bar is, on the other hand, a substantial answer to the action; it is either a *traverse* or a plea *in confession and avoidance*. A plea is said to be a *traverse* when it denies some essential part of the declaration; there are several kinds of *traverses*, the most ordinary is that which may be called a common *traverse*. This consists of a denial by way of express contradiction, in forms of the allegation traversed. A plea is said to be in confession and avoidance, when it admits the facts stated in the declaration to be true, but alleges new facts which obviate or repel their legal effect.

If the defendant admits the cause of action stated in the declaration, he may now, in almost all cases, except actions for assault and battery, false imprisonment, libel, slander, malicious arrest or prosecution, or debauching of the plaintiff's daughter or servant, pay money into court by way of compensation or amends, and plead that such sum is sufficient to satisfy the plaintiff's claim. By 4 & 5 Ann. c. 16, the defendant is at liberty to plead several matters by leave of the court, and by the Common-Law Procedure Act, 1852, § 84, the following pleas, or any two or more of them, may be pleaded together without leave: *A plea denying any contract or debt alleged in the declaration; tender as to part; Statute of Limitations; set off; bankruptcy of defendant; discharge under an Insolvent Act; plene administravit; plene administravit præter; infancy; coverture; payment; accord, and satisfaction; release; not guilty; a denial that the property, an injury to which is complained of, is the plaintiff's; leave and license; son assault demesne.*

By section 86, if several pleas are improperly pleaded together, judgment may be signed. The several pleas should be numbered consecutively.

The General Issue. — There are three pleas usually spoken of as general issues in actions on contracts: *nunquam indebitatus, non assumpsit,* and *non est factum;* but *nul tiel record* might also be mentioned. By rules 8, 12, 17, Trinity Term, 1853, all matters in confession and avoidance must be specially pleaded.

The most common form of the general issue in actions for wrongs is the plea of *not guilty.* By rule 16, Trinity Term, 1853, "In actions for torts, the plea of not guilty shall operate as a denial only of the breach of duty, or wrongful act alleged to have been committed by the defendant, and not of the facts related in the indictment; and no other defence than such denial shall be admissible under that plea, all other pleas in denial shall take issue on some particular matter of fact alleged in the declaration."

The subsequent steps in pleading are the *replication,* containing the plaintiff's answer to the plea; the *rejoinder,* the defendant's answer to the replication; the *surrejoinder;* the *rebutter;* the *surrebutter;* and so on. The pleadings seldom reach the latter, but they sometimes do, and there is nothing to prevent their going beyond it. By section 79 of the Common-Law Procedure Act, 1852, either party may plead in answer to the plea or subsequent pleading of his adversary, that he joins issue thereon, and such shall be deemed to be an issue. Thus the pleadings go on, step by step, till at last the parties come, as they necessarily must, to a direct contradiction. When the pleadings are complete, issue is said to be joined.

Demurrer. — At each step in the proceedings, either party may, if he think fit, instead of pleading replying, &c., *demur* to the last pleading of his adversary; that is, he may say it is not sufficient in law. Special demurrers were abolished by the Common-Law Procedure Act, 1852, therefore *general* *demurrers* alone remain. Either party may, by leave of the court or a judge, plead and demur to the same pleading at the same time.

Equitable Defences. — By section 83 of the Common-Law Procedure Act, 1854, a defendant or plaintiff in replevin may, in any cause in which, if judgment were obtained, he would be entitled to relief against such, on equitable grounds, plead the facts which entitle him to such relief by way of defence; and, by section 85, the plaintiff may reply on equitable grounds.

FORMS OF PLEADINGS IN ACTIONS BY AND AGAINST CARRIERS.

Commencement of a Declaration.

In the Queen's Bench (in the margin), [*or* Common Pleas, *or* Exchequer of Pleas].

The day of A. D. 1872.[1] ———

(Venue.) A. B. by his attorney [*or* in person] sues C. D. for that [here state the special ground of action, commencing a second or subsequent count]. And also for that, &c. [If the plaintiff has any claim recoverable under an indebitatus count, such count should be added to the declaration, commencing] And the plaintiff also sues the defendant for money payable by the defendant to the plaintiff for, &c. [Conclude as follows :] And the plaintiff claims £ .[2]

[1] Every declaration and other pleading must be entitled of the proper court, and of the day of the month in the year when the same was pleaded. Com. Law. Proc. Act, 1852 and 1854. The pleadings should be entitled on the face; entitling them on the back is not sufficient; and if not properly entitled, a pleading may be set aside as irregular. Ripling *v.* Watts, 4 Dowl. 290; Hodgson *v.* Rennell, 4 M. & W. 373; Mills *v.* Brown, 9 Dowl. 151; Newham *v.* Hanney, 5 Dowl. 259. The court or judge may give leave to amend. Com. Law Proc. Act, 1852, § 222.

[2] The plaintiff may join counts in contract and tort, as well as any cause of action, except replevin or ejectment, provided they are by and against the same parties, and in the same rights. C. L. P. Act, 1852, § 41.

FORMS OF DECLARATIONS BY AND AGAINST CARRIERS BY LAND.[1]

(A)

Counts in Contract.

Forms of Indebitatus Counts (by a Carrier).

Money payable by the defendant to the plaintiff for the conveyance of goods by the plaintiff for the defendant at his request.

(B)

For Freight of Goods.[2]

[*Commencement as in page* 703.] For freight ["primage and average" *if claimed*] for the conveyance by the plaintiff for the defendant at his request, of goods in ships, and for money found to be due from the defendant to the plaintiff on account stated between them.

(C)

For Lighterage.

[*Commencement as ante, page* 703.] For the lighterage and the shipping conveyance and landing of goods by the plaintiff for the defendant at his request [*conclude with account stated as ante, form* (B)].

(D)

For the Tonnage of Goods.

[*Commencement as ante, page* 703.] For the tonnage of goods carried by the plaintiff on a certain canal in boats and vessels for the defendant, at his request[3] [*conclude with account stated as in form* (B)].

[1] The common count for work suffices, but if *money* is not to be paid for the carriage of the goods, the above count will not be supported. Bracegirdle *v.* Hincks, 9 Exch. 381; 22 L. J. Exch. 128.

[2] This is the form given by the C. L. P. Act, 1852, but a *delivery* must be proved where it is sought to charge the consignee or indorsee of the bill of lading. Moller *v.* Young, 25 L. J. Q. B. 94. The above form suffices against the indorsee of a bill of lading (Dougal *v.* Kemble, 3 Bing. 383); either the owner or the master may sue for the freight.

[3] 3 Went. 70.

(E)

FOR DEMURRAGE.[1]

[*Commencement as ante, page* 703.] For the demurrage of a ship of the plaintiff, kept on demurrage by the defendant [*conclude with account stated as in form* (B)].

(F)

FOR WHARFAGE AND WAREHOUSE-ROOM.

[*Commencement as ante, page* 703.] For wharfage and warehouse-room for goods provided by the plaintiff for the defendant, at his request [*account stated as in form* (B)].

(G)

FOR PASSAGE MONEY.

[*Commencement as in page* 703.] For the passage of the defendant on board a vessel of the plaintiff, at the request of the defendant [*account stated as in form* (B)].

Against a Carrier for not delivering Goods according to the Direction of the Plaintiff.

For that in consideration that the plaintiff would deliver to the defendant, as and being a carrier of goods for hire, certain goods to be by the defendant carried from to and there delivered according to the directions of the plaintiff, for reward to the defendant, the defendant promised the plaintiff to carry the said goods from to aforesaid, and there deliver the same according to the directions of the plaintiff in that behalf, and the plaintiff delivered the said goods to the defendant, and the defendant received the same for the purpose and on the terms aforesaid, and the plaintiff directed

[1] The above count is sufficient where there is a contract expressed or implied, *not under seal* (Lear v. Yates, 3 Taunt. 389); if no contract, and the defendant has detained the ship longer than is allowed by usage of the port of discharge, the count should be special (per PARKE, B., Horn *v.* Bensusan, 2 M. & Rob. 326; 9 C. & P. 709, and per LORD ABINGER, Kell *v.* Anderson, 10 M. & W. 499). If the detention is *ex delicto* the above form will not be proper. See Harrison *v.* Wilson, 2 Esp. 707.

the defendant to deliver the said goods at a certain place in aforesaid called ; and all conditions were fulfilled, and all things happened, and all times elapsed necessary to entitle the plaintiff to have the said goods delivered by the defendant at the last-mentioned place; yet the defendant did not deliver the said goods at the last-mentioned place, whereby the said goods were lost to the plaintiff (A.), and the plaintiff claims £ .[1]

Declaration against a Carrier for not carrying and delivering Goods (or for not carrying and delivering them within a Reasonable Time).

That in consideration that the plaintiff would deliver to the defendant, as and being a carrier of goods for hire, certain goods to be by the defendant carried from to , and there delivered for the plaintiff, for reward, to the defendant, the defendant promised the plaintiff to carry the said goods from to aforesaid, and there deliver the same for the plaintiff (within a reasonable time in that behalf), and the plaintiff delivered the said goods to the defendant, and the defendant received the same, for the purpose and on the terms aforesaid, and all conditions were performed, and all things happened, and all times elapsed, necessary to entitle the plaintiff to have the said goods carried and delivered as aforesaid, yet the defendant did not carry and deliver the said goods for the plaintiff as aforesaid (within a reasonable time in that behalf), whereby the plaintiff was deprived of the use of the said goods for a long time, and the same were diminished in value, and the plaintiff claims £ .[2]

[1] As to the destination of the goods being altered by the consignee, see London & North-Western Rail. Co. *v.* Bartlett, 7 H. & N. 400; 31 L. J. Exch. 92. A like count will be found in Scothorn *v.* South Staffordshire Rail. Co., 8 Exch. 341.

[2] A count may be added for loss of market, and thereby damage to the plaintiff. See next form. Any special damage sustained by the plaintiff must be averred, or he will not be allowed to give it in evidence. A like count, stating special damage, will be found in Hadley *v.* Baxendale, 9 Exch. 341. As to what damage is remote, see Hadley *v.* Baxendale, and Frances *v.* Gandet, 40 L. J. 121 Q. B., where the declaration is in trover.

Declaration against a Carrier for not carrying and delivering Goods in Time for a Market.

That in consideration that the plaintiff would deliver to the defendant, as and being a carrier of goods for hire, certain goods to be by the defendant carried from to , and there delivered to the plaintiff in time for a market to be held at mid-day, on the day of , A. D. , for reward to the defendant, the defendant promised the plaintiff to carry the said goods from to aforesaid, and there deliver the same to the plaintiff in time for the said market to be so held as aforesaid, and the plaintiff delivered the said goods to the defendant, and the defendant received the same for the purpose, and on the terms aforesaid, and all conditions were performed, and all things happened, and all times elapsed, necessary to entitle the plaintiff to have the said goods carried from to aforesaid, and there delivered to him by the defendant at the time aforesaid, yet the defendant did not deliver the said goods to the plaintiff at aforesaid in time for the said market there held as aforesaid, whereby the plaintiff was deprived of the use of the said goods, and lost the profits which he would have made by selling them at the said market, and the benefit of the expense which he incurred in travelling to aforesaid to meet the said goods, and in preparing to receive the same, and to sell them at the said market, and the said goods were deteriorated and diminished in value, and the plaintiff was and is otherwise damnified, and the plaintiff claims £ .[1]

Declaration against a Railway Company or other Carrier, under a Special Contract, for Non-delivery, or Loss of, or Injury to Goods.

That the plaintiff delivered to the defendant, being a carrier of goods for hire, goods of the plaintiff to be carried by the defendant for the plaintiff from to , and there to be delivered by the plaintiff for reward to the defendant in

[1] Against a carrier on a special contract to forward perishable goods the same evening, Pickford *v.* Grand Junction Canal Co., 12 M. & W. 766.

that behalf, upon and subject to, amongst other terms and conditions agreed upon by and between the plaintiff and defendant, the terms and conditions following, that is to say [*here set out such of the conditions as are material*], and the plaintiff says that he has performed all conditions precedent, &c. [*general averment of conditions precedent, as in page* 706]. And the plaintiff further says, that the defendant did not deliver the said goods for the plaintiff at aforesaid on aforesaid [*this must depend upon the time agreed upon by the terms of the special conditions*], and the said goods, by and through the carelessness and negligence of the defendant, became and were damaged and injured, although the said goods were not damaged or injured by or through, &c. [*here negative any damage or injury to the goods through any of the causes against which the carrier is protected by the terms of the special conditions*], and by reason of the premises the said plaintiff, &c. [*here aver any special damage that the plaintiff has sustained*], and the plaintiff claims £ .

Declaration against a Booking-office Keeper for not taking Care of Goods, and safely delivering them to the Proprietor of the Wagon by which they were directed to be forwarded.[1]

That the plaintiff, at the request of the defendant, caused to be delivered to him a parcel containing goods of great value, and which said parcel was directed to of upon the terms then agreed upon between the plaintiff and defendant, that the said parcel should be taken care of and safely and securely kept by the defendant for the plaintiff until the same could be delivered by the defendant to the proprietor of a certain wagon [*or according to the particular circumstance*], commonly called , or his servant, in order that the same might be safely and securely carried and conveyed in and by the said wagon, from a certain inn [*or otherwise*] called , situate and being to and there be safely and se-

[1] See another form against a booking-office keeper, Gilbart *v.* Dale, 5 A. & E. 543; and see Muschamp *v.* Lancaster & Preston Rail. Co., 8 M. & W. 422.

curely delivered to the said pursuant to the direction aforesaid, for reward, to the defendant in that behalf, and the defendant had and received the said parcel and its contents upon the terms and for the purpose aforesaid [*here aver performance of all conditions precedent, as ante, page* 706], yet the defendant did not, nor would take due or proper care of the said parcel and its contents aforesaid until the same could be delivered, nor did nor would deliver the same to the proprietor of the said wagon, or his servant for the purpose aforesaid, but negligently lost the same, and the plaintiff was and is wholly deprived of the use thereof, and the plaintiff claims £ .

Declaration against a Carrier for Loss of Goods.

That in consideration the plaintiff would deliver to the defendant, as being a carrier of goods for hire, certain goods for the plaintiff, to be by the defendant safely carried from to ,[1] and there delivered for the plaintiff for reward to the defendant in that behalf, the defendant promised the plaintiff that he would safely carry the said goods from to aforesaid, and there deliver the same for the plaintiff as aforesaid, and the plaintiff delivered the said goods to the defendant, and the defendant received the same for the purpose and on the terms aforesaid, and all conditions were performed, and all things happened, and all times elapsed necessary to entitle the plaintiff to have the said goods safely carried from to , and there delivered for him as aforesaid, yet the defendant did not safely carry the said goods from to , and there deliver the same for the plain-

[1] This averment does not seem to be necessary, and, at all events, a variance could be amended at the trial. Where railway companies undertake to carry goods beyond the limits of their own railway, they are liable for the non-delivery (Muschamp *v.* Lancaster & Preston Rail. Co., 8 M. & W. 421, &c.; Bristol & Exeter Rail. Co. *v.* Collins, 7 H. L. Cases, 194), and though the goods are carried partly by water (Wilby *v.* West Cornwall Rail. Co., 27 L. J. Exch. 181), unless they limit their responsibility by special agreement. See also Thomas *v.* Rhymney Rail. Co., 6 Law Rep. Q. B. 266, in error.

tiff as aforesaid, whereby the said goods were wholly lost to the plaintiff, and the plaintiff claims £ .[1]

Declaration against a Railway Company for not providing Trucks to convey Carriages.

The defendants were possessed of a railway from to , and of certain trucks provided by them for the conveyance of carriages on the said railway for hire, and thereupon, in consideration that the plaintiff would deliver to the defendants certain carriages of the plaintiff, to be conveyed upon the said railway of the defendants from to aforesaid for reward to the defendants, the defendants promised the plaintiff to provide trucks for the conveyances of the said carriages, and to convey the said carriages thereon from to aforesaid, and the plaintiff delivered the said carriages to the defendants and they received the same for the purpose and on the terms aforesaid, and all conditions were performed, and all things happened, and all times elapsed necessary to entitle the plaintiff to have trucks provided and the said carriages conveyed as aforesaid, yet the defendants did not provide trucks for the conveyance of the said carriages, nor did they convey the said carriages from to aforesaid, whereby the plaintiff was deprived of the use of the said carriages for a long time, and lost the benefit of the expense which he incurred in delivering the said carriages to the defendants, and was put to expense in conveying the said carriages to aforesaid, and the plaintiff claims £ .

Declaration against a Carrier for Damage done to Furniture in removing it.

That in consideration that the plaintiff would employ the defendant to remove and carry from one place to another cer-

[1] A like count, Syms v. Chaplin, 5 A. & E. 634.

tain furniture of the plaintiff for reward to the defendant, the defendant promised the plaintiff to use due care, skill, and diligence in removing and carrying the said furniture as aforesaid, and the plaintiff employed the defendant for the purpose and on the terms aforesaid, yet the defendant did not use due care, skill, and diligence in removing and carrying the said furniture as aforesaid, and in so doing broke and injured the same, whereby the said furniture was and is much damaged and lessened in value, and the plaintiff claims £ .[1]

Declaration against a Railway Company for not safely keeping Goods left in their Custody at one of their Stations.

That in consideration the plaintiff would deliver to the defendants certain goods of the plaintiff to be by the defendants safely and securely kept and redelivered to the plaintiff on request, for reward to the defendants, the defendants promised the plaintiff safely and securely to keep the said goods, and to redeliver the same to plaintiff on request, and the plaintiff delivered to the defendants, and the defendants received the said goods for the purpose, and on the terms aforesaid, and the plaintiff afterwards, and within a reasonable time in that behalf, requested the defendants to redeliver the same to the plaintiff, and all conditions were performed, and all things happened, and all times elapsed, necessary to entitle the plaintiff to have the said goods safely and securely kept and redelivered by the defendants to the plaintiff as aforesaid, yet the defendants did not safely and securely keep the same and redeliver the same to the plaintiff as aforesaid, whereby the said goods were lost to the plaintiff, and he was put to expense in endeavoring to recover possession of them, and the plaintiff claims £ .[2]

[1] It is not necessary to prove negligence on the part of the carrier, although it be averred (Richardson *v.* London & South Coast Rail. Co., 7 C. B. 839), unless in a case where there is a special contract.

[2] A like count, Van Toll *v.* South-Eastern Rail. Co., 12 C. B. N. S. 75; 31 L. J. C. P. 241.

Declaration against a Railway Company for not forwarding and delivering in due Time the Goods left at one of their Stations to be safely kept and forwarded according to Order.

That the defendants were carriers of goods for hire, and in consideration that the plaintiff delivered to the defendants at certain goods of the plaintiff to be by them kept and returned, or carried and delivered for him at his option as hereinafter mentioned, for reward to the defendants, the defendants promised the plaintiff that they would, at his option, safely and securely keep the said goods for him, and return them to him on request, or carry and deliver them for him to and at such place as he should direct by any order to be given by him to them, and the plaintiff afterwards, and whilst the defendants held the said goods for the purpose, and on the terms aforesaid, directed the defendants, by certain orders given by him to them, to carry the said goods from to aforesaid, and to deliver the same there for the plaintiffs, and all conditions were performed, and all things happened, and all times elapsed necessary to entitle the plaintiff to have the said goods carried from to aforesaid, and there delivered for the plaintiff, according to defendants' said promise in that behalf, yet the defendants did not, within a reasonable time in that behalf, carry the said goods from to aforesaid, and there deliver the same for the plaintiff, whereby the plaintiff was deprived of the use of the said goods for a long time, and the same were deteriorated in value, and the plaintiff claims £ .[1]

COUNTS IN TORT.

Declaration against a Railway Company for negligently injuring Cattle carried under Contract.

That the defendants were the owners of the Railway, and were possessed of engines, horse-boxes, and other mate-

[1] Count for not delivering goods left at a station within a reasonable time after request, Stallard *v.* Great Western Rail. Co., 2 B. & S. 419; 81 L. J. Q. B. 137.

rials for conveying, amongst other things [*here insert the particular sort of animal injured*], on the railway as common carriers, that plaintiff delivered to the defendants a to be carried by them for hire in a certain carriage, van, or other vehicle[1] on the railway from to , subject to certain conditions assented to by the plaintiff, and contained in a notice at the foot of the ticket, or way-bill, of the railway company for the conveyance of the , and which was in these words: This ticket is issued, subject to [*here copy the notice on the back of the ticket or way-bill*]. That whilst the was in custody of the defendants, and through the improper conduct and gross negligence, and from the want of proper care, skill, and diligence on the part of the defendants, the carriage [*or*] was propelled on the railway against certain trucks with so great violence, that the was seriously damaged, and died in consequence thereof, and the plaintiff claims £ .[2]

Declaration against a Booking-office Keeper for losing Goods.

That the defendant kept an office for receiving and booking goods and delivering the same to certain carriers for the purpose of being carried to the places to which the same might respectively be directed, and for keeping and taking care of such goods at the said office until such delivery as aforesaid for reward to the defendant, and thereupon the plaintiff delivered to the defendant at the said office a parcel of the plaintiff to be by the defendant booked and delivered within a reasonable time in that behalf to a certain carrier for the purpose of being carried by him to the place to which the same was directed, and to be kept and taken care of at the said office until such delivery for the plaintiff for reward to the defendant, and the defendant received and had the said parcel for the purpose and on the terms aforesaid, and all conditions

[1] If a horse, put "horse-box."

[2] For a count against a carrier for not taking care of goods after the consignee had refused to accept them, see Hudson *v.* Baxendale, 2 H. & N. 575.

were fulfilled, and all things happened, and all times elapsed, necessary to entitle the plaintiff to have the said goods taken care of and delivered as aforesaid, yet the defendant did not deliver the said parcel to the said carrier for the purpose aforesaid within such reasonable time as aforesaid, and the defendant did not in the meantime, and until such delivery, take reasonable care thereof at the said office, and whilst he had the care and custody of the said parcel for the purpose aforesaid negligently lost the same,[1] and the plaintiff claims £ .[2]

Declaration against a Common Carrier for Injury to Goods.

That the plaintiff delivered to the defendant, and the defendant received from the plaintiff, certain goods to be carried by the defendants as common carriers, from to , and there delivered for the plaintiff for reward to the defendant, yet the defendant so negligently carried the same, that by means thereof the said goods were damaged and spoiled,[3] and the plaintiff claims £ .

Declaration against a Carrier for the Wrongful Detention of Goods.

That the defendant detained from the plaintiff the goods of the plaintiff, that is to say, a [*or if a box, put what it contained*], and the plaintiff claims a return of the said goods, or their value,[4] and £ for their detention.

[1] If there be any reason to suppose that the goods were lost by a misdelivery, through the wilful negligence of the defendant, a count in trover should be added. Wyld *v.* Pickford, 8 M. & W. 443, &c.

[2] A like count, Gilbart *v.* Dale, 5 A. & E. 543.

[3] See Behrens *v.* Great Northern Rail. Co., 30 L. J. Exch. 153; affirmed, 31 L. J. Exch. 299. The plaintiff is entitled to recover the fall in price and deterioration in market value, and is not confined to the parts actually damaged. Collard *v.* South-Eastern Rail. Co., 30 L. J. Exch. 394, where see a form.

[4] The value of the goods must be assessed by the jury, and if several articles are sought to be recovered, the value of each should be separately assessed. Phillips *v.* Jones, 15 Q. B. 780.

Declaration against a Common Carrier for refusing to carry Goods.

That the defendant was a common carrier of goods for hire from to , and the plaintiff, at a reasonable and proper time in that behalf, tendered to him at aforesaid, at his place of business for the receipt of goods to be carried by him as such carrier, certain goods of the plaintiff, and requested the defendant as such carrier to receive the same, and carry them from to aforesaid, and at the last-mentioned place to deliver the same for the plaintiff for hire to the defendant, and the plaintiff was then ready and willing,[1] and offered to pay to the defendant his reasonable hire in that behalf, whereof the defendant then had notice, and the defendant then had sufficient time, means, and convenience to receive and carry and deliver the said goods as aforesaid, and could and ought to have done so, yet the defendant did not, nor would receive and carry the said goods for the plaintiff, and the plaintiff claims £ .[2]

Declaration for not delivering Goods in a Reasonable Time, and for Loss of the Goods.

For that the defendant was a common carrier of goods for hire from to , and the plaintiff delivered to the defendant, and he received as such carrier, goods of the plaintiff [*that is to say, a*], to be carried by the defendant, as such common carrier, from to aforesaid, and there to be delivered by the defendant to the plaintiff

[1] It is not necessary to aver a *tender* of the price of carriage, a readiness to pay is sufficient.

[2] See special damage alleged in Pickford *v.* Grand Junction Rail. Co., 8 M. & W. 372. Also, Johnson *v.* Midland Rail. Co., 4 Exch. 367; Crouch *v.* London & North-Western Rail. Co., 14 C. B. 256; Crouch *v.* Great Northern Rail. Co., 9 Exch. 556. Count, against a railway company for refusing to carry goods except upon unreasonable conditions, Gardton *v.* Bristol & Exeter Rail. Co., 1 B. & S. 112; 30 L. J. Q. B. 273. For refusing to carry a passenger's luggage, Munster *v.* South-Eastern, 4 C. B. N. S. 676; 27 L. J. C. P. 308.

within a reasonable time, in that behalf, for reward, to the defendant, yet the defendant, neglecting his duty as such common carrier, did not safely or securely carry or convey the said goods from to aforesaid, nor safely or securely deliver the same there for the plaintiff, although a reasonable time for doing so had elapsed before the commencement of this suit, but then negligently and improperly lost the said goods, and the plaintiff claims £ .[1]

Declaration against Carriers for not carrying and delivering Goods in Time for a Market.

That the plaintiff delivered to the defendants, as and being carriers of goods [*by railway*] from to , certain goods of the plaintiff, to be by them carried from to aforesaid, and there delivered for the plaintiff in time for a market to be there held, on the day of , A. D. , for reward to the defendants, and the defendants, as such carriers, received the said goods for the purpose, and on the terms aforesaid; and all conditions were performed, and all things happened, and all times elapsed, necessary to entitle the plaintiff to have the said goods carried by the defendants from to aforesaid, and there delivered to him by the defendants at the time aforesaid, yet the defendants did not deliver the said goods for the plaintiff at aforesaid in time for the said market there held as aforesaid, whereby the plaintiff was deprived of the use of the said goods, and lost the profit which he would have made by selling them at the said market, and the benefit of the expense which he incurred in travelling to aforesaid to meet the said goods, and in

[1] See also, as to not carrying within a reasonable time, Wise *v.* Great Western Rail. Co., 25 L. J. Exch. 258; Raphael *v.* Pickford, 5 M. & G. 551. As to the duty to carry within a reasonable time, see Great Northern Rail. Co. *v.* Taylor, 35 L. J. C. P. 210. A like count as to cattle, and injury to cattle by delay, Allday *v.* Great Western Rail. Co., 5 B. & S. 903. A count (including several bailments in one count) for not carrying by a certain hour, Lord *v.* Midland Rail. Co., L. R. 2 C. P. 339.

preparing to receive the same, and sell them at the said market, and the said goods were deteriorated and diminished in value, and the plaintiff claims £ .[1]

COUNTS BY AND AGAINST CARRIERS BY WATER.

In Contract.

Declaration on the Indebitatus Count for Freight.

For money payable by the defendant to the plaintiff for freight for the conveyance by the plaintiff for the defendant, at his request, of goods in ships [*after the word* freight, *add* primage and average, *if claimed*]; and the plaintiff claims £ .

Declaration on the Indebitatus Count for Lighterage.

For money payable by the defendant to the plaintiff for the lighterage, conveyance, shipping, and landing of goods conveyed in lighters and other vessels, and shipped and landed from the same by the plaintiff for the defendant, at his request, and the plaintiff claims £ .

Declaration on the Indebitatus Count for Demurrage.

Money payable by the defendant to the plaintiff for the demurrage of a ship of the plaintiff kept on demurrage by the defendant, and the plaintiff claims £ .

[1] Counts for delay in carrying, charging the loss of market as special damage, Walker *v.* York & North Midland Rail. Co., 23 L. J. Q. B. 73; White *v.* Great Western Rail. Co., 2 C. B. N. S. 7; Hughes *v.* Great Western Rail. Co., 14 C. B. 637.

Declaration on the Indebitatus Count for Tonnage on Canals.

Money payable by the defendant to the plaintiff for the tonnage of goods conveyed by the plaintiff for the defendant, at his request, in barges and other vessels.

Declaration by the Master of a Ship, on the Bill of Lading, against the Consignee of Goods, for not receiving the Goods from the Ship within the Time stipulated by the Bill of Lading.

That the defendant caused to be shipped on board a ship called the , then lying in the port of , whereof the plaintiff was master, goods represented to be in good order and well-conditioned, to be delivered in the like good order and condition at the port of (all and every the dangers of the sea and navigation excepted) unto the defendant or his assigns, he or they paying to the plaintiff certain freight for the said goods, and receiving and clearing the said goods from the said ship within days after notice of the ship's arrival, and the plaintiff received the said goods on board the said ship, and agreed with the defendant to deliver to him the said goods and chattels as aforesaid, and although the said vessel afterwards arrived with the said goods in the said port of , and the plaintiff was always ready and willing to deliver them to the defendant as aforesaid, of which the defendant had notice, and although the plaintiff had performed all conditions precedent on his part, and all things have happened and occurred, and all periods of time have elapsed to entitle the plaintiff to a performance of the defendant's contract, and to enable the plaintiff to maintain this action, yet the defendant did not within the said days, or at any other time, accept or clear the said goods from the said ship; whereby the said ship was for a long time detained at the said port of , and the plaintiff incurred expenses in maintaining the crew of the said ship during the said time, and was deprived of the use of the ship and the profits thereof, during such time. And the plaintiff claims £ .[1]

Declaration by the Indorsee of a Bill of Lading against the Master for not delivering Goods (18 & 19 *Vict. c.* 111, § 1).

That by a bill of lading made on the day of , A. D. , by the defendant, and delivered to G. H., the defendant promised the said G. H. that certain goods of the said G. H. in the said bill of lading mentioned, and then shipped , in the port of should be delivered at (certain perils and casualties only excepted), to the said G. H. or his assigns, he or they paying freight for the same (with primage and average accustomed), and the said G. H. indorsed the said bill of lading to the plaintiff, to whom the property in the said goods passed, and the delivery of the said goods as aforesaid was not prevented by any of the perils or casualties aforesaid, and all conditions were performed, and all things happened, and all times elapsed necessary to entitle the plaintiff to have the said goods delivered to him at aforesaid, yet the said goods were not delivered to the plaintiff at aforesaid, whereby the same were wholly lost to the plaintiff. And the plaintiff claims £ .[2]

Declaration by the Consignee of Goods against the Master of a Ship, on Bill of Lading, for not delivering.

That by a bill of lading made on the day of , A. D. , by the defendant, and delivered to the plaintiff, the defendant promised the plaintiff that certain goods of the plaintiff in the said bill of lading mentioned, and then shipped on board the ship , in the port of should be deliv-

[1] For a form of a declaration by an *owner*, in a special action for the detention of the ship, see Horn *v.* Bensusan, 9 C. & P. 709. See a form by the owner of a lighter for not accepting and unloading goods therefrom, Granger *v.* Dacre, 12 M. & W. 431.

[2] A like count by the indorsee of a bill of lading against the ship-owner, Shand *v.* Sanderson, 4 H. & N. 381.

ered at (certain perils and casualties only excepted[1]), to the plaintiff, he paying freight for the same (with primage and average accustomed), and the delivery of the said goods as aforesaid was not prevented by any of the perils or casualties aforesaid, and all conditions were fulfilled, and all things happened, and all times elapsed, necessary to entitle the plaintiff to have the said goods delivered to him at aforesaid, yet the said goods were not delivered to the plaintiff at aforesaid, whereby the same were wholly lost to the plaintiff. And the plaintiff claims £ .

Declaration by a Carrier against the Shipper upon an implied Warrant that the Goods shipped were not Dangerous.

For Form, see Brass *v.* Maitland, 6 E. & B. 470.

Count against a Carrier by Water on the implied Promise that his Vessel was Seaworthy.

For Forms, see Lyon *v.* Mells, 5 East, 428; and see, as to this cause of action, Shaw *v.* York & North-Midland Railway Company, 13 Q. B. 347.

Declaration against a Carrier for negligently stowing the Goods, whereby they were damaged.

That in consideration that the plaintiff would deliver to the defendant certain goods of the plaintiff to be carried in a ship of the defendant from to for reward to the de-

[1] This will depend upon the terms of the bill of lading; other special exceptions are frequently introduced in the *margin* of the bill of lading, and these should also be mentioned in the declaration. As to the ship-owner's protection against damage or loss by fire or robbery, see 17 & 18 Vict. c. 104, § 503; but the master is not protected against damage or loss by fire or robbery (*ibid.* § 510) unless the exceptions are introduced into the bill of lading.

fendant, the defendant promised the plaintiff to use due and proper care and skill in stowing the said goods on board of the said ship, and to carry the said goods from to as aforesaid (certain perils and casualties only excepted), and the plaintiff delivered the said goods to the defendant, and the defendant received and had the same for the purpose and on the terms aforesaid, and the defendant was not prevented from performing his said promise by any of the perils and casualties aforesaid; yet he did not use due and proper care and skill in stowing the said goods on board of the said ship; whereby the said goods were damaged and deteriorated in value, and the plaintiff claims £ .[1]

Declaration by the Owner of a Ship against the Shipper and Consignee of Goods for not receiving the Goods within a Reasonable Time.

That in consideration that the plaintiff received on board of his ship called certain goods of the defendant to be by the plaintiff carried in the said ship from to and there delivered to the defendant (certain perils and casualties only excepted), the defendant paying freight for the same as agreed upon, the defendant promised the plaintiff to receive the said goods at aforesaid from the plaintiff in a reasonable time after the defendant should have notice of the plaintiff being ready to deliver the same as aforesaid, and the said ship afterwards arrived with the said goods at aforesaid, and all conditions were fulfilled, and all things happened, and all times elapsed, necessary to entitle the plaintiff to have the said goods received by the defendant as aforesaid; yet the defendant did not nor would receive the said goods within such reasonable time as aforesaid, whereby the said ship was detained at for a long time, and the plaintiff was deprived of the use of the said ship, and incurred expense

[1] Like counts, Anderson *v.* Chapman, 5 M. & W. 483. Count for negligence in loading goods on board under a special contract, see Cooke *v.* Wilson, 1 C. B. N. S. 153.

in maintaining the crew thereof during all the time last aforesaid, and the plaintiff claims £ .[1]

Declaration by the Carrier against the Shipper for Freight and Primage, payable in Advance.

That in consideration that the plaintiff would receive on board of his ship called then about to sail from to certain goods of the defendant, to be conveyed by the plaintiff in the said ship from to aforesaid, the defendant promised the plaintiff that he would, two months after the said ship with the said goods on board thereof should have set sail on the said voyage, pay to the plaintiff freight in advance at the rate of £ per ton measurement for each ton of the said goods, and also primage at the rate of £ per cent upon the said freight, and the plaintiff received the said goods of the defendant on board of the said ship for the purpose and on the terms aforesaid; and the said ship with the said goods on board thereof afterwards set sail on the said voyage, and all conditions were performed, and all things happened, and all times elapsed, necessary to entitle the plaintiff to be paid the said freight and primage, yet the defendant has not paid the same. And the plaintiff claims £ .[2]

Declaration against the Captain of a Vessel on the Bill of Lading.

That the plaintiff, at the request of the defendant, caused to be delivered to the defendant divers goods, that is to say [*here specify them*] of the plaintiff, to be carried by the defendant in and by a certain ship of the defendant's, called the , from to and there to be delivered to the plaintiff for freight and reward to the defendant in that behalf

[1] As to this count, see Jesson *v.* Solby, 4 Taunt. 52; Evans *v.* Forster, 1 B. & Ad. 118; Möller *v.* Young, 5 E. & B. 755.

[2] A like count, Tindall *v.* Taylor, 4 E. & B. 219.

(the act of God, the Queen's enemies, fire, and all and every other dangers and accidents of the seas, rivers, and navigation of whatever nature and kind soever excepted),[1] and the defendant then received the same accordingly for the purpose aforesaid; and although the said ship afterwards safely arrived at aforesaid, and no act of God, nor the Queen's enemies, nor fire, nor any danger or accidents of the seas, rivers, or navigation, prevented the safe carriage or delivery of the said goods as aforesaid, yet the defendant did not deliver the said goods to the plaintiff, but so negligently, carelessly, and improperly conducted himself in this behalf, that for want of due care in the defendant and his servants in that behalf the said goods became and were wholly lost to the plaintiff. And the plaintiff claims £ .[2]

COUNTS IN TORTS.

Declaration against the Owners of a Ship for the Loss of a Passenger's Luggage.

That the defendants were owners of the[3] for the carriage of passengers and their luggage, and of goods and chattels from[4] to , and from [*here reverse the places*] for hire, and were common carriers of goods and passengers for hire in the said ship between the places aforesaid, and the plaintiff became a passenger therein to be conveyed from to , with luggage, goods, and chattels, his property, consisting of [*here describe the luggage*] safely and securely to be delivered; and by the negligence of the defendants and their servants the said ship was lost, and the plaintiff's goods and chattels, and the plaintiff was and is wholly deprived of the same. And the plaintiff claims £ .

[1] This must agree with the terms of the bill of lading.

[2] See another form, Colvin *v.* Newberry, 8 B. & C. 66.

[3] State here whether steamship or sailing vessel.

[4] Describe fully the place, so that in case there should be two of the same name, the one intended may be clear.

Declaration against Ship-owners for the Loss of Goods.

That the plaintiff caused to be delivered to the defendants and they received certain goods to be by them shipped on board of the ship and safely and securely carried therein from to , and there delivered for the plaintiff (certain perils and casualties only excepted), for freight payable by the plaintiff to the defendants, and the defendants were not prevented from so shipping, carrying, or delivering the said goods by any of the casualties aforesaid, and all conditions were performed, and all things happened, and all times elapsed, necessary to entitle the plaintiff to have the said goods safely and securely carried and delivered by the defendants as aforesaid; yet the defendants did not safely and securely carry and deliver the said goods as aforesaid, and the same were during the said voyage lost to the plaintiff, and the plaintiff claims £ .[1]

Declaration for Damage to Goods shipped in the Defendant's Ship to be carried.

That the plaintiff delivered to the defendant and the defendant received from the plaintiff certain goods of the plaintiff to be by the defendant safely and securely shipped and carried in the ship on a voyage from to , and there delivered for the plaintiff, for freight payable by the plaintiff to the defendant; yet the defendant so negligently carried the said goods in the said ship on the said voyage, that by reason thereof a large part of them was damaged and rendered of no use to the plaintiff, and the plaintiff claims £ .[2]

[1] See forms, Newberry *v.* Colvin, 7 Bing. 190; Gibbs *v.* Potter, 10 M. & W. 70; Williams *v.* African Steam Co., 1 H. & N. 300. On a bill of lading, see Colvin *v.* Newberry, 8 B. & C. 166. Where the bill of lading described the goods as "one box, containing about 248 ounces of gold dust," it was decided that it was not a declaration of the true nature and value within the Merchant Shipping Act (17 & 18 Vict. c. 104, § 503), so as to render the ship-owner liable for a loss without his actual fault or privity. Williams *v.* African Steamship Co., *supra*.

[2] See Alston *v.* Herring, 25 L. J. Exch. 177; Kay *v.* Wheeler, L. R. 2 C. P. 302.

Declaration for Damage to Goods occasioned by Negligent Stowage.

That the plaintiff delivered to the defendant and defendant received from the plaintiff certain goods of the plaintiff to be by the defendant shipped and stowed on board the ship and carried therein from to for the plaintiff (certain perils and casualties only excepted), for freight payable by the plaintiff to the defendant, and upon the terms that the defendant should use due and proper care in the stowage of the said goods; yet the defendant did not use due and proper care in the stowage of the said goods, and so negligently stowed the same that by reason thereof, and not by reason of any of the excepted perils or casualties, the said goods were damaged, and the plaintiff claims £

Declaration against a Carrier by Water for losing Goods.

See count in declarations by and against carriers by land; and see Gatliffe *v.* Bourne, 4 Bing. N. C. 314. A second count might be added for losing the goods between the place of landing and the plaintiff's place of business, James *v.* Bourne, 4 Bing. N. C. 420.

Declaration against a Carrier by Water for damaging a Cargo.

For a form, see Bennion *v.* Davison, 3 M. & W. 179.

Declaration against a Carrier by the Consignor (with whom the Contract was made), for not giving the Consignee Notice as to the Arrival of the Goods or forwarding them to him.

That the plaintiff, at the request of the defendant, delivered [2] to him certain goods of the plaintiff upon certain terms agreed

[1] See Hutchinson *v.* Guion, 5 C. B. N. S. 149; also, Major *v.* White, 7 C. & P. 41; Anderson *v.* Chapman, 5 M. & W. 483.

[2] A bill of lading is evidence of a shipment, as against a ship-owner in favor of a shipper of goods, or of an indorsee for value. Berkeley *v.* Watling, 7 A. & E. 29.

upon between the plaintiff and the defendant, that is to say, that the said goods should be carried by the defendant in a certain barge or vessel from to , in order that upon their arrival there the goods might be forwarded, or sent, or delivered by the defendant to one at , and there delivered to him for the said plaintiff, or otherwise that the defendant might, upon the arrival of the said goods at or within a reasonable time next following, notify such arrival to the said at for reward to the defendant in that behalf; and although the defendant conveyed the said goods to , and although a reasonable time for forwarding and sending or delivering the same, or notifying the arrival thereof, had elapsed before the commencement of this suit; yet the defendant did not forward, or send, or deliver the said goods for the plaintiff to the said at within such reasonable time, or at any other time, or notify, or cause to be notified to the said within such reasonable time, or at any other time, such arrival of the said goods, but the defendant wrongfully detained the same in his possession for a long and unreasonable time without sending, or forwarding, or delivering, or causing to be delivered the said goods to the said for the said plaintiff, or otherwise notifying, or causing to be notified to the said the arrival of the same, and by reason thereof the said afterwards refused and declined to accept and purchase and pay for the same as he otherwise would have done, whereby the plaintiff hath been deprived of gains and profits which would otherwise have accrued to him and hath lost other opportunities of disposing of the said goods, and the benefit of the profits which would otherwise have arisen therefrom, and hath incurred expenses in endeavoring to obtain the goods, and the same are injured and lessened in value, and the plaintiff claims £ .

Declaration against the Master of a Steam-tug in towing the Plaintiff's Ships.

That in consideration that the plaintiff would employ the

defendant with a steam-tug of the defendant to tow a certain ship of the plaintiff from the port of out to sea, for reward to the defendant, the defendant promised the plaintiff so to tow the said ship in a careful, skilful, and proper manner, and the plaintiff employed the defendant, and the defendant accepted and entered upon the said employment for the purpose and on the terms aforesaid, and all conditions were performed, and all things happened, and all times elapsed, necessary to entitle the plaintiff to have the said ship so towed in a careful, skilful, and proper manner, yet the defendant towed the said ship in a negligent, unskilful, and improper manner, whereby the said ship became and was stranded and damaged, and the plaintiff claims £ .[1]

CARRIERS OF PASSENGERS.

Counts in Contract.

Declaration on the Indebitatus Count by a Carrier for Passage-money.

For money payable by the defendant to the plaintiff, for the conveyance of the defendant in a carriage at his request, by the plaintiff, and the plaintiff claims £ .

Declaration against a Coach Proprietor for not carrying a Passenger.

That the defendant was the owner and proprietor of a certain stage-coach, going and passing from to for the carriage and conveyance therein of passengers and their luggage for hire, and thereupon, in consideration that the plaintiff, at the request of the defendant, would take and engage a place or seat in the said coach of the defendant, to be carried and conveyed therein, as a passenger, from to , together with his luggage, at and for certain reason-

[1] A like count, Symonds *v.* Pain, 30 L. J. Exch. 256.

able hire and reward to be [*or, if already paid, omit* to be] therefore paid by the plaintiff to the defendant, he, the defendant, promised the plaintiff to carry and convey the plaintiff, together with his said luggage in and by the said coach or carriage, from to aforesaid, and the plaintiff saith, that although he did take and engage a place or seat in the said coach or carriage, to be carried and conveyed, together with his said luggage, in and by the said coach or carriage from to aforesaid, and although the plaintiff was ready and willing to be carried and conveyed, together with his said luggage, in or by the said coach, from to aforesaid, and the plaintiff then requested the defendant to carry and convey the plaintiff, together with his said luggage in or by the said coach, from to aforesaid, yet the defendant did not, nor would when he was so requested as aforesaid, or at any other time carry or convey the plaintiff as aforesaid or otherwise, but then wholly neglected and refused so to do, whereby the plaintiff was obliged to procure another conveyance to aforesaid, and was thereby put to great trouble and inconvenience, and to great expense, and was, and is, otherwise greatly injured and damnified,[1] and the plaintiff claims £ .

Declaration against a Railway Company for Delay in a Train.

That the defendants were carriers of passengers in carriages on a railway from to , for reward to the defendants, and thereupon on the day of , A. D. , in consideration that the plaintiff at the request of the defendants would pay them a sum of money as and for the price of their carrying the plaintiff as a passenger in one of the said carriages from to aforesaid, by a train which the defendants advertised in their published train bill and represented to the plaintiff to be a train that would start

[1] Here state accurately any special damage the plaintiff has; also add count for money had and received, to recover back the fare, if any, paid by the plaintiff to the defendant, and on an account stated.

from to aforesaid, at o'clock in the [*afternoon*], and arrive at aforesaid at o'clock in the [*afternoon*] of the said day, the defendants promised the plaintiff that they would use reasonable care and diligence that the said train should start and arrive at the respective times aforesaid, and plaintiff accordingly paid the defendants the said sum of money for the purpose and on the terms aforesaid, and became such passenger to be so carried by the defendants as aforesaid by the said train, yet the defendants did not use reasonable care and diligence that the said train should start and arrive at the respective times aforesaid; and for want of such care and diligence the said train started from aforesaid and arrived at aforesaid respectively at much later times than the respective times aforesaid, whereby the plaintiff was delayed and put to expense and inconvenience, and was prevented from attending to his business at aforesaid as he otherwise would have done, and the plaintiff claims £ .[1]

Count by Husband for Loss of his Wife's Luggage.

That the defendants were carriers of passengers and their luggage (on a railway) from to , and in consideration that the plaintiff caused his wife to become and be a passenger to be carried with her luggage by the defendants (on the said railway) from to aforesaid, within a reasonable time in that behalf, for reward then paid by the plaintiff to the defendants in that behalf, the defendants promised the plaintiff to carry his said wife with her luggage (on the said railway) safely and securely from to aforesaid, and there to deliver to her the said luggage for the plaintiff within a reasonable time in that behalf as aforesaid; and although such reasonable time elapsed, yet the defendants did not safely and securely carry the said luggage from to aforesaid, and there deliver the same to the plaintiff's wife for the plaintiff within such reasonable time as aforesaid,

[1] A like count, Hamlyn *v.* Great Northern Rail. Co., 26 L. J. Exch. 20.

nor until a long time after had elapsed, and during all that time the plaintiff was deprived of the said luggage, and was put to much trouble and expense, and lost much time in endeavoring to obtain the same, and in providing other goods in the place of the said luggage. And the plaintiff claims £ .[1]

COUNTS IN TORTS.

Declaration against a Carrier for refusing to carry a Passenger.

That the defendants were common carriers of passengers for hire from to , and the plaintiff, at a reasonable time and place, and in a fit and proper state, tendered himself to be carried as a passenger from to aforesaid for hire, and was ready and willing and offered to pay the said hire, and the defendants had the means of carrying the plaintiff, and were able to have done so, yet refused to, and did not nor would, carry the plaintiff. And the plaintiff claims £ .[2]

Declaration for Delay in carrying a Passenger.

For a form, see Hamlyn *v.* Great Northern Railway Company, 26 L. J. Exch. 20. (See Form, *ante*, p. 600.)

Declaration against a Carrier for Injury to a Passenger.

That the defendants were common carriers of passengers for hire from to , and received the plaintiff as a passenger to be carried from to for hire, yet the

[1] For form of a declaration against a cab proprietor for the loss of a passenger's luggage from a hired cab, see Powles *v.* Hider, 6 E. & B. 207; Ross *v.* Hill, 2 C. B. 877.

[2] Count for refusing to carry a passenger's luggage, see Munster *v.* South-Eastern Rail. Co., 4 C. B. N. S. 676.

defendants so negligently conducted themselves in and about carrying the plaintiff, that by reason thereof the plaintiff was wounded and seriously injured, and incurred loss of time and expense in and about the cure of his wounds and injuries, and was prevented for a long time from attending to his necessary affairs and business, and was deprived of the gains and profits he would otherwise have derived therefrom. And the plaintiff claims £.

Declaration against a Railway Company for the Loss of a Passenger's Luggage.

That the defendants were carriers of passengers and their luggage upon a railway, from to , for reward to the defendants, and the plaintiff became and was received by the defendants as a passenger, with his luggage, that is to say [a carpet bag, *or as the case may be*], to be by them as such carriers safely and securely carried on the said railway from to aforesaid by a certain train, and the said luggage to be delivered by the defendants to the plaintiff at aforesaid on his arrival there by the said train for reward to the defendants, and a reasonable time for carrying and delivering the said luggage as aforesaid elapsed, yet the defendants did not safely and securely carry the said luggage and deliver the same to the plaintiff as aforesaid, whereby the said luggage was lost to the plaintiff. And the plaintiff claims £ .[1]

Declaration against a Railway Company for not running a Train, as advertised by their Time Tables.

See Count in Denton *v.* Great Northern Railway Company, 5 E. & B. 860.

[1] Like count, Munster *v.* Great Eastern Rail. Co., 4 C. B. N. S. 676; Stewart *v.* London & North-Western Rail. Co., 33 L. J. Exch. 199. For a count for a temporary loss of luggage, see Hearn *v.* London & South-Western Rail. Co., 10 Exch. 793.

Declaration against a Railway Company for Delay in a Train.

That the defendants were carriers of passengers in a railway from to on hire, and the plaintiff came and was received by the defendants, as such carriers, as a passenger to be carried by them, on the said railway, from to aforesaid, for reward to the defendants, by a train which the defendants advertised and represented to the plaintiff, by a published train bill, to be a train starting from aforesaid to aforesaid at o'clock in the [*afternoon*], and as arriving at aforesaid at o'clock in the [*afternoon*], and by reason of the defendants' negligence, default, and want of proper management of their traffic upon the said railway, the said train did not start from aforesaid at the time in that behalf above specified, or within a reasonable time afterwards, and did not arrive at aforesaid at the time in that behalf aforesaid, or within a reasonable time afterwards, whereby the plaintiff was put to expense and inconvenience, and was prevented from attending to his business at aforesaid as he otherwise would have done. And the plaintiff claims £ .[1]

Declaration by the Executor of a Deceased Passenger against a Carrier for Negligence (under 9 & 10 *Vict. c.* 93, *Lord Campbell's Act).*

, executor of the last will and testament of deceased, by his attorney, sues . For that the defendants were common carriers of passengers for hire, from to , and received , since deceased, to be carried from to for hire, yet the defendants so negligently conducted themselves in and about carrying the said , that, by reason of such negligence, the said was injured, and died within twelve calendar months next before this suit, and the plaintiff, as executor as aforesaid, for the benefit of the [*state whom*] [2] of the said , ac-

[1] A like count in McAndrew *v.* Electric Telegraph Co., 17 C. B. 3.

[2] 9 & 10 Vict. c. 93, § 2, directs for whose benefit the action is to be

cording to the statute in such case made and provided, and the plaintiff claims £ .

Declaration against a Carrier of Messages.

Declaration against a Telegraph Company for Negligence in the Transmission of a Message.

That before and at the time of making the agreement hereinafter mentioned, the defendants carried on the business, amongst other things, of transmitting and giving effect, by means of the telegraphs and apparatus of the defendants, and otherwise, to intelligence and messages for certain hire and reward in that behalf, and, therefore, in consideration that the plaintiff would pay to the defendants , the defendants promised the plaintiff that they would transmit correctly for the plaintiff from to the message following, that is to say, and the plaintiff paid to the defendants the said and all conditions (general averment of conditions precedent), yet the defendants did not correctly transmit to the said message as aforesaid, and transmitted to him another and different message [1] in the terms following whereby [*here insert damage*], and the plaintiff claims £ .

PLEAS TO DECLARATIONS FRAMED IN CONTRACT BY AND AGAINST CARRIERS.

Form of a Plea.

In the Queen's Bench [*or* C. P. *or* Exch.]

The day of 18 .

The said defendant by his attorney [*or* in person] says [*here state the matter of defence — see in the various forms*].[2]

brought; and 67, § 4, full particulars of the persons for whom this action is brought, and of the nature of the claim, must be delivered with the declaration. See also 27 & 28 Vict. c. 95, § 1.

[1] This averment must depend upon the circumstances of the particular case.

[2] In the margin, the defendant's name (surname only) is inserted first, then the word "ats" (at the suit of), and then the plaintiff's surname.

Plea of the General Issue — Non Assumpsit.

That he [*or* she *or* they] did not promise as alleged.

Plea of never Indebted, to the Indebitatus Counts.

That he [*or* she *or* they] never was [*or* were] indebted as alleged.

Plea of the General Issue to a Count upon a Deed.

That the alleged deed or bond is not his [her *or* their] deed.

Plea traversing the Delivery and Receipt of the Goods.

That the plaintiff did not deliver to the defendant, nor did the defendant receive from the plaintiff the said goods as alleged.

Plea traversing the Breach.

That he carried the said goods to , and safely and securely delivered the same to [*or* for] the plaintiff within a reasonable time.

Plea of Payment to an Action for the Carriage or Freight of Goods.

That before action he satisfied and discharged the plaintiff's claim by payment.

Plea of Payment into Court.

Brings into court the sum of £ , and says that the said sum is sufficient to satisfy the claim of the plaintiff in respect of the matter herein pleaded to.

Plea of the Statute of Limitations.

That the alleged cause of action did not accrue within six years next before the commencement of this suit.

Plea to an Action against a Carrier charged as a Wharfinger, that the Goods were destroyed by an Accidental Fire.

See Form, Bourne *v.* Gatliffe, 3 Scott, N. R. 1; 7 M. & G. 850.

Plea to an Action by the Consignee of Goods for not delivering them, that the Consignor gave Notice to the Carrier, and stopped the Goods in Transitu.

See Form in Jones *v.* Jones, 8 M. & W. 431.

Plea to an Action for not delivering Goods, that the Defendants could not ascertain to whom they were to be delivered.

That the plaintiff delivered the said goods to the defendants, directed and to be delivered at , to a certain person there, to the defendants unknown, without any information to the defendants, at any time, whereby the defendants could ascertain who the said person was, or where in , or elsewhere, the said goods could be delivered to him, and the defendants, by reason of the premises, not having been able to ascertain who the said person was, or where the said goods could be delivered to him, and the said person having made no application for the same, the defendants, without any default on their part, have been unable to deliver, and have not delivered, the said goods, which is the alleged non-delivery thereof in the said declaration mentioned.

Plea to an Action for the Loss of Goods left in the Cloak-room of a Railway Company, that the Defendants accepted them upon the Condition that they would not be responsible if their Value exceeded £10, and that they did exceed £10.

For Form,[1] see Van Toll *v.* The South-Eastern Railway Company, 31 L. J. C. P. 241.

Plea to an Action for not delivering Goods, that the Goods were seized by the Sheriff under a fi. fa. on a Judgment against a Person who had fraudulently assigned them to the Plaintiff.

That, before the said delivery to the defendants, the said goods were the goods of one , and that while the said goods were his goods, and before and at the time of the bargain and conveyance hereafter mentioned, the said was justly and lawfully indebted to one , in the sum of £ , which sum the said , in the Court of Queen's Bench [*or* C. P. *or* Exch.] by the judgment of the said court, before the committing of the breach of promise in the declaration mentioned, did, in an action by him brought against the said , recover against the said , together with his costs of suit, amounting, with the said debt, to £ , and the defendants say, that before the said delivery to the plaintiff, the said fraudulently, and by collusion with the plaintiff, who knew the premises, bargained and conveyed the said goods to the plaintiff to and for the intent and purpose to delay, hinder, and defraud the said of his said just and lawful debt, whereby the said action and debt of the said were disturbed, hindered, and defrauded. And the defendants further say, that after the said bargain and conveyance, and after the said delivery to the defendants, and before the breach in the declaration complained of, one , then being sheriff of the county of , under

[1] The deposit of goods in the cloak-room of a railway station is not within the Railway and Canal Traffic Act, 17 & 18 Vict. c. 31, § 7.

and by virtue of a certain writ of *fi. fa.* to him directed and delivered at the suit of the said against the said , issued out of the said court, upon and for having execution of the said judgment, commanding the said sheriff to levy of the goods and chattels of the said in his bailiwick the said sum of £ so recovered as aforesaid, seized the said goods and chattels then being in the possession of the defendants as such common carriers, and on the terms aforesaid, the same goods being liable to be seized under the said execution, and kept and detained the same, whereby the defendants, without any default on their part, were prevented from carrying and delivering the said goods within such reasonable time as aforesaid, and were and are prevented from delivering the same to the plaintiff.

Plea by a Railway Company of a Special Condition exempting the Defendants from Liability.

That the said goods were delivered by the plaintiff to the defendants and were received by them to be carried as aforesaid, under a special contract between the plaintiff and defendants, signed by the plaintiff, and subject to just and reasonable conditions contained in the said contract, one of which conditions was,[1] that the defendants would not be answerable for the loss or detention of any goods which might be untruly or incorrectly described in the receiving-note delivered by the plaintiff to the defendants, and at the time of the delivery of the said goods to the defendants, the plaintiff delivered to them a receiving-note, purporting to contain a true and correct description of the said goods, and the defendants received the said goods from the plaintiff upon the faith of the said description, and the said goods were not truly and correctly described in the said receiving-note, and were, without the defendants' knowledge or consent, misdescribed in the said receiving-note, within the meaning of the said condition.[1]

[1] Here describe the condition. As to what are reasonable and what unreasonable conditions, see the body of the work. Like pleas may be found

Plea that the Goods were carried under a Special Contract.[1]
Another Count.

That the said goods were delivered to and received by the defendants to be carried under a special contract signed by the plaintiff [*or* on behalf of the plaintiff], and containing certain just and reasonable conditions, and among others that [*here set out the conditions exempting the defendant*], and [*state facts which show the defendant has acted in accordance with the conditions*].

Plea of a Special Contract repudiating Liability for Loss or Damage unless the Goods were declared and insured according to their Value.

See Form in Wyld *v.* Pickford, 8 M. & W. 443.

Plea that the Goods were carried and tendered to the Plaintiff, who refused to pay for the Carriage.

See Form in Crouch *v.* Great Western Railway Company, 26 L. J. Exch. 345.

Plea by a Carrier by Sea, that the Nature and Value of the Goods were not declared.

See Form in Williams *v.* The African Steamship Company, 1 H. & N. 300.

in Lewis *v.* Great Western Rail. Co., 5 H. & N. 867; Peek *v.* North Staffordshire Rail. Co., E. B. & E. 958. Like pleas as to cattle, Gregory *v.* Midland Rail. Co., 33 L. J. Exch. 155.

[1] As to special contracts, see 17 & 18 Vict. c. 32, § 7. As to effect of this and other statutes upon special agreements, see the body of the work.

Plea that the Goods were received to be carried on the Terms that the Defendants should not be liable unless Bills of Lading were signed, which was not done.

See Wilton *v.* Royal Atlantic Mail Steam Navigation Company, 10 C. B. N. S. 453.

Plea that the Damage was caused by the Goods being of a Dangerous Description, which the Plaintiff well knew, but of which he gave no Notice to the Defendant.

See Form in Hutchinson *v.* Guion, 28 L. J. C. P. 63.

Plea under the Carriers' Act, 1 *Will. IV. c.* 68, *that the Goods were within the Act, and were above the Value of* £10, *and were not declared or insured.*

That the said goods were articles and property of the description mentioned in the first section of the statute passed in the first year of the reign of King William IV., for the most effectual protection of common carriers for hire, and were contained in a parcel which, with the said goods therein contained, was delivered by the plaintiff to the defendant as and being a common carrier by land for hire, at a certain office or receiving-house of the defendant, for the purpose of being by him as such carrier carried for hire [*or*, to accompany the person of the plaintiff as such passenger], as in the declaration mentioned, in a public conveyance, and the value of the said goods then exceeded £10, and at the time of the delivery of the said parcel and goods as aforesaid, there was affixed in legible characters in a public and conspicuous part of the said office or receiving-house, being an office or receiving-house of the defendant, where such parcels were then received by the defendant for the purpose of conveyance, a notice within the meaning of the said statute, whereby the defendant notified that an increased rate of charge in the said notice mentioned was required to be paid to him over and above the ordinary rate of carriage as a compensation for the greater risk and care to be taken for the safe conveyance of articles and property of the description in the first section of the said statute mentioned; and at the time of the delivery of the said parcel and goods at the said office or receiving-house of the defendant as aforesaid for the purpose aforesaid, the value and nature of the said goods were not declared by the person sending or delivering the same, and neither such increased charge as aforesaid, nor any engagement to pay the same was accepted by the person receiving the said parcel and goods.[1]

PLEAS TO DECLARATIONS FRAMED IN TORT.

Plea of the General Issue.

That he is not guilty.

Plea of the General Issue by Statute.

That he is not guilty [*or, if several defendants*, that they are not, nor is either or any of them, guilty].[2]

Plea by a Carrier, denying the Receipt by him of the Goods.

That the plaintiff did not deliver to him, nor did he receive the said goods and chattels from the plaintiff, or any of them, for the purpose alleged.

[1] Forms of like pleas may be found in Machu *v.* South-Western Rail. Co., 2 Exch. 415; Syms *v.* Chaplin, 5 A. & E. 634, and Metcalfe *v.* London & Brighton Rail. Co., 27 L. J. C. P. 205.

[2] State in the margin the words "By statute," and also the year of the reign in which the Act or Acts of Parliament were passed, and also the chapter and section of each of such statutes, and also specify whether they are public or private acts.

Plea to a Count for refusing to carry, denying that the Defendant was a Common Carrier.

That he was not a common carrier of goods [*or* of passengers and their luggage] as alleged.

Plea of Notice and Stoppage in Transitu by an Unpaid Consignor.

See Form in Jones *v.* Jones, 8 M. & W. 431.

Plea to a Count for refusing to carry, that the Plaintiff was not ready and willing to pay the Carriage.

That the plaintiff did not pay, nor was he ready and willing to pay, to the defendant, his reasonable charge for the carriage and delivery of the said goods.

Plea of Payment into Court.

(*If the plea is not pleaded to the whole of the declaration*), as to the first *or* second (and so on) count of the declaration [*or*, so much thereof, &c.], brings into court the sum of £ , and says that the said sum is enough to satisfy the claim of the plaintiff in respect of the matter herein pleaded to.

Plea to a Declaration in Tort for not delivering a Cask of Beer, that the Cask was an insufficient one and burst, whereby the Beer was lost, and could not be delivered.[1]

That at the time the said beer was delivered to him, the same was contained in a certain cask, which was then and at the time of the loss hereinafter mentioned, a bad and insuffi-

[1] This plea is not available under the general issue, but must be specially pleaded.

cient cask, and not properly secured and coopered in that behalf, without any default on the part of the defendant, for which reason the said cask afterwards, and before the defendant could safely and securely deliver the said cask with the beer therein, for the plaintiff as aforesaid, broke, burst, and gave way, and the said beer therein then escaped from the said cask, and was wholly wasted and lost, without the defendant's default, whereby he was prevented from delivering the said cask of beer for the plaintiff, as he otherwise would have done.

Plea denying the Bailment to the Defendant.

That the said goods were not delivered by the plaintiff to the defendant for the purpose alleged.

Plea of Non Detinet to a Declaration for Detention of Goods.

That he did not, and doth not, detain the said goods, or any or either of them, as alleged.

Plea of Accord and Satisfaction.

That he delivered to the plaintiff, and the plaintiff accepted and received from him, certain goods [*describe the articles*] in full satisfaction and discharge of the causes of action in the declaration mentioned.

Plea by Carriers that the Breach was caused by the Plaintiff's own Act and Default.

That when the said goods were delivered to and accepted by the defendants as alleged, the same were, by the negligence and default of the plaintiff, and without any default of the defendants, or any notice or knowledge thereof to or by them, improperly and insufficiently packed and secured, and the defendants were thereby prevented from safely and securely carrying and delivering the said goods as they otherwise would have done, and the same were not delivered to the plaintiff, and were wholly lost to him as alleged by and through his own negligence and default, and not otherwise.

Form of a Replication to a Plea.[1]

In the ——— (*Q. B., C. P., or Ex.*).

The day A. D. 187 .

The plaintiff takes [*or* joins] issue upon the defendant's pleas [*or* all the defendant's pleas, *or* first, second, and third pleas, *as the case may be*].

[1] The surnames of the parties must be inserted in the margin. By C. L. P. Act, 1852, § 53: "Rules to reply and plead subsequent pleadings shall not be necessary, and instead thereof a notice shall be substituted, requiring the opposite party to reply, rejoin, or as the case may be, within four days, otherwise judgment, such notice to be delivered separately, or indorsed on any pleading to which the opposite party is required to reply, rejoin, *or* as the case may be."

For forms of replications in different cases, reference can be made to Bullen and Leake's Precedents of Pleading, and Chitty's Precedents.

INDEX.

INDEX.

A.

H.

I.

J.

L.

M.

P.

S.

T.

V.

University Prsss: John Wilson & Son, Cambridge.